THE BRIDGEST

The Bridgestone

Irish
Food
Guide

JOHN McKENNA - SALLY McKENNA

Estragon Press

FIRST PUBLISHED IN 2009

BY ESTRAGON PRESS

DURRUS

COUNTY CORK

© ESTRAGON PRESS

TEXT © JOHN & SALLY MCKENNA

THE MORAL RIGHT OF THE AUTHORS

HAS BEEN ASSERTED

ISBN 978-1-906927-00-4

PRINTED IN SPAIN BY GRAPHYCEMS

WRITTEN BY JOHN McKENNA

CONTRIBUTING EDITORS:

EAMON BARRETT

ORLA BRODERICK

CAROLINE BYRNE

SABRINA CONNEELY

CLAIRE GOODWILLIE

VALERIE O'CONNOR

JAKKI OWENS

LESLIE WILLIAMS

PUBLISHER: SALLY McKENNA

EDITOR: JUDITH CASEY

EDITORIAL ASSISTANT: EVE CLANCY

ILLUSTRATIONS BY AOIFE WASSER

WEB: FLUIDEDGE.IE

For
Jeffa Gill

THE AUTHORS WOULD LIKE TO THANK

Colm Conyngham, Pat Curran, Grainne Byrne,
Sile Ginnane, George Lane, Frank McKevitt,
Bernadette O'Shea, Margaret Deverell,
Trevor & Barbara Edwards, Eleanor Walsh,
Connie, Sam and PJ McKenna,
Hugh Stancliffe and the crew at GraphyCems,
Chris Carroll, Paul Neilan and all the team
at Gill & MacMillan

Bridgestone is the world's largest tyre and rubber company.

• Founded in Japan in 1931, it currently employs over 100,000 people in Europe, Asia and America and its products are sold in more than 150 countries. Its European plants are situated in France, Spain, Italy, Poland and Turkey.

• Bridgestone manufacture tyres for a wide variety of vehicles from passenger cars and motorcycles, trucks and buses to giant earthmovers and aircraft.

• Many new cars are fitted with Bridgestone tyres during manufacture, including Ford, Toyota, Volkswagen, Mercedes and BMW. Super cars such as Ferrari, Aston Martin and Porsche are also fitted with Bridgestone performance tyres as original equipment.

• Bridgestone commercial vehicle tyres enjoy a worldwide reputation for durability and its aircraft tyres are used by more than 100 airlines.

• In Formula 1 Bridgestone are sole tyre supplier with all the teams now competing on its Potenza racing tyres. Technology developed in the sport has led to increased performance and safety in Bridgestone's road tyres.

- Bridgestone tyres are distributed in Ireland by Bridgestone Ireland Ltd, a subsidiary of the multinational Bridgestone Corporation. A wide range of tyres is stocked in its 6,500 square metre central warehouse and its staff provide sales, technical and delivery services all over Ireland.

- Bridgestone tyres are available from First Stop Tyre Centres and tyre dealers throughout Ireland.

For further information:

BRIDGESTONE IRELAND LTD
10 Fingal Bay Business Park
Balbriggan
County Dublin

Tel: + 353 1 841 0000
Fax: + 353 1 841 5245

websites:
www.bridgestone.ie
www.firststop.ie
www.truckpoint.ie

How To Use This Book

The Bridgestone Irish Food Guide is arranged alphabetically, by county so it begins with County Carlow, which is followed by County Cavan, and so on.

Within the counties the towns are once again listed alphabetically.

Northern Ireland is listed at the end of the book as a separate entity. Note that this is a sterling currency area, though the euro is often accepted, particularly in the border areas.

Many of the places featured in this book are only open during the summer season, which means that they can be closed for any given length of time between October and March. Many others change their opening times during winter. It is always advisable to check the website or telephone in advance if you are using this book in the countryside, out of season.

Finally, we greatly appreciate receiving e-mails with suggestions and criticisms from readers, and would like to thank those who have written in the past, whose opinions are of enormous assistance to us when considering which people, places and products finally make it into this book.

Send feedback to:

www.bridgestoneguides.com

The people described in this book are entitled to display the Bridgestone Best in Ireland plaque. "Best in Ireland" means exactly what it says on the plaque, and if you see an up-to-date plaque displayed by an establishment in this book it is your guarantee that the people involved are providing the very best service possible, whether they are a fishmonger selling at a farmers' market, or a pub with interesting food, a real bakery, or a hip happening restaurant.

The *Bridgestone Guides* are independent and critical guides to Ireland's food culture. There is no payment for inclusion and, unlike many other guide books, which are little more than marketing tools with paid for inclusion, you get into the *Bridgestone Guides* purely on merit.

Introduction

Irish farming is in a state of crisis. The crisis is not merely financial, though that is presently the most potent manifestation of the crisis. But more fundamentally, the crisis in Irish agriculture is a matter of power.

• Quite simply, the Government has ceded control over the fate of Irish agriculture to massive multinational supermarket chains, and in so doing it has sacrificed Irish farming and Irish farmers.

• It has allowed those supermarket chains to acquire and exercise power, but this power is wielded without responsibility, and power without responsibility, as Kipling remarked so long ago, has been "the prerogative of the harlot throughout the ages".

• Are supermarkets harlots, then? Most definitely. They are amoral and destructive, and they dance only to the bidding of the money markets, as a true harlot does. They owe no loyalty, and they know nothing other than submission to their will to profit. They have no culture, and they are mesmerically clever, for how else can one explain why people shop in stores that destroy Irish towns, refuse to disclose their profit margins, and generally act in ways that are totally contrary to the best interests of the country. Above all, that means acting in ways that are inimical to the interests of farmers and farming.

• Ireland has been colonised, one more time. One more time, we are but a pawn in an empire, this time an economic empire.

We need resistance to this economic colonisation, and we need it quickly. That resistance will not come from the government, for the government is intellectually incontinent.

• So the resistance will need to come from the grassroots, and the first step in popular action should come from the realisation that buying imported food in a foreign-owned supermarket in Ireland is, quite simply, a traitorous action.

• But we have another proud tradition to draw on in our popular action. For decades, Ireland was distinguished by its support for the dispossessed and the downtrodden in the developing world. We called for Fair Trade, and we created Fair Trade towns throughout the length and breadth of the country. We saw the morality that needed to be injected into international trade. We behaved with honour and dignity, and we saw through all the guff about GATT and the WTO and all that nonsense. We called for justice, the justice of Fair Trade, where people could control their destiny, avoid exploitation, and have at least a chance of a decent life.

• Now, we need to see that the need for Fair Trade is with our very own farmers. We need to understand that the relationship between supermarkets and farmers is not one of equals, or even one of trading partners, Instead, the relationship is one of master and slave. Irish farmers are powerless. With this imbalance of power has come all the standard consequences: frustration, demoralisation, the stealing of the very culture out of, and from, agriculture.

Fair Trade for Irish Farmers

• Part of the act of resistance, of course, is to use this very book. For twenty years now we have described people who work with food, and whose success, we believe, is pivotal to the very success of Ireland itself, pivotal to the very culture of Ireland itself. The book has got bigger and bigger, and the artisans and food specialists whom we describe have grown organically, successfully, naturally.

• But around this island of success lies a sea of despond, and for the good of the country we must rescue those stranded in that sea of despond. The Government treats the market for food and agriculture as if it is a financial market, and unless something is done the food and agriculture market will go the way of the financial markets. It will collapse, and there will be catastrophe.

• An insistence on Fair Trade for Irish farmers will begin to bring the market back to equilibrium. If that requires state intervention, and it does, then so be it. But even with Government action, we need ourselves to insist on Fair Trade, and the way to do that is in the way in which, and where, you spend your money on foods in Ireland. It's not enough to come up with industry slogans about loving Irish food. Buying local food from local farmers is the responsibility of every citizen. If we accept that responsibility, then we acquire power.

John McKenna   Sally McKenna

Durrus, West Cork 2009

Contents

Contents

Contents

Contents

Contents

County Carlow

Bagenalstown

Country House
● **Kilgraney House**

"It is a thoroughly modern country house hotel", wrote the great food writer Annie Bell, back in 1999 when she first visited Bryan and Martin's Kilgraney House. The cooking, said Ms Bell, "sings with wonderfully clear notes". Spot on, Annie: a great, unique place to stay, and some dazzling cooking explain why Kilgraney has been one of the glories of Irish hospitality for 15 years. Nowhere else is quite like it, nowhere else has such a finely tuned aesthetic in every aspect of the operation, nowhere else has such ageless modernity. (Bryan Leech & Martin Marley, Bagenalstown ☎ 059-977 5283 ✉ info@kilgraneyhouse.com ✉ www.kilgraneyhouse. com – Open Mar-Nov, Wed-Sun)

only in Carlow
Coolattin Cheddar

Ballickmoyler

Country House & Organic Farm
● **Coolanowle Country House Health Spa**

The Mulhall family's amazing adventure is a superlative, sustainable organic farm, and a fine guest house specialising in organically produced food, the essential complement to Coolanowle's health spa. Each week, they service no fewer than seven farmers' markets, bringing their outstanding meat products from the Midlands to Dublin. The Mulhalls practice farming as farming should be practised, and they inspire us with both the organoleptic brilliance of what they do, and with the dignified logic of their farming work. (Eddie & Bernadine Mulhall, Ballickmoyler, Carlow ☎ 059-862 5176 ✉ coolanowle@eircom.net ✉ www. coolanowle.com)

Ballon

● The Forge Craft & Coffee Shop

The hungry traveller would be a happy hungry traveller if every N-route in Ireland had a place as characterful and charming as Mary Jordan's The Forge. It's a real place, with real cooking – country vegetable soup; leg of lamb with mint sauce; baked ham; fruit crumble and cream – and none of that ersatz stuff out of the back of a supplier's lorry. So, pull over, park the car, and sate that appetite, then hit the road, re-charged. (Mary Jordan, Kilbride Cross, Ballon ☎ 059-915 9939 ✆ theforgekilbride@eircom.net – Open 9.30am-5.30pm Mon-Sun)

Country House
● Lorum Old Rectory

"There is a grace and calmness here that is present not only in the fine solidity of the house or its pastoral gardens but mostly in the gracious host, Bobbie Smith." So says Eamon Barrett about Mrs Smith's distinguished country house. And there's more: "She has a natural warmth that makes one instantly feel like you are visiting the grand home of a favourite relative. The rooms all have lovely proportions and dinner at the communal table is never disappointing." Pretty perfect, then. (Bobbie Smith, Ballon ☎ 059-977 5282 ✆ www.lorum.com – Open 1 Mar-30 Nov)

Borris

Hotel
● Step House Hotel

James and Cait Cody's neat boutique hotel is a great address, marrying a lush design style with some very good cooking and some very personable service. The Step House is the sort of place that, after a day's lazy touring, or a day at the horse sales, you can hardly wait to get back to for a drink in the bar, a scrummy dinner, a comfy bed in a commodious, stylish room, and the sleep of the just. Next day, you will want to do it all over again. (James & Cait Cody, Main Street, Borris ☎ 059-977 3209 ✆ www.stephousehotel.ie)

Carlow

Carlow

Butchers Shop
● **Bosco's**

Bosco's has been one of the flagships of Carlow's food culture for more than thirty years now, ringing the changes of shopping styles and purchasing preferences with easeful skill and adaptability, staying true to their metier of great meats, and helpful, calm service. (John Bosco O'Connell, 132 Tullow Street, Carlow ☎ 059-913 1093 – Open 9am-6pm Mon-Fri, 8am-6pm Sat. Unit 3 Fairgreen Shopping Centre, Barrack, Carlow ☎ 059-918 2511 – Open 8am-6pm, till 9pm Thur & Fri, 11am-6pm Sun)

Brewery
● **Carlow Craft Brewery**

The brews of the Carlow Brewery compare to commercial brews as cheese compares to chalk, and the Carlow brews are the big cheeses, the big handmade artisan cheeses. Their brews – O'Hara's stout, critically recognised as the best stout in these islands, thanks to the use of traditional stout hops; the clean, crisp American-style Curim lager; the caramelly, hoppy Molings ale, and the new Leann Follain stout – are a blessed quartet of drinks. All four brews are superb with food, and they stand alongside pot-still Irish whiskey as the real wine of the country. (Seamus & Eamon O'Hara, The Goods Store, Station Road, Carlow ☎ 059-913 4356 ✉ info@carlowbrewing.com ⌂ www.carlowbrewing.com)

Farmers' Market
● **Carlow Farmers' Market**

Look up the website for Coolattin Cheddar and you can click onto some lovely images of the stalwarts of the Carlow Market socialising at their Christmas do. It's a charming collage of smiling faces, from Oracle Farm, from Carlow Cheese, from Newtown Farm, Malone's fruits and on and on. You can feel the social glue that binds marketeers, and makes these precious markets a success. John McKenna's granny, by the by, used to have a little shop, at the front of the family house, on Brown Street in Carlow, many, many years ago, so the connection with trading in Carlow town is deep-rooted. (Potato Market, beside Hadden's Car Park. Sat 9am-2pm)

THE BRIDGESTONE IRISH FOOD GUIDE 23

Deli and Café
● Hennessy's Fine Food Store

Michael and Trish do the good thing in Hennessy's every day, and their shop and café is one of the key Carlow destinations. The level of discrimination in what they cook and what they sell in this fine deli is matched by the exacting standards of everything from the brown bread to the beautiful breakfasts. (Michael & Trish Hennessy, 26 Dublin Street, Carlow ☎ 059-913 2849 – Open 8.30am-4pm Mon-Sat, 7pm-9pm Fri & Sat)

Café Bar
● Lennon's @ VISUAL

Having made Lennon's Café Bar into Carlow's hottest address, Sinead Byrne and chef Gail Johnson have moved to the VISUAL centre for contemporary art, where they will operate the café, with the same scrummy bistro-style cooking that was such a wow! in the original Lennon's. Sinead's son Ross will be running the show, and this glamorous, cutting-edge, recession-bustin' project is some of the most exciting news out of Carlow in quite sometime. (Sinead Byrne, Carlow College, Carlow ☎ 059-913 1575 ✉ lennonscafebar@eircom.net – Open for food day-time. Early evening dinner Thurs & Fri. Kitchen closed Sunday & bank holidays)

Clonegal

Restaurant
● Sha Roe Bistro

Sha Roe has been an unstoppable source of great cook-ing, and a thumping great success, right from the day it first opened its doors in little Clonegal. Henry Stone's cooking is wonderfully efficient and brilliantly managed to play to the strengths of the chef-proprietor, which means that the short menus – six starters, five mains, four puddings – over-deliver on flavour with an unerr-ing accuracy, whether it's a pitch-perfect squash risotto or a lovingly made treacle and macadamia nut tart. The culinary consistency is matched by a charming bohemian calm in the service. So, waiter, bring me sha roe. (Henry Stone, Main Street, Clonegal ☎ 053-937 5636 ✉ sha-roebistro@hotmail.com – Open 7pm-9.30pm Wed-Sat, 12.30pm-3.30pm Sun)

Fenagh

Farmhouse Cheese
● Carlow Cheese

Elizabeth Bradley makes a sweet, Edam-style farmhouse cheese with good raw milk. As with many of the new generation of Irish cheesemakers, the production of Carlow cheese is expert and the result is, in cheese terms, deeply cultured. The Edam style allows the flavours Elizabeth uses – nettles; traditional cumin; funky tomato and basil, amongst others – to shine against a mellow canvas of fudgy, pleasing lactic tastes and aromas. Look out for the Carlow cheese stall at the Saturday Carlow Market, where Elizabeth sells not only her own cheeses but a good selection of other perfectly presented Irish farmhouse cheeses. (Elizabeth Bradley, Ballybrommell, Fenagh ☎ 087-6124452 ✉ ebradley@ gofree.indigo.ie)

Free Range Chickens
● Carlow Foods Limited

Carlow Foods produce excellent free-range chickens, and short of buying one of the organically-reared birds you will find in some parts of the country, Celine and Bertram Salter's fowl are as good as you can get: chickens that cook well, giving moist flesh and a crisp skin, that carve and eat well, and which are a true friend to the cook. You will find them in many of the better butcher's shops. (Bertram & Celine Salter, Kilkea, Fenagh, Carlow ☎ 059-972 7851✉ carlowfoods@ eircom.net ⊖ www.carlowfoods.ie)

Leighlinbridge

Restaurant & Hotel
● The Lord Bagenal Hotel

James Kehoe's hotel has super-smart, super-comfortable rooms. At present, food is served in the traditional Inn, which has been offering good country cooking here for thirty years. When visiting for dinner or the popular Sunday lunch, do give yourself plenty of time to enjoy Mr Kehoe's modern art collection. (James Kehoe, Leighlinbridge ☎ 059-972 1668 ⊖ www.lordbagenal.com)

Cookery School
● Tasteworks Cookery School

Christine Jordan is one of the most dynamic people we
know. When she isn't teaching at Tasteworks, she might
be appearing on the telly in some cook-out, devising
new food products, and all the while rearing a young
family. Phew! But she not only has the energy: she also
has the culinary culture to make her school and her
work successful, thanks to a deep-rooted love of food
and an in-depth appreciation of other food cultures that
helps her focus on the primacy of simplicity in cooking, based on confidence and knowledge. Confidence
and knowledge are what you can expect to discover in
Tasteworks.(Christine Jordan, Rathellin, Leighlinbridge
☎ 059-972 2786 info@tasteworks.net www.
tasteworks.net)

St Mullins

Café & Cottages
● Mullicháin Café

Martin and Emer O'Brien bought one of the ancient
Grand Canal Company grain stores a decade ago, and
have fashioned three pretty guest cottages out of the old
coach house and stables. Most recently, they transformed
the grain store into the Mullicháin Café. It's a space that
suits this idyllic part of the Barrow Valley: hidden, mystical,
friendly, a place apart, a discovery that seems like a revela-
tion. We want to get the kayaks up here to the beautiful Barrow as it twists and bends through this glorious
countryside. (Martin & Emer O'Brien, St Mullins ☎ 051-
424 440 info@oldgrainstorecottages.ie www.
oldgrainstorecottages.ie – 11am-6pm Tue-Sun during high
season. Check off season and bank holidays.)

Tinnahinch

Restaurant
● Boats Bistro

"Nowhere nicer than Boats Bistro on a sunny evening
overlooking the River Barrow". Ah, can't you just see
yourself in Arnie and Georgina Poole's riverside bistro,

glass of wine in hand, appetite primed for some nice cooking, the evening stretching ahead of you... Locals, like our friend Belinda who describes Boats Bistro, are fervent fans of the Poole's relaxed style, and Boats is one of those magical places in this magical river zone. (Arnie & Georgina Poole, The Quayside, Tinnahinch ☎ 059-972 5075 – Open noon-4pm, 6pm-close Tue-Sat, noon-7pm Sun)

Tullow

Cookery School
● **Ballyderrin Cookery School**

Cookery school. Bed and Breakfast. Farm shop. Coffee shop. Farmers' Market stallholder. Hamper and voucher offers. Multi-tasking doesn't come into it, when you consider all the things Pamela Holligan does in Ballyderrin House, but then Ms Holligan used to do that multi-tasking in the corporate world before she relocated to Tullow to this pretty house and began to multi-task all over again. (Pamela Holligan, Ballyderrin House, Shillelagh Road, Tullow ☎ 059-915 2742 ✉ ballyderrinhouse@ eircom.net ⊕ www.ballyderrin.com)

Fruit Liqueurs
● **Boozeberries**

It is Michelle Power's expertise as a herbalist that shines through in her unique Boozeberries liqueurs. Mixing blueberries, cranberries and blackberries with grain spirit is the sort of difficult balancing act that requires supreme skill to accentuate the fruit content whilst keeping the spirit level mellow and tolerable. Ms Power manages this balance with assurance, and she also understands the imperative of making a bottle of Boozeberries look sexy. (Michelle Power, Ballyconnell Lodge, Ballyconnell, Tullow ☎ 059-915 6312 ✉ info@boozeberries.com ⊕ www.boozeberries.com)

Chocolates
● **The Chocolate Garden**

Customers can actually visit this chocolate factory, even without a golden ticket, but you can also buy on line. These chocolates are made by the company which featured in our Guide formerly as Wicklow Fine

Foods, who were in particular known for their fine biscuits - and their promise is to "guarantee to have you in raptures of gourmet ecstasy". Well, bring it on. The company also produces Tipperary Organic Ice Cream. (Jim & Mary Healy, Rath, Tullow ☎ 059-648 1999 ✉ info@chocolategarden.ie ⌂ www.chocolategarden.ie)

Farmhouse Cheese
● Coolattin Cheddar Cheese

Tom Burgess's farmhouse cheese is closest to a territo-rial cheddar cheese in style, yet also has some elements of a Comte-style to it, so it's a true sport of nature. But what is undoubted is the clean alignment of flavours Mr Burgess brings forth, thanks to excellent cheesemaking using his own summer pasture, morning raw milk from happy cows. Coolattin offers sweet notes at the top, a touch of spice, a long, mellow aftertaste that shows the careful maturation of the cheese. Look for it in par-ticular at Elizabeth Bradley's cheese stall at the Carlow Farmers' Market on Saturday morning. A beautiful, elemental farmhouse food. (Tom Burgess, Knockeen, Tullow ☎ 059-915 6189 ✉ tofiburgess@eircom.net ⌂ www.coolattincheddar.com)

Butcher's Shop
● Laz Murphy

The Murphy family butcher's shop in pretty Tullow village is the star of the locale. Local stock from local farms is handled with expert care, so you get proper foods here: their own sausages; spiced beef, good blood puddings, corned beef. "We have a bond with them", is what Mr Murphy says of his local suppliers, so get that solid bond into your life in this wonderful shop. (Laz Murphy, Church Street, Tullow ☎ 059-915 1316 ✉ jimmurphy12@eircom.net – Open 9am-6pm Mon-Fri, 8am-6pm Sat)

County Cavan

Belturbet

Farmhouse Cheese
● **Corleggy Farmhouse Cheese**

Silke Cropp is one of the great Irish cheesemakers, dedicated to the art and craft of raw milk cheesemaking. In addition, she is a pioneer of the farmers' markets system, played a major role in the early days of the Dublin Food Co-Op, and has played a major part in Slow Food Ireland events. Along the way she has also found time to educate nascent cheesemakers in the art form she masters every day in her cheesemaking. She is, in every way, a force for good, but above all it is her cheeses – the soft Quivy and the hard goat's milk cheese Corleggy, the range of Drumlin cheeses made from raw cow's milk – that guarantee her reputation as one of the most outstandng artisans of the last 30 years. There are no other cheeses in Ireland like these, with their sport-of-nature shapes, the open, appealing flavours and textures, their complexities and sense of wonderment, their versatility and sheer goodness. (Silke Cropp, Belturbet ☎ 049-952 2930 ✉ corleggy@eircom. net 🖰 www.corleggy.com)

---

only in Cavan
Drumully Dumpling Boxty

Crêpes
● **Crêpes in the City**

Tina Cropp knows good food, thanks to an upbringing on Corleggy farm. and her crêpe carts and vans have become a staple not just of the Dublin weekend markets, but also of hip music festivals and hip private parties: Tina actually had two crêpe carts at Electric Picnic in 2009! The savoury and sweet crêpes are beautifully conceived, use the choicest of ingredients, and are executed with an epicurean zeal. (Tina Cropp, Coragh, Belturbet ☎ 049-952 4861 ✉ crêpesinthecity@hotmail.com 🖰 www.crêpes.ie)

Blacklion

Cavan

Restaurant with Rooms
● **MacNean House & Restaurant**

Some folk can find heaven in a grain of sand. Neven Maguire is one of those people. Everyday, he will tell you, he thanks his lucky stars that he comes from the wee hamlet of Blacklion. You might think Blacklion is unexceptionable but, for Mr Maguire, it is the centre of the universe, the place where he has the luck to practice his extraordinary skills. Neven Maguire is one of the greatest Irish chefs because he is a generous man, and his cooking exudes that generosity, not least in the exquisite balance and broadness of his incredible tasting menus, where he pays tribute to the taste and texture of superb foods with the fealty of a besotted young man. Staying at MacNean and eating at MacNean is not simply one of the great food experiences, it is one of the great life experiences. (Neven & Amelda Maguire, Blacklion ☎ 071-985 3022 ✉ info@macneanrestaurant.com 🖰 www.macneanrestaurant.com – Open 6.30pm-9.30pm Wed-Sun; 12.30pm & 3.30pm Sun)

Duck and Geese Farm
● **Thornhill Ducks**

To see the full, delicious glory of Ken Moffat's lovely ducks, try the duck plate at the MacNean: confit duck leg, sautéed breast, and foie gras terrine, served with balsamic jelly, local foods ennobled into magnificence, thanks to two great local talents. (Ken Moffat, Thornhill, Blacklion ☎ 071-985 3044 ✉ thornhillfarm@eircom.net)

Cavan

Butcher
● **Barry John Crowe**

BJ Crowe is a serious talent, a serious charcutier who seems to have no limits to both his skills and his ambitions. He has already fashioned one of the most exciting range of specialist sausages that you will find in Ireland, and like the very best butchers he knows that the true skills of a butchers shop shine through in producing good bangers and bacon, good puddings, and properly hung meats. (BJ Crowe, 2 Connolly Street, Cavan ☎ 049-436 2671 – Open 8am-6pm, till 7pm on Fri)

● The Oak Room

Norbert Neylon showed his aplomb as a chef early on in his career – he was winner of the young chefs award back in 1997 – and in the handsome and comfortable rooms of The Oak Room that aplomb is everywhere evident in his gutsy but gracious cooking. He likes classic pairings – fillet of beef with onion compote; roast duck with garlic potato; pan-fried salmon with lemon; brie with red currant compote; chicken with bacon and sage and onion stuffing – and this classical approach suits the elegant textures and tastes he offers in every plate. (Norbert Neylon, 62 Main Street, Cavan ☎ 049-437 1414 ✒ info@theoakroom.ie ☝ www.theoakroom. ie – Open Dinner Tue-Sat from 5.30pm. Bank hol Sundays open 6.30pm-9.30pm)

Cloverhill

● Olde Post Inn

We are serious admirers of the ways in which Tara and Gearoid have developed their quaint and comfortable restaurant with rooms over the last few years. Step by step, piece by piece, they have improved and upgraded, adding a conservatory, improving the rooms upstairs, and yet all the time basing the core of their offer on Tara's superlative service and Gearoid's superlative cooking. Put this pair to work together, and it makes for a dream team, working in what has become a great destination address. The cooking is particularly impressive, deeply rooted in classic techniques – Mr Lynch worked with John Howard in Dublin's legendary Le Coq Hardi, and it shows in the correctness of everything he sends out of the kitchen – but with loads of flavour, flair and organoleptic oomph! In particular, Mr Lynch is a master at orchestrating varying textures in his food, particularly with game dishes, so each dish is wonderfully tactile. It's a great spot to get away to for a few days in lovely Cavan, helped by the fact that the service in the Olde Post is amongst the very best. Great breakfasts too, by the way. (Gearoid Lynch & Tara McCann, Cloverhill, Butler's Bridge ☎ 047-55555 ✒ gearoidlynch@ eircom.net ☝ www.theoldepostinn.com – Open 6.30pm-9pm Tue-Thu, 6.30pm-9.30pm Fri & Sat, 5.30pm-8.30pm Sun)

Cootehill

Deli
● O'Leary's

Niall O'Leary is proud of his shop, proud of the care he puts into his cooking and baking, proud of the business of running a good deli with good things for people to enjoy. That's the way shopkeepers should be, and that's the way O'Leary's is. The shop only has two tables and four chairs, but customers like to loiter, perhaps sitting outside and enjoying a cup of Illy coffee as the cosmopolitanism of Cootehill unfolds before their very eyes. For a small place like Cootehill, this shop is exceptional. There will often be twelve types of home-made salads, home-made breads, quiches still warm from the oven, fresh produce coming from both the kitchen and the locality and some special foods from Europe, like their varieties of olives or the cheese-stuffed chillies. There are wines, ice creams and fresh vegetables. All in all a cornucopia of good things. (Niall O'Leary, 14 Bridge Street, Cootehill ☎ 049-555 2142 - Open 9am-6.30pm Mon-Sat)

Killeshandra

Boxty
● Drummully Boxty

"Boxty is my passion" says Paul Farrelly of the little orbs of potato he makes and sells in the region. "It was actually always a Hallowe'en dish and, like Christmas Pudding, it was never eaten outside of its season." Paul makes his product seasonally, and you can only buy it in the independent retailers and Supervalus and Centras in this locality. It truly is a regional, seasonal speciality.
The type of boxty he mostly sells is his favourite "dumpling boxty", more complex and indeed less economical than the "pan boxty" which is favoured more in the West of Ireland. Boxty is a mixture of raw and cooked potato, moulded into a cylinder. It's a speciality of Cavan, Leitrim, Longford and parts of Fermanagh, where the same product is called a "hurley". Paul's version is suitable for both coeliacs and vegetarians, and we share his passion for this fab food, and salute his determination to maintain its seasonal character and nature. (Paul Farrelly, Drummully, Killeshandra ☎ 049-433 4626)

Organic Meat
● **Irish Organic Meats**

Declan and Deirdre's splendid organic meat stall can
be found at farmers' markets in Carrick-on-Shannon,
Roscommon, Sligo and Boyle, so they tour the north
west selling the foods of the north west, as their organic
beef and lamb comes from Sligo and Roscommon,
and their organic chickens are from Cavan. (Declan &
Deirdre McCarthy, Burren, Killeshandra ☎ 049-433 3915
✉ irishorganicmeats@eircom.net)

Stradone

Chocolate Shop
● **Aine Hand-Made Chocolates**

Ann Rudden has moved to Stradone from her base
in County Meath, and whilst her retail outlet no
longer exists the exceptional quality and luxury brand
appearance of her hand-made chocolates remains
as consistent today as it has been since Ann started
tempering her magic ten years ago. We really like
her new hot chocolate stick, which you whirl and
swirl around your warm milk, building up anticipation
for that first delicious sip. Expert, precise chocolate
artistry. (Ann Rudden, Stradone Village ☎ 049-854 2769
✉ info@aineschocolates.com ⚲ www.chocolates.ie)

Virginia

Preserves
● **Govender's**

Dion and Jane Govender make seriously fine relishes
and chutneys, made with the sort of culinary experience and expertise that places these chutneys as true
heirloom samples. You will find them in Dublin markets
such as Farmleigh, and also in good shops such as Fallon
& Byrne or Supervalu Mount Merrion in Dublin, or more
locally in O'Leary's deli in Cootehill. Once tasted, they
are as essential to an Indian meal as Green Saffron spices.
(Dion & Jane Govender, Ryefield, Virginia ☎ 087-975 6554
✉ sales@govenders.com ⚲ www.govenders.com)

County Clare

Ballina

Restaurant
● **The Cherry Tree**

It's not the lovely lakeside location, or the striking modern dining room, that most characterise Harry McKeogh's restaurant. Instead, through a decade of work, it is the rigorous standards of professionalism, and the subtle and organically-inspired creativity shown by the kitchen, that have made the Cherry Tree such a valuable address. Seasonal local ingredients inspire the kitchen to maintain the highest standards, and smashing service by local ladies plants the cherry firmly on the top of this superb confection of good taste. (Harry McKeogh, Lakeside, Ballina, Killaloe ☎ 061-375688 🖰 www.cherrytreerestaurant.ie – Open 6pm-10pm Tue-Sat, 12.30pm-3pm Sun)

Ballynacally

Farmhouse Cheese
● **Bluebell Falls Goat's Cheese**

Bluebell Falls cheese really does hail from the most blue-bell-bedecked set of waterfalls we have ever seen: visit the farm in May and the place is a veritable colour-field of greeny-purpleness. Paul Keane's pale white cheese is sold very fresh, but the piquant nature of the flavours kicks in straight away, and explains why this cheese is so popular. Don't think Bluebell Falls is only for cooking, either: leave it for a week or two in a cold place and its rapidly maturing pungentness will marry happily with some robust Syrah. (Paul Keane, Ballynacally ☎ 065-683 8024 🖼 bluebellfalls@eircom.net)

only in Clare
Burren Lamb

Ballyvaughan

Farmhouse Cheese and other produce
● Aillwee Cave

If the Johnson family were in charge of signage throughout Ireland, no tourist would ever go astray from their
desired destination. Aillwee cave is the best-signposted
destination in Ireland, and is one of the best destinations in Ireland. It attracts a huge number of visitors,
and as a cave experience and a tourist centre it is hard
to beat, for the professionalism evident here in every
detail gladdens the soul. In the shop, look out above all
for Ben Johnson's cracking Burren Gold cheeses, the
true star of a very fine retail roustabout that boasts lots
of other superb local foods. (Ben Johnson, Ballyvaughan
☎ 065-707 7036 🖱 www.aillweecave.ie – Open 10am-
5pm Mon-Sun)

Cafe
● An Fear Gorta

A sweet and lovely tea rooms in the sweetest, loveliest
little cottage imaginable. Jane O'Donoghue has carried
on the noble tradition of her Mum, Catherine, in serving
superb savouries and superlative teas, and has brought
back to Ballyvaughan the expertise garnered from working in Dublin's Four Seasons Hotel. This is an exciting
new dynamic for one of the great destinations of County
Clare, and one of the most characterful rooms anywhere.
(Jane O'Donoghue, Pier Road, Ballyvaughan ☎ 065-
707 7023 – Open day-time. Open in high summer only)

Farmers' Market
● Ballyvaughan Farmers' Market

Consider this: several editions ago, there were no farmers' markets in County Clare described in the Bridgestone Irish Food Guide. Now, on Saturday morning, you
will find great local foods and crafts in Ballyvaughan,
and also in Doolin and in Newmarket-on-Fergus. On
Fridays, you can get your market fix in Ennis, Kinvara
and Miltown Malbay. Sundays is for Killaloe, and there
is a monthly market in Quin. Thursdays is for the great
market in Kilrush. Local producers selling locally grown
and made foods, and none of it existed less than a decade ago, everything from Maya Fire chilli sauce to Devine
lemon curd to Eve Hegarty's free-range pork to

Una O'Dwyer's salads. Many of the markets also feature splendid crafts, and some even have authors and artists exhibiting and selling. And to think none of this creative dynamic was being expressed only a decade ago! (St John's Hall car park, Saturday 10am)

Shop, Café and Hampers
● Burren Fine Food & Wine

Cathleen Connole's shop is hard by the side of the road as Corkscrew Hill wends its way south out of Ballyvaughan. So, pull into the little car park in front of the shop, have something light and true and tasty to eat if you are hungry, otherwise just buy some excellent wines and hampers of smartly-selected foods and gifts. This is an astute and personal food and wine venture, and we applaud it heartily. (Cathleen Connole, Corkscrew Hill Road, Ballyvaughan ☎ 065-707 7046 📠 info@burrenwine.ie ⬦ www.burrenwine.ie – food served 11am-5pm)

Accommodation & Restaurant
● Gregan's Castle Hotel

Simon and Freddy Haden's house is the most aesthetically inspired destination in the most aesthetically inspired location, hidden by the edge of the road of Corkscrew Hill, looking down on Ballyvaughan, Galway Bay and the limestone magnificence of the north Burren hills. With chef Mickael Viljanen in the kitchen, the aesthetic of the house and the place has been matched by a style of cooking whose complete command of aesthetic beauty is nothing short of breathtaking. Weaving themes and variations around simple local ingredients – Burren lamb; west coast fish; peas; garlic; beetroot; strawberries – Mr Viljanen concocts dishes that are earthy in their depth of taste yet refined to the most poetic sensibility, with every plate as pretty as the most delicate Japanese painting. Gregan's has been enjoying a thunderous renaissance under Simon and Freddy that has made it into one of Europe's leading places to stay and eat, but what has impressed us most is that they simply continue to improve, year in, year out, with every element – food, comfort, design, hospitality – all enjoying upgrades every year. A classic. (Simon Haden, Ballyvaughan ☎ 065-707 7005 📠 stay@gregans.ie ⬦ www.gregans.ie – Open 16 March-27 Nov, Restaurant open 8am-11.30am, 12.30pm-2.30pm, 6.30pm-8.30pm)

THE BRIDGESTONE IRISH FOOD GUIDE

Italian Restaurant
● L'Arco

Ballyvaughan has a funny thing about real Italian food, because it was here that the original Holywell opened up many years ago with its rustic Italian food offer. And now here is another slice of authenticity from the team of Italian chefs in George Quinn's restaurant. What impressed our friend Sile was the fact that the ravioli take a decent while to get served. But that's simply because they're concocting them freshly in the kitchen. And when that spinach and ricotta ravioli, with its butter and sage sauce, finally makes it to the table, it's been more than worth the wait. The pizzas are also very good, and, as you would expect in a decent Italian restaurant, the wines and the coffees are spot on. (George Quinn, Main Street, Ballyvaughan ☎ 065-708 3900 ⌂ www.burrenrestaurant.com – Open from 6pm)

Bar
● O'Loclainn's Bar

"I think you said it is the pub of one's dreams, and we agree!". That's what our friend Maya wrote after a visit to Peter O'Lochlainn's wee pub, just down the pier road out of Ballyvaughan. Actually, it isn't a pub: it's a cocoon, a womb, of good drinks – Maya discovered Green Spot whiskey, always a great day in anyone's life – and a genuinely timeless aesthetic that cannot be found anywhere else in the world. The universe in a pub: here it is. (Peter O'Lochlainn, Ballyvaughan ☎ 065-707 7006 ⌂ drink@irishwhiskeybar.com ⌂ www.irishwhiskeybar.com)

Bunratty

Cookery School
● Bunratty Cookery School

Donna Gregson is one of the movers and shakers of Slow Food in County Clare, and demonstrated impressively at the 2009 Festival in Lisdoonvarna. She is a professional to her fingertips, so anyone who wants to unlock the secrets of the kitchen, and thereby improve their life, could hardly do better than to have Donna to show you how in this attractive and dynamic new school. (Donna Gregson, Manderley House, Deerpark, Bunratty ☎ 061-713500 ⌂ www.bunrattycookeryschool.ie)

Carrigaholt

Clare

● The Long Dock

Tony Lynch's fine old bar is known to locals as "The Dock", and once you have mastered the local patois you can get stuck into some truly special cooking. Fish predominates, along with traditional dishes like liver and bacon, or bacon and cabbage with parsley sauce. Calamari salad is spot on, but pales beside fantastic mussels with white wine, shallots and garlic. Plaice is stuffed with Carrigaholt crab, whilst lemon sole simply has a brown butter, and both are perfect. "Everything tasted of itself", says Valerie O'Connor, who reckons The Dock is nothing less than "a gem". A warning: you will have to be wheeled out if you finish with the chocolate brownie with chocolate ice cream and chocolate sauce. Be ready to be wheeled out. (Tony Lynch, Carrigaholt ☎ 065-905 8106 ⌂ www.thelongdock.com – Food served 11am-11.30am Sun-Thur, 11am-12.30am Fri & Sat)

only in Clare
The Burren Perfumery

Fishmonger
● Sea Lyons Seafood Sales

"We eat, drink and live it" is how Gearoid Lyons describes his involvement and his life with fishing and the fishing industry. He may not work the trawlers any more, but his involvement with fish is still intense, running the factory shop at Carrigaholt as well as a fleet of fish vans that work counties Clare, Limerick and Kerry, as well as a home delivery service. "It's our whole life", says Gearoid. (Gearoid Lyons, Carrigaholt ☎ 065-905 8222)

Carron

Farm Co-operative
● Burren Beef and Lamb Producers Group

A visionary venture that brings together farmers engaged in low-intensity farming, whose animals are

conservation grade, and who are keen to trade sustainably and directly with the consumer. It might sound counter-intuitive to say that if you want to do your best to protect the uniqueness of the Burren that you should consume animals who graze there, but in fact it makes perfect, sustainable – and delicious – sense.
(Ruairí Ó Conchúir, Old School House, Carron ☎ 065-708 9008 ✉ burrenproducers@gmail.com ⌂ www.burrenlife.com)

Café & Perfumery
● The Burren Perfumery

We are in awe of what Sadie Chowan has achieved in the Burren Perfumery, with its gardens, tea rooms and perfumery. But not so much in awe that we don't make sure to visit this unique place every time are in the magical county of Clare, and we strongly advise you to do the same. The aesthetic of the perfumier touches every part of this beautiful enterprise, gifting balance, beauty, and a narcotic sense of otherness to one of the most brilliant places to visit and eat. (Sadie Chowan, Carron ☎ 065-708 9102 ✉ burrenperfumery@eircom.net ⌂ www.burrenperfumery.com – Perfumery open all year. Tea rooms open Apr-Sept, 10am-5pm Mon-Sun)

Pub
● Cassidy's Croide na Boirne

The view of the turlough – will it be there? Will it have disappeared? – is one of the big attractions of Cassidy's, along with some nice food. A lovely place to pause for that oh-so-refreshing pint as you hike the Burren. (Michelle Cassidy, Carron ☎ 065-708 9109 ✉ info@cassidyspub.com ⌂ www.cassidyspub.com – Food served day-time and early-evening)

Cratloe

Farmhouse Cheese
● Cratloe Hills Sheep's Cheese

The mature Cratloe Hills – you will know it by its golden exterior – is a unique sheep's milk cheese, ruddily piquant, superb as a cooking tool where it happily replaces any need for Parmesan, whilst adding tasty lustre all of its own. A summer lasagne of courgettes and basil made with lots of sliced and grated Cratloe Hills: now you are talking the real West Coast cooking! (Sean & Deirdre Fitzgerald, Cratloe ☎ 061-357185 ✉ cratloehills-cheese@eircom.net ⌂ www.cratloehillscheese.com)

Clare

Sheeps milk cheese

Doolin

● The Clare Jam Company

They are true artisans, are David and Vera Muir. The care in their work, the culture in their creativity, combine to help them to make superb jams and marmalades. In a world where so many jams and preserves are concoctions of the ersatz, the Clare jams are the real thing: distinctive, true, unique, and the shop is a don't miss! (David & Vera Muir, Lough North, Doolin ☎ 065-707 4778 ✉ christinemuir@eircom.net)

● Cullinan's Restaurant & Guest House

We guess that the best way to register our respect for what James and Carol Cullinan are doing is to say that they feature in our Bridgestone 100 Best Places to Stay in Ireland books. They are 100 Best material, simple as that, and their house has excellent rooms – the newer ones overlooking the river are the ones to aim for – and the kitchen has earthy, true cooking matched with a professional élan. Happy food in a happy place from a dedicated couple. That's the stuff, isn't it just? (James & Carol Cullinan, Doolin ☎ 065-707 4183 ✉ info@cullinansdoolin.com ⌂ www.cullinansdoolin.com – Open Easter-October 6pm-9pm Mon-Sat, closed Wed)

● **Roadford House**

Frank Sheedy is a tremendous cook, the sort of culinary magician who so delights people that you can expect e-mails from people who have just eaten here, telling you that this guy is one of the best, and be in no doubt about it. We are in no doubt about it at all, especially the incredible desserts that conclude the meal, and which are the tipping point to persuade people that they just have to tell everyone what they have just discovered. To get the most out of the Roadford experience, book a room and don't miss a taste of this brilliance. (Frankie Sheedy, Doolin ☎ 065-707 5050 ✉ roadfordhouse@eircom. net ✆ www.roadfordrestaurant.com – Open 6pm-9pm Mon-Sun)

Clare

● **Stonecutter's Kitchen**

Myles and Karen know what they can do well in the Stonecutters, and well they do it. The ingredients are good, and are cooked with care: good chowder, nice fish cakes, a deep-tasting beef stew, a fresh bowl of soup. You simply can't tire of the good simplicity of this food. (Myles & Karen Duffy, Lough North, Doolin ☎ 065-707 5962 ✉ stonecutterskitchen@eircom.net ✆ www.stonecutterskitchen.com – Open 12.30pm-9.30pm Mon-Sun during high season. Hours vary off season)

Doonbeg

● **Morrissey's Pub**

Hugh McNally has transformed this lovely pub from a traditional Irish bar into a svelte restaurant with rooms, yet he has somehow managed to keep the graceful ambience of the old place, so Morrissey's enjoys a relaxed, timeless feeling. The cooking is modern, flavour-filled and very accessible, so it's a great family get-away, and when the kids have eaten and escape off to the riverside to play, you get a chance to drink in the charms of this singular address. (Hugh McNally, Doonbeg ☎ 065-905 5304 ✉ hughmcnally@hotmail. com ✆ www.morrisseysdoonbeg.com – Open 12.30pm-3pm, 6pm-9pm Mon-Sun)

Ennis

Clare

Chocolate Shop
● Chocolat

Grainne McCormick's Chocolat is a beaut of a shop,
with all the best chocolates you can name and lots of
imaginative gift ideas to seduce your intended with a
blast of the finest narcotic. Best of all, just walking in the
door feels like a treaty treat, just as a chocolate shop
visit should. (Grainne McCormick, Barrack Street, Ennis
☎ 065-686 8599 ✉ chocolatennis@eircom.net – Open
10am-6pm Mon-Sat)

Farmers' Market
● Ennis Farmers' Market

New arrivals into the Friday morning market in Ennis,
such as Annette Minihan, and Eoin McEntee's West
Clare artisan breads, have ensured that this great market
has maintained its mighty dynamic. We think County
Clare has one of the best food cultures in the country,
and to see and buy the proof of the pudding, just turn up
here and marvel in the work of talented – and sociable!
– food people, who just love their work. You, lucky you,
will love it even more. (Upper Market Street, Ennis,
Friday 8am-2pm)

Shop & Café
● Ennis Gourmet Store

Anne Leyden has been the stalwart shopkeeper and
restaurateur in Ennis for some years now – since 1997
in fact – and her little store is – literally – jam-packed
with good things from near and far. For Clare artisans,
the GS is often the first destination when they go to
the marketplace, so look carefully for hot new foods
and brand new arrivals, for this county has one of the
best food cultures in Ireland, and some of the most
impressively creative specialist producers. The bistro
serves excellent cooking, and anyone who wants to
say "Thank you!" to a food loving friend should note
that their regional hamper service is nothing less
than legendary. (Anne Leyden & David Lasblaye, 1
Barrack Street, Ennis ☎ 065-684 3314, ✉ hampers@
ennisgourmet.com ✆ www.ennisgourmet.com – Open
10am-7pm Mon-Sun. In summer open 10am-9pm on
Thur & Fri)

● The Fish Market

Val Egan's shop has simply improved and prospered since Mr Egan opened his doors in 1997. Mr Egan works in prtnership with Garrihy's Seafoods in Doolin, a long-established family firm, so the choice here is always superbly fresh, just the way all the customers like it. (Val Egan, 19 Lwr Market Street, Ennis ☎ 065-684 2424 – Open 9.15am-6pm Tue-Fri, 9.15am-1.30pm Sat)

Traiteur
● The Food Emporium

TJ McGuinness runs a nice space here, just across from the convent, specialising in food-to-go, and everything is always correctly made and served in this amiable traiteur. (TJ McGuinness, 8-9 Francis St, Ennis ☎ 065-682 0554 – Open 9am-6pm Mon-Sat)

Café
● Food Heaven

Noirin's Food Heaven is one busy place, and not just at lunchtime, when the queue stretches back to the door and beyond, and when getting a seat is the tough question. Good tasty modern cooking. (Noirin Furey, 21 Market Street, Ennis ☎ 065-682 2722 ✉ n-furey@yahoo.ie – Open 8.30am-6.30pm Mon-Sat)

Café
● Glor

The café of the theatre in Ennis is a good spot for coffee and light lunches, and do check out their very fine crafts shop which has superb work by Irish artisan producers. (Tom Quinn, Friar's Walk, Ennis ☎ 065-684 3103 - info@glor.ie ✍ www.glor.ie – Open daytime – Open 10am-5pm, lunch served noon-5pm)

Butcher
● Derek Molloy

Derek Molloy is a talented, dedicated charcutier, and whether you shop at his traditional butcher's in the centre of town or the new shop at the shopping centre, you get skill and good service in both places. Shops like Molloys are the backbone of every food culture. (Derek Molloy, Abbey Street, Ennis ☎ 065-682 3296 – Open

9am-6pm Mon-Sat and Roslevan Shopping Centre, Tulla Road, Ennis ☎ 065-686 8350 ✉ molloybutchers@eircom.net – Open 9am-7pm Mon-Fri, 9am-6pm Sat)

Hotel
● The Old Ground Hotel

We are big fans of Allen Flynn's hotel, which seems to us to marry the virtues of an old-style welcome with good comfort, especially in the modern rooms of the hotel. The bar is a good space, the live music is fun at the weekends. (Allen Flynn, O'Connell St, Ennis ☎ 065-682 8127 ✉ reservations@oldgroundhotel.ie ✎ www. oldgroundhotel.com – Open mid Jan-end Dec)

Wholefood Shop
● Open Sesame

Sally Smith's OS was one of the pioneer shops in County Clare – it opened as long go as 1988 – and continues to fly the flag as a driven and dynamic wholefood destination, packed with good things. There is also a second OS in Gort. (Sally Smith, 35 Parnell St, Ennis ☎ 065-682 1480 ✉ opensesame@eircom.net ✎ www.opensesame.ie – Open 9am-6pm Mon-Sat)

Fishmonger
● Rene Cusack

"I want to make shopping here as pleasureable an experience as I can", says Paul Cusack, and there are few in the fish business who know just as well as Mr Cusack how to make the purchase of a few fillets into something elemental and delightful. Cusack's dates all the way back to 1910, and it is one of the proudest brands in Irish seafood. A century of distinguished retailing in Ireland: now, isn't that something to celebrate! (Paul Cusack, Market Street, Ennis ☎ 065-689 2712 – Open 9am-6pm Mon-Sat)

Restaurant
● The Town Hall Café

More bistro than café, perhaps, but whatever you decide about its style, one can't doubt that the THC is one of the key addresses in Ennis, and has been serving consistently excellent food for many years now. It's part of the Old Ground Hotel, and shares the same virtues of consistency, character, and a particularly lovely Clare calmness that we find very winning indeed. (Allen Flynn, O'Connell Street, Ennis ☎ 065-682 8127 ☝ www. flynnhotels.com – Open 10am-noon for coffee, noon-5pm lunch, 6pm-10pm dinner)

Wine
● The Wine Buff

We always have great chats with the owners of the various Wine Buff franchises that operate throughout Ireland, as we meander through the shops and put together a case of wines. The owners are charming, quietly knowledgeable men, guys who avoid the hard sell in favour of making sure that you get exactly the sort of bottle of wine that will have you coming back quickly for another bottle of the same. The shops import wines selected by Paddy O'Flynn, who is based in Bordeaux, and there are many cracking bottles, all offered at very good value indeed. Eamon Cagney flys the flag with distinction in Ennis. (Eamon Cagney, 36C Lower Market Street, Ennis ☎ 065-684 2082 ☝ www.thewinebuff.com)

Ennistymon

Restaurant with Rooms
● Byrne's Restaurant & Townhouse

This handsome townhouse on the main street has been run successfully by Richard and Mary Byrne for more than a decade. There are six suites, and an atmospheric restaurant which has some lovely views of the river. It's a very relaxing room, and there is a lot of style to this operation. (Richard & Mary Byrne, Main Street, Ennisty-mon ☎ 065-707 1080 ✉ enquiries@byrnesennistymon. net ☝ www.byrnes-ennistymon.net – Open lunch during summer, 6.30pm-9.30pm Mon-Sat, reservations recom-mended)

Farmhouse Cheese
● Mount Callan Cheddar

We bought a piece of two-year-old Mount Callan at the 2009 Slow Food Clare festival, drove it safely back home to West Cork, and when we sliced it and ate it we mar-velled at just what a superb cheesemaker Lucy Hayes is. Every fine quality that you hope to find in a mature, hard territorial-style cheese – typicity, sweetness, warmth of flavour, complexity of texture, allied with an endless aftertaste – were all present and correct in what is one of the greatest cheeses in all of Ireland. (Lucy Hayes, Drinagh, Ennistymon ☎ 065-707 2008 ✉ mtcallan@ oceanfree.net)

Clare

Bakery
● Unglert's Bakery

As ageless as the Burren limestone, Unglert's is a sweet and wholesome bakery, with sweet and wholesome breads and cakes. Picture postcard perfect. (Mr Unglert, Ennistymon ☎ 065-707 1217 – Open 9am-6pm Tue-Sat)

only in Clare
Organic St Tola Goat's Cheese Log

Fanore

Restaurant
● Holywell Trattoria

The Holywell Trattoria is one of the four Holywell restaurants, the others are in Ennis, Lahinch and also Galway city. They serve good pastas and pizzas, and wonderful ice creams, and families love them. (Wolfgang Dietl, Fanore, ☎ 065-707 6971 ⌂ www.holywell.net – Open 11am-11pm, evenings only off season)

Restaurant
● Vasco

"Our staff eat here". Ho, ho! There is not just a smart, left-field way of thinking and cooking in Ross Quinn and Karen McGuinness's restaurant and deli, there is wit as well. And Vasco is left-field: flatbread pizza with Lebanese-style lamb; pasta with Tuscan white beans; today's catch a la plancha, and what can you say about "double-fried crumbly pommes frites", other than "Can I have another bowl, please?". One of those sports of nature that County Clare seems so good at conjuring out of the ether, Vasco really is one to watch. (Ross Quinn & Karen McGuinness, Craggagh, Fanore ☎ 065-707 6020 ⌂ www.vasco.ie Open 10.30am-11pm Mon-Sun June-Sept, check their winter hours on their website)

Flagmount

Confectionary
● Bizzy Lizzy Ltd

Helene Gooman's handsome range of sweeties, from Turkish Delight to nougat, fudge and rumballs, can be found in many good Irish delis. (Helene Goomans, Lakefield Lodge, Cahermurphy, Flagmount ☎ 061-921900)

Inagh

Farmhouse Cheese
● Inagh Farmhouse Cheeses

"We all come back to the land and the earth", Siobhan ni Ghairbhith told a Slow Food audience in Lisdoonvarna in 2008, when describing her journey from teaching back to the practice of being a dairy agriculturist and cheesemaker. She also told us that "We all have wishes and ideals, and if you are determined they will come true." Siobhan's wishes and ideals are expressed through her organic raw milk St Tola goat's cheeses, and few ideals about nature, the environment and a creative food culture are expressed at such an artistic pitch. Yes, these goat's cheese have soul, but they have more than that: they have the passion and dedication of the cheesemaker in every bite. In this sense, the St Tola cheeses are nothing less than a life force. "The West Clare land is reflected in the cheeses", says Siobhan. Ms ni Ghairbhith is also reflected in her superlative cheeses. (Siobhan ni Ghairbhith, Inagh ☎ 065-683 6633 📧 info@st-tola.ie 🖰 www.st-tola.ie)

Kilfenora

Free Range Pork
● Burren Free Range Pork

Stephen and Eva Hegarty rear delicious pork which is then transformed into sausages, bacon joints, chops, roasts, hams, belly roasts, and home-cured bacon. Look out for it, sold frozen in all the best Clare country markets. (Stephen & Eva Hegarty, Kilfenora ☎ 065-708 8931)

Gastro Pub
● **Vaughan's Pub**

One of the most famus pubs for music and dancing –
particularly set dancing – in Clare, but those who say
"I won't dance, don't ask me" will be consoled that
the cooking in Vaughan's is as true and as real as the
clatter of heels. (The Vaughan family, Kilfenora ☎ 065-
708 8004)

Kilkee

Bistro and Shop
● **The Pantry Shop & Bakery**

Imelda Bourke has been feeding the locals and visitors
to Kilkee for more years than she may care to remember, but as every new season approaches she once again
brings together the dedication and skillset – and the
enthusiasm and energy – that delights everyone through
the season. Whatever you feel like, you will find it here,
in a restaurant and shop that both pulse with joie de
vivre and a love of good food. (Imelda Bourke, O'Curry
Street, Kilkee ☎ 065-905 6576 🗋 info@thepantrykil-
kee.com 🖱 www.thepantrykilkee.com)

Hotel
● **Stella Maris Hotel**

The Haugh's family's demure and modest hotel is simply
a joyful place to stay, because the emphasis is not on
blinding you with the latest gizmos and whathaveyous.
Instead, the emphasis here is simply on looking after the
guest, cooking nice food, ensuring that you have a lovely
and relaxing time altogether. That will do nicely, thank
you. (The Haugh family, Kilkee ☎ 065-905 6455
🗋 info@stellamarishotel.com 🖱 www.stellamarishotel.
com – Open all year)

Artisan Bakery
● **West Clare Artisan Bread**

Eoin McEntee changed careers mid-stream, transforming himself into an artisan baker having opted out of his
previous life as an engineer. He did courses in Ballymaloe
and UCC's Speciality Food production course, so he is
well versed in practicalities, and has carved an impressve
niche for his breads and cakes, and latterly his relishes

and chutneys. How nice to buy a London Bloomer loaf from Eoin in Kilrush on a fine Thursday morning; that's the sort of globalisation that appeals to us. (Eoin McEntee, The Ferneries, West End, Kilkee ☎ 087-989 2671 ✉ eoin@westclareartisan.com 🖰 www.westclareartisan.com)

Kilkishen

Clare

Bakery
● Sunflower Bakery

Vi Russell's bakery sells to local wholefood shops, but it is her stall at the Limerick Market on Saturday that attracts the crowds, hungry for cheese and onion loaf, rustic baguettes, fine spelt bread, light-as-air scones and tasty pies and pasties. (Vi Russell, Cappalaheen, Kilkishen ☎ 061-367924 ✉ macmcmanus@eircom.net)

only in Clare
Irish Seed Savers Association

Killaloe

Farmers' Market
● Killaloe Farmers' Market

Could there possibly be a nicer place in which to hold a Sunday market than Between the Waters, in Killaloe? Perfect. (Sunday 11am-3pm)

Kilnaboy

B&B
● Fergus View

Mary Kelleher's B&B clings fast to the virtues that made family run B&Bs the staple of Irish hospitality. A bright welcome, delicious cooking, domestic comfort that both relaxes the body, and seduces the soul. Mrs Kelleher makes it look simple, but in reality running a B&B at this standard is an art form, and she is an artist of her own world. (Mary Kelleher, Kilnaboy, Corofin ☎ 065-683 7606 ✉ deckell@indigo.ie)

Kilrush

● Kilrush Farmers' Market

Heading into its seventh year of trading, Kilrush market brings lovely things to the town on Thursday mornings: Clare cheeses, artisan breads, Minihan's amazing baking, Fleur de Sel crêpes, veg from Rahona Roots, pies, snacks and breads from Yellow Cottage, free-range pork from the Burren, and there are some nifty crafts as well from Davy O'Dea crafts. (Town Square, Thursday 9am-2pm)

Artisan Bakery
● Minihan's

Annette Minihan is an amazing talent. Some of her work – the baked vanilla cheesecake; the orange, chocolate and hazelnut tart; the sublime lemon tartlet – seem to us to take artisan patisserie to new heights, with standards far above what you expect from most market stalls. The baking is truly fine, and yet utterly earthy and pure, the work of a woman who truly understands the alchemy of cooking and baking. Ms Minihan sells in Kilrush on Thursday, in Ennis on Fridays and at Bedford Street in Limerick on Sunday. Best get there early, for this work is precious, and work of this standard is rare. Her savoury baking is no less brilliant. (Annette Minihan, Carnacalla, Kilrush ☎ 087- 675 5574 ✉ annette@minihans.com 🖱 www.minihans.com)

Lahinch

Seafood Restaurant
● Barrtra Seafood Restaurant

Respect. That is the mantra of Paul and Teresa O'Brien's lovely cottage restaurant, down towards the shore of Liscannor bay, just south of Lahinch. They grow lots of their own foods in the garden, treat them with TLC in the kitchen, gather up lots of other foods from the shores and seas around them, and the result is a restaurant with a true, enduring and endearing philosophy that respects the foods we source and eat, and the way in which it is best to enjoy them. For more than two decades the O'Briens have done their thing, their way, and we salute their tremendous achievement. (Paul & Theresa O'Brien, Barrtra, Lahinch

☎ 065-708 1280 ✉ barrtra@hotmail.com 🖱 www.
barrtra.com – Open 5pm-10pm Mon-Sun in July & Aug,
Tue-Sun summer, limited hours off-season)

Farmhouse Cheese
● Kilshanny Cheese

Peter Nibbering's Gouda-style cheeses are one of the
great staples of Clare's food culture, and one of the
most enduring. Handsome, rounded hulks of goodness, they don't get much beyond the borders of the
county, bar the Milk Market in Limerick on Saturday – so
their fudgey sweetness and pitch-perfect lactic balance
makes them a vital culinary must-have anytime you are
in the banner county. (Peter Nibbering, Derry House,
Kilshanny ☎ 065-707 1228)

Guesthouse
● Moy House

Moy is one of the dreamiest country houses – dreamy
seaside location, dreamy style and architecture, dreamy
ambience – but beneath all that make-believe, manager
Brid O'Meara and her crew exhibit the sort of dedicated
efficiency that means your dream is never displaced
by the mundanity of anything being less than perfect.
They tread lightly and deftly – and efficiently – for they
know they tread around your dream of the perfect Irish
country house experience. "We even had a turf fire
in our bedroom!", says Eamon Barrrett, impressed by
the stellar standards – and the warm welcome – that
characterises this lovely house. (Brid O'Meara, Lahinch
☎ 065-708 2800 ✉ moyhouse@eircom.net 🖱 www.
moyhouse.com – Open Feb-Dec)

Guesthouse
● Vaughan Lodge

There isn't a more professionally-focused couple in the
hospitality trade than Michael and Maria Vaughan, which
means that the smart Vaughan Lodge is your destination
should you be golfing or surfing in Lahinch. Personally,
we have never forgotten a particularly sweet birthday
party – complete with birthday cake and choruses of
"Happy Birthday To You!" which we enjoyed here just
a few years back, and that sort of thing is the Vaughan's
gift: making something simple into something special.
(Michael & Maria Vaughan, Ennistymon Road, Lahinch
☎ 065-708 1111 🖱 www.vaughanlodge.ie – Open Apr-Oct)

Liscannor

Restaurant with Rooms
● Vaughan's Anchor Inn

Dennis Vaughan cooks some of the best food in County Clare, and he has recently refurbished the upstairs bedrooms above the restaurant and bar to create a proper dinner and duvet experience, which means one can push the boat out with good wines to match his elegant food. Yes, he does the cheffy thing with tasting dishes and ingredients done two- and three- ways, but the discipline in the kitchen lets nothing go astray, and the seafood cooking in particular is right on the money, with vivid flavours captured and precisely delivered. (Denis Vaughan, Main Street, Liscannor ☎ 065-708 1548 🖰 www.vaughans.ie – Open 12.30pm-9pm Mon-Sun. Bar food daily, dinner in restaurant)

Lisdoonvarna

Smokehouse
● The Burren Smokehouse

Twenty years on from when we first met Birgitta and Peter Curtin, and their twin flagships of the Burren Smokehouse and the Roadside Tavern are as vital to the life and soul of Lisdoon' as they have ever been. Mrs Curtin is a major player both with the local Slow Food movement and with the Bord Bia-affiliated Taste Council, so she is both local dynamo and national planner, and there could be no better woman for both jobs, for she has an energy and a sensibility that are profound. The smoked fish the Curtins produce is sublime, and their visitor centre is one of the best organised don't-miss!, destinations in the county. (Birgitta Curtin, Kinkora Road, Lisdoonvarna ☎ 065-707 4432 🖰 www.burrensmokehouse.ie – Open 9.30am-5pm May-Aug, more limited hours off season)

Pub
● The Roadside Tavern

Good drinks, good food, good music, good craic. The four pillars of the culture of the Irish pub pulse hearty and well in this special place run by the Curtin family. (Peter Curtin, Kinkora Road, Lisdoonvarna ☎ 065-707 4084 🖰 www.roadsidetavern.ie)

Hotel
● Sheedy's

Sheedy's is one of those discreet, intimate family hotels that once characterised the hospitality culture of Ireland, but which have become all too rare. But that meticulously maintained, subtle and charming culture lives on here, thanks to Martina Sheedy's polite, shy service, and John Sheedy's utterly lovely, utterly logical cooking. Everything is done by hand, and such care gladdens the heart on every visit.(Martina & John Sheedy, Lisdoonvarna ☎ 065-707 4026 📠 info@sheedys.com 🖑 www. sheedys.com)

Restaurant with Rooms
● Wild Honey Inn

Aidan McGrath has been cooking good food in County Clare for many years, and having got the reins of his own place in the pretty WIld Honey Inn, things are looking good for this talented and self-effacing chef. There is a pretty bar – a very pretty bar – and a neat dining room at the rere, with fourteen simple rooms arrayed around the building, looking over a calm garden. Good cooking and good value accommodation are likely to prove a major draw for the walkers, surfers, botanists and even the romancers of the Burren for years to come. (Aidan McGrath, Kinkora Road, Lisdoonvarna ☎ 065-707 4300 📠 info@wildhoneyinn.com🖑 www.wildhoneyinn.com)

Mountain Lamb

Mountshannon

Cafe
● An Cúpan Caifé

Dagmar Hilty's pretty cottage restaurant is a calm spot, close to the lovely Aistear park, in which to enjoy what Ms Hilty calls "house cooking". That's our type of food; simple, direct, unpretentious, perfectly complemented by some nice wines. (Dagmar Hilty, Main Street, Mountshannon ☎ 061-927 275 ✉ dhilty@eircom.net – Open Wed-Sun from 6pm, 1pm-4pm Sun. Closed Nov and two weeks in Jan)

Newmarket-on-Fergus

Artisan Foods
● Little Red Hen

Katrina Hayes is blessed with a superb organoleptic awareness, as you will discover when you buy her relishes and biscuits at the Limerick Saturday Market. But Ms Hayes also has a wonderful aesthetic sense, so her jars and biccies are beautiful to behold: simple, but gloriously colourful, unfussy, focused. The red pepper, tomato and chilli relish, in particular, is a vital standby for every savoury dish you can think of, so don't miss the LRH stall from 8am on Saturday mornings at the Milk market. (Katrina Hayes, Clenagh, Newmarket-on-Fergus ☎ 061-705354)

New Quay

Farmhouse Ice Cream
● Linnalla Ice Cream

Smart farmers like Brid and Roger Fahy aren't sitting back, worrying about plummeting commodity prices, or what will happen when the CAP ends in 2013. Instead, they have set to making a superb ice cream, Linnalla – swan lake – named for the swans that gather on the flaggy shore at their farm at New Quay. You will find their range in good shops in Clare and Galway and a little further afield, but if you are touring the Burren, do detour and visit the farm to enjoy a cone or three whilst enjoying views of Galway Bay and The Burren. A brilliant enterprise. (Brid & Roger Fahy, New Quay ☎ 065-707 8167 ✉ info@linnalla.com. ⌂ www.linnalla.com)

Pub
● **Linnane's**

A visit to Corcomroe, a walk on the flaggy shore, then a pint of stout in Linnane's ageless little bar. Now you understand the Burren! (New Quay Pier ☎ 065-707 8120)

only in Clare
The Burren Smokehouse

Scarrif

Seed Savers
● **Irish Seed Savers Association**

The ISS is one of the most important troves of Irish agricultural history at work today. If you want to understand just what agriCULTURE means, than you need only look at the work – and buy the seeds and plants – of this visionary chorus of specialists and volunteers. The ISS is inspiring and – ultimately – humbling, and we should all be humbled by the diversity and magnificence of the culture of agrarianism. (Capparoe, Scarrif ☎ 061-921866 ✉ info@irishseedsavers.ie ⌂ www.irishseedsavers.ie)

Shannon

Catering Company
● **Zest**

Zest is the sort of catering company that gives catering a good name. It has grown out of an in-flight catering company based in Shannon, and if you see Ean Malone's bright green boxes and bags or their van and barbecues then you know some good, tasty eating is about to happen. Care and consistency distinguish this zesty company. (Ean Malone, Knockbeg Point, Shannon ☎ 061-475624 ✉ ean@efg.ie ⌂ www.efg.ie)

Sixmilebridge

Clare

Deli & Restaurant
● **Dine & Wine**

Jacques Hubert runs a lovely set up here in little Sixmilebridge. He brings in good wines, he prepares good simple food, and he does everything gracefully and well and
at very keen prices. It's a little bit of la France profonde
in County Clare where you can get a croque Monsieur
or quiche Lorraine and salad served just as it might be
in a little bistro in provincial France. (Jacques Hubert,
The Square, Sixmilebridge ☎ 061-713 900/087-983 2640
📧 dineandwine@eircom.net – Open noon-late Tue-
Sat)

Tuamgraney

Chocolates
● **Wilde's**

Patrica Farrell is a skilled chocolatier, and for more than
a decade now she has been producing chocolate bars
and truffles that are characterised by open, expertly
nuanced flavous and textures, right through the complete range of all five milk and white chocolate bars. A
gorgeous visual aesthetic matches the taste aesthetic
of the chocolate, all of which are both organic and fair
trade. If you see Patricia at farmers' markets, then do try
the fudges she makes specially for the markets. (Patricia
Farrell, Unit 6, Enterprise Centre, Tuamgraney ☎ 061-
922080 📧 wildeirish@eircom.net)

County Cork

● **Arbutus Bread**

Declan Ryan has ascended the peak of his profession not once, but twice in his career. Back in the 1970's, in Cork's Arbutus Lodge, he was the pre-eminent chef of his generation. Today, he is the pre-eminent baker of his generation, though the generation this time is that of the Third Age.

Mind you, to see Mr Ryan at work at the markets, you would no more think he is a guy who should have his feet up, for he acts with the energy of a kid. His energy levels could be explained by his extraordinary breads, breads so good that everyone else's are strictly in second place. Look out for his witty crocodiles, don't miss the red wine and walnut, don't miss the techni- cally perfect sourdough and hearth breads. The staff of life indeed. (Declan Ryan, Unit 2B, Mayfield Industrial Estate, Mayfield, Cork ☎ 021-450 1113 ✉ arbutus@iol.ie 🖰 www.arbutusbread.com)

Tea
● **Barry's Tea**

We drink Barry's tea every day of our lives. These ele- gant teas are staples of one's existence, and whilst great tea blenders have entered the Irish market in recent years, when we want a cup of tea with a splash of milk, then it is to the Barry family's Classic Blend and Earl Grey teas that we turn. (Tommy Barry, Kinsale Road, Cork ☎ 021-491 5000 ✉ info@barrystea.ie 🖰 www. barrystea.ie)

Asian Foods
● **Mr Bell's**

Driss Belmajoub was the man who opened the English Market up to new influences when he started selling and cooking oriental foods in the early 1980's. Back then, however, progress was slow and Mr Belmajoub's cooking was too far out for most market shoppers, so it wasn't

THE BRIDGESTONE IRISH FOOD GUIDE 57

until the 1990's that the zeitgeist caught up with this visionary chef and stallholder. Mr Bell's is today two large stalls in the market, one with Mediterranean foods, the other with Oriental specialities, and both are essential destinations. (Driss Belmajoub, The English Market, Cork ☎ 021-488 5333 – Mr Bell's produce is available in gourmet stores throughout Cork)

Steakhouse
● The Boardwalk Bar & Grill

The Boardwalk is a brash, brassy, bold American-style steakhouse and bar in the newly created dining magnet of Lapp's Quay. It succeeds because John Gately is a driven perfectionist who makes sure it's sourced right, cooked right and served right. The à la carte is a simple page offering, with a few novelties like Alaskan king crab, or the 20oz bone-in rib-eye (gross or what!). What we like about it are the careful touches, like the whipped-up smoked salmon and scallion butter that comes with the good brown bread, or the flourish of crisp fresh herbs on the plate. They understand that with steaks and roasts it's all about the trimmings and the garnishes: the Yorkshire pudding, the gravy, the béarnaise, the crispy onion stack, the hand-cut chips. Staff are well-trained and motivated and the dining space is elegant. So, there'll be a grand piano, maybe a DJ, possibly a crooning Frank Sinatra impersonator, and it'll add up to a whole load of fun and a great night out. (John Gately & Neil Prendiville, Lapp's Quay, Cork ☎ 021-427 9990 ✉ info@theboardwalkbarandgrill.com ⌂ www. theboardwalkbarandgrill.com – Food served noon-10pm Mon-Sat)

only in Cork
Arbutus Bread

Tapas Bar
● Boqueria

A pretty tapas bar, serving the Iberian classic tapas with some ace wines – as we go to press Boqueria has had a change of ownership and hopefully the new energy should see this city centre icon back to its best. (Gerry Callanan, 6 Bridge Street, Cork ☎ 021 455 9049 ✉ tapas@boqueria.ie ⌂ www.boqueria.ie – Open Lunch and Dinner)

● **Brennan & Co**

Brennan's has all your kitchen needs to bring out the inner cook in you, and helpful staff make it an enduring pleasure to shop in this pretty store, buying stuff you may not need, but desperately desire. You can shop online also, and why not book one of their popular cookery courses, and learn exactly how and what to do with all that beautiful equipment you now have. (Denis Collins & Mark Ivers, 7 Oliver Plunkett Street, Cork ☎ 021-427 8283 ✉ letscook@brenco.ie 🖰 www. brenco.ie)

Cork
Central

● **Bresnan and Son**

Bresnan's can trace its market heritage back further than any other stall in the English Market, all the way back as far as 1898, when the family first began to sell their own meat. Today, the traditional methods by which Michael Bresnan and his family work haven't changed at all: superb pastured meats from their own farm, matured to perfection, and sold with quiet good manners.They are famous for their spiced beef, but in truth they deserve to be famous for every piece of meat they sell. (Michael Bresnan, 13/14 Grand Parade Market, Cork ☎ 021-427 1119 – Open daily)

Café
● **Brew**

Anne and Elmarie's café and sandwich bar is pure Cork. It's tiny, simple, and the food has an earthiness and authenticity that makes you smile. "Brew Café: Come on in!" says the sign, and once you go in you will find food like your Granny used to make: lovely leek and onion tart; robust beef lasagne; a Victoria sponge that will take your breath away; great sandwiches, nice salads. The girls' food has their signature style: honest, delicious, and true. Pure Cork, boy. (Anne Dempsey & Elmarie Mulcahy, 21 Paul Street ☎ 021-427 4729 🖰 www. brewcafe.ie – Open all day)

Wine Merchant
● **Bubble Brothers**

Billy Forester's company has a wine shop in the city centre in the English Market, and a second retail outlet at the Marina Commercial Park. Mr Forester and his team sell good wines, and they sell them with sincerity and passion, so a purchase gets you not just the good juice in the bottle, but also the culture and creativity of the winemaker who put it there, and the culture and creativity of the wine merchant who chooses and selects with discrimination and dedication. A model wine company that has developed logically, organically and positively.(Billy Forester, Wine Depot, Marina Commercial Park, Centre Park Road, Cork ☎ 021-484 5198. English market shop ☎ 021-425 4641 ☝ www.bubblebrothers.com)

Café
● Café Gusto

If you need proof that they do everything well in Cork, and do it better than anywhere else, then Café Gusto will suffice to prove your argument. The Gustos do good drinks, and good simple eats, and they know exactly what it is that they do best. The opening of Washington Street for wines and mezze plates, bruschetti and Italian-accented salads at weekends is proof of more logical, smart development as they come up to a decade in business. (Marianne Delaney & Denis O'Mullane, 3 Washington Street, ☎ 021-425 4446 & The Boardwalk, Lapp's Quay, 021-4224099 ☝ www.cafegusto.com – Open Lunch and Dinner at Washington Street, Lunch at Lapp's Quay)

Vegetarian Restaurant with Rooms
● Café Paradiso

Denis Cotter is not just one of the great chefs of his generation: he may well be the most original chef of his generation. He uses no meat nor fish in his cooking, but the culinary completeness and creativity of his work with vegetables, pulses, grains and cheeses is utterly total. The greatest compliment we can pay his cooking is to say that no one could ever copy it – and no one ever has managed to – because it seems to spring from some alternative culinary world, a place where Cotter is sui generis. Marry this amazing cooking to great service, good value, a beatnik ambience and three lovely rooms upstairs to rest your head, and you have the perfect place, the perfect unique place. (Denis Cotter, Lancaster Quay, Cork ☎ 021-427 7939 ☝ www.cafeparadiso.ie – Open Dinner)

Arttisan Chocolates
● The Chocolate Shop

Niall and Rosemary Daly's shop sells chocolates, and the
very best chocolates at that. If you search for Cocoa
Bean from Kerry, or Willie Harcourt-Cooze's extraordinary Peruvian Black San Martin 100% Single Origin, then
it is here. "Chocolate is an affordable luxury", says Niall,
and their range, from Pralus to Skelligs, reveals just how
luxurious chocolate can be. Only brilliant. (Niall and
Rosemary Daly, English Market, Cork ☎ 021-425 4448
🕮 info@chocolate.ie ⬈ www.chocolate.ie – Open
Mon-Sat)

Market
● The Coal Quay Market

For some Corkonians, the CQ Market is the best of a
very good bunch indeed. With everything from fresh
pasta to pristine cheeses to a tumultuous array of home-
grown vegetables and fruit, you can get everything you
could possibly need, along with some coffee as you chat
to everyone about how Cork is, like, the real capital
when it comes to food culture. And if you need to prove
your point, just show the doubters that every stall at
CQ is superb. (Coal Quay, Saturdays 9am-4.30pm Contact Caroline Robinson 🕮 carolinerobinson@eircom.
net ☎ 021-733 0178)

Coffee Shop
● Coffee Central

A marketeer born and bred, Mary Rose has worked in
the English Market for a full forty years. You wouldn't
think it to look at her, mind you, what with her energy
and bonhommie, and her true skill in crafting Coffee
Central into one of the key meeting places in the market, putting the spirit of Cork city into every cup. (Mary
Rose, The English Market, Cork ☎ 021-427 1999 – Open
Mon-Sat)

Coffee Roaster & Coffee Shop
● Cork Coffee Roasters

"Oh no! Are all the sandwiches gone! Oh no!" Wow.
You know you are in one hell of a coffee roastery when
even the daily sarnies are a sell-out, and their absence is
capable of creating such disappointment in a customer.
But then everything John Gowan does is blessed with a

cultured perfectionism that fills us with awe. He roasts great coffees – some of the very best, in fact, and he is a man who learnt his trade well in Seattle, when he wasn't working Alaskan trawlers. He has a super-cool, super-funky shop run by super-cool, super-funky staff. And he even makes amazing sandwiches. Everything about CCR makes your life better, simple as that. (John & Anna Gowan, 2 Bridge Street ☎ 087-776 6322 📧 john-gowan@gmail.com 🖱 www.corkcoffee.com – Open daytime)

only in Cork
The English Market

Restaurant
● Crawford Gallery Café

The loveliest gallery, and the loveliest café. Put one into the other, and you wind up with one of the great Cork destinations, and some of the very best Cork food, cooking that is utterly simple – Ballycotton mackerel; spiced lamb pie; pheasant with bread sauce; pork escallope with cream and lemon – and yet quietly unforgettable. Yes, there is art on the walls of the gallery. But the living art is there on the plate in the café. (Jean Manning, Emmet Place, Cork ☎ 021-427 4415 – Open 10am-4.30pm Mon-Sat)

Restaurant
● An Crúibín

Another new and typically charmismatic arrival on the Cork scene, An Cruibin has a beautiful interior, styled by Simone Kelly of MacCurtain Street's superb Interior Living, with a small restaurant – the Silk Purse, ho ho!! – upstairs. Paul and Frank do good food, right from that perfect ham sandwich at lunchtime – home cooked and hand-carved ham, lovely bread, good butter, a piece of simple perfection – to the weekend dinners upstairs when they open the menu out in the dramatic, intimate space that is The Silk Purse, and where the food fuses Fergus Henderson with a touch of Ferran Adria: artichoke and chestnut mushroom risotto; pork chop with goat cheese and sage polenta; Galloway beef with potato purée; tagine of vegetables with jewelled couscous. Radical. (Paul Lewis & Frank O'Connell, One Union Quay ☎ 021-431 0071 📧 frank@themeatcentre.com 🖱 www.themeatcentre.com – Open 10am-midnight)

● **The English Market**

"It is an historical place that refuses to stagnate and a cultural space that mocks pretension, a jewel of shabby charm and a bulwark against the vulgar tide of homegenising commercialisation".

A jewel, And a bulwark. What apt terms the O'Drisceoil brothers, Diarmuid and Donal, minted when they set to describe the English Market in their superb book, "Serving A City: The Story of Cork's English Market". Some folk don't quite get the shabby charm, of course, but Cork people revel in this aspect of the market, its very imperfection, its wabi-sabi nature, the changing and evanescent complexion that the market presents to its customers each and every day. For us, to enter the market is to enter a self-contained world, a place where the accents are different, the priorities are rearranged, where past and present intersect in a brilliant now, where change occurs in a context of changelessness, the village in the city. The major destinations in the Market are described individually in these pages. In addition to these superstars, here are some of the other highlights of the market:

· K. Noonan Pork & Bacon, for all those finger-suckingly delicious fiddly bits of the pig from Kathleen Noonan's stall (☎ 087 297 1895)· P. Coughlan, for superb meats from Paul Murphy's family-run stall, now into its fifth generation (☎ 021-427 2068) · Stephen Landon, for traditional pork and bacon cuts· The Alternative Bread Company for fine traditional Cork loaves as well as international breads (☎ 021-489 7787) · The Meat Centre for good mutton, a meat as rare as hen's teeth (☎ 021-427 7085) · The Good Food Shop for an excellent range of everything organic (☎ 021-427 9419) · Linda's Flower Shop, for a bouquet for your beloved (☎ 021-427 6917) · Fruit Boost, for a clean fruit hit in a glass (☎ 021-435 8467) · Superfruit, for super fruit (☎ 021-427 5721).

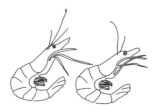

Chocolates
● Eve's Chocolate Shop

People have been making a fuss about salted caramel
recently, particularly the fashion for salted caramel ice
cream. But, down in the little commercial park where
she works, just off Magazine Road, Eve St. Leger has
been mixing salt with caramel for years, in order to
make her unique Corkies. Ms St Leger is not merely a
brilliant chocolatier with a children's dream of a shop.
She is also an innovator, a perfectionist, an artist who
has fashioned her own world through her work. Others
follow fashion: Eve's Chocolates create fashion.(Eve St
Leger, College Commercial Park, Magazine Road, Cork
☎ 021-434 7781 ✍ eve@evechocolates.ie ✌ www.
evechocolates.ie – Open 9.30am-6pm Mon-Fri, 9.20am-
1pm Saturday plus extra hours for holidays)

Sweets
● Exchange Toffee Works

Dan Linehan makes toffee, in a toffee works. Chocolate
may need a factory, but good toffee needs a works in
which to be created, and that is what Mr Linehan does,
superbly. The sweets of your childhood are made here
– clove rock, acid drops, all those sugary gobstopping
chews and crunches – but they are made correctly,
respectfully and sincerely. (Dan Linehan, 37a John
Redmond Street, Mulgrave Road, Cork ☎ 021-450 7791
– Open 9am-6pm Mon-Fri)

Restaurant
● The Farmgate Café

Kay Harte is one of the mighty Cork food women –
Cork's culinary culture is a female one, unlike the rest
of the country – and there is no one more steadfast in
asserting the value and splendour of local foods than
this formidable lady. A recent lunch menu for a visiting
party went like this: potato, thyme and wild garlic soup
(the wild garlic picked by Ms Harte herself); Clare Island
organic salmon; St Tola goat's cheese salad; whiting
with champ; tripe and drisheen; English Market corned
beef; portobello mushroom and Mossfield cheese tart;
apple tart; Milleens cheese; Farmgate bread and butter
pudding. Could there be anything nicer? Truly, we don't
think so. (Kay Harte, English Market, Princes Street,
Cork ☎ 021-427 8134 ✍ farmgatecafe@yahoo.ie –
Open 8.30am-5pm Mon-Sat)

Pizza
● **Fast Al's**

Pizza by the slice doesn't sound like the normal Bridgestone gig, does it? But when the pizzas are Fast Al's, and
are as correctly made and cooked as they are here, then
a little corner joint where you stand up as you munch
your slice is very, very Bridgestone indeed. Alan Gould-
ing is a perfectionist and you taste that striving for perfection, that search for the very best, in every detail of
every slice. With a second shop near to the Post Office,
world domination is steadily underway. (Alan Gould-
ing, 3 Paradise Place, and 2 Pembroke Street ☎ 087-609
9544 – The two Al's are open until 6pm daily, then re-
open from 9.30pm-3.30am on Fridays and Saturdays)

Dips and Marinades
● **Flores Gourmet**

Miriam Flores understands flavours the way Coltrane
understood the tenor sax, or Seamus Heaney
understands pentameter. Time and again you taste her
relishes, her sauces and condiments, or eat her cooking
at the Mahon Point market, and it is the structure and
arrangement of flavours in her foods that knocks you
sideways. Initial flavours will hit first – lime zest, a hit of
chilli – to be followed by the deeper resonant tastes of
spices and complex aftertastes. No one else constructs
flavours quite like this woman, a true wizard of the
kitchen. (Miriam Flores, 14 Pope's Hill, Cork ☎ 085-
139 4037 ✉ rojocatering@yahoo.com)

Brew Pub
● **Franciscan Well Brew Pub**

Shane Long and his team are master brewers, and the
Franciscan Well is the most important brewery and
pub in all of Munster. Their knowledge of how to use
and manipulate hops to add flavours – a Christmas beer
made in 2008 tasted of banana! – makes for beers that
are precious drinks, statements of craftsmanship and
class, as well as organoleptic excellence. If there is a
seasonal brew on offer when you visit, then don't miss
it. Otherwise their classic array of lagers, stout and red
ales are simply superb taste sensations. (Shane Long, 14b
North Mall, Cork ☎ 021-439 3434 ✉ info@franciscan-
wellbrewery.com 🖰 www.franciscanwellbrewery.com
– Open 3pm-11.30pm Mon-Wed, 3pm-midnight Thur,
3pm-12.30am Fri & Sat, 4pm-11pm Sun)

B&B
● Garnish House

Hansi Lucey's house brings out the effusive in guests who stay here. "In Garnish House we felt we were staying with a much loved and loving aunt determined to fatten us up at breakfast and spoiling us with a crazy range of options, each better than the last", a correspondent wrote to us recently, just one in a long line of letters of praise stretching back through the years. Hansi: your much-loved and loving aunt, yes indeed. (Hansi Lucey, Western Road, Cork ☎ 021-427 5111 📖 info@garnish.ie 🖱 www.garnish.ie)

Restaurant
● Les Gourmandises

Pat and Soizic Kelly's restaurant is one of the city's best, with a reputation built on meticulously sourced ingredients and rock-steady, creative modern cookery. Mr Kelly likes to work in the modern style of offering ingredients in several formats and finishes, and his skill brings every dish home safely, gilded with technique and taste. (Patrick & Soizic Kelly, 17 Cook Street, Cork ☎ 021-425 1959 📖 info@lesgourmandises.ie 🖱 www. lesgourmandises.ie – Open 6pm-9.30pm Tue-Thur, 6pm-10pm Fri & Sat, and open Fri lunch)

Patisserie
● Heaven's Cake

Joe Hegarty is the patissier for the English Market, though his lovely baking travels as far west as The Stuffed Olive in Bantry. What we love is that Mr Hegarty's work is confident and professional, yet it's not slick: there is an earthiness to his baking that delivers a slice of heaven here on earth. (Joe Hegarty, English Market, Cork ☎ 021-422 2775 – Open 9.30am-5.30pm)

Café
● Iago

Sean and Josephine Calder-Potts' stall is one of the most aesthetically pleasing in the English Market – architect Alex White picked up a gong for his work on the renovation – and the aesthetic of the stall is matched by the choosy perfectionism that defines this couple. They bring a grace to everything they sell, and to the way they sell it, from their perfectly matured cheeses to their silky, sublime pastas. Aesthete Central, that's Iago. (Sean Calder-Potts, English Market, Cork ☎ 021-427 7047 – Open 9.30am-5.30pm)

Café
● Idaho Café

The McKenna children cannot undertake a trip to Cork city without a visit to Idaho. No way, José, that they aren't going to get in here, in advance of a little serious shopping, for the pancakes, the sausage sandwiches, the fish pie, the shepherdess pie, and then something sweet before they hit the parent's plastic in the city's stores. Idaho is tiny, and more than a little miraculous, an unforgettable piece of Cork culture. (Richard & Mairead Jacob, 19 Caroline Street, Cork ☎ 021-427 6376 – Open 8.30am-5pm Mon-Thu 8.30am-6pm Fri & Sat)

Homestore
● Interior Living

Simone Kelly and Trixie Leahy's beautiful shop is one of the most charismatic and appealing we know. A small selection of classy foods and superstar wines are joined by some of the funkiest homeware goods and furnishings you have ever seen in your life, all of which show that these girls are blessed with the utmost good taste. IL isn't about shopping: it's about culture. (Simone Kelly & Trixie Leahy, 11 MacCurtain Street, Cork ☎ 021-450 5819 🖅 info@interiorliving.ie 🖰 www. interiorliving.ie)

Restaurant
● Isaac's

"Quality at a fair price" is what Canice Sharkey and Michael Ryan promise in Cork city's iconic Isaac's, and that is just what they have delivered ever since they opened their doors, which believe it or not was as far back as the early 1990's. Isaac's first appeared in the *Bridgestone Guides* back in 1993. The cooking is direct, brasserie-accented Mediterranean food with Irish signature notes – chicken wrapped in pancetta with champ is the sort of thing they deliver with confident aplomb – and the room is truly lovely, a classic space with open iron construction beams, a place to relax and enjoy good food and wine. (Canice Sharkey, 48 MacCurtain Street, Cork ☎ 021-450 3805 🖅 isaacs@ iol.ie – Open Lunch & Dinner Mon-Sat, Dinner Sun)

● Jacques

Thirty years in business, and yet Jacques still feels like a teenager of a restaurant, a simple, unpretentious room with really fine Irish ingredients cooked with lots of TLC. The early bird menus in particular represent amazing value for money for food that is sourced and cooked with passionate care. (Jacqueline & Eithne Barry, 9a Phoenix Street, Cork ☎ 021-427 7387 ✉ jacquesrestaurant@eircom.net ⌂ www.jacquesrestaurant.ie – Open 6pm-10pm Mon-Sat; 5pm-9pm Sun)

Cafe & Wholefood Store
● Joup

Cork Central

Rachael Connolly's company has ambitious concepts for their food – they want everything they offer to be healthful, sustaining, environmental, communitarian – but everything is based on the direct and simple deliciousness of what they make and what they sell. The drinks are delicious, the sandwiches, scones, breakfasts and whatnot are all ace. And, of course, supremely healthful. (Rachael Connolly, City End, Ballinlough Road, Cork. Also at Unit 4B Grand Parade, Old English Market, Cork ☎ 021-432 2626 ✉ rachaelconnolly@ireland.com ⌂ www.joup.org – Open 8am-5.30pm Mon-Sat)

Chipper
● Jackie Lennox Restaurant

Cork's classic chipper, and Lennox's is a classic for all the right reasons: great chips, lovely fish, and superb seen-it-all service. (Brian Lennox, 137 Bandon Road, Cork ☎ 021-431 6118 – Open noon-1.30am Mon-Sun. Also in Ballincollig ☎ 021-487 4668 Open noon-late Mon-Fri, 2pm-late Sat-Sun)

Restaurant
● Liberty Grill

Tucked into a narrow room just adjacent to the courthouse, the Liberty is busy, smart, and fun. Actually, make that very smart, for the mix of foods and wines sold here has been artfully thought-through, even down to the McKenna children's favourite mocktail, the Shirley Temple. Whilst Dublin and Belfast have gotten their slew of hip burger joints, the Liberty shows just how Cork city inspires people to originality, for alongside the

beef and lamb burgers in Liberty there are crab burgers
– very, very good – tempeh burgers, nut burgers, tuna
burgers and felafel burgers. The burgers are flanked by
salads and sandwiches at lunchtime, and by grilled meats
and seafood at dinner, including that old warhorse, pork
schnitzel. Kids adore it, of course, but there is much
more to Liberty than just a kid-friendly space. (Marianne
Delaney & Denis O'Mullane, 32 Washington Street,
Cork ☎ 021-427 1049 ✉ dine@libertygrillcork.com
✌ www.libertygrillcork.com – Open 8am-9pm)

Coffee Roasters
● **Maher's Coffee**

Younger, sexier coffee roasters have become superstars
in Ireland in recent years, but Maher's have been doing
the good thing with roasting coffee beans ever since
the new guys were just a twinkle in someone's eye. Fine
coffees, a lovely little shop with all the roast and lots of
coffee paraphernalia and equipment, and a lovely experience all round. (John Mackey, 25 Oliver Plunkett Street,
Cork ☎ 021-427 0008 – Open 9.30am-5.30pm Mon-Sat)

Farmers' Market
● **Mahon Point Farmers' Market**

Mahon is not just one of the country's finest markets, it
is one of the finest distillations of Ireland's food culture
that you can enjoy anywhere. Brilliantly managed by
Rupert Hugh-Jones, the market drops out of the sky
every Thursday morning to confect the most dazzling
array of goodness. How to get the best from it all?
Well, start with a blast of coffee – you have no fewer
than three vendors to choose from – and then navigate
through the assortment of artisans who work here, all
the while thinking about which stall will be your choice
for lunch when the shopping is over. On our last visit,
we began with a hit of Mark Kingston's superb Golden
Bean coffee, speedily spent no fewer than four hours
chatting and shopping for everything from fillets of
john dory to crocodile bread to sushi, and concluded
with a steak sandwich from Gareth Glanville's stall.
Mahon is as much fun as shopping gets. On one visit, we
met a TV producer who asked, incredulously, "What
time in the morning do these guys get out of bed?!"
Early, is the answer. Very early. (Rupert Hugh-Jones,
Thursdays, 10am-2pm ☎ 021-464 6601 ✌ www.
mahonpointfarmersmarket.com

Restaurant
● **Nash 19**

Nash 19 made it into our 100 Best Restaurants in 2009, proof of what happens to food enterprises that are doggedly determined, ambitious, and delicious. Claire Nash has a great team working alongside her, and she has proven over time that she is one of the great Cork meres, those masterly women who manage to understand exactly what food is about. In Nash you get cooking that is deliciously simple, and robustly delicious, served by a team of staff who are as charming as all get out. Somewhat magical, not least their celebrated Christmas pudding, which is rather special. (Claire Nash, 19 Princes Street, Cork ☎ 021-427 0880 🖅 info@ nash19.com 🖰 www.nash19.com – Open 7.30am-4.30pm Mon-Sat (4pm close Sat)

only in Cork
Eve's Chocolate Corkies

Wholefood shop, bakery and café
● **The Natural Foods Bakery**

Ellie and Orla O'Byrne and Roddy Henderson are the mighty trio behind the NFB, and whilst their main base is in Blackrock at their bakery and shop, the original Paul Street address is one of the city's great secrets. It's a destination both to buy their breads and also to enjoy their wholesome, elemental breads, bakes, pies, pizzas, soups and drinks. You will also find the team at markets, in Mahon, Blackrock and Coal Quay. (Ellie & Orla O'Byrne & Roddy Henderson, 26 Paul Street, Cork ☎ 021-427 7244 🖅 ellieobyrne@hotmail.com, orlaobyrne@yahoo.com, roddyhenderson@hotmail.com)

Chocolates
● **O'Conaill Chocolates**

Casey O'Conaill is one of Cork's mighty marketeers – you will find him brewing and selling to ever-present queues of caffeine and chocolate freaks at both Mahon and Midleton – and his coffees are as fine as his excellent chocolates. The city shop is an excellent space for some quite contemplation as you imbibe. (Casey O'Conaill, 16 French Church Street, Cork ☎ 021-437 3407)

● Kay O'Connell Fishmongers

Pat and Paul O'Connell are two of the titans of the English Market, their fish stall a veritable panorama of the ocean's bounty, a cornucopia of fish and shellfish whose splendour is matched by the wit and warmth of their service. Fifty years of trading stands behind the brothers and their team, and you can not only feel that tradition, you can taste it in their superb fish and shellfish. It's nothing less than the Cork culture, boy. Their striving for perfection is evident in every thing they sell, from the city's best sushi to the freshest mackerel, right down to the bags in which they pack the fish. "Saw them once in Barcelona. Took me two years to track them down and to get the right type", says Pat. That's how you get to be the best. (Pat & Paul O'Connell, The English Market, Cork ☎ 021-427 6380 ✉ freshfish@eircom. net ⌂ www.koconnellsfish.com – Open 8am-5.30pm Mon-Sat)

● O'Flynn's

They are gentlemen of the old school, are Simon and Patrick O'Flynn, and an old school politesse and finesse extends to every aspect of their superb charcuterie business. Modesty might lead them to claim that they are simply butchers, but the truth is that their skills create little art works out of every piece of meat they create. Don't expect the punchy manufactured flavours that some younger butchers deal in, when you shop at O'Flynn's. Instead, the brothers are here to coax the natural flavours out of meats, and to abet these flavours with the wisp of smoke, the subtlety of seasoning, the spice of knowledge and experience. Brilliant. (Simon & Patrick O'Flynn, 36 Marlborough Street, Cork ☎ 021-427 5685 – Open 9am-5pm Mon-Thur, 8am-5pm Fri, 8am-4pm Sat)

● O'Keeffe's Artisan Food Store

O'Keeffe's long-established – since 1899! – general store in the triangle at the top of Montenotte Hill in Cork is one of those city stores that offer tins, jams, dry goods and cosmetics, and right beside them, without any fuss or fanfare are plonked a whole load of Ireland's very best artisan food products. It's wonderful! The yogurt is

Glenilen, the apple juice is The Apple Farm, the pies are Taste A Memory, the sausages are O'Flynn's, the bread is Arbutus, the coffee is Cork Coffee Roasters. It's a bit like walking into a gourmet deli like Donnybrook Fair in Dublin, except this is no deli, this is a corner shop with old stone flag floors, wide aisles and good food piled up here and there because why would you buy anything else but good food? (Dan O'Keeffe, St Luke's Cross, Montenotte, Cork ☎ 021-450 2010 ✉ dokeeffe2007@gmail.com ⌂ www.okeeffes-shop.ie – Open 7.30am-10pm)

Cork
Central

Butcher
● On The Pig's Back

Isabelle Sheridan is one of those stallholders whose arrival in the market has enriched it immeasurably. Ms Sheridan and her brilliant staff – where does she get all these funky, switched-on women? – sell great breads, cheeses, charcuterie, drinks and food-to-go, and they make the purchase of everything into an event, thanks to their sense of fun, their discrimination and search for excellence, their joie de vivre. Brilliant. With a new production unit in Douglas at the St Patrick's Woollen Mills, Isabelle is all set to open her second artisan shop, so the next decade is going to be even better than the first. (Isabelle Sheridan, The English Market, Cork ☎ 021-427 0232 ✉ info@onthepigsback.ie ⌂ www.onthepigsback.ie – Open 8am-5.30pm Mon-Sat)

Drisheen and Tripe
● O'Reilly's

Donogh O'Reilly's market stall sells tripe, and drisheen, and has been doing so for four generations. When you taste the two products together, cooked in milk as they serve them in the Farmgate Café, what will surprise you is not the pungency of the foods, but their surprising mellownesss. Many claim the combination of tripe and drisheen has restorative powers, but you should enjoy them simply for their unique tastes and textures. (Donogh O'Reilly, The English Market, Cork ☎ 021-496 6397 – Open 8am-5.30pm Mon-Sat)

Greengrocer
● Organic Garden

The OG is one of our favourite Market stalls, distinguished not just by excellent organic foods of all manner, but also by especially delightful, graceful service, the sort of service you will only find in Cork. Expect to find pristine vegetables and a fantastic selection of dried fruit. It's where we buy dried sour cherries. (The English Market, Cork ☎ 021-427 2368 – Open 8am-5.30pm Mon-Sat)

● The Quay Co-Op

A particularly excellent wholefood store on the ground floor is complemented by the Quay's cosy, ageless wholefood restaurant on the first floor. The Co-Op doesn't change, and it doesn't need to. (24 Sullivans Quay, Cork, ☎ 021-431 7026 ✍ quaycoop@eircom.net ✆ www.quaycoop.com – Open 9am-9pm Mon-Sat)

Cork Central

● The Real Olive Company

Latest news we heard about Toby Simmonds, the mighty tumult of energy who created the Real Olive Co., was that he was planning to buy a small herd of buffalo, in order to make his own mozzarella. As you do. Actually, doing crazy things like that is just what Mr Simmonds does all the time, whether he is fighting for market trading rights, turning Irish people onto olives and the foods of the Mediterranean, or becoming a farmer. The ROC is an inspirational place, not just to buy food, but also to see the beachhead from where Mr Simmonds launched his mighty enterprise. (Toby Simmonds, The English Market, Cork ☎ 021-427 0842 ✍ info@ therealoliveco.com ✆ www.therealoliveco.com – Open 8am-5.30pm Mon-Sat)

● Sowan's Organic Bread Mix

Louise's bread and cake mixes are a staple of our existence. When we want pancakes, when we want richly flavourful breads, when we want chocolate brownies and ginger cake, then we turn to Sowan's brilliantly simple mixes, and we get the deliciousness, the healthfulness, we want, with the minimum of effort. If you feel intimidated by the complexities of baking, but want to have healthful and supremely delicious breads and cakes in your life, you simply can't do without Sowan's. (Louise Delaney-Arrigan, Mount Verdon House, 15 Wellington Road, Cork ☎ 087 662 3998 ✍ info@sowansorganic.ie ✆ www.sowansorganic.ie)

Restaurant
● Star Anise

This quiet little player of Cork's high-quality restaurant circle has the sort of consistent, pleasing cooking that characterises so many of the city's restaurants. The food is modern, with a mix of Mediterranean – chicken saltimbocca; linguine with spinach – and Asian – tiger prawns with chilli; strudel of aubergine – grace notes, and the room positively sparkles. (Lambros Lambrou, 4 Bridge Street, Cork ☎ 021-455 1635 ✉ staranise@eircom.net – Open noon-2.30pm Thu-Fri, 6pm-10pm Tue-Sat)

Café
● Sugar Café & Petits Fours

Christine Girault has fused her café and patisserie business into one smart room, just west of Cork's smart courthouse. Lovely cakes and bakes and lovely daytime savoury eating make for a much-admired destination, a place where everything is done just so, just right. (Christine Girault, 25 Washington Street ☎ 021-480 6530 ✉ petitsfours@gmail.com ◌ www.petitsfours.ie – Open 8am-5pm Mon-Fri. See also Petits Fours, her shop a few doors down the street)

only in Cork
Drisheen

Soup and Sandwich Bar
● Wildways

Maura Roche runs one of the best Cork city places to eat, focusing on organic soups and organic sandwiches and delivering both to stellar standards every day of the week. It's the sort of place that epitomises the Cork approach to cooking and serving food: specialist; devoted, delicious, funky, essential, friendly, and fun. (Maura Roche, 21 Princes Street, Cork ☎ 021-427 2199 ◌ www.wildways.net – Open 7.45am-5pm Mon-Fri, 9am-4pm Sat)

Wine Merchant
● The Wine Buff

Barry Acheson's Washington Street outpost of the estimable WB collection of stores offers good wines,

and good service. There is a quiet character to both
the shop itself and to the collection of wines sold here
that is utterly fetching and winning, (Barry Acheson, 4
Washington Street, Cork ☎ 021-425 1668 ✉ barry@
thewinebuff.com ⚓ www.thewinebuff.com – Open Mon-
Tue 12.30pm-7.30pm, Wed-Sat 10.30am-7.30pm closed
Sun)

CORK CITY SUBURBS

Ballincollig

Greengrocer
● All Organic

We get our organic veggies from Jim and Catriona every
Friday in Bantry, and sometimes on Thursdays in Mahon,
or maybe Saturdays in Midleton. But when they aren't
traversing the markets you will find them in Ballincollig,
selling lots of lovely stuff from the best organic growers such as Horizon Farm of Kinsale or Philip Draper of
Offaly or Narmada Organics of West Cork. Fab. (Jim
& Catriona Daunt, The Old Village Shopping Centre,
Ballincollig ☎ 086 362 2918 ✉ organicrepublic@gmail.
com – Open 10am-5.30pm)

Gluten-free Bakery
● Delicious

Denise O'Callaghan's bakery specialises in gluten and
wheat-free baking, but those strictures don't inhibit
the creativity of this fine baker, who even uses the
honey from her Dad's own bee hives in her baking.
"A restricted diet should not mean a restricted food
experience!", says Denise, so Delicious is also extremely
Precious. (Denise O'Callaghan, Inishmore Ind. Estate,
Ballincollig ☎ 021 487 5780 ✉ info@delicious.ie
⚓ www.delicious.ie)

Fishmonger
● The Good Fish Company

A super new fish shop opened by Denis Good, who
is a long-established and respected fish wholesaler
from Carrigaline. (Ballincollig ☎ 021-437 3917 – Open
8.30am-5.30pm Mon-Wed, 8.30am-6pm Thur-Fri,
8.30am-2pm Sat)

Butcher
● Michael O'Crualaoi

He is a visionary bloke, and a bloody hard worker, is
Michael O'Crualaoi. He is also a fit bloke: we were in a
mini-triathlon that he took part in once, and we were
still struggling towards the finish line when Michael was
strolling back to the start, his medal around his neck. He
brings the same level of commitment – excellent meats,
excellent cooking, excellent service – to his shops in
Ballincollig and Fermoy and lately, Wilton Shopping
Centre and Carrigaline. One-stop-shops for all that is
good. (Michael O'Crualaoi, Ballincollig ☎ 021-487 1205
info@ocrualaoi.com www.ocrualaoi.com – Open
7am-6.30pm Mon-Thu, 7am-7pm Fri, 7am-6pm Sat)

Ballygarvan

Garden Centre Café & Shop
● The Pavilion

The Pavilion seems a lot further than just 8km from the
centre of Cork, with its views over the Owenbue valley
and its pretty garden surroundings. This is a garden
centre, a homestore and a little cafe just off the airport
road south of Cork city. There are jars and biccies and
cakes as well as a selection of wraps and paninis. On
your way out you can buy some Cath Kidston oil cloths
and a cookery book. (Charlie O'Leary, The Pavilion,
Myrtle Hill, Ballygarvan ☎ 021-488 8134 info@
atthepavilion.ie www.atthepavilion.ie – Open day time)

Blackpool

Fishmonger
● Dennehy's Seafood

Tom Dennehy runs the shop that his father, Tom senior,

opened more than 60 years ago, and today he still buys all the fish himself from Union Hall. "I sell the ordinary everyday fish, like whiting, plaice, sole, cod and haddock, rather than the prime fish, and I find there's a great demand for it." A classic fish shop. (Tom Dennehy, 96 Great William O'Brien Street, Blackpool ☎ 021-430 2144 – Open 8am-5.30pm)

Blackrock

Farmers' Market
● Blackrock Village Farmers' Market

Sunday mornings at the car park by the pier is the place to be at 10am to get the best of this small but very fine market which includes baking superstars the Natural Foods Bakery amongst others. (Blackrock, Sunday 10am-2pm)

Blarney

Guesthouse
● Ashlee Lodge

Anne and John O'Leary are the most wonderful hosts, and it is their hospitality – and their incredible energy! – that characterise this smashing place to stay in pretty Blarney. A simply lovely place. (Anne & John O'Leary, Tower, Blarney ☎ 021-438 5346 ✉ info@ashleelodge. com ⌨ www.ashleelodge.com)

Gastro Pub
● Blair's Inn

It is the care shown to every dish sent out from John Blair's kitchen that brings everyone back. This is a man, after all, who goes to the trouble of getting Franciscan Well beer in order to make his bread. Whether you have the simpler bar menu – corned beef and cabbage; lemon sole with lemon butter – or the restaurant – john dory with lemon and thyme beurre blanc; lamb with wholegrain mustard crust; chicken with chorizo mash – everything will be spot on. (John & Anne Blair, Cloghroe, Blarney ☎ 021-438 1470 ✉ info@blairsinn. ie ⌨ www.blairsinn.ie – Food served in bar 12.30pm-3.45pm, 4pm-9pm. Restaurant opens at 6pm)

Carrigaline

Country Market
● **Carrigaline Country Market**

Carrigaline is one of Ireland's most legendary country
markets, bustling along every Friday morning, so get
there early, or suffer the disappointment of seeing
all that you want being carried off by the early risers.
(Carrigaline GAA Pavilion, Fridays 9.30am)

Farmhouse Cheese
● **Carrigaline Farmhouse Cheese**

Pat and Anne have begun making some rather fine
cheese biscuits just recently, a smart and sensible move
to give you something with which to partner the fine
Carrigaline cheeses. The adjectives they use to describe
the Carrigaline cheeses – mellow; delicate; mild – give
you some idea of the zen-like nature of these handmade
cheeses: other cheeses shout at you, but the Carrigaline
cheeses whisper quietly, and they are companionable
foods, special and distinctive. (Pat & Anne O'Farrell,
The Rock, Carrigaline ☎ 021-437 2856 🖑 www.
carrigalinecheese.com)

Fishmonger
● **Good Fish Processing**

Denis Good runs a super wet fish shop as part of his
fish processing business in this specially-designed factory
shop in Carrigaline. (Denis Good, Carrigaline Industrial Park,
Carrigaline ☎ 021-437 3917 🖑 www.goodfish.ie – Open 8am-
5.30pm Mon-Wed, 8am-6pm Thur-Fri, 9am-2pm Sat)

Wine Importer
● **Karwig's Wines**

Last time we passed by Joe Karwig's wine warehouse
we were on our way to paddle twelve miles in a kayak
in the Ocean to City race. But, unless you are travelling
by kayak, don't miss turning off the road between
Carrigaline and Crosshaven and stepping into the shop
to see the lovely wines that Mr Karwig has been selling
to customers for decades now. Joe is one of the great
individuals of the Irish wine scene, his wines chosen with
expert care, in particular the superb Rieslings and Italian
varietals which are closest to his heart. (Joe Karwig,
Kilnagleary, Carrigaline ☎ 021-437 2864 🖑 www.karwigwines.ie)

Crosshaven

Gastro Pub
● Cronin's Pub & Mad Fish Restaurant

Denis Cronin has his finger right on the pulse of modern, fun eating. He has borrowed his Mum Thecla's Seafood Chowder recipe, which he finishes off with a slurp of brandy and cream. He puts a little chilli and lime aioli with his salt and pepper squid, and with Sally Barnes' Woodcock Smokery mackerel, he adds a little balsamic dressing. The sourcing of food in both the Mad Fish Restaurant and Cronin's pub is really spot on, beef from Tom Durcan in the English Market, bread from Hassett's in Carrigaline, smoked fish from Sally Barnes. So whether you are just having a Sean Cronin Special Sandwich or their signature Mad Fish dish of salmon, monk, cod and mussels in a cream and white wine sauce, everything here is right on the money. Denis also runs the Cheese Please stall in the Crosshaven market where he offers a comprehensive selection of Irish artisan cheeses. (The Cronin family, Cronin's Pub, Crosshaven 021-4831829 www.croninspub.com – Mad Fish Restaurant open 6pm-9pm Thur-Sat, Cronin's serves food noon-2.45pm Mon-Fri, noon-3.30pm Sat, 1pm-4.30pm Sun)

Cork
Central

only in Cork
South Coast Day Boat Fish

Farmers' Market
● Crosshaven Farmers' Market

Saturday morning in Crosshaven's pretty village square is the place to get all the good local gear, cheeses from Cheese Please, Mag's baking and local organics. (Village Square, Crosshaven – Open 10am-2pm)

Douglas

Butcher
● Liam Bresnan

A member of the distinguished Bresnan butchering family, which is both the highest compliment and the highest recommendation we can pay to Liam Bresnan's shop. (Liam Bresnan, Douglas Village Shopping Centre ☎ 021-489 1109 ⌂ www.bresnans.ie – Open Mon-Sat 8am-6pm)

● **Douglas Farmers' Market**

This thriving food market was set up in 2004 and features a number of the artisans mentioned on these pages. (Douglas Community Park, Saturdays)

● **Billy Mackesy's Douglas Village Foods**

Billy Mackesy crams a multitude of cabinet freezers into a tiny wee shop in Douglas, and then crams a multitude of hand-made frozen foods into those freezers, and piles a tranche of nice breads and cakes onto the counter. It all makes for high-quality, high-convenience foods, a blessing for those stressed for time. (Billy Mackesy, 1 Tramway Terrace, Douglas ☎ 021-489 0060 – Open 8am-6pm Tue-Fri, 8am-4.30pm Sat)

● **KC's Fish & Chip Shop**

There is nothing nicer than standing in line around the iron room divider in KC's with a gaggle of kids, waiting for your lunch or dinner order – leghorn burger; meat pattie; scampi; chips by 3, please – as the kids scan the posters and writings on the wall and, slowly but surely, begin to see and enjoy all the witty jokes that Wes Crawford and his crew have used to decorate the shop. This is one funny place, and the humour is a match with the smart, good food that KC's offers. It is sort of fast food, but it is properly and – above all – lovingly made and cooked, and it is the fast food that gives fast food a good name. (Wes Crawford, Douglas, Cork ☎ 021-436 1418 ✍ wesc@eircom.net ⌂ www.kcschipper.com – Open 12.30pm-2pm Wed-Fri, 5pm-12.30am Sun-Wed, 5pm-1.30am Thu-Sat)

Rochestown

● **Cinnamon Cottage**

Fifteen years of doing the good thing is the story of Carol and Kieran's legendary deli and traiteur. Whatever it may be that you feel like – chicken in Dijon mustard and tarragon; beef in Murphy's stout; venison with juniper berries; mincemeat crumble; chocolate St Emilion – is all here, cooked to perfection, ready to be brought home and enjoyed for lunch or dinner, along with wines, olive oils, good preserves and other local foods. CC is, literally, a one-stop solution shop for any and every culinary occasion. (Carol Murphy & Kieran Corcoran, Monastery Road, Rochestown ☎ 021-489 4922 ⌂ homepage. eircom.net/~cinnamoncottage ✉ cinnamon@eircom. net – Open 9.30am-6.45pm Tue-Fri, 10am-5.30pm Sat)

Smoked Salmon

NORTH CORK

Ballyvourney

Preserves
● Breheny's Belish

Conall Breheny's market stalls are always one of the highlights of the markets he works, decorated with his great relishes, his lovely sauces, and the other foods he sources from around him. The chef in this food producer shines thorough in the delicacy and skill of his produce: brilliant tomato and carrot soups, the magnificent lemon oil, the sublime rocket pesto, the great relishes and tapenades. Everything is packed with taste, brimful with vigorous textures, bursting with freshness. Only marvellous. (Conall Breheny, Ballyvourney ☎ 087-9477 669)

Preserves
● Folláin

Peadar and Mairín O'Lionáird started Folláin back in 1983, in the teeth of the recession, so they won't be worried by Ireland's current predicament, for anyone who could survive back in 1983 is made of tough stuff. The O'Lionáirds don't need to worry anyhow, because their products are so fine, whether it is their jams, their marmalades or their superb sauces and relishes, and even though you will find them in all the major retailers, these are true artisan products, made with craft and skill. (Peadar & Mairín O'Lionáird, Ballyvourney ☎ 026-45288 ⌂ www.follain.ie)

Buttevant

Fish Smokehouse
● Old Millbank Smokehouse

Geraldine Bass mounts a mightily impressive stall every Thursday at Mahon, selling not just her superb smoked fish, but also a host of other delicious fish products, all of them characterised by the quiet, patient expertise that is the nature of this singular fish smoker. The Millbank signature is a lightness of smoking – the oaky smoky notes are subtle rather than direct, which means the smoked fish pairs superbly with white wines. Geraldine's pâtés, fishcakes and smoked trout are all equally perfectionist. (Geraldine Bass, Willow Pond, Buttevant ☎ 022-23299 ✉ bass3@indigo.ie 🖰 www. theirishsmokehouse.com)

Castlelyons

Country House
● Ballyvolane House

Justin and Jenny Green have opened the Chop House in Lismore as a complement to their superb country house, and the immediate success – and the acute stylishness – of the Chop House give some clue to the meticulous, precise, idiomatic nature of this gifted couple. They understand exactly how to give a destination – whether a country house or a restaurant – just exactly the feeling and ambience that you want. This means that Ballyvolane feels just the way you want a country house to feel: timeless, pristine, cultured, sheerly beautiful, welcoming, hospitable, friendly. One of the very best Irish destinations. (Justin & Jenny Green, Castlelyons, Fermoy ☎ 025-36349 ✉ info@ballyvolanehouse.ie 🖰 www.ballyvolanehouse.ie – Open all year)

Charleville

Farmhouse Cheese
● Clonmore Goat's Cheese

Tom and Lena Biggane only use summer pasture milk to make their fine Clonmore cheese, so it's relatively scarce and you will need to track it down at good cheese specialists, such as Iago in the English Market. It's worth the effort; this is a fine cheese, particularly when it gets to three months old, when all the sparky flavour elements combine. (Tom & Lena Biggane, Clonmore, Newtown, Charleville ☎ 063-70490)

Coolea

Farmhouse Cheese
● Coolea Farmhouse Cheese

Has any other Irish cheese won as many awards as Dick and Sinead Willems's magnificent mature Gouda-style cheese from North Cork? Coolea picked up its first gong in 1983, and has been garnering awards ever since. For us, it is one of the greatest of Irish cheeses, with a sweetness and energy that no other cheese offers, especially when the cheese is matured to 18 months, at which time it is bursting with fudgy, intense, lactic brio. Just one taste is all you will need to realise that every one of those awards has been richly deserved. (Dick & Sinead Willems, Coolea ☎ 026-45204 ᐧᐧ info@ cooleacheese.com. ᐧᐧ www.cooleacheese.com)

Fermoy

Restaurant
● La Bigoudenne

Rodolphe and Noelle's restaurant has been a staple of Fermoy for decades now, renowned above all for their traditional Breton crêpes. But there is also some distinctive and very enjoyable savoury cooking to be enjoyed at both lunch and dinner, and Mr Semeria has a very individual style with his cooking, never slick, always sincere. (Rodolphe & Noelle Semeria, 28 McCurtain Street, Fermoy ☎ 025-32832 – Open Lunch and Dinner)

Farmhouse Cheese
● Fermoy Natural Cheeses

You need some confidence to become a cheesemaker in County Cork. It is, after all, where modern Irish farmhouse cheesemaking began, decades ago. But Frank and Gudrun Shinnick have that confidence, that mettle, and they bring with it a soulfulness that means their cheeses are both of the tradition, and yet simultaneously sports of nature, cheeses that could only be made by this couple, in this place, at this time. The St Brigid and St Gall cheeses are masterly, especially the hard, raw milk St Gall, whilst the Cais Dubh and Cais Rua are fresher cheeses that exhibit the same skill in harnessing the volatile elements of superb milk. The Shinnicks are remarkable in being able to make four distinct cheeses that are each different, yet are united by a directness of taste and texture. Look out for the cheeses on Mark Hosford's market stalls in particular. (Gudrun & Frank Shinnick, Strawhall, Fermoy ☎ 025-31310 ✉ gudrun1@eircom.net)

Restaurant
● Juniper @ The Forge Bar & Restaurant

Daniel O'Leary and Abdou Mounir's restaurant has moved to The Forge, where they offer cooking that is well focused and tastily executed – herb crumbed fish cakes with lemon mayonnaise; lemon chicken with a Thai curry sauce; lamb's liver with a red wine jus; plaice with a tomato and basil butter. The lunch offer has good sandwiches such as harissa-spiced fillet steak with roasted peppers and garlic aioli. (Daniel O'Leary & Abdou Mounir, The Forge Bar and Restaurant, Dunta-heen Road, Fermoy ☎ 025-31284 ✉ juniper.mounir@hotmail.com – Open noon-3pm carvery lunch and sandwich menu, 5.30pm-9pm a la carte, noon-3pm Sun carvery lunch)

Café
● Munchies

Munchies is hugely popular with Fermoy locals, and the food is simple, tasty, generous in flavour and portion. We like the roustabout energy of the room, and the patient, caring service. (Jason & Fiona Hogan, Lower Patrick Street, Fermoy ☎ 025-33653 ✉ munchiesfermoy@gmail.com – Open daytime)

Café
● O Crualaoi Butchers

Michael O Crualaoi's second butcher's shop is no mere meat store. Instead, this glittering addition to Fermoy is a total shopping experience, a mega-store jammed with good things, and a destination characterised by a lively, hospitable ambience that shows standard supermarkets up for the gloomy, gormless places they are. Of course, O Crualaoi's is a great destination for meats, but almost everything else you could possible need – and especially some fine food-to-go – is all here, in a truly dynamic place. (Michael O Crualaoi, 46-48 Patrick Street, Fermoy Tel: 025-49100 - 8am-7pm Mon-Fri, 8am-6.30pm Sat, 11am-3pm Sun)

Restaurant
● **Thai Lanna**

Accessible and enjoyable Thai cooking in an intimate, simply designed room. Good value and approachable. (Brendan Moher, 11 McCurtain Street, Fermoy ☎ 025-30900 ✉ bmoher@eircom.net – Open Lunch Thu & Fri and Dinner)

Kanturk

Farmhouse Cheese and Milk
● **Ardrahan Farmhouse Cheese**

Ardrahan is one of the truly iconic Irish farmhouse cheeses. Mary Burns and her husband, the late Eugene Burns, first began to turn their sublime North Cork milk into a farmhouse cheese in 1983. More than 25 years later, Mrs Burns and her son, Gerald, continue to make one of the great European cheeses, a cheese characterised by refulgent, powerful, buttery flavours, and they have in recent times begun to smoke the cheese, using oak. There is also a truly special milk, Lullaby, which is made using only morning milk, which is naturally high in melatonin, and thus a great aid to restful sleep. Most recently, a semi-soft cheese, Duhallow, has also appeared, so creativity and invention pulse brightly in this remarkable farmhouse industry. (Mary & Gerald Burns, Ardrahan, Kanturk ☎ 029-78099 ✉ ardrahancheese@tinet.ie 🖰 www.ardrahancheese.ie)

only in Cork
North Cork Milk

Butcher
● Jack McCarthy

McCarthy's look like a normal butcher's shop in a normal Irish town. It's no such thing. Cherrywood smoked beef. Duhallow lamb sausage. Guinness and cider spiced beef. A member of the Brotherhood of the Black Pudding. Whiskey dry-cured rashers. See what we mean about not being a conventional butcher's shop? Where else would you see meat treated with such fiendish imagination as in Jack and Tim McCarthy's shop. Tim is the 5th generation of the family to have taken up the butcher's apron, so McCarthy's allies contemporary nous and know how with more than a century of family tradition. And they are always striving to make something new, to take modern ideas and marry them to the best meat they can source. And now, with an online shop, you don't have to make the pilgrimage to Kanturk to get your hands on these exhilarating, exciting foods. Unique. (Jack & Tim McCarthy, Main Street, Kanturk ☎ 029-50178 ✉ info@jackmccarthy.ie ✆ www.jackmccarthy.ie – Open 8.30am-6pm Mon-Sat)

Kilavullen

Market
● Kilavullen Farmers' Market

It takes place in a polytunnel, just beside the Nano Nagle centre, and we have to confess that the Kilavullen Market is one of our favourites. There is such camaraderie between the stall holders, and such intimacy in the setting, that it is just a blast of goodness for the soul and, of course, for the appetite. Truly special, truly Cork. (Nano Nagle Centre, Sat 10.30am-1pm fortnightly, details from ☎ 022-26470)

Macroom

Cheesmonger
● Fiona Burke

Fiona is one of the pioneering marketeers, her cheese stall a feature of many of the best farmers' markets. She also sells Nano Nagle eggs, and Follain Chutney and other good things. (Fiona Burke, Macroom ☎ 026-43537)

● Lynch's Bakery

Humphrey Lynch's wee traditional bakery has good loaves and nice, domestic-style biscuits and cakes. (Humphrey Lynch, South Square, Macroom, ☎ 026-41084 ✉ hlynch1@eircom.net – Open 9am-6pm Mon-Sat)

Oatmeal
● Macroom Oatmeal

Donal Creedon's legendary oatmeal, and his superb coarse-ground flour, are unique. The toastiness of the oats, hand-roasted by Mr Creedon, produces an oatmeal quite unlike any other. We once had breakfast in Ballymaloe House with the novelist and writer Howard Jacobson. Having been persuaded to try some Macroom oatmeal – with cream and brown sugar! – Mr Jacobson took a couple of spoonfuls and then said: "This is porridge? This is nectar!" So, Macroom Oatmeal Nectar: Porridge for the Gods. (Donal Creedon, Kanturk ☎ 026-41800)

Cork
North

Mallow

Country House
● Essink

Paul Ryan is a hard workin' guy, who can be found selling good foods-to-go from his restaurant kitchen at the Kilavullen Market, when he isn't in his normal stomping ground of Essink in Mallow. You can also take his dishes away from the restaurant on Main Street, where Paul serves bar food during the day with an à la carte menu of European-style dishes. (Paul & Claire Ryan, 71 Main Street, Mallow ☎ 022-53257 ✉ essinkfoodcompany@gmail.com – Open 8am-10pm Mon-Sun)

Country House
● Longueville House

In Canada, there is a popular rule of thumb wherein restaurants endeavour to get as much of their produce as they can from within a 100-mile radius.
In Longueville House, William O'Callaghan works on what can only be called the 100-metre principle. What he needs grows outside, in a fabulous walled garden, or else it is reared in the fields outside, or it swims

in the river nearby. Mr O'Callaghan then takes these pristine ingredients – these oh-so-pristine ingredients – and brings to them culinary skills, which are amongst the most lavish and disciplined in the country. Aisling O'Callaghan oversees the house and the beautiful Turner conservatory dining room, the bedrooms are sumptuous, and that, indeed, is the right term for what you experience at Longueville: everything is sumptuous. (William & Aisling O'Callaghan, Mallow ☎ 022-47156 ✉ info@longuevillehouse.ie 🖰 www.longuevillehouse. ie – Open Dinner & Lunch for groups)

Market & Free Range Eggs
● Nano Nagle Centre

The good sisters of Nano Nagle sell their splendiferous eggs, and their salad leaves and veg, at the Kilavullen market in the grounds of this inspiring centre. Happy hens – and boy are they happy! – make for happy eating. (Ballygriffin, Mallow ☎ 022-26411 ✉ nanonaglecentre@ eircom.net 🖰 www.presentationsistersunion.org)

Mitchelstown

Delicatessen & Cafe
● O'Callaghan's

O'Callaghan's is, and has always been, the star of Mitchelstown. Both a great shop and a great place to eat breakfast or lunch, Mary and Pat do the good thing day in, day out. So, ignore the motorway, make the detour into the lower part of town near the traffic lights, take some time and you will find some truly enjoyable cooking. (Mary & Pat O'Callaghan, 19 Lr Cork Street, Mitchelstown ☎ 025-24657 ✉ ocalhansdeli@eircom.net 🖰 www.ocallaghans.ie – Open 8.30am-5.30pm Mon-Fri, 8.30am-5pm Sat)

Newmarket

Organic Meats
● Knockatullera Farm

By their bright green vendor's van shall you come to know John and Olive Forde's brilliant produce, and once you taste this benchmark pork, bacon, lamb and beef, you will be hooked. The Fordes grown their own fodder beet and oats, and farming to organic standards results in meat that is peerless, and amongst the very best you will find anywhere. Back on the farm, John has begun to use horses to plough the fields, back to the future with a vengeance! (Olive & John Forde, Newmarket, ☎ 029-60079)

Watergrasshill

Traiteur
● **Taste A Memory**

We were there when Anne Bradfield sold out of pies at the first Bandon farmers' market, and that has become commonplace for this inspired pie maker: turn up too late and there won't be a steak and kidney, a chicken and mushroom, not even a seafood pie, not to mention a spicy chicken or lamb and feta cheese pasties. These are real pies, with great pastry and stuffed with good fillings. We love to heat the pasties and take them on picnics or camping trips: traditional beef for the boys, lamb and feta for Connie, spicy beef for Sally and spicy chicken for John. Are we happy campers? You bet, for nothing is as nice as pie. Anne has just opened a new Café at the Kinsale Road Commercial Centre, where the pies are sold alongside sandwiches and breakfasts. (Anne Bradfield, Rolls House, Watergrasshill ☎ 086-868 2201 📪 anne@tasteamemory.ie 🖑 www.tasteamemory.ie)

Whitechurch

Farmhouse Cheese
● **Hegarty's Farmhouse Cheddar**

Dan and John Hegarty are dynamic cheesemakers, part of the second wave of cheesemakers who have shown themselves to be able to create cheeses that have as much individuality, personality and typicity as the first blessed wave of Irish farmhouse cheesemakers. Indeed, the style of the North Cork cheeses deserves a special section all unto itself, for just as the West Cork cheeses have a certain overall defining style, so it is that the North Cork cheeses offer a refulgent, direct, whole-some and total cheese experience. A classic example is the brothers' superb cheddar, and also their smoked cheese, which is very fine. But the mature Hegarty's can stand alongside the cream of the crop of Irish cheeses, offering flinty, sweet, territorial typicity, all of it founded on superb quality milk. In a little cookery book of modern Irish recipes we wrote with Paul Flynn, Paul made a risotto of peaches with Hegarty's mature cheddar, so don't just leave this beautiful cheese to the cheese board, for it is versatile and blesses everything it is paired with. (Dan & John Hegarty, Ballinvarrig, Whitechurch ☎ 021-488 4238)

EAST CORK

Ballincurrig

Free-range Pork
● **Woodside Farm**

Noirin and Martin Conroy rear Gloucester Old Spot and saddleback pigs, and then turn them into the most wonderful pork and bacon, thanks to the fact the animals are pure bred, and fed without use of commercial rations. We bought pork and bacon at Midleton market and it just blew us away, it was so fine, so sweet, so true tasting. Frank Murphy of the butchers in town does the slaughtering, and this is a model new food adventure. (Noirin & Martin Conroy, Oldcourt, Ballincurrig ☎ 087-276 7206)

Ballycotton

Restaurant
● **Nautilus**

A little restaurant in a little coastal village serving delicious cooking. Isn't that everyone's dream? Well, Leo and Nessa's Nautilus is the reality, right down to the stripped-back style, the keen prices, and the punchy direct flavours in their pollock 'n' chips, cheddar and leek quiche, plaice with charlotte potatoes, risotto with broad beans. Sweet and lovely. (Leo & Nessa Babin, The Inn by The Harbour, Ballycotton ☎ 021-464 6768 – Open Dinner and Sun Lunch)

Cookery School
● **Rory O'Connell**

A member of the organoleptically gifted O'Connell

clan from Cullahill in County Laois, Rory O'Connell is perhaps best known as a former head chef at Ballymaloe House, but that was only one of many distinguished addresses where he rattled the pans. Today, his house at Snugsboro – what a good place for a house! – is home to a bespoke cookery school, where Mr O'Connell teaches techniques and philosophies that fuse Slow Food principles with classic cookery techniques. (Rory O'Connell, Snugsboro, Ballybraher, Ballycotton ☎ 086-851 6917 ✉ rory@rgoconnell.com 🖱 www.rgoconnell.com)

Day Boat Fish Delivery Service
● **Tadhg O'Riordan**

Tadhg catches the fish on his day boat, and his wife Brenda delivers this freshest of fresh fish. So simple, so good. (Tadhg & Brenda O'Riordan, Ballycotton ☎ 086-170 4085)

Potato Grower
● **Willie Scannell**

Willie's Ballycotton spuds have been one of the pillars of the Midleton market from the day it started, so don't miss these precious esculents, sold by the man himself on Saturdays in Midleton. (Willie Scannell, Ballytrasna, Ballycotton ☎ 021-464 6924/086-830 3625)

Carrigtwohill

Farmhouse Cheese
● **Ardsallagh Goat's Cheese**

Jane Murphy is a hero to everyone who loves good food in Ireland, and her Ardsallagh cheeses reflect not merely the skill of a dedicated cheesemaker, but also the passionate commitment of a dedicated artisan producer. The fact that the Murphys live in Woodstock is apt and appropriate, for there is something of the hippy intellect and idealism in their work with their herd, and their fashioning of lovely goat's milk cheeses. Of course, we can now see, with the benefit of forty years of hindsight, that the hippies were right about many, many things, but producers like Jane Murphy have known that all along, and they are unwavering people, poetic, stardust and golden. (Jane Murphy, Woodstock, Carrigtwohill ☎ 021-488 2336 ✉ jane@ardsallaghgoats.com 🖱 www.ardsallaghgoats.com)

● **Ballintubber Farm**

Every time we buy vegetables from Dave and Siobhan, we feel that we get up close to the Culture of agriCulture. There is a motherlode of pride, experience and expertise in what these farmers do, and their confidence is alluring, the confidence of knowing that your work is valuable, and that your work is valued. Last time we bought one of their new season turnips, brought it home and cooked it, it just blew us away. Blown away by a turnip: that's agriCulture. (Dave & Siobhan Barry, Carrigtwohill ☎ 021-488 3034/086-823 8187)

Cork East

Castlemartyr

Greengrocer and Takeaway
● **The Village Greengrocer**

They have a madly successful take-away traiteur business in the Village Greengrocer, and the success of this part of the business is a key part of what is a brilliant food store. The Village Grocer is really a mini-supermarket, but it's one of those shops where everything has been selected with an expert eye, aiming to provide true, high-quality choices. Sean Walsh began life as a farmer and grower, and this is where his sympathies lie – each vegetable and fruit sold in the shop has the hand-written name of the supplier who grew it, and that, it must be said, is impressive. (Sean & Dorothy Walsh, Main Street, Castlemartyr ☎ 021-466 7655 ✉ thevillagegreengro-cer@eircom.net – Open 7am-7pm Mon-Sat)

Cloyne

Deli & Bakery
● **Cuddigan's Foodstore**

This modest shop in little Cloyne is little more than a counter and a few freezers with cooked food-to-go, but don't let the simplicity blind you to the fact that there is care and consideration in all the things they bake and make. Those white loaves, for instance, are particularly good, as are the jams and preserves and the sweet bak-ing. (Siobhan Cronin, Cloyne ☎ 021-465 2762 – Open 8am-6pm Tue-Sat)

● **Lisanley Honey**

Samuel Leslie Kingston's honey is amongst our favourites: pale golden and clear, the sweetness clean rather
than cloying, the honeys managing to be a summation of
all the energy that nature pours into every pot of this
precious stuff. We are also fans of the pretty labels on
the jars, whose tasteful restraint perfectly captures the
patient, philosophical pursuit of beekeeping and honey
making. (Samuel Kingston, Cloyne ☎ 021-465 2627)

● **Wisteria**

Colm Falvey has been working this eastern neck of the
Cork woods for some years now, beginning at Ballymaloe before heading to Youghal, then Midleton, before
heading back to Cloyne. Wisteria is a very simple room
in the centre of the village, unadorned white walls, simple tables, chairs with cushions, a laminated menu and
a blackboard for the specials. Kidney salad with mushrooms, and prawn cocktail are just dead on, mopped up
with superb house brown bread. Black sole on the bone,
and monkfish with aubergine and tomato and lovage
fondue show just how well Mr Falvey cooks fish, always
one of his strengths. A lovely space, and value is very keen
indeed. (Colm & Kathy Falvey, Cloyne ☎ 021-465 2627 –
Open Dinner Tue-Sun)

Cobh

● **Belvelly Smokehouse**

Frank Hederman is the Mozart of smoke. No one else
manages to compose such a weave of wonderful flavours
from beech wood, flavours that animate like Mozartian
trills. Whatever fish you select – trout; salmon; haddock
– the signature is above all the grace notes of beech
smoke that snake through the fish, concluding with
a long, teasing note on the finish. We have written
before of the legendary smoked mussels, but we have
to reiterate that they deserve their legendary status: no
one anywhere makes anything quite like these. Mind you,
we could say the same about the haddock, supplied by
Love Fish Brenda, which is caught one day, smoked the
next, and in the market the next.

Down at the shop in Belvelly, Caroline makes fish pies, pasties, chowders and cakes, and the shop also has lots of smartly selected good things. Word reaches us as we write that the Hedermans have just re-opened a stall in the English Market, and it's all-systems-go. (Frank & Caroline Hederman, Belvelly, Cobh ☎ 021-481 1089 ✉ shipping@frankhederman.com 🖰 www.frankhederman.com)

Farmers' Market
● Cobh Farmers' Market

Friday morning, 10am, and when the market is held on the seafront during the summer months, it is truly special. (Friday, 10am, Seafront, Cobh)

only in Cork
Rupert's Farm Pale Ale

Organic Prepared Foods
● Just Food

Deirdre and Kevin Hilliard should tweak the name of their company, because rightfully it should be called Just Good Food, as these guys make very, very good food indeed. What's your favourite amongst their organic range? For us the mushroom soup is hard to beat, but we have to say that their lentil soup and their minestrone are both award winners. We love the pâtés and the salads and the relishes and pestos, and we know the growers who supply them, so we know just how careful they are at sourcing. To think it all began with a stall at the Midleton market, and now there is no stopping this dynamic venture. (Deirdre & Kevin Hilliard, Rushbrooke Commercial Park, Cobh ☎ 021-481 5516 🖰 www.justfood.ie)

Guest Accommodation
● Knockeven House

John and Pam spent 29 years in the supermarket business before opening up their lovely house to guests, but that rock-solid professional background goes a long way to explaining why this terrific destination has been such a success. Pam leaves nothing to chance, so concern and comfort are the keynotes for her guests, along with one of the best breakfasts you will find. (Pam & John Mulhaire, Rushbrooke, Cobh ☎ 021-481 1778 ✉ info@knockevenhouse.com 🖰 www.knockevenhouse.com)

● T. H. Continental Bakery

Thomas Hueneberg is a really fine baker, and a jovial, relaxed man, so it's always a treat to buy the breads straight from the baker at the farmers' markets he attends, and to have a chat and set the world to rights. Eating his lovely pretzels certainly puts the world to rights. (Thomas Hueneberg, Cork Dockyards, Rushbrooke Industrial Estate, Cobh ☎ 087-693 2194 🖻 thecontinentalbakery@eircom.net)

Ladysbridge

Organic Farm & Brewery
● Rupert's Farm

Rupert Hugh-Jones is a dynamic presence in the Mahon and Midleton Tuesday markets, but his dynamism isn't confined to growing good foods and organising good markets. He is also growing hops, with which he has begun to make beer on the farm at Ladysbridge, using barley grown by his father-in-law, a couple of miles from the farm. You saw him on the telly, so you know it's all happening, and as we go to press the first few bottles of Rupert's Farm Red Pale Ale have been bottled. If his beer is as good as his vegetables and chutneys and relishes have been, then watch out: we could have a truly significant breakthrough here in terms of true Irish artisan beer. If we were Arthur Guinness, we would be afraid. Very afraid. (Rupert & Lydia Hugh-Jones, Kilcreden, Upper Ladysbridge 🖻 info@rupertsfarm.com 🖱 www.rupertsfarm.com)

Little Island

Wines & Spirits
● Classic Drinks

Hugh Murray's wine company has a very interesting portfolio of wines, with a list that is strong in both New and Old world wineries. From Heavy Metal Shiraz to cutting edge Spaniards such as Palacios Remondo, there is lots of good stuff here. The company also sells many of the leading spirits brands. (Hugh Murray, Unit 5 OC Commercial Park, Little Island ☎ 021-451 0066 🖻 info@classicdrinks.ie 🖱 www.classicdrinks.ie)

Midleton

Organic Chickens
● Dan Ahern Organic Chickens

Buy one of Dan's chickens, and it will make you a gorgeous roast bird for Sunday, and a leftovers chicken pie for Monday, and then the chicken stock made from those healthy bones will bring a voluptuousness to Tuesday's risotto. Three superb dinners for the price of one bird, whilst a trashy, tortured bird from a supermarket will barely even give you enough for a family roast. Chickens aren't the only thing Dan and Nora do, however, for their beef is quite superb also, just as you would expect, and so are their eggs, and so is everything these gifted farmers produce. (Dan & Nora Ahern, Ballysimon, Midleton ☎ 021-463 1058/086-165 9258)

Fishmonger
● Ballycotton Seafood

With a new outlet in the English Market in Cork, BS are a dynamic company, their success founded on sourcing good fresh south coast fish and serving it skilfully and with charm. They also offer some very fine prepared seafood dishes for those a little short of time. (The Walsh family, 46 Main Street, Midleton ☎ 021-461 3122 ✉ ballycottonseafood@eircom.net ⌂ www.ballycottonseafood.ie)

Butcher
● Crowley's Craft Butchers

Jim Crowley is the butcher of choice for many local restaurateurs, which tells you what you need to know about the quality levels of this ambitious butcher. Service levels in the shop match the quality levels of the foods sold, so its win-win for the customer. (Jim Crowley, Mill Road, Midleton ☎ 021-461 3542 ⌂ www.crowleyscraftbutcher.com – Open 8am-6.30pm Mon-Thu, 8am-7pm Fri, 8am-6pm Sat)

Delicatessen and Restaurant
● The Farmgate

Marog O'Brien's much loved restaurant is reached after walking through her utterly singular shop, which is lit as if it is an avant garde boutique crossed with a bespoke design store: this is a funky space, with lovely baking, superb wines and lots of covetable foods. The restaurant is one of the quintessential women's restaurants of County Cork, so the cooking is modest, logical, quite delicious: hake with mussels; roast duck, apple pie, everything beautifully understood, served with a youth and vigour that belies more than 25 years a-cooking. (Marog O'Brien, Coolbawn, Midleton ☎ 021-463 2771 – Open 9am-5pm Mon-Sat, 6.45pm-9.30pm Thur-Sat)

Honey
● **Glenanore Apiaries**

Look out for Michael Woulfe's superlative honeys, in good shops both locally and nationally. Mr Woulfe is both beekeeper and bee teacher, so his expertise and experience are your guarantee of top quality. (Michael Woulfe, Railway House, Midleton ☎ 021-463 1011)

Bread vendor
● **Mark Hosford**

Mark Hosford sells his beautifully minded cheeses at a number of markets, and you can always trust to his judgement. He has a particular fondness for the North Cork cheeses – St Gall; Hegarty's Cheddar; Ardrahan; Clonmore; Coolea – but everything on the trestle table is always good. (Mark Hosford, 6 High Range, Rostellan, Midleton ☎ 086-6351954 ☐ markscheese@yahoo.ie)

Farmers' Market
● **Midleton Farmers' Market**

With a new market on Tuesdays aiming to supplement the original Saturday market, Midleton goes from strength to strength, coursing through its first decade with unstoppable energy. These days, the tents are grand, the setting in the park almost pastoral, so the market has travelled a long way from the ad-hoc-in-the-car-park set-up of ten years ago. The quality and variety of the produce is benchmark: Belvelly fish; Woodside Farm pork; All Organic; O'Driscoll Fish; Ballymaloe School stall; Arbutus Breads; Glenribben Organics; Little Apple Co., the list goes on and on, a testament to the foresight of the founders, and to the hard work of all the stall holders. If you can get out without spending 150 euro, then you are a better man than us. (Contact John Potter Cogan, jpotcog@eircom.net of contact through ☐ www.midletonfarmersmarket.com – Open Sat 9am-1pm)

● **Frank Murphy**

Murphy's is the champion butcher's shop in Midleton, as well as being the simplest and least decorative shop imaginable. The simplicity shows that they concentrate on the important things: good quality meats, properly hung, politely served. (Frank Murphy, 79 Main Street, Midleton ☎ 021-463 1557 – Open 9am-6pm Mon-Sat)

Restaurant

● **O'Donovan's**

Pat O'Donovan's restaurant is the star destination in the town, a place where tasty, beautifully conceived and executed cooking has been blessed with gracious good-mannered service ever since they first converted this former pub into a restaurant. (Pat O'Donovan, 58 Main Street, Midleton ☎ 021-463 1255 – Open 5pm-9.30pm Mon-Sat)

Restaurant

● **Sage**

Kevin Aherne made a special Midleton Food Festival menu for the 2009 fest which used Willie Scannell's spuds, meat from Jim Crowley, Smith & Whelan wines, Ardsallagh and Timo cheeses, Richard Guerin's fish and local organic veg and eggs. So there is not simply culinary skills evident here, but also a sense of the culinary community and the role of the restaurant, which bodes well for this new venture. Classic cooking with imaginative pairings: confit duck with lentil cassoulet, chicken with maple and vinegar sauce, hake with caramelized chorizo and tomato tapenade. (Kevin Aherne, 8 The Courtyard, Main Street, Midleton ☎ 021-463 9682 ✉ info@sagerestaurant.ie 🖱 www.sagerestaurant.ie – Open noon-3pm Tue-Sat, 9am-3pm Sun, 5.30pm-9pm Thu, Fri & Sat)

Wholefood Shop

● **Well & Good**

Jill Bell is one of the Irish wholefood pioneers, and a mighty force for good in Irish food. Mostly, that good is exercised via her judicious sourcing for her splendid shop on Broderick Street, one of those calm, good spaces that make you feel truly alive. (Jill Bell, Broderick Street, Midleton ☎ 021-463 3499 – Open 9.30am-6pm Mon-Sat)

Shanagarry

● Ballymaloe Cookery School & Gardens

Darina Allen is a grandmother, but she has the energy of a grandkid, not a grandmum. She has shown herself to be not just a formidable teacher, inspiring pupils of all ages and backgrounds in her ground-breaking courses at Ballymaloe School. But in the last decade she has also become a fearless polemicist on behalf of good food and good farming. What lies behind her energy, her drive? It seems to us that it is simple: she remains curious, and the curious never age, for there is always something new to inspire you, to motivate you. In this regard, she is just like Alice Waters of Chez Panisse, the two mighty mavens sharing a philosophy of sustainability and simplicity. The Ballymaloe School, with its beautiful gardens, its beautiful market stall in Midleton, and its beautiful aesthetic, is one of Ireland's national treasures, a place where, whilst cooking with ingredients, they also cook with ideas. (Darina & Tim Allen, Shanagarry ☎ 021-464 6785 ⌨ info@cookingisfun.ie ⌂ www. cookingisfun.ie)

● Ballymaloe House

Consider this: what if Ireland had been run, since 1964, on the same philosophical and business lines as Myrtle Allen's Ballymaloe House? When Mrs Allen opened her doors to dinner guests, and later to residents, she established an economic and social model of working that has not changed since that day: produce and source good local foods, pay the people who supply you well, cook the foods with respect, and serve them with good grace in an aesthetically pleasing space. Simple, effective, and sustainable. Ballymaloe is not just the pinnacle of Irish hospitality, a world-renowned address that has often been imitated but has never been equalled. It is also an alternative vision of living and working, and of doing so in a modest, harmonious and ecological way. Would we have a better country if we ran it along the lines of Ballymaloe House? We sure would. In this way, Ballymaloe is nothing less than an idealised Ireland. (Myrtle Allen, Shanagarry ☎ 021-465 2531 ⌨ info@ballymaloe. com ⌂ www.ballymaloe.com – Restaurant Open 7pm-9.30pm Mon-Sat, 7.30pm-8.30pm Sun)

Kitchen Shop and Café
● Ballymaloe Shop & Café

The Ballymaloe empire is so extensive these days, and now includes the sparkling new Grain Store perform-ance-conference space as the latest addition, that it would be easy to overlook Wendy Whelan's shop. It's been here for ever, selling beautiful things, serving beautiful food, and if you don't make the mistake of overlooking it, you will find that it is a true jewel. When Ian and Lorraine wrote to us in summer 2009, after a wonderful gastronomic tour of the country, the Ballyma-loe Café at the End of the Shop was one of their top five memorable destinations. The next letter we received said simply: "I have experienced greatness in the Café". Mrs Whelan has a clear-eyed aesthetic, and it shines through in everything chosen to be sold and prepared in the shop, and to be cooked and served in the café. The baked cheesecake, incidentally, is beyond good. (Wendy Whelan, Ballymaloe House, Shanagarry ☎ 021-465 2032 ⌁ www.ballymaloe.ie – Open Day-time Mon-Sun)

Smoked Salmon
● Casey's Smokehouse

Bill Casey's defining style with his smoked fish is a splen-did lightness and aromaticism, thank to judicious use of oak and beech wood. (Bill Casey, Shanagarry ☎ 021-464 6955 ⌁ smokiec@gofree.indigo.ie)

Ready Meals
● Cully & Sully

Cully & Sully give prepared foods a good name. The con-sistent excellence of their soups and pies is unmatched by anything in the wider commercial market, and they bring both an organoleptic creativity and rigorous self-discipline to the business of producing food on a large scale. The chicken and vegetable soup is the fave of the McKenna children, just in case anyone asks you. (Colum O'Sullivan & Cullen Allen, The Hen House, Shanagarry ☎ sully 086-6058471/☎ cully 086-6076030 ⌁ sully@cullyandsully.com ⌁ www.cullyandsully.com)

Spice Mixes
● Green Saffron

Arun Kapil is a whizz. A whizz with blending spices. A whizz at making superb curries. A whizz at making the

best muesli you ever ate in your life. And, then, to cap it all, he is a whizz at selling his wonderful foods. Honestly, this guy could sell snow cones in northern Alaska, what with all that chat and banter and wisdom he flings out at you as you buy some chatni or some curry for your market lunch. We only wish that the standard of food in Ireland's ethnic restaurants could get even close to what Mr Kapil manages on a simple market stall. His food is so stimulating, so UP, that it stands alone in terms of creativity and deliciousness. "Curry for breakfast? Yes please!" says Valerie O'Connor as she cruises the Limerick Market. Truly, Green saffron is curry for life. (Arun Kapil, Unit 16, Knockgriffin, Midleton ☎ 021-463 7960 📖 eatwell@greensaffron.com 🖰 www.greensaffron.com)

Spice Mixes
● **Wildside Catering**

Here's the kind of bloke Ted Berner of Wildside Catering is: when the Slow Food crew were cooking at Electric Picnic 2009, they not only spit-roasted their hogs, they also built a three-chamber wood-burning stove, on site, on the back of an old agricultural trailer. They used cement flagtones, red bricks and wet sand. The pizzas were awesome, and the Slow Food/Wildside Crew got one of the rare Bridgestone Guide Electric Picnic vendor's awards. So, if you are having that big party/celebration, you need Mr Berner to come along, spit roast that hog, and maybe even build another pizza oven. Wildside is what every well dressed party needs to go with a bang. (Ted Berner, Shanagarry ☎ 086-868 1863 📖 ted@wildsidecatering.ie 🖰 www.wildsidecatering.ie)

Youghal

● Aherne's

The Fitzgibbon family's seafood restaurant with rooms
is a class act, and has been a class act ever since they
opened their doors, a few decades ago now. They have
remained true to the tenets of classic seafood cookery
in the restaurant – scallops with bacon, spinach and
beurre blanc; prawns in garlic butter; baked cod with
Parmesan crust; black sole on the bone – and if you
think you are tired of this food, then the truth is that
you are tired of life, for this cooking is ageless, gracious
and life-affirming. The rooms are excellent, as ageless
and gracious as the cooking, the bar food is superb for
those who want something a little simpler, or who need
to take a detour off the N25 for a break, and Aherne's
is simply the fruit of a noble calling. (The Fitzgibbon
family, 163 North Main Street, Youghal ☎ 024-92424
🖅 ahernes@eircom.net 🖰 www.ahernes.com – Open
all year except Christmas. Bar open noon-10pm, Restaurant open 6.30pm-9.30pm)

● Le Gourmet

Jean-Francois Bernard runs a popular traiteur/takeaway
in the uninviting River Gate Mall where his home-made
brown bread and scones are locally prized. Buy for a
picnic, organise your dinner or book your commun-
ion party. (Jean-François Bernard, 5 River Gate Mall,
Youghal ☎ 024 20000/087-231 9210 🖅 legourmet@
eircom.net – Open 9am-6pm Mon-Sat)

● Oonagh Poynton

Oonagh Poynton is a truly fine cook. What brought
home to us just how accomplished she is was the slice
of bakewell tart we bought one morning at the Mahon
market: reader, it was beyond good, a slice of baking
that was art. Before that, we had enjoyed Ms Poynton's
superb relishes, but this showed that she is as expert
with the sweet as she is with the savoury: a true cook,
indeed. Look out for her cookery classes, or catch her
in either the Mahon market or Lismore market, or many
of the national food fairs. (Oonagh Poynton, Tourig
Lodge, Rhincrew, Youghal ☎ 087-689 9861/024-91838)

● Yawl Bay Seafoods

David Browne's distinctively-packaged Yawl Bay smoked salmon is a classy product that is sold all over the world. Don't miss their wonderful smoked haddock either, one of the best examples you can find. Their factory shop is also a great bet, where their ethos is to buy large, thick fillets and sell them for the best value. (David Browne, Foxhole Industrial Estate, Youghal ☎ 024-92290 ✉ yawlbay@indigo.ie ⊕ www.yawlbayseafood.ie – Open 9am-5pm Mon-Fri, 10am-2pm Sat, closed for lunch Mon-Thur)

Cork
West

WEST CORK

Adrigole

Pub
● Glenbrook Bar

The pub food served here is of a good standard, especially the seafood platters. You'll find it on the side of the road, beside the Hungry Hill Lodge hostel and caravan site. (Adrigole, ☎ 027-60004 ⊕ www.hungryhilllodge.com)

Shop
● Peg's Shop

Originally a post office, this long-established shop sells wine and groceries and is an atmospheric stop on the Ring of Beara. (Adrigole, ☎ 027-60007)

Ardgroom

Pub
● Harrington's Post Office

Internet cafe, post office and general store, the post office of Ardgroom has been in Noralene Ní Urdail's family for generations. Here you will find organic wines, fresh ground coffee and great sandwiches. Come in for a stamp and leave with a bottle of wine and lunch. (Noralene ni Urdall, Ardgroom ☎ 027-74003 ⊕ ardgroom-postoffice@eircom.net)

Ballineen

Cork
West

Café & Shop
● River Lane Café

Walk through this seemingly ordinary shop on a side street in Ballineen and you will notice immediately that it is wonderfully well stocked with loads of West Cork artisan produce. Take a step further into the little back room café and you will get another surprise, for Susan and Tom Fehily have created an extremely pretty little room where they serve pies and quiches and composed salads using loads of Gubbeen produce, as well as farmhouse cheeses and Gairdin Eden salad leaves. There are also choice cakes and some thoughtfully-collected kitchenware to take home. It functions as a bit of an art gallery, as the pictures are something you can take away as well. A lovely addition to this quite sombre part of West Cork. (Susan and Tom Fehily, Bridge Street, Ballineen ☎ 023-884 7173)

Ballinspittle

Café
● Diva

Shannen Keane says that "a café/coffee shop should have a relaxed energy" and this Seattle-born cook has that bohemian joie de vivre that characterises the natives of that vivacious city, and has brought it down to earth in little Ballinspittle. Her baking is truly divaesque, grand, feminine and divinely over-the-top. Everything she makes is memorable and moreish. (Shannen Keane, Ballinspittle ☎ 021-477 8465 ✉ diva.ballinspittle@gmail.com ⌂ www.myspace.com/divacafe – Open 9am-6pm, Wed-Sun 11am-6pm)

Butcher
● Lordan's Family Butcher

Donal Lordan's shop is seriously good, the meat products the work of an expert butcher with his own abattoir and his own way of doing things. The range of sausages, in particular, are worth the trip alone. (Donal Lordan, Ballinspittle ☎ 021-477 8226 – Open 8.30am-6pm Mon-Sat)

Ballydehob

● Annie's

Annie Barry's restaurant is showing the sort of form
these days that made it one of the original West Cork
icons, that unity of great cooking, a unique ambience
and brilliant service that cocoons you in its enviable
warmth and satisfaction. It's a restaurant for everyone,
unpretentious and genuine, the real article, and make
sure to start with a drink across the road in Levis' bar.
Note: Annie is also now making some quite delicious
pork pies, which you can buy at the Gubbeen stalls in
the various West Cork Country Markets. Proper pies
with good hot water pastry. (Annie Barry, Main Street,
Ballydehob ☎ 028-37292 – Open 6.30pm-10pm Tue-Sat)

Italian Restaurant
● Antonio's

Connie McKenna's favourite Italian restaurant is also
a fave of very many other local food lovers. Last time
here we had a dish of spaghetti with fresh crab that was
so, so fine. The pizzas, hot from the pizza oven out
front are very echt and delicious. It's an atmospheric
place, what with M. Pisani hollering out instructions
and orders from the kitchen and the lovable hustle and
bustle of the room itself. A little bit of Italy in West
Cork, Antonio's has very quickly embedded itself into
the heart of community. A true treasure. (Antonio
& Julie Pisani, Main Street, Ballydehob ☎ 028 37139
 antonioristorante@gmail.com – Open 9am-9pm
Mon-Sat, noon-5pm Sun in summer, 9am-5pm Mon-Sat
in winter)

Organic Grower
● Eric's Veggies

Eric has taken to vegetable growing like a duck to water,
and we are lucky enough to be able to buy his glorious
array of vegetables in the Friday Bantry market. He also
operates a box delivery scheme. This year his tomatoes
were superb, we loved his Arran Victory potatoes
(though he says he'll never grow them again – too prone
to blight) and we wouldn't consider buying onions from
anyone else. (Eric Feehely, Derreenaclough, Ballydehob
☎ 086-192 2723 ericfeehely@hotmail.com)

Cork
West

Wholefoood Shop and Café
● Hudson's

Gillian Hudson's shop is a West Cork beacon, bringing good things into this little shop and café, and then radiating them out into the region to complete the success of their journey that began with their makers and bakers and farmers and cheesemakers. The shop is well known, but the café is just as idiosyncratic and authentic, the cooking fine and true, especially the wraps and sandwiches which are amongst the most original you will find anywhere. Yes, that is young Connie McKenna sitting over there, enjoying the soup of the day, wondering about the world. (Gillian Hudson, Main Street, Ballydehob ☎ 028-37565 – Open 9.30am-6pm Mon-Sat)

Free-range Ducks
● Skeaghanore Ducks

We eat and enjoy Eugene and Helena Hickey's scrummy ducks all the time, braising the legs in red wine with olives, cooking the duck breasts pink for the kids, or roasting the whole bird and then shredding it Chinese style to go with pancakes, hoi sin sauce, spring onion and cucumber. Whatever way you cook 'em, the Skeg ducks are downright delicious. (Eugene & Helena Hickey, Skeaghanore, Ballydehob ☎ 028-37428 🖃 skeaghanore-duck@eircom.net)

only in Cork
Washed-rind semi-soft Cheeses

Deli Café
● West Cork Gourmet Store

How lovely to see Joanne's WCGS back in action in 'dehob, selling great foods, great wines – this is the best place to buy wines for miles around, and Joanne knows her Pinot Gris from her Pinot Noir – and doing so in such a happy, commodious space. A little West Cork treasure, nothing less, with delicious daytime food. Do note that groups can book the Gourmet Store for dinner parties, which is rather a nice idea. (Joanne Cassidy, Staball Hill, Ballydehob ☎ 028-25991 – Open 9.30am-6pm Mon-Sat. Dinner by special arrangement)

Baltimore

● Glebe House

We didn't think Jean Perry's Glebe House – one of the most admired of the West Cork icons – could have gotten any better, with its inspirational gardens and delicious home-cooking, but the move into the gallery space, with its dramatic sail-covered patio, part concert space, part evening restaurant, part day-time café, has opened up this gem to more customers and events. The food, whether it's their wholesome breakfasts, light lunches, or seasonal dinners, is all based on what's plentiful, both in the garden and locally, with unique results: lamb with roasted peppers and marjoram; garden salad with Manchego; four fish chowder; lovely kids food such as Rosscarbery bangers with pea and potato mash. Glebe is glorious in every way. (Jean Perry, Glebe Gardens, Baltimore ☎ 028-882 0232 📧 info@glebegardens. com 🖱 www.glebegardens.com. – Open Wed to Sunday, Easter to September)

● Inis Beg

The Boat House designed by architect Tony Cohu for Paul and Georgie Keane's Inis Beg estate has become one of the most referenced modern buildings in Ireland, a classic of modern design that seems to float above the waters at the estate's edge. You can rent it, should you be so lucky, but if the Boat House is already booked, there are other superb cottages for rent in the estate, and the secluded feeling of this little private island is truly special. Chefs Clodagh McKenna and Susan Holland began a new series of guest chef cookery courses in the kitchen at Inis Beg in 2009 – check the website for future courses. (Paul & Georgie Keane, Inis Beg, Baltimore ☎ 028-21745 📧 bookings@inishbeg.com 🖱 www. inishbeg.com)

● Rolf's Country House

Just before school started back at the end of the summer, all the McKennas headed over to Baltimore and had a night in Rolf's. And what a night we had: great fun, lots of rain, a drink in Bushe's bar in the village, then back to Rolf's to enjoy Johannes Haffner's' sparkling sense of humour and the lovely cooking. Rolf's has come a long way from its days as a hostel, and today the accommodation, whilst still simple, is simply lovely, just like the cooking, where the true strength lies in the mittel European specialities such as their stroganoff. But it is the energy and humour of Johannes and Frederike that animates Rolf's, making it a place loved by travellers and beloved by locals. Just smashing. (Johannes & Frederike Haffner, Baltimore ☎ 028-20289 � www.rolfscountryhouse. eu – Open 8am-11pm, noon-2.30pm, 6pm-9.30pm)

B&B
● The Slipway

A favourite little B&B in pretty Baltimore, just across the road from the sea, and with some lovely views. (Wilmie Owen, The Cove, Baltimore ☎ 028-20134 ⌨ theslipway@hotmail.com ⌃ www.theslipway.com)

Bandon

Farmers' Market
● Bandon Farmers' Market

Not only is the Bandon market a superlative farmers' and producers' market, it is also probably the best signposted market anywhere in Ireland. Look out for newcomers like Alan and Zoe's alpha and omega breads amidst other market superstars. (Old Market Yard – car park at the back of the New Spar, Saturday 9.30am-1.30pm)

Butcher
● Carey's Butchers

Martin Carey is one of the leading butchers of his generation, a man whose skills place him right at the top of the charcuterie tree. He begins his quest for the very best quality meat with the careful sourcing of local animals, who are minded as well as could be, and this meticulous animal welfare is then allied to dazzling skill in the preparation and production of the meat. This is a wholly exemplary shop, which is why so many food lovers divert for many miles just to buy their meat from Mr Carey. (Martin Carey, 82 South Main Street, Bandon ☎ 023-884 2107 ⌨ mcarey-ie@yahoo.com – Open 9am-5pm Mon-Sat)

● Curious Wines

Michael Kane's smart wine warehouse on the Bandon
ringroad is home to lots of very fine wines. The shop
shares some sourcing with R&R Wines of Portadown,
and there is real meat here in every section, from quaf-
fers right through to special wines. We use the term
meaty deliberately: Mr Kane likes wines with lots of
body and tactility, from whites such as the Muddy Water
Riesling from New Zealand through to superb house
wines like Château Bauduc from Bordeaux. The website
is efficient, and so is delivery. (Michael Kane, Unit 26
Bypass Business park, Bandon ☎ 023-884 3898 ⏚ www.
curiouswines.ie)

Cork

Butcher
● Maloney's Meat Centre

It's a measure of the level of skill and knowledge that
Dan Maloney brings to his trade that he was one of the
contributors to the Meat Masterclasses given as part of
the Slow Food heritage series in Bandon. Those skills are
put to daily use in his fine butcher's shop on the Main
Street, so if you are an assured cook then you can shop
with confidence, and if you lack that confidence then Mr
Maloney knows exactly how to steer you towards culinary success. (Dan Maloney, 25 Sth Main Street, Bandon
☎ 023-884 4206 – Open 9am-5pm Mon-Sat)

Gastro Pub
● The Poacher's Inn

Barry and Catherine McLoughlin are slowly and steadily
making a name for themselves as being amongst the
leading West Cork players. It's a sign of their standards,
for instance, that Ruth Healy of URRU should choose
the Poacher's as the final dinner destination for her
West Cork food tours, the place where a day's enjoyment of food should be coalesced and concentrated by
Mr McLoughlin's wonderful cooking. The simplest things
are shown utter respect here – a friend once wrote that
the fish pie at lunchtime in the bar was simply perfection
– and our money is on Barry as one of the main players
of the next decade. (Barry & Catherine McLoughlin,
Clonakilty Road, Bandon ☎ 023-884 1159 ⏚ McLaugh-
linbc@hotmail.com – Open for bar lunch Mon-Sat.
Restaurant open Thur-Sat dinner & Sun lunch)

Organic Growers
● **Eddie and Caroline Robinson**

The Robinsons are amongst that inspiring band of
agriculturalists who show how Irish agriculture could
work in an ideal world. They produce wonderful foods
on a small holding, and sell them at Coal Quay Market to
delighted, devoted customers. Sheer goodness, no nonsense. (Eddie & Caroline Robinson, Parkmore, Temple-
martin, Bandon ☎ 021-733 0178 🖅 carolinerobinson@
eircom.net)

Shortbread
● **Seymour's of Cork**

Philip O'Connor's company makes delicious, proper
shortbread: plain, flavoured with cranberry and almond,
and with hazelnut and chocolate. Our favourite is the
traditional, simply because the flavour of the Bandon
Co-Op butter they use shines through in every bite.
Ace. (Philip O'Connor, Cloughsimon Business Park,
Bandon ☎ 086 330 9378 🖅 info@seymours.ie 🖰 www.
seymours.ie)

Wholefood Shop
● **An Tobairin**

Mary Wedel's wholefood shop is amongst that select
band of West Cork stores that set the standard for
wholefood stores everywhere. Beautifully arranged and
commodious, it's a treasure of a destination. Our only
problem is that we always spend far, far too long when
shopping here, chatting to all the staff, setting the world
to rights. Still, someone's got to do it. (Mary Wedel, 79
South Main Street, Bandon ☎ 023-885 2985 🖅 well@
antobairin.com 🖰 www.antobairin.com)

Delicatessen
● **URRU**

URRU is the best, and sells the best, in the best manner
imaginable. Ruth Healy has the most discriminating,
fastidious eye when it comes to choosing what foods
to sell, what books to sell, what sandwiches to make.
It is a mark of merit for every food sold in URRU that
it got onto the shelf in the first place, and that accolade
– choose me! – is your guarantee of greatness. URRU
gladdens our heart on each and every visit we make,
whether it is the quick cup of coffee, or the take-away

sandwich, or the leisurely trawl through the store before the credit card takes a pounding. URRU defines true luxury, selling things that are beautiful, and essential. (Ruth Healy, The Mill, McSwiney Quay, Bandon ☎ 023-885 4731 ✉ info@urru.ie ⌂ www.urru.ie – Open Mon-Sat 9.30am-6.30pm)

Bantry

Cookware Shop
● Bantry Cookware Company

Newly moved to enlarged new premises, Andrew and Maria's cracking store has all your kitchen needs, from groovy gadgets and glamorous gear to the best knife-sharpening service you can find. Precious. (Andrew & Maria Campbell, Bridge Street, Bantry ☎ 027-55651 ✉ info@cookware.ie ⌂ www.cookware.ie – Open 10am-6pm Mon-Sat)

only in Cork
Gubbeen White Pudding

Farmers' Market
● Bantry Friday Market

Teaching a food writing course at the West Cork Literary Festival in 2009, we brought our group of eager students down to the market on a damp Friday morning. We know this market so well – it is our haunt every Friday – that it was a thrill to see how the students, with fresh eyes, reacted to the traders, quizzing them about how to cook Arran Victory spuds from Ballydehob, about how they grew their kohl rabi, spotting the lady in the centre of the square, standing under an umbrella with pots of jam arranged on a stool in front of her. "A pot of jam for your tea, dear?", she asked. Who could resist such an entreaty? And who could resist the charm of this market, not least on the first Friday of each month, when you can buy every thing from a pony to a piece of the best white pudding in Ireland. (Bantry Town Centre, Fridays, with an enlarged market on first Friday of the month when you can buy virtually everything your imagination could imagine)

● Central Fish Market

Colman Keohane revived an old tradition in Bantry
when he opened the Central Fish Market. Colman, with
a family background in fish and shellfish, was just the
man to bring fresh fish to Bantry for the new century.
"My father is in the business, he is involved in Bantry Bay
Seafoods, and I always had a background in fish." The FM
has become one of the essential Bantry addresses, and
a natural progression in 2008 saw Colman and his sister
Ann-Marie open The Fish Kitchen, a lovely fish restaurant
which is – literally – over the shop. "Our ethos in the
restaurant is the same as the shop. Keep it very simple,
very fresh, make it fun and casual, and concentrate on
quality." (Colman Keohane, New Street, Bantry ☎ 027-
53714 – Open 9am-6pm Tue-Fri, Sat 10am-5pm, Mon
9.30am-5.30pm)

Restaurant
● The Fish Kitchen

The FK is both upstairs eating room and a few tables
in the window of the Fish Market, and since they first
opened they have maintained a smart agenda of fresh
fish, treated simply – fish cakes, fish and chips, their
own smoked cod with mustard mash, hake with red
onion, caper and fennel butter – and we have enjoyed
every meal eaten here, whether a family dinner or a
solo lunch. Part of that enjoyment comes also from the
always-excellent service. (Colman & Ann-Marie Keohane, New Street, Bantry ☎ 027-56651 – Open noon-
9pm Tue-Sat)

Organic Growing Supplies
● Fruit Hill Farm

Manfred Wandel's influence on what a dedicated band of
growers, organic farmers and food lovers eat is rather
profound. In early summer 2009, for instance, everyone
was digging their organic Orla potatoes, because we had
all bought our organic Orla seed potatoes from Fruit Hill
Farm. In this quiet way, through his farm supplies and his
most beautiful farm tools, Manfred is a major player in
Irish organics. His work is congratulated by the superb
produce grown on the farm by Eddie, his wife, and which
is sold locally, with every tomato, every courgette, every
lettuce leaf a picture of perfection. (Manfred & Eddie
Wandel, Bantry ☎ 027-50710 ☝ www.fruithillfarm.com)

● Hand-Crafted Knives

Rory Conner's bespoke knives are amongst the best-known signature art works of West Cork. That's right, we called them art works, for whilst they do function – brilliantly – as knives, the purity and profound aesthetic of each and every piece is balm for the heart and the soul. (Rory Conner, Ballylickey, Bantry ☎ 027-50032 ⌂ handcraftedknives@eircom.net)

● Manning's Emporium

Val Manning is one of the pioneer food specialists in Ireland, and long before the current generation of arti-sans were even born, Mr Manning was supporting the fledgling artisan producers in the most elemental way: by stocking their products and selling them with passion-ate conviction. In the autumn of his career, Mr Manning retains that conviction, and the shop is always a lovely, pleasurable detour in West Cork. (Val Manning, Bal-lylickey, Bantry ☎ 027-50456 – Open 9am-6pm summer. Check off season)

Cork
West

● Maughnasily Organic Farm

If we were Minister for Education – or Minister for Agri-culture – then we would mandate that every schoolchild in Ireland pay a visit to Martin and Yvonne's Maughnasilly Farm. Why? Because it is the farm of childhood dreams, of childhood books: ducks waddle around; turkeys caw-caw; children drive blue tractors; cats sleep; willow is fashioned into the most beautiful baskets; glorious vegetables are grown; superb meats are reared. And then on Fridays Martin and Yvonne are in the market in Bantry, selling their produce and baskets, enjoying the craic and the chat. "Food with a face" is their slogan. Truly, this is the Farm with a Face, and a Smiling Face at that. (Martin & Yvonne Flynn, Maughnasily, Kealkill, Bantry ☎ 027-66111)

● O'Connor's Seafood Restaurant

Peter and Anne's handsome seafood restaurant is a warm, comfortable room, with comforting cooking. Seafood dominates the menu, as one would hope to find here on the West Cork coast, but there is also very good meat cookery for those crazy enough not to choose fish and shellfish. Superbly professional and always a pleasure. (Peter & Anne O'Brien, The Square, Bantry ☎ 027-50221/51094 ✆ oconnorseafoods@eircom.net ⌂ www.oconnorseafood.com – Open 12.15pm-3pm Thur-Fri, 6pm-9pm Mon-Sat)

Wholefood Shop, Bakery and Cafe

● **Organico**

West Cork wholefood shops are the best, and Organico may be the best of the best. In both the shop and wholefood café – up the stairs in the building next to the shop – Hannah and Rachel Dare show their imagination and creativity, sourcing superb foods, cooking superb foods, making spaces that are aesthetically pleasing as well as utterly essential for the cook and food lover. Organico is as good as it gets, and it keeps on getting better and better. (Hannah & Rachel Dare, 2 Glengarriff Road, Bantry, shop ☎ 027-51391 cafe ☎ 027-55905 ⌂ www.organico.ie – Open 9.30am-6pm Mon-Sat)

Nursery

● **Peppermint Farm**

Doris Hoffmann's pristine herbs can be bought at the Friday market in Bantry. You will find her beautiful, elemental plants at the stall in front of the Gift Shop. (Doris Hoffman, Toughraheen, Bantry ☎ 028-31869 ⌂ www.peppermintfarm.com)

Home Store

● **Roost**

Emma Ahles's lovely homestore is packed with covetable, collectable goodies, selected with an unerring eye that uncovers the aesthetic in everything. (Emma Ahles, New Street, Bantry ☎ 027-55500 ⌂ www.roost.ie – Open 10am-6pm Mon-Sat)

Beekeeper

● **Tim Rowe Rose Hives**

Tim Rowe's honeys have beautiful labels, especially the Irish Autumn Wildflower Honey, but the packaging can't compare to the contents, for Mr Rowe's honeys are stunning concoctions. The bees enjoy wild rose, clover, may and meadowsweet, heather and charlock, giving the honeys a kaleidoscopic range of flavours. "It is especially good stirred into hot drinks or added to your favourite recipes", writes Mr Rowe, but to be honest, what we use it for most of all is to lather over the breakfast porridge, and when the honey hits the hot oats, there is an alchemy that is only wow! Brilliant honeys, found throughout West Cork. Tim also sells Rose One-Size Box Hives, conducts bee-keeping courses, makes the most lovely beeswax candles (which give the gentlest and most fragrant light) and gives talks on bees and biodiversity. (Tim Rowe, Ballylickey, Bantry ☎ 027-66472 ⌂ www.rosebeehives.com)

Hotel
● Sea View House Hotel

The art and craft of the hotelier is what Kathleen O'Sullivan practices in her gracious hotel, the Sea View. At a time when the hotel industry in Ireland has been compromised by developers availing of tax breaks through building hotels – builders' hotels, we call them, to distinguishes them from proper hotels – Ms O'Sullivan's dedication to her calling seems to us to be ever more vital and valuable. A wonderful place, which many will describe as the best hotel they have ever stayed at. (Kathleen O'Sullivan, Ballylickey ☎ 027-50073 ✉ info@seaviewhousehotel.com ⌂ www.seaviewhousehotel.com)

Pub
● The Snug

As our friend Canon Paul Willoughby tells it, the only problem with The Snug is that as you sit there, enjoying a lip-smacking lunch or dinner, "there will be someone standing there looking at you who is saying to themselves, 'Would he ever hurry up and finish and give me that table!'". This is true: Maurice and Colette's food is so tasty that The Snug is always jammers packed with hungry folk, and there are simply never enough tables. But, of course, patience is a virtue, as the Canon himself might say. (Maurice & Colette O'Donovan, The Quay, Bantry ☎ 027-50057 – Food served noon-8.45pm)

only in Cork
Macroom Oatmeal

Delicatessen
● The Stuffed Olive

Trish and Marjorie get such a blast out of their work
in the 'Olive that it animates this happy room with a
sizzling energy. Bit by bit they track down all the good
things they can find, from Ginger Girl preserves to
Flores syrups to Heaven's Cake patisserie. They make
their own salads and the best rolls and sandwiches in
town, line up lovely wines from Bubble Brothers, cook
excellent food-to-go, and the result is simply the perfect
deli, a space blessed with a whirlygig energy that is glorious. (Marjorie Kelly & Trish Messon, New Street, Bantry
☎ 027-55883 – Open 9am-6pm Mon-Sat)

Cork
West

Restaurant
● Willie Pa's & The Country Store

Christian Barcoe's restaurant is one of the big local
success stories in the zone between Bantry and Drimoleague, thanks to comfortable surroundings and some
fine, fired-up cooking and switched-on service. It's good,
generous cooking, and lately this bright address has
been joined by The Country Store is where Christian's
partner, Helen, sells not only Wille Pa's food-to-go,
but also plants, local foods and lots of other interesting things. It's a symbiotic relationship too, for Willia
Pa's now benefit from her home-grown vegetables and
salads. (Christian Barcoe & Helen O'Brien, Colomane
Cross, Bantry ☎ 027-50392 (Willie Pa's) 027-56080 (The
Country Store) – Open 6pm-10pm Tue-Sat, 12.30pm-
4pm Sun. Open bank holiday Mondays)

Castletownbere

Fishmonger
● Mill Cove Gallery

The Tea Room in the Mill Cove is an unmissable part of
any visit to Castletownbere. The view from the garden
is sublime and the elegant tables and divine crockery all
add up to make this an Experience. Lunch is made up of
a soup and/or a tart, and there are loads of good cakes
and good drinks. Then afterwards there is a sculpture
garden to amble through, as well as their notable gallery.
(John Brennan, Mill Cove House, Castletownbere
☎ 027-70393 ✋ www.millcovegallery.com – Open 11am-
6pm Mon-Sun in season)

● **McCarthy's Bar**

One of the most famous Irish bars, and not just
thanks to the late Pete McCarthy's famous book, for
McCarthy's ticks all of the clichés about Irish country
pubs – groaning shelves, moody light, ebullient service,
a trove of ancient artefacts – but does it all in a very
real way. Your shout, by the way. (McCarthy family, The
Square, Castletownbere ☎ 027-70014 🖃 adrimac22@
yahoo.com)

Delicateseen
● **Taste**

Taste is a deli, wholefood shop and takeaway that is the
first stop for any picnickers taking on the famous Ring
of Beara. We bought some slices of rice, rosemary and
courgette cake which was just about the best picnic food
you could imagine, as well as some Mella's fudge and
some extra mature Gubbeen smoked cheese from their
bulging cheese counter. Perhaps the best day to visit is
Friday, because they make a weekly visit to the Thursday
Mahon market to collect supplies for the shop. This is
a distinctive venture that is a blessing to any traveller
or resident. (Sheila Power, Bank Place, Castletownbere
☎ 027-71842)

Castletownshend

Gastropub
● **Mary Ann's**

One of the prettiest and most atmospheric of the
West Cork destinations, Mary Ann's is a staple of every
traveller's guide book, but with good reason, for MA's is
not a touristic facsimile, but a sound, real working bar
and restaurant. Trish and her crew cook nice food, and
combined with the very special ambiance of the bar and
gallery, it's always rather delightful. (Trish O'Mahony,
Castletownshend ☎ 028-36146 🖃 maryanns@eircom.
net – Open noon-2.30pm, 6pm-9pm Mon-Sun. Closed
Mon off season)

Smokery
● **Woodcock Smokery**

Sally Barnes is one of the supreme fish smokers, with a

Cork
West

signature style that is simply unique, and which has garnered her oodles of culinary prizes over the years. Woodcock smoked fish is up there with the icons of Irish artisan food, with all that punky, idiosyncratic wildness that you expect from a champion West Cork food. Sally uses only local fish, and then either cold smokes or hot smokes the fish – tuna and mackerel are hot smoked, pollock, haddock and salmon are cold smoked. The end result is that blessed unity of smoke, fish and a finishing grace note of salt that delivers culinary bliss. (Sally Barnes, Gortbrack, Castletownshend, ☎ 028-36232 🖃 sally@woodcocksmokery.com 🖰 www.woodcocksmokery.com)

Cork
West

Clonakilty

Gastro Pub
● An Súgán

"It is a genuine place, a million miles away from an Irish theme pub, and the food is unpretentious and delicious." That's how the great Diana Henry, in her *Gastropub Cookbook*, summed up the O'Crowley family's enduring Clonakilty bar and restaurant, and Ms Henry is, as ever, spot on, especially when she advises you towards the good fish cooking. Have the seafood pie, or the salmon and potato cakes. (Sinead O'Crowley, 41 Wolfe Tone Street, Clonakilty ☎ 023-883 3825 🖃 contact@ansugan.com 🖰 www.ansugan.com – Open 12.30pm-9.30pm Mon-Sun)

Restaurant
● Deasy's Harbour Bar

You should just hear our friend Kathy talking about the Thai butternut squash soup that she orders every time she goes for dinner in Billy Blackwell's restaurant in Ring, Deasy's. Honestly, she would have you drooling at the mouth and fainting with the hunger as she goes on and on about the lip-smacking succulence of this starter, and that's before she gets onto talking about the main courses like the roast monkfish or the sweet, saline shellfish dishes and the ace puddings that send you home with a smile on your face. So, we'll have what Kathy's having, please Billy, and thank you very much. (Billy Blackwell, Ring Village, Clonakilty ☎ 023-883 5741 – Open 6pm-9.30pm Wed-Sat, 1pm-3pm Sun)

Hotel & Bistro
● The Emmet Hotel

Marie O'Keeffe does things properly in this quaint local
hotel, sourcing her ingredients carefully, and cooking
everything from scratch, something that can no longer
be counted on in many of the new Irish hotels where
everything – but everything! – comes from the man in
the van. Marie has a particular regard for good offal, so
that's what the smart money searches for on the menu
in the bistro. (Marie O'Keeffe, Emmet Square, Clonakilty
☎ 023-883 3394 📠 emmethotel@eircom.net 🖥 www.
emmethotel.com)

Coffee Shop
● Hart's Coffee Shop

A sweet and lovely spot that is always packed with locals, Aileen Hart's shop fuses coffee shop with café and
informal restaurant in the most splendid – and delicious
– fashion. Both the savoury cooking and the sweet baking are more than good, and the room is always comfy
and welcoming. (Aileen Hart, Ashe Street, Clonakilty
☎ 023-883 5583 – Open 10am-5.15pm Tue-Sat)

Craft Shop
● Etain Hickey Collections

A beautiful craft shop. (Etain & Jim Hickey, 40 Ashe
Street, Clonakilty ☎ 023-882 1479 📠 etainhickey@
eircom.net 🖥 www.rossmorepottery.com)

Shop & Bakery
● Lettercollum Kitchen Project Shop

Con and Karen of Lettercollum have always understood
food in a totally holistic way, right from when they
ran Lettercollum House as a restaurant. Today, in the
Kitchen Project, they show that same aptness, originality
and left-field way of thinking and creating food. There
are breads, cakes, tarts and salads prepared every day,
and masses of classy foods for sale in the shop, along
with brilliant wines. But, it's the individuality of the
Lettercollum Project that sets them apart, the conscious
intelligence that is evident in every delicious thing they
cook, the way in which they have taken the idea of a
traiteur shop and turned it upside down and inside
out. Inspiring. Look out for the local Exploding Tree
chocolate, made by Alison in Inchydoney, just one of

many superb local products. (Con McLoughlin & Karen Austin, 22 Connolly Street, Clonakilty ☎ 023-883 6938 📧 info@lettercollum.ie 🖥 www.lettercollum.ie – Open 10am-5pm Tue-Sat)

Fudge
● **Mella's Fudge**

Mella McAuley's fudge is the best, for a simple reason. Ms McAuley is rigorously self-critical, and she approaches her calling in not just a creative, but in a positively artistic way: this is not just making sweeties, this is making art. The art comes in four styles of fudge – chocolate; rum and raisin; vanilla and walnut – and each one is a mouth riot of buttery richness. Ace. (Mella McAuley, Lisavaird Co-Op, Clonakilty ☎ 086-159 5949 📧 mella@mellasfudge.com 🖥 www.mellasfudge.com)

Craft Shop
● **Michelle Mitton Design Gallery**

We reckon Michelle Mitton understands style, and the architecture and arrangement of style, in a way few others in Ireland do. Just look at her so groovy shop, and you will see what we mean, for its aesthetic is utterly unique. (Michelle Mitton, 28 Pearse Street, Clonakilty ☎ 023-883 5412 – Open 10am-5.30pm Mon-Sat, note, closed lunch 1pm-2pm)

Delicatessen
● **The Olive Branch**

The OB is a great wholefood shop, living up to – if not exceeding – the high standards of these shops in West Cork. Home to organic produce from great producers such as Narmada, Horizon and Devoys, it's a great source for great leaves and vegetables, and then there is also everything else you could ever need. Delightful. (Olive Finn, Andy Beaty, Mark Holland, Spiller's Lane, Clonakilty ☎ 023-883 5711 – Open 9.30am-6pm Mon-Sat)

Bar & Bistro
● **Richy's Bar & Bistro**

Richy's bistro does good, punchy, tasty food, served by enthusiastic staff. You can stick to the conventional modern stuff – the fish and chips, the nachos – but there is actually more to Richy's than this, so the smart money goes for the specials and gets a taste of what a talented and ambitious cook can do. (Richy Virahsawmy, 4 Wolfe Tone Street, Clonakilty ☎ 023-882 1852 ✉ richysbarandbistro@eirom.net 🖰 www.richysbarandbistro.com – Open 5pm-9.30pm Mon-Thur, noon-10pm Fri, 10am-10pm Sat-Sun)

Supermarket
● Scally's Supervalu

Twenty five years of doing the good thing, that's what Eugene Scally and his team have managed to do in Clonakilty. Their modus operandi and their buzzwords are the very polar opposites of how conventional supermarket theory works. Instead, they talk about community, about service, about respect, about the local harvest. This is no surprise. Mr Scally comes from a farming family, one of nine children, and he talks poetically about "the apples, the cream, the great taste of great food produced simply on a farm". So, you see, it's in the blood, it goes down to the bone, and to the very marrow. Scally's offers the poetry of the land, beautifully arranged, artfully sourced. It's not a shop, nor a supermarket. It's a cultural centre. (Eugene Scally, Six Bridge, Clonakilty ☎ 023-883 3088 🖰 www.supervaluclon.ie – Open 8.30am-9pm Mon-Fri, 8.30am-8pm Sat, 9am-6pm Sun)

only in Cork
Mella's Fudge

Butcher's Shop
● Edward Twomey

In 1989, Edward Twomey showed us around 'Clon as, wide eyed and innocent, we worked on our first book. Mr Twomey was not yet famous, but his Clonakilty black pudding would soon make him one of the iconic faces of Irish speciality food. Today, after Edward's passing, the butcher's shop remains an excellent meat store, and Clonakilty black pudding, of course, is a legend unto itself. (Colette Twomey, 16 Pearse Street, Clonakilty ☎ 023-883 3365 – Open 9am-6pm Mon-Sat)

Courtmacsherry

Cork
West

B&B and Catering
● Travara Lodge

We get mails from Richard May every so often, and as
we read them, we roar with laughter, for this man is
one of the most amusing people we have ever met. Add
in Brendan's great cooking to the mix, and you have
a simple, dreamy, idyllic B&B in beautiful Courtmac'.
Food lovers should note that Brendan bakes for the
local Friday market, and that you can also buy his
wonderful cooking at The Chessboard in the village on
Saturday mornings. But you had better get there early!
(Richard May & Brendan Murphy, Courtmacsherry
☎ 023-884 6493 ✉ travaralodge@eircom.net ⌂ www.
travaralodge.com)

Crookhaven

Gastropub
● The Crookhaven Inn

Emma and Freddy's bar has some of the sharpest cooking in West Cork, whether you are just buying a crab
sandwich, enjoying a bowl of chowder sitting outside in
the sun, or settling in for a fun family dinner of beef and
ale stew, smoked salmon and crab quiche, fusilli with
chicken and pesto, or Bantry Bay mussels. Mr Olsson's
cooking is unclichéd and spirited, packed with natural
flavours summoned by his precise skills. Just the right
food, in just the right bar, in just the right village. (Emma
& Freddy Olsson, Crookhaven ☎ 028-35309
✉ crookhaveninn@eircom.net – Open 12.30pm-9pm
Mon-Sun, check off season. Closed Oct-Easter)

Pub
● O'Sullivan's Bar

O'Sullivan's never changes, and there would be a riot if
anyone ever tried to change it. We like the sepia tongue
and groove, the old sailing photographs, the comfy seat
by the window as our place to have a pint and a nice
plate of sandwiches and some of their seafood chowder. (Dermot O'Sullivan, Crookhaven ☎ 028-35319
✉ O'sullivans@crookhaven.ie)

Drimoleague

Dairy
● Glenilen Dairy

Have you seen the funky, colourful new labels on the Glenilen foods? How cool are they? Cool as all get out! Chic as all get out! And to think that we can remember back to the days when the yogurts and creams and cheesecakes of Glenilen Farm were brought by Valerie to the Bantry Boy's Club on Friday mornings in unmarked jars and tubs and containers, when the family business was taking its first, nervous steps. You've come a long way baby, and you've gotten better and better every step of the way. Now, that's how you run a farm business, and how you create a luxury brand: the right people; the right place; truly great products; and passion. (Alan & Valerie Kingston, Drimoleague ☎ 028-31179 ✐ val@glenilenfarm.com, alan@glenilenfarm.com ✐ www.glenilen.com)

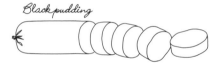

Black pudding

Dunmanway

Bakery
● The Baking Emporium

Andreas Haubold's fine bakery becomes a staple of the West Cork markets during the summer months, but all year long you will find their cakes and breads in good shops and stores throughout the county. These are healthful breads, biscuits and cakes, but they don't lack the pleasure quota either. Do note that the company also has a specialist catering section, for that upcoming big birthday in your life. (Andreas Haubold, Dunmanway ☎ 023-884 5260 ✐ info@bakingemporiumltd.com ✐ www.bakingemporiumltd.com)

● **Coturnix Quail**

Brendan Ross's beautiful quail's eggs are just what your summer salad needs for a crowning touch of colour and succulent, tactile texture. Lovely. (Brendan Ross, Droumdrastil, Dunmanway ☎ 087-206 5067)

Beef
● **Kinrath Dexter Beef**

Paul Johnson rears beautiful Dexter cattle, which are then prepared by the Collins brothers in Dunmanway, and Paul subsequently sells the frozen meat, which is hung for four weeks, from his 1950s Land Rover at the Bandon market (Paul Johnson, Kinrath House, Dunmanway ☎ 023-885 5710)

Patisserie
● **Patisserie Régale**

The king patissier of West Cork has a new brand to his name, for you will now find much R G-L patisserie sold in smart boxes under the Régale label. Whatever you call it, you can only call it one thing: the finest patisserie in County Cork. Great patisserie needs a magic touch, and Richard Graham-Leigh simply has that magic. These cakes and biscuits deliver the sublime, every time. (Richard & Janet Graham-Leigh, Maulanimirish, Dunmanway ☎ 086-086 8183 📧 jandrgrahamleigh@eircom.net)

Durrus

Wine Importer
● **Albatross Enterprise**

Harro Federsen imports a small range of European wines, mainly from his native Germany, and sells them from his beautiful little wine store, just off the main road into Ahakista. Harro and Gisi also organise rip-roaring wine evenings, which are mighty craic altogether. (Harro & Gisi Federsen, Ahakista, Durrus ☎ 027-67248)

Restaurant & Accommodation
● **Blair's Cove**

Richard Milnes has taken up the stoves at West Cork's legendary restaurant, offering a bistro menu alongside the classic dining experience in the magnificent dining room. Right from his first day here, the word was out that this man was cooking some exceptional food, and exceptionally handsome food, and so it is: ham hock terrine with prunes; grilled chicken with tiger prawns; superb john dory with olives; pitch-perfect risotto with cepes; a cherry ice cream which is to die for. Richard's partner Anthea runs the room with grace and ease, and no matter how many times you have been at Blair's Cove, its stunning situation means that every new arrival still takes your breath away. And now, when you get inside, Mr Milnes' cooking will take your breath away also. (Richard & Anthea Milnes, Durrus ☎ 027-62913 ✉ mail@blairscove.ie 🖰 www.blairscove.ie)

Farmhouse Cheese
● Durrus Farmhouse Cheese

Jeffa Gill is one of Ireland's greatest cheesemakers, and Durrus cheese is one of Ireland's greatest cheeses. The milk for the cheese is from a local farm, and each morning it is driven up the hill to Coomkeen to begin the journey into one of the great European raw milk cheeses. Like every other farmhouse cheese, Durrus is a sport of nature, and like every sport of nature it is constantly different, with every factor influencing the original character of the milk and the outcome of the cheesemaking process. This sort of fragility would terrify most people – imagine a working environment where everything, but everything, is volatile, morphing, shape-shifting at all times – but Ms Gill breezes through it, because she trusts to her milk, and she trusts to her craft, and she trusts to thirty years of experience. But it is that volatility, that lightning rod conductivity which the captured flavours of this cheese represent, that most amazes us. Milk is a magic liquid, and Durrus makes magic out of magic. (Jeffa Gill, Coomkeen, Durrus ☎ 027-61100 ✉ info@durruscheese.com 🖰 www.durruscheese.com)

Restaurant and Cookery School
● Good Things Café & Cookery School

Carmel Somer's first book, *Eat Good Things Every Day*, is due to be published as we write, and that publication represents the end of the first stage of the experience of this singular café and cookery school. In that stage, Ms Somers has gone from being an unknown mother of three with no background in West Cork, to being the most respected cook and cookery teacher in the whole region. Her journey has taken determination, but it has allowed her to showcase some of the most artistic and creative cookery skills that West Cork has ever seen. Her food is sui generis: no one else cooks like this, with such a vision and such a level of clear-eyed focus on the simple things, from her classic fish soup to her unique salads. As a teacher, she has shown herself to be supremely confident, and her classes are a blast. She also attracts the glitziest audience of any restaurant in the area. What a journey. What a place. (Carmel Somers, Durrus ☎ 027-61426 ✉ info@thegoodthingscafé.com 🖱 www.thegoodthingscafe.com – Open 11.30am-4pm (lunch served from 12.30pm-3pm), 7pm-8.30pm Thu-Mon. Open Easter, bank hol weekends & from Jun-Sep)

Shop
● **The Village Grocer**

If only every village was so fortunate to have a village store like Eddie Ryan's brilliant shop. Steering a course well away from the franchised brands that now dominate Ireland's towns and villages, Mr Ryan is an independent, and that independence allows him to stock whatever he wants, so all the good stuff from West Cork is here, plus you can also get the newspaper, and an ice cream for the kids. (Edward Ryan, Durrus ☎ 027-61184 – Open 7am-10pm Mon-Sat, 8.30am-10pm Sun)

Enniskeane

Café & Garden Centre
● **The Blue Geranium**

Hosford's is a legendary West Cork garden centre, and their Blue Geranium Café has quickly built a reputation as a don't-miss! destination, whether or not you are planning to buy some seed potatoes or some cacti. Their philosophy is Slow Food inspired, so everything is simple, cooked-from-scratch delicious: potato and ginger soup; Gubbeen bacon with local cabbage; potato cake with Ummera salmon; lemon polenta cake. Everything is done just right here in this fine, child-friendly space. (John Hosford & Olive Brennan, Cappa, Enniskeane ☎ 023-883 9159 ✉ john@hosfordsgardencentre.ie 🖱 www.hosfordsgardencentre.ie – Open 11am-5pm Tue-Sat, noon-5pm Sun)

Country House
● **Kilcolman Rectory**

"Sarah Gornall is someone who not only espouses
perfection, but somehow makes perfection look easy."
That's how the *Irish Examiner's* Mary Leland summed up
Sarah Gornall's modus operandi in this achingly beautiful
19th-century rectory. Ms Gornall has trained as chef,
gardener and interior designer and it's as if all of her
education has been designed to lead her to create this
impeccably beautiful house. She is one of those rare Irish
people who really understands the feng shui of having
the right object in the right place in order to create the
right aesthetic. It all adds up to a wonderful new arrival.
Note, if you want Sarah to cook dinner – and you should
"It's all out of the garden and I love doing it," she says
– then give her a little advance notice. (Sarah Gornall,
Enniskeane ☎ 023-882 2913 📧 info@kilcolmanrectory.
com www.kilcolmanrectory.com)

Farmhouse Cheese
● **Round Tower Cheese**

Nan O'Donovan's farmhouse sweet, mild, gouda-style
cheese is approachable and supremely useful. You will
find it in all the West Cork stores, and many a local
schoolchild's lunchbox. (Nan O'Donovan, Enniskeane
☎ 023-884 7105)

Eyeries

Farmhouse Cheese
● **Milleens Farmhouse Cheese**

Norman and Veronica Steele's cheese has now been in
production for more than thirty years. It is easy, therefore, to take Milleens for granted as one of the icons
of Irish artisan food, but consider this: what would the
landscape of that artisan food world be like if the Steeles
had never made their cheese? And, having made it, stuck
to their principles and their left-field methods of working and selling? The Steeles invented the vocabulary for
Irish speciality food, and we have been speaking their
language ever since. Milleens, nowadays made by Quinlan
Steele, is the Native Tongue. (Quinlan Steele, Eyeries,
Beara ☎ 027-74079 📧 milleens@eircom.net 🖥 www.
milleenscheese.com)

Garinish

Take-away
● The Dursey Deli

It was friends Trevor and Barbara who first alerted us to the Dursey Deli. They raved about the plates of this-morning's-catch, pan-fried mackerel sent forth from what is basically a well-lit caravan on the side of the road, just as you get to the cable car taking you over to Dursey island. On the day we arrived, Marg had sold the last mackerel, which was disappointing – especially after she told the story of the customer who was reluctant to eat the mackerel because it was filleted in front of her (our idea of heaven). Marg had also sold the very last home-made pastie to the smug customer in front of us, who may have deserved it after a long wet walk, but we weren't going to pass up the opportunity to look disgruntled. Fear not, however, for as well as Collins' Beara butcher's burgers, Marg could offer us three portions of extremely fresh haddock – Marg's husband is a fisherman and she buys any further fish straight from the local fishermen's co-op. We watched as she dipped the thick fillets into seasoned flour, and then into her famous beer batter, fried them, and handed them to us on a styrofoam plate, with a generous garnish of salad, to eat in the car in the rain, delighted to be right here, in this place, with this view, and this food. (Marg ☎ 086-1799270, Open Easter to September)

only in Cork
Glenilen Country Butter

Glandore

Gastro Pub
● Hayes' Bar

Declan and Ada Hayes's bar continues its happy, sort of hippy, idiosyncratic existence, with its panjandrum interiors and its fine cooking. (Declan & Ada Hayes, Glandore ☎ 028-33214 ⏱ www.hayesbar.ie ✉ dhayes@tinit.ie – Food served noon-5pm Mon-Sun. No credit cards. Closed 1 September-June)

Goleen

B&B
● Fortview House

For many visitors, Violet Connell's B&B is the ONLY place where they will consider staying in West Cork. Mrs Connell is blessed with good taste, in cooking, in designing a pretty, comforting, calming interior, and her standards have only ever risen through the years. A true one-off, not to be found anywhere else. (Violet Connell, Gurtyowen, Toormore, Goleen ☎ 028-35324 🖅 fortviewhousegoleen@eircom.net 🖱 www.fortviewhousegoleen.com)

Country House
● Rock Cottage

"What a great place it is!", our editor Eamon Barrett wrote about his most recent stay in Barbara Klotzer's lovely, slate-covered lodge, just off the Goleen road. "There is just something magical about Rock Cottage". What explains the magic? Great cooking, great house-keeping, calm comfort, a blissful retreat, that's what. It is meticulous in every detail, and that fastidiousness ex-tends to everything Ms Klotzer does. (Barbara Klotzer, Barnatonicane, Schull ☎ 028-35538 🖅 rockcottage@eircom.net 🖱 www.rockcottage.ie)

Gougane Barra

Hotel and Restaurant
● Gougane Barra Hotel

Neil and Katy's hotel is one of the nicest hotels in Ireland. If you thought that hotels where she cooks and he meets and greets had vanished, then a trip to the lake of Gougane Barra will restore your soul, and your faith in hospitality. Mrs Lucey's food is pure lovely, Mr Lucey is an hotelier of the old school – polite, charming, gracious. We love the simplicity of the rooms, we love especially the Theatre by the Lake in summertime, when a evening of d 'n' d 'n' d – dinner and drama and duvet – is one of the best experiences you can enjoy in Ireland. Priceless, just priceless. (Neil & Katy Lucey, Gougane Barra, Macroom, ☎ 026-47069 🖅 gouganebarrahotel@eircom.net 🖱 www.gouganebarrahotel.com)

Kilbrittain

Restaurant
● Casino House

They almost qualify as West Cork veterans nowadays,
do Michael and Kerrin Relja, for they have been appearing in the *Bridgestone Guides* now since as far back
as 1997. Since those early days, little has changed: the
restaurant is a swish, stylish place, the service from Mrs
Relja is pitch-perfect, and Mr Relja's modern cooking
seems only to have gotten better, more settled and less
intense: strudel of goat's cheese, pine nuts and Swiss
chard; meatballs with sweet and sour cucumber salad;
john dory with prawn wonton. Do note that there is a
picture-postcard-perfect cottage by the entrance that
one can rent, and then it's just a stroll to the restaurant,
and the sea. (Kerrin & Michael Relja, Coolmain Bay,
Kilbrittain ☎ 023-884 9944 ✒ chouse@eircom.net –
Open 7pm-9pm Mon-Sun, closed Wed; weekends only
Nov-Dec. Sun lunch)

Guesthouse
● The Glen

Diana and Guy's house is one of the finest West Cork
addresses, one of those country houses that offers
everything you want in a country house experience,
but which does so in a very novel, winning way. Mrs
Scott is simply one of those people who knows how to
put the right object in the right place, creating classic
country house feng shui, and she is one humdinger of a
cook as well. (Diana & Guy Scott, Kilbrittain ☎ 023-
884 9862 ✒ info@glencountryhouse.com ✜ www.
glencountryhouse.com – Open Easter-Nov)

Kilcrohane

Bistro
● The Grain Store

The sublime, atmospheric O'Mahony's shop and post
office also houses the Grain Store Wine Bar and Bistro
during the season, where Maria O'Mahony fetches
up some fetching food. There is always a very lively,
animated ambience about the Grain Store, and if you
are a holiday visitor it hits that secret West Cork spot

perfectly. (Maria & Frank O'Mahony, Kilcrohane ☎ 027-67001 – Open Lunch and Dinner, June-August)

Kinsale

B&B
● Blindgate House

We have always loved the style of Maeve Coakley's house, and the fact that its conventional exterior hides a superbly designed interior. But style doesn't win out over comfort, and this is a very cosy house to hang out in, enjoying all the best of Kinsale whilst just being far enough up the hill to ensure peace and quiet when the town is at full tilt. (Maeve Coakley, Blindgate, Kinsale ☎ 021-477 7858 ⌨ info@blindgatehouse.com ⌂ www. blindgatehouse.com)

Restaurant
● Crackpots

Carole Norman is one of those women blessed with good taste. Crackpots is, thus, a stylish, singular restaurant, blessed with that special restaurant feel that some rooms have: you just need to lower yourself into a seat here to feel you have made the right choice, and the cooking accentuates that satisfaction: aubergine and feta strudel; john dory with cauliflower and parsley purée; lobster from the tank. The very essence of a Kinsale destination. (Carole Norman, Cork Street, Kinsale ☎ 021-477 2847 ⌨ crackpts@iol.ie www.crackpots.ie – Open 6pm-10pm Mon-Sun (closed Mon-Wed off season)

Café & B&B
● Cucina

Ursula Roncken's café and B&B (bed and bistro) is petite, smart and hip. The cooking is a very well-informed distillation of modern styles that nevertheless reaches back into cooking's classic age, the kind of food that puts us in mind of Bill Granger's style – portobello mushroom burger with red pepper pesto; coronation chicken with mango chutney on ciabatta; smoked chicken Caesar salad with blue cheese croutons. Nice rooms upstairs are great value. (Ursula Roncken, 9 Market Street, Kinsale ☎ 021-470 0707 ⌨ ursula@cucina.ie ⌂ www. cucina.ie – Café open 8am-5pm)

Restaurant & Fishmonger
● Fishy Fishy Café

Martin and Marie Shanahan's restaurant is the hippest
kid on the block, run by the smartest restaurateurs in
Kinsale. Mr Shanahan's fish cooking is so distinguished
that he has to be counted amongst the greatest restaurateurs of his age, yet his greatness is tempered with a
true and affecting modesty. This modesty explains how
his food is so direct and unfussy, devoid of any sort
of grandstanding attempt at greatness, but achieving
greatness by being true, pure, and side-swipingly delicious: the Christy Hurley crab cocktail; casserole of red
gurnard and prawns; grilled skate with balsamic sauce.
There is no other restaurant like Fishy Fishy, which
explains why it is perpetually packed out. And yes, we
are looking forward to Mr Shanahan's television debut,
too. (Martin & Marie Shanahan, Crowley Quay, Kinsale
☎ 021-470 0415 ⌂ www.fishyfishy.ie – Open mid Mar-
mid Oct noon-9pm Tue-Sat, noon-4.30pm Sun-Mon)

Restaurant & Fishmonger
● Fishy Fishy Shop & Chippie

The original Fishy Fishy is now shop, deli and chipper, so
you can buy superb wet fish and prepared fish dishes,
enjoy a lunch in the deli, or take away some crisp, clean
fish and chips. Fish and chips sitting on the wall of the
harbour: bliss! Oh, is it raining? Didn't notice, actually. (Martin & Marie Shanahan, The Guardwell, Kinsale
☎ 021-477 4453 ⌂ www.fishyfishy.ie – Open, shop,
9.30am-5.30pm, chippie noon-4.30pm)

Farmers' Market
● Kinsale Farmers' Market

The Kinsale market is one of the most enjoyable of the
Cork markets, thanks to a picturesque, pastoral location, and a lovely mix of producers who have coalesced
over the last couple of years to form a real community
group. There is a buzz here every Tuesday which is
quite heady and addictive. (Short Quay, Kinsale, Tuesday
mornings)

Restaurant
● Man Friday

Man Friday is one of the longest-established Kinsale restaurants, and Philip Horgan has been serving good food

and making people happy in Scilly, probably for longer than he cares to remember at this stage. MF does a good job well, steers clear of food fashions, and aims simply to fashion a good night out, every night. (Philip & Joss Horgan, Scilly, Kinsale ☎ 021-477 2260 ⏚ www.manfridaykinsale.ie – Open 6pm-10.15pm)

Traiteur & Deli
◆ Mange Tout

Guillaume Lequin's traiteur is compact, and packed with good things, so it's a swift and simple – and hugely pleasurable – process to gather together dinner or a picnic at the drop of a hat. (Guillaume Lequin, Pearse Street, Kinsale ☎ 021-477 2161 – Open 7.45am-6pm Mon-Sun)

Wine Bar
● Max's Wine Bar

Anne-Marie and Olivier's charismatic wine bar and restaurant has always been one of the most characterful of the Kinsale addresses, one of those places whose character and charm – and its air of romance – really makes you feel that you are snug in the beating heart of this dynamic portside village. Olivier's cooking is classic and correct: langoustines with wild garlic butter; rack of lamb with garlic and thyme; sea bream with a basil butter sauce – and the light lunchtime cooking is spot on. (Anne-Marie & Olivier Queva, 48 Main Street, Kinsale ☎ 021-477 2443 – Open Lunch and Dinner. Closed Tues. Open weekends only off season)

B&B
● Pier House

Ann and Pat Hegarty's house is one of the liveliest places to stay that we know. The energy comes from the Hegartys themselves, and also from the fabulous location, right smack bang in the centre of town. (Ann & Pat Hegarty, Pier Road, Kinsale ☎ 021-477 4475 ⏚ pierhouseaccom@eircom.net ⏚ www.pierhousekinsale.com – Open all year)

Delicatessen
● Quay Food Co

David and Laura Peare's deli is one of the vital fixtures of Kinsale, a rustic, dedicated wholefood shop and delicatessen, which is an essential address whether you a are a resident, or maybe a holidaymaker enjoying a spot of self-catering. It's a simple, calm and calming space, and a pleasure to linger in and shop. (David & Laura Peare, Market Quay, Kinsale ☎ 021-477 4000 ✉ quayfood@ hotmail.com 🖰 www.quayfood.com – Open 9.30am-5.30pm Mon-Sat, open till 6pm Sat during summer)

● The Spinnaker

Siun Tiernan's restaurant and bar was one of the original pioneers for good food in Kinsale, and several recent changes have seen this pretty bar and restaurant get re-focused and the creativity in the kitchen is now spot on. (Siun Tiernan, Scilly, Kinsale ☎ 021-477 2098 🖰 www.spinnakerkinsale.com – Open from 10.30am-close Mon-Sun)

● Toddies @ The Bulman

A move from the centre of town down to Summer-cove and the pretty Bulman bar has really reinvigor-ated Pearse and Mary O'Sullivan's work, helping them to achieve a razor-sharp focus with their cooking and service. Mr O'Sullivan's cooking is right on the money – grilled half lobster with beurre blanc; organic sea trout with wild garlic and chervil mayonnaise; home-smoked mackerel with blinis; Parmesan polenta with sage and hazelnut butter. There is up-front tasty food in the bar also, and value is very, very keen indeed. (Pearse & Mary O'Sullivan, Summercove, Kinsale ☎ 021-477 7769 🖰 www.toddies.ie – Open 6.30pm-10.30pm Tue-Sun, Mon-Sun high season. Closed Jan & Feb)

Rosscarbery

● Caherbeg Free-Range Pork

Having garnered prizes galore for their excellent black and white puddings, Avril and Willie Allshire have moved on to create a fine pork pâté to complement the sausages and bacon that comprise the Caherbeg pork portfolio. All are good, with the Caherbeg sausages and the black pudding maybe the cream of the crop. But with standards this high, one can only express personal pref erences about the work of a pair of model West Cork artisans. (Avril & Willie Allshire, Caherbeg, Rosscarbery ☎ 023-884 8474 ✆ caher@caherbegfreerangepork.ie ✆ www.caherbegfreerangepork.ie)

Organics
● **Devoy's Organic Farm**

Sara and John Devoy produce lovely organic veg from their six and a half acres, which we buy from shops and markets in West Cork: the Verity potatoes in early summer of 2009 were particularly fine. The couple have 500 apple trees, are planning to move into organic egg production, and also offer a box delivery scheme which gets their good grub to your doorstep. Brilliant. (John & Sara Devoy, Rosscarbery ☎ 087-235 0900 ✆ jsdevoy@eircom.net)

Cork
West

Restaurant
● **O'Callaghan-Walshe**

Some people don't get the insouciant brilliance of O'C-W. We guess that if you want smart restaurants rather than singular restaurants, and want clichéd service rather than sublime service, then you won't get the point of this iconic West Cork destination. But if you love a certain lugubriousness of style and manner, and if you love great fish and shellfish cookery, then O'C-W will seem to you to be the fish restaurant from heaven. Sean and Martina do what they, and nobody does what they do the way they do it. We applaud this originality, and we crave this superb cooking. (Sean Kearney, The Square, Rosscarbery ☎ 023-884 8125 ✆ funfish@indigo – Open 6.30pm-9.30pm Tue-Sun, Weekends only Oct-May)

Schull

Artisan Ceramics
● **Gourmet Pots**

Mairead and Tony's GP has a superlative collection of artisan ceramics, not just from Ireland but from all points throughout the world. Yes, they are pots, and working pots at that, but actually what they sell here is art, utilitarian art, made manifest in cooking vessels of stunning beauty. (Mairead McAnallen & Tony Barry, Schull mmcanallen@eircom.net)

Guesthouse
● Grove House

Katerina Runske is a dynamo, one of those people
whose elemental energy is astounding to an outsider.
With her smart young son, Nico, handling things in
the kitchen, Ms Runske has moved the lovely Grove
House centre stage in the hospitality culture of Schull.
It's a cliché to say that Grove somehow summarises
the classy bohemianism of Schull, but to tell the truth
Grove somehow summarises the classy bohemianism of
Schull. And watch out for young Nico as he gets more
experience rattling the pots and pans: this is a serious
cooking talent. (Katerina Runske, Colla Road, Schull
☎ 028-28067 ✉ info@grovehouseschull.com 🖰 www.
grovehouseschull.com – Open 7pm-7pm Mon-Sun. Also
open for light lunches outside when the weather is
good)

Farmhouse Cheese
● Gubbeen Farmhouse Cheese

When the CAP payments to Irish farmers stop in a
few years time, there will be a horrendous struggle in
the agricultural community as to how Irish agriculture,
weakened by forty years of EU subsidies, will manage to survive. Gubbeen Farm is the answer. Tom and
Giana Ferguson take every element of their agricultural
practice, and transform them into luxury brands. First
and foremost, of course, the farm itself is a brand. Then
it sells its special location, and its creative dynamic,
in cheesemaking, meat curing, horticulture, and milk
production. Gubbeen represents the biodynamic ideal of
a farm as a total entity, not just self-sufficient, but with
sufficient specialist food production to enable them to
have produce for several farmers' markets every week.
More than anyone else, the Fergusons represent the
culture of agriculture. Even more than that, they represent an economic model of farming that is revolutionary
and yet, strangely, also as ancient as agriculture itself.
(Tom & Giana Ferguson, Gubbeen, Schull ☎ 028-28231
🖰 www.gubbeen.com)

Smokehouse and Charcouterie
● Gubbeen Smokehouse

Since the last edition of this book, Fingal Ferguson and
his crew at the Gubbeen Smokehouse have created the
finest white pudding currently made in Ireland. In itself

this isn't especially dramatic, for these guys are always tinkering, always firing off some new porky product to line up alongside their pristine range of cured and smoked foods. But what is striking about the white pudding is its organoleptic singularity: it's not just a better white pudding, it's simply not like any other white pudding anyone else makes. And this is what makes the GS so amazing: they are creating new food paradigms, rather than just making paradigm shifts with their food products. It's not just their standards that are stellar. It is also their creativity, and their originality. (Fingal Ferguson, Gubbeen, Schull ☎ 028-27824 ✉ smokehouse@eircom.net ⏺ www.gubbeen.com)

Chocolates
● Gwen's Chocolates

Gwendalle Lasserre's stylish, groovy shop is the perfect stage for showcasing this gifted artisan's work with the possibilities and potential of chocolate. There are tastes to be enjoyed here that you have only ever imagined in your dreams: dreamy chocolate heaven. (Gwendalle Lasserre, Main Street, Schull ☎ 086-3171369 ✉ gwenlasserre@hotmail.com – Open 9am-1pm, 2.30pm-6pm Tue-Sat, 9am-1pm Sun and at the Schull Market)

Bar
● Hackett's Bar

Trudy Etchells not only makes brilliant bowls of soup in Schull's hippest pub, she also gives them funky names, so tomato and red pepper, for example, is The Big Red. A bowl of Big Red, a pint of Big Black, and the result is Big Happiness. Seriously wonderful. (Trudy Etchells, Main Street, Schull ☎ 028-28625 ✉ trudyetchells@eircom.net – Food served noon-3pm Mon-Sat, 7pm-9pm Fri & Sat)

Charcutier
● Frank Krawczyk's West Cork Charcuterie

Frank's specialist meats, sausages and pâtés are the cutting-edge of artisan charcuterie, born out of a gifted artisan uniting his Polish background with a flair for creating original West Cork meat products, such as his Corcoppa and the Rebel County smoked beef. The flavours and textures from his cured meats are intense, dreamy and tactile, whether you are serving the

Corcoppa as a starter, or enjoying some of his singular rillettes, or braising his chilli sausages in a stew of beans. We also reckon that one of the greatest treats of the farmers' markets is to have one of Frank's cooked sausages in a roll, with all the gorgeous trimmings, to ward off the hunger pangs as you do the shopping. (Frank Krawczyk, The Barn, Dereenatra, Schull ☎ 028-28579 ✉ westcorksalamis@gmail.com)

● Normandy Ireland Exports Ltd

There is a fish shop at the pier in Schull which sells good fresh fish, and also cooks it with chips in the summertime. Opening hours tend not to be a matter of precise definition. (The Pier, Schull ☎ 028-28599)

● O'Driscoll's Fish

The O'Driscoll brothers are dynamic guys, heading up great market stalls throughout Munster and attracting enormous queues for their high quality and superb value: one morning at Mahon Market the queue must have been thirty yards long, and they hadn't even opened! Recently they have started a cooked fish van at various specialist markets and food events, so look out for this also. (O'Driscoll family, Schull ☎ 028-27569 ✉ olischull@hotmail.com)

● Roaring Water Wholefood Shop

Lisa Davies runs this excellent wholefood shop, which manages to hoover up whatever local specialities are in season, making it a must-visit! whenever you hit Schull. The produce from local growers and producers – and even some experiments from wannabe cheesemakers – makes its way here, to a key West Cork address. (Lisa Davies, 47 Main Street, Schull ☎ 028-27834 – 9.30am-6pm Mon-Sat & Sun during the summer)

● Schull Market

Resident in a variety of places throughout the village, but usually in the Pier Road car park, the Schull market is home not just to local heroes like Gubbeen Smokehouse and Frank Krawczyk, but also to visitors like Breheny's

Belish and locals like Yummy Tummy, Eithne McCarthy's baking, Knockeen honey and fruit, Mella's fudge and other classy artisans. It's what Sunday morning is for. (Pier Road, Sundays 10am-3pm)

Farmhouse Cheese
● West Cork Natural Cheese Company

Bill Hogan and Sean Ferry have been making cheese at the Newmarket Co-Op for the last few years, and the quality of their Gabriel and Desmond cheeses remains stellar, two thermophilic, super-hard cheeses that are unlike any others. Gabriel and Desmond are amongst the finest Irish cheeses to cook with, gifting everything from fondues to gratins with sublime sweet notes and ruddy tactility. Mr Hogan is hoping, as we write, to get a little cheese school started, and it would be a mighty day indeed for Irish cheesemaking if this brilliant artisan were able to pass on a lifetime of skills, knowledge and experience to a new generation. (Bill Hogan & Sean Ferry, Dereenatra, Schull ☎ 028-28593 ✉ bh@wcnc.ie ✍ www.wcnc.ie)

Skibbereen

Organic Seeds
● Brown Envelope Seeds

Madeleine McKeever's brilliant, witty seed company is our seed company of choice, and you will see her wondrous selection of good things to grow in local wholefood stores and other outlets in West Cork. Ms McKeever's mission is simple: "To help people grow their own food". You never had such a fine ally as this talented plantswoman. (Madeleine McKeever, Ardagh, Church Cross, Skibbereen ☎ 028-38184 ✉ madsmck-eever@eircom.net ✍ www.brownenvelopeseeds.com)

Restaurant & Cookery Courses
● Island Cottage

John and Ellmary's unique restaurant on beautiful Heir Island is one of the most singular of West Cork's iconic addresses. Mr Desmond works with local fish, duck and lamb, bakes excellent bread, conjures wonderful salads, and makes some truly fine desserts. Ms Fenton serves this divine food in the room of their simple cottage, with good wines, and great camaraderie amongst all the guests who number no more than twenty at each evening's sitting. Heir Island is experiential: no matter what we write about it – and we have written about it for many, many years – can even begin to capture what an adventure it is to have dinner here. (John Desmond & Ellmary Fenton, Heir Island, Skibbereen ☎ 028-38102 ✉ info@heirislandcottage.com 🖳 www.islandcottage.com – Open Dinner Wed-Sat. No credit cards. Closed 15 Sept-15 June)

only in Cork
Brown Envelope Seeds

Restaurant
● Kalbo's Café

Siobhan O'Callaghan's café is Connie McKenna's Skibb favourite, and Connie is not alone. For a dozen years now Siobhan has been conjuring up the pleasure, cooking good things with deft grace, like Connie's fave butternut squash soup, and good salads based on leaves grown by husband Anthony, and then amongst the good fish dishes and meat dishes there are ace sweety things with which to end either lunch or a weekend dinner. True, honest, simple and delicious. (Siobhan O'Callaghan, 48 North Street, Skibbereen ☎ 028-21515 – Open breakfast and lunch, dinner Fri & Sat)

Restaurant
● Over The Moon

Francois Conradie is a brilliant cook, Jennifer Conradie is one of the best f-o-hs we have ever seen. Put them together and you have the sublime OTM. We love the cooking here: sea trout gravadlax with blinis; lamb shank with mash and spinach; dover sole with Oriental broth; pistachio chocolate brownie, all of it beautifully and artfully realised, and served with the sort of true hospitality and sincerity that you dream of finding. It all makes OTM the star of Skibb. (Francois & Jennifer Conradie, 46 Bridge Street, Skibbereen ☎ 028-22100 ⌂ www.overthemoonskibbereen.com – Open noon-3pm, 6pm-10pm Mon-Sat, 5.30pm-8pm Sun. Closed Tues)

Restaurant
● Riverside Café

You would never have known the River Ilen runs dramatically down the back of North Street in Skibb, until the Riverside cleverly opened up an informal bistro with a bright window facing the river, and a couple of chairs on a deck to take advantage of any summer sunshine. Clever exploitation of the locality also extends to the food, where local charcuterie and cheese are used to make up the various platters they serve along with their home-made bread. The Riverside has quickly become The meeting place for Skibb residents, who value its easy style and smart cooking. (Majella & Shane O'Neill, North Street, Skibbereen ☎ 028-40090 – Open 9am-5pm Mon-Sat, 6pm-9.30pm Wed-Sat)

Farmers' Market
● Skibbereen Saturday Market

It's a busy, buzzy place on Saturday morning, the Skibb fairfield. Organic growers like Devoys, Gairdin Eden and Tim and Fiona York are here with splendiferous stuff. There is home baking at the Kingston's trestle table, as well as Dunmanway's Baking Emporium. Lakeside Poultry has good eggs, Tom Ferguson is on the Gubbeen stall, there is fine fresh fish caught by day boats – we bought mackerel, a fine orange-spotted plaice and some prawns that were still twitching – and there is chocolate for sale, and plants and Tara's Organic Foods, and a host of lovely craft stalls give the market a broad scope of colour. "Everything is homemade, including myself" quips one stallholder. Well, yes indeed. (Fairfield, Skibbereen, Saturdays 10am-2pm)

Herb Preserves
● West Cork Herb Farm

Rosarie O'Byrne is an alchemist who manages to bring out the essence of the herbs you will find in her much

Cork
West

treasured herb products such as basil oil, rosemary and garlic oil, sweet pepper relish and geranium jellies. Every time you meet Rosarie she is talking about some new project. This year it was trying to understand what went into the original 1640 marshmallow (egg white, sugar and mallow sap apparently). Her West Cork Herb Farm jars are available in specialist food shops, buy them when you find them. (Rosarie O'Byrne, Church Cross, Skibbereen ☎ 028-38428)

Timoleague

Café Bar
● Dillon's Restaurant

John and Julie Finn have taken over the reins at the charmingly quixotic Dillon's, long one of West Cork's best destinations. They've been jammers since they opened, selling morning coffees with home-made scones, informal lunches and smart dinners. John is a right-on-the-money chef - the fish cookery here is sublime – and Julie was born to play the role of front of house. The restaurant has a great holiday feel that syncs sublimely with this most beautiful village. So, turn up, turn up for poached hake in white wine with champ and a whole-grain mustard and prawn cream; lamb burger with leaves and new potatoes; cod with crispy polenta and rocket; homemade apple pie. Cream with that? (John & Julie Finn, Mill Street, Timoleague ☎ 023-884 6390 – Open Lunch & Dinner from 6.30pm-9.30pm Wed-Sun)

Smokehouse
● Ummera Smokehouse

There is almost forty years of smoking experience at work in Anthony Creswell's Ummera smokehouse, forty years of care in sourcing and smoking the best fish they can find. Along with their acclaimed smoked salmon – regarded by many food lovers as the best you can buy – there is also smoked chicken, smoked bacon and smoked silver eel, though the continued supply of eel is now in doubt. We love the way in which the smoky-salty-sweet trilogy of key flavour notes, from oak smoke, brine and sugar, animate the Ummera foods, giving them the most singular organoleptic qualities. There is magic at work here, nothing less. (Anthony Creswell, Inchybridge, Timoleague ☎ 023-884 6644/087-2027227 📖 info@ummera.com 🖐 www.ummera.com)

Union Hall

● The Coffee Shop

One of the best ways to enjoy Carol Noonan's Coffee Shop is to take a dawn kayak trip with Atlantic Sea Kayaks down at Reen Harbour, and then scoot up here afterwards for breakfast. But even if you have other ways of building up an appetite when in the area, make sure to end up right here. Carol makes a lovely range of home-made cakes and cookies, fantastic home-made bread sandwiches and great soups and this light room, displaying an abundance of local art as well as the workings of the kitchen, is the ideal place to find oneself in, in this archetypal seaside village. (Carol Noonan, Main Street, Union Hall ☎ 028-34444 – Open daily 9am-5pm, shorter hours off season)

● The Fish Shop

"Everything is local" boasts Peter Deasy proudly – "except for the tuna, which we can sometimes get locally, the boats are fishing for it now, and the salmon, which is organic and comes from Galway". Talk to this wise man for a few minutes and you know Peter knows every detail of every fish he sells, and that is why The Fish Shop is a superb shop. It also operates as a wholesaler, but confines its customer base to the very best local restaurants. The display of fish is jaw droppingly spiffing, with tips on how to cook it, and even what type of wine to drink with it. A classic store. (Peter Deasy & Anthony Walsh, Main Street, Union Hall ☎ 028-33818 📧 info@glenmarshellfish.com – Open daily, 9am-5pm, Sat 9am-1pm)

County Donegal

Ardara

Donegal

B&B
● **The Green Gate**

Paul Chatenoud's idiosyncratic B&B is the sort of place where you might expect to find someone like Leonard Cohen staying there, after you drive up the hill and get out of the car. It is simple, spartan, adored by many, detested by others. The secret is that you must surrender to its simplicities, its aesthetic, and let go of your preconceptions. Do that, and you just might find your piece of heaven. (Paul Chatenoud, Ardvally, Ardara ☎ 075-954 1546 – Open all year. No credit cards)

Bar
● **Nancy's Bar**

A legendary local pub. Step in the door, step back in time, so surrender yourself to the intoxication of the rooms, the pint, and the exotic Louis Armstrong sandwich. (Front Street, Ardara ☎ 074-954 1187)

Café
● **The West End Café**

Freshly battered and fried fish, freshly fried chips, a steaming mug of tea, and isn't Charlie and Philomena's café just the best? Of course it is. (Charlie & Philomena Whyte, Main Street, Ardara ☎ 074-954 1656 – Open 9.30am-10pm Mon-Sun)

Bridgend

Bar & Restaurant
● **Harry's Restaurant**

Harry's made it into our 100 Best Restaurants in Ireland in 2009, which says it all about the ambition and determination of Donal and Kevin Doherty and their crew. These guys are fired up and they are hitting their best, with superb cooking based on the most careful sourcing imaginable: Donegal pasture beef; Greencastle fish; Whiteoaks organics, Thornhill ducks; Braemar farm ice cream; Ariosa coffee. Their distinguished suppliers can only be delighted with the respect these young men show to their food: john dory with mussel and Malin crab risotto; red gurnard with chorizo, fennel and butterbean ragoût; dry-hung, bone-in rib-eye steak; Inisowen lamb neck to shank. This is really exciting stuff, the sort of cooking that is at last making a reputation for Donegal as culinary heaven. (Donal & Kevin Doherty, Bonemaine, Bridgend, Donegal ☎ 074-936 8544 – Open noon-4pm, 4pm-late Mon-Sun. More limited hours off season)

Buncrana

Donegal

Bar & Restaurant
● The Beach House Bar & Restaurant

Claire McGowan's restaurant is the sort of classy, professional destination that you dream of stumbling upon, a place which makes the most of its gorgeous location by bringing great food and great service to a truly spectacular setting. There is a hipness, a knowingness, to everything Ms McGowan does, from the intelligence to source their meats from Maurice Kettyle to knowing just how to orchestrate a room to make it feel glam and grand to knowing that what kids really – really! – want for dessert is jelly and ice cream. A class act, through and through. (Claire McGowan, Swilly Road, Buncrana ☎ 074-936 1050 ✍ www.thebeachhouse.ie – Open lunch from noon, dinner from 5pm Mon-Sun, more limited hours off season)

Bistro & Bar
● The Laurentic

Named for the White Star liner that sank at the mouth of Lough Swilly in 1917, carrying 3,211 gold bars! the Laurentic today is an atmospheric bistro and bar and the cooking is sound and offers good value. Their secret is cooking everything to order and sending it out on smart white plates which beautifully frames Declan Burke's cooking. It's a lovely spot and very popular with locals. (Denis & Monica McLoughlin, Linsfort, Buncrana, ☎ 074-932 4019 – Open 5pm-9pm Thu & Fri, 3pm-10pm Sat, 12.30pm-9pm Sun)

Carrigart

Restaurant and Bar
● The Olde Glen Bar

The Olde Glen is ancient – they can trace its origins back to 1750 – and is quite a secret in Donegal, though the secret is spreading, thanks to the good food being served in the restaurant by Thomas and Marietta McLaughlin. This is one of the archetypal Irish bars. (Thomas & Marietta McLaughlin, Glen, Carrigart ☎ 074-915 5130)

only in Donegal
Hook Head Mackerel

Culdaff

Restaurant and Bar
● McGrory's

The Inisowen legend that is McGrory's powers on through the years, with siblings Ann, John and Neil ladling out the hospitality as to the manner born. There is something so very generous about this trio as they go about their business, managing the bar, the restaurant and the rooms, so generous with their time, their energy, their knowledge and experience, that it animates the entire place. The music sessions held here are the stuff of legend, of course, but McGrory's is special whether you can pick with a plectrum or not. (Ann, John & Neil McGrory, Culdaff ☎ 074-937 9104 ⌨ info@mcgrorys.ie ⌂ www.mcgrorys.ie – Food served in bar and restaurant Mon-Sun. Bar food served all year 12.30pm-8.30pm. Restaurant hours can vary according to season, so it is wise to check.)

Donegal

Coffee Shop and Mini Bakery
● Aroma Coffee Shop

Tom and Arturo's restaurant is on an unstoppable roll, and sure why wouldn't it be, when you consider that the

President herself, Mrs McAleese, is one of their cheer-leaders, a devotee of Tom's unbelievably delicious brown bread. And you can add super chef Clodagh McKenna to that list of devotees, and everyone else who has turned up to this modest little space in search of some of the county's finest food. Whilst Tom's baking is peerless, Arturo's savoury cooking is every bit as fine, and the simple dishes are realised with a perfectionist zeal that both these guys share. The proof of their greatness is the fact that in the teeth of the recession, Aroma has sailed serenely, ambitiously on, busier than ever, believe it or not. We believe it. (Tom Dooley, The Craft Village, Donegal Town ☎ 074-972 3222 – Open 9.30am-5.30pm Tue-Sat, lunch served noon-4pm, 7 days in high season)

only in Donegal
McGettigan's Sausages

Tearoom
● The Blueberry Tearoom

The Blueberry is usually humdingingly busy, packed not just with tourists but also with locals who enjoy both the generously flavourful cooking and the friendly serv-ice from keen, efficient staff. Worth the detour, as they apparently say in some guidebooks. (Brian & Roberta Gallagher, Castle Street, Donegal ☎ 074-972 2933 ✉ birchill88@hotmail.com – Open 9am-7pm Mon-Sat)

Farmers' Market
● Donegal Farmers' Market

Every third Saturday morning of the month is the date for the Donegal market. There are also markets in Letterkenny, on the last Friday of the month, and in Ballybofey, each Friday. (The Diamond, Donegal, 3rd Saturday 10am-2pm)

Butchers
● McGettigan's Butchers

McGettigan's have actually won the Craft Butcher's of Ireland sausage making competition no fewer than four times over the last ten years, a simply extraordinary record in competitions that are marked by ferocious creativity. But Ernan McGettigan and his team seem to be able to spin new ideas out of the ether with ease. If it's not a sausage that's on your mind, then everything else in the shop shows the same creative energy. (Ernan McGettigan, The Diamond, Donegal ☎ 074-972 1461)

Bar & Restaurant
● The Olde Castle Bar & Restaurant

A minute's walk away from the Diamond, and the Olde Castle bar and restaurant is home to unpretentious, gimmick-free local seafood, with the sort of menu that every Donegal destination should offer: Killybegs seafood pies; Lily Boyle's fishcakes; seafood chowder; cod in breadcrumbs; grilled lobster; seafood platter. "This is a must for visitors and locals", said Caroline Byrne, after enjoying the largesse of the platter: Bruckless crab meat; Donegal Bay oyster; poached and smoked salmon; crab claws; baby prawns and a nice wee pot of marie rose sauce. This is smart cooking, and a model lesson in offering the sublime bounty of the county's coastline. Red Hugh's restaurant upstairs is more formal, the cooking enjoys equal panache. Service is incredibly speedy, and the food for children is especially thoughtful. (Seoirse & Maeve O'Toole, ☎ 074-972 1262 ⁑ www.oldecastlebar. com – Open for bar lunch 12.30pm-4pm, restaurant open 6pm-9.45pm)

Wholefood Shop
● Simple Simon Natural Foods

The Simple Simon in Donegal's Diamond is one of four stores in the county operated by this smart little chain, the others being in Letterkenny, Ballyshannon and Dungloe. Good baking and good local produce make the stores a valuable resource. (Robbie & Mick Gillen, The Diamond, Donegal ☎ 074-972 2687 ⁑ simplesimon@ eircom.net. Simple Simon Living Food, Oliver Plunkett Road, Letterkenny ☎ 074-912 2382; Castle Street, Ballyshannon ☎ 071-982 2737; Supervalu, Dungloe ☎ 074-956 1982 ⁑ www.simplesimondonegal.com)

Dunfanaghy

Wholefoods & Wines
● The Green Man

Eileen Gallagher and Neil Hougardy collate the finest local Donegal foods with great wines and imported Fair

Trade foods in this smashing shop on the main street, a truly important addition to the far north west. (Eileen Gallagher & Neil Hougardy, Main Street, Dunfanaghy ☎ 074-910 0800 🖰 www.greenmandunfanaghy.com – Open 9.30am-6pm Mon-Sat, 10am-2pm Sun)

● The Mill Restaurant

Derek and Susan Alcorn have blazed a path of glory ever since they opened their doors in the beautiful restaurant with rooms that is The Mill, and they have blazed this path thanks to doing everything just right. It has always fascinated us to see customers at rest and play here, treating The Mill like an old friend, relaxing in the utter comfort, totally chilled out, and dreaming of dinner to come: salad of chorizo, broad beans, olives and soft boiled egg; leek and asparagus risotto; Horn Head lamb with basil mash; chocolate torte with chocolate and thyme ice cream. Derek Alcorn is a singular cook, devoted to local foods to which he shows the ultimate respect. Simply perfect. (Derek & Susan Alcorn, Figart, Dunfanaghy ☎ 074-913 6985 🖰 www.themillrestaurant. com – Open Easter-Halloween, Restaurant open 7pm-9pm Tue-Sun)

Dunkineely

● Castle Murray House

Consistency, consistency, consistency. That's what you get in Marguerite Howley's Castlemurray House, and that's why Castlemurray House has been in the *Bridgestone Guides* ever since our first book, back in 1991. Part of their success is explained by the fact that Remy Dupuy has been in the kitchen since 1994, cooking house classics such as prawns and monkfish in garlic butter, tartare of Inver sea trout with blinis, or ravioli of Donegal crab. And, since 1991, we have been writing that the views from the dining room are amongst the most captivating in the entire county, and this is a county that does views everywhichway. The rooms are simple and comfortable, the hospitality genuine and fetching. (Marguerite Howley, Dunkineely ☎ 074-973 7022 🖰 www. castlemurray.com – Restaurant open 6.30pm-9.30pm Mon-Sat; 1.30pm-3.30pm, 6.30pm-8.30pm Sun)

Donegal

Glenties

Donegal

Biodynamic Grower
● Thomas Becht

For more than twenty years, Thomas and Lucia Becht have managed their farm according to the bio-dynamic principles of Rudolf Steiner. Over that time, they have created not just an ideal farm, but an ideal agricultural working environment. Sustainable in a true sense, dignified in a true sense, productive in a true sense and nutritional in a true sense, the Bechts farm in the way farming should be practiced, using the gift of good land to produce wondrously fine food, which they even deliver to your door by means of their box delivery scheme. They are practical people, and hard-working people, and they are animated by the possibilities and potential of the culture of agriculture. Truly, truly inspiring. (Thomas & Lucia Becht, Doorian, Glenties ☎ 074-955 1286 ✉ donegalorganic@hotmail.com ⏚ www.donegalorganic.ie – Shop open 8.30am-8pm Mon-Sun)

Preserves
● Filligan's Preserves

"Small is the philosophy behind our business". Isn't that a lovely thing for a duo of artisans to say about their business? We know small is beautiful, we know small works, we know small is sustainable, but so many get seduced by the idea of endless expansion that small often gets lost. Not with Philip and Sara Moss of Filligan's. Since they started in 1997, they have grown, a wee bit, but what they do is make jams, preserves, relishes and chutneys by hand, and the hands that make them are their own, and those of their little team, so expansion and mechanisation are out of the question. And that's the reason why the Filligans' products are so fine, so next time you open one of their pretty jars, just reflect on the hands that stirred and created what you are enjoying. (Sara & Philip Moss, Tullyard, Glenties ☎ 074-955 1628 ✉ moss@filligans.com ⏚ www.filligans.com)

only in Donegal
Mulroy Bay Scallops

Glenveagh

Restaurant
● The Tearooms

No one who goes to Donegal should miss Glenveagh
Park, and no one who goes to Glenveagh Park should
miss its tearooms and restaurant, shining examples
of how to serve great food without compromise in a
self-service setting. Michelle Hunter and her crew do
a fabulous job, serving homemade, tasty, smart cooking every day in the tea rooms, and during the summer
season in the restaurant also. Salads are fresh and crisp,
sandwiches are wholesome, the tarts and quiches are
imaginative and beautifully cooked, and the tray bakes
hit the spot every time. "It's just simple home baking",
Michelle says modestly, but it's simple home baking as
simple home baking should be: honest, soulful, delicious.
And a little tip: make sure to have that insect repellent
ready so the midges don't make a meal of you. (Michelle
Hunter, Churchill, Letterkenny ☎ 074-913 7090
🖰 www.glenveaghnationalpark.ie – open all year)

Donegal

Greencastle

Restaurant
● Kealy's Seafood Bar

Tricia Kealy's super bar, just across from the pier, is
home to good, friendly food, and is a legendary address
in this far-flung neck of the woods. Both the bar and
the dining room are calm, atmospheric places to eat,
and whilst there are menu choices for meat eaters, you
would want to be crazy not to choose the excellent
fish and shellfish cookery. (Tricia Kealy, The Harbour,
Greencastle ☎ 074-938 1010 – Open 12.30pm-2.45pm
7pm-9.30pm Tue-Sun)

Mountain Lamb

Laghey

Donegal

Restaurant and Accommodation
● Coxtown Manor

Edward Dewael's house is one of the nicest places to stay in Ireland. That's what our friends tell us, not that we didn't know it ourselves, having stayed here many times since we first found this calm, calming country house, just a few miles south of Donegal town. Our friends – and us! – love the good food, the comfort, the fascinating fellow guests you meet, and we love the way in which Mr Dewael piulls all the elements of Coxtown together, like a master puppeteer. Sublime. (Edward Dewael, Laghey ☎ 074-973 4574 📧 coxtownmanor@oddpost.com 🖥 www.coxtownmanor.com – Open mid Feb-end October)

only in Donegal
Aroma Brown Bread

Letterkenny

Butcher
● McGee's Butcher's

The location in the shopping centre isn't ideal, but McGee's is a serious butchers shop, with fine meat from their farm in County Tyrone. (Joe McGee, Unit 29 Letterkenny SC, Port Rd, L'kenny ☎ 074-917 6567 📧 mail@mcgeesfood.ie 🖥 www.mcgeesfood.com – Open 9am-6pm Mon-Wed, 9am-8pm Thur & Fri, 9am-7pm Sat, noon-6pm Sun)

Rathmullan

Restaurant
● An Bonnan Bui

Simple things can make you famous. Martin Kelly and Monica Santos's lovely, simple An Bonnan Bui is famous for: the chocolate cake. They could describe the cake as

Bonnan Bui Chocolate Cake

"the world famous chocolate cake". But that's not their style. Instead it's described as "a very good chocolate cake". But it is much more than that, as indeed is everything this talented pair cook and serve. Monica's Brazilian background shows itself in the menus, but whether she is preparing her native dishes or more conventional fare such as rack of lamb or Mulroy Bay scallops, the cooking is precise, expert, superbly defined. Pure darling. (Martin Kelly & Monica Santos, Pier Road, Rathmullan ☎ 074-915 8453 ✉ bonnanbui@yahoo.ie ⌐ www. anbonnanbui.com – Open 5.30pm-9.30pm Mon-Sun. Weekends only off season)

Country House
● **Rathmullan House**

Mark Wheeler and his crew, with chef Ian Orr at the helm, brought their cooking van to Electric Picnic in 2009 and snapped up the Eco award, for cooking sustainably sourced fish. Lucky Picnickers, able to get a taste of the dynamic cooking of this team so far away from Rathmullan's home in northerly Donegal. Mr Orr is proving himself to be the latest, and perhaps the greatest, in a line of kitchen talent that has lifted Rathmullan into the superstar territory amongst Irish country houses, and Mr Orr is going to be one of the leading talents of the next decade, for he brings judgement and modesty in his cooking of the most sublime ingredients: oak-smoked Fermanagh chicken with shaved fennel and pea and mint purée; fritto misto of local scallops and Portavogie prawns; Greencastle monkfish with peperonata; Silverhill duck with pea and asparagus risotto cake. Amazing food, gorgeous house, superb hospitality, a true star. (Mark Wheeler, Lough Swilly, Rathmullan ☎ 074-915 8188 ✉ info@ rathmullanhouse.com ⌐ www.rathmullanhouse.com – Open all year, apart from mid Jan-mid Feb)

County Dublin

DUBLIN CENTRAL

Farm and Café
● **Airfield House**

The only working urban farm in Dublin is managed by
a private trust, and hosts many gardening and growing
events through the year. There is a fine café and shop in
which to enjoy some tasty, simple food whilst relishing the peculiarity of an agricultural oasis in the 'burbs.
(John O'Toole, Upper Kilmacud Road, Dundrum, D14
☎ 01-298 4301 ✉ info@airfield.ie 🖰 www.airfield.ie –
Open 10am-5pm Mon-Sun)

Restaurant
● **Ananda**

Even hell – for which read the ghastly Dundrum Shopping Centre – can have an oasis of calm and creativity,
and in the DSC that oasis is Ananda. Asheesh Dewan
has fashioned new standards of creativity and achievement for Indian cooking here, in a beautiful room that is
one of the treasures of the southside. Don't come here
to eat the conventional dishes: push out the boat with
chicken with rose petal, or Robata pork with apple-
infused cider, and you will have an experience unlike any
other. Parents should note that the kid's menu is only
fabulous, and the room is gorgeous. (Sunil Ghai, DSC,
Sandyford Road, Dublin 15 ☎ 01-296 0099 ✉ info@
anandarestaurant.ie 🖰 www.anandarestaurant.ie –
Open 5.30pm-11pm Mon-Sun. Open from 4pm on Sat &
Sun)

Restaurant
● **Anderson's**

Noel Delaney is one of the most imaginative and gifted
of Dublin restaurateurs, a man who opened up a café,
food hall and wine shop in Glasnevin when everyone else
thought it was a graveyard, and who proved that serving
great cooking in a great room would work on any side of
the river. Anderson's is cosmopolitan, mannered and fun,
with every element of their food well-considered and
well-executed. A little slice of la dolce vita in Dublin 9.

(Noel Delaney, 3 The Rise, Glasnevin, D9 ☎ 01-837 8394 ✆ info@andersons.ie 🖰 www.andersons.ie – Open 9am-7.30pm Mon-Wed, 9am-9pm Thur-Sat, 10am-7.30pm Sun)

Crêperie
● Anderson's Crêperie

Noel Delaney designed and executed his Drumcondra crêperie with just as much flair and panache as he brought to the original Anderson's in Glasnevin. The room is both café and crêperie, but for us it's the buckwheat crêpes and the Breton cider that are the stars of the show, especially if there is a plash of jazz playing, as there is on Wednesday evenings. Another super-cool success story that takes you from the Northside to somewhere close to Saint Pol-de Léon. (Noel Delaney, 3 Carlingford Road, Drumcondra, D9 ☎ 01-830 5171 ✆ info@andersons.ie 🖰 www.andersons.ie – Open 9am-7pm Mon-Sat, Fri open till 9pm, 10am-7pm Sun)

Deli-Café-Bistro
● Angel Park Eatery

"Big thumbs up!", says Caroline Byrne of Tanya McGouran's deli-café-bistro, just off Dublin's gracious Merrion Square. But, says Caroline, be prepared to queue if you are buying from the deli, for the crush here at lunchtime as the APE gets saturated with staff from all the nearby offices means it gets mighty crowded. The wait is worth it; this is good, freshly made food, with excellent salads to go – satay noodle; lentille de Puy and chick pea; good tabouleh – and you can piece together ingredients to make your own fave sandwich, or go for the girls' take on classics, such as their rumplestiltskin, with baked ham, wilted cabbage, wholegrain mustard and melted cheese on brown bread. Nice cooking in the café. Excellent. (Tanya McGouran, 5 Lower Mount Street, D2 ☎ 01-676 3010 – Open 7.30am-4pm Mon-Fri)

Café and Bakery
● Arnott's

The La Brea Bakery in Arnott's has now been joined by the third branch of Dunne & Crescenzi's cracking L'Officina restaurants, which is in the Jervis centre branch. Serving only guaranteed origin products from Italy, the Officina addresses meld delicious food with big, bright busy rooms that are a sheer pleasure to be in. Real smart, which is exactly what you feel when you choose to eat here. The Abbey Street entrance is home to the La Brea bakery and café. (Henry St, D1 ☎ 01-805 0400 ⏱ www.arnotts.ie)

● Asia Market

Everything you could possibly need for successful Asian cooking under one unflatteringly-lit roof. The Asian staff are impassively quiet, the Western staff are awesomely funky. (Helen Pau, 18 Drury Street, D2 ☎ 01-677 9764 – Open 10am-7pm Mon-Sun)

● Avoca

Avoca is one of Ireland's leading luxury brands, up there in the stratosphere with Ballymaloe, Gubbeen, The Tannery and other singular stalwarts of Ireland's food culture. Strangely enough, we had an accidental little part in their development, for we wrote many years ago in a newspaper about an embarrassing episode when John McKenna tried to be a modern Dad and feed his (then) babies at Kilmacanogue, when it was one of only a couple of Avocas. McKenna failed miserably to feed the kids, but wrote about how great the food was – what little he got to try – and how brilliant the staff were. Avoca took that little shot of praise and, like champions, they geared up and, like the best icons, they never rested on their laurels, always getting better and better. We have called in the past for Simon Pratt, the brains behind the food, to be a Tsar for Food Standards, Actually, we think he should be Taoiseach. (Simon Pratt, Suffolk Street, D2 ☎ 01-672 6019 ✉ info@avoca.ie ⏱ www.avoca.ie – Open 10am-6pm Mon-Fri, open till 8pm Thur, 10am-6.30pm Sat, 11am-6pm Sun. Also in Rathcoole, Naas Road, Co Dublin, and Counties Wicklow, Cork and Galway)

● Il Baccaro

Abandon all critical perspective, all ye who step down the stairs into Il Baccaro. You are here for the craic, and for more wine. Much more wine. Tomorrow be damned, and isn't it great to be young and in Dublin! (Meeting House Square, Temple Bar, D2 ☎ 01-671 4597 ⏱ www.ilbaccaro.com – Open 5.30pm-10.30pm Mon-Sun, noon-3pm Sat)

Restaurant
● Bang Café

Lorcan Gribbin is a great chef, and a great ambassador
for pure, stylish modern Irish restaurant cooking. He
has held the reins of Bang steady now for an impressive
span of years, and being the quiet, thoughtful man
from County Laois that he is, he doesn't make a song
and dance about the fact that he is one of the city's
best chefs, and cooks some of the city's best food. It's
our job to tell you that, and now you know. (Lorcan
Gribbin, 11 Merrion Row, D2 ☎ 01-676 0898 ⁿ www.
bangrestaurant.com – Open 12.30pm-3pm Mon-Sat
(open till 4pm Fri & Sat); 6pm-10.30pm Mon-Wed; 6pm-
11pm Thu-Sat. Closed Sun)

Restaurant
● Bar Italia

David Izzo and Stefano Crescenzi's Bar Italia serves
Italy's greatest gastronomic hits, and does everything
well, from good pastas and panino to some of the
most carefully-crafted coffee in the city. There is a
second branch in the IFSC, further down the river from
Ormond Quay. (David Izzo, 26 Lower Ormond Quay,
D2 ☎ 01-874 1000; Unit 2, IFSC D1 ☎ 01-670 2887
ⁿ www.baritalia.ie – Open 8am-10.30pm Mon-Fri,
10am-10pm Sat. Also at Bloom's Lane, 26 Lower
Ormond Quay, D1 – Open 8am-11pm Mon-Fri, 9am-
11pm Sat, 9.30pm-10pm Sun)

only in Dublin
Shop Easi Anwar Ratols

Restaurant
● Base

According to our man Leslie Williams, Shane Crilly and
Aengus Lacey make the best pizzas in the country. Not
just the best in Dublin, but the best in Ireland. What do
they do right in Base? That name says it all. They start
with the right type of flour to make the perfect thin,
crispy base, they use a wood-fired oven imported from
L.A, and they heat it with ash, and then they let their
imaginations roam, piling on good ingredients as if they
hailed from Naples. Base, with its purity and discipline

– there are only a couple of silly ingredients used – may just be the pizza heaven Dublin has waited decades for. (Shane Crilly & Aengus Lacey, Terenure Road East, D6 ☎ 01-440 4800 ✉ info@basewfp.ie ⏱ www.basewfp.ie – Open noon-11pm Mon-Sun)

Restaurant & Accommodation
● Bentley's

Richard Corrigan's Dublin counterpart to his successful London restaurant has already entered local mythology as the place where gossip coalesces, urban myths begin, and trends and examples are set. Even Ross O'Carroll-Kelly, arbiter of everything that is ghastly about modern Ireland, felt moved to note that "not everyone in this town is suddenly eating the Bentley's early bird and using public tranport". As usual, Ross is wrong; smart people go by bus and they do eat the Bentley's pre-theatre menu, enjoying croquettes de jamon with avocado and melba toast, veal liver with shallot mash and devil sauce, and poached apricot with coconut sorbet, all for 25 euro. Mr Corrigan's cooking is classic and cautious, and whilst it is very different to the wild work of his youth when we first ate it in London twenty years ago, it is still supremely enjoyable. There are attractive rooms for lodging up above the restaurant, and the location on St Stephen's Green can't be beat. (Richard Corrigan, 22 St Stephen's Green, D2 ☎ 01-638 3939 ✉ info@ bentleysdublin.com ⏱ www.bentleysdublin.com – Open 7am-10.30am, noon-2.30pm, 5.30pm-11pm Mon-Fri, 7am-11am, noon-3pm 6pm-11pm Sat & Sun, closed 10pm Sun)

Restaurant
● Bianconi

The Macari family's long, bright room is always a good spot for accessible and very tasty Italian cooking, straight from the textbook: antipasto misto; pizza Margherita; ricotta and spinach tortelloni. (Tony Macari, 232 Merrion Road, Ballsbridge, D4 ☎ 01-219 6033 – Open 9.30am-10pm Mon-Fri, 10.30am-10pm Sat, 10.30am-9pm Sun)

Restaurant
● Bijou

Bijou is a rock-solid, rock-steady neighbourhood restaurant, of the sort every neighbourhood in the city should have, and of the sort that is patronised by smart, food-loving locals who enjoy the modern food and the assured, confident tone of the room. They have been doing the good thing for more than a decade now, for devoted customers, and plans to add a deli to their bistro and restaurant offer are in development. (Linda Smith, 47 Highfield Road, Rathgar, D6 ☎ 01-496 1518 🖃 bijourestaurant@eircom.net 🖰 www.bijourathgar. ie – Bistro open noon-late, restaurant open from 5pm Wed-Fri, from 6pm Sat, 12.30pm-5pm Sun)

Restaurant
● Bistro One

A staple address of the Foxrock scene, Bistro One has been sending out good, French-influenced cuisine for many years. Mark Shannon does things right: good tablecloths, good glasses and good wines by the carafe, cosy bentwood chairs, and properly sourced food, from Connemara hill lamb to West Cork double cream to John O'Reilly's 28-day dry-aged rib-eye. A restaurateur's restaurant. (Mark Shannon, 3 Brighton Road, Foxrock Village, D18 ☎ 01-289 7711 🖃 dining@bistro-one.ie 🖰 www.bistro-one.ie – Open noon-2.30pm, 6pm-10pm Tue-Sat)

Restaurant
● The Blackboard Bistro

Jean and Pierre's little basement on Clare Street is a place of which they are quietly proud, and so they should be. It's a cosy space for couples, a fun room for a group, and the Mediterranean/Provençal notes of the cooking are a sure-fire hit: chicken with couscous and grilled vegetables; burger with mash, fried onions, red wine sauce and a fried egg; smoked bacon and leek risotto; passion fruit sorbet. Quietly classy and expert, and quite lovely. (Jean & Pierre Heyraud, 4 Clare Street, D2 ☎ 01-676 6839 – Open 12.30pm-2.30pm Tue-Fri, 5.30pm-9.30pm Tue-Sat)

Deli and Bakery
● Blazing Salads Food Company

Lorraine, Joe and Pamela Fitzmaurice put the expertise shown in their fine "Blazing Salads Cookbook" into deli-cious, tactile reality every day in their bustling deli and shop, and via their splendid naturally leavened breads, which are also sold in other outlets apart from the Drury Street shop. There are two generations of skill and understanding behind everything they make and bake. (The Fitzmaurice family, 42 Drury Street, D2 ☎ 01-671 9552 📠 info@blazingsalads.com 🖱 www.blazingsalads.com – Open 9am-6pm Mon-Fri, 9am-5.30pm Sat)

Restaurant
● Bleu Bistro Moderne

Eamonn O'Reilly's second restaurant – close to the more formal One Pico – is a smart, bright room with smart, bright cooking that is symptomatic of this fine chef's expert understanding of what people like to eat: mushroom and tarragon risotto; rib-eye burger with smoked Knockanore cheese; herb-crusted lamb with carrot and star anise purée; fillet of beef with duck fat potatoes and bearnaise. Grown-up cooking, and value is very, very keen. (Eamonn O'Reilly, Joshua House, Dawson Street, D2 ☎ 01-676 7015 🖱 www.bleu.ie – Open noon-11pm Mon-Sat, noon-9pm Sun)

Restaurant
● Bóbós

When Leslie Williams conducted an extensive survey of the new generation of Dublin hamburger restaurants for www.bridgstoneguides.com, he gave Bóbós the highest rating of all: 9 out of 10. How do you score that high? Top quality meat from a great butcher, toasty crusty buns, good mushy peas, chocolatey chocolate shakes, and very good berry juice. In short, attention to detail, and when you throw in a lot of ironic design icons – TK lemonade; Saxa salt on the table, wow! – then you are well ahead of the rest. "When are we coming back?" asked Leslie's son, Grellan. It's what everyone asks. (Jay Bourke, 22 Wexford Street, D2 ☎ 01-400 5750 📠 info@bobos.ie 🖱 www.bobos.ie – Open 9am-11.30pm Mon-Fri, noon-11.30pm Sat, 1pm-10pm Sun)

Wine Merchant
● Brechin Watchorn

A cracking local wine shop, and Stuart and Gavin are lively and enthusiastic oenophiles. (Stuart Brechin & Gavin Watchorn, 29 Dunville Avenue, Ranelagh, D6 ☎ 01-491 1763 📠 info@brechinwatchornwine.com 🖱 www.bwwine.com – Open 11am-8pm Mon-Fri, 11am-7pm Sat, 2pm-9pm Sun)

● Bretzel Bakery

If you have not ridden your bike up to the doors of the
Bretzel on a weekend morning and joined the queue to
buy bagels, challah. and onion bread, then you cannot
call yourself a true resident of Dublin. Buying bread here
is a rite of passage for all who come to the capital, and
as long time devotees, we are delighted that under owners Cormac Keenan and William Despard The Bretzel
is, today, busier and better than ever. You can get their
breads in other outlets, but make no mistake that the
pilgrimage to Lennox Street is part of the whole caboo-
dle, especially since a brilliant refurbishment brought
traditional design elements of the shop back into focus.
(William Despard, 1a Lennox Street, Sth Circular Road,
Portobello, D8 ☎ 01-475 2742 ⌦ www.bretzel.ie –
Open 8.30am-6pm Mon-Fri, 9am-5.30pm Sat, 9am-1pm
Sun)

● Browne's Deli and Café

Peter Bark's coffee shop and deli by day becomes a
French-style bistro by night, and even folk with Sandy-
mount-sized negative equity can enjoy it, thanks to the
very keen prices. Moules marinieres; lamb with flageo-
lets; scallops with Puy lentils; confit duck leg; Toulouse
sausages and mash are the sort of classic dishes over
which the kitchen shows complete control. It's a busy
place at any time of day or night, so don't turn up hoping
for a table. (Peter Bark, Sandymount Green, D4 ☎ 01-
269 7316 ⌦ pbark@eircom.net – Open 7.30am-9.15pm
Mon-Fri, 9am-9.15pm Sat, 10am-5pm Sun)

● The Bull & Castle

Part of the FXB group, the B&C is important because
– unlike almost all Irish pubs – it is home to many good
Irish-made brews, so call for a pint of Galway Hooker
or O'Hara's Stout, or Blarney Blonde. Excellent. (Christ
Church, Dublin 2 ☎ 01-475 1122 ⌦ www.bullandcastle.ie)

● Buns.ie

In front of the Bank of Ireland in College Green one
morning, Paula and Ger Coyne sold 1,000 cup cakes in a
few hours. 1,000! "Truly delicious!" is how Leslie

Williams described Paul and Ger's baking, so to get hold of these little marvels of taste, hunt Buns down at Mespil Road every Thursday, at Howth market on Sunday, and Newbridge on Saturday. You can also order online, and the only problem is: what bun? A Bunny? A Hummingbird? An Old fashioned? Ah, the paradox of choice! (Paula & Ger Coyne, North King Street, D7 🖰 www.buns.ie)

Restaurant
● Cafe Bar Deli

Jay Bourke's cheep'n'cheerful eateries offer simple Mediterranean-style food at good prices, which explains why the Dublin originals have been joined by branches down the country. (Jay Bourke, 12 South Great Georges Street, D2 ☎ 01-677 1646 🖰 georgesstreet@ cafebardeli.ie 🖰 www.cafebardeli.ie – Open 12.30pm-11pm Mon-Sat, 2pm-10pm Sun. Also 62 Ranelagh Village ☎ 01-496 1886 🖰 ranelagh@cafebardeli.ie – Open 12.30pm-11pm Mon-Sat, 12.30pm-10pm Sun)

Restaurant & Cookery Classes
● Café Fresh

Mary Farrell's restaurant is one of the staples of Powerscourt, and one of the staples of Dublin vegetarian cooking. Mary's deli on Leeson Street, Deli Fresh, offers the restaurant's signature dishes to take away, another smart aspect of an operation that includes cookery classes, a catering wing, and Mary's own Café Fresh cookbook. (Mary Farrell, Top Floor, Powerscourt Townhouse Centre, D2 ☎ 01-671 9669 🖰 info@cafe-fresh. com 🖰 www.cafe-fresh.com – Cafe Open 9am-6pm Mon-Sat, Deli Open 7.30am-3.30pm Mon-Fri)

Café
● The Cake Café

The CC isn't a café: it's a legend. We suspect that it may be just about the favourite place of *Bridgestone's* Dublin editors. "It has a secret garden quality", says Elizabeth Field. "One of the churches of the laid-back, boho-chic inhabitants of the too-cool-for-school Portobello to Dublin 8 neighbourhood", says Caroline Byrne. Add this mysterious bohemianism to knock-out cooking, and you have the true stuff of legend. Owner Michelle Darmody is, for us, one of the most singular talents at work in the capital today, and we will queue up anytime for parsnip and celery soup (what a good combination); butternut squash, chilli and chickpea hotpot and then a chocolate brownie with a properly made cup of tea. Are we happy? We sure are. (Michelle Darmody, 62 Pleasant's Place, D8 ☎ 01-478 9394 ✉ thecakecafe@gmail.com ⌂ www. thecakecafe.ie – Open 8.30am-6pm Mon, 8.30am-8pm Tue-Fri, 9am-5.30pm Sat)

Bar
● The Cellar Bar

One of the best bars in Dublin in which to eat, and manager Damian Corr's energy and enthusiasm, and his wine expertise, are hard to beat. (Damian Corr, Merrion Hotel, Upper Merrion Street, D2 ☎ 01-603 0600 ⌂ www.merrionhotel.com – Open noon-2.30pm, from 6pm Mon-Sun)

Restaurant
● The Cellar Restaurant

Ed Cooney has cooked in the Cellar ever since they opened, and he is a modest, generous cook whose understated manner is in contrast to what we find the overstated manner of much of the Merrion Hotel. Mr Cooney's cooking is mature and vivid: sugar-cured Galway salmon with hazelnut crème fraîche; Tipperary lamb with Lusk apple balsamic; Castletownbere scallops with sauce ravigote; McLaughlin's rump steak with portobello mushroom. Mr Cooney's sourcing is meticulous, such a contrast to the anonymous food offer of so many hotels. (Ed Cooney, The Merrion Hotel, Upper Merrion Street, D2 ☎ 01-603 0600 ⌂ www.merrionhotel.com – Open breakfast 7am-10.30am Mon-Sun, lunch 12.30pm-2pm Mon-Fri (no lunch Sat), brunch 12.30pm-2.30pm Sun, dinner 6pm-10pm Mon-Sun)

Whiskey Shop
● The Celtic Whiskey Shop

Ally Alpine's shop-of-two-halves – one half whiskey, one half wine – is one of our favourite haunts. If you love whiskeys of all manner, then this is the Holy Grail, for they are here in all their serried magnificence, their desirability making us behave just like kids in a sweetie shop. The wines are chosen with the same smart discrimination as the whiskeys, and the expertise of the staff warms the heart as surely as a tot of Redbreast. (Ally Alpine, 27-28 Dawson Street, D2 ☎ 01-

675 9744 ✉ info@celticwhiskeyshop.com 🖰 www.
celticwhiskeyshop.com – Open 10.30am-8pm Mon-Sat,
12.30am-6pm Sun and bank hols)

Restaurant
● **Chameleon**

Twenty years ago, Carol Walsh opened The Cellary in
Fownes Street, and in 1994 transformed the restaurant
into the Indonesian-influenced Chameleon. Other
Temple Bar restaurants have been around as long, but
none continue to embody the bohemianian spirit that
characterised this district in the early days of the late
'80's and early 1990's. Carol and Kevin continue to do
just that, cooking generous, simple Indonesian-style
food in characterful rooms, with personal, spirited
service. Bless 'em. (Carol Walshe & Kevin O'Toole,
1 Fownes Street, Temple Bar, D2 ☎ 01-671 0362
✉ book@chameleonrestaurant.com 🖰 www.
chameleonrestaurant.com – Open from 5pm Tue-Sat
and Sat lunch)

Restaurant
● **Chapter One**

When most chefs get their photograph taken, they try
to look moody and serious. Anytime you see a photo
of Ross Lewis, he is smiling like a sandboy. Sure, why
wouldn't he be laughing. With his partner, Martin Corbett, Mr Lewis runs what is probably the most beloved
restaurant in Dublin, not to mention perhaps the most
successful. His cooking is a wonder – nuanced, personal,
vigorous, utterly Irish – and yet informed by every food
style that surrounds him. Chapter One is the restarant
where you go to celebrate the good things in life,
because the rooms and the food and the service seem
like nothing other than a pure celebration of the genius
of Irish cooking. The new chef's table lets six customers
eat right in the heat and heart of the action. Personally, if
we had to eat off the floor it would still be a treat to get
the chance to enjoy such animated, delicious cooking.
(Ross Lewis & Martin Corbett, 18-19 Parnell Square, D1
☎ 01-873 2266 🖰 www.chapteronerestaurant.com –
Open 12.30pm-2pm Tue-Fri; 6pm-10.30pm Tue-Sat)

only in Dublin
Chapter One Charcuterie Trolley

Deli & Wine Shop
● The Cheese Pantry

Aidan McNeice and Karen McHugh's deli and café has
settled nicely into the Drumcondra way of life, with a
really useful store of good foods and wines, and lots of
nice things to eat in the café at the back of the shop.
Their cheese selection is unmatched in this part of
town. (Aidan & Karen McNeice, 104 Upper Drumcondra Road, Drumcondra, D9 ☎ 01-797 8936 🖃 aidan@
thecheesepantry.com 🖱 www.thecheesepantry.com –
Open 9am-8pm Mon-Tue, 9am-10pm Wed-Sat, 10am-
4pm Sun)

Restaurant
● Chez Max

Everyone's favourite little French eaterie has become
such a success that they have opened a second branch
on Baggot Street. There isn't an original dish on the
menu, and hooray! for that. You are here for Piaf, and
steak frites, Brel, and moules, Brassens, and boeuf
bourguignon. Their secret is that there is no artifice to
the food, no campness, no irony, no retro: they love
this sort of cooking, and so will you. The new Baggot
Street destination has the same cosy, clubby, banquet-
tey, bentwoody feel, and the same classic fare, so settle
in for Toulouse sausage with lentils, beef cheek terrine,
and moules frites. (Max de Laloubie, 1 Palace Street,
D1 ☎ 01-663 7215; 133 Baggot Street, ☎ 01-661 8899
🖱 www.chezmax.ie– Open 8am-midnight Mon-Fri,
11am-midnight Sat-Sun)

Chinese Restaurant
● China Sichuan

When Kevin Hui's China Sichuan relocated to new
premises in Dublin 18 in 2008, it raised the bar for
standards of ethnic cooking in Ireland, and quickly took
top spot for Chinese food from the Belfast restaurants
that previously enjoyed the most exciting cooking. The
dishes simply don't miss: aubergine and tofu in hot ginger
and garlic sauce; monkfish in black bean; king prawns in
duck egg yolk; camphor tea smoked duck. The room is
luxurious, the service swift and polite, and whilst you
can spend serious money with the à la carte, set menus
are marvellous value. (Kevin Hui, The Forum, Ballymoss
Road, Sandyford, D18, ☎ 01-293 5100 🖱 www.china-
sichuan.ie – Open noon-10pm Sun-Fri, 6pm-10pm Sat)

Café

● **Cobblers**

Eilis Davy's popular café on Leeson Lane has been doing the good thing for a couple of years now, with nice
daytime food that pulls in the office workers and grind
students who spill out of Stephen's Green and Leeson
Street every day. (Eilis Davy, 4 Leeson Lane, D2 ☎ 01-
678 5945 – Open daytime)

Coffee Stall

● **Coffee Angel**

Karl Purdy is an autodidactic perfectionist, so whenever
you come across a Coffee Angel coffee cart, you are in
for a caffeine-fuelled experience that navigates via the
sublime through to the narcotic. Every year at the Irish
barista championships, Mr Purdy's crew do exceptionally
well, inspired by the dedication – and sheer hard work
and vision – of their boss. You will find carts at CHQ
and also in Dun Laoghaire and at many events. (Karl
Purdy, CHQ, D1 ✉ info@coffeeangel.com ⊕ www.
coffeeangel.com)

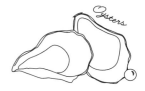

Restaurant

● **Coppinger Row**

Having fashioned a success with the South William
lounge just around the corner, the Bereen brothers,
Conor and Marc, have stepped up to the restaurant
plate with Coppinger Row, imaginatively sited in Coppinger Row, one of those thoroughfares that everyone
walks down but where no one lingers. Well, there is
cause to linger now: CR has good Med-fashioned food
at good prices, and it's the sort of offer where you can
have a snack of little plates or something more substantial. It's still early days yet for this kitchen, but the brothers have shown in the South William that they

know how to tweak and alter to get a signature style, and the room has all the energy it needs to be a solid destination. (Conor & Marc Bereen, Coppinger Row, D2 ☎ 01-672 9884 ⌂ www.coppingerrow.com – Open noon-11pm Tue-Sat, 1pm-8pm Sun)

● The Corkscrew

A huge range of wines from all over the world have been brought into this tiny space on Chatham Street, so what-ever it is that takes your fancy, you will find the bibulous object of your desires on their crowded shelves. (Colm Douglas, Peter & Paul Foley, 4 Chatham Street, D2 ☎ 01-674 5731 ⌂ www.thecorkscrew.ie – Open 10.30am-7pm Mon-Sat, 10.30am-8pm Thur, 12.30pm-5.30pm Sun)

● The Corner Bakery

Cara Lloyd and David Brown's bakery is a vital slice of Dublin 6W. There is a true, unswerving individuality to their baking which flies in the face of the uniformity and blandness of mainstream baking. But then, this is real baking, and it comes with a real sense of the culture and history of bread and sweet baking. "The Corner Bakery evolves" says Mr Brown, and indeed it does, developing more specialities, and getting better and better at what they do. So, fill that bag with Irish sticks, a brace of cup-cakes, a cinnamon bar, some pizza slices and a chocolate buttercream cake, and finally a Liberty Bakery's soda bread. Only brilliant. (David Brown & Cara Lloyd, 17 Terenure Road North, D6W ☎ 01-490 6210 – Open 8am-5.30pm Mon-Sat, 9am-1pm Sun)

● Cornucopia

We had the great honour of being asked to launch the Cornucopia Cookbook, *Cornucopia at Home*, back in late 2008, and were delighted that it went on to enjoy richly deserved success. Like the restaurant, the book is about much more than food. It is a narrative, of eating and learning, of work and family, of cooking and enjoyment, a work in progress both for body and soul. Deirdre McCafferty's restaurant is more than a restaurant because it hasn't simply fed people for more than 25 years, it has sustained them. For us it is one of

Dublin
Central

the great Dublin addresses, and the enlargement of the
original restaurant into a funky new space bodes well
for the next twenty five years of Cornucopia. (Deirdre
McCafferty, 19-20 Wicklow Street, D2 ☎ 01-677 7583
⌨ cornucopia@eircom.net ⌂ www.cornucopia.ie –
Open 8.30am-9pm Mon-Fri, 8.30am-8pm Sat, noon-7pm
Sun)

Restaurant
● La Corte del Caffè

With branches in Powerscourt, The Epicurean Mall and
the IFSC, La Corte, a collaboration between David Izzo
and Stefano Crescenzi, is a solid sender of good food
and truly superb coffee, the art and craft of coffee at
its very zenith. (Epicurean Food Hall, 13 Lower Liffey
Street, D1 ☎ 01-873 4200 ⌂ www.lacortedelcaffe.
ie – Open 9am-6pm Mon-Sat, Thurs 'till 7pm, 11am-
6.30pm Sun. Also IFSC, Custom House Square, D1
☎ 01-672 1929 – Open 7.30am-5pm Mon-Fri. Also
Powerscourt Shopping Centre, South William Street, D2
☎ 01-633 4477 – Open 10am-6pm Sat, 10am-7pm Thur,
10am-5pm all other days)

Bakery
● Craft Bakery

The rye and sourdough bread are what attract local residents and *Bridgestone* editor Leslie Williams to
Rathmines's handsome bakery, where Eugene Davis will
also, interestingly, sell you bread dough to bake in your
own oven, so here's one you made earlier, sort of. "No
artificial preservatives, no trans-fats, no pre-mixes, no
improvers" they proudly announce, so get the true stuff
and staff of life here. (Eugene Davis, 8 Upper Rathmines
Road, D6 ☎ 01-412 6154 – Open 8am-5.30pm Mon-Sat,
9am-1pm Sun)

Restaurant
● Dax

"The food's always good and they're very relaxed and
friendly". Well, if you wanted to summarise the charms
of Olivier Meissonave's delightful restaurant, you
couldn't do much better than our friend Fiona's one
line appraisal. Mind you, she might also have added that
the wines are only fab, and that the care shown in M.
Meissonave's selection shows not just his expertise, but
is also symptomatic of the TLC shown in every detail

Dublin
Central

of a restaurant that is, in fact, one of the Bridgestone editors' favourite in the entire city. (Olivier Meissonave, 23 Upper Pembroke Street, D2 ☎ 01-676 1494 ✉ info@dax.ie ✆ www.dax.ie – Open 12.30pm-2pm Tue-Fri, 6pm-11pm Tue-Sat)

Delicatessen
● Delizia Italian Delicatessen

Mina Fusco's shop is a good stop for hot sandwiches for lunch and for take-away foods for dinner. (Mina Fusco, 4 The Mart, Leopardstown Road, D18 ☎ 01-207 0408 ✉ delizia@eircom.net – Open 9am-6.30pm Mon-Fri, 10am-6pm Sat)

Shop and Restaurant
● Donnybrook Fair

Joe Doyle's shop is a marvellous trove of culinary treasures, a slick and stylish parade of the best artisan foods, great wines, and you can even get the newspaper whilst you are picking up a Morrin & O'Rourke pie or some of Ed Hick's sausages. DF attracts new food producers, and supports them by placing their goods for sale alongside the icons of Irish specialist food. Mr Doyle does all of this modestly, charmingly, daringly, and he has shown himself to be someone who reads the needs of his customers well. There is a pretty restaurant upstairs from the shop with good, straight-ahead cooking, and, of course, new branches have opened on Baggot Street, and in Greystones in County Wicklow. (Joe Doyle, 91 Morehampton Road, Donnybrook, D4 ☎ 01-668 3556 ✉ info@donnybrookfair.ie ✆ www.donnybrookfair. ie – Shop open 7am-10pm Mon-Sat, 9am-10pm Sun. Restaurant open 7.30am-10pm Mon-Thur, 7.30am-10.30pm Fri-Sat, 9am-10pm Sun. Also 13 Baggot Street, ☎ 01-668 3556 – Open 7am-9pm Mon-Fri, 8am-10pm Sat, 9am-6pm Sun. Also Grattan Court, Greystones ☎ 01-287 6346 – Open 7am-8pm Mon-Thur & Sat, 7am-9pm Fri, 8am-8pm Sun)

Butcher
● John Downey & Son

John and Mark Downey's shop is one of the city's leading butchers, and there is an almost torrential energy to the work of this father and son team, a feverish creativity that enlivens every aspect of their charcuterie calling. They hold organic certification, and are especially

Dublin
Central

valuable as a source of game, right down to Irish-bred buffalo. (John & Mark Downey, 27 Terenure Rd East, D6W ☎ 01-490 9239 🖑 www.organicfoodsireland.com – Open 8.30am-5.30pm Mon-Sat)

Co-Op and Market
● Dublin Food Co-Op

The Saturday market at the DFC is one of the great food events of the capital, and has been for more than 25 years now. Whilst their old stomping ground of Pearse Street is now occupied by the Super Natural food market, the move to Newmarket has been smooth and successful, and the Saturday buzz that this unique co-op offers is as addictive as ever. There are organic foods and wines, Greek cooking, Belgian waffles, Indian specialities, Moonshine dairy products, Natasha's Living Foods, George Heise's breads, and Dream Delights baking are just some of the stall-holders and stalwarts, and you can find many of the Saturday traders also at their Thursday market. A dream delight, indeed, and simply unmissable. (John de Courcy, 12 Newmarket, D8 ☎ 01-454 4258 🖑 www.dublinfoodcoop.com – Open 9.30am-4pm Sat)

Farmers' Market
● Dundrum Farmers' Market

The market takes place in the Dundrum Centre's Pembroke District from noon on Sunday. (Dundrum Town centre, Dundrum, Sunday, noon-4pm)

Restaurant
● Dunne & Crescenzi

Ten years of doing the food thing, the good thing, the right thing. That's what Eileen (Dunne) and Stefano (Crescenzi) have brought to Dublin in the last decade. And in that time they have made themselves amongst the most significant players in the city's food culture, marrying D&C to the Bar Italia, Nonna Valentina and L'Officina concepts. What they do is, basically, simple: they create nice places in which they serve nice foods and wines with the help of nice staff. To be honest, they are curators as much as restaurateurs, and what they do is to curate the elements of an authentic experience, then bring them to you. They are gifted people, they run great places, and you can feel the heartbeat of the city in every one of them. (Eileen Dunne & Stefano Crescenzi,

22 South Frederick St, D2 ☎ 01-677 3815 – Open
7.30am-11pm Mon-Thu, 7.30am-midnight Fri & Sat,
9am-9pm Sun and bank hols. Also 11 Seafort Avenue,
Sandymount D4 ☎ 01-667 3252 – Open 8.30am-late
Mon-Sat, 9.30am-late Sun and bank hols. ⌁ www.
dunneandcrescenzi.com)

Restaurant
● **Eatery 120**

120 does just what you want it to do. "A solid local
restaurant" is what the solid burghers of D6 say about
this favourite spot in Ranelagh. "A really reliable local
eaterie" is how another describes 120's unpretentious
cooking and adept sourcing of ingredients. The lack of
pretension is what makes 120 work, along with a truly
logical system of running a restaurant: they buy good
stuff from good producers and they show it respect.
Plus, they have a sense of irony, like offering 1980's
prawn cocktail, and duck a l'orange, this time as confit
duck leg with orange jus. Smart. Really smart. (Eoin &
Brian Lennon, 120 Ranelagh, D6 01 470 4120 ⌁ www.
eatery120.ie – Open 12.30pm-2.30pm Tue-Fri, 10am-
3pm Sat, Sun and bank hols, and from 5.30pm till late
Mon-Sun)

Restaurant
● **L'Ecrivain**

"Keeping It Simple" is the title of Derry Clarke's second
book, and it's a mantra he has adopted during twenty
years of L'Ecrivain. Okay, so L'Ecrivain seems grand and
complicated, but actually if you look closely, you see that
Derry and Sallyanne actually run a simple show: they
cook superb food, serve it with true grace and professionalism, and they are true to their calling as restaurateurs. Our most recent dinner was described by Leslie
Williams as "Virtually (no, actually) perfect", and so it
was, from Dublin Bay prawns with brick pastry, wild
halibut with black pudding and mustard velouté, through
suckling pig with pearl barley broth to Westmeath Hereford beef with beetroot vinaigrette to chocolate silk
cake with liquorice ice cream and caramelised bananas.
Twenty years of being perfect: now just how many
restaurateurs do you know who can claim a record like
that? (Derry & Sallyanne Clarke, 109 Lower Baggot
Street, D2 ☎ 01-661 1919 ⌁ enquiries@lecrivain.com
⌁ www.lecrivain.com – Open 12.30pm-2pm Mon-Fri;
6.30pm-10.30pm Mon-Sat)

Restaurant
● Eden

Eden has been unpredictable in recent times: John McKenna and Leslie Williams had a so-so lunch there one afternoon, but the next time Leslie was back the food was simply knock-out: classic smokies to begin; great lambs's sweetbreads, beautiful brill with mushrooms, top-notch city cooking in one of the loveliest rooms in Temple Bar. Eating outside in Meetinghouse Square is one of the city's delights. (Jay Bourke, Meeting House Square, Temple Bar, D2 ☎ 01-670 5372 ⌨ eden@edenrestaurant.ie ⌂ www.edenrestaurant.ie – Open 12.30pm-3pm Mon-Sun, 6pm-10.30pm Mon-Sat, 6pm-10pm Sun, noon-3pm brunch Sat & Sun)

only in Dublin
Coffee Angel

Restaurant
● Ely CHQ Brasserie

CHQ is the principal restaurant destination of the trio of Elys. "Providers of good times" is how the *Financial Times* described these characterful cellars and the airy wine bar. That is thanks, once again, to superb staff, and to punky modern cooking that is precisely executed: scallops with black pudding and walnut butter; Lough Neagh eel with verjus; poached salmon with molasses bacon and tarragon cream. The little people's menu, incidentally, may well be the best in the city. (Erik & Michelle Robson, IFSC, D1 ☎ 01-672 0010 ⌨ elychq@eircom.net ⌂ www.elywinebar.ie – noon-late Mon-Fri, 5pm-late Sat)

Restaurant
● Ely HQ Gastro Pub

ELY classic signature dishes are the order of the day in the Gastro Pub, where we would love to see some more of the modern Irish artisan ales on the list. A great room for chilling out after work. (Erik & Michelle Robson, Hanover Quay, Docklands, D2 ☎ 01-633 9986 ⌂ www.elywinebar.ie – Open noon-11.30pm Mon-Wed, noon-12.30am Thur-Fri, 4.30pm-late Sat & Sun)

● Ely Wine Bar

Ely celebrates a decade in business at the very end of
2009, a decade during which Erik and Michelle Robson's
wine bar has become, for many, one of the key destinations in the city. You can talk about their magnificent
wines, and their lovely, simple food, but for us Ely is
characterised by its staff, who are upfront, upbeat,
classy and friendly, and it is from these young folk that
the energy of this radiant place emerges. Proof of the
Ely pudding is the fact that having gotten the format in
design, drinks and food right whenever they opened, the
Robsons have barely had to tweak the formula. Happy
birthday baby. (Erik & Michelle Robson, 22 Ely Place,
D2 ☎ 01-676 8986 ⌨ elywine@eircom.net ⌂ www.
elywinebar.ie – Open noon-11.30pm Mon-Thu, noon-
12.30pm Fri, 5pm-12.30am Sat)

● Ennis Butchers

Our editor Leslie Williams is just one of many Dublin
residents who are devoted fans of Ennis Butchers, and
who consider Derek Bolger's shop to be amongst the
leading places to buy superb meat in the city. Whilst
the meticulously minded and properly hung beef is one
of the main attractions, Ennis's is also a first-class shop
with lots of artisan and organic foods from many of
Ireland's leading producers, and there are brilliant wines
as well. Mr Bolger hangs his meat for 28 days at 3°C, so
this is Irish beef as Irish beef should be aged, handled and
prepared, dark in colour with creamy yellow fat. Quite
brilliant. (Derek Bolger, 463 South Circular Road, Rialto,
D8 ☎ 01-454 9282 – Open 8am-7pm Mon-Sat)

● Enoteca delle Langhe

Here is what Caroline Byrne reckons about Mick Wallace's neat wine bar: "Enoteca delle Langhe in our little
Italian quarter on the quays by the Morrison Hotel, is
my favourite Italian wine bar, and probably my favourite
wine bar, on a par with the cellar at Fallon & Byrne.
Great, affordable Italian wines and real Italian cheeses, it's
just brill." Mr Wallace also runs the Enoteca Torino at
another of his developments on Grattan Crescent in Inchicore, and we admire a builder who builds apartments
that have shops and cafés as an integral part of

the development. (Mick Wallace, Blooms Lane, opp. Millennium Bridge, D1 ☎ 01-888 0834 ✉ enoteca@ wallace.ie. Also Grattan Crescent, Inchicore ☎ 01-453 7791 – Open 12.30pm-11pm Mon-Sat)

Wine Merchant
● Enowine

A pair of stylish shops in both the IFSC and Monkstown, with a tea room in Monkstown – Yvonne's – and a wine bar in the IFSC is the full complement of Yvonne and James Connolly's wine and food business. Eno is a total wine organisation, with wine classes, winemaker dinners, a newsletter, an online service, a wine tasting centre that uses the Enomatic system, and a lot of clever think-ing has gone into creating a seamless, smart business with superb wines on offer. The Eno wine bar is a very convenient location if you are going on to a gig in the O2. (James & Yvonne Connolly, Custom House Square, IFSC, D1 ☎ 01-636 0616 ✉ info@enowine.ie ⌾ www. enowine.ie – Winebar open Lunch and Dinner Mon-Sat; Also at 23 The Crescent, Monkstown, Co Dublin ☎ 01-230 3500 – Yvonne's Cafe open 10am-6pm Mon-Sat)

Food Mall
● Epicurean Food Mall

The EFM sails on as a source of good stalls at which to eat. The addition recently of David and Dee Coffey's Pie Kitchen, brings super pies like root veg and cheddar, or wild venison or steak and stout, to the public. Long-term residents like Itsabagel and La Corte are here, along with food from just about every corner of the globe. We like the fact that it's clamorous, and not slick. (Middle Abbey St, D1 – Open 10am-6pm Mon-Sat)

Restaurant
● Expresso Bar

Ann-Marie Nohl's restaurant is as rock-steady as they come, and whilst the cooking at first glance is all mod-ish and modern – it's like eating Bill Granger's greatest hits, whether it's breakfast, lunch or dinner, in a very Bill Granger room, come to think of it – it's never fake, and the room always has a good, calm, feminine feel. Expresso is a very popular place, and deservedly so. (Ann-Marie Nohl, 1 St Mary's Road, Ballsbridge, D4 ☎ 01-660 0585 – Open 7.30am-9pm Mon-Fri, 9am-9.30pm Sat, 10am-5pm Sun)

Crêperie
● **Fafie's**

At Fafie's they make their own buckwheat batter, using
organic eggs and fashion them into the most beautiful
crêpes, filled with good cheeses, syrups or sugars. We
love the names – Les Simples, Les Modestes, or, if you're
feeling hungry Les Prospères. We chose "The Goat in
the Ocean", or smoked salmon in cream, goat cheese,
chives and lemon, from the Les Prospères menu. As
for the sweet pancakes, you can choose between Les
Douces, Les Legères, but don't tell us you won't opt for
Les Volupteueuses. It's hard to overlook the crêpes, but
you can also choose toasted tartines, including a classic croque Monsieur. A little slice of Brittany. In Kevin
Street, where else? (Ann-Sofie Laidain, 2 Lower Kevin
Street, D8 ☎ 01-476 3888 ✉ info@fafies.com ⏚ www.
fafies.com – Open 9am-10pm Tue-Fri, 11am-11pm Sat,
12.30pm-4.30pm Sun)

Restaurant & Shop
● **Fallon & Byrne**

Our last visit to F&B was a speedy scoot through the
ground floor to pick up some things before we caught
the train back to Cork. If we had been catching a
freight train, we could have filled it – easy! – with all
the good things that you find here and that you simply
must have. There isn't a carelessly chosen item on the
shelves, there isn't a carelessly chosen bottle of wine on
the basement shelves, and upstairs remains one of the
greatest dining rooms in the city, a place to experience
all the nervy, noisy energy of Dubliners at play. F&B is
one of the greatest achievements of Dublin city. (Fiona
McHugh, Exchequer Building, 11-17 Exchequer Street,
D2 ☎ 01-472 1010 ✉ feedback@fallonandbyrne.com
⏚ www.fallonandbyrne.com – Open 12.30pm-3pm,
6pm-10pm Mon-Sun, open till 11pm Fri & Sat)

Farmers' Market
● **Farmleigh House**

Farmleigh is home to some of the very best farmers
markets to be found anywhere in the city, and a summer
Sunday spent shopping and eating here is a true, special
family treat. Do look out also for special events such as
An Bord Bia's annual artisan beer festival, which draws
huge crowds of the curious, and the thirsty. (Phoenix
Park, D7 ☎ 01-815 5900 ⏚ www.farmleigh.ie)

● **The Foodie Buddha**

Claudia Marion had a stall in the George's Street Arcade
for many years, and has now transplanted her judicious
sourcing and cooking to the South Circular Road. It's
a pretty shop, characterised by a lovely old pharmacy
counter, and there are salads, sarnies and drinks as
well as great foods, including what may well be the best
spelt brownie in the known universe. You can quote us
on that. (Claudia Marion, 12 South Circular Road, D2
☎ 087-967 3322)

● **The Food Room**

Alison and Barry Stephens run a really great shop on
the main Clontarf Road – the Donnybrook Fair of
D3 is what locals like to think – and Barry's cooking
draws in queues of locals, especially at lunchtime
when the place is jammers. Excellent. (Barry & Alison
Stephens, 46 Clontarf Road, D3 ☎ 01-833 2258 ⬥ www.
thefoodroom.ie – Open 8am-7pm Mon-Fri, 9am-6pm
Sat & Sun)

Dublin Central

● **Fothergill's**

A Dublin 6 legend for decades now, and yet the energy
and enthusiasm of the crew in Fothergill's remains as
youthful as ever. It's not an old-style deli, it's an ageless
deli, with ever-reliable sweet baking and lots of excellent savoury foods, and it's part of the very fabric of life
around here. Glorious. (Tom O'Connor, 141 Rathmines
Rd Upr, D6 ☎ 01-496 2511 – Open 9.30am-6pm Mon,
9am-6.30pm Tue-Fri, 9am-6pm Sat)

● **Roy Fox Gourmet Foods**

"If I were the nation's boss, one of the things I'd love
to see is that every town and village across the country
had a little 'Roy Fox's' in it". That's Domini Kemp of *The
Irish Times* writing about her – and very many other's –
favourite specialist deli, one of the city's great stores,
tucked just off the main strip of Donnybrook. So, let's
make Domini boss, shall we? (Joanne Donnelly, 49a Main
Street, Donnybrook, D4 ☎ 01-269 2892 ✉ sales@
royfox.ie – Open 9am-7pm Mon-Sat, 10am-6pm Sun)

Restaurant
● The French Paradox

Simple plates of good food and some zinging wines
make up the rock-steady formula of Tanya and Pierre
Chapeau's original and intriguing eaterie. The FP is in
a paradoxical position, somewhere between a French
deli and a wine bar, but it works superbly, with tasty
food spurring on the desire to order another glass of
wine. The wine shop downstairs is terrific. (Tanya &
Pierre Chapeau, 53 Shelbourne Road, Ballsbridge, D4
☎ 01-660 4068 ✆ wineshop@thefrenchparadox.com
✆ www.thefrenchparadox.com ✆ www.chapeauwines.
com – Open noon-3pm, 6pm-10.30pm Mon-Fri, noon-
10.30pm Sat. Amuses gueules served from 3pm-7pm)

Restaurant
● Les Frères Jacques

Stick with the set menus – the carte is very pricey – and
you can have an affordable and quintessentially French
experience in the ageless Les Frères Jacques, one of
those valuable restaurants that ignores fashion in favour
of classic cookery and polite service. (Jean Jacques Cail-
labet, 74 Dame Street, D2 ☎ 01-679 4555 ✆ info@
lesfreresjacques.com ✆ www.lesfreresjacques.com
– Open 12.30pm-2.30pm, 7.30pm-10.30pm Mon-Fri,
7.15pm-11pm Sat)

Supermarket
● Fresh – The Good Food Market

With four stores across the city – Smithfield, Camden
Street, Grand Canal Square and Northern Cross –
Fresh has lots of chances to live up to its name, and it
does that with gas in the tank. These are great stores,
and they stock and sell what you want to buy and eat,
whatever it might be. Yes you can buy ordinary stuff
here – they are supermarkets after all – but if you want
the good stuff, then it is here also, and it's not just stuff
to treat yourself with: Fresh do the staples from breads
to soups to meat to fish to sausages to little sweet
tarts from Crossmaglen, and do it all well. You might
call them the Waitrose of Dublin. Excellent. (Noel
Smith, Smithfield Village, Unit 5, Block F, Smithfield, D7
☎ 01-485 0271; Also Unit 3B, 4 Grand Canal Square, D2
☎ 01-671 8004; Also Unit 5 Northern Cross, Malahide
Road, D17 ☎ 01-848 9280; Lower Camden Street, D2
✆ www.freshthegoodfoodmarket.com)

Restaurant
● Furama

Rodney Mak's Chinese restaurant has been a reliable and consistent destination for two decades now. (Rodney Mak, Ground Floor, Eirpage House, Donnybrook Main Road, D4 ☎ 01-283 0522 ☝ www.furama.ie – Open 12.30pm-2pm Mon-Fri, 5.30pm-10.30pm Mon-Thu till 11pm Fri-Sat)

Patisserie
● The Gallic Kitchen

Sarah Webb's ageless bakery has been a staple of the *Bridgestone Guides* for the last twenty years, but age does not stall them, and the company is opening a new shop in lovely Abbeyleix in September 2009 as we write this book, also a new kitchen in Durrow, Co Laois, and are developing an organic farm. Phew! They also work nine farmers' markets each week, as well as the lovely wee shop in Francis Street. All of this food empire is based on delicious baking, and consistency, and sheer hard work, and it gladdens our heart to see them achieve so much, and to see them bring good food to so many people. And to think that it is all based on pastry, surely the most secure foundation in the world. (Sarah Webb, 49 Francis Street, D8 ☎ 01-454 4912, ☝ www.gallickitchen. com ✉ galkit@iol.ie – Open 9am-4.30pm Mon-Sat)

Shop
● Get Fresh

Niall Dermody's shop is a terrific place. Whatever you might need for cooking and entertaining, it is all here, and it is all beautifully presented and packaged, with everything dolled up and polished up with lots of TLC. Their array of fresh fruit, vegetables and herbs is worth anyone's detour to the Rosemount Centre, so set the satnav to Get Fresh and be prepared to go Wow! (Niall Dermody, Unit 6, Rosemount S.C., Marian Road, Rathfarnham, D14 ☎ 01-493 7148 ✉ getfresh6@eircom. net – Open 9am-6pm Mon-Fri, 8am-6pm Sat)

Restaurant
● Good World Chinese Restaurant

One of the true stalwarts of ethnic eating in Dublin, the Good World has one of the best dim sum offers in town, but make sure to hand them back the English

menu and tell them you are looking for the real thing.
(18 South Great Georges Street, D2 ☎ 01-677 5373 –
Open 12.30pm-midnight Mon-Sun)

Restaurant
● Gourmet Burger Co.

The last time PJ and John McKenna were in GBC, PJ was
having the burger and fries as a late lunch, to take away
as we headed home from our little mini-tour of 2009.
The food took a reassuringly long time to appear, and
when it did, we were blown away not just by the burger,
which was superb, but also by the fries, which were
pitch-perfect perfect. So, abandon any idea that this is
fast food, because it is actually fine food cooked slowly,
and it is brilliantly done. (Jonathan Dockrell, 97 Ranelagh
Road, D6 ☎ 01-497 7821 🖑 www.gourmetburgercom-
pany.ie – Open noon-10pm Mon-Thu, noon-11pm Fri &
Sat)

Restaurant
● Green 19

Green 19 has become one of the city's hottest destinations, a place that pushes all the right buttons, straight
from that welcoming cocktail – Green Mexican for me,
please – and then onto food from chef Adam Dickson
that is in-your-face delicious, and amazing value, at least
for the main courses such as chicken supreme with
mushroom and tarragon cream with lemon zest mash.
The sarnies are good – though not such great value
– and the atmosphere is funky and relaxed, especially
after a couple of those decadent cocktails. Make sure
you book for the evening time, because chances are
the place will be packed. (Stephen Murray, 19 Camden
Street Lower, D2 ☎ 01-478 9626 🖑 www.green19.ie –
Open 10am-11pm Mon-Sat, noon-6pm Sun)

Restaurant
● Gruel

Gruel reminds us of the *New Yorker* cartoon where one
urbanite says to another "I like the fact that everything is
mis-matched, I just wish it was mis-matched differently."
You might want to redecorate Gruel, if you don't have a
taste for jarring contrasts and clashing colours, but the
sort of short order cooking that the kitchen fires out
brooks no complaints, tasty, in-your-face modern grub.
Weekend brunch is a right of passage for Dublin resi-

Dublin
Central

dents in their twenties. (Ben Gorman & Mark Harrell, 67 Dame Street, D2 ☎ 01-670 7119 📠 info@mermaid.ie – Open 8am-10.30pm serving breakfast, lunch and dinner)

Restaurant
● L'Gueuleton

"I left with a pain in my stomach from eating too much, but I couldn't help it: everything was so good there was no way I was leaving anything behind!" So, that's the funky L'Gueuleton for you: so good you can't leave anything on the plate. For many Dubs, this is one of the best places in the city. The food is punky and always tastes improvised, as if they just thought of a new way to finish a dish, and that makes for exciting eating: Carlingford oysters Rockefeller; chicken chasseur with cèpes and tarragon; suckling pig with Lyonnaise potatoes. The room is moody and magnificent, and value is excellent. (Declan O'Regan, 1 Fade Street, D2 ☎ 01-675 3708 🖰 www.lgueuleton.com – Open 12.30pm-3pm, 6pm-10pm Mon-Sat, 1pm-3pm, 6pm-9pm Sun)

Restaurant
● Restaurant Patrick Guilbaud

A staple of fine dining in Dublin for decades now, RPG has the confidence of always being run by the same kitchen and management team. It is grand and expensive and for many people personifies the very essence of bourgeois dining. (Patrick Guilbaud, The Merrion Hotel, Upper Merrion Street, D2 ☎ 01-676 4192 🖰 www.merrionhotel.com – Open 12.30pm-2.15pm, 7.30pm-10.15pm Tue-Sat)

Restaurant & Delicatessen
● Harvey Nichols

Just as Henry Harris made his name cooking at Harvey Nicks in London, so Robert Haughton has made his name cooking at Harvey Nicks in Dublin. Mr Haughton has the kind of skills that allow him to put a dish like cappuccino of butternut squash with pan-fried scallops and a curried aïoli and make the whole thing seem as if the ingredients were born to be together. This is serious cooking and prices are decent for such an adventure in the culinary arts. (Robert Haughton, Dundrum Town Centre, Sandyford Road, D16 ☎ 01-291 0488 🖰 www.harveynichols.com – Open 12.30pm-3pm Mon-Fri, 12.30pm-3.30pm Sat, 12.30pm-4pm Sun, 6pm-10pm Tue-Sat)

Fish Shop & Restaurant
● Hemmingway's

With just 14 seats, Hemmingway's is a northside cult
address. "A fish shop gone wild" is what Brian Creedon
calls his hip shop and eatery, and that's just what this
fish traiteur is. Great if you want wet fish, brilliant if you
don't want to cook at all, when the take-away seafood
dishes will hit the spot, ideal if you want a glass of good
wine and a piece of fish cooked for you. A new model
fish business. (Brian Creedon, Vernon Avenue, Clontarf,
D3 ☎ 01-833 3338 – Open 1pm-8pm Mon, 11am-8pm
Tue-Thur, 11am-9pm Fri-Sat)

Restaurant
● Hole in the Wall

Martin McCaffrey's famous pub has a fine wine shop,
with over 600 bottles on the shelves, in the centre of
this meandering, comfy pub, and you can buy a bottle
and take it into either the pub or into the restaurant,
where there is some serious cooking taking place. This
is cheffy work: oxtail tartlet; scallops with piperade;
oysters tempura; fillet of beef with chorizo hash brown,
tarte tatin, but it's well accomplished and value is
keen. Do note that Sunday lunch is strictly first-come,
first-served. (Martin McCaffrey, Blackhorse Avenue,
D7 ☎ 01-838 9491 – Open 2pm-10pm Mon-Thu, 2pm-
10.30pm Fri, noon-10.30pm Sat, noon-10pm Sun)

Café
● Honest to Goodness

One of the George's Street Arcade specials, HTG lets
Darragh Birkett and Martin Ansbro get all funky with
their fine, freshly baked breads, producing everything
from proper breakfasts to popular sandwiches and
panini at lunch, along with good soups and salads. A
cult destination. (Darragh Birkett, 25 Market Arcade,
South George's Street, D2 ☎ 01 633 7727 ↻ www.
georgesstreetarcade.ie – Open 9am-6pm Mon-Sat,
noon-4pm Sun)

Wholefoods
● The Hopsack

Jimmy and Erica Murray's pioneering wholefood shop is
thirty years old, yet three decades have not served to
diminish the pioneer spirit that has brought energy to
this shop right from the day it opened, when John

McKenna actually lived just up the road and was a law student at UCD. (Erica & Jimmy Murray, Swan Centre, Rathmines, D6 ☎ 01-496 0399 ⌕ www.hopsack.ie – Open 9am-7.30pm Mon-Wed, 9am-9pm Thu-Fri, 9am-6.30pm Sat, 1pm-6pm Sun)

Restaurant
● Hô Sen

Crispy spring rolls; rice paper rolls; pancakes stuffed with pork and shrimp; tofu with Vietnamese spices; talapia in fish broth, that's the sort of lean, crisp, clean Vietnamese cooking Ho Sen offers and Tim and Tuan seem to have gotten it just right, and service and value all chime with the cooking in being hip to the trip, and great, great fun. (Tim Costigan, 6 Cope St, Temple Bar, D2 ☎ 01-671 8181 – Open 5pm-11pm Mon-Sat, 12.30pm-3pm, 5pm-9pm Sun)

only in Dublin
Porterhouse Oyster Stout

Restaurant
● Hugo's

Great wines and innovative cooking – roast blossom and plum-stuffed tenderloin of pork; tortellini with truffle and artichoke cream sauce, served with a simple rocket and Parmesan salad; scallops with a saffron butter sauce and tomato confit, accompanied by angel hair and cep mushrooms - have helped make Gina Murphy's restaurant a quiet, cult choice amongst food lovers. Ms Murphy is a professional to her fingertips, and her confidence and panache are your guarantee of good food and good times. (Gina Murphy, Merrion Row, D2 ☎ 01-676 5955 ✉ info@hugos.ie ⌕ www.hugos.ie – Open noon-3pm, bites served 3pm-5pm Mon-Fri, brunch served 11pm-4pm Sat and Sun, dinner 5pm-11pm Mon-Sun)

Pizzeria
● Il Fornaio

Formerly a well-kept Northside secret until it opened a branch in the IFSC in the financial quarter, Il Fornaio has always done good pastas and pizzas, and contented itself with doing them right, just the way an Italian restaurant in Italy would. The pizzas are classic and crisply crunchy, the pastas are ace, again sticking to classic dishes and making sure they are true and precise. The coffee, of course, is also excellent. (Bruno Cinelli, 55 Kilbarrack Road, Raheny, D15 ☎ 01-832 0277 ✉ info@ilfornaio. ie ⚲ www.ilfornaio.ie – Open 8.30am-10pm Mon-Thu, 8.30am-11pm Fri, 10am-11pm Sat, 10am-10pm Sun. Also at 1b Valencia House, Custom House Square, D1 ☎ 01-672 1852)

Restaurant
● Imperial Chinese Restaurant

One of the most senior of Dublin's ethnic restaurants – Mr and Mrs Cheung opened up back in the dog-days of 1983, and survived! – The Imperial continues to offer good conventional Chinese food, and some excellent dim sum at weekends, which is our favourite time to enjoy the spacious, bright room. In 2008 they opened a sister restaurant in Leopardstown, where they also include some Asian – Japanese, Malaysian, Vietnamese and Thai – dishes on the menu, along with a dim sum selection. (Mr & Mrs Cheung, 12a Wicklow Street, D2 ☎ 01-677 2580. Also Unit 3a Leopardstown Shopping Centre, Ballyogan Road, Leopardstown D18 ☎ 01-294 6938 ⚲ www.imperialchineserestaurant.com– Open noon-11.30pm Sun-Thu, noon-midnight Fri & Sat)

Markets
● Irish Village Markets

Tara Dalton and Des Vallely's company runs markets in Dublin city – Ranelagh, Tallaght and Mespil Road – as well as Sandyford, The Spawell and Whitewater SC in Newbridge. The Ranelagh market has just opened as we write, opposite the Luas station, and a cracking line-up is at work: Buns.ie; Terryglass Organics; California Market Bakery; Sitha Moorthy's Tasty Indian Food; Poulet Bonne Femme; Suha's Felafel and many, many more. Great news for D6! These are great markets with truly superb produce of every manner and style, even wines! (Des Vallely & Tara Dalton ☎ 01-284 1197 ✉ info@ irishvillagemarkets.com ⚲ www.irishvillagemarkets.com)

Bagel Bar
● Itsabagel

Domini and Peaches Kemp's pioneering bagel bar goes from strength to strength. And, like many devotees we still love joining the lunchtime queue in the Epicurean, and the expectant waiting in line as you try to make up your mind as to what bagel it is going to be today. So what will it be: the Club Bagel? The Deluxe? The Itsareuben? The Gourmet Veggie? Go on, make your mind up! (Domini & Peaches Kemp, Epicurean Food Hall, Lwr Liffey Street, D1 ☎ 01-874 0486; Fitzwilliam Lane, laneway Adjacent to the Merrion Hotel, D2 ☎ 01-644 9941; Unit 56a Blackthorn Road, Sandyford Industrial Estate, Sandyford, D18 ☎ 01-293 5994; The Pavilion, Royal Marine Road, Dun Laoghaire, Co Dublin ☎ 01-236 0644 🖰 www.itsabagel.com)

Restaurant
● Itsa4

Meticulous care in sourcing top-notch ingredients – their roll call of suppliers is a veritable who's who of great Irish artisans – means Itsa4 never puts a foot wrong. Add in great value, fine service and a happening room, and you have Sandymount Culinary Central. The Star menu at weekends is amongst the best value in the city. The Kemp sisters really understand how to make a room, and exactly how to train staff, so you need only add those physical and human ingredients to superb culinary ingredients, and you have a hit, a palpable hit. (Domini & Peaches Kemp 6A Sandymount Green, D4 ☎ 01-219 4676 🖰 www.itsabagel.com – noon-3pm Tue-Fri, 5.30pm-10pm Tue-Sat, noon-3pm Sat, noon-8pm Sun)

Coffee Roasters
● Java Republic

David McKiernan's amazing, state-of-the-art, megamillion coffee roastery at Ballycoolin just takes your breath away. Architects Douglas Wallace have designed an über-cool industrial space where you can buy coffee, try coffee, and get something nice to eat. We have known Mr McKiernan since he first started JR – we wrote the first ever piece about him – and he is dynamic, dedicated and driven, and we have no doubt that when it comes time to write the next edition of this book, the Java Republic brand will be global. In the meantime, there are great coffees and very nice food to be enjoyed in a truly amazing space that is worth anyone's detour to Ballycoolin. (David McKiernan, 510 Mitchelstown Road, Northwest Business Park, Ballycoolin, D15 ☎ 01-880 9300 🖰 www.javarepublic.com – Open 7am-4.30pm Mon-Fri)

Restaurant
● Jo'burger

Jo'B is the funkiest incarnation amongst the generation
of burger-barrier-breakers who have made minced meat
in a patty hip as all get out. Join the queue to get your
mitts on the Zola, the Zondi, the Pure, the Molapo
and all the energy of the vibe, the staff, the sounds and
the room. A blast, though the staff have a wee bit too
much attitude sometimes. (Joe Macken, 137 Rathmines
Road, D6 ☎ 01-491 3731 ✉ info@joburger.ie ⌂ www.
joburger.ie – Open noon-11pm, closes later on Fri & Sat,
Mon-Sun)

Restaurant
● Juniors

A blackboard menu, the tiniest wee room imaginable,
and two brothers doing their damndest: Juniors is
our kind of place. The food has Italian grace notes
rendered in a gutsy way, so the dishes have a Tyrolean
capaciousness but a Ferrari sensibility, which might
sound somewhat dyspeptic, but we assure you it isn't.
Don't miss the cheesecake for pud, and enjoy what Paul
and Barry are achieving here in Beggar's Bush. (Paul and
Barry McNerney, 4 Bath Avenue, Ballsbridge ☎ 01-
664 3648 ⌂ www.juniors.ie – Open all day)

Café
● Keshk Café

We lived right across the street from Keshk, in the
basement of a Georgian house, many years ago now,
and we just wish this simple, inexpensive, b-y-o café had
been operating then. What you do is first buy a bottle
at the Louis Albrouze wine shop just a few yards up the
road, then sit down for felafels with tahini, hummus,
lamb meshe with rice, baklava with pistachios, earthy
Middle Eastern cooking which suits this informal space
perfectly. (Mustafa Keshk, 129 Upper Leeson Street, D4
☎ 01-668 9793 ⌂ www.keshkcafe.ie – Open noon-late)

only in Dublin
Ray

Café
● KC Peaches

KC Peaches is one of the hippest destinations in Dublin,
run by one of the hippest crews. There is an energy
about this room, right from early in the day, that is
addictive, the energy of people at work getting the big
buzz from cooking great food. They are famous for their
cup cakes – amongst the best you can get anywhere,
and they were baking them before the cupcake storm
swept over the country – but then you could say the
same about the weekend brunches, or the daily frittata,
or even the simple sides such as the sesame sugar snaps.
Everything we have ever eaten in Katie Cantwell's bustling room has been utterly delicious. (Katie Cantwell,
Unit 10A Trinity Enterprise Centre, Pearce Street, D2
☎ 01-677 0333 🖅 thekitchen@kcpeaches.com ⌑ www.
kcpeaches.com – Open 9am-6pm Mon-Sat)

Deli Café
● Kennedy's of Fairview

Dublin
Central

"The kind of food shop/deli/café which planners should
require builders and developers to open" is how Leslie
Williams summed up the pivotal local position which
Sarah Kennedy's destination provides in Fairview. Ms
Kennedy has bucked every trend ever since she opened:
she offered value when everyone was expensive; she
expanded into upstairs at a time when everyone else
was contracting, and she has done this by simply cooking
good food and doing it at excellent prices. So, whether
it's breakfast, a quick lunch, or an inexpensive dinner,
Kennedy's is the one. (Sarah Kennedy, 5 Fairview Strand,
D3 ☎ 01-833 1400 ⌑ www.kennedysfoodstore.com –
Bistro open 6pm-9.30pm Tue-Sat, Shop open 9am-8pm
Mon-Sat, 10am-4pm Sun)

Korean Restaurant
● Kimchi@ The Hop House

"This is a shining light on the Korean scene. It's the best
one I've eaten in, and they've still kept the old bar" says
Valerie O'Connor of Kyoung Hee Lee's hip and happening restaurant, pub and music venue. The Old Shake-
speare pub is now home to tofu broth with seafood,
beef with sweet potato noodles, pork with chilli sauce,
and of course you must have some kimchi on the side,
and a shot of soju. Lovely. (Kyoung Hee Lee, 160 Parnell
Street, D1 ☎ 01-872 8536 – Open Mon-Sun)

● **Kinara**

Everyone's favourite Northside Indian restaurant, Kinara
has built a formidable local reputation and a formidable local audience by delivering Indian and Pakistani
specialities that show genuine authenticity. They also use
organic chicken, lamb and beef, and the tandoori cooking is very fine. Keema aloo with paratha bread, please,
some dal Kinara and beef lobia, and we are back in those
happy days of the back pack and the Karakoram High-
way. Ah, remember that? (Sean Collender, 318 Clontarf
Road, D3 ☎ 01-833 6759 ✉ info@kinara.ie 🖰 www.
kinara.ie – Open noon-4.30pm, 4.30pm-11pm Mon-Sun)

● **Kish Fish**

Brothers Bill, Tadgh and Damian run the business of
Kish Fish with their mother, Fedelmia, and Kish is as
hip and slick a food business as you will find anywhere.
Their astuteness is evident in their two retail shops.
The original Kish, in Smithfield, is very near to where
many Dubliners will remember the location of the old
Dublin fish market. In Coolock they have a large modern
premises where the displays are large enough to display
whole fish – a great confidence booster for the customer. Kish Fish – named after the Kish Lighthouse – is
a fabulous mix of the traditional – "Our filleters all come
from the stock that worked the market" – and the modern. These are community shops that attract visitors
from everywhere, and this is a family business that is as
professionally run as you can find.(Bill, Tadgh, Damian
or Fedelmia O'Meara, 40/42 Bow Street, Smithfield, D7
☎ 01-854 3900– Open 9am-4.30pm Tues-Fri, 9am-1pm
Sat, Malahide Road Industrial Park, Coolock, Co Dublin
☎ 01-854 3925 – Open 8am-5pm Mon-Fri, 8am-2pm Sat
🖰 www.kishfish.ie)

Dublin
Central

● **Kitchen Complements**

Your first port of call when any serious baking beckons
should always be Kitchen Complements, where Ann has
been stocking Rolls Royce equipment for many happy
years. (Ann McNamee, Chatham Street, D2, ☎ 01-
677 0734 🖰 www.kitchencomplements.ie – Open
10am-6pm Mon-Sat, till 7pm Thur)

● Koh Restaurant and Cocktail Lounge

It's the Pho Bo in KOH that will be bringing you back to this slick, hip room in the Millennium walkway. A big bowl of beef broth with rib-eye beef, glass noodles and a shower of spring onion, sweet basil and mint, it's the kind of fast-food-soul-food combo that hits the spot. Elsewhere, KOH has Asia's greatest hits — Thai curries; noodle dishes — and there is even a rib-eye for the timid. Witty, very hip, and repeat after us: Pho Bo KOH. (Conor Sexton & Conor Kilkenny, 6-7 Jervis Street, Millennium Walkway, D1 ☎ 01-814 6777 ✉ enquiries@koh.ie ✉ www.koh.ie – Open noon-5pm Mon-Sun, 5pm-10.30pm Sun & Mon, 5pm-11pm Tue-Thur, 5pm-11.30pm Fri & Sat)

● Konkan

The secret of Konkan is to make sure to order the southern Indian dishes the restaurant specialises in, which concentrate on fish dishes cooked with coconut. So go for the Mangalori fish and crab gassi, the prawns with mango, the Jardaloo boti from Bombay, and the chicken Chettinad. Do note that their take-away is also excellent. (Bala Nayak, 46 Upper Clanbrassil Street, D8 ☎ 01-473-8252 ✉ info@konkan.ie ✉ www.konkan.ie – Open 5.30pm-11.30pm Mon-Sun)

● Lawlor's Butchers

A recent expansion of this fine butcher's shop, and the addition of a good fish shop, has made it an even more vital element of the Rathmines village. Lots of good beef and birds, lots of game and good sausages, and knowledgeable service. Lawlor's also operate the meat section in Morton's superb deli and supermarket in Ranelagh. (James Lawlor, Upper Rathmines Road, D6 ☎ 01-497 3313)

● Lennox Café

Everyone's favourite neighbourhood café is an always-cosy and warm space, and vies with Anderson's of Glasnevin as one of the city's best spots for brunch. It's

Dublin Central

furnished almost like a doll's house, with dainty cups
and old black and white photos of the area, but there is
nothing dainty about the food, which has the sort of deliciousness that encourages you to get stuck in: chicken
quesadilla; organic scrambled eggs with wild mushrooms; salad with Parma ham, warmed figs and caramelised walnuts. A cult address, for food lovers of all ages.
(Huibrecht Luykx, 31 Lennox Street, D8 ☎ 01-478 9966
– Open 9am-5pm Mon-Sat, 9.30am-5pm Sun)

Bakery
● Liberty Bakery

Tommy is a third-generation baker, and it's to the Liber-
ties that you go for great soda bread and all the Dublin
classics such as gur cake and apple puffs. Ageless. (42
Meath Street, D8 ☎ 01-454 7725)

Delicatessen
● Lilliput Stores

"It's where I buy my weekday sandwich when I'm making
deliveries", says a classy artisan producer, so you need to
know that Brendan O'Mahony's Lilliput Stores is where
the artisans choose to shop. A lot of good things are
packed into one tiny store, from veg to bread to wine to
charcuterie, and if only it had been here when we lived
in Stoneybatter, way back when. (Brendan O'Mahony,
Arbour Hill, Stoneybatter ☎ 01-672 9516 – Open 8am-
7.30pm Mon-Fri, 8am-6.30pm Sat, 9am-4pm Sun)

Delicatessen
● Liston's

If they haven't got it, then you actually don't need it.
Everything that you do need, however, you will find in
Karen Liston's exemplary deli, cum traiteur, cum wine
store, an address which is distinguished by particularly
wonderful service. (Karen Liston, 25 Camden Street, D2
☎ 01-405 4779 ⌨ listonsfood@eircom.net ✆ www.
listonsfoodstore.ie – Open 8am-6.30pm Mon-Thu, 8am-
7pm Fri, 10am-6pm Sat)

Restaurant/Takeaway
● Little Jerusalem

Abraham Phelan has brought great food to every place
he has cooked in Dublin and Little Jerusalem is no ex-

ception. The Palestinian and Lebanese cooking has wonderful new tastes, such as Mulihea Pilaranp – a form of spinach which is cooked with rabbit, onion, garlic and olive oil or Arayess, where Lebanese bread is filled with minced lamb, onion, garlic and tomatoes. High standards all round make for a vital new address. (Abraham Phelan, 3 Wynnfield Road, Rathmines, D6 ☎ 01-4126912/087-9717196 📧 littlejerusalem@live.ie – Open 1pm-11pm Tue-Sun)

Restaurant
● The Lobster Pot

Tommy Crean, John Rigby and chef Don McGuinness have been doing good fish and shellfish cookery for years, and serving this good food with good wines, and it ain't broke and they sure ain't gonna fix it. Charming, fashion-free, so let's have sole bonne femme and coquilles St Jacques and some Chablis and off we go. (Tommy Crean, 9 Ballsbridge Tce, Ballsbridge, D4 ☎ 01-668 0025 🌐 www.thelobsterpot.ie – Open 12.30pm-2pm Mon-Fri, 6pm-10.30pm Mon-Sat)

Restaurant
● Locks

Chef Troy Maguire likes rich, hearty cooking, and in dishes such as black pudding tarte tatin, or saddle of lamb with Sarladaise potatoes and sweetbreads, he is firing out trencherman food that is, however, as delicate as a dancer. A swish room, decent pricing and loads of ambition bodes well for the newest star of Portobello, a restaurant that, even in its short life, has become many people's favourite place to eat in the entire city. (Teresa Carr & Kevin Rynhart, 1 Windsor Tce, Portobello, D8 ☎ 01-454 3391 📧 info@locksrestaurant.ie 🌐 www.locksrestaurant.ie – Open noon-4pm Sat & Sun, 5.30pm-10.30pm Mon-Thur, 5.30pm-11pm Fri-Sat)

Cupcakes
● Lolly & Cooks

Utterly addictive cupcakes – coffee; coconut and raspberry; lemon with sprinkles – explain why Lolly & Cooks is going down a storm in the George's Arcade. (Laragh Strahan, Drury Street Entrance, George's Arcade, D2 ☎ 01-675 0865 📧 laragh@lollyandcooks.com 🌐 www.lollyandcooks.com – Open 9am-6.30pm Mon-Sat, 'till 9pm Thu, 10am-6pm Sun)

● Louis Albrouze

A wonderful array of specially sourced French wines is the key note of this very stylish shop. LA is also where you get your takeaway bottle when eating at Keshk Cafe just down the street. (Nathalie Hennebert, 127 Upper Leeson Street, D4 ☎ 01-667 4455 ✉ leesonstreet@louisalbrouze.com ✌ www.louisalbrouze.com – Open 10.30am-9pm Mon-Sat)

● Mad Hatter's Tea Party

Not once, but twice have Sharon and Ann-Marie's unique, crazy, brilliant Mad Hatter's Tea Party won the Bridgestone Electric Picnic Style Awards. If we were having an event we would want these girls there and we expect to see them making cameo appearances in Tim Burton's upcoming movie. (Sharon Greene & Ann-Marie Durney, 52 Synge Street, D8 ☎ 087-653 0456/087 937 0312 ✉ queensofneon@gmail.com)

Dublin
Central

● La Maison

Having made a great success at Vaughan's pub in Terenure, Olivier Quenet has transformed La Maison into a stylish, seriously good French restaurant. The menu, strangely, is written first in French, then English, but this doesn't get in the way of extremely accomplished cooking: the terrine plates are a good place to start, with excellent terrines and quenelles of duck liver pâté served with pickles, before pan-roasted cod with morels, rocket and gnocchi, or tarte Provençale or the keenly-priced mixed seafood platter. Crisp linen, crisply attired waiters, and a nice slice of La France profonde in central Dublin. (Olivier Quenet, 15 Castle Market, D2 ☎ 01-672 7258 ✉ www.lamaisonrestaurant.ie – Open 12.30pm-3pm Tue-Sat, 6.30pm-10.30pm Tue-Wed, 6.30pm-1am Thur-Sat)

● The Market Bar

A tapas menu in this big, busy bar in the George's Street complex has been a hit ever since they first opened their doors, and an impressive consistency - and an impressive simplicity - has kept everything running smoothly.

Gets mighty busy after work. (Jay Bourke, Fade Street, D2 ☎ 01-613 9094 ⌂ www.marketbar.ie – Tapas noon-9.30pm Mon-Thu, noon-10.30pm Fri-Sat, 3pm-9.30pm Sun)

● Matthew's Cheese Cellar

There is actually more than forty years of cheese whole-saling experience underpinning the wonderfully authen-tic shop that is Matthew's. The cheeses are pristine and the hamper offers particularly cherishable. (Annie McEvoy, 17 Upper Baggot Street, D2 ☎ 01-668 5275 ⌂ annie@matthewscheesecellar.com ⌂ www.matthewscheesecellar.com – Open 11am-6pm Mon-Fri, 10.30am-2.30pm Sat)

● McHugh's Off Licence

McHugh's is a hugely respected wine shop and never a year goes by without them deservedly garnering more awards. Their new Bistro and Café in Raheny has, as you would have hoped, a really good wine list, which offers terrific value for money. (57 Kilbarrack Road, D5 ☎ 01-839 4692, 25e Malahide Road, Artane, D5 ☎ 01-831 1867 ⌂ good-drinks@mchughs.ie ⌂ www.mchughs.ie – Open 10.30am-10pm Mon-Sat 12.30-10pm Sun. McHugh's Wine & Dine, 59 St Assams Park, Raheny, D5 – Open noon-3pm, 5pm-10pm Mon-Sat, noon-8pm Sun)

● The Mermaid Café

Ben Gorman and Mark Harrell's restaurant is one of that small but select group of Irish restaurants that have no obvious antecedents, and no obvious points of comparison to their colleagues in the restaurant game. Mr Gorman sees things differently from other cooks; his approach is oblique, bookish, intellectual, so he puts smoked paprika oil with grilled ox tongue, sage and mustard mash with Angus rib-eye steak, beetroot but-ter with sea bass, potato and duck cake with foie gras. Intriguing work, and if the improvisations are occasion-ally erratic, that's OK. Sunday brunch is one of the great metropolitan rites of passage. (Ben Gorman & Mark Har-rell, 69/70 Dame Street, Temple Bar, D2 ☎ 01-670 8236 ⌂ www.mermaid.ie – Open 12.30pm-2.30pm, 6pm-11pm Mon-Fri, 6pm-11pm Sat, noon-3.30pm, 6pm-9pm Sun)

● The Merrion Hotel

Recessionary times may mean that your cash availability for afternoon tea is a little less than it was at the height of the boom, but if you do have money to splash and somebody special to meet then afternoon tea at the Merrion is a textbook example of honouring and respecting this great tradition. (Peter MacCann, The Merrion Hotel, Upper Merrion Street, D2 ☎ 01-603 0600 ☝ www.merrionhotel.com)

Micro Brewery
● Messrs Maguire

Their four craft-brewed drinks from brewer Cullan Loughnane are what makes Messrs Maguire stand out in the city, so head here for Plain Porter, Weiss, Haus and Rusty Red Ale, and feel sorry for the folk drinking dull Guinness up in the Storehouse, inexplicably Ireland's most popular tourist destination. (Cullan Loughnane, 1-2 Burgh Quay, D2 ☎ 01-670 5777 ☝ www.messrsmaguire. ie – Open 10.30am-12.30am Mon-Tue, 10.30am-1.30am Wed, 10.30am-2.30am Thu-Sat, noon-midnight Sun)

Wine Merchant
● Mitchell & Son

Mitchell's is one of the blue chip Dublin wine institutions and before they moved north of the river they had actually traded in Kildare Street since 1886. Strangely enough when CHQ originally opened in 1820 it was used as a bonded warehouse, so the tradition of great wines in Mitchell's has gone even further into the past. The selection of wines is superb and their very own Green Spot Whiskey, one of the only remaining bonded Irish whiskeys, is one of the great Irish drinks. (Peter Dunne, CHQ building, I.F.S.C. Docklands, D1 ☎ 01-612 5540 ☝ chq@mitchellandson.com – Open 10.30am-7pm Mon-Fri, 11am-6pm Sat. Also at 54 Glasthule Road, Sandycove, Co. Dublin ☎ 01-230 2301 ☝ glasthule@mitchellandson.com – Open 10.30am-7pm Mon-Sat, 12.30pm-5pm Sun. Also at Grange Road Retail Centre, Grange Road, Rathfarnham, Co Dublin ☎ 01-493 3816 ☝ grangeroad@mitchellandson.com – Open noon-7pm Mon, 11am-8pm Tue-Thu, 11am-8.30pm Fri, 10.30am-8.30pm Sat, 12.30pm-8pm Sun ☝ www.mitchellandson.com)

Dublin
Central

● Monty's of Kathmandu

Shiva Gautam's Monty's has a handsome new restaurant in Rathgar, joining the great Temple Bar stalwart where Shiva and his team have been offering unique Nepalese cooking since 1997. Monty's is one of the few stars of Temple Bar, a restaurant with vividly lovely food, and the refurbishment of the room has made it an even better space in which to enjoy some unique cooking. We have always had truly terrific Nepalese cooking in here, their tandoori specialities are spectacularly fine, and the authenticity of the food is echt. Out in Rathgar, the setting is plusher – this is a lovely tabernacle of a room, dark and welcoming, lined with wine bottles – but the cooking is equally true and fine and the dedication to service and high standards in Monty's is exemplary. (Shiva & Lina Gautam, 28 Eustace Street, Temple Bar, D2 ☎ 01-670 4911, 88 Rathgar Road, D6 ☎ 01-492 0633 shiva@tinet.ie www.montys.ie – Open noon-2.30pm, 6pm-11.30pm Mon-Sat, 6pm-11pm Sun)

Shop
● Morton's

The Morton family have been busy of late, opening new stores at Park Place, just off Hatch Street, as well as a convenience store at the Beechwood stop of the LUAS in Ranelagh. This is good news for Dublin food lovers, but like many folk we still cherish any visit to the original store on Dunville Avenue, for us one of the pivotal destinations for Dublin food. Everything – but everything – that they sell in here is superb, right down to the splendid displays of flowers. The butchery section run by Morton's of Rathmines is reason alone to visit. But you will find that filling a trolley with good things is never easier, nor more pleasureful than in this classic supermarket. (15-17 Dunville Avenue, Ranelagh, D6 ☎ 01-497 1913 info@mortons.ie www.mortons.ie – Open 8am-8pm Mon-Fri, 8am-6.30pm Sat, 11am-4pm Sun. Also at Park Place, Hatch Street ☎ 01-478 2758)

Fish & Game
● Thomas Mulloy

Mulloy's is a long-established, city-centre shop whose specialisation in excellent prime fish and shellfish is matched by an equal expertise in the selling of seasonal game birds. The company is presently expanding, with imminent plans to open a shop along the West Pier in Howth. (Tommy & Ross Mulloy, 12 Lower Baggot Street, D2 ☎ 01-661 1222 ✉ info@mulloys.ie 🖰 www.mulloys. ie – Open 9am-5.30pm Tue-Fri, 9am-3.50pm Sat)

Raw and Living Food Company
● Natasha's Living Foods

The first taste we had of Natasha's Living Foods blew us clean away. It was a raw, sprouted chickpea hummus with cumin and coriander, and it was amazing. Then we met Natasha at Electric Picnic, where she got the Healthy Buzz Award for her foods, such as Bomb in a Bag granola, and Love Apple Kisses, and her incredible spicy kale snacks. We need raw foods in our diet, but no one else is making raw foods as provocatively, teasingly delicious as these. A new star, and a vital resource for your kitchen. You can find her foods in farmers' markets, including Dublin Food-Co-op, Temple Bar and Dun Laoghaire, and in various independent shops. (Natasha Czopor, North King Street, Stoneybatter D7 ☎ 01-617 4807 🖰 www.natashaslivingfood.ie)

Wine Merchant
● Nectar Wines

John McGrath and Carl Byrne are passionate about their wines, and source from exciting winemakers. They hunt down good producers from France, Italy, Spain and Australia, and keep the list short and special. We love these wines, with their slightly feral wildness and freshness, their lack of self-consciousness and naturalness. Excellent. (John McGrath & Carl Byrne, 3 Sandyford Village, D18, ☎ 01-294 4067 ✉ sales@nectarwines.com 🖰 www.nectarwines.com)

Chinese Restaurant
● New Millennium Chinese Restaurant

The NM is one of the best destinations for dim sum in Dublin city: prawn dumplings; char siu puffs; crispy squid rings; cheung fun; crispy fried bean curd. Don't let them give you the western menu that is ritually handed out to diners: ask for the special menus that the Chinese customers get and that show what they can really do. (Colin Tang, 51 South King Street, Dublin 2 ☎ 01-635 1525 Open – noon-11pm Sun-Thu, noon-midnight Fri & Sat)

● **Nolan's**

The star of Clontarf has been selling great foods for years now, and remains the first choice for artisans looking for sympathetic outlets for their foods. They find that sympathy and understanding here, in a wonderful independent supermarket where it is always a pleasure to shop, precisely because the staff and owners enjoy that sympathy and understanding. (Richard Nolan, 49 Vernon Avenue, Clontarf, D3 ☎ 01-833 8361 – Open 9am-7pm Mon-Wed, 9am-9pm Sat, 11am-4pm Sun)

Restaurant

● **Nonna Valentina**

Nonna Valentina is dedicated to cucina casalinga – Italian home cooking – and, if it doesn't seem a contradiction in terms for such simple food, the results are spectacular. They use the Italian term "curato" to describe the food, meaning dishes that are properly nurtured, sourced and cooked, and curato is what you get from the cuisine. Don't miss the panzerotti with pheasant ragu. (Stefano Crescenzi, 1-2 Portobello Road, D8 ☎ 01-454 9866 dunneandcrescenzi@hotmail.com www. dunneandcrescenzi.com – Open 10am-3pm, 6pm-10.30pm Mon-Thur, 10am-10.30pm Fri & Sat)

Café

● **Nude**

Norman Hewson's Nude stores were the first to offer fresh, high-quality, high-energy, healthful foods and drinks, and the formula remains as crisp and attractive today as ever. (Norman Hewson, 21 Suffolk Street, D2 ☎ 01-672 5577 info@nude.ie www.nude.ie.– Open 7.30am-9pm Mon-Sun)

Restaurant

● **O'Connell's in Ballsbridge**

Tom O'Connell is a most generous man, and that is why he is one of the great modern restaurateurs. When he goes on a little jaunt, a food lover's tour around the country, we will receive an e-mail on his return to Dublin 4, singing the praises of something new and interesting he has discovered, or relishing some old timer who is still doing the good thing. He is a champion of the good, and nowhere more so than in his splendid restaurant,

Dublin Central

where care, generosity and consistent innovation all marry to produce some of the city's most pleasureful, delicious cooking in one of the city's best restaurants. (Tom O'Connell, Lansdowne Road, Ballsbridge, D4 ☎ 01-665 5940 📧 info@oconnellsballsbridge.com 🖰 www.oconnellsballsbridge.com – Open 7am-10.30am Mon-Fri, 7.30am-1am Sat, 8am-11.30am Sun, noon-2.30pm Mon-Sat, 12.45pm-3.30pm Sun, 5.30pm-10pm Mon-Sat. Closed Sun dinner)

Restaurant
● L'Officina

Dunne & Crescenzi's original L'Officina has been joined by a second city branch in the Arnott's centre in D2. L'Officina works to a formula – approved denomination Italian foods served by vigorous staff in handsome big rooms – and if only every formula was as consistent, successful and pleasureful as this one. The discipline evident here is incredible, the achievement is considerable. (Eileen Dunne & Stefano Crescenzi, Dundrum Town Centre, D16 ☎ 01-216 6764 – Open 9.30am-10pm Mon-Wed, 8.30am-10.30pm Thu, 8.30pm-late Fri & Sat, 11am-10pm Sun. Also at Unit 35 Nurney Road, Kildare Town, Kildare – Open 9.30am-6pm Mon-Wed, 9.30am-8pm Thur-Sat, 10.30am-7pm Sun. Also at Arnott's, Jervis Centre, D1 – Open 9am-6.30pm Mon-Wed, 8.30am-10.30pm Thu, 8.30am-11pm Fri & Sat, 10.30am-7pm Sun)

Restaurant
● Oliver's Eatery

Olivier Quenet has fashioned a triumph from his cooking in Vaughan's Eagle House pub in Terenure. Leslie William's list of stonkingly good dishes is typical of what many could write about the cooking: "grand big bowl of whitebait; good minute steak sandwich; perfect Guinness pie with decent puff pastry; generous shin of beef pot au feu with a big marrowbone to pick out and spread on toast; very good mackerel; excellent chips; good ice cream". Anything else, Leslie? "Great pints of Guinness and Beamish served by happy, friendly staff". A neighbourhood star. M. Quenet also has the fine Breton restaurant, La Maison in Castle Market in the city centre. (Olivier Quenet, Vaughan's Eagle House, Terenure ☎ 01-490 1251 📧 info@oliverseatery.ie 🖰 www.oliverseatery.ie – Open noon-10pm Mon-Sun)

● One Pico

Eamonn O'Reilly got on top of the recession before any
other Dublin restaurateur, sending out ace cooking at
amazing value, and winning a new audience who had,
perhaps, had him pigeon-holed as a pricey destination.
The only price consideration in One Pico these days is
to wonder how such fine food can be cooked at such
keen prices, and fine food it is: ham hock terrine with
anise girolles; hake with Peking duck; sea bream with
black bacon, and some perfect puddings to finish. Excellent. Mr O'Reilly himself is also rattlin' the pots and pans
at Bleu, his bistro on Dawson Street. (Eamonn O'Reilly,
5-6 Molesworth Place, D2 ☎ 01-676 0300 ⌂ www.one-
pico.com – Open 12.15pm-2.30pm, 6pm-11pm Mon-Sat)

Restaurant
● 101 Talbot

Neal and Jenny were chef and manager of 101 before
assuming the mantle of owners and operators of one of
the northside's most iconic addresses. The transition has
been smooth, the tradition of serving great 101 Talbot
food – smoked trout and almond tart; vegetable and
peanut curry with pea rice; sirloin with whiskey cream
sauce – continues with modest aplomb. The room has
an awesome energy when full, the service is great, and
101 has always been one of the best choices for vegetarian cooking in the city. (Neal Magee, 101 Talbot Street,
D1 ☎ 01-874 5011 ⌂ www.101talbot.com – Open 5pm-
11pm Tue-Sat)

Butcher
● O'Toole's Butchers

Everyone knows Danny O'Toole as the pioneer butcher
in Ireland when it comes to sourcing organic meats,
but customers of Terenure also know Kenn O'Toole,
Dernán O'Toole and Aoife O'Toole, so this is a family
business and not just a one-man show. And what a family
business, as the third generation of O'Tooles stamp their
claim to running the best butcher's shop in town! They
marry superb sourcing with dextrous charcuterie skills, and
finish off the package with the sort of service that you could
only find in Dublin: witty, charming, capable and polite. A
once and for all star. (Danny O'Toole, 138 Terenure Road
Nth, D6W ☎ 01-490 5457 ⌂ otoolebutcher@eircom.net –
Open 9.30am-6pm Mon-Sat)

● Out of the Blue

The East Coast Inshore Fishing Company act as
commission agents for fishing boats, sourcing fresh
fish direct from the boats and distributing them to
independent fishmongers and shops, and supplying their
own renowned market fish stalls in the various city and
south city Dublin farmers' markets. Their fish vans trade
under the name Out of the Blue, and no visit to the
Leopardstown, Temple Bar or Naas farmers' markets
should be undertaken without buying fish from these
notable sellers. The company East Coast actually dates
back to 1942, and has been in the O'Callaghan family
since 1971. (Unit 28 Millennium Business Park, Cappagh
Road, D11 ☎ 01-864 9233 Leopardstown Friday Market,
Temple Bar and Naas Saturday Market)

● Panem

Location should always have counted against Panem –
it's kind of in-between-the-bridges on Ormond Quay –
but quality has won out over location, and Ann Murphy's
little Italian-style bakery and café is a destination address
in the middle of nowhere, and has been since 1996. Little
has changed in that time, and what hasn't changed is the
attention to detail and the high quality of the baking and
the care in fashioning superb drinks. A filled focaccia, a
sunny day on the boardwalk, all is well with the world.
(Ann Murphy, 21 Lwr Ormond Quay, D1 ☎ 01-872 8510
– 8am-6pm Mon-Fri, 9am-6pm Sat, 10am-4.30pm Sun)

● Pearl Brasserie

Pearl has become many people's favourite old friend
in the city centre, a rock-solid, rock-steady brasserie
where Kirsten and Sebastian cook splendid food, serve
it with stunning efficiency and charm, and offer it at very,
very keen prices. Crispy prawns in filo with mango and
black pepper; hake with celeriac mousse; lamb kebab
with couscous; pistachio ice cream; passion fruit and
blood orange sorbet. These guys simply have not put
a foot wrong for the last few years. (Kirsten Batt &
Sebastian Masi, 20 Merrion St Upr, D2 ☎ 01-661 3572
info@pearl-brasserie.com www.pearl-brasserie.
com – Open noon-2.30pm Mon-Fri, 6pm-10.30pm Mon-
Sat)

Dublin
Central

● Pembroke Town House

A beautiful location on tree-lined Pembroke Road is
the major asset of the PT, though the exceptionally
fine staff match the place and grandeur of the house.
The bedrooms are calm and very comfortable, the
public rooms are cosy and a nice place to help yourself
to a drink from the bar. Last time we stayed a gaggle
of marathon runners all descended for breakfast at
the same time, which put the kitchen under a lot of
pressure, and though the staff responded brilliantly, they
could sharpen the breakfast offer a little. (Fiona Teehan,
90 Pembroke Road, Ballsbridge, D4 ☎ 01-660 0277
🖰 www.pembroketownhouse.ie)

Restaurant
● Peploe's

One of the city's busiest brasseries, and a room that
always has a gaggle of people eating and relaxing, no
matter what time of day it is. Barry Canny understands
his audience very well: they want to enjoy good wines,
good service and straightforward food in a nice room –
it's the Chris King and Jeremy Corbin restaurant mantra
brought to Dublin – and it works a treat. (Barry Canny,
16 St Stephen's Green, D2 ☎ 01-676 3144 🖅 info@
peploes.com 🖰 www.peploes.com – Open noon-midnight Mon-Sun)

Restaurant
● Pichet

A fusion of talents between chef Stephen Gibson and
sommelier Nick Munier, Pichet has hit the ground running at this big wrap-around-the-corner spot in between
Dame Street and Exchequer Street. The only over-the-
top element is the gaudy chairs, but otherwise Pichet
is lean and mean. They call it a café/bar/restaurant, so
the food is both informal and direct, bistro cooking with
big, bold bistro flavours: veal bolognaise with rigatoni;
Hereford rib-eye with bearnaise; confit suckling pig
with Puy lentils; crispy hen's egg with Serrano ham. The
concision and intelligence of the menus is fantastic, and
the wine list is simply a masterpiece. (Stephen Gibson
& Nick Munier, 14-15 Trinity Street, D2 ☎ 01-677 1060
🖅 info@pichetrestaurant.com 🖰 www.pichetrestau-
rant.com – Open 8am-10.30pm Mon-Fri, 10am-11pm
Sat, noon-9pm Sun)

Dublin
Central

Cookery Classes
● Pink Ginger

What you need to know about Eimer Rainsford is simply
that she was head chef of Avoca for more than a decade.
Head chef of Ireland's leading luxury food brand is as
good as it gets, so if you want to know how Eimear
made all that magic for more than ten years, you need to
enrol for one of the classes she holds in her own home.
(Eimer Rainsford, 4 Serpentine Road, Sandymount, D4
☎ 087-986 4964 ✆ www.pinkginger.ie)

Restaurant
● Pinocchio

Pinocchio is part of a truly dynamic organisation that runs
this bustling Ranelagh address, Campo de Fiori in Bray,
as well as a cookery school, a catering company, and a
travel company. They also send out very amusing e-mails
to people like us, which are always stuffed with cheery,
sunshiney best wishes. And cheery, sunshiney best wishes
is what you will be feeling yourself after some of their
echt cooking, and the very echt wines which they import.
It's great to take a seat and order the salami or seafood
plates with a glass of wine to have a simple grazing of
food, or else to make an evening of it with some precise
Italian cooking. They do just what you want, the way
you want it. (Marco Roccasalvo, Marco Giannantonio &
Maurizio Mastrangelo, Luas Kiosk, Ranelagh D6 ☎ 01-
497 0111 ✆ www.pinocchiodublin.com – Open 7.30am-
10.30am Mon-Fri, 9.30am-11pm Sat, 11am-10pm Sun)

Dublin
Central

Café
● Phoenix Café

Helen Cunningham was one of the original pioneers
in Temple Bar, running Blazes restaurant for sixteen
years before finding herself up in the wonderful Phoenix
Park. The Phoenix is the sort of place that gives visitor's
centres a good name. It's charming, stylish and the food
is real – caramelised onion, white cheddar and thyme
tart; baked salmon with fennel seeds, sea salt and a
lemon crust; organic beetroot salad with blood orange
and balsamic dressing; brown rice with butter beans,
pomegranate and feta. Whether your appetite has been
sharpened by a run or just a brisk walk, this is the place
in which to satisfy it in style. (Helen Cunningham, Phoenix Park Visitor's Centre, D8 ☎ 01-677 0090 – Open
9.30am-4pm Jan-Dec, 9.30am-5pm Oct-Mar)

● Plan B

Plan B is Class 1 when it comes to seriously fine Italian cooking. Order the simplest of things in Linda Madigan's little place – bresaola salad with rocket; spaghetti with courgettes and chilli – and you see the glory of Italian cooking in perfectly created and cooked ingredients that shine because of the fundamental respect for simplicity shown by this kitchen. The room may not look like much, but there is a magic at work here, and it is accentuated by wonderful, relaxed service that gets you right into the groove of this peachy place. (Linda Madigan, Manor Place, Stoneybatter, D3 ☎ 01-670 6431 ✉ lindmadigan@hotmail.com – Open 12.30pm-late)

● Poppadom

With branches in Limerick and Sligo, and a fine take-away at Newland's Cross, Amjad Hussain's excellent Indian restaurants have enjoyed great success ever since they opened in Rathgar with a wow! impact, more than a decade ago now. But the standards set then have been maintained, and whilst other ethnic food chains have stolen much of the recent limelight, Poppadom remains a star destination for excellent food and service. (Amjad Hussain, 91a Rathgar Road, D6 ☎ 01-490 2383 ✆ www.poppadom.ie – Open 6pm-midnight Mon-Sun. Also Unit 5B Newland Cross, D22 ☎ 01-411 1144)

● Porterhouse Brewing Co.

The Porterhouse is quite an empire these days, with the original Temple Bar Porterhouse joined by branches in Nassau Street, Bray, Glasnevin and Covent Garden in London. Their success has been founded on superb brewing skills, and their range of beers is simply brilliant, thanks to their dedicated – ha, obsessive! – search for the right hops, the right malt, the right yeasts, out of which they fashion three stouts, three ales and three lagers. Taste their trio of stouts – Oyster; Plain and Wrasslers – and you can see and taste the brilliance at work here, the understanding of the culture of brewing, the ability to extract and conjure flavours, like magic. An essential part of any visit to Dublin. (Liam La Harte & Oliver Hughes, Parliament Street, D2 ☎ 01-679 8847 ✆ www.porterhousebrewco.com)

Dublin
Central

● The Port House

The Port House has been a wowee! hit ever since this
little tapas bar in a basement opened its doors. The
paella is ace, the calamari is fab, the patatas bravas are
yum, the chorizo in red wine is everyone's favourite, and
just to show their Basque side they also do some good
pintxos. No reservations, so be prepared to wait, with
a glass of good fino. Their second branch, Bar Pintxo,
at Eustace Street in Temple Bar, is equally fine. (Lee
Sim, 64a South William Street, D2 ☎ 01-677 0298 ✉ info@
porterhouse.ie ⌂ www.porthouse.ie – Open 11.30am-
11pm Mon-Fri, 12.30am-midnight Sat & Sun)

Restaurant
● Punjab Balti

Gursharan Singh has shifted the emphasis in the cooking
in Ranelagh's PJ more in the direction of the tandoor
oven, and away from the balti-style dishes, though
their classic dishes like Balti lamb remain, and are as
consistent and precisely delivered as ever. The starters
offer delights such as Aloo chop – potato and minced
lamb coated in gram flour and deep-fried; a very good
prawn peri peri coated in semolina, and a spot-on lamb
shish kebab. Finish with some superb homemade kulfi,
bring in a couple of bottles from Redmond's brilliant
wine shop just down the street, and all is well with the
world. (Gursharan Singh, 15 Ranelagh Village, Ranelagh,
D6 ☎ 01-496 0808 ✉ gsingh@punjabbalti.ie ⌂ www.
punjabbalti.ie – Open from 5pm Mon-Sun)

Restaurant
● Queen of Tarts

Yvonne and Regina Fallon are the business. Having
conquered Cork Hill over the last decade with their
sumptuous baking, they have opened up branch two –
princess of tarts, perhaps? – in Temple Bar, on Cow's
Lane, a great room in a charming naive French style with
a great terrace. The new QoT also has lots of excellent
meat-free dishes, at both breakfast and lunch, whilst
back in the original, the superb tarts and cakes that have
made these girls legends in their own lunchtimes continue to wow! the populace. (Regina & Yvonne Fallon,
Cork Hill, D2 ☎ 01-670 7499. Also at Cow's Lane, Dame
Street, D2 ☎ 01-633 4681 ⌂ www.queenoftarts.ie –
Open 7.30am-7pm Mon-Fri, 9am-7pm Sat & Sun)

● Redmond's of Ranelagh

One of the best wine shops and off licences in the city and the country, Jimmy Redmond's store is one of the essential food fixtures of Ranelagh, and was a major Dublin player long before Ranelagh began to become the gourmet ghetto which it has slowly but surely emerged as in the last five years. When he was last visiting the Punjab Balti, Leslie Williams picked up a 2005 Arneis from Seghesio in Sonoma in California and "a strange but wonderful Portuguese Baga from Luis Pato, delicious stuff and perfect with the food". Delicious stuff, then, and always perfect with whatever food you are having. (Jimmy Redmond, 25 Ranelagh Village, D6 ☎ 01-496 0552 – Open 10.30am-10pm Mon-Sat, 1pm-10pm Sun)

Market

● Red Stables Food Market

Red Stables is one of the great Dublin markets, with everything from Omega beef to Corleggy Cheese to Hemmingway's ready meals, to Burke Farm ice cream, and there are even gourmet dog biscuits for that special someone in your life. (Red Stables, St Anne's Park, Mount Prospect Avenue, D3 ☎ 01-222 7377 ⌨ info@ redstables.ie ⌂ www.redstables.ie – Open Sat 10am-5pm, till 4pm in winter)

Restaurant

● Residence

When you get an email from a friend who is married to one of Ireland's leading chefs describing "an outstanding lunch in Residence" then you know that Graham Neville is really doing something interesting in Restaurant Forty One in Residence, a club on St Stephen's Green. Mr Neville spent several years with Kevin Thornton before walking across the Green. But it's not so much Kevin Thornton that his cooking reminds us of, more the legendary Basque chef Andoni Luis Aduriz, of Mugaritz, in San Sebastian. Like Aduriz, Mr Neville is on the hunt for the pure essences of his ingredients: foie gras with salt; hazelnut sauce with chicken; oxtail essence with beef fillet; passion fruit mousse encapsulated in chocolate. This is very exciting cooking indeed, and it's good value too. (Simon & Christian Stokes, 41 St Stephen's Green, D2 ☎ 01-662 0000 ⌂ www.residence. ie – Open for lunch Wed-Sat, dinner Tue-Sat)

Restaurant
● **Restaurant 1014**

1014 is owned by CASA, the Caring and Sharing Association, and caring and sharing is just what they do
at Gareth Smith's terrific restaurant. "The restaurant
reminded me of the kind of great places you find outside
the centre of Paris, where real Parisians go out to eat",
says Caroline Byrne, and if you come here for, let's say,
Sunday lunch, then what you see is the clientele of a
neighbourhood restaurant, and all of them having a ball.
Mr Smith sources carefully and cooks everything from
scratch, and it's demon food: chowder with soda bread;
hake with bacon and shallot mash; calamari with sweet
chilli sauce; Connemara lamb with champ. "Everything
was perfect", says Caroline. "Simple, faultless and the
best of Irish". Wow! (Gareth Smith, 324 Clontarf Road,
D3 ☎ 01-805 4877 ⏁ www.restaurant1014.com –
10.30am-10pm Mon-Sat, 12.30pm-10pm Sun)

Restaurant, Café
● **Roly's**

People take Roly's for granted now, but it truly was a
revolutionary project when it opened, six weeks before
Xmas in 1992, when the Celtic Tiger wasn't even a
Celtic Kitten. Today chef Paul Cartwright fires out
super-consistent brasserie food to super-enormous
numbers of people, and the clamour of the room
remains one of the most vividly enjoyable in the city.
When people talk about restaurants that have been
pivotal in building Dublin's food culture, remember that
Roly's has been one of the most important addresses,
for it offered affordability, glamour, and it was one of the
first places where tables of women friends felt comfortable eating together. A feminist hero, then? Yes indeed.
(John & Angela O'Sullivan, Paul Cartwright, 7 Ballsbridge
Tce, Ballsbridge, D4 ☎ 01-668 2611 ⏁ www.rolysbistro.
com – Restaurant Open noon-4pm, 5.45pm-10pm, Cafe
Open 7am-10.30pm Mon-Fri, 9am-10.30pm Sat-Sun)

Restaurant
● **Saba**

Paul Cadden is a dynamic young guy, and he has fashioned one of the city's best ethnic restaurants in Saba,
both in terms of exciting Thai and Vietnamese cooking,
and also with its exuberant decor and sexy ambience.
Any time of day, we are game ball for the soft-shelled

crab, or the hake in banana leaf, or their excellent pad thai noodles. The room works best when you are with a bunch of people, in which case the intoxication of this zesty, chilli-rich food soon leads to intoxication of another sort. Only excellent, and a new Saba To Go on the Rathgar Road in Rathmines means southsiders have this classy food on their doorstep. Quite essential. (Paul Cadden, 26-28 Clarendon Street, D2 ☎ 01-679 2000 📠 feedback@sabadublin.com 🖰 www.sabadublin.com, www.sabatogo.com – Open noon-late Mon-Sun)

Mexican Foods and Cooking Classes
● Sabores de Mexico

Gus and Theresa make the real thing, Mexican cooking with true zing and authenticity. You will find their wonderful foods at Temple Bar, Sat 10am-5pm, Leopardstown, Fri 10am-2.30pm, Brooklodge every 1st Sunday, Brockaugh Centre, every 2nd Sunday, and there is nothing – nothing! – finer than a burrito or a fajita made by Gus and which uses their superlative Don Theresa salsas. They also organise cookery classes in Great Strand Street and in Killiney, and conduct culinary holidays to Mexico. (Theresa & Gustavo Hernandez, 3 North Great Strand Street ☎ 01-282 4614/086-353 4369 📠 mail@meromeromexico.com 🖰 www.meromeromexico.com)

Restaurant
● Seagrass

Sean Drugan made his name in Il Posto before moving to South Richmond Street, where he continues to offer serious cooking at decent prices. The food is modern Irish, so there are risottos, lamb casseroles, hotpots, and tasting plates which let you sample the different things the kitchen in working through each day. The room is comfortable and calming, and everyway professional. (Susannah Jackson & Sean Drugan, 30 South Richmond Street, Portobello, D2 ☎ 01-478 9595 📠 info@seagrassdublin.com 🖰 www.seagrassdublin.com – Open noon-5pm, 5pm till late Tue-Sun)

Fishmonger
● Sea Pearls

There is nothing else in the south city quite like Sea Pearls, where cracklingly fresh fish is sold at really keen prices. (South Richmond Street, Portobello, D6 ☎ 01-478 9134)

Dublin
Central

Restaurant
● Seven

Seven feels like a private house, but staff are professionally turned out and the food is slick. Well-achieved dishes such as leg of lamb with green lentils and sweet potato, or whole sea bass with lemon and caper butter, strike the right note, though prices are kinda high for a neighbourhood place. (Darius Sadri, 73 Manor Street, D7 ☎ 01-633 4092 🖰 www.sevenrestaurants.ie – Open noon-2.30pm, 5.30pm-9.30pm Mon-Sat. No lunch Sat, but Sun brunch from noon and Sat lunch planned for high summer season)

only in Dublin
Gur Cake

Restaurant
● Shanahan's

It's the poshest steak in town, and the price of dinner for a party might force you to sell the house, but there is no lack of charm about Shanahan's, so long as you can afford it. Service is great, the steaks are unquestionably fab, arguments about value are beside the point. (John Shanahan, 119 St Stephen's Green, D2 ☎ 01-407 0939 🖰 management@shanahans.ie 🖰 www.shanahans. ie – Open for Fri lunch from 12.30pm, dinner Mon-Sun 6pm-10pm)

Cheesemonger
● Sheridan's Cheesemongers

It all started with a market stall, and today Sheridan's is a little empire of food quality, with two shops in Dublin, a shop in Galway and in Waterford, a new cheese centre in Athboy, and a pub and restaurant in Galway city, along with their position as one of the mainstays of farmers markets. Everything is superb, and is served by the best staff in the business: Seamus and Kevin Sheridan and Fiona Corbett should be in demand as speakers on how to recognise great staff, and then motivate them to be dynamic and assertive masters of service. Sheridan's is as pivotal to modern Irish food culture as Ballymaloe or Chapter One: original, cultured, an organisation that is an enrichment of its society. (Kevin & Seamus Sheridan, Fiona Corbett, 11 Sth Anne Street, D2 ☎ 01-679 3143

info@sheridanscheesemongers.com ⌐ www.
sheridanscheesemongers.com – Open 10am-6pm Mon-
Fri, 9.30am-6pm Sat)

Ethnic Shop
● **Shop Easi**

Shop Easi is THE place to go for mangoes. They fly in ten
to twelve different varieties from March to September,
and these are perfumed wonders that smell of jasmine,
rose petals and unearthly delights. Leslie Williams makes
a bee-line in particular for the Anwar Ratols in June and
July. "I'm off to get the Anwar Ratols, darling. I may be
some time". (Kashif Mahmood, 63 Clanbrassil Street,
D2 ☎ 01-473 3565 – Open 10.30am-9.30pm Sat & Sun,
11am-9.30pm Mon-Fri)

Restaurant
● **Silk Road Cafe**

Abraham Phelan cooks some of the most flavourful and
complete cooking that you will find in any Dublin café.
The space is informal – it's a pretty, bright self-service
café where you pick up a tray – but the cooking is
perfectly realised, focused largely on vegetarian dishes,
though that is not an issue for the omnivores who come
here because the food is so fine, the place so gracious.
Lovely, lovely work. And speaking of self-service cafés,
if you haven't seen Eddie Izzard doing Darth Vader in
the Dark Star café, you haven't lived. (Abraham Phelan,
Chester Beatty Museum, Dublin Castle, D2 ☎ 01-407 0770
⌐ silkroadcafe@hotmail.com ⌐ www.silkroadcafe.
ie – Open 10am-4.30pm Mon-Fri, 11am-4.30pm Sat,
1pm-4.30pm Sun)

Cafe
● **Simon's Place Coffee Shop**

The hippies were right, you know, and the hippysome
flavours and feeling of Simon's is just right, too. Step in
here, and step back to a gentler Dublin, with food that
seems to console the soul as much as it satisfies the
appetite, in the kind of room that everyone feels they
own a part of, the kind of room you don't want to leave.
So, some vegetable soup, some brown bread, maybe a
hearty egg sandwich, and certainly some cinnamon buns
with coffee. And time to linger, time to linger. (Simon
McWilliams, George's Street Arcade, D2 ☎ 01-679 7821
– Open 8.30am-5pm Mon-Sat)

● **Soup Dragon**

Fiona and Niamh's SD is almost a decade in business,
during which time they have served superb soups to
queues of hungry people, developed things other than
soups – quiches, curries and stews, a couple of pies, nice
cakes and bakes. But it's the soups that ring our bell:
broccoli and blue cheese; chicken and corn chowder;
vegetable gumbo, every one a meal unto itself. (Fiona
Fairbrother, 168 Capel Street, D1 ☎ 01-872 3277
✆ events@soupdragon.com ⬥ www.soupdragon.com
– Open 8am-5pm Mon-Fri, 10am-4pm Sat)

● **South William**

They cook eight different pies in this funky pub, and
that's it. Which is great, because it's one for each day of
the week, with one left over. Which one will you forego
this week, then? Wicklow venison? Bacon and cabbage?
Goat's cheese and spinach? Hmm. It's never easy, is it?
Their sister establishment, Coppinger Row, is just back
down the street and around the corner. (Marc & Conor
Bereen, 52 South William Street, D2 ☎ 01-672 5946
✆ info@southwilliam.ie ⬥ www.southwilliam.ie – Food
served noon-10pm Mon-Thur, noon-9pm Fri & Sat)

Dublin
Central

● **Spiceland**

Abraham's Spiceland is perhaps the very best shop for
sourcing Middle Eastern foods, and it is packed with
good things, from long beans to superb baklava. The
quality of fruit and vegetables is also very high, and there
is a halal meat counter amidst all the oher necessities of
life. (Abraham Ali, 4 Sth Richmond Street, Portobello,
D2 ☎ 01-475 0422 – Open 10am-9pm Mon-Sun)

● **Supervalu Mount Merrion**

There is a great sense of pride in the local neighbourhood about the sheer quality of Damien Kiernan's singular supermarket, and it is richly deserved. Mr Kiernan's
USP is simply that he sells more Irish artisan foods than
you would expect in a supermarket and, interestingly, his
artisan suppliers speak of him in the highest regard. "It's
gone out of its way to be different, and the difference

in this case really is Irish!" is how Caroline Byrne sees Mr Kiernan's modus operandi, and it makes this a peach of a store. They try harder, and they succeed. (Damien Kiernan, 27 The Rise, Mount Merrion, D6 ☎ 01-288 1014 – Open 7.30am-8pm Mon-Fri, 8am-6pm Sat)

● Sushi King

The care and craft that Rodney and Audrey bring to the art of sushi has been rewarded by the opening of a second store, on Dawson Street, to join the original take-away on Baggot Street. There are seats in Dawson Street, so you can enjoy this splendid food away from the office. They make everything fresh every day, so don't turn up before 11 am, and then simply agonise over the choice of fascinating Asian dishes: massaman beef curry; salmon teriyaki on rice; california maki; duck with hoi sin sauce. Ace food, and healthy as a spring day. (Rodney & Audrey Gargan, 146 Lower Baggot Street, D2 ☎ 01-644 9836. Also at Dawson Street ☎ 01-675 2000 ⊕ www.sushiking.ie – Open Mon-Fri, 8am-6pm)

● Sweeney O'Rourke

They are so helpful in Sweeny O'Rourke. Ring them up, or drop into Pearse Street with some query, and if they don't stock or sell the part, gizmo, widget or whatever that you want, they will tell you who does, and probably find the 'phone number for you. Such service! Such politeness! Such charm! That's why all the professionals shop here for their serious kit. (Shane & John O'Rourke, 34 Pearse Street, D2 ☎ 01-677 7212 ⊕ info@ sweeneyorourke.com ⊕ www.sweeneyorourke.com – Open 9am-5pm Mon-Fri)

● Sweeney's Wine Merchants

Finian Sweeney has crammed more than 1,000 wines into his smart shop at Hart's Corner, so whatever you seek, you will likely find it here. The beer selection is as capacious as the wine offer, and all the other elements of a great wine shop – a delivery service, tastings, wine appreciation classes, a party service – are all present and correct. (Finian Sweeney, 6 Finglas Road, Hart's Corner, D11 ☎ 01-830 9593 ⊕ www.sweeneyswine.ie – Open 10.30am-10pm Mon-Sat, 12.30pm-10pm Sun)

● Temple Bar Market

There is nowhere else quite like it. We were here on the
very first Saturday the TB Market set up its stalls, and
its flourishing success has been one of the great delights
of contemporary Dublin life. Today, you can turn up
and get some spit-roasted Arklow pig from the Goode
Life Food Company, you can get Florence and Damien's
excellent breads, Gus and Theresa's superb Mexican
foods, Karuna's treats, David Llewellyn's brilliant juices,
olives, magnificent coffees, freshly dug organic vegetables, and on and on and on. TB was the pioneer market,
and everything else that has transformed market retailing throughout Ireland owes a debt to this visionary
venture. (Meeting House Square, Saturdays ⌂ www.
templebar.ie)

● Terroirs

"We wanted to create a boutique shop selling only the
very best" is how Sean and Françoise Gilley explain their
decision, and determination, fifteen years ago, to open
the relentlessly stylish Terroirs. For fifteen years they
have flown the flag for great wines and great speciality foods, and also for excellent service and the sort
of ambience that you positively relax into. In fact, you
don't even need to walk into Terroirs to get a taste for
how this couple work: just look at Françoise's uncan-
nily brilliant window displays and you will see a supreme
aesthetic at work. The wines are great, especially their
Loire selection, in fact they are particularly strong on
France. (Sean & Françoise Gilley, 103 Morehampton
Road, Donnybrook, D4 ☎ 01-667 1311 ✉ info@
terroirs.ie ⌂ www.terroirs.ie – Open 1pm-7pm Mon,
10.30am-7pm Tue-Sat)

● Thomas's Delicatessen

A legendary deli for the last twenty five tears, Thomas
Murphy's inspiring deli is one of the defining destinations of Foxrock. Mr Murphy is a Slow Food acolyte, and
the philosophy of SF translates into stocking the best
organic, naturally produced, delicious foods you can ever
desire, sourced from many of the leading Irish artisans.
When the foods are not Irish, they are international
brands of the highest calibre, and when it comes to wines

the selection is superlative. There is such an exuberant passion for good food here that it makes every visit into a food lovers adventure. Here's to the next 25 years. (Thomas Murphy, 4 Brighton Road, Foxrock, D18 ☎ 01-289 4101 🖰 www.thomasoffoxrock.ie – Open 8am-7.30pm Mon-Sat, 9am-4pm Sun)

Restaurant
● Thornton's

Kevin Thornton has opened a second restaurant, Menu, in Belfast, continuing the practice of superstar chefs of having more than one outlet for their creativity. And Mr Thornton is one of Ireland's superstar chefs, and has been ever since he opened up in the tiny Wine Epergne in Rathmines twenty years ago. Whilst Thornton's has a reputation for being expensive, you can access this dazzling, technically perfect food at decent prices if you try the tapas menu served at the bar, or go for the good value lunch menus, which offer superb value for such stellar cooking. The room isn't the most atmospheric, but food of this quality is a cultural miracle. (Kevin & Muriel Thornton, Fitzwilliam Hotel, St. Stephen's Green, D2, ☎ 01-478 7008 🖰 thorntonsrestaurant@eircom. net 🖰 www.thorntonsrestaurant.com – Open 5.30pm-10.30pm Tue & Wed, 12.30pm-2pm, 6pm-10.30pm Thu-Sat)

Deli & Sandwich Bar
● Toffoli

It's a box-sized place, but Elaine McArdle's little room has echt pizzas and very interesting piadina sandwiches where they take good breads and pack them with tasty ingredients, and they really hit the spot. (Elaine McArdle, 34 Castle Street, D2 ☎ 01-633 4022 – Open 9.15am-5.45pm Tue-Fri)

Italian Restaurant
● Da Tommaso

Wear your Barca football shirt in here, and they'll slag you off. But it's a small price to pay for the very genuine crack and the friendly service in Da Tommaso. It's all clichéd right down to the check tablecloths and the movie star photos. But the best cliché of all is that the food is authentic and really tasty, whether you're having spaghetti with clams or a pizza Tommaso. (Tommaso Stennato, 24 Fairview Strand, D3 ☎ 01-887 5939/087-294 3750 – Open 5pm-11pm Tue-Sun)

Bakery
● Traditional Polish Bakery

Karl Tracz's bakery supplies the multiple stores as well
as Polish, Russian and East European shops, and their
own shop on Capel Street. We like the 100% rye flour
brown bread, and the cheese pastry. (Karl Tracz, 85
Capel Street, D1, Ballymount Industrial Estate, Walk-
ingstown, D12 ☎ 01-408 9992 ✉ info@polishbakery.eu
🖱 www.polishbakery.eu)

Restaurant
● Tribeca

Omelettes. Burgers. Noodles. Sandwiches. Salads. It
sounds obvious, but Tribeca do this upfront food with
good grace and good service, which is why it is always
buzzing. They also run the Canal Bank Café on Leeson
street. (Ger Foote & Trevor Browne, 65 Ranelagh, D6
☎ 01-497 4174 ✉ info@tribeca.ie 🖱 www.tribeca.ie –
Open noon-11pm Mon-Sun)

Karaoke Music Bar
● Ukiyo Bar

There is probably a time in everyone's life when, for
reasons we won't go into here, you feel the need
to sing, "My Heart Will Go On" in front of all your
closest friends. Should discretion fail to get the better
of you, then Ukiyo is the place in which to reveal your
inner Celine. Make sure to have lots of nice Japanese
and Korean food and their Rack of Sake – all the nine
varieties that they stock – before you pick up the
microphone. (Duncan Maguire, 7 Exchequer Street, D2
☎ 01-633 4071 🖱 www.ukiyobar.com – Open noon-
4pm, 7pm-11pm Mon-Thur, noon-3.30pm, 5pm-2.30am
Fri-Sun)

Bakery & Café
● Il Valentino

Owen Doorly's bakery is one of the most significant
openings in Dublin in recent years. The stunning quality
of his Italian-influenced breads is a cause for rejoicing;
breads where flour, yeast, salt and water combine into
mellifluous culinary magic, bound in a loaf of Tuscan
bread, or superb ciabatta or focaccia. "Bread is not just
bread, it's a world" says Mr Doorly, and few other bakers show just how splendid and complete a world that is.
The Valentino breads are pivotal as your daily bread, but

they are also made into the most wonderful treats here in the café. Bliss. (Owen Doorly, 5 Gallery Quay, Grand Canal Harbour, D2 ☎ 01-633 1100 – Open 7am-7pm Mon-Fri, 9am-6pm Sat, 9am-3pm Sun)

Restaurant
● Venu

It might seem like a back-handed compliment, but one of the things we like about Venu is the fact that they make the most superb chips. Not only that, but they are determined to make the best chips in the city. We admire that ambition as much as we admire their perfect, dry, slightly crunchy frites. The cooking here has been consistently good since they opened, and whilst opinions on the room – it's an always-lit basement – are divided, a taste of Clogherhead crab salad, or a tender rib-eye of beef, or some organic salmon with noodles, will have you well focused on the plate. (Charles Guilbaud, Anne's Lane, D2 ☎ 01-670 6755 ⊕ www.venu.ie – Open from 6pm Tue-Sat, brunch on Sat from noon)

only in Dublin
Bretzel Bakery Onion Bread

Wine Merchant
● The Vintry

One of the most highly regarded and critically acclaimed wine shops in the capital, Evelyn Jones's The Vintry is a consistent prizewinner for the excellence of the shop's wine offer, and the knowledge and expertise of the service. If you don't know Gamay from grand cru, they are here to help you master the arcane world of wine. (Evelyn Jones, 102 Rathgar Road, D6 ☎ 01-490 5477 ⊕ vintry@vintry.ie ⊕ www.vintry.ie – Open 10.30am-10pm Mon-Sun)

Shop
● Wilde and Green

Carmel and Denise's hip shop is partly a lifestyle destination – they have candles and tableware and skin-care products – but it is the food selection here that will have you returning again and again to Milltown, with everything from Fixx coffee to Craft Bakery breads on sale along with the choicest deli goods imaginable and great foods-to-go. But one gets the sense that these ambitious women are only beginning, and that many new ideas and developments lie ahead for this classy venture. (Carmel O'Callaghan & Denise Begley, St Anns, Milltown Road, Milltown, D6 ☎ 01-268 3333 🖰 www.wildeandgreen. com – Open 8am-6.30pm Mon, 8am-7pm Tue-Fri, 9.30am-6.30pm Sat, 10am-6.30pm Sun)

Restaurant
● The Wild Goose Grill

As the name suggests, Kevin McMahon's origins as a sommelier play a large part in the Goose's offering, with a huge, smart list of wines available. The food offer is very savoury – cote de boeuf for two; rack of lamb; duck breast; dry-aged steak, even the risotto has Gorgonzola and they do a blue cheese potato gratin. Big food, which suits big bottles, but it's not a macho place, and women like the neat room above McSorley's pub, possibly because of echoes of upstairs at Roly's Bistro. You need to take it easy with those big bottles, however, or the bill will stack up. (Kevin McMahon, 1 Sandford Road, Ranelagh D6 ☎ 01-491 2377 Open 5.30pm-late 7 days, Sun 12.30pm-3pm)

Dublin Central

Restaurant
● Winding Stair Bookshop & Café

As part of the Thomas Read group, the mighty Winding Stair has been embroiled in the group's commercial difficulties, but let's not let that distract us from the simple fact that TWS continues to be one of the most unmissable places to eat in Dublin city. Their take on contemporary Irish cooking is robustly delicious —– smoked pollock poached in milk with cheddar mash; boiled collar of bacon with parsley sauce; Lough Neagh trout with boiled spuds; parsnip and shallot tart with Gubbeen cheese – and utterly distinctive. But then everything about TWS is distinctive: the wines, the style, the service and the clamour of voices when the room is rockin'. (Elaine Murphy, 40 Lwr Ormond Quay, D1 ☎ 01-872 7320 🖰 restaurant@winding-stair.com 🖰 www. winding-stair.com – Open 12.30pm-3.30pm Mon-Sun, 6pm-10.30pm Tue-Sat, 6pm-9.30pm Sun)

Fishmonger
● Wright's of Marino

"If it swims - we have it!!" is the famous logo of Wrights of Marino, and this smart piece of sloganeering is no idle boast. Wrights specialise in selling exotic fish. So if you are looking for yellowfin tuna or line-caught sea bass, this is the place to start. As with so many other Irish fishmongers, it has taken generations of expertise and commitment to build Wrights of Marino into the seafood wholesaler that most of Dublin's restaurateurs turn to when sourcing fresh fish. They also operate a smokehouse, producing and selling not only smoked salmon but also smoked cod, haddock, coley, mackerel, trout and cured gravadlax. At the heart of the business, however, is the Wrights of Marino shop, which has been selling fresh fish to Dubliners, from the same spot, for nearly 100 years. (John Wright, 21 Marino Mart, Fairview, D3 ☎ 01-833 3636 ✉ info@wrightsofmarino. com 🖰 www.wrightsofmarino.com – Open 10.30am-2.30pm Mon, 9am-5pm Tue-Thu, 9am-5.30pm Fri, 10am-3.30pm Sat)

Oysters

NORTH COUNTY DUBLIN

Finglas

Fishmonger
● Stevie Connolly's Seafood

"Dublin is a great place to sell fish," says Stevie Connolly. "the locals understand fish. They buy it regularly." Stevie's shop is in the old Dublin village of Finglas, and the location is part of the reason for the success of the shop. "In working class areas, people always bought fish," he adds. It's historical, it's cultural, with its animus often leading back to religious practices, as well as economic factors. "My busiest days are still Wednesday and Friday." (Stevie Connolly, Unit 3 Finglas Main Shopping Centre, D11 ☎ 01-856 8564 – Open 8am-6pm Tue-Fri, 8am-2pm Sat)

Howth

● **Aqua**

Blessed with a room with some of the finest views of the sea imaginable, Aqua has been doing the good thing ever since they opened in 2000. Ten solid years of fine cooking – oysters with shallot vinegar; lobster with potato salad and leaves; sole meunière; hake with basil beurre blanc; cod with courgette Provencale. You can't argue with this sort of classic fish cookery – save that it is relatively expensive for the à la carte – but the professionalism and what we have called the restaurantness of Aqua make it a safe bet every time. (Richard Clery & Charlie Smith, 1 West Pier, Howth ☎ 01-832 0690 ✉ dine@ aqua.ie ☞ www.aqua.ie – Open 12.30pm-3pm Tue-Fri, 12.30pm-3.30pm Sat, noon-5pm Sun, 5.30pm-10pm Tue-Sat, 5pm-8.30pm Sun)

Fishmonger
● **Beshoff's the Market**

"We're proud to be traditional fishmongers supplying the freshest, best-quality seafood available, naturally and responsibly," says Alan Beshoff. With Beshoff's the Market they've taken this imprimatur a step further. Next to a superbly stocked fish counter you will find fresh organic fruits and vegetables, wines, oils and sauces. There is a coffee bar, an oyster bar and a critically-regarded restaurant. They have utensils for the kitchen, flowers for the table. "I want people to be able to come in, have a cup of coffee, buy *The Irish Times*, maybe get some flowers, and some mackerel," says Alan. Beshoff's is an essentials shop, and everything is ethically sourced, organic or wild, and beautifully presented. (Alan Beshoff, 17/18 West Pier, Howth ☎ 01-839 0766 ✉ sales@beshoffs.ie ☞ www.beshoffs.com – Open 8am-6pm Mon-Sat, 9am-6pm Sun)

Café, Deli and Bakery
● **The Country Market**

Downstairs you will find the CM deli, with lots of organics, good baking and plenty of food to go. Upstairs in their cosy café chef Lindsey Cooney fashions goat's cheese crostini, fisherman's pie, chicken and broccoli crumble, home-made meatballs and lots of tempting salads, and then gets stuck into the nice sweet stuff like carrot and banana cakes. An excellent venture. (Joseph Dogherty, 16 Main Street, Howth ☎ 01-832 2033 – Cafe Open 8am-6pm Mon-Sat, 8am-5pm Sun. Shop open 7am-7pm Mon-Sat, 7am-5pm Sun)

● Doran's on the Pier

Sean Doran says: "At Doran's we select only the best and freshest seafood from directly off the local boats, and literally from Malin Head to Mizen Head. And with the changing cultural spectrum and the demands for more exotic types of fish, we fly in twice weekly fish such as sea bream, swordfish, fresh sardines, catfish, tilapia and carp to name but a few. So if you are looking for a traditional cut of cod or long ray, want to have that special dinner with black sole, turbot or monkfish or maybe something more exotic like baked seabass or tuna for the barbecue, Doran's on the Pier is the place to come." Doran's on the Pier also run a website - www.seafood2go.ie - which is open to both the trade and the public, as well as running the very fine Oar House restaurant, right next door to the shop. (Sean Doran, 7 West Pier, Howth ☎ 01-839 2419 ⌐ www.lettdoran.ie – Open 9am-6pm Mon-Sat, 10am-5pm Sun)

● Ella Wine Bar

Aoife Healy's restaurant is just lovely: lovely room, lovely food, lovely atmosphere, lovely value for your money. They enjoy themselves with the cooking here – smoked chicken cannelloni; crab and crayfish mornay; shoulder of lamb with champ; tempura of Dublin Bay prawns - and their enjoyment is infectious, and will have you smiling. Lovely wines complete the picture of loveliness. (Aoife Healy, 7 Main Street, Howth ☎ 01-839 6264 ⌐ info@ellawinebar.com ⌐ www.ellawinebar.com – Open 12.45pm-2.45pm Thur-Sat, 6pm-late Mon-Sat)

● The House

"The House ticks all the boxes. It's friendly and offers good service to all customers, including children. The atmosphere is lively yet laid back, the food is fantastic and made from the freshest, high-quality local ingredients, and it's clear that every attempt has been made to offer all of this for very good value. The House is everything you'd want from a restaurant for dinner with friends and family during the week, or brunch at the weekend." Some restaurants make it easy for *Bridgestone* reviewers, and in this case Caroline Byrne just had to turn up at The House, enjoy wonderful food and service, and then deliver her verdict: The House ticks all the boxes. (Karl Dillon & Ian Connolly, 4 Main Street, Howth ☎ 01-839 6388 ⓘ info@thehouse-howth.ie ⓦ www. thehouse-howth.ie – Open 9am-9.30pm, lunch served noon-5pm, dinner 6pm-9.30pm. Open till 10.30pm Sat & Sun. Brunch 11.30am-5pm Sat & Sun & bank hols)

Restaurant
● Ivan's Oyster Bar & Grill

Ivan's is the restaurant gig of the Beshoff family, legendary fishmongers of Dublin, and adjoins their Market emporium. There is both an oyster bar and a grill bar, and sparklingly fresh seafood is what you get in this slick room. They keep the cooking simple: fruits de mer seafood plate; sashimi tuna carpaccio; Ivan's Niçoise with an olive dressing; pan-roasted brill – and they rarely put a foot wrong. (Alan Beshoff & Aidan Meyler, West Pier, Howth ☎ 01-839 0285 ⓘ info@ivans.ie ⓦ www.ivans.ie – Open 12.30pm-9.30pm Sun-Thur, 12.30pm-10pm Fri & Sat. Oyster bar open noon-close)

Restaurant
● King Sitric

One of the longest established restaurants in all of Dublin, and how splendid that Aidan and Joan continue to fly the flag for good seafood cookery and great white wines. (Aidan & Joan MacManus, East Pier, Howth ☎ 01-832 5235 ⓘ info@kingsitric.ie ⓦ www.kingsitric. ie – Open from 6.30pm Mon-Sat, 1pm-7pm Sun. Closed Tues and bank hols)

Fish Shop
● Nicky's Plaice

Four generations of the McLoughlin family have played their part in establishing Nicky's Plaice as an iconic destination in Irish fish retailing, with Martin McLoughlin now heading the business. The location – at the very end of Howth Pier, makes it the archetype of what a fish shop should look like and what it should offer. "The location has huge impact. It's unique, you feel you are coming back to the home of fish. The history attached to it is older than any of us, but the expertise and knowledge still stands. We are still working on improving that today," says Martin. This is a proud shop with a real sense of mission. and Martin McLoughlin makes much of his respect for the sea. "Fish is one of the last things that man has gone out to hunt." (Martin McLoughlin, West Pier, Howth ☎ 01-832 3557 – Open 10am-1pm Mon, 9am-6pm Tue-Fri, 9am-8pm Thur, 9am-1pm Sat)

only in Dublin
Spice Burger

Restaurant
● The Oar House

Catch of the day means catch of the day in The Oar House - fish directly from the trawlers on the pier - and it has meant that this is one of the northside's hottest tickets. It can be hard to get one of the 40 seats in here even midweek, so powerful is the mix of sharp seafood cookery and truly excellent pricing. The smart local money always goes for the daily specials, whilst the fish'n'chips are knock-out. (Sean Doran, West Pier, Howth ☎ 01-839 4562 ⌂ www.oarhouse.ie – Open noon-10.30pm Mon-Sun)

Fishmonger and Smoked Salmon
● Ocean Path

With more than 42 years in the industry, Alan Ecock's Ocean Path are the largest processors of fresh seafood in Ireland, supplying Superquinn, M&S, Supervalu, Centra and Dunnes amongst others with a vast range of fresh seafood, frozen fish and value-added seafood products, and their traditionally smoked salmon, Dunns of Dublin.Their shopfront for retailing to the public can be found in Ireland's seafood Mecca, the West Pier at Howth, where you will find a superb range of Irish fish, deep-sea fish, shellfish and exotics. This is nothing less than the oldest fish company in Ireland – established back in 1822, and it is still family-run. (Alan Ecock, West Pier, Howth ☎ 01-839 8900 ⌂ www.dunns.ie – Open 9am-6pm Tue-Fri)

Lusk

● Llewellyn's Orchard Produce

David Llewellyn now has ten years of masterminding
the fruit of orchards and in that time he has fashioned a
unique range of drinks from artisan apple juice to real,
proper, cider to a balsamic cider vinegar, and when he
isn't plucking the apples he is, believe it or believe it not,
making red and white wines, using cabernet sauvignon
and merlot and sauvignon blanc and chardonnay grapes.
You will find David at lots of farmers' markets and on
any cold morning you can sort yourself out with one
of his warmed apple juice drinks. (David Llewellyn,
Quickpenny Road, Lusk ☎ 01-843 1650 ⌨ pureapple@
eircom.net)

Malahide

Dublin
North

Restaurant
● Bon Appetit

Oliver Dunne is creating one of the city's glories in BA.
His food is involved, precise, challenging to both the
senses and the intellect, and very, very expert: warm
salad of rabbit, globe artichokes, broad beans and cep
vinaigrette, or pan-fried brill with roasted cauliflower
and lime purée, celery gnocchi and red wine sauce, are
typical of his improvisations with texture and flavour,
and the food never misses a beat. Prices are very fair,
and the cooking downstairs in Cafe Bon is also deliciously achieved and very fine value. (Oliver Dunne, 9
St James Terrace, Malahide ☎ 01-845 0314 ⌨ reserva-
tions@bonappetit.ie ⌂ www.bonappetit.ie – Open 7pm-
9.30pm Tue-Sat, 1pm-8pm Sun)

Restaurant
● Café Bon

The more informal café space run by Oliver Dunne's
Bon Appetit restaurant offers a simpler menu, but no
less ambition or precise professionalism in the execution
and service of the dishes. (Oliver Dunne, 9 St James
Terrace, Malahide ☎ 01-845 0314 ⌨ info@bonappetit.ie
⌂ www.bonappetit.ie – Open 6pm-10.30pm Tue-Sat,
1pm-8pm Sun)

● Foodware Store

When she isn't fashioning really good Ballymaloe
accented food for her store Aisling Boyle puts on the
trainers and runs marathons. Presumably, we imagine,
in order to relax! The Foodware team, with Jill Sloan,
another ex-Ballymaloe school, as head chef, have made
the shop a staple of chichi Malahide for many year's
now and it's a really charming space. (Aisling Boyle, Old
Street, Malahide ☎ 01-845 1830 🖅 aislingfood@mac.
com 🖰 www.foodwarestore.com – Open 9.30am-6pm
Mon-Sat)

Café & Garden Centre
● Garden Works

There are two Garden Works stores, here at Mabestown, and at Clonee out in deepest County Meath, and
they are beloved amongst keen gardeners, not just for
being excellent plants people, but also for having exceptionally good food halls and cafes in which to shop and
eat. "We are immensely proud of our cafés and the daily
miracles they produce." Well, when you get gardeners
talking like that about cooking you know that it is as big
a priority for them as their plant life. That's the secret
of the two Garden Works cafés, and it's why no self-
respecting gardener would ever turn up here without a
good appetite. (Mabestown, Malahide ☎ 01-845 0110.
Also at Dunboyne, Co Meath ☎ 01-825 5375 🖅 info@
gardenworks.ie 🖰 www.gardenworks.ie – Open
9.30am-5pm Mon-Fri, 9.30am-5.30pm Sat, noon-5.30pm
Sun & bank hols)

Wine Shop
● Gibney's Fine Wines

Gibney's is a famous Northside pub, but for the
purposes of the *Bridgestone Guides* what you need to
know is that their wine shop is one of the most highly
regarded in the entire country, and tends to waltz
away with several awards every year. (New Street,
Malahide ☎ 01-845 0606 🖰 www.gibneys.com – Open
10.30am-11.30pm Mon-Thu, 10.30am-12.30am Fri & Sat,
12.30pm-11pm Sun)

Farmers' Market
● Malahide Farmers' Market

You will find the food outside the Malahide Market at

the GAA club, whilst inside is a nice bevy of crafts and crafts people. On average there's 30 stalls each week, so there's lots to choose from. (Saturday 10am-4pm, Church Street, side of St Sylvester's GAA hall, Malahide www.irishfarmersmarkets.ie)

Naul

Organic Herb Nursery
● The Herb Garden

Denise Dunne is the herb guru you need if a bounte-ous herb garden is what you want to see every time you look out the window. Denise not only grows and sells the herbs but designs herb gardens and offers a consultancy service. All her work is organically certified. (Denise Dunne, Forde-de-Fyne, Naul ☎ 01-841 3907 info@theherbgarden.ie www.theherbgarden.ie – Visitors strictly by appointment only)

Organic Vegetables
● McNally Family Farm

Long before it was fashionable or profitable Jenny and Patrick McNally were farming the way nature intended. Today they produce beautiful salad leaves, herbs and crops and you'll find them at Temple Bar and Leopardstown markets. (Jenny & Pat McNally, Balrickard, Ring Commons, Naul ☎ 01-841 3023)

Newcastle

Butcher
● Lett's Craft Butchers

John Lett opened a fish counter in his excellent butch-er's shop "because I wanted to sell everything fresh". So along with award-winning sausages, artfully butchered locally-sourced meat and organic chickens, you can buy the freshest and most professionally prepared seafood fillets. The fish is supplied by Kish Fish, and it matches the superb quality and stylishness that this shop exudes. This is a gem of a shop, a mixture of artisan craftmanship and a sophisticated design ethic. (John Lett, Main Street, Newcastle www.lettscraftbutchers.com – Open 9am-6.30pm Mon-Sat)

Portmarnock

Wine Shop
● Jus de Vine

Jus de Vine should be called Mondo Vino, because the first time you walk in the door of Tommy Cullen's shop you'll find it hard to believe that he hasn't brought the entire world of wine to a single store and then opened that store in Portmarnock. This place is beyond belief. And yet its defining characteristic is the modest knowledge of the staff, rather than any bumptiousness, that makes them so good and helps them win so many awards. So you can expect incredible wines and really great service. (Tommy Cullen, 7 Portmarnock Town Centre, ☎ 01-846 1192 – Open 10.30am-10.30pm Mon-Sat, 12.30pm-10.30pm Sun)

Skerries

Fishmonger
● Egan's Ocean Fresh

Tony Gunnery, a third generation fishmonger, runs this quaint little shop in the picturesque area of Strand Street, next to the fishing harbour. "We're just here to sell fish" says Mr Gunnery, and that's what they do: good-quality flat fish, chunky fillets of turbot, brill and John Dory, plenty of plaice and mackerel. (Tony Gunnery, 85a Strand Street, Skerries ☎ 01-849 5244 ⏀ www.egansfreshfish.com – Open 9am-6pm Tue-Sat, 11am-3pm Mon)

Deli & Cafe
● Olive

"We have great pride and confidence in the business we have created together," is how Deirdre Fahy describes the singular deli and cafe that she and Peter have created in Skerries. "It's a great town. The locals are fantastic and very loyal", says Deirdre. The reason why the locals are so loyal is because the foods on the shelves and foods in the café are both so good. They keep things very simple and they do things very correctly. (Peter Doritty & Deirdre Fahy, 86 Strand Street, Skerries ☎ 01-849 0310 ⏀ sales@olive.ie ⏀ www.olive.ie – Open 8.30am-6pm Mon-Sat, 9.30am-5pm Sun)

● The Red Bank

Terry McCoy has been one of the pioneers of modern Irish cooking, wielding the pots and pans and transforming his local foods ever since he opened up the Red Bank back in 1983. The Red Bank's reputation has been built on Terry's magnificent seafood cookery, though there are meat dishes on the menu. The Red Bank also has comfortable rooms, and the hospitality since 1983 has always been genuine and true. (Terry McCoy, 5-7 Church Street, Skerries ☎ 01-849 1005 ⌁ www.redbank. ie – Open 6.30pm-9.45pm Mon-Sat, 12.30pm-4.30pm Sun)

Wine Merchant
● Red Island Wines

Dougie Stewart's shop is a place for serious wine lovers and many of the bottles on the shelves are regularly chosen by the weekend wine writers as particularly peachy objects for your attention and your Saturday night dinner. (Dougie Stewart, 64 Church Street, Skerries ☎ 01-849 4032 ⌁ info@redislandwine.com – Open noon-8pm most days, till 9pm Fri)

Gastropub
● Stoop Your Head

You want to find an archetypal seafood restaurant in a coastal town like Skerries, and fortunately Stoop Your Head will deliver your achetypal needs with solid sender confidence. It's a simple spot, and you'll probably have to wait for a table, but those Moules marinière, Dublin Bay prawns, dressed crab, prawns Marie Rose all have your name on them. (David May, Harbour Road, Skerries ☎ 01-849 2085 – Food served noon-3pm, 5.30pm-9.30pm Mon-Thu, noon-3pm 5.30pm-10pm Fri-Sat, 12.30pm-3pm, 4pm-8pm Sun)

Swords

Bakery
● La Boulangerie Francaise

Last time we were in Swords we went all the way to Applewood Village to get some breads and some lunch at Florence and Damian's place. Once we had found the shop and stood in line to order we got soups, sandwiches, bread, croissants. But as all the tables were taken we wound up having lunch in the car. No matter: everything was delicious and isn't it brilliant to see a him and her place doing so well in a zone where the big brands dominate. (Florence & Damian Cusack, Unit 77, Applewood Village Square, Swords ☎ 086-102 2786 ⌂ www.laboulangeriefrancaise.ie – Open 9am-5pm Mon & Sat, 9am-6pm Tue-Fri and Temple Bar Market on Saturdays)

Roadside Take-away
● The Chuck Wagon

You'll have to turn off the M1 onto the old N1 to access Martin Crosby's truckers paradise, and few detours are so worth the detour. The sausage and bacon soda bread still has no peers for a fix of proteins and carbs to get your motor running. (Martin Crosby, Turvey Hill, Swords ☎ 085-702 5446 – Open 7.30am-5.30pm Mon-Sat)

The Ward

Chocolates
● Chez Emily

It's great fun to visit the three Chez Emily shops, especially with some kids in tow, but if you can't make it up to North Dublin and Meath you will find these really fine chocolates in lots of the best Dublin and east coast delis. These are classy chocolate concoctions, and they reveal craftsmanship and care married to a lovely aesthetic. (Ferdinand Vandaele & Helena Hemeryck, Cool Quay, The Ward ☎ 01-835 2252, Also at Main Street, Ashbourne, Co Meath and 68 Main Street Swords ✉ Helena@chezemily.ie ⌂www.chezemily.ie)

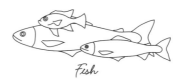

Fish

Blackrock

Market
● **Blackrock Market**

There are a few nice food stalls amongst the arts and
crafts of the weekend market, one of the longest running in Dublin. (19a Main Street, Blackrock, Co Dublin ☎ 01-283 3522 manager@blackrockmarket.com
🖱 www.blackrockmarket.com – Open 11am-5.30pm
Sat, noon-5.30pm Sun, 11am-5.30pm bank holiday Mons)

Wine Importer
● **Burgundy Direct**

"It was stunning!" is how Leslie Williams described a
recent tasting led by Conor Richardson of Burgundy
Direct, one of those small, independent, bespoke wine
companies whose survival should give us all cause to
celebrate. Mr Richardson sources wines from people
who are pretty much like himself: quiet; confident;
understated; interested in quality, not flashiness. And if
you think that anything from Burgundy requires a hedge
fund manager's salary, think again, for there are some
really great value wines here, amongst others that are
for special occasions. It's not all Burgundy too: Conor
sources well from Italy, Germany and regional France.
There isn't a bad bottle on the list. (Conor Richardson,
8 Monaloe Way, Blackrock ☎ 01-289 6615 📧 info@
burgundydirect.ie 🖱 www.burgundydirect.ie)

Traiteur
● **The Butler's Pantry**

"It's so much better for welfare and well-being to eat
food like you might have cooked at home," Eileen Bergin
told *The Irish Times* a couple of years ago in an interview. And there, in a single sentence, you have both the
modus operandi, and the reason for the success, of The
Butler's Pantry, a business that now extends to nine
stores in Dublin and Wicklow, as well as their Events
catering service. Other business people might talk
about profit, or market share, but Ms Bergin talks about
"welfare and well-being", and that is what you get in this
food, you get the wellness and well-being that real food
brings, but you get it without needing to make it yourself, and you get great food without any compromise

in quality. We all need a BP in our lives at many times, for many reasons, and we think that Ms Bergin's amazing company is one of the leading Irish luxury brands, no less. (Carol at 53 Mt Merrion Avenue, Blackrock ☎ 01-288 5505; Michael, 2B Vernon Avenue, Clontarf, D3 ☎ 01-833 3314; Also Helen at 97B Morehampton Road, Donnybrook, D4 ☎ 01-660 8490; Karolina at 99 Rathgar Road, Rathgar, D6 ☎ 01-492 9148; Mary at 3 Sandymount Green, D4 ☎ 01-215 1700; Michelle at 1a Montpellier Place, Temple Hill, Blackrock, Co. Dublin ☎ 01-284 3933; Helen Abbey Street, Wicklow ☎ 0404-66487; Alison at Church Road, Greystones, Co Wicklow ☎ 01-201 0022; Julie at 19 Sandycove Road, Sandycove, Co. Dublin ☎ 01-230 1624 ⌂ www.thebutlerspantry.ie)

● Cakes & Co

A pretty pink cottage houses one of Ireland's most amazing cake companies. In fact, you look at the cottage and wonder to yourself if it, like all their incredible cakes, is deliciously edible, as well as being superbly handsome. Us? Well, we secretly crave the classic VW campervan cake. Oh, guess it's not a secret anymore. Unbelieveable work. (Rosanna Mulligan & Joannie Langbroek, Jane Cottage, Newtownpark Avenue, Blackrock ☎ 01-283 6544 ✉ joannie@cakesandco.com, ✉ rosanna@cakesandco.com ⌂ www.cakesandco.com – Open 9.30am-5.30pm Mon-Sat)

● The Dublin Cookery School

"I wanted a wow! factor from the minute people walk in the door," Lynda Booth told food writer Marie-Claire Digby. Boy, did Lynda ever get that Wow! factor! The DCS is stunning, the inspired work of architects Studio M and builder Paul Oatway, and it's just the right place for Lynda to develop her skills as a teacher in a logical development of the school that builds on from the classes she originally held in her nearby home. Ms Booth has food teaching in her blood, and communicates brilliantly, and she marries this with the very best guest chefs – a who's who of hot talent – and a fantastic range of courses. Superb. (Lynda Booth, 2 Brookfield Terrace, Blackrock ☎ 01-210 0555 ✉ info@ dublincookeryschool.ie ⌂ www.dublincookeryschool.ie)

Wine Merchant
● McCabe's

McCabe's is one of the glories of Irish wine retailing,
a dynamic shop with a huge range – more than 1500
wines – and ever-helpful, pleasant staff. Their second
shop in Foxrock also has a restaurant, and you can buy
a good bottle in the shop to take in to lunch or dinner,
with only a modest corkage charge. (John McCabe,
51/55 Mount Merrion Avenue, Blackrock ☎ 01-288 2037
🖅 value@mccabeswines.ie ✆ www.mccabeswines.ie –
Open 10.30am-10pm Mon-Sat, 12.30pm-8pm Sun)

Supermarket
● The Organic Supermarket

A smart, retro-style shop houses Darren Grant's
amazing array of organic products. Mr Grant opened his
doors "on the day the recession was announced", but
like many addresses in this book, quality and a keen eye
on service has seen his business blossom: he's up 45%
in 2009, and for a simple reason; if you pick up a lettuce
in the OS, chances are it was picked in Wicklow at 6am
that morning, and driven the few miles to Blackrock
to be on Darren's shelves at 8am. Good food, smart
solutions, organics for ther people, and you know it not
only makes sense, it is also better for you, and better
for the planet. (Darren Grant, 2c Main Street, Blackrock
☎ 01-278 1111 🖅 contact@organicsupermarket.ie
✆ www.organicsupermarket.ie – Open 8am-8pm Mon-
Fri, 10am-8pm Sat, 11am-6pm Sun)

only in Dublin
Green Spot Whiskey

Crumlin

Fishmonger
● JL Fitzsimmons Fish Shop

A great place to buy ray – Dublin's favourite fish. Ask
Philip Fitzsimmons how to cook it and he will tell you:
"Flour it and fry it in a bit of butter, or bake it. Or, if you
have time, dip it in a bit of batter and eat it doused in
salt and vinegar. If we didn't have ray we'd have to shut
the place!" he adds. (Philip Fitzsimmons, 183a Kimmage
Road West, Crumlin Cross ☎ 01-455 4832 – Open
10am-5.30pm Tue-Fri, 10am-4pm Sat)

Dalkey

Farmers' Market
● Dalkey Farmers' Market

We love the atmospheric hall in which they hold the
Dalkey Market, for it gives a taste of what Dalkey was
like in the old days, when it was a seaside village and not
just an outpost of bourgeois Dublin. Great foods and
lovely stallholders complete the picture. (Jackie Spillane,
Heritage Centre, Main Street, Dalkey ☎ 087-957 3647
🖅 market@dlrcoco.ie 🕙 www.dlrcoco.ie/markets – Open
Fri 10am-4pm)

Café
● Idle Wilde Cafe

IW is a good, buzzy neighbourhood café. (Ruan Healy,
20 St. Patrick's Road, Dalkey ☎ 01-235 4501 – Open
8am-5pm Mon-Sun)

Restaurant
● Nosh

Nosh is for everyone. Come in for a quiet dinner with a
friend, and it's ace. Send a bunch of friends and family in
who are on a visit to the city, and they will tell you that
it was ace. The Farrell sisters - like the Kemp sisters of
Itsabagel - just know how to do the right thing, and how
to keep on doing it with consistent excellence. The food
has an open, feminine, modern style, and like the best
female proprietors they always manage to have exactly
what you feel like eating. (Sacha & Samantha Farrell, 111
Coliemore Road, Dalkey ☎ 01-284 0666 🖅 comments@
nosh.ie 🕙 www.nosh.ie – Open noon-4pm, 6pm-late Tue-
Sun, brunch served 11am-4pm Sat & Sun)

Wine Merchant
● On the Grapevine

Gabriel and Pamela Cooney opened in Dalkey on St.
Patrick's Day, 1999, so there is more than a solid decade
of service to the people of Dalkey – and latterly Mount
Merrion, where they have a second store – from this
dedicated couple. "A shining example to all who want to
run a neighbourhood wine shop: an interesting range of
wines, reasonable prices, a few foodie titbits, and knowledgeable, friendly service". That's how John Wilson of
The Irish Times summed up this pristine independent

wine operation. (Gabriel & Pamela Cooney, 21 St
Patrick's Road, Dalkey ☎ 01-235 3054 🖅 sales@
onthegrapevine.ie 🖰 www.onthegrapevine.ie – Open
11am-8pm Mon-Sat)

Restaurant
● Ouzos

Ouzos moved around town a few times before pitching
their tent out southside in the bourgeois heartland of
Dalkey, where a comfortable room and comforting food
has really struck a chord with the fussy, well-informed
locals. The logic and simplicity of their seafood cookery
puts us in mind of Kinsale's Fishy Fishy Café – hot, lively,
salty, top of the mouth tastes, whether it's mussels
cooked with crab meat and lobster, or lemon sole with
citrus butter, or haddock in a tempura batter with hand-
made chips. There are steaks and meat dishes, but the
fish and shellfish is where the smart money gets spent.
(Fionnuala Quirke, 22 Castle Street, Dalkey ☎ 01-
285 1890 🖅 reservatioins@ouzos.ie 🖰 www.ouzos.ie
– Open noon-10pm Mon-Sat, noon-9.30pm Sun)

Pizzeria
● Ragazzi

Who cares about clichés when the clichés are as well-
delivered, and delivered with such ironic sincerity, as
they are in Fabio Perozzi's legendary Ragazzi. Legendary?
Well, it's a local legend for good Italian cooking – especially the pizzas – and lively service. So, go on and have
that spag bol you secretly crave, and of course a glass
of Sambucca to finish. Sambucca, did you say?! Hold me
back! (Fabio Perozzi, 109 Coliemore Road, Dalkey ☎ 01-
284 7280 🖅 ragazzi109@yahoo.com 🖰 www.ragazzi.
ie – Open 5.30pm-10.30pm Mon-Sat)

Wholefood Shop
● Select Stores

Oliver and Mairead McCabe have a real sport of nature
here, a great vegetable, fruit and wholefood shop that
also has a juice bar and a small range of healthy foods to
eat in. Select Stores is at the centre of Dalkey in every
way: literally, socially, and foodwise. These are witty, fun
guys, and this is a witty, fun place to get the good stuff.
(Oliver McCabe, 1 Railway Road, Dalkey ☎ 01-285 9611
🖰 www.selectstores.ie – Open 7.30am-6.30pm Mon-
Fri, 8am-6pm Sat, 10am-4pm Sun)

Restaurant
● Thai House

Tony Ecock's Thai House restaurant is a model of good cooking, great service, consistent consistency and customer satisfaction. Attention to detail with both food and service has allowed the Thai House to build a core audience who enjoy excellent Thai cooking, along with its necessary counterpart, which is superb value for money. A model restaurant, focused on service and satisfaction, and do note that there is a great takeaway menu available each evening, for those nights when you just want to put your feet up. (Tony Ecock, 21 Railway Road, Dalkey ☎ 01-284 7304 🖫 www.thaihouse.ie 🖅 tony@thaihouse.ie – Open 6pm-10.30pm Tue-Sun, till 11pm Sat)

Delicatessen
● Thyme Out

Dublin
South

Amongst the testimonials to their excellence arrayed on their website, we like the one from the customer of Thyme Out who reckons that it is worth travelling to Dalkey just to buy their coleslaw. Coleslaw! Now, doesn't that tell you everything you need to know about this pristine deli? When you take care of the coleslaw, then you know that everything else will be well taken care of also. From such simple, quotidian things are mighty reputations built, and David and Berna have built a mighty reputation since opening almost a decade ago. But it's not a reputation they ever coast on: each day they begin anew, they begin again, the coleslaw is made fresh. (David & Berna Williams, 2a Castle Street, Dalkey ☎ 01-285 1999 🖅 thymeout@eircom.net 🖫 www.thymeout.ie – Open 8.30am-7pm Mon-Sat)

Restaurant
● Wine Not

A cousin of the popular Ragazzi, Winenot is much more echt, and much less theatrical, in its offer of Italian cooking, which can run from pappardelle with wild boar ragu, to prawns wrapped in smoked pancetta, to ravioli of porcini mushrooms. Team this beautifully delivered food with their superb collection of Italian wines and you have one classy destination. (Gabriele Carioni, Fabio Perrozzi, Vincenzo Celentano, 1 Coliemore Road, Dalkey ☎ 01-235 2988 🖅 winenot@eircom.net 🖫 www.winenot.ie – Open 6pm-midnight Mon-Sun (from 2pm Sun)

Dun Laoghaire

Restaurant
● Alexis Bar & Grill

Onion soup with cheddar gratinée. Panfried veal liver,
pancetta, crispy onions, creamed potato, red wine jus.
Organic sirloin with chips and bearnaise. Peppered
duck with confit potatoes. Smoked haddock risotto
with poached egg. Jane Russell's sausages with mash and
onion gravy. It's back to the future time, folks, in the
company of Alan O'Reilly and his brother, Patrick. Retro
food done exquisitely, and at the best value for money
pricing on the east coast. So, the only problem is getting
a table. On no account miss their exquisite fries. (Alan &
Patrick O'Reilly 17-18 Patrick Street, Dun Laoghaire
☎ 01-280 8872 ✆ info@alexis.ie ✆ www.alexis.ie –
Open 12.30pm-2.30pm, 5.30pm-10pm Tue-Fri, 5.30pm-
10pm Sat, 12.30pm-3pm, 5.30pm-9pm Sun)

Cookery School
● Cook's Academy

If you are looking for recreational cooking then Tim and
Vanessa Greenwood's Academy has more than enough
courses to satisfy every tastebud. If you want to step up
to the bar, however, and wield the pots and pans professionally, you can also do an intensive one month's course
that should set you out on the road of the professional
chef. Cook's Academy rings all the current bells from
cup cakes to sushi to men only cooking. (Vanessa & Tim
Greenwood, 2 Charlemont Terrace, Crofton Road, Dun
Laoghaire ☎ 01-214 5002 ✆ info@CooksAcademy.com
✆ www.cooksacademy.com)

Farmers' Market
● Dun Laoghaire Farmers' Market

The biggest of the Dublin CoCo markets is also one
of the very best markets in the country. On a sunny,
summery day some 10,000 – yes 10,000! – happy eaters
will make their meandering way through the People's
Park, both to buy produce from an amazing array of
stall-holders, artisans and producers, but also to feast on
the best array of food-to-graze that you will find at any
market. The mix of food to buy and food to eat creates
a quite unique ambience, so it can feel as if it's a festival
more than a farmers' market. Yes, a festival of food,
that's just what Dun Laoghaire market is. (Jackie

Spillane, Dun Laoghaire-Rathdown County Council, The People's Park, Dun Laoghaire ☎ 01-205 4700 ☎ 087-957 3647 ✉ market@dlrcoco.ie ⌂ www.dlrcoco.ie/markets – Open Sun 11am-4pm. Also at Dalkey, Fri 10am-4pm; Marlay Park Sat 10am-4pm)

● Gourmet Food Parlour

Lorraine and Lorraine have bravely gone where so many southsiders fear to tread and crossed the river and opened up the second GFP in busy Swords, and a cafe in The Grange at Ballyboughal. Their expansion was always on the cards for the Gourmet Parlour offering is a twenty-four carat good food production, and it's as hip as all get out, which explains why the Dun Laoghaire address was a success from day one. A wine bar, a cafe and a traiteur all in one, their formula is to keep everything simple and spot on, as with their tapas menu that offers Spain's greatest hits in a series of small and delicious plates, from pan Catalan to meatballs with rustic bread. (Lorraine Byrne & Lorraine Heskin, 7 Cumberland Street, Dun Laoghaire ☎ 01-280 5670 ✉ dunlaoghaire@gourmetfoodparlour. com – Open 8.30am-5pm Mon-Thu, 8.30am-late Fri, 10am-5pm Sat, noon-4pm Sun. Also at Unit 2 St Fintans, North Street, Swords ☎ 01-897 1496 ✉ swords@ gourmetfoodparlour.com – Open 8am-5.30pm Mon-Thu, 8am-late Fri, 10am-5.30pm Sat, noon-6pm Sun. Also at The Grange, Oldtown Road, Ballyboughal ☎ 01-807 8888 ✉ info@gourmetfoodparlour.com – Open 9.30am-5.30pm Tue-Fri, 10am-6pm Sat & Sun ⌂ www. gourmetfoodparlour.com)

● J Hick & Sons

You might think you already know everything you possibly could about Ed Hick's prize winning sausages and his jaw-droppingly fine puddings – about which we once actually wrote a poem. But did you know that when Mr Hick is concocting his sausages he is looking at them not just from an organoleptic point of view, but also in terms of their seasonality. So, there is wild venison for the winter and then a slightly sweeter apple and pepper during the summer months. Mr Hick is the man who started the real sausage revolution in Ireland, and every time you buy a proper hand-made sausage it owes a debt to this quiet and authoritative artisan. Ed's bacon, by the way, is dry cured for six weeks before being smoked over beechwood. It's beyond good. (Ed Hick, 15A, George's St Upr, Dun Laoghaire ☎ 01-284 2700 ⌐ www.thepinkpig.com)

Fishmonger
● The Ice Plant

In what was the old Ice Plant on Dun Laoghaire pier, you will find a great fish shop, selling the day's catch, plus fish to feed the seals. (Coal Quay, Dun Laoghaire Pier ☎ 01-280 5936 – Open Tue-Sat mornings)

Restaurant
● Real* Gourmet Burger

RGB is a star, and produces star hamburgers, made with superb ingredients that elevate the simple staple into stellar eating. Only hassle is managing to bag a table, for southsiders have taken to this hip operation with alacrity. Brilliant. (Dave Larcan, The Pavilion, Dun Laoghaire ☎ 01-284 6568. Also at Ballsbridge, Sweepstakes Centre, Ballsbridge D4 ☎ 01-667 0040 ⌐ info@realgourmetburger.ie ⌐ www. realgourmetburger.ie – noon-9.30pm Mon-Thurs, noon-10pm Fri & Sat, noon-9pm Sun)

Dublin
South

Glasthule

Restaurant
● Caviston's Deli & Seafood Restaurant

The gloom on Dublin's southside, what with NAMA and Anglo Irish and every other SNAFU you can think of all arriving in the one recession, has called for a light at the end of the tunnel. Caviston's have shone the beacon by opening up on Friday and Saturday evenings. So if you have never managed to get there during the day, now there is a chance to sample some of the country's finest seafood cooking at the weekend. In fact, Caviston's have shone the beacon for decades now, first with their peerless delicatessen and wet fish counter, and then with the copperfastened cooking that has made the restaurant into one of the best loved places to eat. The cooking is both pure and earthy: monkfish with O'Doherty's black bacon, marinated tuna with wasabi and coriander mayonnaise, Clare Island salmon with watercress and beurre blanc. Unchanging, because it's

perfect. (David & Lorraine Caviston, 59 Glasthule Road
☎ 01-280 9245 🖱 www.cavistons.com – Restaurant
open three lunch sittings per day: noon-1.30pm, 1.30pm-
3pm, 3pm-5pm Tue-Sat; 6pm-8.15pm, 8.15pm-close Fri
& Sat)

Butcher
● **Danny O'Toole**

The southside branch of the O'Toole's family's famous
butchery business is superbly run by Tom O'Connor,
and it is one of the food lovers' fixtures of Glasthule.
Great food, fantastic service. (Tom O'Connor, 1
Glasthule Road ☎ 01-284 1125 – Open 9am-12.30pm
Mon, 9am-6pm Tue-Sat)

only in Dublin
Hick's Sausages

Restaurant
● **Rasam**

Nisheeth Tak's slinky Indian restaurant, up above the
Eagle Pub, is a classy operation. A large and very stylish
room offers dishes collected from the subcontinent
- Baigun cheese bhaja frok Kolkotta, tandoori quail
from Haryana, gosht awadh from Awadh, safaed maans
from Rajasthan - and the result of this cherry picking
is a menu that is far removed from the conventional,
inauthentic Indian cooking which is so widespread.
(Nisheeth Tak, Eagle Pub, 18/19 Glasthule Road ☎ 01-
230 0600 🖱 www.rasam.ie – Open 5.30pm-11pm
Mon-Sun)

Deli & Wine Shop
● **64 Wine**

Whilst 64 has won a high profile on account of its
fanatastic range of wines, what you will also find here
is a great array of great foods, many of them chosen
for their suitability in terms of matching with wine. So
if you need that mature Cashel Blue for some claret,
or a buttery Coolea for a Pinot Blanc you can get both
here. (Gerard Maguire & Richard Moran, 64 Glasthule
Road, Glasthule ☎ 01-280 5664 ✉ info@64wine.com
🖱 www.64wine.com – Open 9.30am-7pm Mon-Wed,
9.30am-8pm Thur-Fri, 9.30am-7pm Sat)

Glenageary

● **The Bombay Pantry**

In the last *Bridgestone Irish Food Guide* there were
four Bombay Pantrys. Today there are no fewer than
seven dotted north and south of the city. All of them
proving that top-notch Indian food can provide the
best takeaway meal of them all. The BP formula works
because the cooking is done from scratch and it really
understands how to marry the complexities of Indian
cookery with the Irish love of vivid front-of-the-mouth
flavours. We have been eating Bombay Pantry food
right since they opened in 1997, and we have never
had so much as one dud dish in all that time. (Vivek
Sahni, Emma & John Sheehan, Glenageary Shopping
Centre, Glenageary ☎ 01-285 6683. Also at 14 Rathgar
Road, Rathmines, D6 ☎ 01-496 9695; 107 Clonskeagh
Road, Clonskeagh ☎ 01-260 7885, 38 Philipsburgh Ave,
Fairview ☎ 01-884 0033, Unit 6, Rathbourne Village,
Ashtown, D14 ☎ 01-899 6688; 6 Castle Street, Bray,
Co Wicklow ☎ 01-270 0700 Unit 2a Retail Centre,
Grange Road, Rathfarnham, D16 ☎ 01-493 2222 – Open
5pm-10.30pm Tue-Sat, 5pm-10pm Sun. Glenageary and
Rathmines open Mondays ⌒ www.bombaypantry.com)

only in Dublin
Queen of Tarts

Goatstown

● **Bin No 9**

Andy Kinsella has such a stellar range of great wines
in Bin No 9 that he is a staple of the weekend wine
columns with numerous wines selected as the best and
best value in their category. Mr Kinsella is no snob, so
whilst he does have big names, what really rings his bell
is to find something curious, unlikely and joyful to quaff.
And those are the kind of bottles you'll find here. (Andy
Kinsella, 9 Farmhill Road, Goatstown ☎ 01-296 4844
⌒ Andrew@BinNo9.com ⌒ www.binno9.com – Open
10.30am-10pm Mon-Sat, 12.30pm-8pm Sun)

Killiney

Tea Merchant
● Kingfisher Tea

Colm Hassett offers seventy varieties of tea from Assam to Nettle to Rooibos Orange Eucalyptus in his portfolio and it is no exaggeration to say that every single one of them can offer an organoleptic experience of the highest order. Mr Hassett is a master tea importer and his deep understanding of the labyrinthine and endlessly complex world of tea offers the tea lover an experience that is both sensual and spiritual. (Colm Hassett, 121 The Sycamores, Shanganagh Road, Killiney ☎ 01-272 1856/087-662 5189 ✉ info@kingfishertea.com ☝ www.kingfishertea.com)

Leopardstown

Dublin South

Farmers' Market
● Leopardstown Organic Market

Leopardstown is a great, great market, with every stall seemingly a cornucopia unto itself, from Duncan Healy's organic veg to Jackie's brilliant sweet cakes to the gracefully delicious work of market stalwarts such as Sheridan's, McEvoys, the Gallic Kitchen and Out of the Blue. All you need – all you could possibly need! – is here, and served by a dedicated crowd of talented people, all of whom seem to be having just as good a time as you are. Smashing. (Sean McArdle, Racetrack, Leopardstown ☎ 086-3826377 ✉ info@irishfarmersmarkets.ie ☝ www.irishfarmersmarkets.ie – Open Friday 11am-7pm)

Markets
● Sean McArdle Markets

Sean runs lots of markets throughout Dublin and the east coast, but he ain't finished yet, and plans for another city centre market to join Harcourt Street are in place, along with Trinity College, Dublin Zoo, Athlone, Drogheda, and elsewhere. Does this guy ever sleep? Doesn't look like he needs to. (Sean McArdle ☎ 087-611 5016 ✉ www.irishfarmersmarkets.ie ☝ www.irishfarmersmarkets.ie)

Monkstown

Wine Merchant
● Enowine

The original branch of Enowine has a trove of wonderful wines to entice you through the doors, but the addition of Yvonne's Café adds another reason to get down to Monkstown. The menu is short and sweet, but it cleverly has all those things that you feel like eating, and they do nice things for the kids, so make it a family trip, with a few bottles in the bag after you have had something to eat. (James & Yvonne Connolly, The Crescent, Monkstown ☎ 01-230 3500 ☏ info@enowine.ie ☝ www. enowine.ie – Yvonne's Cafe open 10am-6pm Mon-Sat)

Gastropub
● The Purty Kitchen

The Purty Kitchen does as good a pub lunch as you will get anywhere in Ireland, which explains why this ancient bar is perennially packed to the rafters, and why they opened a branch in Temple Bar in the city centre. The cooking hits the spot, whether you have fish and chips or even an old warhorse like surf'n'turf, where good shelled prawns come on top of a sirloin with a plate of shallow-fried garlic potatoes. Next door to the Kitchen they run the Food & Wine Emporium, where you can take away a selection of the dishes offered on the menu. (Conor Martin, Old Dun Laoghaire Road, Monkstown ☎ 01-284 3576 ☏ info@purtykitchen.com ☝ www. purtykitchen.com – Food served 12.30pm-10pm. Also 34/35 Essex Street, Temple Bar ☎ 01-677 0945)

Restaurant, Café & Bar
● Seapoint

A handsome bistro run by Shane Kenny and chef Nick Clapham, Seapoint has the sort of modern, easy cooking that seems de rigueur southside – tuna with avocado wasabi; warm duck salad with new potatoes; wild mushroom risotto with rabbit; lamb with ratatouille; lime and ginger crème brûlée. "Seapoint stands out for all the right reasons," says Caroline Byrne. (Shane Kenny & Nick Clapham, 4 The Crescent, Monkstown ☎ 01-663 8480 ☏ info@seapointrestaurant.com ☝ www.seapointrestaurant.com – noon-3pm Tue-Sat, 6pm-10.30pm Mon-Sat, noon-9pm Sun)

Dublin South

Wine Merchant
● Searson's

Searson's may be a Dublin wine firm of a distinct
pedigree and an impressive vintage, but there is nothing stuffy or old-school about Charles Searson and his
team. These guys are passionate about wine, about wine
culture, about wine and food, and it is the customer who
gets the benefit of all this wine energy and savvy. In fact,
we can borrow some of their own words to best describe what they do: writing about the 2002 Domaines
Ott, Chateau Ramassan from Bandol they write that
it is "Utterly characterful but not brutish". Searson's
wouldn't let a brutish wine in the door, and believe us
that the wine world these days is filled with wines that
are not just brutish, but foul-mouthed as well. None of
those guys here: just the good stuff, just the best stuff.
(Charles Searson, Monkstown Crescent ☎ 01-280 0405
📧 sales@searsons.com 🖱 www.searsons.com – Open
10.30am-6pm Mon-Wed, 10.30am-8pm Thu & Fri,
10.30am-7pm Sat)

Dublin
South

Restaurant
● Taste

Jakki and Ingrid's bistro is winning quite a local
reputation, and bringing some of the lustre back to
Monkstown, a village that has at different times been
home to many good restaurants. The restaurant is above
the Spar shop – which Jakki runs – and it's a rock-steady
proposition: a swish, feminine, modern room with swish,
Bill Granger-style cooking: panzanella salad; crabmeat
salad with Parma ham; lemon pepper calamari; salmon
with white bean ratatouille; pork belly with mustard
mash. Modern-conservative cookery, perhaps, but it's
done with style and energy. (Jakki & Ingrid Murphy,
1-2a Monkstown Crescent, Monkstown ☎ 01-284 1249
📧 info@tastemonkstown.ie 🖱 www.tastemonkstown.
com – Open from 6pm-late, Sunday brunch from
11.30am-late)

Mount Merrion

Shop and Café
● Michael's Food & Wine

"Every neighbourhood should have a Michael's to call
their own" said *Food & Wine* magazine about Michael

Lowe and Mary O'Keeffe's brilliantly idiosyncratic little sport of nature, up on Deerpark Road. Deli, wine shop, casual restaurant, it's the sort of place that works as the Caviston's of MM, always packed with folk who simply adore the place. A lot of what they love is the modesty of the place, and the modesty of the owners, but the truth is that Michael and Mary know how to cook well and choose well, despite their protestations that it's not about them. It's not about their egos, but it is all about their hospitality, and their lovely, Italian-accented food. Pure darling. (Michael Lowe & Mary O'Keeffe, 57 Deerpark Road, Mount Merrion ☎ 01-278 0377 – Open 9.30am-6pm Mon-Thu & Sat, 9.30am-10.30pm Fri)

Rathcoole

Restaurant & Shop
● Avoca

Avoca is where we, and everyone we know, stop if we are en route from Cork to Belfast. For locals, it's not simply the best stop-over on the main road, it's none other than a Godsend in an area deprived of good food. You need nerve to pour a pink concrete floor in a big store: Simon Pratt has that nerve, and he has the nous to serve superb, moreish food in both the self-service restaurant and the lovely Egg Café. All in all, Avoca is simply an experience that lifts your spirits. Everytime. (Simon Pratt, N7 Naas Road, Rathcoole ☎ 01-257 1800 Egg Cafe Reservations ☎ 01-257 1810 ⊕ www.avoca. ie – Store open 9.30am-6pm Mon-Sat, 10am-6pm Sun. Cafes close at 5pm. Also in Suffolk Street, Dublin 2 and counties Wicklow, Cork and Galway)

Stillorgan

Korean and Chinese Restaurant
● Gong

The wonderful, affable Tim, one of the figureheads of Chinese eating in Dublin thanks to many years in the original China-Sichuan, mans front-of-house in Gong, so that is a good intro to a friendly neighbourhood ethnic restaurant, that offers a fairly voluminous array of Sichuan, and some Korean, dishes. (Mr Lee, 8 Lwr Kilmacud Road, Stillorgan ☎ 01-278 3328 – Open noon-3pm, 6pm-11pm Mon-Sun)

Dublin South

● Fenelon's Craft Butchers

Cliff Lenehan's shop is one of the cornerstones of the SSC, a trove of good meats, good advice, and true, honest service. It's a much-beloved shop, and with good reason, for they give real service and live up to their reputation of craft butchers with every piece of meat they sell. (Cliff Lenehan, 6 Stillorgan S.C., Stillorgan ☎ 01-288 1185 ⌂ www.fenelons.ie – Open 8.30am-6pm Mon-Wed & Sat, 8.30am-8pm Thu & Fri)

Tallaght

Theatre Cafe and Bar
● Interval Bistro @ the Civic Theatre

"Finally, the 250,000 people in the South Dublin County Council area have a place where they can eat home-cooked food in a properly run restaurant, by people that care, and want you to come back". That's how important Leslie Williams reckons Jimmy and Beverley Dunne's Interval Bistro is. And boy do these guys show that they care: virtually everything is made on-site, and made with TLC: have those lamb shanks for lunch, placed in a thyme and red wine jus, and enjoy slow-cooked meat that just falls off the bone. The spuds will be new season Queens, the veg is crisp and fresh, and whilst a lot of the offer seems similar to what you might find elsewhere, it isn't: this food comes from the heart, and not from the man in the van. Only wonderful. (Jimmy & Beverly Dunne, Civic Theatre, Tallaght, ☎ 01-462 6532 ⌂ www.civictheatre.ie – Open 10am-7.30pm, Mon-Sat)

Coffee & Tea
● Irish Village Markets

Des and Tara were brave to open up a market in Tallaght, a place otherwise seemingly dedicated to indifferent food, and hopefully their foresight will be rewarded. (Des Vallely & Tara Dalton, South Dublin Tallaght Market, Civic Plaza, Tallaght, Friday 11am-4pm ⌂ www.irishvillagemarkets.com. Also markets at Mespill Road, D4, Thur 11am-2.30pm, Newbridge Co Kildare, Wed 9am-4pm, Carmanhall Road, Sandyford, Fri 11am-2.30pm, Spawell Car Boot Sale, Sun 11am-3pm, Ranelagh Village Market, 10am-7pm Thu, 10am-6pm Fri-Sun)

County Galway

GALWAY CITY

Café and Take-away
● **Anton's**

People double park out front whilst they rush into Anton's to grab soup or a focaccia or brown bread sandwich, and that's no surprise. The food is simple, but it's true, fresh and good, with fine pastries to enjoy either in this little room, which is bedecked with the work of local painters, or to take away. Anton's is a job well done, a classy neighbourhood space packed with regulars, with everyone a happy customer. (Anton O'Malley, 12a Father Griffin Road, Galway ☎ 091-582067 – Open day time Mon-Fri)

Restaurant
● **Ard Bia, Nimmo's & The Long Walk Market**

"I just love it... it is the proprietor who uses the word 'Darling' a lot when talking to customers, which is exactly what this restaurant is – room, staff, food – all pure darling". Our friends Conor and Sile know the good places where you get welcomed in the most affectionate terms, and they are dead right about Aoibheann McNamara's legendary restaurant: it is pure darling. Ms McNamara and her partner Patrick O'Reilly have a unique aesthetic, and they sprinkle it like fairy dust on everything they touch – their restaurant, their cooking, their service, even their cottage – Moorehall – which you can rent, out on the shores of Lough Carra. Ard Bia isn't just a place to eat, for with its gallery, its market, its breast-feeding mornings, its Steiner School, its fashion shows and club nights, it's actually a community, a universe, unto itself. Oh, and the grub is mighty, only mighty. (Aoibheann McNamara, 2 Quay Street, Galway ☎ 091-539 897 ✉ ardbia@gmail.com ✆ www.ardbia.com – Ard Bia Cafe open noon-3pm Wed-Fri, 10am-3.30pm Sat, noon-3.30pm Sun. Ard Bia upstairs restaurant open 6pm-10pm Fri & Sat. Nimmo's open 6pm-10.30pm Mon-Sun. The Long Walk Market open 11am-6pm Sat)

Galway
City

Restaurant
● **Artisan**

Matt Skeffington's restaurant above Galway's legendary Tigh Neactain's pub is the latest of a series of interesting and somewhat left field culinary tenants for this always-enjoyable room. (Matt Skeffington, 2 Quay Street, Galway ☎ 091-532 655 ✉ artisanrestaurant@gmail.com 🖰 www.artisangalway.com – Open lunch and dinner Mon-Sun)

Asian Tea House
● **Asian Tea House Restaurant**

You can get a flavour of more than a thousand years of Asian history in Terry Common's Tea House, where the ancient tradition of the Tea House has been brought to –where else? – Galway. As well as a broadly based, pan Asian menu, the key attraction here is a range of super-lative teas including a range of specialist blossom teas. A sip of Jasmine Fairy or maybe a sip of Love At First Sight and you will suddenly understand the Japanese con-cept of wabi-sabi, the philosophy of evanescence and of capturing the fleeting moment which the Japanese con-structed around the essence of the tea ceremony. (Terry Commons, 15 Mary Street, Galway ☎ 091-563749)

Café and Food Hall
● **Sam Bailey's**

Noel Reidy is doing good stuff in Sam Bailey's. The room looks like a posh American diner, and they do quotid-ian things – good granola for breakfast; a fine vegetar-ian breakfast; proper Cobb salad; roast beef sarnie on ciabatta; a New York-style cheesecake – really properly and correctly. It may be the best choice for breakfast in town, and motivated, friendly staff round out a picture of a carefully crafted business. (Noel Reidy, Eglinton Street, Galway ☎ 091-507123 ✉ info@sambaileys.com 🖰 www.sambaileys.com – Open 7am-7pm Mon-Sun)

Café and Flower shop
● **Budding Café**

Walk through the flower shop and walk into a tiny café with eight tables, a blackboard menu with the day's dishes, and some truly lovely food. The Budding Café is really the Blooming Café, so let's enjoy some earthly delights: the savoury tart of the day for you, some nice crostini for me, chocolate chip cookies and some punky ice cream for the children. Ah, lovely. (Ellen & Frank Heneghan, Sea Road, Galway ☎ 091-588821 – Open 9.30am-6pm Mon-Sat)

Wine Warehouse
● Cases

Peter Boland has been bringing good wines to the folk of Galway for the past two years, kicking off his smart wine warehouse in 2007 with a hip portfolio of good bottles. It is the biggest place to buy wine in the West, and the list keeps them right up there with the many other good places in Galway in which you can buy excellent wines. We like the way in which Mr Boland does clever, analytical things like sorting out which of his wines have garnered gongs at the big international tastings – more than fifty of his bottles got medals and commendations at the 2009 Decanter Awards – and the fact that he is interested in biodynamic wines, and that sort of nous is exactly what you need from a smart wine merchant. If you know wines, Cases is a delight. If you don't, then fear not, for you are in good hands. (Peter Boland, Riverside Commercial Estate, Tuam Road, Galway ☎ 091-764701 ✉ peter@cases.ie ◌ www.cases.ie – Open 10am-7pm Mon-Sun)

Galway
City

Spanish Restaurant & Tapas Bar
● Cava

So, here's how Sabrina Conneely got the best out of an evening in Cava: "I asked them to bring an array of tapas to us and they delivered: marinated olives, cubed roast potatoes with spicy aioli, prawns and garlic, mussels in manzanilla sherry, Catalan tomato bread with manchego cheese, roast pork belly with apple confit. All these dishes were mouth-watering, but my favourite was the salted cod cakes with lemon (they salt their own cod here)." Well, that will do nicely, and Cava is working hard to summon up and offer that peculiarly Iberian insouciance which marks out a confident and driven food enterprise. JP McMahon and Drigin Gaffey have done their research, and from atmosphere to music to the sharp cooking and the all-Spanish wine list Cava is a hot ticket. (JP McMahon & Drigin Gaffey, 51 Dominick Street Lower, Galway ☎ 091-539884 ✉ blasfoods@ gmail.com ◌ www.cavarestaurant.ie – Open noon-4pm, 6pm-10pm, tapas all day, Sat & Sun brunch 11am-5pm, late opening Fri & Sat)

● The Cobblestones Cafe

Kate Wright's cosy kitchen-like Cobblestones Café
has just the food you crave in just the sort of room
you need in order to lose a couple of hours in foodie
reverie. A true freshness is the signature of the cooking,
from clean light soups via Med-style vegetable and salad
plates through to moreish puds. Moreish, indeed. (Kate
Wright, Kirwan's Lane, Galway ☎ 091-567227 🖸 kate-
wright@eircom.net – Open 9.30am-6pm Mon-Sat,
11.30am-6pm Sun)

Butcher

● John E Colleran & Sons

Raymond Colleran is the third generation in his family to
front up one of Galway's busiest butchers. They are also
renowned suppliers to many of Galway's best restaurants. (Raymond Colleran, 18 Mainguard Street, Galway
☎ 091-562582 – Open 8am-6pm Mon-Fri, 7am-6pm Sat)

Restaurant

● Da Roberta & Osteria da Roberta

Salthill's solid sender does it two ways, vis the iconic da
Roberta, one of the fave Galway Italian food addresses,
and via the almost-next-door Osteria da Roberta,
where there is slightly simpler, lighter cooking, but no
less energetic and heartfelt. The format ain't broke
– just witness the waiting queues at weekends – so
they don't tinker with it, they just get on with making
Italian classics and serving them with brio. (Sandro &
Roberta Pieri, Da Roberta, 161 Upper Salthill, Galway
☎ 091-585808 – Open noon-11pm Mon-Sun, Osteria
da Roberta, 157 Upper Salthill, Galway ☎ 091-581111
🖸 daroberta@eircom.net – Open 5pm-11pm Mon-Sat,
12.30pm-11pm Sun)

Restaurant and Lunch Box Take Out

● Da Tang Noodle House

Ireland is awash with ersatz Chinese food, so thank
heavens for Du Han Tuo's brilliant noodle house and its
exciting excursions into the treasures of Northern Chinese cooking. The noodle dishes are actually only one
element of the offer – there are also soups, tofu dishes,
hot pots, spare ribs and so on – but give us a dish of
pan-fried noodles with roast duck, ginger, peppers and
spring onions, and maybe a bottle of China Pearl, and

we are the happiest bunnies in the city. (Du Han
Tuo & Catherine O'Brien, 2 Middle Street, Galway
☎ 091-788638 info@datangnoodehouse.com ⌂ www.
datangnoodlehouse.com – Open noon-3pm Mon-Fri,
6pm-11.30pm Mon-Fri, noon-11pm Sat)

Fishmonger
● Deacy's Fish Shop

Michael Deacy is the fourth generation of his family to
run Deacy's Fish Shop and his children have just started
to work with him, so a fifth generation will take over
this Galway institution in time. Deacy's has been on High
Street since 1915, a street where traditionally fish was
sold from stalls. In fact the premises that is now Deacy's
Fish Shop was originally a record and music shop, with
a fish counter outside, and the family lived upstairs
above the shop. There would have been a number of
fish counters running the length of the street, so this is
a place of historical significance for fish selling in Galway.
(Michael Deacy, 11 High Street, Galway ☎ 091-562515 –
Open 9am-6pm Mon-Sat)

only in Galway
Galway Native Oysters

Café
● Delight Gourmet Food Bar

David and Paula Lawrence's Delight food bars, in Abbeygate Street and at the Kingfisher Club in Renmore, are
places where smart people cook and serve smart food,
and do so with style and wit. They have a Hunter Salad,
for example – turkey, ham and bacon with mayo, stuffing, cheddar, tomato and red onion (phew!) – and they
follow this gargantuan effort with the Gatherer Salad –
mixed leaves, cherry tomatoes, sprouted beans, seeds,
apple, carrot, and cranberry couscous with a hazelnut
and balsamic dressing. Smart or what! Lovely stuff,
and consistency and service are their signature. (David
& Paula Lawrence, 29 Upr Abbeygate Street, Galway
☎ 091-567823 ✉ delightgfb@eircom.net ⌂ www.de-
light.ie – Open 8.30am-4.30pm Mon-Fri, 11am-4.30pm
Sat. Also at Delight Health Cafe, The Kingfisher Club,
Renmore Avenue, Renmore, Galway – Open 8.30am-
4.30pm Mon-Fri, 10am-3pm Sat)

● Devon Dell

Devon Dell is, quite simply, a lovely B&B and, unlike
other places in Galway which seesaw in terms of quality
and consistency with unconvincing regularity, Berna
Kelly does a superb job each and every day. Modest and
meticulous, and the breakfast is one of the finest served
anywhere. (Berna Kelly, 47 Devon Park, Lower Salthill,
Galway ☎ 091-528306 📠 devondell@iol.ie 🖰 www.
devondell.com Open Feb-Oct. No credit cards.)

Craft Butcher
● Martin Divilly

Martin Divilly is an ambitious guy, one of those younger
generation butchers whose skills marry superbly with
sourcing and marketing to produce a spiffing total
charcuterie effort. The hand-picked Angus and Hereford
beef, in particular, are superb, but they truly have everything you need here. (Martin Divilly, Unit 9/10 West-
side Shopping Centre, Galway ☎ 091-523947 – Open
8.30am-7pm Mon-Thu, 8.30am-8pm Fri, 8am-6pm Sat)

Fishmonger
● Duane's Seafood

The scope and variety of fish sold here stems from
the fact that they wholesale to over 100 hotel and
restaurant customers in the West of Ireland region,
so customers at Duane's newly acquired Henry Street
shop can take advantage of the huge selection thanks
to the many whims and demands of their many cheffy
customers. (Thomas Duane, 67 Henry Street, Galway
☎ 091-586641 – Open 7am-5pm Mon-Sat)

Fishmonger
● Ernie's Fish Stores

Ernie Deacy opened Ernie's Fish Stores some 34 years
ago, selling a comprehensive range of seafood at the
stellar standard that you could and would expect from
someone born into a family of seafood experts – Ernie's
great grand aunt, Mary Joe Conroy, was the biggest
exporter of herrings in Ireland, way back in the 1890s.
In the last decade Ernie's has changed to cater for the
demands of a changing audience. Along with Fair Trade
goods and organic wines and produce, there is now a
huge selection of specialist teas and coffees to

Galway
City

choose from, as well as a range of spices and herbs. Ernest Deacy is adept at reading his audience, and adept at changing with the times when it's needed. And, in keeping with family tradition, the next generation has already started work at Deacy's, with both Ernie's son and daughter working alongside him. And, more than a century after the family started the business, you can still buy herring. (Ernie Deacy, Sea Road, Galway ☎ 091-586812 – 9am-6pm Mon-Sat)

Hotel

● The G Hotel & Matz at the G

The G is one of the ultimate symbols of Ireland's Celtic Tiger years, a bling-bling temple of over-the-top design styles that showcase Philip Treacy's work at its most arch and iconoclastic. We love it, even though the tiger has turned into a sickly kitten and Fianna Fail doesn't even do the Builder's Tent at the Galway races anymore. But never mind the Tiger, for the G stands as a fin de boom intoxication in all its contradictory glory, as crazy as a Bordeaux chateau or a baronial mansion. The great Stefan Matz has charge of the kitchens and it is enough to say that no one else would make a dish like lasagne of local monkfish loins with turmeric cream, or polenta and boxty potato of spinach and Mossfield gouda with a smoked paprika-scented broth of leeks. (Gerry Barrett, Wellpark, Galway ☎ 091-865 200 🖰 www.theghotel.ie – Open 7am-10am Mon-Fri, 7am-11am Sat-Sun, 6.30pm-9.30pm Sun-Thu, 6pm-11pm Fri-Sat, 1pm-3pm Sun)

Market

● The Galway Saturday Market

They are all heroes, and legends, the traders of the Galway market. Pick any one – Gourmet Offensive; BoyChik Donuts; Sheridan's cheesemongers; Madras Curry; Gannet Fish; Brekish Dairy; Cait Curran; Dave Holland's Bread Stall; Kappa-ya sushi, and on and on – and they are not merely people selling foods that they have made and grown themselves, they are cornerstones of the Galway food culture, and cornerstones of Galway culture, period. Brekish Dairy have been selling here for twenty years, and other traders with crafts and vegetables go back just as far, and some go back for fifty years or more. It's a whirlygig, a hullabub, and yes we miss Mia's Muffins too, but hopefully they will be back after a sabbatical. All in all, the Galway Saturday market is probably the most exhilarating place to shop in Ireland. And now, up the stairs in Sheridan's for lamb

Galway City

and barley stew and a glass of La Ferme St Martin Cotes-du-Rhone. Do you mind carrying the bags? Thanks. (Beside St Nicholas's Church ✉ galwaymarket@eircom. net 🖱 www.galwaymarket.net – Open 8.30am-4pm Sat, 2pm-6pm Sun)

Fishmonger

● Gannet Fish Pantry

"People lose their head a bit when they see what we do," says Stephane Griesbach, accurately describing his joyful customers on first sight of his fantastic presentation of fish. And no wonder, there's sometimes up to 500kg of fish on display, much of it sold on the bone. For Parisian-born M Griesbach understands that you eat first with the eyes. Stephane Griesbach is an unusual entity in the fish business, for he's a first-generation fishmonger. He has, however, very quickly established a reputation as a superlative seller of fresh fish. "It's enthusiasm," he says, "people realise we are very serious about what we are doing. We work hard. We give cooking tips, and we have good prices." As we go to press Stephane has opened in the Eyre Square Shopping Centre. (Stephane Griesbach, 32 Dun Ri, Athenry ☎ 086-3488591. Also Eyre Square Shopping Centre – Open 9am-6.30pm Tue-Sat. Also selling at markets in Ballinasloe, Fri 9am-1pm; Loughrea, Thu 9am-1pm; Oranmore, Thur noon-6pm; Moycullen, Fri noon-6pm; Gort, Fri 10am-2pm; Claregalway, Sat 10am-2pm, Galway, Sat 9am-6pm)

Bakery

● The Gourmet Tart Company

Michelle and Fintan Hyland's GTC has been in rapid expansion mode in recent years, opening their most recent branch in the Galway Shopping Centre, following on from their lovely shop in Abbeygate Street, which made outlet number three after Salthill and Henry Street. Like Dublin's Gallic Kitchen, the GT guys simply understand the need for savoury food to have a tactile bite, followed on by a salty, savoury moreishness that draws you in, and the need for sweet baking to have a yielding, tender nature, so that you cannot resist that sweet temptation. They deliver on both counts, big time, every time. (Michelle & Fintan Hyland, 65 Henry Street, Galway ☎ 091-5883847 – Open 8am-6.30pm Mon-Sat, 9am-6pm Sun. Also Lower Abbeygate Street, Galway, Salthill & Galway Shopping Centre)

● **Goya's**

Emer Murray has a slick, smart deli now alongside her indispensable Goya's bakery and café. It's another space in which Ms Murray can demonstrate her total mastery of the culinary world, for she is not just a brilliant baker – at which she is one of the country's finest – she is quite simply a master gourmet, whose signature style is found in everything she makes, from potato gratin to carrot cake. We might describe that signature style as bringing a delicate richness to everything she does, an appreciation of the tactility of cooking and eating that ladles on sensual pleasure. Luxury, nothing less. (Emer Murray, 2/3 Kirwans Lane, Galway ☎ 091-567010 ✆ info@goyas.ie ✆ www.goyas.ie – Open 9.30am-6pm Mon-Sat)

Bakery

● **Griffin's Bakery**

Can you believe that there is a baking history stretching back more than 130 years in Griffin's? It would be so easy, as you ask once again for a batch loaf or a St Nicholas seed bread, to take the wonderful hurly-burly of the shop for granted, to overlook the fact that Griffin's is one of the most important addresses in the city. So, we are here to tell you that every loaf, every cake, every bun, every whiskey brack, is part and parcel of the city around you, and of the people of that city. Jimmy Griffin is one of those bakers who has bread in his blood, and it is through his baking that he expresses himself and his passion for the breads not just of Ireland, but of the global baking community. Fantastic. (James Griffin, 21 Shop Street, Galway ☎ 091-563683 ✆ sales@griffinsbakery.com ✆ www.griffinsbakery.com – Open 8am-6pm Mon-Sat)

Galway City

B&B

● **The Heron's Rest**

"We were at the Film Fleadh in July and stayed in the Heron's Rest. We left wondering whether it would be possible to clone Sorcha and lots of little Heron's Rests throughout Ireland – because we'd probably never stay anywhere else! The breakfast was incredible – the menu alone meant our expectations were high, but they were left in the dust – simply perfect – and ne'er a rasher or sausage in sight! And of course the location was perfect too – overlooking the Corrib with The Claddagh across the way, and a stone's throw from Ard Bia and Tigh Neactain's. Perfect, perfect, perfect for Galway." That's our friend Sile's response to this sublime place, and we can't top it at all. (Sorcha Molloy, 16a Longwalk, Spanish Arch, Galway ☎ 086-337 9343 ✉ msorcha@gmail.com ✆ www.theheronsrest.com)

Pub/Restaurant
● The Huntsman Inn

There isn't a smarter, slicker enterprise in the West than the Huntsman. From breakfast to bedtime, they have what you need – restaurant, bars, bedrooms – all managed and overseen with a professionalism that gladdens the heart. As with the best Irish enterprises, they know what they are good at and they are good at what they know, from the snappy, simple lunch menus – smoked haddock sandwich; cod and chips with chive mayonnaise – to the dinner menus – Huntsman fish cakes; hake with haricot bean purée; chicken on tarragon mash. Housekeeping is meticulous, service is svelte, and the only problem – especially at lunchtime – is getting a table. (Stephen Francis, 164 College Road, Galway ☎ 091-562849 ✆ www.huntsmaninn.com – Open 8am-9.30pm Mon-Sun)

only in Galway
Cait Curran

Restaurant
● Kappa-Ya

Junichi Yoshiyagawa's cooking floats between culinary boundaries like a dream: squid noodles with bacon and cabbage; seared tuna and grapefruit salad; duck with dashi and cep sauce; ox tongue stew with hokkaido, fennel and chestnut mash; grilled lamb with miso and blue cheese. This is not just umami-rich cooking, this is Umami Heaven, and there is nothing else quite like it anywhere in Ireland. Step in the door of this little room, and step into the cooking of your dreams. Phew! (Junichi Yoshiyagawa, 4 Middle Street Mews, Galway ☎ 086-3543616 ✉ kappaya@eircom.net – Open noon-6.30pm Mon-Sat, 7pm-10.30pm Fri & Sat)

Café and Flower shop
Kashmir

The Kashmir delivers a consistently good standard of Indian food and when you find your favourite dishes, stick with them and enjoy the excellent service and the excellent value for money. The chicken and lamb dishes, in particular, are great. (Kilderry House, Lower Fairhill Road, Galway ☎ 091-520099 ✉ kashmirindian@gmail. com 🖰 www.kashmir.ie – Open 5.30pm-11.30pm Mon-Thu, 5pm-midnight Fri-Sun, 1pm-3.30pm Sun)

Restaurant
The Malt House

Now with the smart new livery that its proper, respectful food always deserved, Mary and Paul Grealish's Malt House is set to underline its reputation as one of the very best restaurants in Galway. The room may have changed, but the cooking from Brendan Keane and his team remains direct and true – Malbay crab claws with garlic butter; Slaney Valley lamb with organic carrots and chard; West coast lobster and chips – and it is served with great good grace thanks to friendly, efficient staff. This is a dynamic new chapter for a fine place. (Mary & Paul Grealish, Olde Malt Mall, High Street ☎ 091-567866 ✉ info@themalthouse.ie 🖰 www. themalthouse.ie – Open noon-2.30pm, 6pm-9.30pm Tue-Sat)

Galway
City

Shop
McCambridge's

Imagine being such an iconic address that geniuses like the Murphy brothers of Dingle create a brand new ice cream in your name and in your honour. Well, that's just what the Murphy boys did in 2009 when they crafted the McCambridge's Brown Bread Ice Cream specially for Eoin, Natalie and Norma McCambridge's legendary shop. Everything that is good in the west makes its way to this shop, and has been doing so for eighty-five years. In all that time they have never stood still, and the re-fit of the shop and the addition of cutting-edge foods, such as Goya's cakes, Friendly Farmer meats and McGeough's charcuterie show a shop that remains right at the cutting edge itself. (Eoin McCambridge, 38/39 Shop Street, Galway ☎ 091-562259 ✉ retail@mccambridges.com 🖰 www.mccambridges.com – Open 8.30am-7pm Mon-Wed, 8.30am-9pm Thu-Sat, noon-6pm Sun)

Wine Bar
● Martine's Quay Street Wine Bar

Martine's survives and thrives in the bustle of Galway's busy culinary marketplace. They source carefully, they cook carefully, the service always enjoys that expansive Galway bravado, and together these make for a mighty cocktail. (Martine McDonagh, 21 Quay Street, Galway ☎ 091-565662 ⌁ www.winebar.ie – Open 4pm-10pm Mon-Fri, 1pm-10pm Sat-Sun)

only in Galway
Sheridan's on the Docks

Restaurant & Fish'n'Chip bar
● McDonagh's Seafood House

Galway is one of those cities where everybody with any sort of a history in retailing claims to be not just a shop, but a veritable institution. In fact, McDonagh's genuinely is an institution in the city. A fish restaurant which also has a fish and chip bar, McDonagh's combines simplicity and reliability in their fish cookery to make not just a veritable institution, but also an essential address. (Colm McDonagh, 22 Quay Street ☎ 091-565001 ⌁ fish@mcdonaghs.net ⌁ www.mcdonaghs.net – Restaurant open 5pm-10pm Mon-Sat, Fish and Chip bar open noon-11pm Mon-Sat, 4pm-10pm Sun)

Shop
● Morton's of Galway

Eric Morton's shop is the only shop you need. Everything that graces the shelves of this sublime food hall is there on merit, and the quality levels in every department of the shop, from baking to wines, from butcher to seafood counter, is nothing less than stratospheric. It is no exaggeration to say that shopping here makes you feel better both during the experience and afterwards when you enjoy the sumptuous haul of good things that you've brought home. (Eric Morton, Lower Salthill, Galway ☎ 091-522237 ⌁ sales@mortonsofgalway.ie ⌁ www.mortonsofgalway.ie – Open 9am-7pm Mon-Sat, 10am-5.30pm Sun)

● Olio & Farina

Liam and Maria Payne's O&F may be part of a franchise, but they have brought to the franchise the joie de vivre of Galway, and the energy of two very experienced food practitioners. Don't miss the Lite Bites Cafe at the rear of the shop. (Liam & Maria Payne, 50 Upper Abbeygate Street, Galway ☎ 091-539742 ⁀ www.olioefarina.com – Open 9.30am-6.30pm Mon-Thur, 9.30am-8pm Fri, 9.30am-6.30pm Sat)

● Oscar's

Even though Michael O Meara has years of experience in various kitchens, those experiences haven't limited his imagination or his visual brio when it came time to open up his own place. Oscar's is like a sport of nature, a place where the decor feels like a stage set and where it seems as if the food has sprung, newly formed, from the chef's imagination, just before the dish makes its way out to you. This sense of spontaneity gives Oscar's a real thrill and the always imaginative twists on good local ingredients and global influenced dishes is a blast. Sinead Hughes does service the way service should be done. (Michael O Meara & Sinead Hughes, 22 Upper Dominick Street, Galway ☎ 091-582180 ⁀ oscarsgalway@ eircom.net ⁀ www.oscarsbistro.ie – Open 7pm-late Mon-Fri, 6pm-late Sat)

Galway City

● Park Room Restaurant

Eamon Doyle understands what makes an hotel work: it's the staff. "Staff make it!" is the sort of comment you hear about the Park House, for almost 35 years a fixture in Galway. This is the way Irish hotels used to be: trustworthy, genuine, real, natural, relaxed, whether they are checking you in, or serving you dinner in the sparkling dining room, the Park Room. The care lavished by the staff on this hotel comes into its own in the restaurant, where venerable culinary classics – consommé; prawns thermidor; fillet steak au poivre – are shown tender loving care everytime. "We simply like people" says Mr Doyle. It shows. (Eamon Doyle, Park House Hotel, Forster Street, Eyre Square, ☎ 091-564 924 ⁀ parkhousehotel@ eircom.net ⁀ www.parkhousehotel.ie – Open daily for breakfast, lunch and dinner)

● Providence Market Kitchen

"My favourite place to eat lunch in Galway", says Sabrina
Conneely, which is quite a statement considering how
many other excellent lunchtime choices there are in
the city. What's to love? Well, for a start, Orla Fox and
her crew use leaf tea here – Campbell's – and not tea
bags, so that gives an idea of the extra effort invested in
getting everything right. They start baking at 5am, firing
out the fruit scones – don't miss the cranberry scones
– the carrot cakes, the Victoria sponge – ah, Victoria
sponge! – and then at lunch there are excellent mezze
plates. "Love the menu, everything is fresh, homemade
and staff are very welcoming", says Sabrina. PMK has
been such a wow! that there is already a second branch
in Clarinbridge. Incidentally, the work of local artists
is always on show in the room. Brave guys, competing
with the art that is on every plate. (Orla Fox, corner
of Abbeygate and St Augustine Street ☎ 091-533906
⌒ www.providencemarketkitchen.com – Open 8am-6pm
Mon-Sat)

● Seafood Centre @ Galway Bay Seafoods

The Seafood Centre developed organically from the
thriving wholesale business of Galway Bay Seafoods.
People would turn up at the door of the factory and
plead for some of their very fresh fish. In response the
family put out a little table, which turned into a little
corner shop. This facility got busier and busier and
developed into a factory shop. Then in 2007 it was
transformed into a professional, modern shop "designed
from our own heart and head to get every aspect of
quality fish", says Noel Holland. "We're very proud
of our quality" he adds, "it's our first, second and last
thought of every day." (Noel Holland, New Docks,
Galway City ☎ 091-563011 – Open 8.15am-5pm Mon-
Wed & Sat, 8.15am-7.30pm Thu & Fri)

● Sheridan's Cheesemongers

Galway does great shops and great shopkeepers and
Sheridan's belong right up there at the summit of this
mercantile greatness. What fascinates us is the way in
which every member of staff is as efficient and charming
and helpful as every other member of staff.

But Sheridan's have shown right from when they started with a little trestle table in the market, that their working methods are different, and better than everybody else. This isn't just a shop it's a temple to the culture of good food. Upstairs the wine bar is the cutest space with simple, tasty cooking and classy wines. (Seamus Sheridan, Kevin Sheridan, Fiona Corbett, 16 Church Yard Street, Galway shop ☎ 091-564829, wine shop ☎ 091-564832 ⁀ www.sheridanscheesemongers.com – Shop Open 9.30am-6pm Mon-Fri, 9am-6pm Sat, (and 1pm-6pm Sun June-Aug only), Winebar open 2pm-9pm Tue-Fri, noon-8pm Sat)

only in Galway
Solaris Botanicals

Gastro Pub & Restaurant
● Sheridan's on the Docks

The food reads like a menu from Fergus Henderson's St John's restaurant – soused mackerel with cucumber and baby beetroot; giant puffball, salsify, Mount Callan and radish salad; St Tola goat's cheese croquette with new potatoes and rainbow chard; guinea fowl with butternut purée, barley and pickled apple; dark chocolate delice with malted barley ice cream – and Enda McEvoy's food eats like food for the gods: creative, cutting-edge, yet utterly rooted in the logic of sourcing and pairing sublime ingredients. Mr McEvoy and Seamus Sheridan – who cut his teeth cooking in a Galway restaurant, The Blue Raincoat, aeons ago – are firing out some of the most exciting food you can enjoy anywhere. If the food upstairs is a thrill, the food downstairs may be less risk-taking, but it is no less enjoyable, and the pub is one of the best in the country, with proper drinks from beers to wines to coffees. A landmark address, in every respect. (Enda McEvoy, Seamus Sheridan, New Docks, Galway city ☎ 091- 564905 ✉ info@sheridansonthe-docks.com ⁀ www.sheridansonthedocks.com – Open for pub food nightly, Mon-Sat, and the restaurant opens 6pm-10pm Tue-Sat)

Pub
● Tom Sheridan's Bar

Kenneth Connolly had a great success when he ran the Old Schoolhouse out in Clarinbridge. Today in Tom

Sheridan's the same instinct for clean tasting and crowd pleasing dishes is evident. Roasted rare-breed pork with thyme and garlic stuffing, spinach and ricotta tortellini, rocket, prosciutto and Parmesan pizza. Mr Connolly also runs his own bakery company, so sandwiches and desserts have real integrity. (Ken Connolly, Clybaun Road, Knocknacarra, Galway ☎ 091-525315 🖱 www. tomsheridans.com – Open 9am-late)

Tea Blenders
● Solaris Botanicals

Jorg Muller and Karin Wieland's Solaris teas are amongst the new generation of iconic products in Ireland. Beautifully packaged – would you have guessed the packaging was developed on a shoestring? Thought not. Their teas are stupendous examples of meticulous sourcing and blending, married to an holistic vision of the healthful nature of proper teas. Their jasmine tea, for instance, is so superior to the stuff sold in Chinese stores as to be completely unrecognisable, whilst their green tea is simply the best on the market, top-grade sencha tea with crushed cardamoms, lemon and orange peel and cloves and star anise. In truth, you could say that about every one of their ten varieties. So go on: make your own tea ceremony with Solaris, and get a glimpse of both the majesty of tea, and the sacredness of the art of tea. Simply outstanding. (Jorg Muller & Karin Wieland, 30 Portacarron, Ballymoneen Road, Knocknacarra, Galway ☎ 091-586443 🖱 info@solarisbotanicals.com 🖱 www. solarisbotanicals.com)

Butcher
● C.R. Tormey & Sons

John Tormey is a scion of the mighty Tormey charcuterie family, and that really says just about all you need to know about the levels of meat quality and service that you will find here in the Headford Shopping Centre. The aesthetic beauty of preparation of every cut and dish is matched by the sheer quality of the family's own meats. As good as it gets. (John Tormey, Unit 17 Headford Shopping Centre, Headford Road, Galway ☎ 091-564067 🖱 info@crtormeys.ie 🖱 www.crtormeys.ie – Open 9am-6pm Mon-Wed, 9am-7pm Thu, 9am-8.30pm Fri, 9am-6pm Sat, 9am-5.15pm Sun. Also at Harbour Place, Mullingar ☎ 044-9345433; Bridge Street, Tullamore ☎ 057-932 1426)

Restaurant
● Tulsi

It's the friendliness of the service in Tulsi that is the most immediately arresting factor of this simple ethnic restaurant. The warmth of the welcome is indicative of the effort they make and the food backs up that comfort feeling with quiet aplomb. (Mukther Ahmmed, 3 Buttermilk Walk, Middle Street, Galway ☎ 091-564831 ⌂ www.tulsigalway.com– Open noon-2.30pm, 6pm-11pm Mon-Sat (closed 11.30pm Fri & Sat), 1pm-10pm Sun)

only in Galway
The Galway Saturday Market

Restaurant
● Vina Mara

Eileen Feeney's restaurant is a model of professionalism, with Joe Flaherty's inviting modern cooking under-scored by the owner's hospitality. There are some nice ideas in Mr Flaherty's work– confit shoulder of lamb; smoked haddock and leek tortellini – and he likes sweet, welcoming flavours and textures, and the food goes very well with an excellent wine list. (Eileen Feeney, 19 Middle Street, Galway ☎ 091-561610 ⌂ info@vinamara.com ⌂ www.vinamara.com – Open from 12.30pm lunch, from 6pm dinner, Mon-Sat. Opens 5.30pm Sat)

Japanese Café
● Wa Café

Yoshimi, formerly of Kappa-ya, has opened the small and perfectly formed Wa Café. Wa means four things: Japan; Japanese; Harmony; and Circle. All are appropriate for this lovely venture, for if you are new to Japanese food, this is a smashing place to get an introduction to Japan and all things Japanese. Secondly, Yoshimi's food will show you the harmony of ingredients which is so important in Japanese food. Finally, the circles of sushi, of rice balls, of miso bowls demonstrate the hypnotic aesthetic which this cookery revels in, the hidden and the exposed, the surrounded and the open. "A really cute, intimate setting... loved it!" says our girl Sabrina. So, see you there for aduki bean roll, miso with rice balls, salad with umeboshi dressing and a Gammo to go. The hippest address in the west. (Yoshimi

Hayakawa, 13 New Dock Street ☎ 091-895850 📠 info@
wacafe.net 🖰 www.wacafe.net – Open 11.30am-9pm
Mon-Sun)

Wine Shop
● The Wine Buff

Tony and Eleanor Grealy were the seventh Wine Buff
to open in Ireland, and when you consider that that
number of outlets has now doubled, you can see that
the WB is doing something right. That something is
rock-solid wines at very good prices, and as such they
are a pivotal counterpoint to the blandness of what
is sold in supermarkets as wine. WB wines are hand-
made, carefully sourced, individual and interesting, and
all present terrific value for money. Ok, it's a formula,
of sorts, but it's a mighty good one. (Tony & Eleanor
Grealy, The Promenade, Salthill, Galway ☎ 091-586550
📠 tony@thewinebuff.com 🖰 www.thewinebuff.com –
Open 1pm-8pm Mon-Wed, noon-8pm Thur, noon-9pm
Fri, 11am-8pm Sat)

Café
● Wild Nettle

The Wild Nettle is the café of the HipKidz fitness
complex and, as you might hope with a café in a fitness
centre, their food focus is on healthy dishes, though that
doesn't mean you can't have cream with your porridge,
or gravy with your bangers and mash. If you are heading to the airport, it's also a convenient place to grab a
good, light bite before you take to the skies. (Patricia
Flaherty, Hipkidz, Unit 7, Briarhill Business Park, Briarhill, Galway ☎ 091-381653 🖰 www.hipkidz.ie – Open
9am-5pm Mon-Fri, 10am-5pm Sat, noon-5pm Sun)

Wine Shop
● Woodberry's

Declan and Sandra Owens' shop is one of the best
wine destinations in the west, and we love the slightly
cloistered, packed-from-floor-to-ceiling atmosphere of
the shop, which seems to make the hunt for that special
bottle even more special. Declan and Sandra also have
a witty blog, which wears its knowledge lightly and with
amiable humour. (Declan & Sandra Owens, 3 Middle
Street Mews, Middle Street, Galway ☎ 091-533706
📠 woodberrys@eircom.net 🖰 woodberrys.blogspot.
com – Open 10.30am-7pm Mon-Fri, 10am-7pm Sat)

Aran Islands – Inis Meáin

● Inis Meáin Restaurant and Suites

Ruari and Marie-Therese de Blácam are the coolest cats
on the island, and their suites and restaurant already
enjoy a cult status that few addresses ever achieve,
never mind places that have only been open for a few
seasons. Their secret is simple: they are blessed with
a shared aesthetic that has fashioned something brand
new – their beautiful restaurant and state-of-the-art trio
of suites – and yet staying and eating here feels like you
have come to a place that is ageless and ancient. This fusion of modernity and timelessness doesn't exist in many
places and, along with Mr de Blacam's thunderously fine
cooking, it makes for one of the great Irish hospitality
experiences. Once in your lifetime, make it over to here.
(Ruari & Marie-Therese de Blácam, Inis Meain ☎ 086-
826 6026 🖱 www.inismeain.com – Open 1 May-30 Aug)

● An Dún

Shop, restaurant and B&B, Teresa Faherty's welcoming
house – hard by Synge's cottage – is a good place, run
by a very smart lady. The rooms are simple – pine
furniture, understated design – and the cooking is
modest and excellent; we had a lovely breakfast of
Colleran's bacon and scrambled eggs whilst PJ McKenna
wolfed down the French toast. Teresa is the kind
of lady who would, we suspect, make you toast of
whatever nationality your heart desired. Just right.
(Teresa and Padraic Faherty, Inis Meain, Aran Islands
☎ 099-73047 🖅 anduninismeain@eircom.net 🖱 www.
inismeainaccommodation.com)

Aran Islands – Inis Mór

● Kilmurvey House

Treasa Joyce runs the most special B&B you can find,

Galway
County

and on the four evenings of each week that she cooks
dinner, Mrs Joyce shows herself to be a simply brilliant
cook, so when you are booking to stay in this jewel
of a destination, make sure that you include at least
one – no, two! – nights when you can enjoy this special
food in a great, humming dining room. Mrs Joyce's
cooking has a domestic generosity and a professional
elan, whether you are having roast loin of pork or a
bowl of the loveliest garden potatoes you ever did eat.
The team who work with Tresa are as good as it gets,
and Kilmurvey is simply one of the best places to stay
not just on Aran, but anywhere in Ireland. (Treasa &
Bertie Joyce, Kilmurvey, Inis Mór, Aran Islands ☎ 099-
61218 📠 kilmurveyhouse@eircom.net 🖰 www.
kilmurveyhouse.com – Open 1 Apr-16 Oct)

Guesthouse
● Mainistir House

Joel d'Anjou is a one-off, and if you happen to click with
this one-off individual, then you will treasure every
moment spent in Mainistir and every bite eaten of Joel's
legendary vegetarian buffets. But, some people don't
get on the Mainistir wavelength, and don't get caught
up in the club-like atmosphere of the place. If you feel
you could catch the wave – a working knowledge of
Glyndebourne helps, as does an appreciation of the
late, great singer Lorraine Hunt Lieberson, to give you
a couple of tips – then you will find a soulmate here on
Aran. (Joel d'Anjou, Kilronan, Inis Mór, Aran Islands
☎ 099-61351 📠 mainistirhouse@eircom.net 🖰 www.
mainistirhousearan.com)

Guesthouse & Restaurant
● Man of Aran Cottage

Joe grows the vegetables and leaves in his handsome
garden, Maura transforms them into special culinary
creations in the kitchen, and Man of Aran is one of the
key defining points of any visit to Inis Mór. There isn't
anything nicer than to stay in one of their three guest
rooms for a few days, letting the spirit of this extraordinary island seep into your bones, letting the elegant
and natural simplicity of the Wolfes' work settle you to
rights, remind you of how life should, and maybe could,
be lived. (Joe & Maura Wolfe, Kilmurvey, Inis Mór,
Aran Islands ☎ 099-61301 📠 manofaran@eircom.net
🖰 www.manofarancottage.com – Open Mar-Oct)

Galway
County

Aran Islands –Inis Oirr

● Radharc an Chlair

Everyone loves Brid Poil's B&B. It's the right house on
the right island with just the right feel, and we love it
too. (Brid Poil, Inis Oirr, Aran Islands 📖 bridpoil@
eircom.net ☎ 099-75019)

● South Aran Guesthouse & Restaurant

You could go to Enda and Maria Conneely's quietly
inspiring guesthouse and restaurant just to stay and eat
and enjoy the island and Enda's terrific cooking. Or you
could do a powerboat course, or learn about macrobiot-
ics, or do some pilates. You could also do the Transformation Game, a life coaching course they teach. But, to
tell you the truth, you only need to stay and eat with
these amazing people to undergo transformation in your
life. They are holistic people, quietly spiritual, and genuinely inspiring in the most modest way. (Maria & Enda
Conneely, Fisherman's Cottage, Inis Oirr, Aran Islands
☎ 099-75073 📖 foodwise@eircom.net 🖰 www.
southaran.com)

Athenry

● Foods of Athenry

Siobhan and Paul Lawless's bakery is one of the very best
in Ireland. As bakers they are able to mix an earthiness in their breads with a delicacy in their finishing and
execution that makes them utterly lovable. You could
pick any of their bread and cake range – all right then,
let's choose the tea brack – and it will simply blow you
away with goodness, with that true staff-and-stuff-of-life
essentialism. Their secret, we reckon, lies in their in-
quisitiveness, their need to push their own boundaries in
order to see what new ideas emerge. Intellectually fascinating, and yet as fundamental as curiosity and creativity
itself, they are a shining star. (Siobhan & Paul Lawless, Old-
castle, Kilconieron, Athenry ☎ 091-848152 📖 siobhan@
foodsofathenry.ie 🖰 www.foodsofathenry.ie)

Galway
County

● The Friendly Farmer

Ronan Byrne is our sort of farmer. "Our ethos is based around farming with traditional breed, slow-maturing animals and selling our produce locally... One of the methods, we use is the 'Pasture Poultry' model, which is based around the principle of making sure our chickens, ducks, geese and turkeys go outside and eat *fresh grass* as part of their daily diet." Why is that important? Simply because the most dynamic farmers in modern agriculture all see themselves as grass farmers. As Michael Pollan wrote in his masterly *The Omnivore's Dilemma*, discussing the farming practices of Joel Salatin's Polyface Farm in the United States: "The animals come and go, but the grasses, which directly or indirectly feed all the animals, abide, and the well-being of the farm depends more than anything else on the well-being of its grass." So, Mr Byrne is ahead of the posse when it comes to understanding grass and its impact on what we eat, and how you use it to produce wonderful food. Of course, one of the books that influenced Mr Byrne was a book on poultry by... Joel Salatin! Wheels within wheels, or maybe even corn circles within corn circles. (Ronan Byrne, Knockbrack, Athenry ☎ 087-620 3765 ✉ thefriendlyfarmer@gmail.com 🖰 thefriendlyfarmer. blogspot.com)

● Sweetie Pies of Galway

In everyone's idealised dream world, there is a granny who bakes you lovely, sweet, crumbly, domestic cakes and goodies. This dream world doesn't exist, of course. In the real world, thankfully, there is Maureen and Jennifer's Sweetie Pie bakery and tea rooms at The Old Barracks in Athenry, and there are those lovely, sweet, crumbly domestic cakes and goodies, just like in your dreams. Except they are better. Made with real butter, simply packaged, a joy to behold and to eat, they can be enjoyed here but are also sold in local stores in and around Galway county. Sweetie Pie cakes are dreamy, blissful, and don't miss their ace mince pies at Christmas time. (Maureen Foley & Jennifer Griffin, The Old Barracks, Cross Street, Athenry ☎ 091-877492 ✉ info@ sweetiepiesofgalway.com 🖰 www.sweetiepiesofgalway. com – Open 9.30am-5pm Mon-Sat. Also at Millennium House, Westbridge, Loughrea ☎ 091-880746)

Ballinafad

● **Ballynahinch Castle**

They understand hospitality at Ballynahinch, they
understand how to draw down, how to trigger, the
archetypal images and memories in your mind about
what hospitality means. The fire is always lit as you come
through the door; the bar always has a gregarious mix
of drinkers; the dining room says elegance, romance,
the charm of nature outside the window captured for
your gaze. Patrick O'Flaherty and his team seem to us to
not merely be people who never put a foot wrong, but
who instead know with every action how to put every
foot right: they dance the dance of hospitality better
than almost anyone else, and that is why Ballynahinch
is so special. So, open the wine, and bring on venison
terrine, and wild mushroom soup, and McGeough's
beef with red wine sauce, and let's live for every
moment in this magical world within the world. (Patrick
O'Flaherty, Ballinafad, Recess, Connemara ☎ 095-31006
bhinch@iol.ie www.ballynahinch-castle.com)

Ballinasloe

● **Beechlawn Organic Farm**

Isn't it just so right, so poetic, that Padraig Fahy and
Úna Ní Bhroin, the human dynamos behind the brilliant
Beechlawn Farm, should have met at the Organic College at Drumcollogher when they were both studying for
their diplomas! Diplomas turned into action when they
started their first, half-acre garden in 2001, and a year
later they were in commercial production. Today, you
see them here, there, and everywhere, their magnificent
organic produce the bedrock of local farmers' markets as well as a stall in Eyre Square in Galway, in local
Supervalu stores and via a local box delivery scheme.
Beechlawn today is home to 16,000 square feet of poly-
tunnels, gangs of eager volunteers, and an annual Farm
Open Day. Just pay a visit, and see what these incredible
people achieve: the west's awake, alright. (Padraig Fahy
& Úna Ní Bhroin, Ballinasloe ☎ 090-964 6713 info@
beechlawnfarm.org www.beechlawnfarm.org)

Galway
County

● **Killeen Farmhouse Cheese**

Marion Roeleveld is a great cheesemaker, and her goat's milk mature gouda cheeses are amongst the best of their kind in Ireland. Marion is the cheesemaker who brought Mossfield cheeses to prominence, and there is a profound wealth of knowledge in all her work, so it comes as little surprise that Ms Roeleveld is a teacher of cheesemaking as well as a cheesemaker. Even though the milk is pasteurised, she ushers a wealth of sensuous textures and taste from her cheeses, and the paste is beautifully formed and lush. Snap up the goat's cheese wherever you see it. There is also a cow's milk cheese. (Marion Roeleveld, Killeen Millhouse, Ballyshrule, Ballinasloe ☎ 090-974 1319 📖 haske-marion@iolfree.ie)

● **Kylemore Acres**

We have to 'fess up and say that we don't just write about Richard and Diana Murray's herb mixtures, we also use them all the time in the kitchen. There is an acuity and a culinary appreciation in every one of these pretty sachets, and whether you are roasting a leg of lamb, or adding oomph to your Bolognaise these artful mixes give a dish more focus and a more panoramic taste experience. Happily you find them in many good shops throughout the entire country. (Diana & Richard Murray, Kylemore, Laurencetown, Ballinasloe ☎ 090-965 5857 📖 sales@kylemoreacres.com 🖰 www.kylemoreacres.com)

Ballyconneely

● **The Connemara Smokehouse**

The Connemara Smokehouse pride themselves in being specialists in wild, organic and environmentally sustainable products. They sell smoked salmon, mackerel and trout, and, when available, kippers and smoked cod. Graham Roberts still hand fillets every fish, and everything is extra carefully produced. "I like to keep my hand on everything, because that's where quality comes from." The internet is now a large part of the business, with customers able to buy online, and as well as that they open the smokehouse to the public. Often customers will start by calling in to buy for a picnic, and follow up with mail order. (Graham & Saoirse Roberts, Bunowen Pier, Ailebrack, Ballyconneely ☎ 095-23739 ✉ info@smokehouse.ie ⌂ www.smokehouse.ie)

only in Galway
Inis Meáin Roosters

Bearna

Restaurant
● O'Grady's on the Pier

O'Grady's does what it does – cooking seafood in an atmospheric bar and restaurant – and it does it well, with consistent cooking, smashing views out over the water, and buzzy, personable staff who know their job inside out. Ultra-professional. (Michael O'Grady, Seapoint, Barna, Galway ☎ 091-592223 ✉ ogradysonthepier@hotmail.com ⌂ www.ogradysonthepier.com – Open from 6pm daily. Sun lunch 12.30pm-2.45pm)

Hotel
● The Twelve

Whilst its location on the side of road does not feel very luxurious, the Twelve is coming together as a destination, thanks to good staff and some very good value for money. The bedrooms are very glam and very spacious. (Fergus O'Halloran, Bearna Village, Galway ☎ 091-597000 ✉ enquire@thetwelvehotel.ie ⌂ www.thetwelvehotel.ie)

Claregalway

Farmers' Market
● Claregalway Farmers' Market

Saturday morning at County Galway's favourite traffic jam is the site for the market. Get there early for the fresh fish. (Sat 10am-2pm)

Clarinbridge

● Claire's Tearooms

Claire Walsh is a legend out west and in the early days
when we began to write Bridgestone Guides, Ms Walsh
was recognised as one of the great idiosyncratic restaurateurs of her generation. Her idiosyncracy, which is really another way of saying that she has oodles of style, is
as manifest today as it was twenty-five years ago, and the
same ability to make simple food into a special occasion
is something she does in Claire's Tearooms every week.
Upstairs, Claire's daughter Kiersey McGrath runs a craft
shop which proves that style is in the blood. (Claire
Walsh, Clarinbridge ☎ 091-776606 – Open 10.30am-
5pm Tue-Sat, Sun 1pm-5pm)

Pasta
● Magnetti Pasta

Five years down the line and Marco and Sean Magnetti's
lovely range of fresh pastas has become a staple of many
delis and shops – luckily we can even buy them in our
local store down in deepest West Cork. The pastas,
raviolis and sauces all have a rustic and tactile richness,
so you get a real sense of an artisan product made
carefully. The family also run the Trattoria Magnetti
on Quay Street in Galway city, where you can get
their pasta, along with pizzas, in a quaint, enjoyable
space. (Marco & Sean Magnetti, Unit 1A Clarinbridge
Business Park, Clarinbridge ☎ 091-776580 ✉ pasta@
magnettifoods.com 🖰 www.magnettifoods.com.
Trattoria Magnetti, 12 Quay Street, Galway ☎ 091-
563910)

Cleggan

Seaweed Relishes and Seafood
● Cleggan Seaweed Company

The Cleggan Company isn't just seaweeds, for they also
have a Seafood company which sells the catch of the
day and will even deliver it to your door. Make sure to
ring in advance to check that there is fish. The seaweed
range is distinguished by its luxury brand packaging and
by the fact that the sea vegetables are hand harvested

and naturally air dried. If you don't have kombu and spaghetti de mer in your lifestyle then this is the most elegant way of getting these most elemental ingredients into your life. (Shane Forsythe, Cleggan Fishing Village, Connemara ☎ 095-44649 📠 info@clegganseaweed. com 🖰 www.clegganseaweed.com)

Clifden

Shop
● **The Connemara Hamper**

There is nowhere else quite like Eileen and Leo Halliday's deli. It's quite a simple place – the design sensibility is almost Shakerish in its modesty, almost monastic – and yet there is a relish for food here that is anything but self-denying, though it may be somewhat monastic. They have the gift to be simple, and the gift to make utterly wonderful brown bag lunches, amongst a trove of delightful ingredients that you want to take from their hamper and put straight into yours. (Eileen & Leo Halliday, Market Street, Clifden ☎ 095-21054 📠 info@ connemarahamper.com 🖰 www.connemarahamper.com – Open 10am-5.30pm Mon-Sat)

Country House
● **Dolphin Beach**

A dreamy, delightful country house, which enjoys the most jaw-dropping location out on the Sky Road, the Foyle family's home is a real peach, a more-than-magical, super-stylish place to stay that somehow summons up all the intoxications of Connemara. The house is beautiful, the hospitality fulsome, and memories of various times spent here over the years remain preciously vivid. (The Foyle family, Lower Sky Road, Clifden, Connemara ☎ 095-21204 🖰 www.dolphinbeachhouse.com 📠 stay@dolphinbeachhouse.com)

Fishmonger
● **Duane's Fish Shop**

Crab is the summer speciality if you are holidaying in Clifden and John Duane's Fish Shop is the place to get it, along with lots of other good piscine specialities. (John Duane, Main Street, Clifden ☎ 095-21804 – Open 10am-6pm Mon-Fri, closed Mon off season, 10am-5pm Sat)

Galway
County

Restaurant
● Mitchell's

"The most consistent restaurant I know from annual visits from the past five years." That statement, from a friend who is also an industry professional, tells you all you need to know about why Mitchell's has survived and thrived in Clifden since 1991. So many restaurateurs come and go in this town because they lower standards in order to make more money, but Mitchell's do the good thing and the result is simply that this is the destination choice for many visitors to Clifden. (JJ Mitchell, Market Street, Clifden ☎ 095-21867 – Open noon-close, with dinner sittings at 7pm & 9pm Mon-Sun. Closed Hallowe'en-March)

only in Galway
Connemara Lamb

Guesthouse
● Quay House

"Ten out of ten". That's the sort of rating your friends relay back to you after staying with Paddy and Julia Foyle in their world-class Quay House. Not only is Quay House ten out of ten in terms of class, it is also ten out of ten in terms of value, and offers an idiosyncratic luxury that only an iconoclastic bloke like Paddy Foyle could conjure up out of furnishings and fire places and a strange obsession with both Napoleon Bonaparte and Marlene Dietrich. Unique. (Paddy & Julia Foyle, Beach Rd, Clifden, Connemara ☎ 095-21369 ✍ res@ thequayhouse.com ✇ www.thequayhouse.com)

B&B
● Sea Mist House

"No major changes, just improving and maintaining what we have." Such is the patient and dedicated approach to hospitality of Sheila Griffin, and what a contrast Ms Griffin's philosophy makes in comparison to the ghastly and ghostly modern hotels that now litter Ireland. This lovely Victorian house is a peach of a place and the breakfast is one of the most creative and enjoyable in the West. (Sheila Griffin, Clifden, Connemara ☎ 095-21441 ✍ sgriffin@eircom.net ✇ www.seamisthouse.com)

● **Steam**

If you want to know why the cooking in Claire and Alan's café is so right on and rock steady, it could be because Claire's Mum, Eileen, is one of Clifden's legendary cooks, and her Dad, Hugh, is one of Clifden's legendary kitchen gardeners. The influences of her childhood are shown every day in Steam: Spanish chicken and chickpea casserole, confit of duck with celeriac and roasted vegetables, goat's cheese lasagne. They have improved the food offer every year since they opened and the lunch special brings in loads of locals, whilst their catering business for folk with holiday homes is on the up and up. Claire's Mum, Eileen, also does some home catering from her home in High Moors (☎ 095-21342). (Claire Griffin & Alan King, Station House, Clifden ☎ 095-30600 – Open 10am-6pm Mon-Sat)

Furbo

Hotel
● **Connemara Coast Hotel**

"It's like an escape, a mini world of its own." That's what our girl Valerie O'Connor felt like after just a few days in Charles Synnott's excellent Furbo hotel. Mr Synnott is probably best known for running Brook's Hotel in Dublin, which we rate as the best in the capital. Out here in Connemara, he shows the same appreciation for comfort, for great works of art and for delivering sincere hospitality. So follow Valerie O'Connor's advice and "switch off and get lost." (Charles Synnott, Furbo, Galway ☎ 091-592 2108 ✉ info@connemaracoast.ie 🖱 www.connemaracoast.ie)

Gort

Market
● **Gort Farmers' Market**

If it's Friday morning then the traffic jam today in Gort is being caused by the farmers' market. So simply park the car, pick up a bag and go and do some shopping rather than sitting fuming behind the wheel. (Town Centre, Gort – Open Fri 10am-2pm)

● **Kettle of Fish**

"If you're looking for fresh fish and chips with a good dash of vinegar this is the place to go" says Sabrina Conneely. KOF is a tiny chipper with a seating area. It's very clean, with lovely staff. So order up scampi and chips, or calamari and chips, or monkfish with tartar sauce and what you will get is sparkling fish and perfect dry, crisp moreish chips. For your inner Glaswegian they also deep fry battered Mars bars. We'd stick to the fish and chips if we were you. (Siobhan Fahey, The Square, Gort ☎ 091-630300)

Kilcolgan

Oysters
● **Michael Kelly Shellfish**

The Kelly family oysters are the crème de la crème of the ocean. As if that wasn't enough Diarmuid Kelly's company is also outstandingly efficient and it takes no more than one telephone call and before you know it there is a man at your door with a beautiful crate of oysters. It is essential therefore to always have the Guinness or the Chablis ready at the right temperature. (Diarmuid Kelly, Tyrone, Kilcolgan ☎ 091-796120 ✉ kellyoysters@eircom.net ✇ www.kellyoysters.com)

Kinvara

Health Food Shop
● **Healing Harvest**

Sian Morgan is a registered homeopath, as well as being proprietor of a splendid healthfood shop. Ms Morgan runs classes in homeopathic first aid, so take a look at her site, www.sianmorgan.com, for more details. Healing Harvest's website also allows you to order all their products online. (Sian Morgan, Main Street, Kinvara ☎ 091-637176 ✇ www.healingharvest.ie)

Pub
● **Keogh's Bar**

Keogh's is one of the best-known pubs for food in Galway, and it's easy to see why this traditional bar in such a popular choice, for it's hugely atmospheric and along with the food they even do dancing and traditional music. The food rings all the bells as well, and they aptly describe it as a "simple menu of quality". Spot on. (Michael Keogh, The Square, Kinvara ☎ 091-637145 ⬡ mikeogh@eircom.net ⬡ www.kinvara.com/keoghs – Food served 9am-10pm Mon-Sun)

Smokehouse
● Kinvara Smoked Salmon

Declan Droney is one of the sharpest tools in the shed, a bloke whose masterly minding of his smoked salmon company is a textbook example of how you turn an artisan product into a luxury brand. Just one look at his impossibly glamorous packaging, with its resonant colours and evocative imagery, immediately places this smoked fish in the company of *Vogue* or *How to Spend It*. Then you open the packet and the organic fish tastes even better than it looks, a teasing symphony of smoky grace notes abetted by a lush, buttery texture. Kinvara is worth the company of your very best white wine, and your very best friends. (Declan Droney, Kinvara ☎ 091-637489 ⬡ info@kinvarasmokedsalmon.com ⬡ www.kinvarasmokedsalmon.com)

Galway
County

only in Galway
Connemara Air-Dried Lamb

Leenane

Country House
● Delphi Lodge

"Grilled Killary mackerel (caught this morning by David)". Now, do you want to eat that mackerel, when you see it described like that, as part of the dinner menu in Peter Mantle's legendary house? Of course you do, and such a sure, witty description perfectly summarises the earthy, sporty, companionable nature of this most singular house, and it also shows the care devoted to the cookery. The wine list is something to get lost in, deeply lost in, though do bear in mind that you will be fishing again tomorrow at some ungodly early hour. (Peter Mantle, Leenane ☎ 095-42987 ⬡ res@delphilodge.ie ⬡ www.delphilodge.ie)

Letterfrack

Galway County

Craft Shop & Café
● Avoca

Every time you walk into an Avoca store, your life gets better. Letterfrack Avoca, with its cracking location just across from the sea at Ballinakill Bay, is one of those blessed stores, and even the briefest browse around all their must-have homegoods is fun, especially with a pause to get something good to eat in the café. Whilst your life gets better, however, we can't promise that your credit card may be somewhat weaker upon exit. (Simon Pratt, Letterfrack ☎ 095-41058 ✉ info@avoca.ie ⌂ www.avoca.ie – Open 9am-6pm Mon-Sun. Closed Jan 15-Mar 15)

Country House
● Renvyle House Hotel

Ronnie Counihan and chef Tim O'Sullivan run one of Ireland's best destinations, out here on the westerly shores, in a house that is a place and a passion unto itself. It is hard to know who loves Renvyle more: McKenna adults? Or McKenna children? Guess we will have to just take another trip to this magical little universe and then argue the toss one more time. Mr O'Sullivan's cooking, in particular, is amongst the finest country house cooking anywhere in Europe, both hugely disciplined and yet enjoying a free-form energy that makes it seem as if he has just dreamt it all up. That is quite a feat, and it makes for quite a treat. (Ronnie Counihan, Letterfrack, Connemara ☎ 095-43511 ✉ info@renvyle.com ⌂ www.renvyle.com)

Country House
● Rosleague Manor

Mark Foyle's pretty pink country house ticks all the boxes. Its location overlooks Ballinakill Bay and the Twelve Bens. Its gardens cascade down to the sea. The house is elegant and yet charmingly understated and you could say exactly the same about the food served in the restaurant. It is romantic yet it's never twee and it's stylish but never OTT. For all these reasons, and most especially Mr Foyle's cordiality, Rosleague is one of the shining lights of Irish hospitality. (Mark Foyle, Letterfrack, Connemara ☎ 095-41101 ⌂ www.rosleague.com – Open Mar-Nov)

Loughrea

Café Deli
● **Fare Green Food**

FGF is only excellent, a tiny deli and shop that has all
the things you want and need and none of the things
you don't want or need. Maureen and Irene source with
care, and they are food lovers to their fingertips, so
everything comes graced with care that it should give
the maximum pleasure, whether it's a quickly-grabbed
Americano or a lazy lunchtime plate of good things.
(Maureen Fynes, Westbridge, Loughrea ☎ 091-870911
🖰 maureenfynes@yahoo.co.uk– Open 8am-6.30pm
Mon-Fri, 9am-6pm Sat, open Sun seasonally)

Market
● **Loughrea Market**

Local heroes, such as Padraig Fahy of Beechlawn Farm
and Stefan Griesbach of Gannet Fish, and the Lawless
family of the Foods of Athenry are just some of the
blue-chip artisans who make this little market special.
(Barrack Street – Open Thurs 9am-2pm)

Moycullen

Traiteur & Deli
● **Enjoy**

Enjoy is the new offspring of local heroes Kevin and Ann
Dunne, of White Gables restaurant. Walk in the door
and you are assailed by the waft of fresh breads arranged
on the old table, then hum and haw over what food-to-
go you would like, the dishes all characterised by Kevin's
love of the culinary classics and his precise and correct
rendering of those classics, from boeuf bourguignonne
to chocolate mousse. As with the restaurant, everything sparkles, everything is as good as it can possibly
be. (Kevin & Ann Dunne, Moycullen ☎ 091-868200
🖰 info@whitegables.com 🖰 www.whitegables.com –
Open 10.30am-8pm Tue-Sat, 10.30am-5pm Sun)

Wine Merchant
● **Mad About Wine**

Ivan Edwards is another of those sommeliers-turned-
wine sellers whom you seem to find in Galway, and his

Galway
County

experience in the world of wine and his appreciation of the culture of wine shines through the list, and also the finely chosen goodies that the shop stocks. (Ivan Edwards, Main Street, Moycullen ☎ 091-868882 📧 ivanedwards@eircom.net – Open Tue-Sat)

● Moycullen Farmers' Market

Gannet Fish and Beechlawn Organic Farm are just two of the producers who animate the Friday afternoon market in Moycullen. (The Forge – Open Fri noon-6pm)

Restaurant
● White Gables

Don't you just love it when someone has the courage and the confidence to say that their cooking is "focused around seafood, with time-warp classics such as seafood cocktail Marie Rose, poached fresh halibut Veronique and scallops mornay...." Oh, bring on the Cordon Bleu! And don't you just love it that Kevin and Ann Dunne would have cooked those dishes twenty years ago when they opened, and that they cook them today with the same exactitude and finesse that distinguishes every element of this pristine restaurant. "White Gables is such a treat!", says Sabrina Conneely, and indeed it is, thanks to the family's determination that eating here should always be special, and should be special every single time. (Kevin & Ann Dunne, Moycullen Village ☎ 091-555744 📧 info@whitegables.com 🖱 www.whitegables.com – Open 7pm-9.30pm Tue-Sun 12.30pm-3pm Sun)

Oranmore

Restaurant
● Asian Fusion

Charlie Chan is a pioneer of ethnic cooking way out west, and continues his confident embrace of classic Chinese cooking in the lovely space of Asian Fusion. (Charlie Chan, Castle Court, Castle Road, Oranmore ☎ 091-790823 – Open 5pm-11pm Mon-Thu, 5pm-11.30pm Fri & Sat, 3pm-10pm Sun)

Restaurant
● Basilico

"Loved this place, and could not find a fault" was the reaction of our friend Sabrina on her first visit to

Galway County

Basilico. It's the restaurant of the Coach House Hotel, a 16-bedroom set-up in the centre of Oranmore, a busy but somewhat anonymous suburb of Galway. There is a pizza menu and a good selection of pastas alongside the à la carte, and Paulo Sabatini's cooking is spot on: calamari fritti is baby squid and courgette in a light batter with marinara sauce; a house salad is ripe tomatoes with buffalo mozzarella. Mains of pearl barley risotto with salmon and cherry tomatoes is as good as strips of beef fillet with fennel seed, wild mushrooms and new potatoes. Fabiano Mules' staff are courteous and sharply dressed, and Basilico is a excellent arrival. (Paulo Sabatini, ☎ 091-788367 ✉ basilico.oranmore@yahoo.ie, 🖰 www.coachhousehotel.ie – Open breakfast, lunch and dinner)

Market
● **Oranmore Farmers' Market**

Get your Foods of Athenry breads and cakes and your Coolfinn Organic gardens baking, your vegetables from Beechlawn Organic Farm along with lots of other choice Galway produce, at the Thursday afternoon market. (Open Thur noon-6pm)

Deli
● **Susan & Alan's Kitchen Pantry**

There are oodles of good things in Alan and Susan's pantry, from the best specialist artisan products from all over the island and rarities from further afield such as Terra Rossa olive oils – and their olive oil and thyme blend – Zaramama popping corn, and really choice wines from around the globe. A good new arrival. (Susan Hynes, Castlecourt, Castle Road, Oranmore ☎ 091-788705 ✉ info@susanandalan.ie 🖰 www.susanandalan.ie – Open 9am-6pm Mon-Sat)

Oughterard

Butcher
● **Roger Finnerty's & Sons**

Finnerty's is a classy, creative butcher's shop, and they do those things that mark out the true butchers' shops – excellent sausages, special black and white puddings, great beef – every bit as well as it can possibly be done. Creative and dedicated. (Billy Morgan, Main Street, Oughterard ☎ 091-552255 ✉ finnertysbutchers@iolfree.ie – Open 8am-6.30pm Mon-Sat, 'till 7pm Fri)

● McGeough's Butchers

He's pretty much the superstar of the younger generation of Irish butchers, James McGeough, his air-dried
beef and lamb products now in many shops away from
his own calm, quiet shop in little Oughterard. So it's a
good time to reflect on the fact that Mr McGeough got
where he is by virtue of the 10,000 hours, to borrow a
popular modern theory. Travel back in time, to when he
worked with his dad, and then his six years of study in
Germany, and then the many, many hours inventing and
elaborating and perfecting his recipes, and you will tot
up the same number of hours of work that made The
Beatles great and made Bill Gates rich. Mr McGeough
makes it look easy, and his modesty belies all his graft,
but make no mistake as you savour that unmistakable
slice of a McGeough luxury charcuterie product, that
what you are enjoying is time dedicated to you.
(James McGeough, Barrack Street, Oughterard
☎ 091-552351 ✉ fougheast@iol free.ie ⌂ www.
connemarafinefoods.ie)

● Probus Wines

Paul Fogarty's shop is a cult address. Writing on the
occasion of the shop's tenth anniversary, John Wilson
of *The Irish Times* praised Probus as being an archetype
of the "slightly maverick enterprises that buck the
trend towards corporate blandness, and succeed with a
different kind of wine shop... The shop is small, but full
of different quirky wines". Indeed it is, and many happy
returns to Probus on hitting a decade in business. We
have said before that one of the things that distinguishes
Mr Fogarty as a wine buyer is not just his appreciation
of wine, but also his knowledge of food, so his wines
are subtle, complex and multi-dimensional, and it's a
pure treat to turn up here with an empty mind and a
thirst for something good.(Paul Fogarty, Camp Street,
Oughterard ☎ 091-552084 ⌂ www.probuswines.ie)

● The Yew Tree

Eric Japaud is a talented baker, and he has upped the
reputation of the much-loved Yew Tree since taking over
a couple of years back. The breads range from Norwegian rye to cheddar and jalapeno, via soda bread

Galway
County

and a pain de campagne, and there is a moreish range of savouries and cakes. Confident, evocative work, and a vital address. (Eric Japaud, Main Street, Oughterard ☎ 091-866986 – Open 9am-6pm Mon-Sat)

Recess

Country House
● **Lough Inagh Lodge**

Oh boy, but wouldn't a spot of fly fishing in Maire O'Connor's demure country hotel be just the ticket? That's the sort of thing you find yourself saying to yourself as you work through a big book like this, dreaming of a boat on the lake, the wisp of the fly in the air, the utterly magnificent away-from-it-all location of Lough Inagh. Or wouldn't a spot of walking with that great guide, Michael Gibbons, be just the thing to straighten out that back and sort out those office lazy legs. And then dinner in the dining room and the unique peace of a good night's sleep in Connemara. Ah. (Maire O'Connor, Recess, Connemara ☎ 095-34706 📠 inagh@ iol.ie 🖱 www.loughinaghlodgehotel.ie – Open Mar-Dec)

only in Galway
Killeen Farmhouse Cheese

Roscahill

Garden & Tea Rooms
● **Brigit's Garden**

Jenny Beale and her team like to say that "Kindness is contagious – pass it on!". They should also say: "Brilliance and a lot of culinary creativity belong together so share the news!" Brigit's is one of Ireland's most individual, imaginative gardens, and the garden café has exactly the sort of slowly made, nourishing, true cooking that you crave after an encounter with myriad garden wonders. So pass on the good news: Brigit's is one of the stars of the West! (Jenny Beale, Pollagh, Roscahill ☎ 091-550905 🖱 www.galwaygarden.com – Café opens 10.30am-5pm May-Sept. Open Sundays in April. Tea always available Oct-Apr)

Roundstone

● The Angler's Return

Lynn Hill's house is one of those places that lodges in
your memory. There is something archetypal about this
sporting lodge, something that makes it a sporting lodge
that is a sport of nature in its uniqueness, its specialness.
Quite, quite lovely. (Lynn Hill, Toombeola, Roundstone,
Connemara ☎ 095-31091 ◌ www.anglersreturn.com –
closed Dec-Jan)

Bar & Restaurant
● O'Dowd's Seafood Bar & Restaurant

O'Dowd's is the destination in Roundstone for an
atmospheric pint and some nice seafood, either in the
bar, where there is a mix of sandwiches, toasties and
seafood, or for more expansive seafood cookery in the
restaurant. They also have some self-catering accommodation, if you are planing more than a brief visit, and they
even sell their own T-shirts. Changeless, which is just
fine by us. (O'Dowd family, Roundstone ☎ 095-35923
◌ odowds@indigo.ie ◌ www.odowdsbar.com – Open
10am-9.30pm all year)

Mushrooms

County Kerry

Annascaul

Black Pudding
● **Ashe's Black Pudding**

Thomas Ashe has made a formidable reputation with his
famous black pudding – the pudding of choice for many
restaurateurs – but he is only beginning, as a new white
pudding and fine pork sausages prove. The sausages are a
classic example of peppery porky perfection, the spicing
subtle, the texture firm, and the highest compliment we
can pay them is to say that they compare to the best
sausages made by butchers in Northern Ireland. The
white pudding has a much softer texture than the black
– back bacon and cooked gammon ends are used in place
of blood – but again it's quixotic, interesting and hugely
enjoyable. Just remember to pack that freezer bag when
it's time to visit Tom Crean's old stomping ground of
Annascaul, for you will want to bring home a haul of
these hand-made beauties. (Thomas Ashe, Annascaul
☎ 066-915 7127 📖 info@annascaulblackpudding.com
🖲 www.annascaulblackpudding.com)

Ballinskelligs

Chocolate
● **Cocoa Bean Artisan Chocolates**

Emily and Sarah are the kind of girls who, having made
an ace bar of chocolate such as their gin and tonic
chocolate bar, then start to work on it to improve
it and make it even more unique. Anyone else would
just say: Hallelujah! I have just made a superb bar of
chocolate!, but Emily and Sarah instead start tinkering
with all manner of things – sherbet; popping candy –
before discovering that a fine powder of dried Persian
limes gives a sweet and sour lime flavour with a tongue-
tingling sensation. So, there is the difference between
Cocoa Bean and the rest: they work and work until
they discover that dried Persian lime powder is the
way they need to go. Phew! (Emily Webster & Sarah
Hehir, The Glen, Ballinskelligs ☎ 066-947 9119 🖲 www.
cocoabeanchocolates.com)

Kerry

Chocolate

● Skelligs Chocolate Company

Colm Healy may well be the Willy Wonka of Irish
artisan chocolate. He has a little chocolate factory, the
most westerly in Europe, to which you can bring your
children so they can watch chocolate being tempered
with bug-eyed wonder. He also runs chocoholics
competitions, and we're guessing that somewhere along
the line there is a golden ticket involved. In between
times he makes excellent truffles, fruit clusters, hot
chocolate and even little chocolate gifts for new
mothers. (Colm Healy, The Glen, Ballinskelligs ☎ 066-
947 9119 ✎ info@skelligschocolate.com ✍ www.
skelligschocolate.com – Open to the public 10am-4pm
Mon-Fri Sep-Dec, Feb-May, 10am-5pm Mon-Fri Jun,
10am-5pm Mon-Fri, noon-5pm Sat & Sun Jul-Aug)

Blackwater

Tearooms

● The Strawberry Field

Margaret and Peter make exceptionally good crêpes.
And when you pull up to this traditional cottage, when
touring the peninsula, and order up a flour crêpe with
some ice cream and a cup of tea you realise just what
an appropriate snack this is for the hungry traveller, not
to mention the hungry traveller's children. (Margaret
& Peter Kerssens, Moll's Gap-Sneem Road, Blackwater
☎ 064-668 2977 ✎ info@strawberryfield-ireland.com
✍ www.strawberryfield-ireland.com – Open 11am-6pm
Mon-Sun)

Bonane

Chocolatier

● Benoit Lorge

Last time we were coming back from Kenmare to West
Cork, we pulled over at the old post office in Bonane
where Benoit Lorge weaves his magic, and where we
always pull over when driving this road. And, truth be
told, as usual we enjoyed the charm of the shop almost
– almost! – as much as we enjoyed the lovely chocolate
truffles we bought. M. Lorge is a very good chocolatier.

282   THE BRIDGESTONE IRISH FOOD GUIDE

(Benoit Lorge, Releagh Cottage, Bonane, Kenmare
☎ 064-667 9994/087-991 7172 ☐ info@lorge.ie
🖑 www.lorgechocolate.com)

Caherdaniel

Kerry

Farmers' Market
● Caherdaniel Market

Local baking hero Jane Urquhart is one of the key
players and providers to the fun Caherdaniel Market,
where you will also find good local crafts as well as more
handmade local foods. (Blind Piper, Caherdaniel – Open
12.30pm-6pm Sundays, May-Oct, weather permitting)

Guesthouse
● Iskeroon

Two bed-and-breakfast suites and a self-catering
apartment form the core of Iskeroon, but saying that is a
bit like saying Rembrandt was a guy who painted. What
you need to know about David and Geraldine's Iskeroon
is that its location is other-worldly wonderful: set in
acres of semi-tropical gardens that run down to the sea,
you feel you are in a world apart when you are here,
and it's a feeling that stays with you always. (Geraldine
& David Hare, Iskeroon, Caherdaniel ☎ 066-947 5119
☐ res@iskeroon.com 🖑 www.iskeroon.com)

Cahirciveen

Farmers' Market
● Cahirciveen Market

If you are down on your holliers in Kerry in July and
August then head down to the Cahirciveen market for
some nice local foods. (Community Centre, Thurs 11am-
2pm, high season)

Bar & Restaurant
● The Point Seafood Bar (O'Neill's)

The Valentia ferry leaves from just by O'Neill's, but
before you make the crossing make sure to enjoy some
fine seafood in Michael and Bridie's pub. They have won
a fine reputation, built on cooking fresh seafood simply

and with respect. (Michael & Bridie O'Neill, Renard Point, Caherciveen ☎ 066-947 2165/087-2595345 – Open Lunch Mon-Sat, Dinner Mon-Sun during high season. Telephone first off season, especially if visiting during months Nov-Mar)

● **QC's**

With their fish and shellfish supplies coming straight from Quinlan's Fish at Renard's Point, Kate and Andrew Cooke's restaurant is on a roll even before they fire up the grill and start sending out brill with toasted garlic or sizzling prawns or their own, crisp fish and chips. This is a really smart, hip place, with smart, hip cooking. (Kate & Andrew Cooke, 3 Main Street, Caherciveen ☎ 066-947 2244 ⌨ info@qcbar.com ✆ www.qcbar.com – Open for food 12.30pm-2.30pm Mon-Sat, 6pm-11.30pm Mon-Sun with more limited hours off season)

● **Quinlan's Kerry Fish**

Quinlan's Kerry Fish is quite an operation. First of all there is smoked salmon, a fine organic example of smoked salmon that is always very good value for money. Then they have their four Kerry shops, and finally there is a nationwide delivery service, usually to customers from the Midlands who visit the Quinlan brothers whilst on holiday, and then, having experienced the quality of fish they sell, order them on-line in €100 boxes, which are delivered overnight. (Fintan & Liam Quinlan, Main Street, Caherciveen ☎ 066-947 2686. Also The Square, Killorglin ☎ 066-976 1860. Also 1 The Mall, Tralee ☎ 066-712 3998. Also Park Road, Killarney ☎ 064-663 9333 – Open 10am-6pm, Mon-Fri, 10am-2pm Sat ✆ www.kerryfish.com)

Castlecove

● **Westcove Farmhouse Shop**

Jane Urquhart is a baker, and what you need to know about Castlecove is that should you be travelling the Ring of Kerry, you can turn off the road, between

Caherdaniel and Castlecove, and enter a world of
Norwegian chocolate cake, or lemon and cream tart,
or chocolate and walnut brownies. Jane sells at many
of the Kerry markets, but we advise a visit to the shop,
where you will also find excellent crafts, and where you
can take a look at the tasty self-catering accommodation
that is part of this smashing set-up. (Jane Urquhart,
Westcove Farmhouse, Westcove Road, Castlecove
☎ 066-947 5479 ✉ westcovefarmhouse@oceanfree.net
🖰 www.westcove.net)

only in Kerry
Diliskus Cheese

Castlegregory

Farmhouse Cheese
● Dingle Peninsula Cheese

Maja Binder's cheeses – Diliskus; Beenoskee and Kilcummin – are unique. Flavoured with sea vegetables, and
rubbed with salted whey, they reflect an earlier age
when Irish cheeses were more improvised and less commercial than they are at present. Ms Binder's originality
is matched by an acute understanding of the ways of
milk and these are wonderfully satisfying and invigorating
cheeses. (Maja Binder, Kilcummin Beg, Castlegregory
☎ 066-713 9028)

Seafood, Relishes and Charcouterie
● On The Wild Side

Olivier Beaujouan is the significant other of Maja
Binder, the previous entry in this book, and one can
only imagine what the dinner table conversation
must be like in their house. For they match each
other in terms of wild, almost eccentric creativity,
with Ms Binder working with milk, and M. Beaujouan
working with sea vegetables, fish and charcuterie. On
The Wild Side sea vegetables are amongst the most
precious of Irish artisan foods, but everything Olivier
sells at his various farmers' markets is crafted with
exactitude and embellished with joie de vivre. (Olivier
Beaujouan, Kilcummin, Castlegregory ☎ 066-713 9028
✉ seatoland@hotmail.com)

Castlemaine

Organic restaurant
● **The Phoenix**

Here's the kind of message Billy and Lorna at the
Phoenix are prone to send to us: "June 19th, French
gypsy band Txutxukan, Cuban salsa class every Thursday.
Phoenix annual fund raiser with fabulously tasty Phoenix
buffet and a great night of dance and fun." When they
aren't organising these raucous evenings, or selling their
vegetables at the beautiful Milltown Church market,
they somehow manage to run a B&B and a vegetarian
wholefood restaurant. Wonderfully left field. (Billy
& Lorna Tyther, Shanahill East, Castlemaine ☎ 066-
976 6284 ✉ phoenixtyther@hotmail.com ⌂ www.
thephoenixorganic.com)

Mutton pie

Cromane

Pub and Restaurant
● **Jack's Coastguard Station**

The proof of the cult status of Brian and Grainne's
restaurant is the fact that local seafood specialists will
give you the tip that it's the kind of place you should
take yourself to when in Kerry. If you do make your
way to this beautifully maintained stone-fronted building
and head through the bar into the formal dining room,
you will discover classic bourgeois fish cookery: sole on
the bone with chive and lemon beurre blanc, hake with
caramelised baby fennel and tapenade, crisp salmon with
braised leeks and caper and sorrel vinaigrette. Chefs
Helen Vickers and Patricia Teahan concoct elegant,
intelligent food, and if the prices are in effect city prices
it's because the food is worth the money. (Grainne &
Brian Keary, Cromane Lower, Killorglin ☎ 066-976 9102
✉ jackscoastguardstation@yahoo.ie ⌂ www.
jackscoastguardstation.ie – Bar open noon-11.30pm,
till 12.30am Fri & Sat, Restaurant open 6pm-9pm, till
9.30pm weekends. Closed Tues all year, & Weds during
low season)

Dingle

● Bee's Teas

Bee's Teas observes the First Commandment of all tearooms – loose tea is thy God and thou shalt have no teabags on thy premises. Mind you, it also gets the Fourth Commandment – thou shalt have mismatched crockery – and the Ninth – thou shalt have delicate cupcakes with splodges of cream on the top and collars of coconut flakes. So, prepare yourself for a Damascene conversion when you take a seat and peruse the menu in this happy, girly tea loft. (Bee, Dick Mack's Yard, Green Street, Dingle)

Dairy
● Bric Farm

Mae and Tom Bric run a classic dairy in the Gaeltacht area outside Dingle. They produce a semi-hard cow's cheese, Tairgi Feirme An Daingean, (Dingle Farm Products) and also sell real milk – Dingle Farm Milk – which is available in Siopa Ui Glaithearta (O'Flaherty's Londis) Baile an Mhuilinn, Dingle and other shops in the locality. (Tomas & Mae Bric, Baile na nGall ☎ 066-9155218)

Seafood
● Ted Browne's of Dingle

We buy Ted Browne's smoked salmon and his prepared crab meat all the time. The smoked fish is sublime, whilst the quality of the crab meat and the crab claws simply has no equal in Ireland. Mr Browne is also a supreme ecologist, using his waste to create the darkest, finest compost you can imagine. Pristine foods, and sustainable production: that's why Mr Browne's company is such a model business. (Ted Browne, Ballinaboula, Dingle ☎ 066-915 1933 ✉ tbrowne@indigo.ie)

Accommodation
● Castlewood House

Helen and Brian Heaton worked in various top-notch Irish hotels before they realised their ambition to run their own place. They have brought the standards of the best hotels and married it to a spontaneous Dingle hospitality in Castlewood House. There is luxury here in every detail and in particular their breakfasts,

Kerry

where porridge has a shot of Cooley whiskey, Dingle kippers are paired with scrambled eggs and the buffet selection is a smorgasbord of early morning delights. (Brian & Helen Heaton, The Wood, Dingle ☎ 066-915 2788 ☏ castlewoodhouse@eircom.net ☝ www.castlewooddingle.com)

Restaurant
● The Chart House

With chef Noel Enright, the Chart House fire has truly come alive in recent times. The cooking relies on local sourcing, and savvy, unpretentious delivery that isn't afraid to make a powerful statement: Glenbeigh oysters with goat's cheese butter; shoulder of Staunton's pork with crackling and creamed potatoes; Dingle Bay crab-meat with shellfish bisque; Blasket Island lamb with black olive sauce. Mr Enright ennobles his fine local ingredients with deftness and a sense of true savour, and that combination is further over-delivered by the excellent wine list, with some choice South African stars that Mr McCarthy imports himself. (Jim & Carmel McCarthy, The Mall, Dingle ☎ 066-915 2255 ☏ charthse@eircom.net ☝ www.charthousedingle.com – Open 6.30pm-10pm Mon-Sun, closed Mon & Tue off season)

Market
● Dingle Local Produce and Craft Market

It's at the height of the summer and the height of the season when the Dingle market is rockin' at its best. And then there can be as many as thirty stalls selling every manner of food and craft that local ingenuity can bake, cook and fashion. (The Harbour, Dingle, Fridays 10am-3pm)

Fish & Chips
● Dingle Reel Fish & Chip Shop

"The best fish and chips in Ireland" is what the locals say about the fish and chips in Mark Grealy's fast-becoming-a-legend chipper. Of course, the locals are biased – we are in Kerry, remember – but they are right to be biased, for Mr Grealy seems to have hit on the perfect formula for perfect fish and chips, and he is doing the good stuff, with fish from day boats being cooked the right way to make "proper, real food". It's real, alright. (Mark Grealy, Holy Ground, Dingle ☎ 066-915 1713 – Open 1pm-10pm)

● Emlagh House

Emlagh is a grand and beautiful house, and to complement their superb home, Marion and Grainne have opened equally superb self-catering accommodation, Water's Edge House, for those who want to make a Dingle holiday into a major family stay-over. The same breathtaking standards of housekeeping and attention to detail that characterise Emlagh are evident here: this is sumptuous accommodation, with each apartment sleeping six people. Emlagh, meantime, has been in our *Bridgestone 100 Best Places to Stay* book ever since it opened, which says it all, really. (Marion & Gráinne Kavanagh, Emlagh, Dingle ☎ 066-915 2345 📧 info@emlaghhouse.com 🕯 www.emlaghhouse.com – Open Mar-mid Nov)

● Gorman's Clifftop House

Comfort and confidence are the hallmarks of Gorman's, though we shouldn't overlook their stunning location, looking out over Smerwick Harbour. But inside, the public areas and the bedrooms are super-comfortable, and the cooking from Vincent is calm, classic and confident: scallops with coriander butter; sirloin with champ and brandy and mushroom sauce; chicken with chorizo and sauté potatoes. Breakfast is just as good as the evening meals, so try to get a little stroll or a cycle ride in before the porridge and the scrambled eggs. (Vincent & Sile Gorman, Glaise Bheag, Ballydavid, Dingle ☎ 066-915 5162 📧 info@gormans-clifftophouse.com 🕯 www.gormans-clifftophouse.com – Food served 6.30pm-9pm Mon-Sat. Reservations only off season. Closed Nov-Mar)

● Greenmount House

Refurbishments and extensions over recent times have increased the Curran family's handsome house into a twelve bedroom luxury guesthouse. It's pretty, and comfortable and the views over Dingle Harbour are as fine as the breakfasts, served in the conservatory, which have won a host of awards going back over twenty years. (John & Mary Curran, Upper John St, Dingle ☎ 066-915 1414 📧 greenmounthouse@eircom.net 🕯 www.greenmount-house.com)

Kerry

● An Grianan

With a pretty lunchtime space in the shop now adding
to the desirability of this pivotal Dingle address, Fanny
and Michelle power on in the pretty, pinky An Grianan.
There are fresh juices, organic salads and good curries,
cracking sandwiches – Dingle cheese with avocado and
sun-dried tomato on nigella seed focacia; homemade
hummus with roast vegetables and leaves on brown spelt
soda – and the organic breakfast is the business. Ace.
(Fanny Binder & Michelle Flannery, Green Street, Dingle
☎ 066-915 1910 ✆ dinglehealthfoodshop@eircom.net
– Shop open 9am-6pm Mon-Sat, Café open 9am-5pm
Mon-Sat)

Accommodation
● Heaton's Guest House

Caroline Byrne had a wonderful time staying in Heaton's, and the pleasure of the experience she ascribed
to the fact that "Cameron and Nuala kept a constant
presence should we ever have needed anything, and any
request was instantly obliged", Fantastic, and when you
add in the comfort of the rooms and the truly special
breakfast, you can see why Heaton's is such a hot ticket
for a Dingle destination. (Nuala & Cameron Heaton,
The Wood, Dingle ☎ 066-915 2288 ✆ heatons@iol.ie
✆ www.heatonsdingle.com)

Kerry

only in Kerry
Blasket Island Lamb

Butcher
● Jerry Kennedy

"Blasket Island lamb sausage with rosemary and garlic".
In just an instant, reading about this sort of award-
winning sausage, you get the measure of Jerry Kennedy's
creativity. Famed in town as the man whose Blasket
Island lamb has no peers – Atlantic pré salé lamb, just
consider it! A friend who picked up some from the
shop called it "the best I've found in the country" – Mr
Kennedy is also a master charcutier, and in addition to
his immaculately presented meats, look out also for local
heroes such as Annascaul black pudding. (Jerry Kennedy,
8 Orchard, Dingle ☎ 066-915 2511 – Open 8am-6pm
Mon-Sat)

● Milltown House

Mark Kerry's house has a fabulous location, hard by the water looking across at Dingle and its harbour. It's a lovely place to stay, and a great refuge should you be in Dingle during the season, for its just-out-of-town location means it is peaceful when Dingle is raucous. The Kerrys are professionals to their fingertips, and they do things well, and they do things right. (Mark, Anne & Tara Kerry, Milltown, Dingle ☎ 066-915 1372 🖃 info@ milltownhousedingle.com 🖰 www.milltownhousedingle. com)

only in Kerry
Murphy's Ice Cream

Ice Cream
● Murphy's Ice Cream

Sean and Kieran Murphy are amongst the major players in modern Irish food, and two of the defining artisans of their time. That they have achieved their status through producing superb ice creams is paradoxical in a country where people used not take ice cream seriously. But the Murphy brothers, via their charm and their utter dedication to excellence, have made the Irish take ice cream very seriously indeed, and their work is magnificent. Everything they make is great, but to show you the nature of this business, we need to look away from the ice cream at two facts of the company. Firstly, Kieran Murphy is the Irish food blogger par excellence, his blog being witty, modest and smart. Secondly, last time the McKenna boys, Sam and PJ, went into the Dingle shop to buy ice cream, they didn't have enough money on them. "No problem", said the lovely lady behind the counter. "Sure, take the cones and when you find your Dad, come back with the difference." Ah! Brilliance, and generosity. There is also a summertime shop in Tig Aine's in Graig, Ballyferriter. (Sean & Kieran Murphy, Milseoga Uí Mhurchú Teo, Sráid na Trá, An Daingean ☎ 066-915 2644 🖃 sean@murphysicecream. ie 🖰 www.murphysicecream.ie – Open 11am-10pm Mon-Sun, closes early evening off season)

Kerry

Restaurant
● Out of the Blue

"Fishy ideas and tastes". That's how Tim Mason describes the work of himself and his crack crew in OOTB. It's an apt phrase, for the cooking in OOTB, whilst always succulent and delicious, does come across as very considered, cerebral, well thought through. So, there is a little counterpoint of tapenade along with the sea bass and lemon butter sauce, there is rosemary with cod, and cream and chives to accent the sweetness of pollock. It's superb cooking, wonderfully invigorating and pleasing, and the room is as great as the wine list, which is one of the great wine lists.(Tim Mason, Waterside, Dingle ☎ 066-915 0811 ⌨ outoftheblue@ireland.com ⌂ www.outoftheblue.ie – Open 12.30pm-3pm, 6.30pm-9.30pm Thu-Tue; noon-3pm, 6pm-8.30pm Sun. Closed Nov-Feb. Open Wed high season)

Pies
● Píog Pies

The Piog Pie Collection has grown, from four mouth-watering (really) pies, to half a dozen Bespoke Beauties, with a shepherd's pie and a free-range chicken pie joining the original quartet of Kerry lamb; beef and Guinness; seafood, and lentil and root vegetable. We are using the language of fashion for Brid and Steven's pies because they are, in truth, couture cooking, every pie fashioned like a one-off piece of design. The savvy sourcing of the best ingredients is completed by the expert care lavished on everything that Piog produces, and we would rate these as highly as any other pie being made today. You will find them at farmer's markets in Dingle, Listowel, Limerick and the summer Castlegregory market, in fish shops in Tralee, Kenmare and Dingle, and do not miss them. (Brid ni Mhathuna & Steven Neiling, Dingle ☎ 087-794 4036 ⌨ sales@piogpies.com ⌂ www.piogpies.com)

Café
● Garden Café

They really enjoy cooking in the GC, and you might find a spinach and Stilton tart as the choice of the day, or maybe Jerry Kennedy's Blasket Island lamb sausages with mash, or even a rabbit stew concocted by chef Ruggero. As well as the food they exhibit local art, sell local crafts and enthusiastically throw their support behind the local

Kerry

festivals. So it's a café as community endeavour as well as for culinary delights. (Green Street, Dingle ✆ www.thegardencafedingle.eu – Open 10am-5pm Mon, Wed-Sat, noon-4pm Sun)

Café
● Goat Street Café

"Slow Food and Fast Service" is a good mantra for any restaurant, and they put it into practice in the Goat Street, sourcing local organic produce and then keeping things simple and respectful with the cooking: vegetarian tagine with couscous, duck confit with poached plums, smoked salmon and feta cheese frittata. There's a good vibe about Laurence and Ed's café, especially the week-end dinners. (Laurence Wetterwald & Ed Mulvihill, Main Street, Dingle ☎ 066-915 2770/086 8264118 ✆ www.thegoatstreetcafe.com – Open 10am-5pm Mon-Sun, 6pm-9pm Thur-Sat)

Restaurant
● Global Village

"Fab food". "Really impressed". That's the sort of feedback happy travellers to Dingle report about the classy finesse of Martin Bealin's cooking in Global Village. The shop-like exterior gives little indication of the seriousness of Martin's cooking, though the white linen tablecloths spell out that the culinary arts are practised here. Of course, the fish cookery is always the primary option, sourced from local boats, but whatever you choose will be graced with both smart, intuitive creativity – Cromane oysters with caramelised shallot and blue cheese ice cream; peppered tuna with tarragon and onion polenta cake – and superb service from the team. "Brilliant", says Caroline Byrne of the Bridgestone parish. (Martin Bealin & Nuala Cassidy, Upper Main Street, Dingle ☎ 066-915 2325/087 917 7700 ✉ admin@globalvillage.com ✆ www.globalvillagedingle.com – Open 5.30pm-10pm Mon-Nov)

Restaurant
● Fish at The Marina

Alex Barr is progressing patiently and organically in Fish at the Marina. After their fifth summer, they now have plans to open in the summer evenings, so get here for the salt and chilli squid, the tuna burger with tomato and olive chutney, local fish and chips, scallop and chorizo salad or simple, luxurious lobster Thermidor. Part of his cooking experience took Alex to Australia and the zingy zesty flavours he learnt whilst Down Under suit the Dingle waterfront just as much as they do the Sydney waterfront. (Alex Barr, Marina Buildings, Dingle ☎ 086-378 8584 – open day time and planning to extend to evenings in 2010. Closed during the winter months)

only in Kerry
Fenit Mussels

Kenmare

Restaurant
● The Breadcrumb

Like many proper bakers Manuela Goeb's ambition with her breads is to offer not just the culture of baking, but the culture of good health. Her German background has gifted her with the knowledge of the importance of bread for health, and she puts that into delicious action six days a week. Recently she has focused increasingly on breads for people suffering from wheat and gluten allergies, but aside from these the rye, the sourdough, the soda and the olive baguettes are outstandingly good and they are matched by sweet specialities which manage to be wholesome as well as wholly indulgent. (Manuela Goeb, O'Shea's House, New Road, Kenmare ☎ 064-664 0645 ⌨ info@thebreadcrumb.com ⌂ www.thebreadcrumb.com – Open 8am-6.30pm Mon-Sat, 8.30am-3pm Sun)

Hotel
● Brook Lane Hotel

"They do things well and they do things right" is how our friend Bernadette summed up Dermot and Una Brennan's boutique hotel on the edge of town. She might have added that they also do things in an understated and unpretentious way, as you would expect from a bunch of real professionals. Happily the bar and restaurant menus include dishes like Irish lamb stew, Kenmare seafood platter, fish pie, and braised Kerry lamb, which means that either the bar food or the restaurant food is always a good choice. (Dermot & Una Brennan, Kenmare ☎ 064-664 2077 ⌨ info@brooklanehotel.com ⌂ www.brooklanehotel.com)

● An Cupan Tae

Dainty. How often do you get the chance to use a word like "dainty" nowadays? But Mary O'Leary's tea room at the easterly end of Kenmare is dainty, and has dainty things to eat – little biteens of scones and sweet cakes and dainty sandwiches – and fine china cups that make the simple business of a cup of tea into an adventure in elegance. Fifteen minutes in here, perusing the 'papers, sipping tae, spreading butter and jam on your scone, is like a day at a spa. Ah. (Mary O'Leary, 26 Henry Street, Kenmare ☎ 064-664 2001 ✉ cupantaekenmare@gmail.com ✆ www.cupantaekenmare.com – Open 9am-6pm Mon-Sun, from 10am-5pm off season. Closed Jan-Mar)

Juice and Coffee Bar
● Fruit and Bean

Fresh juices, fresh coffees and a fresh soup of the day is Vanessa Foley's calling card in F&B. (Vanessa Foley, Henry Street ☎ 064-664 2106 – Open 9.30am-5.30pm Mon-Sun)

B&B
● Hawthorn House

Noel and Mary O'Brien run a nice little B&B just as you come into town from the Glengarriff side. (Noel and Mary O'Brien, Shelbourne St, Kenmare ☎ 064-6641035 ✉ hawthorn@eircom.net ✆ www.hawthornhousekenmare.com)

Bar
● The Horse Shoe Bar

By its flower bedecked exterior shall you know Paul Bevan's pub, and once you get a taste of their good bar food, you will want to know it even better. Horseshoe burger, Horseshoe spare ribs, Horseshoe steak, they aren't rewriting the culinary book, they are just doing things right. (Paul Bevan, 3 Main Street, Kenmare ☎ 064-664 1553 ✆ www.horseshoebarkenmare.com – Open noon-3pm Mon-Fri, 5pm-9.30pm Mon-Sun)

Café
● Jam

He is a power in the town and the county is James Mulchrone, and ever since he opened Jam in 2002, after

Kerry

a spell working as a chef in the town, he has developed slowly and carefully to achieve greater and greater things. All those great things are based on really fine baking, and true to form they have recently upped their game once again with the introduction of a dedicated baking unit. Us, we would walk over the hill from West Cork just for the sausage rolls. (James Mulchrone, 6 Henry Street, Kenmare ☎ 064-664 1591 ✉ info@jam. ie ✍ www.jam.ie – Open Mon-Sat 8am-6pm. Also in Ballyseeds, Tralee ☎ 066-719 2580 and Old Market Lane, Killarney ☎ 064-37716)

Restaurant
● An Leath Phingin Eile

The most atmospheric room in town is now under the capable management of Dermot Brennan, who also runs the Brook Lane Hotel, just outside town. Stone walls, bent wood chairs and crisp white napkins set an unclichéd tone and the food riffs on classic dishes in some very exciting ways, adding coconut and Thai spices to a bouillabaisse, a crab samosa to monkfish, or their own concoction of Irish stew. A fruit jelly and vanilla ice cream dessert was one of the nicest things we ate all year. (Dermot Brennan, 35 Main Street, Kenmare ☎ 064-664 1559 ✉ info@leathphingineile.com ✍ www. leathphingineile.com – Open 6pm-10pm Wed-Mon)

Restaurant
● Mulcahy's

"Dined recently in Bruce Mulcahy's. It is all you say and it is more: he deserves every accolade. Bruce is uncompromising when it comes to quality and presentation, and the food is served to the highest standards". Our friend Billy knows exactly the measure of Bruce Mulcahy's cutting-edge cooking, and the key word here, surely, is "uncompromising", for nothing comes out of this kitchen unless it is perfect, and over the last several years, ever since he trimmed back the fusion elements of his cooking, every dish that has come out of the kitchen in Mulcahy's has been perfect: scallops with tempura of cauliflower; black sole with tomato and brown butter sauce; crispy duck confit with shredded duck leg salad. Perfect service magically brings all this good stuff together. (Bruce Mulcahy, Henry Street, Kenmare ☎ 064-664 2383 – Open 6pm-10pm Mon-Sun, closed Tue & Wed off-season)

● O'Donovan's

You will find locals eating in Gerry Foley's pub enjoying simple food that is well executed and is very good value for money. (Gerry Foley, Henry Street, Kenmare ☎ 064-664 2106 – Food served noon-9pm Mon-Sun, closed Thu off season)

● Packie's

Martin Hallissey's brilliance as a chef is to confect his culinary spell from the simplest of ingredients. Other chefs use up-front flavours and cheffy techniques to impress you, but Mr Hallissey just cooks the ingredients as he finds them and presents them as simply as possible, and the result is, well, spellbinding. His cooking puts us in mind of cucina casalingua – Italian home cooking – in its respect for simplicity and freshness, And from this Mr Hallissey brings forth a profound goodness: not to put too fine a point on it, but eating in Packie's is a balm for the soul, as well as a blessing for the appetite. This is not just thanks to the food, but also to the service – amongst the very best – and the room, which is quite sublime. 24-carat classic. (Martin Hallissey, Henry Street, Kenmare ☎ 064-664 1508 – 6pm-10pm Mon-Sat. Weekends only Nov-Dec. Open one week before Christmas. Closed mid Jan-mid Feb)

● The Pantry

The Pantry is one of the great wholefood shops, a treasure trove of local goodies, and a vital larder for quality wholefoods and essential ingredients. Only smashing. (Hugo Speykebrood, Henry Street, Kenmare ☎ 064-664 2233 ⌨ hugokenmare@eircom.net – Open 9am-6pm Mon-Sat, 11am-3pm Sun)

● The Park Hotel

Francis and John Brennan have been introduced to a television audience via their RTE series *At Your Service* and there is no better duo to advise people in the hospitality industry on how to get it right than this, justly famous, band of brothers. When people talk about the high culinary standards of a town like Kenmare, what they mean is that for the last few decades practitioners such as the Brennan brothers fashioned world-class standards of hotel keeping and have maintained those standards with fastidious attention to detail. Whilst The Park is as world famous as Cork's Ballymaloe House, it shares with that iconic destination a fundamental modesty: yes it is grand, but there is a very humble sense of service underpinning every part of the team's work. (John & Francis Brennan, Kenmare ☎ 064-664 1200 ✉ info@parkkenmare.com 🖰 www.parkkenmare.com)

Wine Importer
● Mary Pawle Wines

The pioneer specialist importer of organic wines continues to unearth fabulous new discoveries from organic European and Southern Hemisphere winemakers. If there is a signature to the wines Mary chooses to bring into Ireland it is that she likes a refinement of texture allied to a core sweetness. Both of which are evident in particular in her Italian and Spanish wines. You will find Mary Pawle Wines in many of the best wholefood shops throughout the country. (Mary Pawle, Gortamullen, Kenmare ☎ 064-664 1443 🖰 www.marypawlewines.com)

Gastro Bar
● The Purple Heather

Grainne O'Connell has been working wonders in the sublime Purple Heather since 1975. Back in those days, most Irish pub cooking consisted of ham sandwiches and Nescafé, but the O'Connell family have always been different, and like the Allen family of Ballymaloe they have always done their own thing, and always done it superbly. In the PH you will enjoy proper, home-made, hand-made food, from soups to puds, and it will put a smile on your face as surely as your head and your heart will be saying that maybe there is time for a second pint? or another glass of wine? and sure what's the rush? Can't we linger in this tabernacle of a room just a little longer? We can? Good. (Grainne O'Connell, Henry Street, Kenmare ☎ 064-664 1016 ✉ oconnellgrainne@eircom.net – Open 11am-7pm Mon-Sat)

Guesthouse
● Shelburne Lodge

When you talk about Maura and Tom Foley's contribution to Kerry tourism you have to think in a different and hugely elongated time frame. Tom and

Maura are heading towards fifty years of world-class service in Kenmare. The beech tree in the garden of Shelbourne Lodge has been there for two centuries and the pine trees are just fifty years behind them. Just as timeless is their superlative understanding of the arts of hospitality and cooking and their devotion to their calling. Shelburne Lodge is one of the nicest places to stay in Ireland. (Maura & Tom Foley, Killowen, Kenmare ☎ 064-664 1013 ✉ shelburnekenmare@eircom.net ⌂ www.shelburnelodge.com – Open Mar-mid Dec)

Traiteur
● **Truffle Pig Fine Foods**

Andrew and Lindsey Hill's excellent traiteur has moved into the centre of Kenmare, which is where it belongs, along with the other icon addresses of the food lovers' capital. It's a vital address for good foods to go of every hue and cry, all served with a charming smile. (Andrew & Lindsey Hill, Henry Street, Kenmare ☎ 064-664 2953 ✉ aghill1@msn.com – Open 9.30am-6pm Mon-Sat)

Wine Shop
● **Vanilla Grape**

We had such a great chat and such a fun time on our last visit to Alain Bras' wine and card shop. M. Bras talks about his wines as some folk talk about their children – fondly, knowledgeably, patiently – and it was great craic to put together a case of his suggestions, and even more fun to enjoy them back at home. He has sourced quixotic, quirky, personality-led wines from all over the globe, and that's no surprise, really, for he's a pretty quixotic, quirky, personality-led bloke himself. Vanilla Grape is just the sort of wine shop a town like Kenmare needs and demands. (Alain Bras & Christine Arthur, 12 Henry Street, Kenmare ☎ 064-664 0694 ✉ vanillagrape@eircom.net ⌂ www.alainbras.com – Open 8.30am-6pm Mon-Sat)

Chipper
● **Wharton's**

Wharton's is traditional inside and out, with a traditional stone façade and old pine tables, and then legendary traditional fish and chips inside. Kenmare natives, despite years of familiarity with the chipper, talk about it in proud and reverential and possessive tones. (Main Street, Kenmare, ☎ 064-664 2622 ✉ info@whartonskenmare.com)

Killarney

● Arbutus Hotel

The Arbutus is a modest, old-style hotel, and we like
it. It has the right feel for a centre-of-town destination,
the same sort of ageless feel you get in Courtney's tea
rooms just up the street, and if it doesn't have the mega-
specification of some of Killarney's other destinations, it
is still a lovely, cosy, family-run hotel. They cook dishes
like chicken Florentine, and duck with herb stuffing
and orange glaze, and salmon with lemon butter sauce,
and it is just what we want. No fashion, just hospitality
and nice food. (Seán & Carol Buckley, College Street,
Killarney ☎ 064-310 37 ✉ stay@arbutuskillarney.com
🖰 www.arbutuskillarney.com)

only in Kerry
Miss Courtney's Tearooms

Restaurant
● Bricin

They do "traditional" food upstairs at Bricin, so you
can enjoy boxty with chicken and tarragon, or seafood
chowder or Kerry lamb with rosemary, and just as the
cooking is a welcome counterpoint to the prevailing
modernism, so the cloistered style of the dining rooms
is pleasingly old fashioned. (Paddy & Johnny McGuire, 26
High St, Killarney ☎ 064-663 4902 ✉ bricin@eircom.
net 🖰 www.bricin.com – Open 12.30pm-3pm, 6pm-9pm
Tue-Sat)

Restaurant
● Cellar One Restaurant

The cooking in the basement restaurant of The Ross
Hotel is as funky and fashionable as the design: Skegh-
anore duck wontons; boudin of Clonakilty black pudding; cajun-spiced calamari; fillet of salmon with red
pepper risotto. It may be fashionable, but it is correctly
done and service is friendly and apt. (Padraig & Janet
Treacy, Town Centre, Killarney ☎ 064-663 1855 🖰 www.
theross.ie – Open for breakfast, 7.30am-10am, and dinner, 6.30pm-9.30pm Mon-Sun)

Tea Rooms
● Miss Courtney's

Four generations of women have run Miss Courtney's,
ever since they opened their doors in 1909, a century
of service to the town. Today, the gleam in this room
makes you smile from the second you walk through
the door – only the Killarney Park Hotel rivals Courtney's for housekeeping – and the ambience and setting
of Sandra Dunlea's tearooms is ageless and graceful.
When Sam and PJ McKenna sat down here one Saturday morning, they quickly proclaimed it one of their
favourite places, and that before they had even eaten
a smoked salmon sandwich or a cup cake. After our
friend Françoise had been, she told a Killarney boat man
the next day that they had enjoyed the vegetable soup
and the chicken sandwich and the tea, and he replied:
"Ah sure, I remember it well. My mother used to bring
me there when I was a boy and they had lovely éclairs
there." See: a visit to Miss Courtney's is a memory
for ever. (Sandra Dunlea, 8 College Street, Killarney
☎ 087- 610 9500 📖info@misscourtneys.com, 🖰 www.
misscourtneys.com – Open 10am-6pm Mon-Sat

Restaurant
● The Europe Hotel

You are swimming in the outdoor part of the Europe's
amazing swimming pool, looking down at the lakes,
and above them the tops of the mountains are dusted
with snow. Phew! Is this a dream? No, it's just Easter
in Killarney, and it's pretty mind-boggling, actually. The
Europe Hotel has been here for aeons, but a massive refurbishment over recent years has seen this icon address
step into the new century with aplomb. Nowhere else
rivals the Europe in terms of the pool and the spa, but
the other elements of the hotel are working smoothly
also, in particular the cooking, which has always been
good but which has, in tandem with the hotel's refit,
stepped up a gear or two. We liked the way in which
they are so relaxed about cooking for children in the
Brasserie, and how the food is unpretentious. Incidentally, John McKenna once gave a talk in The Europe, at
a potato conference. His title: "Making Potatoes Sexy".
The McKenna children, needless to say, were mortified.
They have since recovered. (Michael Brennan, Fossa,
Killarney ☎ 064-667 1300 📖 reservations@theeurope.
com 🖰 www.theeurope.com)

Kerry

Restaurant
● Gaby's

Geert Mais is a fine cook who works in the European classical tradition, a tradition of cooking which is nowadays relatively hard to find. His food is precise, correct and formal; he isn't afraid to use booze and cream and he doesn't waste time and energy on silly reductions and squirt sauces and other signatures of modern, clueless cooking. So, you come to Gaby's for rich food, in particular the chef's special lobster dish, or the prawns with tagliatelle, or some sole meunière, with a glass or two of Chablis, of course. You can call it bourgeois, but we just call it classy. Nice atmospheric rooms. (Geert & Marie Mais, 27 High Street, Killarney ☎ 064-663 2519 ᐱ www. gabysireland.com – Open 6pm-10pm Mon-Sat)

Butcher
● The German Butcher

We wouldn't dream of a visit to Killarney without calling in to Armin Weise's shop to get the best German-style sausages you can buy in Ireland, along with excellent meats, and a nice cup of coffee to sip whilst we gather our thoughts and relax. So, will we get some kassler as well? Ah, we will. (Armin Weise, Aghadoe, Killarney ☎ 064-663 3069 ᐱ info@germanbutchershop.com ᐱ www.germanbutchershop.com – Open 8am-6pm Mon-Fri, 8am-4.30pm Sat)

Café
● Jam

The Killarney destination of James Mulchrone's Kenmare deli, bakery and café room is serviced by the same kitchen so standards and consistency are only excellent. Jam has been operating in Killarney since 2002 now, and you don't stay in business that long unless you know how to do the good thing, each day, every day. That's what they do here. (James Mulchrone, 77 High Street, Killarney ☎ 064-663 1441 ᐱ info@jam.ie ᐱ www.jam. ie – Open 8am-5pm Mon-Sat)

● Killarney Park Hotel

Padraig and Janet Treacy own two other hotels in Killarney, with the boutique The Ross and the grand The Malton, along with the Killarney Park. Each is different, and each will have its own admirers, but for us the all-round excellence of the KP just shades it. This is, we think, one of the jewels of Irish hospitality. Why? Because every element of running an hotel, from housekeeping to cooking to the spa, is practiced as an attempt at perfection. They don't just want to be the best they can be: they want to be the best. And so, from the food in the bar to the style of the rooms, the KP is a masterpiece of the art of hospitality. (Padraig & Janet Treacy, Kenmare Place, Killarney ☎ 064-663 5555 ⏱ www.killarneyparkhotel.ie)

Bar
● The Lane Café Bar

A glam spot for some good daytime food. (Padraig & Janet Treacy, The Ross, Town Centre, Killarney ☎ 064-663 1855 ✉ info@theross.ie ⏱ www.theross.ie – Open 11am-9pm)

Hotel
● The Malton

Padraig Treacy's third hotel used to be the venerable Great Southern Hotel, but as soon as he took over Mr Treacy began to establish the style and service signatures that have made him Killarney's leading hotelier. The McKenna family enjoyed a fine dinner here on our last visit, in the Garden Restaurant, and whilst sweeping changes have been successfully made, the scale of The Malton means that this will be an exciting work-in-progress for a little while longer. (Padraig Treacy, Killarney ☎ 064-663 8000 ⏱ www.themalton.com)

Ice Cream Parlour
● Murphy's Ice Cream

The Killarney outcrop of the Murphy brothers' mighty empire of ice cream. Everything they do is done in the very best way that they can do it. (Séan & Kieran Murphy, 37 Main Street, Killarney ☎ 066-915 2644 ✉ sean@ murphysicecream.ie ⏱ www.murphysicecream.ie – Open 11am-10pm Mon-Sun, closes early evening off season)

Kerry

● **The Ross**

Cool School meets Old School in The Ross. The Cool
is the design, which is freakily wonderful and successful.
The Old is the standard of service in the hotel and the
Cellar Restaurant and the Lane Café Bar, service that
is rooted in traditional values of hospitality, discretion
and charm. It's a wonderful mix of values, and one that
very few manage to pull off successfully. (Padraig & Janet
Treacy, The Ross, Killarney ☎ 064-663 1855 ✉ info@
theross.ie 🖰 www.theross.ie)

Fishmonger
● **Spillane's Seafood**

Nowadays this long-established fish institution is first
and foremost a fish processing and wholesaling enterprise, but regulars know that if you turn up at their shop
in the factory there will be probably 50 or 60 different
species of fish on offer, all of it as fresh as they would
expect, and good value. (Paudie Spillane, Lackavan,
Killarney ☎ 064-663 1320 – Open 9am-6pm Mon-Fri
(closed for lunch), 9am-1pm Sat)

Killorglin

Restaurant
● **Giovanelli's**

We like the fact that Daniele prepares five starters and
five main courses for his little Italian eating house and
deli, and we like the Italian specialities which he sources
and sells over the deli counter. There's plenty to like in
this archetypal and unpretentious slice of Italy. (Daniele
Giovanelli, Lower Bridge Street, Killorglin ☎ 066-
979 6640 – Open lunch 12.30pm, dinner 7pm-9pm Tue-Sat)

Deli and Bakery
● **Jack's**

"Lovely place!" was how our friend Barbara summarised
Jack and Celine Healy's bakery and deli in pretty Killorglin. "Bought bread and cheese: excellent". Barbara didn't
say if the bread was one of Jack's traditional Irish loaves
– a nice chewy batch loaf, maybe, or some crumbly,
warm brown soda – or whether they bought one of his
newer styles like San Francisco sourdough to go with

Kerry

the excellent farmhouse cheeses minded in the deli by
Celine. Whatever it was, however, we can assure you
that it was good, for this is a great bakery, and a great
shop, and it's a delight to visit Jack's. (Celine & Jack
Healy, Lower Bridge Street, Killorglin ☎ 066-976 1132 –
Open 8am-7pm Mon-Sat, 8am-5pm Sun)

Restaurant
● Nick's Restaurant

Nick and Anne Foley's legendary restaurant is a staple of
Kerry hospitality, thanks to generous, flavourful cooking
that revolves around classic dishes, and warm, maternal
service that you can never tire of. (Nick & Anne Foley,
Lwr Bridge St, Killorglin ☎ 066-976 1219 – Open 5pm-
10.30pm Tue-Sun)

Restaurant
● Sol y Sombra

Clíodhna Foley first performed a magnificent act of
renovation and restoration to bring Killorglin's old
Church of Ireland back to life as a place in which to
house her wine and tapas bar. Then she completed the
circle of success by establishing a focal hub for the town
based around great food and great wines, in the process
echoing the work of her parents, Nick and Anne, whose
Nick's Restaurant is one of the pillars of the town.
There are lovely dishes here – piquillo filled with black
pudding; grilled baby squid with garlic; cod and bechamel
croquettes – and the wines are a class act: just have a glass
of that Mantel Blanco Verdejo Sauvignon with some potato
tortilla or a cazuela of prawns and we guarantee you that
you won't stop at a single glass. Fab. (Clíodhna Foley, The
Old Church of Ireland, Killorglin ☎ 066-976 2357 ⌐ www.
solysombra.ie – Bar open 5pm, Food served 6pm-10.30pm)

Farmhouse Cheese
● Wilma's Killorglin Farmhouse Cheese

Wilma O'Connor's gouda-style cheese doesn't make
it far beyond the Kingdom of Kerry, which is a pity
because this expertly crafted cheese deserves a much
bigger reputation than it currently enjoys. The mature
cheese in particular showcases the raw milk of their own
Fresian herd in a palette of sweet perfection. You can
buy the cheese direct from the farm, which is just off the
Caragh Lake road. (Wilma O'Connor, Ardmoniel, Killorglin ☎ 066-976 1402 ⌐ killorglincheese@eircom.net)

Listowel

Bistro & Accommodation
● Allo's

Armel Whyte's beautiful pub and bistro has been one of the most distinctive Kerry addresses for many years now, yet every time you walk into this sublime bar it feels fresh as a daisy, endlessly renewed, and the cookery has a youthfulness and vigour that make it always appealing. There are also very good rooms available upstairs for those wanting to get to know lovely Listowel better. (Armel Whyte, 41 Church Street, Listowel ☎ 068-22880 – Open pub hours, food served noon-9pm Tue-Sat)

Farmhouse Cheese
● Béal Lodge Dairy Farm

Kate Carmody's organic farm is a proper farm, a place where organic milk makes organic cheese, where rare-breed pigs roam, chickens cluck (and hopefully lay eggs!), and lambs chew the grass and the weeds. But it is the Wensleydale and Cheddar-style cheeses Kate makes that are the true stars of the show, and they just ooze star-quality milk, and the skill of a cheesemakers, who, in our opinion, has simply gotten better and better ever since the farm converted to organic status a dozen years ago. Wonderful. (Kate Carmody, Asdee, Listowel ☎ 068-41137 ✉ cait@eircom.net ⌂ www.kerryorganics.ie)

Deli
● John R's

Pierce Walsh really chose well when it came to stocking his refurbished bakery and deli on Church Street. Aside from Kate Carmody's brilliant local cheeses, the rest of the selection is sourced from Sheridan's. Wines come from Italian winemaster Enrico Fantasia's Grape Circus and other top-notch wineheads. And the foods that three generations of the family have been making – their baked hams, the soda breads, the rhubarb tarts – are proudly present and as distinguished as ever and their wooden crated hampers are crammed with good things. A great renewal, so bring on the next generation! (Pierce Walsh, 70 Church Street, Listowel ☎ 068-21249 ✉ pwalsh@johnrs.com ⌂ www.johnrs.com)

Farmhouse Cheese
● Kerry Farmhouse Cheese

It is apt that every year's cheesemakers bring their cheeses to the Listowel Food festival in the hope of winning the Sheila Broderick Memorial Cheese Competition. Mrs Broderick was a pioneer cheesemaker, and today her daughter, Eilish, continues this distinguished family tradition of hand-crafting excellent territorial-style cheeses. (Eilish Broderick, Coolnaleen, Listowel ☎ 068-40245 🖂 kerrycheese@netscape.net)

Farmers' Market
● Listowel Farmers' Market

Friday morning is the time to be here for the good stuff. (Fridays 10am-1pm 🖱 www.listowelfoodfair.com)

Milltown

Market
● Milltown Organic Market

What a lovely Saturday morning the McKenna boys had on their last visit to Milltown, the sort of lazy meander around this beautiful old church, unearthing one beautiful local food after another, that finally provokes the McKenna children to say "Dad, do you have to talk to absolutely everyone!". But, of course, John McKenna has to do pretty much just that, as he gossips away with Sarah Caridia of the brilliant Callinafercy Organics – check out that Angus beef and Kerry lamb, and do think about that Xmas turkey from Sarah if you want something special. Lorna is here from The Phoenix, Manuela from The Breadcrumb, there is paella cooking – has that been adopted as a Kerry dish? – and aside from the locals, the shelves are packed with good organic things, like the peerless produce of Philip Dreaper. This is one of the loveliest shopping experiences in all of Ireland. (Mary O'Riordan, Milltown Organic Store, Old Church, Milltown ☎ 066-976 7869 – Open Saturdays 10am-2pm)

Kerry

only in Kerry
Dingle Pies

● Milltown Organic Store

Aside from the fabulous Saturday market, the Milltown store is a great shop at any time of the week. (Old Church, Milltown ☎ 066-976 7869 ✉ info@milltownorganicstore.com 🖱 www. milltownorganicmarket.com – Open 10am-6pm Mon-Fri, 10am-2pm Sat)

Portmagee

Bar, Restaurant & Guesthouse
● The Moorings @ The Bridge Bar

There is a lot going on in Portmagee these days. Not only are Gerard and Patricia Kennedy continuing their distinctive, individualistic ways with seafood cookery in their restaurant, keeping up with their hospitable inn-keeping in the bar, and generously providing comfortable bedrooms for the happy and sated traveller. This would be more than enough for most folk, but an intriguing new string has been added to the Kennedy family bow, as Kevin Kennedy has begun to import Japanese Koyu matcha tea, the green powder tea that is one of the cornerstones of not just Japanese tea culture, but Japanese food culture. Look up Kevin's site – 🖱 www. koyumatcha.com – for details on how to access this tea powerhouse. On a more local note, anytime you are in Portmagee, then Kennedy's is your only man, not simply a piece of quintessential Kerry hospitality and generosity, but a stylish, classy destination. (Patricia & Gerard Kennedy, Portmagee ☎ 066-947 7108 ✉ moorings@iol.ie 🖱 www.moorings.ie – Restaurant open 6pm-10pm, Bar open noon-9pm. Restaurant closes Oct-Mar, bar open all year)

Sneem

Butcher
● PJ Burns

Annascaul pudding may garner more attention as the quintessential Kerry-style, cake-style black pudding these days, but the little butcher's shop that is PJ Burns has been making this unique Kerry food for decades, and so the shop is a must visit! They mix pinhead oatmeal with sheep fat, onions, spices and whatnot and then bake the pudding in a large tray. When it's ready, they slice your piece straight from the baking tray, and your breakfast or dinner is set. If you are heading to Sneem but miss the shop, just knock on the door and someone will sell you whatever you need. Smashing. (Kieran & Anne Burns, Sneem ☎ 064-664 5139 📖 sneemblackpudding@hotmail.com – Open 9am-7pm Mon-Sat)

Farmhouse Cheese
● Dereenaclaurig Farmhouse Cheese

There are a few farmhouse cheeses in Ireland that are purely local cheeses – one thinks of Carrowholly in Mayo, or the much-missed Carraig in West Cork – and Harry van der Zanden's Dereenaclaurig is one of those lactic sports of nature. At the height of summer Harry makes about twenty pounds of cheese a day from the milk of his cows, flavours some with cumin, some with garlic, and leaves some sweet and plain. Some cheeses are held for up to a year, but after most of the little truckles have reached four months, Harry will sell them at local markets around the Ring of Kerry. It's what every dairy farmer should be doing, of course, but so few of them actually do it. Thank heavens that Harry does, for the Dereenaclaurig cheeses are only wonderful, and their scarcity makes them even more precious. (Harry van der Zanden, Derreenaclaurig, Sneem ☎ 064-664 5330)

Kerry

Tralee

Bar & Restaurant
● Duinin Seafoods

Paddy O'Mahony knows fish, and, listening to his lyrical Kerry tones, one senses an epicurean gourmet at the heart of all his many business endeavours. The O'Mahony's shop in Market Place in Tralee has sold fish for the last 22 years and Paddy O'Mahony is positive about the fish he can sell. "Fish is handled better now. Irish fishermen today know more about handling than they ever used to. So even though we used to be able to buy from day boats, where the fish was only a couple of hours out of the water, but now they have to travel hours to get the fish, they cool it down immediately it is caught – it's handled properly on the boat. The first couple of hours after a fish is caught is the most important. And if it's handled well then it keeps fresh." (Paddy O'Mahony, Market Place, Tralee ☎ 066-712 1026 – Open 9am-6pm Mon-Fri)

Shop
● Kingdom Food & Wine

Local heroes like Piog Pies, or West Cork heroes such as Glenilen dairy products, are just some of the choice things that navigate their way to Maeve Duff's fine deli and wine shop, a lovely space that is crammed choc-a-bloc with fine foods. They have a very busy sandwich and food-to-go offer, and whatever deli or cookery product you could imagine or desire will be found in here, making it Tralee's one-stop-solution-shop. (Maeve Duff, Oakpark, Tralee ☎ 066-711 8562 🖰 www. kingdomstore.ie – Open from 8am-7pm Mon-Sat)

Butcher's shop
● Aaron O'Connell

Aaron O'Connell has won the white pudding award in the annual Craft Butchers competition not once, but twice. Consecutively. That says all you need to know about the competitiveness and creativity of this excellent butcher, who also tends to take home medals for both his sausages and his black puddings, and who notably took the most recent award for his drisheen, that crème de le crème of boudins. (Aaron O'Connell, 22 Upper Castle Street, Tralee ☎ 066-712 6661)

Restaurant
● Val's Bar & Bistro

Renowned Kerry chef David Norris has taken the culinary helm at this well-loved Tralee restaurant, uniting Tralee's best chef in what is probably Tralee's most atmospheric restaurant. His back-to-basics menu puts a strong emphasis on local ingredients: the best Kerry beef, the best Fenit mussels, the best vegetarian food. Under the control of owners Bobby and Seamus O'Halloran, Val's has been doing things properly for the last fifteen years (they even employ a mixologist to blend their cocktails) so this uniting of good cooking and good style is a very positive step for Tralee. (Bobby & Seamus O'Halloran, David Norris, Bridge Street, Tralee 066-712 1559 – Food served 5.30pm-10pm Wed-Sat)

Valentia

Café
● The Lighthouse Café

If you go into Danny O'Brien's photoblog – www.
porchfield.com – and scroll back to June 2009, you
will see the most amazing shot of Paul and Paula Duff's
Lighthouse Café on Valentia Island. Just down from the
lighthouse, and with a yacht dissecting the bay in full sail,
it's an incredible portrait. "Don't go to Valentia without
dropping in. The food is organic and salivating!!" writes
Danny, and indeed that is just what Paul and Paula do.
She makes the chowders and stews and the baking, he
looks after the garden and its produce and sorts out the
fish they will cook. That's how you do it, and that's how
the Duffs have done it since taking over this simple space
in 2005. (Paula & Paul Duff, Dohilla, Valentia ☎ 066-
947 6304 ⌂ www.thelighthousecafe.ie – Open Mon-Fri
noon-6pm, Sat noon-10pm, Sun noon-6pm)

Ice Cream
● Valentia Island Farmhouse Ice Cream

"We face south; it's good grass, it's good land. Happy,
healthy cows produce happy, healthy milk." That's how
Joe Daly explained the modus operandi of Valentia
Island farmhouse ice cream to *The Irish Times*, and it's
pretty much all you want to hear from a farmhouse ice
cream maker. They produce a rake of flavours – white
chocolate; hazelnut and pistachio; Madagascan vanilla –
and they relish the challenge of being asked to make any
manner of flavoured ice or sorbet. The very best way
to enjoy the ices, of course, is to make your way to the
tiny shop they have established in an old parlour of the
farm on Valentia, buy up a few Calum's Cups or Tetra
Pods, and sit on the wall while the view wipes your eye
with its magnificence. An ice cream world less ordinary.
(Joe & Caroline Daly, Kilbeg, Valentia Island ☎ 066-
947 6864 ✉ valentiaicecream@eircom.net ⌂ www.
valentiaicecream.com – Icecream Parlour open 11am-
7pm Mon-Sun. Closed 1 Sept-31st May)

Kerry

County Kildare

Athy

Farmers' Market
● **Athy Farmers' Market**

The Athy market is home to terrific foods of every hue and cry, and also to some very interesting crafts, so you can buy a willow basket in which to bring home your fresh fish, your freshly-baked bread, delicious dry-cured bacon, zingingly fresh Moyleabbey organics, hearty Gallic Kitchen pies, delicious Castlefarm relishes and vegetables, and whatever your tummy desires. And, then, maybe a little stroll along the Grand Canal, before you head home to start the dinner with that lovely palette of good things to inspire you. (Emily Square, Athy – Open 10am-3pm Sunday)

Organic Farmshop
● **Castlefarm Shop**

Welcome to the most important couple in contemporary Irish agriculture. Jenny and Peter Young are not just farmers, they are revolutionary farmers. In Castlefarm they have a created a mixed-use organic farm, with a superlative farm shop, and they have recently created a series of allotments. They make cheese with the milk of their herd of Friesians and Jersey-cross cows. They have planted an orchard. They keep bees. They orchestrate tours and farm walks. Each week we receive a newsletter telling us what is going on, what is new, what new foods they have produced to sell in the shop, what event they have organised for the local community, what festival or jamboree they are working at or supporting. In short: they communicate, a skill that virtually every other Irish farm has lost. They practice farming as farming is meant to be practised, and we are in awe of what they have achieved in just a few short years. So, make a pilgrimage to the shop, rent an allotment, bring the kids for a tour, and see the Culture of Agriculture at work. Simply outstanding. (Jenny & Peter Young, Castlefarm, Narraghmore, Athy ☎ 087-678 5269 ✍ jenny@castlefarmshop.ie ⌂ www. castlefarmshop.ie)

Kildare

Ballymore Eustace

Restaurant & Gastropub
● Ballymore Inn

"Welcome to the homepage of The Ballymore Inn. We're glad you're here. We look forward to sharing our passion for great food with you next time you're in town." The O'Sullivan family's hospitality extends even beyond the handsome walls of the ground-breaking Ballymore Inn and into cyberspace, for they welcome you to their website with the same unabashed relish as they welcome you to their restaurant and bar. Georgina O'Sullivan is, for us, one of the great cooks, her work having the same stubborn quality as Myrtle Allen and the same flourish as Bernadette O'Shea. She works the great canon of ingredients and Irish cooking history, but everything is rewritten according to her aesthetic: Duncannon smoked salmon with red grapefruit; Mc-Geough's Connemara ham with roasted tomatoes and Caesar dressing; McCormack farm salad leaves with avocado, orange and spiced pecans; Slaney lamb with harissa dressing; West Cork sirloin with smoked paprika and garlic dressing. This is astonishing food, but in a quiet way, not a flash way, and the Ballymore Inn is one of Ireland's greatest culinary destinations. (Georgina & Barry O'Sullivan, Ballymore Eustace ☎ 045-864 585 📬 osullivan@ballymoreinn.com 🖰 www.ballymoreinn. com – Open 12.30pm-9pm Mon-Sun)

only in Kildare
Jane Russell's Black Pudding

Kildare

Ballysax

Organic Chicken
● Ballysax Organic Chicken

Margaret McDonnell and her husband, Jim, are the pioneers of organic chicken production in Kildare, though it's lovely to see that they have been joined by the free-range Hubbard birds of Carbury chickens, which kind of makes Kildare the quality chicken capital of Ireland right now. Margaret's birds are simply beautiful, a joy for the cook for they behave properly in the oven, a joy for the carver as the meat is dense and muscular, a joy for the eater who gets tactile, sexy chicken for dinner. The birds are available from the farm, and the last one we bought, from the Castlefarm shop, and cooked, was one of the finest chickens we have ever eaten. (Margaret & Jim McDonnell, Martinstown Rd, Ballysax, The Curragh ☎ 045-442 4735 ✆ magmcdonnell@eircom.net)

Carbury

Chickens
● Sandra Higgins' Carbury Chickens

Sandra Higgins runs a free-range chicken farm with her Dad, in Carbury, where she farms Hubbard chickens and, a local food lover writes "They are as good as any we have tasted. They are quite big and have proper strong legs with the great treat being all the meat in and around the carcass that the carver gets to have when no-one's looking!" Sandra supplies quite a few local Kildare restaurants – including the K Club where the chef happens to be Finbar Higgins, who is indeed married to Sandra – and also sells from her farmgate for a very modest ten euro per bird. This is a brilliant new venture that is moving quickly in the right direction. (Sandra Higgins & Eddie McKeon, Carbury Chickens, Rathmore, Carbury ☎ 087-663 9008)

Farm Shop
● Deirdre and Norman O'Sullivan

Kildare's irrepressible organic farmers are mainstays of the Dublin Organic Food Co-Op, and have been bringing great food to the people of the capital for yonks, after establishing themselves here in Carbury on fourteen acres in 1990. Their produce is simply beautiful: beautiful to behold, beautiful to cook with, beautiful to eat, and oftentimes it seems that you are also mainlining the goodness and optimism of this pair as you enjoy the fruits of their labours. Their farm has vegetables, hens' eggs, honey bees and a farm shop, and they also sell in Trim at the market on Fridays. From a beautiful farm comes beautiful, healthful food. "You have to learn to communicate with the nature spirits, seek their help and come to an agreement with them", Deirdre told the great grower and writer, Cait Curran. "And you have to be grateful for their help. Because I feel that my

Kildare

intention and energy is good, I will be sustained for as long as I need and I feel that my future is secure". That, ladies and gentlemen, is nothing less than the Prayer of Agriculture. (Deirdre & Norman O'Sullivan, Carbury ☎ 046-955 3337 ✉ organicveg@eircom.net – Shop open Friday afternoon)

Castledermot

Café
● Mad Hatter Café

Alice Cope's baking is attracting lots of attention in little Castledermot. Her cupcakes have Eat Me! written all over them, whilst the coffees have serious Drink Me! appeal. The wraps are named after Wonderland characters and are the stuff of legend, precision-cooked, lightly-toasted and whizz-bang wonderful. (Alice Cope, Unit 1, Keenan's Lane, Castledermot – Open 9am-6pm Mon-Sat, 10am-4pm Sun)

Clane

Café
● Zest Café

Mark Condron and his crew are cool cats, and they have been doing good stuff just off the main strip of Clane for years now. The food hits all the modern pleasure points – Zest burger with Cashel Blue; chicken with wild mushroom and chorizo cream; Caesar salad; salmon with lime and coriander cream – and it's the cooking of people who like to cook, so the food has that edge of creativity, rather than the ghost of cliché. The room is simply lovely, and this is a textbook modern café and restaurant that is dedicated to service. (Mark Condron & Alan O'Regan, Unit 6/7, Clane Shopping Centre, Clane ☎ 045-893 222 ✉ info@zestcafeandrestaurant. ie ⌂ www.zestcafeandrestaurant.ie – Open 8.30am-4.30pm, 5.45pm-10pm Mon-Sat, 1pm-9pm Sun)

Kildare

Kilcock

Organic Pie Maker
● Morrin O'Rourke Farm Foods

Harry Morrin O'Rourke has the right pedigree to be a great pie maker, for he is the son of Mary Morrin whose superb baking was a feature of the *Bridgestone Guides* for many years. Well, Harry has restarted the Morrin O'Rourke pie business, and last time we were in Dublin we bought an organic beef and cider pie in Donnybrook Fair. It was mega! and left us wanting a taste of the lamb and cumin pie, the pear and caramelised red onion and goat's cheese tart, and the chicken and ham pie. Organic produce comes from local superstars such as Deirdre O'Sullivan and Margaret McDonnell, and the skill in the baking pays due and proper respect to these superlative organic ingredients. Look out for Harry at Temple Bar Market and snap up the pies in good delis, like Donnybrook Fair and Fallon & Byrne. Superb. (Harry Morrin O'Rourke, Belgard, Kilcock ☎ 01-628 4411/086 320 8940 ✆ morrinoh@yahoo.ie ✆ www.morrinorourkefarmfoods.com)

Kilcullen

Cafe
● Fallon's Bar & Cafe

It's in the evening time when Fallon's, a handsome stonecut room in Kilcullen, really comes into its own, with no-nonsense deliciousness fired out in dishes such as Ted Browne's crispy prawns with sweet chilli and lime dressing, or Sandra Higgin's Hubbard chicken with herb stuffing and a carrot and parsnip purée, or a really fine dry-aged sirloin with fries and bearnaise. The daytime cooking isn't as punchy or daring as it has to try to balance the kitchen's bravado with a conservative clientele, so to get the best of Fallon's make it an evening trip and then revel in some up-front, zinging food. (Brian Fallon, Main Street, Kilcullen ☎ 045-484681/086-2079958 ✆ www.fallonb.ie – Open 12.30pm-11pm Mon-Sun)

Restaurant
● The Riverside Restaurant

Literally on a riverside boardwalk, and tempting you to eat al fresco, The Riverside is a hip operation offering modern cooking consciously supplied by producers who work within a ten km radius: James's beef, Margaret's chickens, Nicolas's organic vegetables and Jenny's cheese. This is a great place to go on a Saturday night and order prawn cocktail and then steak, and then go again in the week and order blackened organic

Kildare

salmon, or mussels in Thai red curry sauce. Note: in the adjacent building they also have The Italian Kitchen @ the Riverside, where simple Italian dishes are served authentically and with great value. (Peter Dunlea, Kilcullen ☎ 045-482966 ✉ info@theriverside. ie ⁀ www.theriverside.ie – Open 5pm-10pm Mon-Fri, 10am-10pm Sat & Sun)

Butcher
● **Nolan's**

James Nolan is one of the greatest Irish butchers, and he runs one of the greatest Irish butcher's shops. Year after year his charcuterie products win awards, day after day droves of happy customers leave Nolan's with produce that will make their mealtimes happy events, after having enjoyed a retail experience that is always a happy event, for Mr Nolan's staff are so switched on it's almost not true. In many respects, Nolan's is the classic example of the modern Irish butcher, a place where high standards of service meet high standards of creativity, working with superb natural ingredients. Bring lots of shopping bags for all you will buy to take home. (James Nolan, Main Street, Kilcullen ☎ 045-481 229 ⁀ http:// nolansofkilcullen.tripod.com – Open 8am-6pm Mon-Sat)

only in Kildare
Ballysax Organic Chickens

Sausages
● **Jane Russell's Original Irish Sausages**

As we write, Jane Russell is launching a brand new black pudding, the latest addition to her fantastic range of speciality sausages and dry-cured bacon. Ms Russell is one of those producers who never sits still, and it always comes as a shock to realise that she only started her company in 2004. Who else has acquired such a profile in five short years, but that profile has been built on hard work and creative ingenuity, driven by a relentless perfectionism that allies with a hungry epicurianism. Splendid. (Jane Russell, Link Business Park, Kilcullen ☎ 045-480100 ✉ jane@straightsausages.com ⁀ www. straightsausages.com)

Kildare

● L'Officina

Kildare Village seems to us to be nonsensical – it has no logical reason to exist – but the logic the centre so conspicuously lacks is made up for, in spades, by L'Officina. Excellent Italian foods are cooked with passionate care by a truly swish crew, and as the room fills up on a weekend lunchtime, it takes on an energy that is simply transformative. Suddenly the illogicality of the location is replaced by the logical deliciousness of this modern Italian food, and on our last visit the McKennas ate fantastic gnocchi, an excellent lasagne, first-class mushroom risotto, and before we left we spent a silly amount of money on the lovely things they sell in the shop. We'd do it all again tomorrow. (Eileen Dunne & Stefano Crescenzi, Unit 35 Kildare Village, Nurney Road, Kildare ☎ 045-535850 ✆ www.dunneandcrescenzi.com – Open 8.30am-10pm Mon-Wed, 8.30am-10.30pm Thu, 8.30am-11pm Fri-Sat, 10.30am-7pm Sun)

Deli
● Mary-Kathryn's Deli

Mary-Kathryn Murphy has a Ballymaloe school and Cathal Brugha Street background, as solid a foundation as you can get for making proper, properly prepared food. "Great home cooking" is how Mary-Kathryn describes her ambition in the deli, and all the baking and cooking here is lovingly made from scratch, and it not only shows, for you can also taste it in every bite. (Mary-Kathryn Murphy, 6 Academy Street, Kildare ☎ 045-530588 ✉ marykathryn@campus.ie – Open 8.30am-5pm Mon, 8.30am-6pm Tue-Fri, 8.30am-3pm Sat)

Maynooth

Wine Merchant
● Mill Wine Cellar

The Mill is a super wine shop, and a unique one, also, for the charm of its traditional exterior is continued inside with a charming, casual shop, where you can also rent a DVD! But, DVDs aside, it is wine you are here for, and Berna Hatton's selection is superb, and congratulated by a judiciously selected range of specialist beers. It's laid-back and a perfectly lovely place in which to buy good wines. (Berna Hatton, Maynooth ☎ 01-629 1022 ✉ info@millwinecellar.ie 🖱 www.millwinecellar.ie – Open 8am-10pm Mon-Fri, 9am-10pm Sat, 12.30am-10pm Sun)

Moyvalley

Pub
● Furey's of Moyvalley

A popular just-off-the-main-road spot for a bite to eat for travellers. (Charleen Sammon, Moyvalley, Broadford ☎ 046-955 1185 – Food served noon-7.50pm Mon-Sat)

Naas

Ice Cream Parlour and Coffee Shop
● Missy Moo's Ice Cream

Jaffa cake ice cream! Hoo hoo! How Homer Simpson is that! Siobhan Woods understands that ice cream is all about abandon, so abandon self-restraint all ye who enter Missy Moo's, and get ready for Minty Golfballs, or Cookies'n'Cream, or Mud Pie, or Chocolate Fudge Brownie. There are 18 splendiferous flavours on offer, all hand-made, all delicious. If for some curious reason you do not want to have a chocolate fudge brownie ice you can get a cup of coffee and a slice of apple pie in the café, and get some of Siobhan's hummus, and her cranberry confit to take away. (Siobhan Woods, 2 Chapel Lane, Naas ☎ 086-309 9406)

Farmers' Market
● Naas Farmers' Market

Siobhan Popplewell has powered the Naas market to success for more than five years now, creating a mix of specialist marketeers along with hot new arrivals that has created a particularly devoted following amongst shoppers. There are Choc O'Neill's truffles, Sheridan's cheeses, olives, a quartet of bread stalls, French wines, Castleruddery organics from Wicklow, fresh fish from Out of the Blue. Bring the kids along for a treat of Missy Moo's ice cream and, bags full, it's time to head home. (Friary Lane, beside Storehouse – Open Sat 10am-3pm)

Deli, Café & Hampers
● Harvest Kitchen

Harvest Kitchen is both kitchen which serves paninis, wraps, sandwiches and drinks, and Harvest Hampers, where Marie Leacy chooses top notch ingredients and makes it extremely simple to say "thank you" or perhaps "please forgive me" to that special person in your life. (Marie Leacy, 1 Sallins Road, Naas ☎ 045-881793 ⌨ www.harvestkitchen.ie – Open 9am-5pm Mon-Thu, 9am-6pm Sat)

Wine Importer
● Tyrrell & Co

Simon Tyrrell is not just the leading expert of the wines of the Rhone Valley, he is also one of the most distinguished explicators of the world of wine we have ever met. He wears tremendous learning and expertise with extreme lightness and modesty, carefully explaining why a particular wine is the way it is. He selects wines from people he respects, and whose wine-making methods he respects, and his list is, quite simply, amongst the best you can find. The day you encounter these wines is the day your life just got a whole lot better, and you can make that day today by clicking on www.thestoreroom.ie, where Simon and Emma retail their wines online. Otherwise, good restaurants and good wine shops sell these magnificent drinks. (Simon & Emma Tyrrell, Rathernan, Kilmeague, Naas ☎ 1890-252 624/045-870882 ✉ thestore@thestoreroom.ie ⌨ www.thestoreroom.ie)

only in Kildare
Castlefarm Shop

County Kilkenny

Bennettsbridge

Apple Juice
● **Mosse's farm Apple Juice**

Tiina Mosse's lovely juice is brand new, yet it was one
of the star turns of the 2009 Savour Kilkenny Festival.
Using the Karmine apple gives the juice crisp acidity
and freshness, and it is really special, so here's hoping
we see a lot more of Mosse's in the future. (Tiina
& Simon Mosse, Bennettsbridge ☎ 056-772 7790
✉ tmosse@eircom.net)

Pottery & Café
● **Nicky Mosse Pottery**

Nicky Mosse's famous spongeware is based in a fine
old mill that has a fine young tea room with lots of
rather nice things to eat. Somewhat sadly, everything
you behold in this handsome store rapidly becomes
something you wish to possess, so the credit card can
take a hammering. (Nicholas Mosse, Bennettsbridge
☎ 056-772 7105 ✉ sales@nicholasmosse.com ✇ www.
nicholasmosse.com – Café Open 11am-5pm Mon-Sat,
1.30pm-4pm Sun)

Castlecomer

Café and Crafts
● **Jarrow Café**

At the second Savour Kilkenny Festival, Anna and Evan
fashioned stunning dishes in the Jarrow Café with the
produce of featured Kilkenny artisans: smoked Goatsbridge trout paté; Kylemore beef braised in Guinness;
Knockdrinna goats' cheese tart with tomato and thyme;
Dunedin sticky apple pudding. Fascinating food, and a
truly lovely space, especially as the Estate Yard is home
to a panjandrum of wonderfully gifted craftspeople,
including Rosemarie Durr, one of our favourite potters.
(Anna & Evan Stewart, Castlecomer Discovery Park,
Estate Yard, Castlecomer ☎ 056-444 0019 ✇ www.
discoverypark.ie – Open 10am-5.30pm Mon-Sun)

Kilkenny

Cramer's Grove

Ice Cream
● **Cramer's Grove Ice Cream**

"Since the 1950's ice cream has been made commercially and I think we've forgotten what the real thing tastes like", Nigel Cramer told Mick Kelly of *The Irish Times* back in 2007, two years after Nigel and Carol had started to make Cramer's Grove Ice Cream. "Commercial production uses the by-products of dairy as opposed to dairy itself. Because we have the herd here, we only use fresh milk." Now you know why Cramer's Grove is so good, and why commercial ice creams are so vile. Cramer's Grove is the real thing: ice creams made from the full milk of a happy herd of Holstein-Friesian cows by the very people who mind and milk the cows. Accept no substitute, and if you have forgotten what real, true, genuine, artisan ice cream tastes like, just get a tub of cinnamon ice cream, or their incredible Bailey's and brown bread ice cream, and dig a spoon into depthless, delightful flavours. (Nigel & Carol Harper, Cramer's Grove, Kilkenny ☎ 056-772 2160 ✉ icecream@cramersgrove.com ☝ www.cramersgrove.com)

Cuffesgrange

Organic Apple Juice
● **Highbank Organic Orchards**

Not too many orchards also stage masked opera, so Highbank is a little different from the norm. When they aren't staging some favourite Commedia dell'Arte, then Julie and Rod Calder-Potts are busy making a superlative single vintage apple juice, which you can buy from the farm shop and from Iago in Cork's English market. It's a beauty, with only a touch of ascorbic acid added for preservation. (Julie & Rod Calder-Potts, Cuffesgrange, Kilkenny ☎ 056-772 9918 ✉ highbank@eircom.net)

Cookery School
● **Ryeland House**

If you haven't heard of Anne Neary's cookery school, it's because, for the last 20 years her cookery classes have filled up simply by virtue of word of mouth. That speaks

Kilkenny

volumes for Mrs Neary's aptitude and intelligence as a
cook. And you can see that aptitude and intelligence in
her fine book *A Country Kitchen*, which Anne published
at the end of 2009. It's a lovely collection, and very
practical and useful, just like the cookery courses
themselves. (Anne Neary, Cuffesgrange ☎ 056-
772 9073/086-276 7656 ✍ ryelandhouse@gmail.com
🖰 www.ryelandhousecookery.com)

Ferrybank

Apples and Apple Juice
● Vogelaar's Apple Farm

Fine apples, from Discovery to Coxs, and fine juices
from those fine apples, are sold from Kees and Aneke's
farm shop. When the apples are eaten and the juices
sold, they shut up shop, and we wait happily until next
year. (Kees & Aneke Vogelaar, Mullinabro, Ferrybank
☎ 051-872544/087-2527829 ✍ vogelaar@eircom.net)

Gathabawn

Farmhouse Ice Cream
● Gathabawn Farmhouse Ice Cream

Using the milk and cream from their own farm, Anthony
and William Brennan have begun making highly regarded
ice creams and sorbets. You will find their flavours,
such as Baileys and brown bread, or honeycomb and
chocolate chip, on the menus of good restaurants, and
it is noticeable that those restaurants state the source
of the ice cream, such is the cachet in having Gathabawn
ice creams. An ideal family farm enterprise, producing
beautiful things to enjoy. (Anthony & William Brennan,
Gathabawn, Kilkenny ☎ 086-3516880)

Kilkenny

Graiguenamanagh

Country House
● Ballyogan House

They are doing the good thing in Ballyogan House, are
Robert and Fran. "The level of hospitality had me smiling
all the way: beautiful house and lovely people", writes
Eamon Barrett of his encounter with this gem in the

heart of one of Ireland's most beautiful areas, the Barrow Valley in and around Graiguenamanagh. The house is a smart, compact farmhouse with bay windows and a coffee-cream colouring, looking out over tree-lined rolling lawns and manicured gardens. The four rooms are lovely, the sitting room and conservatory places to plop down in and look forward to tea and cakes. Boats Bistro nearby is a good dining choice, and this region is one of our favourite places to be. (Robert & Fran Durie, Graiguenamanagh ☎ 059-972 5969 ✉ info@ballyoganhouse.com ✎ www.ballyoganhouse. com – Open 1 Apr-31 Oct and for St Patrick's weekend)

Restaurant
● Boats Bistro

Arnie and Georgina Poole's Boats Bistro has a fantastic location, looking out over the river Barrow with cruisers moored on the water. There is a small room downstairs with a larger room above, and the menu changes most nights and fits on an A4 sheet, "always a good sign I think!", says Claire Goodwillie. The cooking is spot on: smoked salmon wrapped around velvety smooth crème fraiche with chopped spring onions, with a potato cake; tian of crab and avocado; swordfish with asparagus and potatoes is exactly what you want it to be. Desserts are a selection of ice creams from Cramer's Grove; ricotta and cinnamon tart; chocolate and hazelnut loaf, all excellent. Friendly service and "if you discovered this place whilst on holiday you would think: what a gem!", says Claire. (Arnie & Georgina Poole, High Street, Graiguenamanagh ☎ 059-972 5075 – Open Lunch noon-4pm, Dinner from 6pm Tue-Sat, noon-7pm Sun with more limited hours off season)

only in Kilkenny
Goatsbridge Trout

Restaurant and B&B
● Waterside

Simple accommodation and clean, simple cooking in a lovely riverside mill. (Brian & Brigid Roberts, Graiguena-managh ☎ 059-972 4246 ✉ info@watersideguesthouse. com ✎ www.watersideguesthouse.com – Open Dinner from 6.30pm. Open seven nights in summer, and Sunday lunch, weekends only in winter)

Inistioge

Restaurant
● Bassett's At Woodstock

Mijke and John's Bassett's place has a charm and a signature that is all its own, the sort of country restaurant
that enriches the culture of any county, and of any country. It has the most wonderful location, in the Woodstock demesne, and the beauty of the room is matched
by the beauty of Mijke's cooking: cream of garlic soup
with aged Parma ham and a slick of balsamic; pan-fried
foie gras with onion, vanilla and cumin relish; veal with
tuna cream; monkfish with risotto and beetroot purée;
whilst grilled Wexford lobster is served so simply, with
its own bisque and some fresh peas, that it quite takes
your breath away, just the sort of grown up cooking that
you expect here, fusing culinary intelligence with a singular style. Don't miss the Saddle Hill lamb, from James and
Chrissie Murphy. Brilliant. (Mijke Jansen & John Bassett,
Woodstock Gardens, Inistioge ☎ 056-775 8820 ✉ info@
bassetts.ie ⌂ www.bassetts.ie – Open noon-4pm Wed-
Sat, 1pm-5pm Sun, Dinner from 7.30pm Wed-Sat)

Kilkenny

Delicatessen and Take-away
● Blueberry Larder

The first time we ever walked past Will and Kerry
Fitzgerald's BL, it was the array of serious, well-
thumbed cookery books that the kitchen was using that
caught our eye. Then we looked at their lovely food
and quickly forgot the texts. But the books show how
this fine traiteur works: they take an idea, then they
riff on it until they have a Blueberry dish all of their
own. So their dishes have conventional titles – Irish
stew; shepherd's pie; beef stroganoff; salmon fishcakes;
chocolate raspberry roulade – but Mr Fitzgerald's
experience means that nothing ever tastes clichéd, so
the cooking is precise and invigorating, and if you have
little time for the kitchen, or little skill when you get
there, then Blueberry is your home from home. (Will
& Kerry Fitzgerald, 2 Market Yard, Kilkenny ☎ 056-
776 1456 ⌂ www.blueberrykilkenny.com ✉ info@
blueberrykilkenny.com – Open 8.30am-6pm Mon-Wed
& Sat, 8.30am-7pm Thu-Fri)

Kilkenny

● Café Sol

With a new branch, Bistro Sol, now open in Thomas-town, Noel McCarron's Sol team are showing that their formula of good, accessible cooking in attractive, calm rooms is a winning one. The cooking concentrates on delivering straight-ahead flavours and textures, and dishes such as pasta with crab, chilli, tomato and garlic, or Kilkenny beef with braised oxtail and potato rosti, or Lavistown sausages with colcannon, are no-nonsense cooking at its best, designed to hit the taste recep-tors with maximum impact. You might call it culinary kapow! (Noel McCarron, William Street, Kilkenny ☎ 056-7764987 ✉ info@cafesolkilkenny.com 🖰 www.cafesolkilkenny.com – Open 11.30am-10pm Mon-Sat, noon-9pm Sun)

● Campagne

"Back in Campagne last night for another faultless meal", writes Eamon Barrett. "Campagne still flawless", writes Claire Goodwillie. Faultless. Flawless. How many res-taurants garner those special words of praise? And yet, ever since they opened their doors, one has not heard anything but these terms of praise for Garret Byrne's cooking and Brid Hannon's service, and as we write in late 2009 Campagne has enjoyed a year of extraor-dinary success. Funny thing is, they have made it look easy to open a beautiful room with impeccable cooking, and boy is that cooking impeccable: brill with girolles, pancetta and braised lettuce; duck breast and confit leg with mushroom polenta; cod with tomato ravioli and fennel purée; chicken with foie gras mousse, spinach and smoked bacon; Mount Callan cheddar rarebit with pick-led walnut; lime parfait with strawberry soup. Dazzling food in a dazzling room, but do make sure to book at evening time or you won't manage to get a table to enjoy this magic. (Garret Byrne & Brid Hannon, 5 The Arches, Gashouse Lane, Kilkenny ☎ 056-777 2858 ✉ info@campagne.ie 🖰 www.campagne.ie – Open 12.30pm-2.30pm Fri & Sun, 6pm-10pm Wed-Sat, 6pm-9pm Sun)

● Carrigan's Liquor Bar

A beautiful reinvention of a classic Marble City bar. (2 High Street, Kilkenny ☎ 056-770 3979 🖰 www.langtons.ie – Food served 9am-8.30pm Mon-Sun)

Kilkenny

Wine Merchant
● Le Caveau

"A modest but intelligent man, with a real passion for wine." That's how John Wilson, wine writer of *The Irish Times*, described Pascal Rossignol, when he wrote a piece celebrating the tenth anniversary of Pascal and Geraldine's shop, which Mr Wilson called "one of the finest wine businesses in Ireland". Right on both counts, John. Le Caveau is a gem, one of those tardis-like shops that is tiny, and which unveils its wine portfolio slowly, steadily, delightfully. They import 180 wines from more than 75 producers, and yet they never rest, always looking for new wines, new bargains, new frontiers, most recently their wonderful array of Italian wines. Talk to Pascal and Geraldine – like her husband, equally modest and intelligent – and they always stress the need for wines to show "character and authenticity". Add in the need for good value in these straitened times, and Le Caveau delivers at every point. Ten more years, please, ten more glorious years. (Pascal & Geraldine Rossignol, Market Yard, Kilkenny ☎ 056-775 2166 ✉ secure@lecaveau.ie ✍ www.lecaveau.ie – Open 10.30am-6.30pm Tue-Sat)

Café
● Chez Pierre

Pierre Schneider's sweet little dining space has lots of attitude, and the sort of dishes you will find chalked on the blackboard include confit of quail with black pudding and chestnuts, or beetroot salad with goat's cheese and a yogurt dressing, turbot with potatoes, or mushroom risotto or wild sea bass with petits pois. The puds, like apricot pudding with ice cream, are very fine. (Pierre Schneider, 17 Parliament Street, Kilkenny ☎ 056-776 4655 ✉ chezpierrerestaurant@hotmail.com – Open 10am-5pm Mon-Sat)

Restaurant
● Fléva

Kayrin Connery's restaurant is a beaut, thanks to the boss's wondrous joie de vivre, and to Michael Thomas's smart, punky cooking. Add in a vivid upstairs room, great sounds and an ever-changing array of modern art, and you have one of the jewels of Kilkenny city. Mr Thomas does some things straight – rib-eye with portobello mushrooms, grilled tomato, Fléva fries and

Kilkenny

bearnaise; Dick Dooley's Ballyraggett lamb with mint and pistachio crust and dauphinoise potatoes – but with other dishes his eye wanders from the straight and narrow, so Caesar salad has crab and baby shrimp, or salmon will have a crab and chive polenta (he likes crab, it seems). Sharp, precise cooking, and one of our favourite rooms. Fléva is New Orleans slang for "What's happening now!' Fléva is happening now. (Kayrin Connery, 84 High Street, Kilkenny ☎ 056-777 0021 ✉ flevarestaurant@eircom.net ✆ www.fleva.ie – Open 12.30pm-2.30pm Tue-Fri, 12.30pm-3pm Sat & Sun, 6pm-9.30 Tue-Fri, 5.30pm-10pm Sat, 6pm-8.30pm Sun)

Restaurant
● **Foodworks**

Peter Greany has serious form in serious restaurants stacked up on his CV, so it was no surprise that he attracted attention right from the out. His food has the sort of chutzpah you would expect of someone with time spent in good kitchens in London and Sydney, so right from a croque monsieur for breakfast or a lunchtime saffron risotto with lemon and thyme marinated chicken, this food speaks for itself, and it's no wonder that Claire Goodwillie will call Foodworks "a great place for lunch". So, creamy fish pie with potato for me, and smoked trout with rocket for you, then a bread and butter pudding to share. A great place for lunch indeed and, hopefully, a great place for dinner in the future. Food works is a hot spot. (Peter Greany & Maeve Moore, Unit 4, Gas House Lane, The Arches, Kilkenny ☎ 056-777 7696 ✉ foodworkscafe@gmail.com – Open 9am-noon, breakfast, noon-5pm lunch Mon-Sat)

Delicatessen
● **The Gourmet Store**

Padraig and Irene Lawlor's shop can appear, at lunchtime, to be feeding not just Kilkenny city but the whole of Kilkenny county, as this handsome food store is besieged with folk wanting wraps and paninis and sandwiches and whatnot. So, sharpen up your elbows and join the throng. Away from lunch hour, the shop is more sedate, and is a cracking space in which to browse for nice things. (Padraig & Irene Lawlor, Main Street, Kilkenny ☎ 056-777 1727 ✉ gourmetstore@hotmail.com ✆ www.thegourmetstorekilkenny.com – Open 9am-6pm Mon-Sat)

● **Kilkenny Design Centre**

"Our food philosophy is very simple", says Kathleen
Moran. "Make good food!" That's what Kathleen
and her crew do in the classic space that is the
Kilkenny Craft Design Centre. Here you will find true,
unpretentious cooking: cherry tomato, roast shallot and
feta tart; cottage pie with celeriac mash; beef burger
with rosemary focaccia and potato wedges; beef and
Guinness casserole with mustard mash; Joan's raspberry
and cream sponge cake. The harmony of the room and
the assurance of the food makes for a happy space, a
space it's always a joy to return to. (Kathleen Moran,
Castle Yard, Kilkenny ☎ 056-772 2118 📠 info@
kilkennydesign.com 🖲 www.kilkennydesign.com – Open
10am-6pm Mon-Sat, 11pm-6pm Sun and bank hols)

only in Kilkenny
Knockdrinna Whey-fed Pork

● **Kilkenny Farmers' Market**

There are almost twenty stalls manned by enthusiastic
artisans for you to choose from every Thursday morning
in Kilkenny. (The Market Yard, Kilkenny – Open Thursday morning)

● **Kilkenny Ormonde Hotel**

It's no exaggeration to say that if he ran his own place,
with his name over the door, rather than cooked in
an hotel, then Mark Gaffney would be one of the best
known chefs in the country. But Mr Gaffney is modest
and unassuming, and he does a superb job in the
Ormonde, so there is no ego to gratify, and he simply
cooks great food in this fine hotel and pleases everyone
who enjoys his cooking. It goes without saying, of
course, that Mr Gaffney does not cook "hotel" food:
he cooks Mark Gaffney food, in an hotel; food that is
hip, light, perfectly in the culture, modern and utterly
convincing. (Mark Gaffney, Ormonde Street, Kilkenny
☎ 056-772 3900 📠 info@kilkennyormonde.com
🖲 www.kilkennyormonde.com)

Kilkenny

● Marble City Bar

A very stylish part of the Langton group, who operate
many bars and restaurants in the city. Very funky, and
a good lunchtime spot. (The Langton family, 66 High
Street, Kilkenny ☎ 056-776 1143 🖰 www.langtons.ie –
Food served 10am-10pm)

Tea Rooms
● Marble City Tea Rooms

The Langton family opened these tea rooms, at the rere
of the Marble City bar, back in 2005, and they are a
lovely spot in which to take tea and maybe meet a friend
to catch up on the gossip. (The Langton family, 66 High
Street, Kilkenny ☎ 056-776 1143 🖰 www.langtons.ie –
Open 9am-9pm Mon-Sun)

Restaurant
● Rinuccini

Here is the measure of Rinuccini and its hospitality:
a friend and his wife are having dinner in Rinuccini
with our friend's brother, his wife and their son, who
is severely autistic. Recounting the dinner later, our
friend marvels at the attention the staff lavished on his
brother's son, the care, the solicitude, the charm and the
humour, all in order that everyone at the table should
have a wonderful evening. That's called over-delivering
in the business, and over-delivering is what they have
been doing in Antonio Cavaliere's Rinuccini restaurant
for many years now, cooking good Italian food, offering
comfortable accommodation and, above all, taking care
of everyone who comes through the door, and especially
taking care of those who need the most care. A story to
bring a smile to your heart. Fabulous. (Antonio, Marion
& Riccardo Cavaliere, 1 The Parade, Kilkenny ☎ 056-
776 1575 🖃 info@rinuccini.com 🖰 www.rinuccini.
com – Open noon-3pm Mon-Fri, 5pm-10pm Mon-Sat,
noon-3.30pm Sat & Sun, 5pm-9.30pm Sun)

Asian Delicatessen
● Shortis Wong

Mary and Chris's shop marries the hugger-mugger of the
ethnic store with the calm of the old Irish grocery store,
and it's both a unique synthesis and an unbeatable combination. Everything you could possibly need or want is

here, from won ton wrappers to Lavistown sausages, arranged with an aesthete's eye, and sold with the wisdom of the gifted grocer. Chris and Mary were the winners of the first Savour Kilkenny award, and to say that they won by acclamation, and that their win was greeted by local delight, is exactly right. Part and parcel, fixture and fabric of the culture of the city. (Mary Shortis & Chris Wong, John Street, Kilkenny ☎ 056-776 1305 – Open 9am-7pm Mon-Sat)

Coffee Shop
● The Two Dames

Tracie and Lavinia Daly are "born, bred and buttered John Street Women", for they grew up just down the street from where they have opened The Two Dames. When our mate Richard was up in the city for the arts festival and all that highbrow stuff, he was initially attracted by the sign saying "man crêche", but he got a lot more than a place to park the hubby when he stepped in the door of TTD. "Roast pepper and tomato soup with chunky garlicky croûtons, and a "Surprise" – my request for a sandwich – the best sandwich I've had in yonks: good seedy wholemeal toasted and then sliced down the middle and crisped slightly ...think French toast without the curl!!! filled with chicken and a stuffing so good the granny had to have a hand in it ... with some chopped green grapes and lightly melting brie all served with a crisp dressed green salad ... all that and a mineral for not much more than a tenner." Girls, Richard will be back. And so will we. (Tracie & Lavinia Daly, 80 John Street, Kilkenny ☎ 085-175 5005 ⌂ thetwodames. blogspot.com)

Wine Merchant
● Vendemia Organic Wines

Helen and Urs Tobler stock one of the best selections of organic wines in Ireland. There are real beauties to be discovered here, wines of distinctiveness and deliciousness. (Helen & Urs Tobler, Hebron Road, Kilkenny ☎ 056-777 0225 ✉ info@vendemiawines.com ⌂ www.vendemiawines.com – Open 9am-5pm Mon-Fri)

Wine Merchant
● The Wine Centre

The O'Keeffe family call their wine accessories business Wine Obsessed, and that's just about right on the ball for what they do here in John Street. The Wine Centre has a must-be-seen-to-be-believed selection of wines crammed into a series of atmospheric rooms, and it's the easiest and nicest thing in the world to fritter away time hunting down perfect bottles to bring home. (Edmond O'Keeffe, 15 John Street, Kilkenny ☎ 056-776 5900 ⓣ www.wineobsessed.com – Open 10.30am-10pm Mon-Sat)

Restaurant & Townhouse
● **Zuni**

The Zuni crew always manage to stay ahead of the bunch. Their latest re-invention has seen the bar converted into an all-day café, where you can breakfast in the morning and share some Zuni tapas at night. Maria Raftery's cooking in the glamorous restaurant offers archetypal modern Irish food: Gubbeen antipasti plate, deep-fried Bocconcini Mozzarella with crisp pancetta; scallops with saffron asparagus and shrimp risotto; salmon with pink grapefruit hollandaise. Last time Claire Goodwillie dropped in for a cup of coffee in the café she asked if they had the day's newspaper. It appeared a few minutes later, after a member of the staff had run down the road to the newsagents to get it specially. Now, that's service. (Paul & Paula Byrne, 26 Patrick Street, Kilkenny ☎ 056-772 3999 ⓓ info@zuni.ie ⓣ www.zuni.ie – Open 12.30pm-2.30pm, 6.30pm-10pm Mon-Sat; 1pm-3pm, 6pm-9pm Sun)

only in Kilkenny
Blackberry Café Brandy Cake

Kilmacow

Bakery
● **Harney's Bakery**

We're not sure how they feel about it locally here on the Kilkenny/Waterford border, but Denis Harney was awarded a Eurotoques gong for his Waterford Blaa, the crusty squidgey white bread roll which is the signature bakery product of county Waterford. We have no doubt the locals took the news well, and bought up their blaa for breakfast like they do every day. (Denis Harney, Kilmacow ☎ 051-885118)

Lavistown

Farmhouse Sausages, Burgers & Study Centre
● Lavistown Farmhouse

Olivia Goodwillie makes four varieties of her utterly
unique Lavistown sausages. There is the breakfast sausage which is lightly spiced; the Lavistown chilli, which
has red pepper and a kick of chilli; and the garlic sausage,
which also brings a raft of cumin. Olivia's most recent
innovation, along with some really nifty new packaging,
is the Italian-style cocktail sausage, packed with the flavours of fennel, paprika and garlic. When the Goodwil-
lies aren't looking after their piggywigs, they run a series
of fascinating annual classes in the Study Centre, and
have been doing so for the last thirty years. So whether
you want to identify lichens, bake bread or finally get
to grips with mushrooms or foraging, then one of these
one- or two-day courses will equip you with the holistic
expertise that the Lavistown Centre enshrines. (Olivia
Goodwillie, Lavistown ☎ 056-776 5145 ⌨ courses@
lavistownhouse.ie ⌂ www.lavistownhouse.ie)

Piltown

Apple Juice
● The Little Irish Apple Co.

Mark, Philip and John Little's Little Irish Apple Company
isn't actually that little, for they have a total of sixty
acres of orchards from which to produce excellent
apples and really, really fine apple juices. You'll find them
at good farmers' markets and specialist retailers. (Mark,
Philip & John Little, Clonmore House, Piltown ☎ 051-
387109)

Honey
● Mileeven

The second generation of the Gough family has joined
this exemplary artisan company with Sarah Gough now
working alongside her mother Eilis as they build their
portfolio of honeys, preserves and Christmas goodies.
For more than twenty years Eilis Gough has demonstrated the most acute organoleptic excellence in every
product she has fashioned, and the Mileeven's range
always seem to capture the essence of whatever ingredient they are working with, whether it's the tang of

Kilkenny

a raspberry, or the burn of a drop of Jameson whiskey. The foods are as beautifully packaged as they are composed. (Eilis & Sarah Gough, Owning Hill, Piltown ☎ 051-643368 📧 mileeven@indigo.ie 🖱 www.mileevenfinefoods.com)

Artisan Bakery
● A Slice of Heaven

Mary McEvoy is one of the greatest bakers we have ever met. Many years ago, when working in the Kilkenny Ormonde after she had returned from her position as head pastry chef in L'Ecrivain, she made us a crème brûlée that was, quite simply, perfection. Perfection, and unforgettable. Today, she bakes cup cakes and cakes, and her cakes are perfection. We brought her awesomely decorated cup cakes home to the kids last time, and the children were struck into silence by their magnificence, by their grace and art, every bite a slice of heaven. Incredible work. (Mary McEvoy, Ballygown, Piltown ☎ 087-953 3870 📧 mary@asliceofheaven.ie 🖱 www.asliceofheaven.ie)

Stoneyford

Farmhouse Cheese, Pork, Preserves
● Knockdrinna Farmhouse Cheese & Lavistown Farmhouse Cheese

Helen Finnegan won the judges award in the 2009 Bridgestone Electric Picnic awards for this reason: she farmed the grass that fed the cows that made the milk that made the cheese that made the whey that fed the pigs that made the sausages that Helen cooked at her Electric Picnic stall. This isn't from soup to nuts, this is from grass to gourmet. Mrs Finnegan has been one of the most significant arrivals in Irish artisan food in the last five years, and both the Knockdrinna and Lavistown Cheeses that she fashions are benchmark specialist foods. What is extraordinary, however, has been the speed at which Helen has developed not just new cheeses, but also expanded logically into pork production and into running a farm shop alongside her participation at farmers' markets. The cheeses exhibit the generosity and can-do mentality of the cheesemaker, whether it's the delicate Knockdrinna Snow, the sheeps' milk Knockdrinna Meadow, or perhaps most surprisingly her

Kilkenny

ability to carry on the tradition of the Caerphilly-style Lavistown Cheese, which Helen has been making since 2008. A archetypal artisan. (Helen Finnegan, Stoneyford ☎ 056-772 8446 ✉ hlanders@esatclear.ie ☝ www. knockdrinna.com)

Farm Shop
● Knockdrinna Farm Shop

Every farm should have a farmshop, and every farmshop should be like Knockdrinna where you can buy the cheesemaker's cheese, the farmer's pork, and the cook's bread, relishes, preserves and salads. (Helen Finnegan, Stoneyford ☎ 056-772 8446 ✉ hlanders@esatclear.ie ☝ www.knockdrinna.com – Open 10am-6pm Tue-Sat)

Thomastown

Café
● The Blackberry Café

Déja Vu? Yes, you think you have seen the outside of Jackie Moyne's beautiful café, and indeed you have, in those Failte Ireland adverts where they hope to convince tourists that every shop front in Ireland is as beautiful as this. If only! Every detail here, from colours to craftsmanship, is lovingly, tenderly, affectionately rendered, making for a classic café in the old style. Jackie's food, then, drives home a message of timeless goodness, using local speciality foods and her own vividly creative baking. A slice of that apple brandy cake and a cup of tea, my friend, and you are in heaven. (Jackie Moyne, Market Street, Thomastown ☎ 087-053 7858)

Trout Farm
● Goatsbridge Premium Irish Trout

If you produce a fine trout, as Margaret and Gerard Kirwan do, then what sort of a dream must it be when an outstanding chef such as Garret Byrne, of Campagne in Kilkenny, invents a dish like this to celebrate your product: 'Cured Goatsbridge trout, cucumber gazpacho, horseradish potato salad'. Whew! Boy but that tells you that you have arrived with an amazing fish, and that is just what Goatsbridge trout is. You will find it whole, portioned and in fillets, and also hot smoked, at good fish counters. (Margaret & Gerard Kirwan, Thomastown ☎ 086-818 8340/086 254 4906 ✉ info@ goatsbridgetrout.ie ☝ www.goatsbridgetrout.ie)

Kilkenny

● **Kylemore Farm produce**

Martin Lyng rears superb Angus and Hereford beef, fresh farm lamb, and some chickens and free-range turkeys, with the animals prepared for his market stall by Christy Byrne of Camolin. The quality is outstanding, so look out for Martin at markets in Carrick, Clonmel and Ardkeen. (Martin Lyng, The Rower, Thomastown ☎ 051-423647)

Delicatessen

● **Sol Bistro**

"It's already very popular", says Claire Goodwillie of the Thomastown outpost of Café Sol. Noel McCarron and his team have brought a somewhat similar style of food and menu down from the city and it's proving to be just what Thomastown needs. The food is accessible in style, in price and in flavour, and we don't expect that this will be the only Sol offspring. (Noel McCarron, Thomastown ☎ 056-775 4945 ✏ info@cafesolkilkenny.com ✐ www.cafesolkilkenny.com – Open noon-4pm 5pm-close Mon-Fri, noon-close Sat & Sun)

only in Kilkenny
Drumeen Farm Rapeseed Oil

Homebaking

● **Two Little Cooks**

We first met Roseann and Eadaoin at the Discovery Park in Castlecomer when they were part of the launch of new artisan products in the 2009 Savour Kilkenny Festival. They wowed! us with their bakewell tarts, lush sweet, fruity concoctions of sheer and simple delight, and also with their incredible presentation. They did a two-hander, talking about their foods, with all the élan of French & Saunders, really sharp and witty and, thus, just like their foods and themselves. Look out for this terrific baking at markets in Kilkenny, Thomastown, Castle Lynch and Killian Hill. Bakewells are their signature creations, but we should, really, re-christen these wonderful cakes Bakebrilliantlys. (Roseann O'Brien & Eadaoin Walsh, Friars Hill, Thomastown ☎ 086-345 3193)

Kilkenny

● **Truffle Fairy**

Each and every individual chocolate that the Truffle Fairy
sprinkles on the tip of your tongue is fashioned by hand
by Mary Teehan. So the next time you have a spiced
rum truffle, or a white chocolate Baileys Irish Cream
truffle you can reflect happily on the fact that you have
your own, your very own, truffle fairy. (Mary Teehan,
Thomastown ☎ 056-779 3375 ✐ mary@trufflefairy.
com ✍ www.trufflefairy.com)

Wine Academy

● **Wine Academy Ireland**

Mary Gaynor is one of Ireland's most experienced
wine educators, and holds an MBA in Wine from the
Bordeaux School. Mary now undertakes her own
courses to W.S.E.T. Advanced Certificate level as well
as wine appreciation classes and wine training. (Mary
Gaynor, The Quay, Thomastown ☎ 056-772 4894
✐ marygaynor99@eircom.net ✍ www.wineacademy.ie)

Tullaroan

Bakery

● **Oldtown Hill Bakery**

"The wholesome home-made taste of old," that's what
Joy and James Moore aim to capture in their breads and
tarts. The milk for the soda bread is from their own
herd, the apples for their apple tart are local Bramleys,
and their dedicated hands-on production means that
these bakery products positively sing with goodness.
Unlike commercial baking the Moores prepare
everything from scratch, so the only "improver" that you
find in Oldtown Hill breads and cakes is mother nature
herself. (Joy & James Moore, Oldtown Hill, Tullaroan
☎ 056-776 9263 ✐ oldtownhill@mail.com)

Kilkenny

only in Kilkenny
A Slice of Heaven

Urlingford

Organic Farm
● Drumeen Farm

Charlotte and Ben's farm is the original pioneer,
the longest-established organic farm in Ireland, and
they are heading towards thirty-five years of sane,
sustainable food production. They rear chickens,
turkeys, beef and lamb and process them in their own
abattoir, and if you call ahead you can buy direct. So
now you know exactly where to get that Xmas turkey.
The most exciting new development from the farm is a
cold-pressed rape seed oil, and once you have a taste
of this – you might enjoy it in Chapter One Restaurant
in Dublin, for example, drizzled over an amuse of clams
with roasted tomatoes – then those pricey European
olive oils are going to be replaced immediately by
Drumeen Farm rape seed oil. It's a superlative product,
and one of the most exciting new culinary innovations
in years. (Kitty, Charlotte & Ben Colchester, Islands,
Urlingford ☎ 056-883 1411 ⬛ charlottecolchester@
hotmail.com)

Blaas

Kilkenny

County Laois

Abbeyleix

Café
● Café Odhrán

Now that Abbeyleix is going to be by-passed, the good
places are quickly opening up in advance of the town
regaining its soul after years of traffic torture. Patricia
Ward's Café Odhrán is a place where you will often
see some of the McKennas, usually buying something
delicious to take away and feed all the family as we head
either north or south. We like the domestic style of
both the room and the cooking, which is honest, true
and generous and which always manages to have just
exactly what you feel like right now. (Patricia Ward,
Main Street Abbeyleix ☎ 057-875 7380 – Open 9.30am-
5.30pm Mon-Sat)

Bakery & Café
● The Gallic Kitchen

The mighty Gallic Kitchen comes to Abbeyleix with
a new shop in the centre of the village to showcase
the bakery products of the Dublin dynamo. Anytime
we have a GK double-banger sausage roll – with Janet
Drew's red pepper relish, of course – or a crisply tender
potato cake is a time when life is good, when life is very
good. The only thing more impressive than the Gallic
Kitchen's quality levels are their levels of consistency,
which have never dipped in more than twenty years
of baking. Vital. (Sarah Webb, Main Street, Abbeyleix
☎ 057-875 7431 ⊕ www.gallickitchen.com – Open
10am-6pm Tue-Sat)

Jams, Preserves & Relishes
● G's Gourmet Jams

Jam is a product very like bread. The standard stuff you
see everywhere is simply not worth bothering with,
for the ambition of most manufacturers is to make the
cheapest product possible and then to sell it at a high
price. Jam makers like Helen Gee, on the other hand,
come at the business of jam-making from the opposite
angle: they want to preserve the character and class of

Laois

their fruit via jam making, they want to showcase the quality of the fruit, they want to grandstand the glory of blackberries, the nobility of loganberries, the acidity of rhubarb. They do not disguise it with cheap sugar and additives. So, each jar of Mrs Gee's jams is like a shock of fruit, a tasty glimpse into the individuality of each fruit. You do this by doing things in the simplest way possible: good fruit; an open pot, a big wooden spoon, and sheer hard work and discrimination. Terrific stuff. (Helen Gee, Ballypickas, Abbeyleix ☎ 057-873 1058 ✉ gsgourmetjams@eircom.net ⌂ www.gsgourmetjams.ie)

Ballacolla

Farmhouse Cheese
● **Abbey Organic Cheese Co.**

Pat Hyland was just beginning to make his Abbey Brie and Abbey Blue cheeses when we were writing the first Bridgestone Guide, and his hard work and hunger to succeed means that today Pat is a stalwart producer for several farmers' markets, selling not just their own cheeses, including the St Canice goat's milk cheeses, but also a range of European cheeses that he sources. There is much more to Pat's stall than just cheese, however, so take a close look the next time you see the Paddy Jack stall. (Pat Hyland, Cuffsborough, Ballacolla ☎ 057-873 8599 ✉ abbeycheese@eircom.net)

Killenard

Hotel
● **The Heritage**

Under Donagh Davern's stewardship, The Heritage made it into the *2009 Bridgestone 100 Best Places to Stay in Ireland*. Now, when you consider that this is a great big hotel built around a golf course, and that both hotel and golf course seem to have dropped out of the sky into County Laois, and that we don't do golf courses – excepting, of course, the much-missed Shanks – it is a measure of what Mr Davern and his crew have pulled off here in Killenard, The staff are the bee's knees, right from the team of concierges – everyone of them a star

Laois

– through to the reception staff and the restaurant staff. Robbie Webster's cooking is as fine as ever – you may recall Robbie as chef at Ballynahinch Castle where he made a terrific reputation for logical, modest, modern Irish food – and food and service fit hand in glove. And, finally, a confession: yes, we did the golf. We did. And if you find five or six stray golf balls, they're ours. (Donagh Davern, Killenard ☎ 057-864 5500 ✉ info@theheritage.com ✆ www.theheritage.com)

Restaurant
● **Sol Oriens**

Sol Oriens is the Italian restaurant in the grounds of The Heritage, and a very popular and busy place it always seems to be, at least whenever the McKennas are there having a family dinner. It's text book bourgeois Italian in style and ambience and in the cooking, and that is just what everyone wants. (Donagh Davern, Killenard ☎ 057-862 3822 ✉ info@theheritage.com ✆ www.theheritage.com – Open Dinner Wed-Sun)

Mountrath

Country House
● **Roundwood House**

Back in the seventeenth century the estate that is today known as Roundwood was actually called Friendstown. That's a name that is as appropriate today for Frank and Rosemary Kennan's rambling Paladian house as it was a couple of centuries ago because the bonhomie in Round-wood is utterly infectious and the stranger you meet for dinner at 7.30pm in the evening will be your new best friend by breakfast the following morning. Friendstown indeed. (Frank & Rosemary Kennan, Mountrath ☎ 057-873 2120 ✉ roundwood@eircom.net ✆ www.roundwoodhouse.com – Open all year, except Christmas)

only in Laois

Paddy's O'Granola

Laois

Portlaoise

Wholefoods
● The Fruit'n'Nut Place

Dick Wellwood and his family have been doing the good stuff here in Portlaoise for nigh on twenty-five years and their experience is one of the key elements of this excellent wholefood shop, a repository of everything that is good in the locality. (The Wellwood family, 1 Lyster Square, Portlaoise ☎ 057-862 2239 – Open 9.30am-6pm Mon-Sat)

Town House
● Ivyleigh House

Dinah Campion's house enjoys some of the most pristine housekeeping we have enjoyed anywhere in Ireland, and it is amazing how good it makes you feel, and how luxurious it feels to stay in a house that is the recipient of such intense TLC. That intense TLC is also obvious when Mrs Campion cooks breakfast in the morning, with every dish prepared and finished fresh for the table. This is where you stay in Portlaoise. (Dinah Campion, Bank Place, Portlaoise ☎ 057-862 2081 ✆ www.ivyleigh. com)

only in Laois
The Heritage Room Service

Restaurant
● The Kingfisher

Khurshid Googee's Kingfisher Restaurant enjoys one of the best culinary reputations of any ethnic restaurant away from the capital. That reputation has been built on twelve years of rocksteady cooking and service during a time at which Portlaoise has been transformed from a sleepy midlands town to a far-flung outpost of the capital city. The Kingfisher team have navigated the changes in town well, from introducing early bird eating to offering the entire menu as a takeaway. (Khurshid (GooGee) Anwar, Main Street, Portlaoise ☎ 057-866 2500 ✆ inquiries@kingfisherrestaurant.com ✆ www. kingfisherrestaurant.com – Open noon-2pm Wed-Fri, 5.30pm-11.30pm Mon-Sun)

Laois

Restaurant & Food Store
● The Kitchen & Food Hall

Jim Tynan has been cooking for almost all his life,
learning at the apron strings of his mother and
grandmother, and opening his own place in Laois
when he was a raw twenty-two year old. After almost
thirty years in the kitchen his modus operandi and
his aesthetic have neither altered nor dimmed and
the Kitchen & Food Hall is one of the most glorious
destinations in the Midlands. It's invidious to single out
any one particular element of Jim's work, but the quality
of sweet baking in the Food Hall is rarely matched in
Ireland. And best of all it is a very distinctive style of
Irish baking that owes its provenance to the women
who taught Jim how to cook. (Jim & Sarah Tynan, Hynds
Square, Portlaoise ☎ 057-866 2061 ✉ jimkitchen@
eircom.net ⌂ www.kitchenfoodhall.com – The Kitchen
open 8.30am-5.30pm, The Foodhall open 9am-5.30pm)

Granola
● Paddy's O'Granola

Patrick O'Connell began fashioning his granolas when
he was a student as a means of earning a few bob. It
was probably a student idea to come up with his slogan
which is "Nick Nack Paddy Whack. Get yourself a
tasty snack!" Hmmm. The granola provokes no such
ambivalence, for it's a fantastic, toasty, rich, cluster
of health. At Electric Picnic 2009 we enjoyed the
O'Granola with Glenillen Farm Yogurt and Wexford
Strawberries, and it was a breakfast for the gods.
(Patrick O'Connell, Cullahill, Portlaoise ☎ 086-397 6215
✉ paatrickoconnell@live.ie)

Restaurant & Food Store
● Seasons Restaurant

After a detour out of town that took up a couple of
years, Kevin Hennessy is back where he belongs, running
a restaurant, up above a pub in the centre of Portlaoise,
which is how he made his reputation. With an all-female
crew in the kitchen and Kevin himself in confident control out front, this is an understated room with modest
and very good-value cooking: deep-fried Camembert
with tomato jam, braised lamb shank with mash and mint
gravy. (Kevin Hennessy, 24a Market Square, Portlaoise
☎ 057-868 0809 – Open 12.30pm-2.30pm, 6.30pm to
late Tue-Sun)

Laois

County Leitrim

Ballinamore

Cakes
● Cannaboe Confectionery

Sharon Sweeney is a sugarcraft wizard. Her cakes, from glamorous wedding cakes to her mini cup cakes, have to be seen to be believed, such is her expertise, and what she doesn't know about almond paste, or sugar paste or royal icing or piping figures isn't worth knowing. If there is some special event that demands a special cake, then Sharon is your only sugarcraft girl. (Sharon Sweeney, Willowfield Road, Ballinamore ☎ 071-964 4778 ✉ info@cacamilis.com ⊕ www.cacamilis.com – Open 9.30am-5.30pm Mon-Sat)

Carrick-on-Shannon

Accommodation
● Ciúin House

Fiona and Barry Reynold's stylishly contemporary house, with its emphasis on cool luxury, is a vital counter-point to the bland hotels that are littered throughout the country now. Unlike those hotels, Ciúin House is motivated by the calling of good service, nice cooking, and individual attention from the owners. (Fiona & Barry Reynold, Hartley, Carrick-on-Shannon ☎ 071-967 1488 ✉ info@ciuinhouse.com ⊕ www.ciuinhouse.com)

Country House
● Hollywell Country House

Rosaleen and Tom may be hanging up the aprons in the lovely Hollywell some time soon, so it's time to wish the next generation of Mahers well in their stewardship of this noble house, and time to praise Tom and Rosaleen for their light-hearted, witty, selfless hospitality over the course of many years. People like the Mahers may not be famous, but they are something altogether better: they are legendary. (Rosaleen & Tom Maher, Liberty Hill, Carrick-on-Shannon ☎ 071-962 1124 ✉ hollywell@ esatbiz.com – Open 1 Mar-31 Oct)

● **Market Yard Farmers' Market**

Donegal Fishermen. French bakers. Tattie Hoakers.
Cheese Etc. My goodness but the world and his wife
are all here in the gorgeous Market Yard on a Thursday
morning. So come along and say Hi! to Steve and Mary
and Eileen and Lisa and Sean and Declan and all the guys
with all the good stuff. And when all the bags are full,
time for a coffee and a sit-down in The Larder Café as
you plan tonight's dinner. (Market Yard, Carrick-on-
Shannon ⌕ www.themarketyardcentre.com – Open
Thurs 10am-3pm)

● **The Oarsman**

Ronan and Conor Maher are amongst the leading
restaurateurs in the North West, their Oarsman bar
and restaurant a shining example of how to run a smart
business that serves its community and its visitors.
We have said it before, and it is worth stating again:
the brothers get their gift in the blood, for their Mum
and Dad, Tom and Rosaleen of Hollywell, just over the
bridge, are steeped in the culture of hospitality, and this
is what animates these two driven young men. Hospitality, and great food, sourced with care from great
producers such as Maurice Kettyle, Pat O'Doherty, Ken
Moffat, Sheridan's Cheesemongers, Gubbeen Smokehouse, Tattie Hoaker organics to name just a few. And
don't worry if you can't get a seat in the restaurant, for the
cooking served in the bar is zappy and intense: Moroccan spiced Tom Beirne's lamb with minted pea couscous,
smoked paprika vegetables and cucumber crème fraiche, or
organic salmon and coriander pattie, on toasted brioche,
with rocket and fennel salad and pont neuf potatoes. Bar
Food? Oarsman Bar Food! (Ronan & Conor Maher, Bridge
Street, Carrick-on-Shannon ☎ 071-962 1733 🖾 info@
theoarsman.com ⌕ www.theoarsman.com – Food served
noon-8.30pm Tue-Sat)

Dromahair

● **Cheese Etc**

Trevor and Myra Irvine have brought the world of farmhouse cheeses to Dromahair, with their shop at Main

Leitrim

Street now bringing the experience and expertise of this gifted couple to this pretty town. Away from home, Trevor and Myra are amongst the leading marketeers in many farmers' markets, from Carrick to Belfast selling the best cheeses minded to their peak of culinary perfection. You need a good wine merchant when buying wine, but a good cheesemonger when you are buying cheese is even more important, and if you want to see how Ireland's farmhouse cheeses offer a taste and a glimpse of the sublime, you need Cheese Etc as part of your weekly shopping. (Trevor and Myra Irvine, Main Street, Dromahair ☎ 086-265 4675 ✆ cheeseetc@ eircom.net. Also at the following markets: Johnstown Court, Sligo Wed 10am-2pm, Carrick-on-Shannon Thur 10am-2pm, Manorhamilton Fri 10am-2pm, St Georges Belfast Fri, 6am-2pm, IT College Sligo Sat 9am-1pm, St Georges Belfast Sat, 9am-3pm, Tullywood Farm, Keadue 11.20am-3.30pm, as part of farm shop)

Restaurant
● **The Riverbank**

"The locals love it!" is how a local friend describes John Kelly's cooking in Dromahair's Riverbank Restaurant. The restaurant adjoins the family pub, the Club House, and Mr Kelly graduated via the Fermanagh College and Neven Maguire's MacNean restaurant, as well as spells in Clevery Mill and Cuisto Perigord, and that's as blue-chip a c.v. for a young man working in food as you can get in this area. Early days yet, but their own good breads, good dishes with Thornhill duck, and modern classics like prawns in ketaifi pastry bode well for the future. (John Kelly, The Club House, Dromahair ☎ 071-916 4590 Tue-Sat 6.30pm-10pm, Sun 12.30pm-3pm)

Farmhouse Cheese
● **Tullynascreena Goat's Farm**

Michael and Marika Tolksdorf picked up a silver medal for their raw milk goat's cheese in olive oil at the 2009 British Cheese Awards, and that accolade shows the sort of quality these cheesemakers not only aspire to, but succeed in achieving. The Tullynascreena cheeses aren't the easiest to find – though Cheese Etc is a good place to start – but they are well worth any food lover's detective hunt, for they are clean, vibrant, wonderfully fresh and loaded with clean, lactic brilliance. (Michael & Marika Tolksdorf, Dromahair ☎ 071-916 4934)

Leitrim

Dromod

Bakery
● Dromod Homemade Boxty

The age of the rediscovery of boxty is dawning and Timmy Faughnan is right there, ready for the deluge of interest in this most quixotic of potato products. Dromod boxty features potatoes, flour, milk and salt, and when you bring it home we suggest you fry a slice or two of it in the fat left by some good bacon, and get a taste of one of the ageless Irish classics. Timmy also makes breads, potato breads and pancakes, and you'll get them in local Supervalus. (Timmy Faughnan, Station Road, Dromod ☎ 071-963 8535)

Drumshanbo

Bakery
● Jinny's Bakery

You are a lucky food lover if you live within the distribution circle of Sinead and Pascal's cutting-edge artisan bakery. After only six years Jinny's has established itself as one of those companies that wins gold medals as often as the rest of us have a hot dinner. The brown breads in particular are simply an essential staple of good eating, though that doesn't mean to say that we are going to pass up on the scones and the carrot cakes if we are offered. Having access to bread of this quality should be a constitutional right of every Irish citizen. (Sinead McGuire & Pascal Gillard, Carrick Road, Drumshanbo ☎ 071-964 1033 ✉ sinead@jinnysbakery.com ✆ www.jinnysbakery.com)

only in Leitrim
Dromod Boxty

Jamestown

Restaurant
● The Cottage

Sham Hanifa is making some good things to eat in this handsome room, which readers may recall as formerly being Al Mezza. A handsome building and a handsome room, and handsome food on the plates: seared scallop

Leitrim

with shredded pork belly and apple and cider foam; Vietnamese salad with Kearns organic leaves, sesame beef, ginger and spring onion dressing; sirloin with mushroom and beef marrow crumble; double chocolate biscuit cheesecake with white chocolate curl. One to watch, closely. (Sham Hanifa, Jamestown ☎ 071-962 5933 ✉ info@cottagerestaurant.ie ⏱ www.cottagerestaurant.ie – Open 6pm-10pm Thurs-Sun, noon-4pm Sun)

Kinlough

Restaurant with Rooms
● The Courthouse

Piero Melis is a serious cook, and if he worked away from the tiny hamlet of Kinlough he would be better known for his robust, rich Sardinian cuisine. But then, if he didn't work in lovely little Kinlough, you wouldn't have the pleasure of coming to this sweet place, staying overnight, enjoying some good wines imported by the man himself, and then enjoying the coup de grâce which is this fine food: crab linguini with garlic and chilli; courgette, pepper and goat's cheese penne; veal saltimbocca with mozzarella; fillet steak with rocket, Parmesan shavings, rosemary and olive oil. Wine buffs should look out in particular for the rare Sardinian wines that Piero imports, and which lend the final note of authenticity to a little slice of Sardinia in lovely Leitrim. (Piero Melis, Main Street, Kinlough ☎ 071-984 2391 ✉ thecourthouserest@eircom.net ⏱ www.thecourthouserest.com – Restaurant open 6.30pm-9.30pm,'till 10pm high summer), noon-2.30pm Sun)

Manorhamilton

Shop
● The Co-Op Shop

Small, lovely and unchanging, The Co-Op Shop is one of our favourite places to shop in the north west. They sell the peerless produce of local producers, arrayed around a shop that looks and feels like every Irish grocery store looked and felt back in 1966, and that timelessness is an apt metaphor for what the Co-Op Shop does: it offers a timeless service, and timeless goodness. (Manorhamilton ☎ 071-985 5609 – Open 9.30am-6pm Mon-Sat)

Leitrim

● **Manorhamilton Farmers' Market**

There is a fine little market held at the Bee Park on Fridays, where you will find local beeswax candles, porter cakes, local organic fruit and veg, cheese, fresh fish and lots of good domestic baking. (Bee Park, Fridays 10am-2pm)

Rossinver

Herbs
● **Eden Plants**

Rod Alston is an early music specialist, and a herb-growing specialist, and the two things seem to us to harmonise beautifully together, indeed to belong together. So the next time you order some of Mr Alston's beautiful herbs, and when it is time to plant them, play a little Purcell, or Telemann, and think of Mr Alston, out there in the hilly fields of his farm surrounded by the beauty of herbs, a line of William Byrd or Couperin running through his mind. (Rod Alston, Rossinver ☎ 071-985 4122 ✉ rodalston@eircom.net)

Organic Centre
● **The Organic Centre**

They ring the changes of the seasons in The Organic Centre, simply by preparing for them. As autumn 2009 was setting in, you could attend courses here on mushroom hunting – timely – preserving and storing vegetables and fruit – timely – remedies for the winter months – timely – planning and planting your garden – timely – as well as super-informative courses on growing and sprouting wheatgrass, growing trees from seed, wine making and growing your own mushrooms. It's because of this mix of timeliness allied to forward-planning that the OC is so important for good food and sustainablility in Ireland. Hans Wieland does a fabulous job as administrator, and the energy that the tutors bring to the courses is unflagging and inspirational. Haven't done an OC course? You haven't lived! (Hans Wieland, Rossinver ☎ 071-985 4338 ✉ organiccentre@eircom.net 🖰 www.theorganiccentre.ie)

Leitrim

County Limerick

Adare

Restaurant
● **White Sage**

Tony Schwarz has cooked in and around Adare for some years, including a stint in the Mustard Seed, so getting the keys to his own place in Ireland's prettiest village was always on the cards. Even before you get in the door this thatched cottage will have charmed you, and the cooking then completes the task: slow roast pork with white sage stuffing, choucroute and charcuterie sauce is the sort of signature dish chefs would kill for; duck confit with black pudding, apples and prunes is classic robust brasserie fare. Desserts show the skill of gifted pastry chef: pear and frangipane with yogurt, cream cheese and honey ice cream is already a classic, and standards like crème brulée are shown appropriate respect. (Tony Schwarz, Main Street, Adare ☎ 061-396004/087 9450254 ✆ thewhitesagerestaurant@hotmail.com ⌂ www.thewhitesagerestaurant.com – Open 5.30pm-10pm Tue-Sat)

Restaurant
● **The Wild Geese**

David and Julie have been at the helm of the beautiful Wild Geese for nigh on a decade, and have done nothing more during that time than get better and better and better. Their success is simple: the alliance of their respective talents is a mighty achievement, she at front-of-house, he in the kitchen, and we mean it when we say there isn't a better him 'n' her team in the country. Put this lovely food and service with the most romantic dining space, and you have magic. The food reads somewhat fussy, but its rigorous logic makes for great eating, so bring on the fillets of seabass with crab wontons, the lamb with rosemary and thyme potato gratin, the perfection of pineapple and mango compote with passion fruit ice cream. (David Foley & Julie Randles, Rose Cottage, Main Street, Adare ☎ 061-396451 ✆ wildgeese@indigo.ie ⌂ www.thewild-geese.com – Open 6.30pm-10pm Tue-Sun (closed Sun off season)

Annacotty

● Copper & Spice

The village branch of Brian and Seema Conroy's city star, with true ethnic cookery and affable service. (Bryan & Seema Conroy, The Mill Bar, Annacotty Village ☎ 061-338791 ✉ copperandspice@eircom.net 🖰 www.copperandspice.com – Open 5pm-10.30pm Tue-Sat, 12.30pm-4.30pm Sun)

● Ponaire Coffee

As part of Tommy and Jennifer Ryan's plan for world domination through coffee, the couple have just expanded their business from a small unit in Tipperary to a deli and bright, open roastery in Annacotty business park. They eventually plan to have a shop and deli in Limerick city, so the world domination plan is proceeding apace. Tommy does the marketing and distribution, while Jennifer does the roasting and packaging. World domination is assured because their coffees are so superb. Like the best of the new generation of roasters, the Ryans are alive to the organoleptic potential of their beans and their roasts. They understand the volatility of the beans and the roasting process, and in playing with the process and mastering it, they capture not only the flavour and the essence of the bean, but somehow manage to package its very energy also. These are not mere drinks: these are life support machines, with goodness in every cup, and they are savoured at Bridgestone Central, especially the clove and black pepper notes of the Connoisseur blend, with its mix of Indonesian and Columbian beans. Magnificent artisanship, nothing less. (Thomas & Jennifer Ryan, Unit E1 Annacotty Business Park, Annacotty ☎ Roastery 061-339799 ☎ Coffee Shop 061-339801 🖰 www.ponaire.ie)

Ballingarry

● The Green Apron

Theresa Storey has been a busy producer since our last edition. As well as selling her preserves in the Limerick market, she now mans a stall at the local Ballingarry market on the first Tuesday of each month. Back at the ranch, Theresa has begun to run kitchen gardening courses – home-preserving; backyard chicken keeping; organic growing; hedgerow foods, herb gardening and growing under cover – are just some of the delightful introductions to the really good life. Ms Storey is an inspiring artisan: anyone who can dream up a "Partridge in a Pear Tree" chutney is simply pure Bridgestone. (Theresa Storey, Derryclough, Ballingarry ☎ 069-68524 ✉ storeytd@tinet.ie ✉ storeytd@thegreenapron.ie ✆ www.thegreenapron.ie)

Restaurant & Country House
● The Mustard Seed

Dan Mullane is a poet of the aesthetic world, a man whose grasp of design, comfort and style is matched by few others in Ireland. Both Echo Lodge, the country house, and its Mustard Seed restaurant, are blessed with the sort of classic charm that makes you think of Garbo, Gable, Bogart and Bacall, a timeless summit of style that makes you swoon with feverish delight. As with design, so it is with the cooking in The Mustard Seed, the sort of elegant country cooking that uses lots of modern methods – tempura; vegetable foams, confit – but which always serves forth food that is nothing other than Mustard Seed cooking, just the way we all love it. A balm for the soul, no less. (Dan Mullane, Echo Lodge, Ballingarry ☎ 069-68508 ✉ mustard@indigo.ie ✆ www. mustardseed.ie – Open all year, except first two weeks in Feb)

only in Limerick
Limerick Ham

Drumcollogher

Organic College & Market
● Organic College & Market

If you are going to write a Mission Statement, then do it like this: "The Organic College affirms the right of people to produce and use health-giving food, without damage to the environment. It provides a range of courses and support services towards sustainable farming and co-operative rural living." Two sentences that push all the buttons: the right to produce, to use, the right to health, the respect for the environment, the need for sustainability, the dream of co-operative living in the country. Beautiful. No wonder the courses at the College are always over-subscribed.(Drumcollogher ☎ 063-83604 ✉ oifig@organiccollege.com ◌ www.organiccollege.com)

Hospital

Smoothies and Juices
● **Wild Orchard**

So, whilst Innocent sold out to Coca-Cola, Diarmuid and his team have kept on doing the good thing, making healthy Wild Orchard drinks the proper way, and doing it in a manner that is as refreshing as a WO blackberry and blueberry smoothie. "We squeeze our fruit gently", they say, and they do that, and everything else, with a smile. Excellent. (Diarmuid Crowley, Enterprise Centre, Hospital ☎ 061-383930 ✉ diarmuid@wildorchard.ie ◌ www.wildorchard.ie)

Kilcornan

Preserves
● **Nature's Bounty**

"It is the flavours and textures that will surprise the most, I think, and the realisation of to just what extent the cultivation and mass production of food have muted our taste experiences." Richard Mabey wrote that in the original edition of his ground-breaking book, *Food For Free*, back in 1972. He went on: "There is a whole galaxy of powerful and surprising flavours preserved intact in the wild stock: tart and smoky berries...."
Colette O'Farrell collects hedgerow fruits for her jams and preserves, and in so doing she shows us – truly – the bounty of nature, the galaxy of powerful and surprising flavours in the wild stock. She has planted an orchard with heritage varieties, so the link is with both wild nature and historical nature, and tuning in to this endless food chain is a wonderful, startling, food experience. (Colette O'Farrell, Cowpark, Kilcornan ☎ 061-393942)

Farmhouse B&B, Rare Breed Pork Products

● Rigney's Farmhouse Bed and Breakfast

Caroline Rigney is not just a benchmark-standard pork producer, who sells from her smart farmshop at her house. She also utilises the house as an extremely capable B&B hostess. But for the purposes of this book, it is Mrs Rigney's skill as a rearer of rare-breed pork and a skilled processor of that same meat that we come to applaud: Curraghchase is magnificent pork meat, right up there with the very best in the country, and nothing is nicer than a trip to Kilcornan to load up the freezer box with packets and packets of rashers and sausages and the best pig's trotters in the country. When Caroline first wrote to us, she noted that: "I love all the animals that I keep. The pigs put me in good humour...". And that's the secret: happy animals, superlative foods. (Caroline Rigney, Curraghchase, Kilcornan ☎ 061-393988 ✉ info@ rigneysfarm.com ⌐ www.rigneysfarm.com)

Killonan

Artisan Confectionery

● Pandora Bell

As soon as we had eaten our first ever Pandora Bell salted caramel, we unwrapped and ate another one. Several minutes later, we ate another, and we want you to know that this is atypical behaviour for us. But, it's not everyday that confectionery like Nicole Dunphy's comes into your life. Astonishingly, Ms Dunphy trained herself as a chocolatier whilst on a career break, before heading to the Valrhona School and then the Italian Culinary Institute. Her caramels and her Tim Burtonish lollipops and her nougats are the stuff of dreams, and not just kid's dreams, but the dreams of anyone who loves great confectionery made with pure ingredients. "Faking it is just not an option," says Nicole, and here is a bright new star. (Nicole Dunphy, Killonan, Ballysimon ☎ 086-824 1823 ✉ info@ pandorabell.ie ⌐ www.pandorabell.ie)

Limerick City

● Alchemist Earth

Michaela Maguire's natural remedy shop is also home to
good wholefoods and the brilliant Gingergirl range from
Helen Keown. (Michaela Maguire, 10 Sarsfield Street,
Limerick ☎ 061-404218 – Open 10.15am-5.45pm Mon-
Thu, 10.15am-6.30pm Fri, 10am-6pm Sat)

Café
● Café Noir

Pat O'Sullivan, of Moll d'Arby's, has fashioned a great success in Café Noir, a good looking room with well-chosen
food, from neat breads – white; baguette; cheese and
onion, and lots of pretty pastries – to daily staples like
James McGeough's magnificent lamb and pork sausage
rolls, steak and Guinness pie; good eggy quiches and nice
bespoke salads. The formula is simple, the discipline considerable, and it doesn't miss a beat from pastry-topped
onion soup to lemon meringue pie. (Pat O'Sullivan,
Robert Street, Limerick ☎ 061-411222 – Open 8am-6m
Mon-Sat)

Asian Superstore
● Cheong Heng Hong Oriental Supermarket

It's big, it's chilly, it's characterless, and it's got everything you need for every conceivable ethnic dish. Make
sure to get a Chinese lantern to light at your next
garden party as darkness falls: locals will be sure to
report it to the Gardai as a UFO! (95-96 Henry Street,
Limerick ☎ 061-316868 – Open 11am-7pm Mon-Sun)

Restaurant
● Chocolat

An off-shoot of the Tsang family's family of restaurants,
Chocolat has a French name, Asian food, and a sexy,
glossy, black interior. But value is super-keen, especially the
early-bird menus when you can feed the family at decent
prices. The Asian dishes work best – Chinatown roasted
duck; wasabi sirloin; General Tsao's chicken – so these
are by far the smarter choices than the Mediterranean-
style dishes. (The Tsang family, 110 O'Connell Street,
Limerick ☎ 061-609709 ✆ www.chocolatrestaurant.ie –
Open 10am-10.30pm Mon-Sat, noon-10pm Sun)

THE BRIDGESTONE IRISH FOOD GUIDE   355

Restaurant
● Ciaran's Café

When Valerie O'Connor ordered the shepherd's pie in Ciaran's Café, what she got was a perfect plate of food: a pie of lentils topped with celeriac, with lemony, buttery carrots, shredded beets dressed with sesame seeds; garlicky kale, and simple, plain quinoa. Now, that is how to do vegetarian food, and with some poppy seed and lemon cake to finish, and after a trip to the ace farmers' market at UL on a Tuesday morning, you are talking sweet satisfaction. Ciaran has a lot of theories about food and its consumption, but he knows the greatest theory of them all is deliciousness, and doing it right. (Ciaran O'Callaghan, Drumroe Village, University of Limerick, Castletroy ☎ 061-338787 ✉ info@ciarans.ie ⟨ www.ciarans.ie – Open 9am-5pm Mon-Fri)

Restaurant
● Copper & Spice

Bryan and Seema Conroy's wonderful ethnic restaurant offered stellar new standards in Limerick when they first opened, and they have maintained those standards with impressive consistency, successfully opening a second branch at Annacotty. C&S is particularly important as a source of imaginative, true vegetarian cookery, but authentic and deeply-understood culinary expertise underlies all they do. (Bryan & Seema Conroy, 2 Cornmarket Row, Limerick ☎ 061-313620 ✉ copperandspice@eircom.net ⟨ www.copperandspice.com – Open 5pm-10.30pm Tue-Sun)

Restaurant
● Cornstore

Dark, shiny, plush and luxurious, Cornstore is a stunner, and chef Maura Baxter backs up the charm of the room with some really charming cooking. It's worth mentioning that their children's food is quite inspired – proper burgers, real goujons, fluffy mash, crisp fries and proper puddings are all artfully and carefully made, and they will even give baby a bowl of mash and puréed vegetables with Parmesan for free. So, whilst the kids are happily tucking into delicious, proper, healthful food, you can enjoy the punch of dishes like sea bream with green and black olives, or 12-hour pork belly on mash with apple purée and cider jus, and then finish with a fine Eton Mess, and excellent coffee. Cornstore knows what it wants to do, and it knows exactly how to do it. A gem. (Maura Baxter, 19 Thomas Street, Limerick ☎ 061-609 000 🖰 www. cornstorelimerick.com – Open noon-3pm Sat & Sun, 5pm-late Mon-Sun)

Delicatessen
● Country Basket

Choc full of great wines, veggies, artisan bread, local preserves, cheeses, hams, Ponaire coffee, Pandora Bell chocolate and all manner of good things. This bright new store, opened by chef Simon Wilkinson, has been described as the Fallon and Byrne of Limerick, and is a great addition to the city. (Simon Wilkinson, Thomas Street, Limerick ☎ 061-319621 – Open 10am-7pm Mon-Sat)

Deli
● La Cucina

Bru and Lor run a great place, the sort of place that is always great, and which doesn't really get enough attention for just how good it is, how important it is to the goodness of the scheme of things in a city like Limerick. Bruno's Italian cooking is true and to the point: take simple things, understand them, now make them delicious. His cooking is so rock-steady that plans to expand La Cucina have been on the cards for a while, and will hopefully be realised soon, bringing this soulful food to even more happy eaters, along with some wine. Right now, for great savory dishes, salads, flatbread sarnies, punchy coffees and great food to go, La Cucina can't be beat. (Bruno & Lorraine Fanneran, 5 University Court, Castletroy ☎ 061-333980 🖰 http://italianfoodies.ie – Open 11am-9pm Mon-Fri, noon-9pm Sat, 5pm-9pm Sun)

Fishmonger
● René Cusack

The fish shops now known as René Cusack began life as the Grimsby Fish Stores, started by Michael Cusack in 1910. Today, the business is in the hands of the affable Paul Cusack, and there are four René Cusack stores, all hosting a fantastic display of fish. The fish processing business is in Raheen, where they process fish and smoke salmon in the traditional way. The philosophy behind the stores hasn't changed. "I want to make shopping here as pleasurable an experience as I can," says Paul Cusack. "Anybody can buy whiting and put it on a counter, but if you have a good approach to the customer, if you personalise it, and give time to your customers, then it becomes a cultural thing." If you're in Limerick on a Saturday morning, don't miss the Saturday morning market, and René Cusack's fish counter. As Paul Cusack says, "It's a fun place, it's buzzing!" (Paul Cusack, St Alfonsus Street, Limerick ☎ 061-440054 – Open 9am-5.30pm Mon-Sat. Also at The Limerick Milk Market, ☎ 061-408011– Open 10am-6pm Tue-Sat. Also at 9 Market Street, Ennis ☎ 061-6892712 – Open 9am-6pm Mon-Sat. Also at Belhavel, Athlone ☎ 0906-420355 – Open 10am-6pm)

Café
● Ducartes at the Hunt Museum

A pretty riverside terrace is just one of the attractions of Ducartes, always a nice place to share good food. (Hunt Museum, Rutland Street, Limerick ☎ 061-312662 ⌂ www.huntmuseum.com – Open 10am-5pm Mon-Sat, 2pm-5pm Sun)

Wine Shop
● Fine Wines

The Fine Wines group now comprises no fewer than 18 stores, from their birthplace in Limerick, south to Cork, east to Dublin, and north to Galway. (Vintage House, 48 Roches Street, Limerick ☎ 061-417784 ⌂ www. finewines.ie – Open 10.30am-11pm Mon-Sun)

Butcher
● Jim Flavin

Flavin's may have an unremarkable location, adjacent to the petrol station, but don't let this distract you from the fact that this is a super serious destination for food lovers. Aside from winning rafts of medals annually at the butchers' competitions, which shows that the nuts and bolts of Jim Flavin's business are carefully attended to, their special USP is the fact that they finish their own beef on their own farm. This explains why Flavin's beef is the meat of choice for leading local chefs. Elsewhere the company is eternally improving, expanding their range, and over the last couple of years they have transformed the shop into a one-stop culinary solution shop. But that brilliant beef is the product that you simply must not miss. (Jim Flavin, Dublin Road, Castletroy, Limerick ☎ 061-331977 – Open 7am-7pm Mon-Sat)

Artisan Producer
● Forbidden Food

Connie Devlin's delicious soups, felafels, hummus, samosas and dips are almost completely vegan, but it is their sheer deliciousness, rather than any dietary framework, that marks out the work of this gifted cook. Get them at both the UL market and the Milk Market, and make your life even better. (Connie Devlin, 6 Reidy Park, Clancy Strand, Limerick ☎ 086-104 4443 ✉ dollydevlin@yahoo.co.uk)

Restaurant
● Freddy's Bistro

"This place is gold," said Valerie O'Connor after her last visit to Liz Phelan's bistro on Glentworth Street. Val isn't alone: "The best meal we had in Ireland" wrote two visting Americans – Jerry and Barbara – after they got back home, in a mail to Bridgestone Central. So, Ms Phelan is onto something good, based mainly on classic dishes from which she extracts the maximum of tactile pleasure: duck pâté is smooth, musky and earthy; mussels in white wine are juicy, plump and peachy sweet. Sea bass in lime leaves will send you to Vietnam on a cloud, whilst rack of lamb with roasted pumpkin is pure comfort cooking. Desserts are rustic and robust, pricing is good and service does just what it needs to do in an atmospheric room powered by the energy of a fired-up kitchen. (Liz Phelan, Theatre Lane, Lower Glentworth Street ☎ 061-418 749 ᗏ www.freddysbistro.com – Open from 5.30pm-late Tue-Sat)

Restaurant
● The French Table

In a nice site on Steamboat Quay, The French Table has already notched up a year of cooking and serving fine, classical French food in a simple, clean room. Toulouse sausage and wild mushrooms with a smoked garlic dressing is nothing less than a mini cassoulet, whilst a cassolette of pan-seared prawns with lemon butter is straight out of the 1980's, and all the better for such confident timelessness. Crispy lamb shoulder with grilled lamb cutlets is hearty fare, whilst trio of fish and shellfish with a champagne beurre blanc is light and clean. The dessert plate is one of the preferred ways to ascend to heaven direct from Steamboat Quay, an explosion of sorbets, mousses, tarts, brulées that will sweep you up to the cumulus. Value is good, and they look after their customers as guests, which says it all. A good choice for lunch as well, when value is sharp as a nail. (Thomas & Deirdre Fialon, 1 Steamboat Quay, Limerick ☎ 061-609 274 ⏚ www.frenchtable.ie – Open Lunch from noon Tue-Sat, Dinner from 6pm Tue-Sun)

Butcher
● Garrett's Speciality Butchers

A funky charcuterie shop, and a showcase for the sort of work that the newer generation of butchers in Ireland are doing. In Garrett's, virtually everything is done for you: the meats are cut to order, marinaded this way and that, trussed, prepared, stuffed, and – effectively – ready to roll. Butchers like Garrett Landers know the limitations of their customers – a very small set of cooking skills – but they turn this weakness into their own strength, a brilliant response to market demand for meat-based meals that are simple to finish in the domestic kitchen, but which have all the qualities and virtues of hard work and skill. The hard work and skill is Mr Lander's: the credit is all yours. (Garrett Landers, Unit 16 Racefield Shopping Centre, Dooradoyle ☎ 061-305734 ✉ garrett@ garrettsbutchers.com ⏚ www.garrettsbutchers.com – Open 7am-7pm Mon-Fri, 7am-6pm Sat)

Artisan Producer
● Gingergirl

"I have a pot of gooseberry and elderflower simmering... my customers have gone nuts for this: it sells out at every market and one shop has just re-ordered after a delivery four days ago. I'm thrilled".
That's Gingergirl, aka Helen Keown, red-headed dynamo, maker of jams, chutneys, preserves and other mercurial brews that folk go nuts for. Taste any of them – take the plum preserve we have in the kitchen and which is almost completely finished – and you will understand why: Ms Keown captures the essence of the fruit. Her cooking is a high-wire act of balancing, extracting, preserving, concocting. delirious. (Helen Keown, Sunnyside, Rosbrien, Punches Cross, Limerick ☎ 087-611 6360 ✉ helen@ gingergirl.ie ⏚ www.gingergirl.ie)

Cheese Shop and Deli
● Greenacres

Marie's day-to-day shop opens out on Saturday to

include a market stall, but at any time it's a place for lively banter, and great foods and drinks. (Marie Murphy, Limerick Milk Market ☎ 087-247 5478)

Wholefood Shop
● The Grove

Limerick's wholefood diamond has a simple thesis: make it fresh, sell it all, then close shop and go home. Then come back tomorrow and do it again. The blackboard menu spells out what is on offer – veggie pizzas; cheese and curry pie; lentil bake; shepherdless pie – all served with slaws and waldorfs. "They deserve a mention and a handshake" says Valerie O'Connor. Done. (Sue Hassett, 11 Upper Cecilia Street ☎ 061-410084 – Open 8.30am-3.30pm Mon-Fri)

Delicatessen
● Ivan's of Caherdavin

The star of Caherdavin, on the western edge of the city, Ivan's is a fail-safe source for good foods, and is especially popular with locals for properly prepared food-to-go. (Ivan Cremins, Caherdavin, Limerick ☎ 061-455766 ✉ ivanssupermarket@eircom.net – Open 8am-11.30pm Mon-Sun)

Restaurant
● Jasmine Palace

The JP is one of the food staples of Limerick city centre, popular and unchanging, with Chinese food cooked for Irish appetites, which is just how their copious queues of customers like it. (O'Connell Mall, O'Connell Street, Limerick ☎ 061-412484 ✉ info@jasminepalacerestaurant.com ⌂ www. jasminepalacerestaurant.com – Open 4pm-11pm Mon-Thu, 12.30pm-11.30pm Fri & Sat, 12.30pm-10.30pm Sun)

Market
● Limerick Milk Market

As we go to press the Limerick Milk Market is closed to facilitate the building of a roof to cover the entire complex. This will make a good thing even better. Just to give you a taster, here is a report from Valerie O'Connor about a visit to the market before the roof was in place.

Green Saffron: Curry for breakfast? If Arun Kapil has concocted it, with his wondrous array of spices, then yes please! Green Saffron has become one of the major market players over the last four years, best known not only for their superb spice mixes, but also for their cracking curries: channa masala packed with ginger; creamy and rich chicken korma, punchy lamb rogan josh. €30 gets a superb curry dinner with naan breads and rice, one of the best bargains going. **Kilshanny Cheese:** Pete Nibbering has been selling his hand-made Gouda at the Limerick market for 20 years. It's simple, he turns up, wheels out the cheese, sells up and goes home. He makes cumin gouda, the best one, then pepper, garlic, herb, plain, and he sells a few rounds of the neighbouring St Tola goat's cheese too. The milk comes from his neighbour's cows, as cheese is meant to be, smooth, smooth, smooth. (☎ 065-7071228) **Marie's Cheese Shop:** Marie's Cheese Shop has really upped its game. Not content with getting all the shoppers sitting in her café Marie has hugely expanded her repertoire and now so many cheeses adorn her tables. It's a feast for the eyes and the love handles too. Wheels of French brie, Gorgonzola, slabs of Cheddar and doorsteps of feta are here. Rounds of salsa cheese and Wensleydale are selling like hot (cheese) cakes. Great to see Marie thriving at this time, and she is a character to be reckoned with. Oh and her prices are really good. (☎ 087-247 5478)

On the Wild Side: The incredibly talented Olivier makes the trip from Kerry to Limerick to bring his wares to a devoted Limerick following. He makes his own merguez, venison sausages, smoked salmon salads, tapenade of sea veg, sea spaghetti with garlic and ginger and the kind of food Henry VIII would have lopped his own head off for. He also sells goodies from the home of Gubbeen and various Spanish sausages and dried meats. Did I say Henry VIII? I meant Bilbo Baggins. (☎ 066-713 9028) **Piog Pies:** Brid Ni Mathuna set up this business with her husband one year ago and has firmly established herself on the list of must-haves for Limerick foodies. Her pies are simple, delicious and consistent. Beef and Guinness, Kerry lamb, Shepherd's, Free Range Chicken are all yum. The kids loved the shepherd's pie the most, my lamb one was full of tender meat and veggies with a just-right crust. Piog also sell in Listowel, Dingle and Mallow. (☎ 087-794 4036)

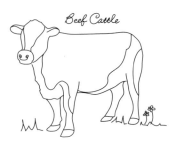

Beef Cattle

The Real Olive Company: These guys are bastions of the markets in Ireland. There is always a queue and they always sell out. The anchovies are just the best, the olives do what they say on the tin and their feta and olive salad is worth the queuing, as is their black olive tapenade. You can even do housekeeping here with super affordable lavender oil and dried lavender for cents. Nice soaps and dried fruit make you feel like you're just back from Provence, a good call when it's really Limerick in the rain. (🖰 www.therealoliveco.com) **Relihan's Farm Shop:** Adare man Tommy Relihan knew what he was doing when he decided to stick a pig on a spit and roast it at the crack of dawn every Saturday morning. This pig is hogged by mid day, in baps or in foil to take home and heat up for dinner. It has the best crackling too. Open one year, Relihans do a healthy trade in sausages, rashers, lamb and gourmet sausages. Their beef is mature Aberdeen Angus, reared on their farm in Adare. To support local food-trepeneurs they also sell Natures Bounty, Ponaire Coffee. The kids spent half an hour watching a butcher go to work on a beef carcass and then told me all about cuts and how to hang meat etc. Dinner and a show. (☎ 061-609607) **Sunflower Bakery:** The Sunflower Bakery is the one woman venture of Vi Russell. Known as the 'organic baker' as all her ingredients are organic, she really makes the best real bread you will taste. Cheese and onion loaf packs a punch, baguettes are rustic and gnarly. Her spelt bread is a great seller and she is passionate about it due to its high protein content. Carrot cake and lemon cake vie (sorry) for space with veg pasties, scones and pies. (☎ 086-220 7790) (Limerick Town Centre – Open Saturdays)

Butcher's Shop
● Brendan Loughnane

Loughnane's is a good, serious butcher's shop, the sort of folk who make good sausages and puddings, the staples of the breakfast table. (Brendan Loughnane, Upper William Street, Limerick ☎ 061-414213 – Open 8am-7pm Mon-Fri, 8am-5pm Sat)

Restaurant
● Market Square Brasserie

A classy, intimate room is part of the MSB formula for success, along with smart staff and good cooking, and it all makes for a successful combination. (Ronan Branigan, 74 O'Connell Street, Limerick ☎ 061-316311 – Open 6pm-9.30pm Tue-Sat)

Restaurant
● Moll d'Arby's

Pat O'Sullivan and chef Denis Cregan have run a good show in Moll d'Arby's over the last several years, and the refurbishment being undertaken as we write this book augurs well for their future ambitions. (Pat O'Sullivan, George's Quay, Limerick ☎ 061-411511 ✉ molldarbys@ eircom.net 🕆 www.molldarbys.com – Open 12.30pm-3pm Mon-Fri, 5.30pm-10pm Mon-Wed, 5.30pm-11pm Thur-Sat)

Restaurant
● Munchy Munchy

The destination for Limerick's own Chinese community, and a particularly good spot if you cherish dim sum, along with the slithery, gloopy outer-reaches of ethnic cooking. (1-2 Glentworth Street, Limerick ☎ 061-313113 – Open 12.30pm-2.30pm, 5.30pm-11.30pm Mon-Sat, 12.30pm-10.30pm Sun)

Butcher
● O'Connell's Butchers

Ask about a cheap cut for the family dinner in O'Connell's and Paul Crughan and his team might interest you in some lamb bellies, then tell you how to stuff them and exactly how to cook them. Ah: a real butcher's shop! Skilled charcutiers who know how to spice beef, make a sausage, and sell it to you with charm. O'Connell's is an old-style shop: old-style design, old-style expertise, old-style charm. (Paul Crughan, Little Catherine Street, Limerick ☎ 061-414 819)

Deli
● Olio & Farina

Susan Mulvihill runs a lovely shop, part of the excellent
O&F franchise, in a vividly pretty store in the city. The
Olio & Farina range shows the sort of tasty integrity that
underpins Italian artisan foods and crafts, and with 300
items for sale in the shop, Susan has everything you need
for that classic antipasto plate to the swishest pasta dinner. (Susan Mulvihill, 2 Little Catherine Street, Limerick
☎ 061-319133 ✉ limerick@olioefarina.com
🖰 www.olioefarina.com – Open 9am-6pm Mon-Sat)

Butcher's Shop
● Michael O'Loughlin

Good meat, great service. That's the mantra of Michael
O'Loughlin's shop, where you can source everything
from mature Birdhill beef to wild rabbit to pork and
apple sausages. The names of the farmers Michael
sources from are chalked on the 'board, and the shop
is also an excellent outlet for game during the season.
You can even get the spuds and the turnips here. (Michael
O'Loughlin, Upper William Street, Limerick ☎ 061-414102)

only in Limerick
The Milk Market

Hotel & Restaurant
● One Pery Square

Very quickly, No 1 Pery Square seems to have established
itself as the epicentre of Limerick's food culture. Patricia
Coughlan's boutique hotel and restaurant has been one of
the most completely conceived and delivered destinations
in Ireland in recent years, and from the moment they
opened their doors, the place was buzzing. The rooms are
beautiful, the cocktails are great, and the food is right in
step with the hip, knowing and genuine engagement that
you find here, from wild boar sausage with sauerkraut
to sea bream with cauliflower to chargrilled lamb rump.
These are big dishes and bold with flavour, delivered with
the confidence that this place exudes. Ms Coughlan is
a maverick, a person with a very clear vision and a soul
full of determination, and it all shows here in the star of
Limerick city. (Patricia Coughlan, 1 Pery Square, Limerick
☎ 061-402402 🖰 www.oneperysquare.com)

Restaurant
● La Piccola Pizzeria

La Piccola is actually two restaurants, both being fed by the same kitchen, and it has been in Limerick longer than you would believe. But, never mind the longevity, just feel the energy and the generosity: it's the kind of place where everyone sings Happy Birthday! to you when it's your big day, and that is just A-OK with us. So, tuck into specials like veal-stuffed mushrooms, or creamy mussels in a scallop dish with piped potato, or a good, rich lasagne with deep-flavoured ragu. You could call it a cliché, what with the waxy fiascos for candles and the movie star photos, but La Piccola is actually easy-going, casual dining at its best. 30 more years, we say. (Gareth Grimes, 56 O'Connell Street, Limerick ☎ 061-313899 – Open 5pm-10.30pm Mon-Sun)

Restaurant
● Poppadom

The Poppadom group set new benchmark standards for Indian cooking when they first opened in Rathgar in Dublin, and the small number of restaurants in the chain maintain consistent standards of delicious excellence and reliability. (Amjad Hussain, 2c Robert Street, Limerick ☎ 061-446644 – Open 5.30pm-11.30pm Mon-Sat)

Restaurant
● The River Bistro

Diarmuid O'Callaghan's first chef-patron venture has proven to be a huge success story for this talented cook, a man who first made waves many years ago when he cooked in the great Green Onion Café, when it was the brightest light in town. Today, his aim is just as true as back then: rack of lamb with crispy rosti; pork belly with black pudding; monkfish with pea bombs, autumn berry crumble. The cooking is generous in every way – sensuous, earthy, real and satisfying. (Diarmuid O'Callaghan, 4 George's Quay, Limerick ☎ 061-400990 ✉ riverbistro@eircom.net 🖰 http://theriverbistro.ie – Open 6pm-10pm Tue-Sat)

Market
● Riverside Market

Local heroes such as Helen Keown's Ginger Girl are amongst the Bedford Row stalwarts on a Sunday morning, selling lovely things in a lovely spot. Lots of good brunchy style cooking will keep you awake as you peruse the arts and crafts that are also for sale from local craftspeople. (Bedford Row, Sun, noon-5.30pm)

Fish & Game
● John Sadlier

The history of Sadlier's is long and distinguished: John's parents, Jim and Susan, opened the original shop on Henry Street back in 1948, moving four years later to Roches Street where they have been ever since. John Sadlier himself came into the business in 1974, a "young gossoon of 16", and has developed the business to a point where sales and turnover have increased steadily and successfully year-on-year. Today, cod and salmon are the best sellers, "but with people travelling there is also demand for sea bass, swordfish, tuna". Former best-sellers such as whiting have declined in popularity, but John says a keen cost-consciousness is seeing people choose haddock and other sometimes overlooked fish. (John Sadlier, Roches Street, Limerick ☎ 061-414232 – Open 8.30am-5.45pm Tue-Sat)

Café
● The Sage Café

Bright, buzzy, busy, and hugely successful right from the day it opened, the Sage thrives because of a vital curiosity in the way they cook what they cook. There is always some tweaking going on in their presentation of dishes, so that you can turn up day after day and order the same thing, except it won't be quite the same as the last time. This creativity runs right through the menu, from the breakfast muffins to the savoury hits like lambs' liver with cider jus to the truly sublime puddings – the carrot cake may be the very best you can get. Essential. (Mike & Siobhan Hogan, 67-68 Catherine Street, Limerick ☎ 061-409458 ✉ info@thesagecafe.com 🖰 www.thesagecafe.com – Open 9am-5pm Mon-Sat)

Artisan Market
● The UL Market

Established in September of 2008, and gathering momentum ever since, the UL Market brings out staff, students and locals to buy the beautiful produce of superstars like Gingergirl, as well as Stephen Joyce with fresh fish from Kinsale; Connie Devlin of Forbidden Foods with smashing soups, falafels, samosas and hummus; Dave and Nora from the fine Sallymills Bakery; Fran and John's funky Fruit and Nut Bakes; Roy from Plant Life with organic and health foods; Patricia comes down from Tuamgraney with her brilliant Wilde's Chocolate; that most gifted cheese-maker Marian Roeneveld has her superlative Killeen Farmhouse Cheese; Elaine and John from Good & Green have freshly dug produce from their small-holding; Loaf have their homemade dinners to go; there is good sushi from Gem Sushi; El Chilli Loco lay on the salsa dancing with chilli jams and salsas; Rose Cottage have fruits and fruit juice; and Tony Gerahy from the splendid Lough Boora Farm has organic beef, lamb, poultry, fruit and vegetables down from Offaly. Only brilliant. (University of Limerick ☎ 061-202700 – Open noon-5.30pm Tue)

Café
● The Wild Onion

We love the Wild Onion. We love the food, of course, those ever-reliable staples like the Chicago burger or the Reuben or the giant cookies and the great cheese cake. But we also love the hang-dog, shuffle-butt sort of style and ambience of the place, that feeling of a little bit of the Windy City in Ireland. Just ace. (Bob & Ruth Di Girolamo, High Street, Cornmarket, Limerick ☎ 061-440055 ✉ eat@wildonioncafe.com 🖰 www. wildonioncafe.com – Open 8am-4pm Tue-Fri, 9am-3pm Sat)

Wine Shop
● The Wine Buff

Ever-reliable Limerick outpost of the Wine Buff chain, and indeed the first of the franchise to open in Ireland. (Mike O'Mara, 17 Mallow Street, Limerick ☎ 061-313392 🖰 www.thewinebuff.com – Open 10.30am-7pm Mon-Sat, 10.30am-8pm Fri)

County Longford

Aughnacliffe

Artisan Chocolates
● ChocOneill

Choconeill were formerly associated with County Kildare, but Jamie and Beatrice have moved lock, stock and chocolate to Longford, where a shop is planned where chocoholics can visit to see exactly how these faberge class chocs are fashioned by these gifted chocolatiers. We love their boite en chocolate, where your selection of truffles, pralines and fresh chocolates are placed in a box that is made of... chocolate. You eat the chocolates, then eat the chocolate box. If that isn't foodie heaven, then we don't know what foodie heaven is. Their single origin chocolates are of superb distinction, their sea salt milk chocolate caramels are a beautiful twist on a classic. (Jamie & Beatrice O'Neill, The Hollow, Dunbeggan, Aughnacliffe ☎ 086-212 8067 info@chocooneill.ie www.choconeill.ie – Open by appointment)

Longford

Restaurant
● Aubergine Gallery Café

Stephen Devlin's restaurant has been the Longford leader for a good few years now, a simple, lean room with lively modern food that is meticulously managed by the Devlin family. It's human energy that explains the success of the Aubergine, an energy that starts with the funky room and the service, and then comes through in spades in Stephen's hip, direct cooking. The day's dishes are detailed on the blackboard menu and show Stephen's loving execution of modern classics: smooth chicken liver pâté; calamari; popcorn shrimp; lamb shank with root veg; confit duck with red wine sauce; rhubarb crumble. Lovely. (Stephen & Linda Devlin, 1st Floor, The White House, 17 Ballymahon Street ☎ 043-48633 aubergine@eircom.net – Open noon-5pm Tue-Thur, 6pm-8pm Wed-Thur, noon-4pm, 6pm-9.30pm Fri-Sat, 2pm-7.30pm Sun)

Butcher's Shop
● Herterich's Butchers

We used to stop in Herterich's to buy sausages and sausage rolls many years ago, en route from Dublin to Sligo. When we stop in Herterich's today, we still buy the bangers and the sausage rolls, but we would also be able to get everything we might need to feed the 5,000, for the shop has grown steadily, surely and importantly, and hasn't it been great to see this traditional store prosper. (Louis Herterich, 38 Ballymahon Street, Longford ☎ 043-46597 – Open 9am-6.15pm Mon-Thur, 8am-6.15pm Fri & Sat)

Market
● Longford Farmers' Market

Kearns' organic veg, O'Halloran's free-range eggs, Matthews' jams and chutneys, O'Connor's home baking, York's home grown vegetables, and Niall Byrne's Ireland West Seafare, all make for a lively market in Longford on Fridays. (Market Square, Fridays 9.30am-2pm)

Chocolate Shop and Café
● Torc Café and Food Hall

Torc is deservedly famous for its truffles, but Ruth and her team feed more than your sweet tooth in this bright, modern room. There is lots of proper savoury food served through the day, and this is a kitchen that cooks with relish, so it's poached egg, bacon and bagel for breakfast, chicken and mushroom pie for lunch, and then let's meet at six and have a stone-baked pizza and a glass of wine. Or two. Lovely, just lovely. (Ruth McGarry-Quinn, New Street, Longford ☎ 043-48277 ✉ info@torccafe.com 🖰 www.torccafe.com – Open 9.30am-6pm Mon-Sat. Tea menu served Fri & Sat, 5pm-8pm)

Restaurant & Country House
● Viewmount House

"Not only should it be in your 100 Best Places to Stay, it should be in the 10 Best Places to Stay." That's the sort of enthusing recommendation that Gary O'Hanlon's cooking has been winning in Beryl and James Kearney's Georgian house. It's not just the cooking in the VM restaurant, however, that is winning plaudits. The extension of the house to create new rooms and the out-in-the-out-house restaurant has been beautifully achieved, and with Beryl's hospitality and Mr O'Hanlon's cooking, it turns VM into a don't-miss! destination. The restaurant feels like an old coach house, with stone walls, good white tablecloths, pretty flowers and superb service. Mr O'Hanlon cooked in Boston for a while, and it shows. 'It's like an Upstate menu" is how our friend Bernadette described the autumn menu, but if it's upstate, it's superbly sourced upstate cooking, with the best foods of local artisans put to stunning use. A VM fall tartlet of butternut squash, Serrano ham, fig and Crozier Blue is awesomely delicious, whilst grilled milk-fed veal with soufflé potato and celeriac purée is nothing other than divine. The cheeseboard is beautifully presented, puds like dark chocolate ganache with raspberry and peppermint ice cream are wow! and this is the hottest destination Longford has seen in years. (Beryl & James Kearney, Dublin Road, Longford 043-334 1919 📖 info@ viewmounthouse.com 🖱 www.viewmounthouse.com)

Mushrooms

County Louth

Annagassan

Fish Smoker
● Coastguard Seafoods

Terry Butterly's smoked fish has a terrific reputation amongst restaurateurs, so if you come across a very nice piece of smoked salmon in a good restaurant somewhere on the east coast, there is a good chance that Mr Butterly caught it and smoked it. Terry has been doing the good thing for more than 35 years, and his expertise in marine conservation should see the next 35 years taken care of. (Terry Butterly, Harbour Road, Annagassan ☎ 042-937 2527)

Ardee

Butchers and Delicatessen
● Callaghan's Butchers and Deli

Peter's Ardee Gold sausages or his prize-winning black pudding may be the USP product that brings you here, but the high quality of all the meat will have you bringing home the bacon and the beef as well as the sausages. Peter is a fourth generation butcher, and a man who walks the fields in his wellies to select the best beef cattle, which he then ages for up to 28 days. A classic butcher's shop, where their creative charcuterie shines brightly. (Peter Callaghan, 58 Market Street, Ardee ☎ 041-685 3253 – Open 9am-6pm Mon-Thu, 9am-7pm Fri, 9am-6.30pm Sat)

Restaurant
● Fuchsia House

Sarah and Sarajit's menus offer dishes from all over the globe, but the interesting thing about Fuchsia is that they make this polyglot international style work, and they make it work successfully for a conservative local audience, so they're smart restaurateurs. So you could come for Sunday lunch and have darne of salmon, or sirloin of beef with mash and gravy, whilst on a Friday night you could be eating a thali plate of Indian food, with a mixture of curries and paratha, and on Wednesday you might have the cracking value special and follow some onion bhajis with lemon and herb chicken and a Bailey's cheesecake. Sarah runs the room superbly. (Sarah Nic Lochlainn & Sarajit Chanda, Dundalk Road, Ardee ☎ 041-685 8432 ✉ sarah@fuchsiahouserestaurant.com ⌂ www.fuchsiahouserestaurant.com – Open noon-3pm, 6pm-11pm Tue-Sat, noon-9pm Sun & bank holiday Mons)

Takeaway
● Indish Indian Takeaway

Indish is the take-away of the Fuchsia House restaurant, but focuses exclusively on Indian and Bangladeshi cooking, including excellent tandoor dishes. So, one sheekh kebab, one tandoori mackerel, one prawn bhuna, one palak paneer and paratha times two, all of it cooked in front of you as you wait, bringing back memories of those back-packing days in the Karakorams. (Sarah Nic Lochlainn & Sarajit Chanda, Bridge Street, Ardee 041-687 1111/687 1122 ✉ sarah@indishindiantakeaway.com ⌂ www.indishindiantakeaway.com - 5pm-11pm Mon-Sun)

only in Louth
Bellingham Blue Cheese

Carlingford Peninsula

Guesthouse
● Beaufort House

Michael Caine is a Yachtmaster, so he is one serious sailor, and he is also a superb cook, so if you fancy some time learning to sail in the Carlingford Sailing School, followed by good eating in a handsome, professional B&B in this loveliest of villages, then Beaufort is for you. Sure sounds like a rather good way to spend five days to us. (Michael Caine, Ghan Road, Carlingford ☎ 042-937 3879 ✉ michaelcaine@beauforthouse.net ⌂ www.beauforthouse.net)

Café
● Dan's Stonewall Café

Dan's is opposite PJ O'Hare's famous pub, and it's the choice of smart food lovers for a salad, a brie and bacon sandwich, a club sandwich on home-made bread, home-made soups, so it's always a busy place. Some weekends Dan opens a little later and serves tapas. (Dan McKevitt, The Square, Carlingford ☎ 042-9383797 – Open 9am-6pm Mon-Sun, with evening openings for tapas at weekends)

only in Louth
Carlingford Lough Oysters

Delicatessen
● Food For Thought

TJ runs one of the stars of the village in this well-established deli and traiteur in Carlingford, and it's a key address in the town. There are nice things to buy in the deli and to eat in the deli, and equally tasty, comforting foods to bring home. So, take care of lunch with a bumper-filled baguette and a pot of good tea or some proper soup, whilst that fresh lasagne and salad will take care of dinner. Sorted. Thank you very much, TJ. (Tom Hayes, Trinity Mews, Dundalk Street, Carlingford ☎ 042-938 3838 ⌨ tjhayes@iol.ie – Open 9am-7pm Mon-Sat, 10am-7pm Sun)

Guesthouse with Restaurant
● Ghan House

The question everyone has been asking us as we worked on this book throughout all of 2009 is; "How is the recession affecting restaurants and places to stay in Ireland?" And we reply, to people's amazement, that some places have barely noticed the recession at all. Ghan House is one of those places, and that doesn't surprise us one bit, for Paul Carroll and his team have polished and perfected their offer of food and accommodation in this modest country house over the last decade, and they have created a vivid, charismatic destination that brings guests back time and again. The cooking is rock-steady country cooking – shoulder of Cooley beef with wild mushroom ragoût and fondant potatoes; pork cooked in Calvados with apples and herbs; Sichuan roast quail with chilli and soy. The strength of Ghan House, however, is the totality of the experience, where service, comfort and cooking all align, perfectly. (Paul Carroll, Carlingford ☎ 042-937 3682 ᗧ ghanhouse@ eircom.net ᗧ www.ghanhouse.com – Open lunch by arrangement, dinner 7pm-9.30pm. Booking essential for lunch and dinner)

Louth

Bistro
● Kingfisher Bistro

Siblings Mark and Claire Woods actually describe themselves as a "brother and sister team", which is rather sweet. They have recently upped their game in the Darcy McGee centre, doubling the size of the restaurant when they refurbished, fitting a new kitchen, getting a restaurant licence and devising new menus and wine list, a very apt vote of confidence as they come into a decade of service. Mark likes to accent some dishes with Asian notes – star anise with duck; roast curry oil with belly pork; a Nobu-style Asian cod with potato rosti – whilst other dishes sail straight ahead: roast chicken with champ and spring onion and bacon velouté; shank of Cooley lamb with celeriac mash. The wine list is concise and appealing. (Clare & Mark Woods, Darcy McGee Court, Dundalk Street, Carlingford ☎ 042-937 3716 ᗧ info@kingfisherbistro.com ᗧ www. kingfisherbistro.com – Open 6.30pm-9pm Tue-Sun, 12.30pm-3pm Sun)

Pub
● PJ O'Hare's

O'Hare's is a famous and famously atmospheric bar and restaurant, where the cooking is sound and logical: Carlingford Lough chowder, steak, Guinness and oyster pie, Slaney lamb with red wine and thyme, Annagassan smoked salmon. (Michael & Bernadette Heaney, Whitestown, Carlingford ☎ 042-937 3730)

Bistro and Accommodation
● The Oystercatcher Lodge & Bistro

Comfortable rooms and savoury bistro cooking using fresh fish and shellfish from the bay, and lamb and beef from the Cooley hills, are the Oystercatcher formula, and it's a formula that has been working successfully for many years now. (Brian & Denise McKevitt, Market Square, Carlingford. Accommodation ☎ 042-937 3922

Dining ☎ 042-937 3989 ✉ info@theoystercatcher.com
🖱 www.theoystercatcher.com – Food served 6pm-
9.30pm Mon-Sun, Thur-Sun off season, open for lunch
during high season only)

Castlebellingham

Louth

Farmhouse Cheese
● **Bellingham Blue**

Peter and Anita Thomas make a brilliant raw milk blue
cheese, one of the most difficult callings in the world of
specialist cheesemaking. Anita has the dairying background, whilst Peter is a printer by trade, and this union
of differences is surely what makes Bellingham so interesting and different. You could compare it to an English
Stilton, maybe even a mature Gorgonzola, but of course
the truth is that it is both those things and yet none of
them, for the Thomases have fashioned something quite
unique, "Strong blue cheese, mottled rind, strong rustic
flavour" is how Ross Lewis of Chapter One in Dublin
describes Bellingham on his menu, and that's just right.
Bellingham is a member of the Slow Food Ireland raw
milk cheese presidium (Peter Thomas, Mansfieldtown,
Castlebellingham ☎ 042-937 2343 ✉ glydefarm@
eircom.net)

Farmers' Market
● **Castlebellingham Farmers' Market**

A good farmers' market is held in quiet Castlebellingham
on the first Sunday of each month. (1st Sunday in the
month, 11am-5pm)

Drogheda

Restaurant
● **Borzalino Restaurant**

Dominic and Filomena's friendly family place is where
you head to to feed the kids pizza whilst you enjoy some
ravioli with smoked salmon and ricotta or a classic like
saltimbocca alla Romana. It's been a good destination for
more than a decade now, so the locals like what they
do and the way they do it, and everyone comes

back. (Dominic & Filomena Borza, 20 Loughboy, Mell, Drogheda ☎ 041-984 5444 ✆ www.borzalinorestaurant. com – Open 5.30pm-10.30/11pm Mon-Sun)

Wine Bar
● D'Vine

Sonia Micallef has really pulled off a success here in the quirky D'Vine. She keeps things simple: there are plat-ters such as antipasto misto or the grand board to share which will get any bunch of mates off to a great start, then there are bruschetta, then salads, and the black-board has the cooked dishes of the day, and the wine list has the best selection of bottles in the county. Here is a cook who knows exactly what she wants to do and does exactly what she does best – tartiflette; Lyonnaise salad; cod in tomato and red pepper; a demon orange cake. The food is ruddy and real, the mix of dishes and service is right on the money. (Sonia Micallef & Damien Leddy, Patrickswell Lane, Off Narrow West Street, Drogheda ☎ 041-980 0440 – Open noon-3pm Mon-Fri, 6pm-late Wed-Fri, noon-late Sat, 5pm-late Sun)

only in Louth
Glebe Brethan Cheese

Hotel
● Eastern Seaboard Bar & Grill

We first came across Reuven Diaz many years ago when he started cooking in Louth, but then lost touch with this genial guy until he upped and opened the slick Eastern Seaboard with his wife, Jenni Glasgow. These cool cats have created a funky, swish space, albeit in an unlikely setting in an industrial estate out of town, in which to enjoy Reuven's cooking. The menu is lengthy, but choice ingredients and sane, level-headed New York-style cooking, as well as good value, means the food hits the spot: crab cakes in ciabatta with lime mayo; lemon grilled swordfish; beer-battered haddock; portobello "steak" with slow-roast tomatoes and roast garlic butter. This is clever work, clever cooking, and a whole new cool school for County Louth. (Jenni Glasgow & Reuven Diaz, 1 Bryanstown Centre, Dublin Road, Drogheda ☎ 041-980 2570 ✉ info@easternseaboard.ie ✆ www.easternseaboard.ie – Food served noon-10pm daily, till 8pm Sun)

Fishmonger
● The Fish Cart

Peter Kirwan was a fishmonger who sold fish in the centre of Drogheda from a pony and cart, and today his son, Patrick Kirwan, continues this proud family tradition in the centre of Drogheda, selling fish in The Fish Cart – named after his father's cart. Patrick also started selling fish from a cart in the town, before opening his shop in 1996.During the time the shop has been open, Drogheda has blossomed as a city, with many more people choosing to live in this east coast town. "When we started, we sold on the street and we used to sell for just three days. Now the shop is open for five days a week, and we're busy." (Patrick Kirwan, 55 Lawrence Street, Drogheda ☎ 041-983 0622 ✆ – Open 8am-6pm Tue-Sat)

only in Louth
Cooley Lamb and Beef

Restaurant with Rooms
● Scholars Townhouse Hotel

In a country that has endured a tsunami of modern design in brand new hotels, how refreshing to enjoy the comforting old style of Scholars. This twenty bed hotel attracts devoted followers who cherish its warm welcome and unpretentiousness, and last time John McKenna was here he ate well in the restaurant, enjoying smoked chicken Caesar salad and then some fall-off-the-bone lamb shank with champ and a lightly minted gravy, and then some old-style apple pie. (Glenn McGowan, King Street, Drogheda ☎ 041-983 5410 ✆ info@scholarshotel.com ✆ www.scholarshotel.com)

Delicatessen
● Stockwell Artisan Foods

Gwen Fearon and Orlaith Callaghan's Stockwell deli, on Stockwell Street is a one-stop solution to any culinary quest in the Drogheda area. The deli has taken over the shop next door and now has five tables, where they operate a "retro funky deli". You can call in here for breakfast, when they sell around one hundred scones per day, with their home-made jam. Lunch on a vegetarian soup, perhaps a slice of their deep delicious fritattas maybe, and then take away a brie and spinach lasagne, or a Thai chicken curry with brown rice for dinner. You can even bring in your serving dishes to them, and they'll make food for your dinner party – and not tell anyone! Secret dinner parties, they call it. Everything is Fairtrade, home-made and local. (Gwen Fearon & Orlaith Callaghan, 1 Stockwell Street, Drogheda ☎ 041-9810892 ⌨ info@stockwellartisanfoods.ie ⌂ www.stockwellartisanfoods.ie – Open 9am-5pm Mon-Wed, till 6pm Thur-Sat)

Dundalk

Wine Shop
● Callan's Wine Shop

Mary and Kevin Callan maintain an excellent range of wines, and a complementary range of specialist beers, in this tidy, busy store. (Mary & Kevin Callan, Park Street, Dundalk ☎ 042-933 4382 ⌨ info@callans.ie – Open 10.30am-11.30pm Mon-Sat, 12.30pm-11pm Sun)

Frozen Fish Catering
● Celtic Fish Caterers

Ian was a fisherman and, according to Antoinette "knows by looking at something whether it's good or not". This has been one of the reasons for the early success of Celtic Fish Caterers, a new venture in the north east which operates from a small factory just outside Tallinstown. There's haddock in breadcrumbs, calamari, monkfish, prawns in garlic butter, cod cakes and crab cakes. But their real speciality is hand-produced dressed crab, presented properly in the shell with a mixture of delicious seasonings. All the food is cooked in the little unit beside their house. They've converted a third of an acre for parking and they sell to the public straight from the factory. (Ian & Antoinette Lawrence, Tully, Corcreaghy, Dundalk ☎ 042-938 4445 – Open 10am-6pm Mon-Sat)

Farmers' Market
● Dundalk Farmers' Market

The Dundalk market takes place in the town centre each Friday with a selection of up to fifteen stalls, all run by local producers. This is a splendidly seasonal market with cheese, vegetables and preserves direct from the people who make them, which is how it should be. (Peter Thomas ☎ 087-277 8538, Market Square Fri 10am-3pm)

Bar & Restaurant
● Fitzpatrick's Bar & Restaurant

The Fitzpatrick family have been doing the good thing for nigh on sixteen years now, in their array of bar rooms and restaurant in Jenkinstown. The pristine maintenance of the gardens and the exterior sets the tone for a beautifully maintained traditional premises, and the care of the building shines through in the care of the staff. The cooking riffs on modern classics – scallops with black pudding; grilled cod with seafood velouté; tempura of langoustine; hot chocolate fondant – and there is a generosity and spiritedness here that gives the place a huge buzz. (Danny Fitzpatrick, Rockmarshall, Jenkinstown, Dundalk 042-937 6193 ✑ admin@ fitzpatricks-restaurant.ie ✆ www.fitzpatricks-restaurant.ie)

Café
● Mizu House Café

Nuala King runs a spa in the beautifully restored Georgian house that is Mizu, but for food lovers it is the café that is of interest here, a luxe space in which to enjoy healthful salads and savoury main dishes. (Nuala King, River Lane, Dundalk ☎ 042-933 0833 ✑ info@mizu. ie ✆ www.mizu.ie)

Fishmonger
● Johnny Morgan

Colm Morgan is the fourth, or maybe he's the fifth, generation of his family to sell fish in County Louth. "It goes back as long as anyone can remember," he says simply. The Morgan forebears began by "fishing for herring in Carlingford Lough - the real horse and cart thing. My grandfather and his father started selling herring in Dundalk. It all started from there." This progressed to "buying a wee van back in the thirties" when Colm's father got involved. And both father and son started a fish stall in the town, just outside the Ulster Bank. Today, the shop is in Eimer Court in Dundalk. It's a tiny shop, with a great aesthetic and sense of style. Their policy is, quite simply, the very best for selling fish: "We try to get rid of everything each day, and then start again the next. We strive to re-stock on a daily basis." (Colm Morgan, 7 Eimer Court, Market Square, Dundalk ☎ 042-932 7977 – Open 9am-5.30pm Tue-Fri, 9am-3pm Sat)

Beer Importer
● Noreast Beers

David McIlherron's company imports fine Continental beers and ciders, which are distributed throughout the country to bars and off licences. (David McIlherron, Coes Road Industrial Estate, Dundalk ☎ 042-933 9858)

Restaurant
● No. 32

Good local food in a good room with good service and value. Susan Heraghty's restaurant ticks all the boxes, and has been doing so for years now, riding the changes through that time, tweaking the offer to suit the changing lifestyles and budgets, but always delivering tasty grub: coriander, lime and honey chicken with savoury rice; spinach and ricotta roulade with herb pesto; lamb burger with cucumber raita. The food has a very feminine lightness of execution and the tastes hit home directly and pleasingly. (Susan Heraghty, 32 Chapel Street, Dundalk ☎ 042-933 1113 ✉ info@no32.ie ⦿ www.no32.ie – Open from 5.30pm Mon-Sat)

only in Louth
Annagassan Crab

Wine Shop
● Quintessential Wines

Seamus Daly learnt his wine whilst on the road for Paddy Keogh's Wines Direct, which is wine boot camp par excellence in Ireland. In Quintessential has amassed many characterful bottles and he sells them in a funky, fun way, designated according to their fundamental nature, so on the right is Juicy, for easy drinking, over here is Fruit Driven for smooth, dry, voluptuous wines, and try a taste of Crisp – fresh and zesty – or spoil yourself with Something Special. Great fun, and it makes Quintessential quite essential. (Seamus Daly, 9 Dublin Road, Drogheda ☎ 087-274 5204/041-983 0960 ✆ sales@quintessentialwines.ie ✆ www.quintessentialwines.ie – Open 11am-8pm Mon-Sat, till 9pm Thu & Fri)

Restaurant
● Rosso

Louisa Gilhooley runs the room whilst head chef Conor Mee rattles the pans, and Rosso has been a star destination ever since they opened. Mr Mee's food is ace: Annagassan white crab and avocado cocktail with sauce gazpacho; scallops with braised ham hock; duck pastillas with curry and soy dressing; chicken Kiev '09 with garlic cream. The food is classical – chicken Kiev! – but it's a classical style that has not so much been sharpened up as roughed up a bit, and it shows a team that is hungry, ambitious and on top of their game. Prices are good for such fine ingredients and such careful cooking, and vegetarians should note that there is a proper menu of vegetarian choices. (Louisa Gilhooley, 5 Roden Place, Dundalk ☎ 042-935 6502 ✆ www.rossorestaurant.com – Open 12.15pm-2.30pm, 6pm-9.30pm Tue-Fri, 6pm-9.30pm Sat, 12.30pm-7pm Sun)

Café
● Simply Rosso Café

The glam, pinky, arty first-floor room of Rosso, overlooking the cathedral, is where you take breakfast and afternoon tea. Meet you there for a slow roast pork sandwich on Keelan's sliced pan bread and a pot of tea. Would we like a waffle with banana and vanilla ice cream? We would, you know. (Louisa Gilhooley, 5 Roden Place, Dundalk ☎ 042-935 6502 ✆ www.rossorestaurant.com – Open 10am-5pm Mon-Sun)

Dunleer

Farmhouse Cheese
● Glebe Brethan Cheese

David Tiernan's cheese is amongst the most exciting and creative of the new era of Irish farmhouse cheeses. Coming out of four generations of dairying clearly gave the Tiernans not only the confidence to realise exactly what they wanted to create, but also gave them the vision to create something markedly different from what any other Irish cheesemaker was doing. So, what they do is to take the raw milk from Montbeliarde cows, all of whom have appropriately French female names!, and fashion a Gruyere-style thermophilic cheese. But using the term Gruyere is misleading, for Glebe Brethan isn't flinty and dry like Swiss-style cheeses. Instead, thank to lush pastures, it is nutty and agrestic, mustardy and umami, which might sound impossible in single cheese, but we can assure you Glebe Brethan manages all these taste contortions, and as the cheese ages to 18 months it becomes even more quixotic and perplexing. One of the great modern Irish cheeses. (David Tiernan, Glebe House, Dunleer ☎ 041-685 1157 ⬛ dtiernan@iol.ie ⬛ www.glebebrethan.com)

only in Louth
Termonfeckin Turkeys

Termonfeckin

Farm Shop
● McEvoy's Farm Shop

David McEvoy's shop has a particular reputation for Christmas turkeys, fine birds that are properly reared and fed and prepared – but all of the meat and fowl that this committed farmer and butcher produces is of superlative quality. Chickens are reared to 80 days, pork is free-range from Middle White pigs, lamb is dry-aged for three weeks, beef is dry-aged for three weeks and they make wonderful sausages. (David McEvoy, Nunneryland, Termonfeckin ☎ 041-988 1242 – Open 9am-6pm Mon-Sat)

County Mayo

Achill

Café
● The Beehive

Patricia and Michael's Beehive buzzes like crazy during
the summer season on Achill, but it's worthwhile joining
the queue because the cooking here is very good, especially the nettle soup and their traditional home baking.
As well as food there are lots of interesting things to buy
in the shop. (Patricia & Michael Joyce, Keel, Achill Island
☎ 098-43018 ✉ joycesbeehive@msn.com – Open
9.30am-6pm Mon-Sun. Closed Nov-Easter)

Guesthouse
● Bervie

It's the little wicket gate that leads from the garden
directly onto the sands of the beach that characterises
John and Elizabeth Barrett's happy house. It's the gate
from your childhood dreams and your childhood books
and it makes Bervie feel like both *The Enchanted Garden*
and *Where the Wild Things Are.* (John & Elizabeth Barrett,
Keel, Achill Island ☎ 098-43114 ✉ bervie@esatclear.ie
🖰www.bervieachill.com)

Surf School, Bicycle Hire, Coffee, Ice cream & Chocolate
● Blackfield

They are serious about life's great pleasures in Blackfield,
so this is where you come to get a serious cup of coffee,
some serious ice cream, some serious chocolate, not to
mention a board and a suit, so you can head off and ride
a tube on the Achill waves. (Gerry Brannigan, Closhreid,
Achill Island ☎ 098-43590 ✉ info@blackfield.com
🖰 www.blackfield.com – Open Easter until Oct,
10.30am-5.30pm Mon-Sat, 11am-5.30pm Sun)

only in Mayo
Putóg

Butcher

● Calvey's Master Butchers

If you want to enjoy two of the great secrets of Achill you first of all eat the local lamb with its unique pré salé flavours in Calvey's restaurant. Then, when it is time to bid farewell to Achill you purchase the largest freezer box you can and you buy Achill organic and mountain lamb in Calvey's butchers. Months later, as you defrost and cook this sublime food you will be brought right back to the smell and taste of the Achill surf. (Grainne Calvey, Keel, Achill Island ☎ 087-290 8129 🖱 www.calveysofachill.com)

Mayo

Restaurant

● Calvey's Restaurant

We would drive all the way to Maeve Calvey's restaurant just to eat organic Achill lamb. If that seems rather far fetched then let us assure you that one taste of this peerless meat will persuade you back to Achill at the first opportunity. Ms Calvey and her team also cook excellent fish dishes and have the shortest possible chain of supply, so the quality of fish is wonderful also. But that Achill lamb! (Maeve Calvey, Keel, Achill Island ☎ 098-43158 🖱 www.calveysofachill.com – Open 11.30am-5pm, 5.30pm-9.30pm Mon-Sun)

Restaurant

● The Chalet

Fresh fish and shellfish, shown proper respect are the first choice in Julie Hassett's little restaurant. (Julie Hassett, Keel, Achill Island ☎ 098-43157 – Open May-Nov 6pm-9pm Mon-Sun, sometimes open from noon during July and August)

Ballina

Fish Smokery & Delicatessen

● Clarke's Salmon Smokery

Clarke's started life in 1945, when Jackie Clarke opened the business in Ballina, selling not only fish, but rabbits and chickens as well. The proximity of the salmon-stocked River Moy led the shop to go more and more in the direction of selling salmon, and in the eighties Clarke's became solely a fish retailer. The smokery was started in the sixties, and is just one of the reasons for Clarke's eminent reputation. The smoking still takes place today in the rear of the seafood deli in Ballina, using Jackie's original recipe. Today the business is run by Jackie's sons, John, Dara, Peter and Kevin, and the business has taken a fresh turn in the new millennium with the rise of internet shopping, and exporting salmon through this medium is a substantial part of the business. Their online shop sells and exports not only smoked salmon, but also barbecued salmon, smoked silver eel and sea vegetables. Their two attractive stores stock a range of convenient, value-added, carefully made foods, including fishcakes, seafood lasagne, seafood pie, salmon en croute and various pâtés. The enterprising Clarke brothers have moved with the times, and the two Clarkes shops are two of the most dynamic retailing spaces in Ireland. (Kevin, John, Peter & Dara Clarke, O'Rahilly Street, Ballina ☎ 096-21022 ✎ info@clarkes.ie ⌂ www.clarkes.ie – Open 9am-6pm Mon-Sat. Also at Peter Street, Westport, Co Mayo)

Bar and Restaurant
● Crockett's on the Quay

Crockett's is a big, fun, lively bar with a restaurant, with lots of music, card tournaments, quiz nights, some rooms upstairs (do bear the music in mind if you are staying), and some tasty food in both the bar and the cosy restaurant. The cooking is kind of modern European greatest hits, and the locals lap it up, then have another pint. (Alan & Paul Murphy, David Smith, Ballina ☎ 096-75930 ✎ info@crocketsonthequay.ie ⌂ www.crocketsonthequay.ie – Open for bar food 12.30pm-9pm Mon-Sun. Restaurant opens 6pm-9.30pm Mon-Sun)

Wine Shop
● Fahy's

Fahy's is one of those wine shops that gets checked virtually every weekend in the newspapers as being the place to get hold of whatever bottle the wine writers are raving about right now. It is a great shop, one of the best in the country never mind just being one of the best in the West, and they have the nose and the instinct to hunt all the good bottles, which now amount to a stock of more than 800 different wines. Excellent. (Teeling Street, Ballina ☎ 096-22143 ✎ fahywines@hotmail.com – Open 11am-11pm Mon-Thu, 11am-11.30pm Fri & Sat, 6pm-11pm Sun)

Butcher, Bakery, Deli & Café
● Heffernan's Fine Foods

Geraldine and Anthony Heffernan transformed their butchery and deli business in late 2007, creating a deli, a bakery, a café and a butcher's shop from their original premises. These smart people take their culinary cues from the best influences, the menu writings of Neven Maguire, Rachel Allen, Avoca and Darina Allen, so the cooking is clean tasting and logical – chicken vol-au-vent with salads; beefeater sandwich with roast beef, red onion, tomato and horseradish mayo; home-baked gammon and cheddar cheese melt with Ballymaloe relish; home-made Cumberland sausages with mash and onion gravy. The selection of bakes and cakes in the deli is fab, and having their own abattoir in Rathduff is simply the best guarantee you can get of superb meat. Another great Mayo destination. (Geraldine & Anthony Heffernan, 4 Market Square, Ballina ☎ 096-21218 – Open 9am-6pm Mon-Sat)

only in Mayo
Achill Organic Lamb

Restaurant with Rooms
● The Ice House

They are sure doing the good stuff in The Ice House, and they have patiently taken their time since they opened to get the details right. Seat hard by the banks of the River Moy, a few minutes walk from town, the building is visually stunning, which it has to be to rival the views downriver. Manager Dara Cruise oversees an excellent crew, and in the Pier restaurant Gavin O'Rourke is producing elegant, 100-Best-Quality cooking, and the food is particularly eye-fetching, with starters like tempura of monkfish with black ketchup and salsify dazzling you with its good looks before the tastes of the combination dazzle you one more time. Halibut with saffron and a ragout of creamed leeks, mussels and smoked salmon is a perfect piece of fish with a fantastic ragout of leek whilst a plum tarte tatin has pitch-perfect pastry. The rooms are gorgeous, and everything in The Ice House is perfectly chilled. (Dara Cruise, The Quay, Ballina ☎ 096-23500 ✉ chill@theicehouse.ie 🖰 www.theicehouse.ie)

Kettles
● Kelly Kettle Co

Patrick and Seamus Kelly are the fourth generation of the Kelly family to manufacture the world-famous Kelly Kettle, a storm kettle that lights using anything from dried seaweed, to twigs to cow dung, and with this fuel can boil water in 3-5 minutes. The design of the kettle has changed very little since it was first introduced in the 1890's, and it is still the cooking implement of choice for many anglers, kayakers, hill walkers, adventurers and explorers. Note: If you are interested in fishing on Lough Conn, contact Padraic Kelly on ☎ 096-22250. (Patrick & Seamus Kelly, Newtown Cloghans, Knockmore PO, Ballina ☎ 087-286 4321 – Office hours 9.30am-5.30pm GMT Mon-Fri)

Restaurant
● Market Kitchen

You hear nothing but raves about Ballina's new Market Kitchen, upstairs above Brennan's Lane pub. Great staff, great value, and, importantly, a genuine attempt to prepare gluten-free dishes for coeliacs, through starters, main courses and puddings. They use good local foods, make gluten-free battered fish and chips, and have a Bailey's and Toblerone cheesecake that will mean you will have to be wheeled out, but sure that's not a problem. A real happening place. (Susan Walshe, Garden Street, Ballina ☎ 096-74971 marketkitchen@gmail.com www.marketkitchen.ie – Open 3pm-late Tue-Sat, 2pm-9pm Sun, open bank holiday Mons)

Ballinrobe

Market
● Ballinrobe Food & Craft Market

Mayo's emergence as a hub of thrillingly good food isn't confined to its restaurants, hotels and shops, but is also evident in markets like the Ballinrobe market, held at the parish centre every Saturday. Mixing local foods with local crafts creates a brilliant synergy of local energy, and you can feel the fizz and crackle of that creative energy here every week as you pile your basket high with good things. (Jean Cross, Parish Centre, Cornmarket, Ballinrobe ☎ 094-952 0887 – Open 10am-1pm Sat)

Ballycastle

Coffee House
● Mary's Bakery

We love Ballycastle – it was this little village and the paintings of Stuart Shills that first showed us the wabi sabi beauty of County Mayo – and we love Mary's Bakery, halfway down the street. Irish bakery-cafés should all be like this – domestic, calm, wafted with sweet and savoury odours and the babble of chat, and the sighs of contented folk enjoying the lovely food, Ah, take us back to Ballycastle. (Mary Munnelly, Main Street, Ballycastle ☎ 096-43361 – Open 10am-6pm Mon-Sun, with more limited hours off season)

only in Mayo
Carrowholly Cheese

Shop and Bar
● Polke's

A wee shop in front to get the 'papers, the milk and the bread and the butter, and a wee pub in the rere to get a pint and a half 'un of Power's Gold Label. Shopping as it should be! Polke's is a beauty of a bar, thanks to superb housekeeping, and a changeless charm. (Brian Polke, Main Street, Ballycastle ☎ 096-43016)

Country House
● Stella Maris

When we first wrote about Terence McSweeney and Frances Kelly's country house back in 2003, we predicted it would be one of the stars of the decade. For once, we were right. Stella Maris is recognised as one of the best places to eat and stay in Ireland, and it has gained that reputation thanks to the devotion and discipline of this couple, a pair of fastidious hotel keepers. Ms Kelly's cooking, in particular, is simply amazing: modest and lovingly executed in – literally! – every detail. It is food that comforts, consoles and delights, and it reminds us in many ways of the cooking of Ballymaloe House, country cooking ennobled by classy ingredients. Superb. (Terence McSweeney & Frances Kelly, Ballycastle ☎ 096-43322 ⌂ www.stellamarisireland.com – Open dinner for non-residents, 7pm-9pm Mon-Sun, 'till 10pm weekends)

Castlebar

Mayo

Café
● Café Rua

Café Rua is the original McMahon stronghold, opened
originally by mum Ann McMahon, now run by daughter
Colleen McMahon whilst Aran McMahon conquers the
West on Spencer Street in the brilliant Rua. If we haven't
said it before, then what you need to know about Café
Rua is that it is the friendliest place in the West. And
we don't mean that the staff are friendly – they are,
of course – we mean that it's a place where the other
customers are incredibly friendly. Why so? Because this
is one busy place, so sharing tables is essential, and when
you share a table with someone and you are both having
scrummy food, then how could you not get around to
asking about their health, and their dog, and have they
seen Pixar's UP and which is their fave Pixar anyhow? So,
salmon and potato cakes with Stephen Gould's leaves for
me, and roast loin of pork with champ and red cabbage
for my new best friend, and what did you say your name
was? (Colleen & Aran McMahon, New Antrim Street,
Castlebar ☎ 094-902 3376 ✉ aran@iol.ie ✌ www.
caferua.com – Open 9.30am-6pm Mon-Sat, with one-off
Friday night openings often on the last Friday of the
month)

Deli & Café
● Rua

Aran McMahon's deli is the brightest star in the West.
The impact Rua has had in its first years of business
has been extraordinary, gifting a great new address to
Castlebar, and complementing perfectly the superb Café
Rua which the McMahon family have run for many years.
Mr McMahon is simply the sharpest tool in the shed, so
if you can imagine Bandon's URRU crossed with Fallon
& Byrne and with a slice of Avoca, then that's what you
get in Rua. Plus, they do the funkiest newsletter, which
makes them a bit like Zingerman's of Ann Arbor. You'll
note we are using luxury brand addresses to compare to
Rua, and that's how it should be: Rua is a luxury brand
address, a place where everything is done their way, and
that's the best way. Brilliant. (Aran McMahon, Spencer
Street, Castlebar ☎ 094-928 6072 ✌ www.caferua.com
✉ aran@iol.ie – Open 9am-6pm Mon-Sat and evenings
on the last Friday of the month, booking essential)

● Sheila's

The Butler family's butter-making business uses pasteurised milk which they ripen in order to give a distinctive and richer country flavour. They also make an excellent buttermilk and a pro-biotic butter, which contains friendly bacteria. You'll find them in all good supermarkets. (Tom & Sheila Butler, Shraheens, Balla, Castlebar ☎ 094-903 1425 ✉ sheilasmayo1@eircom. net ⌂ www.cuinneog.com)

Claremorris

Tea Shop, Apiary & Farmhouse Cheese
● Derrymore Farmhouse

Vincent and Manita used to run the smallest shop in the west, which showcased their honey, cheese, eggs, knits and vegetables in a space that was about a square metre. They have expanded since then and today you can shop for the Derrymore products whilst also having a slice of home-baked cake and a cup of tea looking out over their lovely gardens. "Honest quality hand-made produce of which we are proud" is what they aim to achieve and what they do achieve. (Vincent & Manita van Dulmen, Derrymore, Partry, Claremorris ☎ 094-9543173 – Open 10.30am-6pm Mon-Sun. Closed Sept to Apr)

Butcher
● The Food Store

Niall Heffernan's Food Store has gotten the key of the door, having turned twenty-one years old in 2009, and having spawned the second Food Store in Claremorris the previous year. That's been two decades of continual, self-critical improvement, and it has made the Food Store into one of the best shops in the West. Their Mayo Angus beef is merely one USP of a shop that is both butchery, deli, bakery and general store. Service levels match quality levels all the way. They built a by-pass around Claremorris a few years ago. No, we never use it either. (Niall Heffernan, Ballyhaunis Road, Claremorris ☎ 094-936 2091 ✉ thefoodstore@eircom. net – Open 7.45am-6.30pm Mon-Thu, 7.45am-7pm Fri-Sat. Also at Silverbridge Shopping Centre ☎ 094-937 7788 – Open 9am-6.30pm Mon-Thur & Sat, 9am-8.30pm Fri)

Cong

Café
● **Hungry Monk Café**

Fiona McMahon's pretty cafe in pretty Cong is one of the key destinations of the town. Ms McMahon does things right from soups to salads, from lemon cake to Fairtrade coffee. Don't miss it. (Fiona McMahon, Abbey Street, Cong ☎ 094-954 6886 – Open 9.30am-6pm Mon-Sat, 11am-5pm Sun)

Hotel
● **Lisloughrey House**

Sister hotel to Ballina's Ice House and Glasson's Wineport Lodge, Lisloughrey has the most gorgeous location on the doorstep of Cong, and with views out across Lough Corrib. Wade Murphy's cooking in their Salt restaurant is packed with successful modern flourishes: polenta-crusted skate wing with citrus brown butter vinaigrette; monkfish tail and lobster with watercress and rhubarb risotto; year-old Connemara ham with watermelon and mint gelée; pork, cider and apple sausages with Durrus whipped potatoes and caramelized onion jus. This is exciting work and the swagger of Lisloughrey is really captivating. (Ray Byrne, The Quay, Cong ☎ 094-954 5400 ✉ lodge@lisloughrey.ie 🖱 www.lisloughrey.ie)

Foxford

Fishmonger and Fishing Tackle
● **Tiernan Brothers**

The Tiernan Brothers' association with fishing and the River Moy can be traced back to Michael and PJ Tiernan's great-great grandfather Martin Tiernan, one of the foremost Fly-Tiers in Ireland, and his great-great grandsons are today synonymous with angling in County Mayo. The shop began as a butcher, fish tackle shop and fishmonger, and remained a fishing tackle shop in the hands of the senior Tiernan brothers. In the mid 1990's Michael and PJ re-opened the tackle shop in Foxford, and the now-flourishing business spawned a fish shop. Tiernan's is a traditional shop – "We have very little in

the freezer, just fresh fish" says Martin. And alongside
the fish shop they have a busy internet online store
selling tackle, and they can also be found selling in local
country markets: Foxford Woollen Mills, Sat 9am-
2.30pm; Charlestown, Murphy's Londis, Tues 9am-
2pm; Swinford Main Street, Thurs 9am-2pm; Castlebar
Market Square, Fri 9am-5pm. (Main Street, Foxford
☎ 094-925 6731 ⌖ www.themoy.com – Open Mon-Sun
during the summer season, 8am-6pm. Off season hours
9am-6pm Mon-Sat)

Louisburgh

Café
● Hudson's Pantry

"Had a couple of cracking meals in Hudson's Pantry",
writes a friend after a few weeks out west. "The menu is
very much Spanish/Moroccan and simply executed and
well priced", writes another, and we quote our mates
just to show that Hudson's is the sort of place that
people write to tell you all about once they have been
there to eat. Richard and Tricia Hudson are famous, of
course, for running Hudson's in Navan for many years,
but their re-invention out here in Louisburgh, a wee
parish of about 400 souls, has been the talk of the west
for the last year or so. Richard isn't the sort of cook
to work the way others do, so there might be braised
shank of lamb, but here it will have been shaken up with
cumin and paprika, and that sort of Moorish seasoning
runs through the food, from the preserved lemon in
lentil soup to their zarzuela fish stew with almonds and
saffron to the harissa with grilled salmon. If you like the
food of Moro, then Hudson's is your only man, a slice of
Iberia in little Louisburgh. Lucky Louisburgh. (Richard &
Tricia Hudson, Long Street, Louisburgh ☎ 098-23747 –
Open 6pm-9.30pm Wed-Sun)

only in Mayo
Clew Bay Shellfish

Mulranny

Hotel
● The Mulranny Park Hotel

The resurrection by Tom and Kathleen O'Keefe of the old Great Western Hotel in Mulranny has been one of the great achievements of Irish hospitality over the last decade. Whilst some of the original team have moved on from Mulranny, changes have been handled smoothly, and the hotel has already acquired its own culture and service ethic. It's a great place for families as you can stay in their two-bedroom apartments, and there is such an air of relaxation here that you quickly tumble into a state of blissful relaxation, dreaming of dinner in the lovely Nephin Restaurant after a long walk on the beach. (Tom & Kathleen O'Keefe, Mulranny, Westport ☎ 098-36000 🖰 www.mulrannyparkhotel.ie – Bar lunch served 12.30pm-9pm. Restaurant open 7pm-9pm Mon-Sun)

Newport

Relishes
● A Taste of Days Gone By

Patti Moss fashions fabulous and unusual relishes from traditional recipes discovered in the cookery notebooks of her grandmother, some of them dating back to the 1920's. These are real sports of nature: banana butter; Susie's strawberry and rhubarb jam; Grandmother's apple jam, terrific queer gear and a real taste of the old that is like the shock of the new. (Patti Moss, Furnace, Newport ☎ 087-753 8055)

Butcher
● Dominick Kelly's Butchers

If you were to ask us – and you were just going to weren't you? – to explain the emergence of Mayo as a food destination that suddenly has all this exciting stuff going on – Rua, Knockranny, Cabot's, Sage, Hudson's, LoTide, Ice House, Clarke's, Carrowholly, An Port Mor, to name just a few dynamic addresses – we would put the responsibility on the shoulders of Sean Kelly of Newport. Mr Kelly is the Mayo champion, a man who has tirelessly worked to put Mayo on the culinary map, and a man whose own work has been the very best example to all those who have followed him into the Mayo Food Brotherhood. Kelly's is one of the best butcher's shops in Ireland, a place where Mr Kelly melds tradition with innovation in the charcuterie arts, not least with his brilliant putog, where he cooks a black pudding in a sheep's stomach. But everything in Kelly's reflects care, pride, and above all, pride in place, this place that is Mayo. Give this man the Freedom of Croagh Patrick. (Sean F Kelly, Main Street, Newport ☎ 098-41149 – Open 8.30am-7pm Mon-Sat)

Café
● **Kelly's Kitchen**

Sean and Heidi's café has the great advantage of being able to source their meats from Kelly's Butchers next door, so that gets them off to a flying start. Mr Mohan then works hard to complete the picture, making everything in-house, and showing terrific culinary nous: pot of Clew Bay mussels with fennel cream; beer-battered fish with Puy lentil purée; Newport beef with Yorkshire pudding; smoked haddock with leek sauce; scallops with Kelly's black pudding and boxty. This is generous, logical, inviting cooking, and it's a real treat, so make sure that any trip to Newport includes a visit to the Kitchen. (Sean & Heidi Mohan, Main Street, Newport ☎ 098-42720 – Open 10am-5pm Oct-Feb, 10am-6.30pm Mar-June, 10am-9.30pm July-Sept)

Country House
● **Newport House**

Newport is the utter archetype of the Irish County house, and it offers the archetypal Irish country house experience. Grand, gracious, ageless, it's a slice of the past, but happily existing in the present, and there is no other house quite like it. John Gavin's cooking is as classic and measured, and luxurious, as the house, built on the harmonious use of garden and river ingredients: you eat a dish of john dory with garden spinach and a white wine and basil sauce and it is perfection, nothing less. We once even pushed the boat out here one morning and had eggs Benedict, and it was the most perfect eggs Benedict we ever had, as well as being the richest. Kieran Thompson's wine list is deservedly legendary, and also offers great value. (Kieran & Thelma Thompson, Newport ☎ 098-41222 🖰 www. newporthouse.ie)

Westport

Mayo

Restaurant
● An Port Mor

Frankie Mallon made his name cooking out in Cronin's
Shebeen in Rosbeg, though his CV extends back to time
spent working in Belfast's legendary Roscoff when that
restaurant was at its dazzling peak. Now in his new An
Port Mor, his stylish food has lots of punky attitude,
seen in dishes like warm salad of roasted pig's cheeks
with Kelly's black pudding and apple and vanilla sauce, or
cumin and raisin blinis to go with Connemara smoked
salmon, or shrimp butter with turbot, or buttermilk
pannacotta. The long rooms have a sweet, almost
domestic style to them, and here is another element of
the Mayo renaissance, courtesy of a man from Armagh!
(Frankie Mallon, Brewery Place, Bridge Street, ☎ 098-
26730 ⁻ www.anportmor.com – Open 6pm-10pm Tue-
Sat, 6pm-9pm Sun)

Wine Merchant
● Cabot & Co

Liam Cabot has been making wine in Slovenia. Now,
most wine merchants focus simply on selling wine, but
Mr Cabot is different. He wants to get his wellies on.
He wants to get his hands dirty. That's the kind of bloke
he is, and the kinds of wines he sells are those made
by people who get their wellies on and get their hands
dirty. He is a true maverick, a renegade intellectual with
an aesthete's perception, and a sense of humour. His
wines are superb, every one of them, and every one of
them represents both a journey – by the winemaker and
the wine merchant – and an holistic choice – by the winemaker and the wine merchant. Life enhancing! (Liam
& Sinead Cabot, 4 Cloghan, Westport ☎ 098-37000
⊞ sales@cabotandco.com ⁻ www.cabotandco.com)

only in Mayo
Clarke's Smoked Moy Salmon

Restaurant
● Cabot's Source

Redmond Cabot's restaurant is a place with wit and style, and no little personality. In short, it's the kind of place you dream about stumbling across when holidaying in Westport, and it has all the local foods you dream about enjoying: Clare Island salmon smoked by Jerry Hassett on Achill Island; Clew Bay mussels harvested by Padraig Gannon; Seamus Hawkshaw's Mayo lamb with dauphinoise potatoes; hake with watercress; homemade strawberry cheesecake. Other top-notch suppliers include McGeough's of Oughterard, Sheridan's Cheesemongers and Fingal Ferguson of Gubbeen. The room in The Linenmill is big and beautiful, the wines are only deadly, and whilst it can be a bit beatnik and left-field at times – jazz on Wednesday evenings, poetry readings on Thursday, not quite the standard thing – it's pretty smashing. (Redmond Cabot, The Demesne, Westport ☎ 098-50546 ✆ info@cabotssource.com ✆ www. cabotssource.com – Open 6pm-11pm Wed-Sun)

Restaurant
● Carrowholly Cheese

Andrew Pelham-Byrne is the Mayo cheesemaker par excellence, producing a small range of Gouda-style cheeses from the raw milk of local farmers, but doing it in the way in which Irish cheesemakers used to work back in the early days, with small-scale production and very limited distribution, thereby gifting us with a true local speciality. Andrew actually sells most of his cheese himself, setting up a stall twice a week in Westport, part of his determination that specialist food should be sold by the producer in order to keep prices super keen. These are lovely cheeses, especially the 9-month-old plain cheese, when the stored-up-sunshine of milk from summer grasses shines through. Don't leave Mayo without some. (Andrew Pelham-Byrne, Carrowholly, Westport ☎ 098-28813)

Fishmonger and Delicatessen
● Clarke's Seafood Delicatessen

The Clarke brothers' Westport store is both an excellent wet fish shop, and a smarter-than-smart seafood deli. This family quartet is a superb team of operators, and a confident, urbane aura surrounds everything they do, so shopping here is a luxury experience even before you get those luxury fish dishes home for dinner. Pure class. (John, Dara, Kevin & Peter Clarke, Peter Street, Westport ☎ 098-24379 ✉ info@clarkes.ie ⌂ www.clarkes.ie – Open 9am-6pm Mon-Sat)

Hotel & Restaurant
● Knockranny House Hotel

Seamus Commons is one of the great chefs of his generation, and his cooking in Knockranny is going to cement his reputation as one of the most gifted cooks at work in Ireland. He is a culinary auteur: every dish he sends out is a Seamus Commons dish, shaped to his instinct, his personality, his vision, and that vision is complete and total, and is founded on sheer hard work: Mr Commons puts more detail into a single dish than most chefs put into an entire dinner menu, yet his food isn't fussy. Instead he is seeking out affinities and connections. Look what he does with Mayo lamb, for example: he slow cooks the shoulder, sears the loin, cooks the sweetbreads, and pairs these elements with peas, polenta and sweet fennel. With Killala lobster, he butter poaches the tail, serves the claws with mayo, makes lobster tortellini and collects samphire to garnish a shellfish minestrone. Analysing his tasting menus – "I was completely blown away with the food!" a local friend said after an October evening's feast – could occupy five or six pages of this book. As hot as it gets, simple as that. (Adrian & Ger Noonan, Westport ☎ 098-28600 ⌂ www.khh.ie)

Restaurant
● The Lemon Peel

Back in the centre of town after a temporary relocation, Robbie McMenamin does good food at decent prices and so his success as one of Westport's best restaurateurs is no surprise. He is quite a traditionalist as a cook, with Cordon Bleu classics such as chicken liver pâté with Cumberland sauce, or roast duck with Grand Marnier or sirloin steak with garlic butter as staples of his menus, though he does throw in the occasional modern touch – chicken with chorizo and wild mushroom sauce; roast vegetable risotto; Cajun shrimp with salsa. Clean, clever food, and a lively, simple room that offers great value for both food and wine. That's how you survive and thrive for nearly fifteen years! (Robbie McMenamin, The Octagon, Westport ☎ 098-26929 ✉ robbie@lemonpeel.ie – Open 5pm-11pm Tue-Sun. Open Sundays in high summer)

Mayo

● Lotide Fine Foods

Seamus Moran is the Sun King of sea vegetables. He puts
them in sausages, he puts them in pasta, he puts them
in black and white puddings, he puts them in relishes,
and everywhere he puts them he creates great culinary
magic. Mr Moran has a truly sharp organoleptic sense,
perhaps explained by his time as a chef, but every time
he launches a new sea vegetable product – most recently
his pasta range – he gets it right, right from the start.
We would rate his sausages as being amongst the best
in Ireland, and our kids would rate then higher than
that. You will find Lotide products in the best shops in
Ireland, and that is where they belong. (Seamus & Carmel Moran, Moyna, Kilmeena, Westport ☎ 098-42616
✉ info@lo-tide.com ✆ www.lo-tide.com)

● Market 57

Colm McLoughlin's shop has some fantastic wines
alongside classy deli produce and smart homeware so
it's a don't miss in Westport, a one-stop destination for
people who want to buy the ingredients and also buy
the wok/rolling pin/delph to cook eat it with. (Colm
McLoughlin, Westport ☎ 098-27317 – Open 9am-7pm
Mon-Sat, 11am-6.30pm Sun)

● Marlene's Chocolate Haven

From toffee turtles to sweet nuts, dark pineapple to pra-
line and hazelnut shell, Marlene's handmade chocolates
are a little bit of heaven in a chocolate haven. And when
you've finally made up your mind, sit yourself down and
have yourself a cup of classy hot chocolate. (Marlene,
The Courtyard, James Street, Westport ☎ 098-24564 –
Open 9am-6pm Mon-Sat)

● Sage

Sarah Hudson is one of the Hudson's of Louisburgh,
whilst her partner Davide Dannaloia is from Sardinia,
and in Sage they are creating some fascinatingly fine, and
authentically echt, Italian food. Mr Dannaloia will, for
instance, cook belly of pork for two days, and serve it
with his own handmade pasta, and the herb-infused

meat will be food for the Gods, true and simple, a taste of the divine. Sage is truly exciting. (Sarah Hudson & Davide Dannaloia, 10 High Street, Westport ☎ 098-56700 – Open 5.30pm-close Tue-Sat)

Restaurant
● Sol Rio

Sinead and Jose's Sol Rio has a pretty extensive menu offering, from pizzas to fish to pastas and meat dishes. So they aim very clearly to give something for every member of the holiday families who fill up this room. Meat from McCormick's and seafood from Clarke's underpin tasty popular cooking. (Sinead Lambert & Jose Barroso, Bridge Street, Westport ☎ 098-28944 ✉ solrio@iol.ie ⌘ www.solrio.ie – Open noon-3pm, 6pm-10pm Tue-Sun)

Country Market
● Westport Country Market

The Westport market is one of the longest established markets in Ireland, and it is one of the nicest markets in Ireland. Packed with good things from locals who make and bake and cure and farm and brew and collect and grow and nurture, the market has all you need, from goat's milk cheeses to flowers to country butter, from herbs to eggs. And then there is time for a cup of tea and a chat before you bring all these lovely things home, culinary ideas bouncing around in your head. (Town Hall, Westport, Thursday, 10am-2pm)

Hotel
● Westport Plaza Hotel

Excellent staff are the USP of the Plaza, and when we say excellent, and when we say Unique Selling Point, we mean it: these guys are the bee's knees of hospitality and they transform a night in the hotel or dinner in the restaurant into a little treasure of good feelings. Quite excellent. (Joe Corcoran, Castlebar Street, Westport ☎ 098-51166 ⌘ www.westportplazahotel.ie)

only in Mayo
Killala Lobster

County Meath

Ashbourne

Coffee
● **Ariosa Coffee Roasting Boutique**

Some guys want to be the best they can be. And some
guys just want to be the best. Michael Kelly is one of the
latter type of guys, and when it comes to coffee roasting, he just wants to be the best there is. He is well on
his way, having learnt his craft in New York and Sydney,
a craft he seeks to improve on with every roast. Ariosa
is one of the glories of modern Irish food, a product that
fuses ambition and execution in perfect alignment, all the
better to make sure that your cup of coffee is the best
it can possibly be. That's why there is such a big queue
every Saturday morning at the Temple Bar market, as
shoppers get – there is no other way to put this – their
fix, their hit, their narcotic. Ariosa is coffee as narcotic,
your social drug for the new decade. (Michel Kelly, Race-
hill, Ashbourne ☎ 01-835 3078 ✉ info@ariosacoffee.
com 🖰 www.ariosacoffee.com)

Chocolate Shop
● **Chez Emily**

One of three chocolate boutiques from the
extravagantly talented Helena Hemeryck and Ferdinand
Vandaele, Chez Emily is home to exquisitely fashioned
truffles and sweeties and florentines and orangettes and
liqueur chocolates and everything the child still residing
in your culinary DNA could possibly desire. The other
stores are in Swords and The Ward in County Dublin.
(Helena Hemeryck & Ferdinand Vandaele, Main Street,
Ashbourne ☎ 01-835 2252 ✉ info@chezemily.ie
🖰 www.chezemily.ie)

Butcher
● **Hugh Maguire**

Hugh Maguire is the big cheese of Irish craft butchers.
He is a quiet man, but determined, and he has served
as chair of the Craft Butcher's Association. In his shop
in Ashbourne – readers may recall the shop in Navan,
which has now moved here – he proves the greatness

Meath

of his aptitude as a butcher day in and day out. His bacon, sausages and puddings – three pork standards by which you judge the creativity of any butcher – are peerless, and they reflect not just precise skills, but also an agrestic, country-smart character. These are, after all, the traditional foods of Ireland, and what fascinates us about Maguire's is how Hugh interprets and re-interprets them for the modern age. Otherwise, the beef and lamb are superbly handled, and the modern prepared dishes for time-poor folk in Ashbourne are of benchmark standard. A true classic. (Hugh Maguire, Unit 3-4 Ashbourne Town Centre ☎ 01-849 9919 ✆ hughmaguirebutchers@eircom.net – Open 8am-7pm Mon-Wed, 8am-9pm Thu-Fri, 8am-6pm Sat)

only in Meath
Hugh Maguire's Black Pudding

Fishmonger
● Nick's Fish

Nicholas Lynch's renowned wholesale business opened this flagship shop in 2007. Nick's Fish sells an eclectic selection of fish, including the award-winning Loch Duart salmon, and a range of organic wines. One of their specialities, and indeed one of their most popular items, is their epicurean seafood mix, which uses premium fish, all carefully deboned. The fishing industry is part of Mr Lynch's heritage: his mother was from Inis Meain in the Aran Islands. "The sea was their only option" he says of his maternal family. "It took a huge toll in those days, my mother lost many relatives to the sea." Nick's Fish is now a vital addition to Ashbourne, a pristine, superbly run outfit that is worth going out of your way to visit. (Nicholas Lynch, 9 Town Centre, Ashbourne ☎ 01-835 3555 ✆ www.nicksfish.ie – Open 10am-6pm Mon-Fri, 10am-5pm Sat)

Athboy

Butcher
● Brogan's Butchers

Niall Brogan's shop is simple, but don't let the simplicity blind you to the fact that this is a place for serious meat, beautifully prepared – and charmingly served – by the man himself. (Niall Brogan, Main Street, Athboy ☎ 046-943 2122 ✉ brogansbutchers@hotmail.com – Open 9am-6pm Mon-Sat)

Bakery
● Doreen's Bakery

A charming local bakery with all the jammy, squidgy sweet things your kiddie heart desires, as well as some very good breads. (Main Street, Athboy ☎ 046-943 2054 – Open 9am-6pm Mon-Sat)

Ballivor

Fudge
● Man of Aran Fudge

Tomás Póil is an Aran Islander and he makes wildly colourful hunks of fudges in all manner of flavours, and sells them with a happy smile and affable chat at farmers' markets. Stop him and buy some. (Tomás Póil, Station House, Ballivor ☎ 086-256 6542 ✉ info@ manofaranfudge.ie 🖰 www.manofaranfudge.ie)

Carnaross

Restaurant
● The Forge

Pauric White's restaurant, housed in a pretty traditional forge, is a simple space in which to enjoy the chef-proprietor's respectful, idiosyncratic cooking. (Pauric White, Potteragh, Carnaross ☎ 046-924 5003)

Cheese Warehouse
● Sheridan's Cheesemongers

The mighty Sheridan's have opened a brand new shop in the former station house of the Great Northern Railway, beside their main offices and affineur rooms in Athboy. Alongside Irish and continental cheeses at their peak of organoleptic perfection you will find all the deli products that Sheridan's have made their own, along with their complete range of wines. Take a peek into the maturing room and see the Glebe Brethans and Durruses and Giorgio's Parmesans steadily inching their way towards perfect maturity, and get a glimpse into the search for perfection that animates this entire organisation. It's a particularly lovely space, fitted out in Sheridan's inimitable, simple, bricolage style.(Franck le Moenner, Whitegate Cross, Carnaross ☎ 046-943 0373 ⌐ www.sheridanscheesemongers.com)

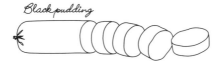

Clonee

Garden Centre Cafe
● Garden Works

Garden Works is as much homestore and café as garden centre, but howsoever you want to describe this top-notch company, what counts is that they do serious food in their cafés and shops, here and in Malahide. (Piercetown, Dunboyne, Clonee ☎ 01-825 5375 ⌐ info@gardenworks.ie ⌐ www.gardenworks.ie – Cafe open 9.30am-5pm Mon-Fri, 9.30am-5.30pm Sat, noon-5.30pm Sun)

Kells

Restaurant
● Cross Street Bistro

A new address in Kells, run by chef John O'Rourke and his sister-in-law Louise O'Rourke, and an exciting one at that, which is already generating much heat amongst local food lovers. They bake their own bread and sound and thoughtful cooking is complemented by an excellent range of gluten free dishes. Meath has needed CSB for a long time.(John & Louise O'Rourke, Cross Street, Kells ☎ 046-924 1702 ⌐ crossbistro@eircom.net – Open 9.30am-3.30pm Tue-Sat, 5.30pm-9pm Wed-Fri, 6pm-9.45pm Sat, closed Sun & Mon & Tues evening)

Farmhouse Cheese and Yogurt
● Glenboy Goat Products

Gordon and Ann make goat's cheeses and very fine smoothies and yogurts. (Gordon & Ann Hugh, Balgeeth, Kells ☎ 046-924 9624)

● **Kells Farmers' Market**

Kells has both a country market, on Fridays, and a weekly farmers' market, on Saturday. (Saturday, 10am-2pm, FBD Insurance Ground, Kells)

Soft cheese, buttermilk, cream, cheesecakes

● **Kilbeg Dairy Delights**

Kieran and Jane Cassidy's company is shaping up to be the Glenilen Dairy of the Midlands. They make excellent cream, buttermilk, quark, yogurts and cheesecakes, using the pasteurised milk from their herd of Holsteins. These are proper milk products, reflecting good pastures and good herdsmanship, bringing grassy, rich, lactic flavours into beautifully natural products. Try these creams and buttermilks and you won't go near a homogenised, bland milk product again. (Jane & Kieran Cassidy, Horath, Carlanstown, Kells ☎ 046-924 4687 ✆ www.kilbegdairydelights.ie)

Restaurant

● **Vanilla Pod Restaurant**

A stand-alone restaurant, housed in the well-known Headford Arms Hotel and very different in style to the hotel, this is a place for straight-ahead modern food, and in particular for some very good wines, an area they have a particular interest in. There is a good, dedicated team at work here, and they source carefully, using local foods like Glenboy Cheese and sourcing fish from Nicholas Lynch, so pair some goat's cheese fritters and their signature seafood platter with a good bottle and the night is already young. (Olivia Duff, Kells ☎ 046-924 0084 ✉ info@headfordarms.ie ✆ www.headfordarms.ie – Open 5.30pm-10pm Mon-Thu & Sun, 5.30pm-11pm Fri & Sat, noon-close Sun)

Laytown

Farmers' Market and Ecology Centre

● **Sonairte National Ecology Centre**

There is a farmers' market here every second Sunday of the month. The produce of the organic gardens is available from the shop and there are many interesting courses for those who want to learn about growing. (The Ninch, Laytown ☎ 041-982 7572 ✆ www.sonairte.org)

Navan

Hotel & Restaurant
● Bellinter House

Jay Bourke's Bellinter is the only Meath address to make
it into our annual 100 Best Places to Stay in Ireland.
The house has been beautifully restored, and as such
is a contrast to so many other fine country houses in
Meath that have simply had modern hotel wings tacked
onto them, thereby wrecking the aesthetic of the house.
Bellinter is different: the house lives for the modern era
thanks to the subtle use of technology, and thanks to
fantastic service, an amazing pool, and good food in the
Eden restaurant. Hip, knowing, and lovely. (Jay Bourke,
Navan ☎ 046-903 0900 ✉ info@bellinterhouse.com
🖰 www.bellinterhouse.com – Eden Restaurant serves
breakfast and dinner. Food served in Drawing Room and
Bellinter Bar all day.)

only in Meath
Kilbeg Buttermilk

Fish Shop
● Connolly's Seafood

The Connolly family history in seafood comes from their
long experience in fishing, and today the family still all
work as fishermen. For the last eight years they have
been selling the best and freshest fish in Navan, and
their audience is there for them. "People are eating a lot
more fish" says Noleen Connolly. "They are more aware
of their diets, and there were never as many cookery
programmes. More people are cooking at home, and we
see the result of it." (Kieran & Noleen Connolly, Navan
Shopping Centre, Navan, ☎ 046-907 2233 – Open
8.30am-5.30pm Tue-Fri, 8.30am-1pm Sat)

Gastro Pub
● O'Brien's Good Food and Drink House

Tim O'Brien is partner in another successful restaurant in Meath – Franzini O'Brien's in Trim – and he has
brought the same professional, modern, no-nonsense
approach to O'Brien's, keeping prices keen for the
commuter-belt crowd and their children. So enjoy zippy

Meath

food like good burgers and pizzas, and some nice wines. (Tim O'Brien, Johnstown Village, Navan ☎ 046-902 0555 – Open 5.30pm-10pm Mon-Sat, 1pm-9pm Sun)

● Ryan's Bar

Michael Ryan's pub is a landmark in Navan, a beautifully maintained pub and wine shop, and a very popular place to eat. They serve good food each day, focusing on a bread-related offer in the shape of sandwiches, filled rustic breads, classic bagel combinations and tasty wraps. A bowl of chowder, a ham open sandwich on brown soda bread with salad, and all is well. (Michael & Anne Ryan, 22 Trimgate Street, Navan ☎ 046-902 1154 ✉ enquiries@ryansbar.ie ✆ www.ryansbar.ie – Morning coffee served, and bar food served noon-3pm Mon-Fri)

Ratoath

Cookery School
● Fairyhouse Food & Wine School

Billie O'Shea is one of those amazing can-do women who run cookery schools throughout Ireland. Like Darina or Carmel or Catherine or Christine or Linda, she has mighty energy, and that prized autodidactic ability that allows her to master anything she wishes. She offers everything from corporate classes to cooking for kids and simpler demo courses, all informed by a sharp wit and a capacious skill. (Billie O'Shea, Ratoath ☎ 01-689 6476 ✉ info@fairyhousecookeryschool.com ✆ www.fairyhousecookeryschool.com)

Slane

Patisserie and Delicatessen
● George's Pastisserie and Delicatessen

With a new shop opened in the town centre in Drogheda, and with his Poet's Rest restaurant humming along, and with his farmers' market stalls, George Heise is becoming the King of the Midlands. It all began here a decade ago, with rock-steady patisserie forming the core attraction, and giving everyone reason to visit Slane. Along with superb sweet and savoury baking, the shop has a charming, unfazed feel, and George Heise brings in lots of good local foods. Excellent. (George Heise, Chapel Street, Slane ☎ 041-982 4493 ✆ reservations@ georgespatisserie.com 🖰 www.georgespatisserie.com – Open 9am-6pm Tue-Sat)

Restaurant
● The Poet's Rest

"An attractive eccentricity is in evidence", wrote Aoife Carrigy in *Food & Wine* magazine when she visited George Heise's The Poet's Rest. It's an eccentricity we like, slightly time-warped, slightly humorous, and extending into menus that are cherishable for their lack of fashion-following: warm chicken and black pudding roulade; sea bream with potato scales and bean cassoulet; roast salmon in filo pastry; pumpkin and ginger pie with cinnamon ice cream. The retro feel of the food on their hugely popular Sunday lunches is just darling: chicken consommé with tarragon dumplings; beef stroganoff with basmati rice and garden vegetables; bread and butter pudding with vanilla sauce. Almost enough to make you order a bottle of Hirondelle. The restaurant also opens for breakfast, so porridge with G's jam, please, and then a mushroom omelette and we are ready for anything. (George Heise, Chapel Street, Slane ☎ 041-982 4493 ✆ georgheise@eircom.net 🖰 www. georgespatisserie.com – Open 8am-10.30pm Tue-Sat, noon-5.30pm Sun)

Country House & Restaurant
● Tankardstown House

Brian and Patricia Conroy's magisterial house is both accommodation – six rooms in the house and seven cottages in the yard – and eating destination, with a bistro in the basement and a just-opened restaurant, Brabazon, created out in the old cow shed. Still early days, but reports from our friends who have stayed are universally positive, so this pristine address is shaping up just so. (Brian & Patricia Conroy, Slane ☎ 041-982 4621 🖰 www.tankardstown.ie)

only in Meath
Burke's Farm Applepie Icecream

Tara

Ice Cream
● Burke's Farm Ice Cream

Bernadette Burke grabbed a bronze medal for her
Belgian chocolate ice cream at the Dingle food awards
late in 2009, proof not just of the fineness of her work
with ice creams and flavourings, but also of her hunger to compete alongside the best in the business, for
Mrs Burke had grabbed the gold medal the previous
year with her amazing apple crumble ice cream. They
produce 15 flavours in total, using milk from a small herd
of Jersey cows, so lushness and luxury are right here.
(Bernadette Burke, Corbalton, Tara ☎ 087-953 2656
burkefarmicecream@eircom.net)

Trim

Restaurant
● Franzini O'Brien's

Sister restaurant to O'Brien's in Navan, and with the
same ethos of modern, accessible cooking that suits
everyone from children upwards, and good keen
prices. (Alex Mills, French's Lane, Trim ☎ 046-943 1002
franziniobriens@live.ie – Open 6pm-10pm Mon-Sat,
1pm-9pm Sun)

Organic Market
● Trim Visitor Centre Organic Market

The Friday afternoon market is a good one, and the
centre itself has a good coffee shop, Ramparts, with
some nice things to eat. (Trim Visitor Centre 3pm-6pm
Fri trimvisitorcentre@eircom.net)

County Monaghan

Ballybay

● **Ballybay Farmers' Market**

The Ballybay Farmers' Market alternates each Friday
between the Square in the centre of Ballybay, and the
Riverdale Car Park. It is a producer-run market with
organics, shrubs, home-baking and the produce of the
local Camphill community. (Ballybay Square & Riverdale
Car Park – Open 10am-noon Fri)

---

only in Monaghan
Lucy Madden's Wild Garlic Soup

Carrickmacross

Hotel & Restaurant
● **Nuremore Hotel**

You might reckon you know what a panna cotta is. You
are, after all, a *Bridgestone* user. But when Ray McArdle
serves a panna cotta with broccoli, as part of a dish of
scallops that also includes daube of beef, you might not
be so sure all of a sudden. And when your duck foie gras
sandwich has ice cream to go with it, you might wonder
if you know anything at all. Mr McArdle is still pushing
the envelope of cookery's possibilities and potentials,
and it gives his cooking great motivation and youthfulness – he is still hungry, to explore, to learn, to get
better, so settle in and settle down for tempura of john
dory with potato gnocchi; the three-hour squab with
sautéed artichokes and pigeon jus; the splendid celebration of Fermanagh Old Spot pig; the autumn pear martini
with Viognier granita. The food will be crisply, perfectly
executed, a statement of the art, and the possibilities of
the art. (Ray McArdle, Carrickmacross ☎ 042-966 1438
⌨ nuremore@eircom.net ⌂ www.nuremore.com
– Restaurant open 12.30pm-2.30pm, 6.30pm-9.30pm
Mon-Sun, no lunch on Sat, last orders 9pm Sun)

Castleblayney

Cured Meats
● **Malone Foods**

Whilst Malone's is a meat company of a much larger scale than those who feature in the *Bridgestone Guides* there is an artisan sensibility about their work and some of their specialities, like stout-cured beef and Monaghan dry-cured ham, are extremely interesting. The range are always very well packaged and presented. (Des Malone, Lough Egish, Castleblayney ☎ 042-974 5102 📠 manager@malonefoods.ie 🖳 www.malonefoods.ie)

Clones

Country House
● **Hilton Park**

We once met an eighth generation sake maker in Galway, and were utterly astonished that one family could maintain such a lengthy attachment to one profession. Well, eat your heart out Japanese sake makers, because the ninth generation of Maddens, Fred and Joanna, have now joined the eighth generation, Johnny and Lucy, in one of Ireland's grandest country houses. There is a lot of energy in Hilton, and a lot of interaction with the local community via film festivals, book club weekends and arts festivals. But anyone who simply wants to enjoy the epitomisation of the country house experience simply has to stay and eat here, enjoying food that comes from the garden straight to the plate, via the kitchen: wild garlic soup, roast duck breast, damson jus, balsamic radicchio and pommes Écrasés, blackcurrant leaf bavarois, blackcurrant coulis and honeycomb. (Johnny & Lucy Madden, Fred & Joanna Madden, Scotshouse, Clones ☎ 047-56007 📠 mail@hiltonpark.ie 🖳 www.hiltonpark.ie)

only in Monaghan
Malone's Dry-cured Monaghan Ham

Emyvale

Monaghan

Butcher
● Silver Hill Foods

The Steele family's company is renowned for high-quality duck production, but they go the whole hog in every way with their work, and so you can get a Silver Hill feather duvet, or pellets of duck manure. This holistic view of large-scale food manufacturing is extremely impressive, and it explains why a commercial company like Silver Hill can work successfully alongside Sheridan's cheesemongers to produce Sheridan's amazing duck leg confit. The McKenna children, keen fans of duck with pancakes and hoi sin, are already taking care of the next generation of Silver Hill ducks. (Stuart Steele, Emyvale ☎ 047-87124 ⌨ silverhill@eircom.net ⁀ www.silverhillfoods.com)

Glaslough

Country House, Cookery School and Hunting Lodge Hotel
● Castle Leslie

Castle Leslie isn't just a 1,000-acre estate any longer, it has virtually become an independent republic of food and cookery. With accommodation and hospitality in the castle as well as in the Hunting Lodge, there is also a cookery school and somehow they manage to get time to produce a range of top-class relishes and preserves. Whilst the Castle is really an adult-only zone the Hunting Lodge is very family friendly. (Sammy Leslie, Glaslough ☎ 047-88109 ⌨ info@castleleslie.com ⁀ www.castleleslie.com)

County Offaly

Ballinahown

Honey
● **Meadowsweet Apiaries**

Andrew McGuinness is a trained chemist but, if he
doesn't mind us saying so, he approaches bee-keeping
not as a science, but as an art, and as a beekeeper he is
an artist of the genre. His terroir honeys are superlative
things, the heather honey from the Clara bog intense
and louring, the summer honeys lighter, brighter, cleaner.
The beeswax products Mr McGuinness makes are just
as classy as his honeys, so do not miss these peerless
foods, the very foundation of life on earth. (Andrew
McGuinness, Doon, Ballinahown ☎ 086-884 4938
✉ andrewmcguinness@hotmail.com)

Banagaher

Artisan Bakery
● **Coolfin Gardens Organic Bakery**

Jonas and Layla's organic bakery bake ruddy, rustic, seed-
packed breads for the Lough Boora box scheme, as well
as farmers' markets in Galway, Oranmore, Tullamore
and Thurles. Look out for the rye and sourdough breads
in particular, real breads packed with organic goodness,
breads that are allowed lots of time to develop structure
and flavour. Layla worked with Sheridan's Cheesemongers for several years, so customer skills are as top
notch as their wheaten rye with pumpkin, linseed and
sunflower seed bread. Very good indeed. (Jonas Hein &
Layla O'Brien, Coolfin House, Banagher ☎ 087-204 5593
✉ coolfin@gmail.com)

Offaly

only in Offaly
Slieve Bloom Cranberries

Birr

Offaly

● The Chestnut

A lovely bar, just off the square in the centre of town.
Look out for their full moon market in their courtyard
every third Saturday of each month, and their summer
barbecues. (Clodagh Fay, Green Street, Birr)

Tea Room
● Emma's Cafe & Deli

The prettiest shop front in town is the design prelude to
a pretty room with a handsome counter and tables and
chairs and some nice modern cooking. (Adrian Shine &
Debbie Kenny, 31 Main Street, Birr ☎ 057-912 5678 –
Open 9am-6pm Mon-Sat, 11am-5pm Sun)

Organic Dairy Products
● Mossfield Organic Farm

More than almost any other organic farmer in Ireland
Ralph Haslam's work over the last decade has unleashed
the holistic power of organics. Switching from conventional agriculture has empowered this innovative and
creative farmer in a truly Damascene way. Today the
farm not only produces some of Ireland's finest organic
dairy products, from cheese to yogurts to buttermilk
and ice cream, but it does all of this in a fashion that uses
the farm's own energy, and thereby reduces its carbon
footprint. Mossfield is a model of how organics mean so
much more than simply unadulterated food, and shows
how it stands for empowerment and dynamism, and
the most wonderful Irish foods that you can possibly
discover. (Ralph Haslam, Clareen, Birr ☎ 057-913 1002
📠 info@mossfield.ie 🖥 www.mossfield.ie)

Organic Store
● The Organic Store

Jonathan Haslam's shop is a shining star of good organic
foods. He has organic produce from superstar locals
such as Philip Dreaper, and cheese from his dad's farm,
of course, but there is so much more besides, and everything is always so beautifully handled and presented that
the flourish of goodness is everywhere evident. Superb.
(Jonathan Haslam, Main Street, Birr ☎ 057-912 5881 –
Open 9.30am-6.30pm Mon-Fri, 10am-6.30pm Sat)

● Prue & Simon's

All the classy shops in Dublin stock Prue & Simon's. So if you are in Supervalu in Mount Merrion, or Thomas's in Foxrock, then these wonderful sausages and bacons are waiting there with your name on them. Simon has been busy in the last while, fashioning the perfect breakfast roll, using P&S bangers and bacon, and it's this passion for getting everyday things to the peak of their potential that has always characterised the Rudd family. (Prue & Simon Rudd, Busherstown, Moneygall, Birr ☎ 0505-45206 ✆ prue@prueandsimons.com ⌂ www. prueandsimons.com)

● Andrew Rudd Food Group

Andrew Rudd has become well known thanks to his appearences on TV3, and when he's not in front of the cameras, Andrew is busy sourcing good European products and distributing them to the best delis throughout the country. (Andrew Rudd, Syngefield, Birr ☎ 057-912 5646 ⌂ www.andrewrudd.ie)

● Slieve Bloom Foods

Ciara Morris has her own cranberry farm, and there aren't many people in Ireland who can say that. In fact Ciara and her partner Michael Camon are the only people in Ireland who can say that. Because since acquiring the farm in 2006 they have become specialist suppliers of cranberries to some of the leading restaurants in Ireland as well as using them in their own range of preserves. (Ciara Morris, Clareen, Birr ☎ 057-913 1372 ✆ info@slievebloomfarmhousefoods.com ⌂ www. slievebloomfarmhousefoods.com)

● Spinners Town House and Bistro

Clare O'Sullivan's bistro with rooms is perhaps the best known address in town, and it's a confident, professional destination with snappy tasty food in the bistro and comfortable rooms to lay your head upstairs. (Clare O'Sullivan, Castle Street, Birr ☎ 057-912 1673 ⌂ www. spinnerstownhouse.com – Open 6.30pm-9pm Sun-Mon, Wed-Thu, 6.30pm-10pm Fri-Sat, 12.30pm-2.30pm Sun. Early bird 4pm-7pm)

Offaly

Cloghan

Offaly

Organic Soup
● Clanwood Farm

Orla Clancy makes organic soups using the produce from her organic farm, where in addition to good healthy vegetables she also rears Limousin cattle. The soups are colourful, rooty and wholesome, and of course they are absolutely so convenient. Let Orla do it for you. (Orla Clancy, Cush, Cloghan ☎ 087-649 4477 ✆ clanwoodfarm@eircom.net ✆ www.clanwoodfarm. com)

only in Offaly
O'Donoghue's Rock Buns

Organic Farm
● Lough Boora Farm

Tony Garahy operates one of the most successful box schemes in Ireland, bringing his own and other organic products to a huge network of happy eaters. We love, in particular, the beautiful carrots that Tony's light, sandyish soil brings forth. So if you want to get your hands on them, sign up. (Tony Garahy, Cloghan ☎ 057-934 5005 tonygarahy@eircom.net)

Coolnagrower

Organic Farm
● Philip Dreaper

Philip Dreaper isn't just one of the biggest organic grow-ers and processors in Ireland, he is also one of the best. We are lucky to be able to get his products at the mar-ket in Bantry in West Cork on a Friday, and everything that comes out of the farm seems to enjoy the most ex-treme level of perfection, whether it's an Offaly potato or an Offaly parsnip. Peerless growing, so look out for Philip's label on bags of good things in organic stores and farmers' markets. (Philip Dreaper, Coolnagrower, Fortal, Birr ☎ 057-912 1562 ✆ coolnagrower@eircom.net)

Fernbane

Tea Rooms
● Maidin Gheal

Serbane Spollen has taken over the business started by her mother. Maidin Gheal is Irish for "bright morning" and this draws reference to the early morning baking that goes on here. As well as a small bakery they cook all their dishes carefully each morning, serving curries, goujons, omelettes and pastas. "Small but fresh" is their motto, and it's spot on, so if you are traveling anywhere near to Fernbane, this is your stop for coffee and something sweet, or a light and energy-filled lunch. Sweet. (Serbane Spollen, Main Street, Fernbane ☎ 090-645 4665 – Open 9am-6pm Mon-Sat, with more limited hours off season)

Killeigh

Organic Dairy
● Glenisk Organic Dairy

The Cleary brothers continue to innovate with their range of organic dairy products, recently adding in yogurts with granola to join a splendid range that takes up an acre of space in the McKenna fridge. Even though the Glenisk range has gone for low fat in all its products, the sheer quality of the milk gives a richness and satisfying totality to all of these products, from their cow's milk through to their strong woman yogurt. (Vincent Cleary, Newtown, Killeigh ☎ 057-934 4000 📧 info@glenisk. com 🖥 www.glenisk.com)

Portarlington

Blueberries
● Derryvilla Farm

John and Belinda Seager's blueberry tonic is one of the finest health drinks made not just in Ireland but anywhere on the planet. If PJ McKenna, aged 11, can cash in all the superfood goodness of all the bottles of Derryvilla Blueberry tonic that he has consumed in his short life, then we expect him to be leppin' around the place in 2110. There are also excellent preserves, and those who want to get these beautiful berries for their breakfast

muesli, and for the underside of their crème brûlée
can visit the farm and get them straight from the bush.
(John & Belinda Seager, Derryvilla, Portarlington ☎ 057-
864 2882/087 246 6643 ⌨ info@derryvillablueberries.
com 🖱 www.derryvillablueberries.com)

only in Offaly
Derryvilla Blueberries

Sugarcraft
● Sweet Creations

Miriam Pearson is one of Ireland's leading speciality cake
bakers and designers and her work has to be seen to be
believed. (Miriam Pearson, Pinewood, Cushina, Portarlington ☎ 086-405 1555 ⌨ sweetcreations@eircom.net
🖱 www.sweetcreationsireland.com)

Tullamore

Cakes and Relishes
● Annaharvey Farm Foods

Rachael Deverell is the fourth generation of her
family to turn Annaharvey Farm into a productive
dynamic destination. A range of biscuits, breads,
cakes and relishes ushers forth from the Annaharvey
kitchens, all of them blessed with goodness. (Rachael
Deverell, Tullamore ☎ 057-934 3544 ⌨ foods@
annaharveyfarmfoods.ie 🖱 www.annaharveyfarmfoods.ie)

Café & Deli
● Delicious Caffé

Anne William's café, traiteur, wine shop and all-round-
good-spot is a key destination in Tullamore. There is
a lovely feel to the space – bright, open, relaxed – and
the food, whether you are grabbing a daytime bite to
eat, or grabbing some food to take home for dinner, or
grabbing a bottle of wine to enjoy with that dinner, is
just spot on. (Anne Williams, Harbour Street, Tullamore
☎ 057-932 5943 ⌨ shop@deliciouscaffe.com 🖱 www.
deliciouscaffe.com – Open 8am-7pm Mon-Sat)

Beef and Lamb
● Farm Factory Direct

Robert, Margaret and Ivor Deverell specialise in Hereford beef and Offaly lamb, and since the last edition of this book, their lamb has been one of the most outstanding things that we have cooked and eaten. When you taste a product as distinctive and distinguished as FFD lamb, you realise that this company has the ability to take meats to a level of epicurean perfection that very few people can actually achieve. The beef, of course, is splendiferous too, beautifully butchered and prepared, and capable of making even the most inexperienced cook into a culinary master. (Ivor & Margaret Deverell, Kilcruttin Business Park, Tullamore ☎ 057-932 9405 📩 info@farmfactorydirect.ie 🖰 www.farmfactorydirect.ie)

Beef and Lamb
● Hanlon's

"There is a lovely door-case in Hanlon's butchers shop in Patrick Street", wrote the 2009 Tidy Towns judges in their report on Tullamore. They went on: "This building is obviously much loved by its owners, with a riot of colourful baskets full of colourful flowers". Doesn't that just tell you all you need to know about Michael Hanlon's shop: a riot of colourful baskets full of colourful flowers. And inside, excellent charcuterie, which enjoys the same lavish attention as the shop itself. (Michael Hanlon, Patrick Street, Tullamore ☎ 057-935 1534)

Offaly

Farmhouse Cheese
● Mill House Sheep's Cheese

Elfie and Beni Gerber deserve greater prominence for their excellent range of sheep's milk cheeses, and the cheeses ideally might travel beyond their modest distribution in the Midlands. But maybe if they became more organised and professional, something might be lost of the serious but amateurish way in which cheesemaking is part of their farm work rather than their entire and only focus. So, you will have to hunt down the hard Millhouse cheese, and the soft, flavoured Pastorello will really bring out the culinary detective in you, but we assure you these cheeses are really worth the effort to find them, for they are rather special. (Beni & Elfie Gerber, Killeenmore, Tullamore ☎ 057-934 4334 🖰 www.millhouseireland.com)

● O'Donoghue's Bakery

Cathal O'Donoghue's best-selling bread is his batch loaf. Every one of those loaves requires eight hours, from start to finish. Eight hours. Consider that supermarket breads are "baked" in minutes, and you see immediately the difference between what Mr O'Donoghue does and what the big boy bakers do. In short, he does it right, and because he does it right, it takes time. Time to develop flavour, and structure, and crust, and crumb. Time dedicated to you, lucky customer who lives near to Tullamore and who can get their hands on these superb rock buns, and bloomers and brown soda breads, and good white pan loaves. (Cathal O'Donoghue, Kilcruttin Centre, Tullamore ☎ 057-932 1411 ✉ bread@odonoghuesbakery.ie)

Butcher

● Tormey's Butchers

The Tullamore outpost of the celebrated family butchers, who also have pristine addresses in Mullingar and Galway. Tormey's beef is as good as it gets, but then everything they prepare and sell is as good as it gets. (Tormey family, Bridge Street, Tullamore ☎ 057-932 1426 ✉info@crtormeys.ie ✆ www.crtormeys.ie – Open 9am-6pm Tue-Sat)

Offaly

Sheeps milk cheese

County Roscommon

Ballaghaderreen

Coffee House & Art Gallery
● Meet You Here Café

When Pauline Harper opened Meet You Here right at the end of 2008, people said of the cottage, that "anyone that lived here were very successful in life." Well that success is on-going, for Ms Harper has made a great splash with her baking, her cooking and her brewing. "Possibly the most charming cafe in the country" said Sarah Marriot in The *Irish Times*. There are comfy sofas and lots of paintings and art works for sale, but what you need to know is that Pauline's baking is a local legend and that nobody in Roscommon would think twice about walking through a downpour to have lemon tart with home-made pistachio and raspberry ice cream. (Pauline Harper, Gates of St Nathy's College, Cathedral Street, Ballaghaderreen ☎ 086-300 3803 – Open 8am-10pm Mon-Sat, 2pm-6pm Sun)

---

only in Roscommon
Castlemine Beef & Lamb

Boyle

Farmers' Market
● Boyle Farmers' Market

The Boyle Market is a wee beauty, so turn up for good organics from the Kearns family, fresh fish from Peter, who also turns his cheffy hands to sushi and barbecued salmon, fresh juices from Marion, eggs from Brid, cakes from Patricia and Violet, chutneys and oils from Siobhan and John, cakes and soda bread from Maureen, alpaca knitwear from Louise, and more besides. A lovely setting only adds to the pleasure of shopping at its best. (King House, Main Street, Boyle, ✉ unabhan2@eircom.net, Saturday 10am-2pm)

Castlemine

Farm Shop
● Castlemine Farm

Castlemine is a very important and radical project by
the Allen brothers, Brendan and Derek. Over the last
couple of years, since taking over the farm from their
dad, Sean, they have revised almost every detail of how
Castlemine works, but they have hung onto one incredible USP: "Our farm is based in a limestone region. My
father has always been of the opinion that this limestone
creates a sweet grass and hence a sweet flavour on the
meat. We now believe the same as our beef and lamb
has a very consistently sweet flavour", writes Brendan. Is
it true? It sure is: Castlemine beef and lamb are superb,
meat products that reflect the terroir from which they
emerge. Best of all, the brothers have created a farm
shop where you turn up to get this wonderful food,
another vital step forward, and they also sell on line, and
at local markets. Smart, innovative, and how fantastic
to see farmers looking to the land to give their foods
uniqueness and character. When they opened the shop
in August 2009, they hoped they might attract 150
people. 300 turned up. The people are voting with their
appetites. (Derek & Brendan Allen, Castlemine ☎ 090-
662 9886/087 2231202 ✉ info@castleminefarm.ie
🖰 www.castleminefarm.ie – Open 10am-6pm Fri & Sat)

only in Roscommon
The Hooker Brewery

Keadue

Farmers' Market
● Tullywood Farm

Not just farm to fork, but pork to fork is the mission of
the Delaney family. They specialise in rearing rare breeds
– Tamworths, Saddlebacks and Gloucester Old Spots,
the blessed trinity of porkers – and it's a happy day when
you turn up at the farm shop to discover pork of this
amazing quality, both fresh pork and bacon and in the
guise of their ace sausages. You will also find Tullywood
pork at local farmer's markets, but do try to visit the

shop, where you may also be tempted by their beautiful hen houses, and by their pig keeping courses, or decide that you want to study sausage making with Joe. Pork to fork, indeed. (Joseph & Julie Delaney, Tullytawen, Keadue ☎ 071-964 7905 ✉ tullywoodfarm@eircom. net ☝ www.tullywoodfarm.com – Farmshop open every Sun, 11.30am-4.30pm)

Roscommon

Food and Wine Shop
● Gleeson's Artisan Food & Wine Shop

Mary and Eamonn Gleeson are the pivotal protagonists of what is turning into a little Roscommon culinary revolution. Alongside the other entries in this county, their food and wine shop and townhouse shine as a beacon of distinguished and distinctive thinking about food, about how to make it, how to serve it and what that making and serving does for a local community. The alliance of their own fresh baked breads and hams, along with high-quality food to go, and the best Irish artisan products makes Gleeson's worthy of whatever detour you have to make to get here. A bright new star. (Mary & Eamonn Gleeson, The Manse, Market Square, Roscommon ☎ 090-662 6954 ✉ info@ gleesonstownhouse.com ☝ www.gleesonstownhouse. com – Open 9am-6pm Mon-Sat)

Townhouse & Restaurant
● Gleeson's Townhouse & Manse Restaurant

The original enterprise of Mary and Eamonn Gleeson is a comfortable townhouse and a restaurant which is open from breakfast through to dinner. (Mary & Eamonn Gleeson, The Manse, Market Square, Roscommon ☎ 090-662 6954 ✉ info@gleesonstownhouse.com ☝ www.gleesonstownhouse.com – Open daily for breakfast, lunch and dinner)

Craft Brewery
● The Hooker Brewery

Good beer is a health food, or more specifically a health drink. And bad beer is toxic. If you want to put this theory to the test, go into one of the pubs or restaurants that serve Hooker – Tobergal Lane in Sligo, maybe, or Bierhaus in Cork, or Bull & Castle in Dublin, or Sheridan's in Galway – and order a pint of Hooker Ale. Drink half of it. Now, don't you feel better. Now, drink the remaining half. Don't you feel even better. This is not just the alcohol getting to you. This is the result of a properly made drink, made with good ingredients, offering a palette of flavours to your palate, and connecting your brain cells with your pleasure principle. Now, waste some money and order a commercial "lager". Take a sip. Isn't it awful? You have just had one of the great organoleptic lessons of your entire life. Now, aren't you grateful to Ronan and Aidan, grateful that they don't pasteurise their ale, that they don't use chemicals and preservatives to make the ale last forever, that they envisage their brew as something that is truly, truly good for you. Some lessons are more fun than others. So, the next time you clink a glass with a friend and say "Your good health!", make sure that you mean it. (Aidan Murphy & Ronan Brennan, Racecourse Road, Roscommon ☎ Aidan Murphy 087-776 2823 📖 aidan@ galwayhooker.ie ☎ Ronan Brennan 087-236 6186 📖 ronan@galwayhooker.ie 🖰 www.galwayhooker.ie)

Restaurant & Guesthouse
● Jackson's Restaurant & Guesthouse

Jackson's is the sort of place about which you receive unsolicited emails which will tell you that, for example, there is nowhere in Galway producing food of the quality that Geraldine Garvin is firing out here in Market Square. Ms Garvin likes clean, distinct flavours in each dish, such as a warm duck salad that boasts a saffron poached pear and pitted green olives. There's personality and confidence here. (Michael Hopkins & Geraldine Garvin, Market Square, Roscommon ☎ 090-6634140 📖 info@jacksons.ie 🖰 www.jacksons.ie)

Organic Shop
● Tattie Hoaker

Tattie Hoaker is a cracking specialist organic shop and a distributor of organics throughout the region, as well as a major market player in the region. It's a great store, a place where everything exudes sheer healthfulness and goodness. (Aidan Gillan & Maureen Brosnan, 14 Goff Street, Roscommon ☎ 090-663 0492 📖 tattiehoaker@ gmail.com – Open 10am-6pm Mon-Sat)

Shannonbridge

● The Old Fort

What a place for a restaurant! The Old Fort was built
in 1810 as part of the Shannonbridge Fortifications,
designed to keep Napoleon at bay. Modern day
Napoleons and Josephines, however, turn up to enjoy
good, modern cooking in an atmospheric enclave:
deep-fried goat's cheese with beetroot sorbet; toasted
oysters with lime and ginger butter; fillet steak with a
garlic and whiskey sauce; squash and prune tagine with
chickpea couscous. Great value, and great fun. (Fergal &
Linda Moran, Shannonbridge ☎ 090-967 4973 📖 info@
theoldfortrestaurant.com 🖱 www.theoldfortrestaurant.
com – Open 4pm-9.30pm Wed-Sat, 12.30pm-3pm Sun)

Roscommon

County Sligo

Ballymote

● **Temple House**

A gargantuan and gracious country house, now run by the newest generation of the distinguished Perceval family, Roderick and Helena. (Roderick & Helena Perceval, Ballymote, Sligo ☎ 071-918 3329 ✉ mail2007@templehouse.ie ⌐ www.templehouse.ie)

Castlebaldwin

Guesthouse & Restaurant
● **Cromleach Lodge**

Christy and Moira have been welcoming guests to Cromleach for more than thirty years, so they are true pioneers of hospitality and classy cooking in the North West. Moira's cooking in her eponymous restaurant is – and has always been – correct and classical: scallops on pommes anna with herb de Provence dressing; pistachio and herb crusted rack of Sligo lamb; ragoût of lobster and prawns with fennel. Simpler lunches are served in the bar – garlic mushroom vol au vent; beef casserole with mash; sirloin with sautéed onion, mushroom and pepper sauce. The rooms are comfortable, the views are quite astounding. (Christy & Moira Tighe, Ballindoon, Castlebaldwin, Boyle ☎ 071-916 5155 ⌐ www. cromleach.com)

Curry

Organic Pasta & Pasta Sauce
● **Noodle House Pasta**

We buy and eat Ingrid Basler's pastas all the time, and our daughter, Connie, can somehow manage to use half a jar of Noodle House pasta sauce every time she makes a dish of pasta for herself. So, if Ingrid could only get every devoted customer to work on a ratio of one jar NH sauce to 2 servings HN pasta, untold riches await. Connie's more portion-control-conscious parents doesn't use as much sauce, but they do eat the NH pastas with equal frequency, and have been doing so for more than a decade now. A new range of jams has just been launched, the children have joined Ingrid and Alois in the business, and there is a skip in the step of Noodle House pasta. (Ingrid Basler, Rathmagurry, Curry ☎ 071-918 5589 🖰 www.noodlehouseorganics.ie)

---

only in Sligo
Kilcullen's Sea Water Baths

Enniscrone

Victorian Seaweed Bathhouse
● Kilcullen's Hot Sea Water Health Baths

Sligo is seaweed country, home to pioneers like Carraig Fhada sea vegetables, and Prannie Rhattigan, who is due to launch her seaweed cookery book as we write, is a native of the area. The true seaweed pioneers however are the Kilcullen family, and their amazing sea water health baths in Enniscrone. If your bones ache from too much surfing on the strand, sink them into one of these sea water baths with plenty of seaweeds and sit for twenty minutes in a steam bath and you will emerge a new surfer dude! Simply brilliant. (Enniscrone ☎ 096-36238 🖰 www.kilcullenseaweedbaths.com)

Rathlee

Sea Vegetables
● Carraig Fhada Seaweed

Hand-collected and air-dried on the beach, Frank Melvin's sea vegetables are the premier cru of the genre, superb and vital sea products that bring health with every bite and nibble. You will find them in good wholefood shops, and don't miss them. (Frank Melvin, Cabra, Rathlee, Easky ☎ 096-49042)

Sligo

Sligo

Restaurant & Bar
● Coach Lane @ Donaghy's

Andy Donaghy's restaurant prides itself on a signature
dish of steak and chips, and they do it to perfection,
every time. There is food in the bar from mid-afternoon
– potato skins; barbecued ribs, fish'n'chips, beef and
Guinness stew – and upstairs that perfect steak frites,
with perfect onion rings! is calling to you. (Andy & Orla
Donaghy, 1-2 Lord Edward Street, Sligo ☎ 071-916 2417
🖰 www.coachlane.ie – Open restaurant from 5.30pm-
close Mon-Sat, from 4.30pm Sunday, bar opens 10.30am,
serving food from 3pm Mon-Sun)

Country Grocer
● Cosgrove's

This is a really special shop, and as you step in the door
you step back through the years, to a time when all
shops were like this, manned by kindly gentlemen and
ladies who know every detail of what they are selling,
and whose craft is the true craft and art of being a shopkeeper. Priceless. (Cosgrove family, Market Street, Sligo
☎ 071-914 2809 – Open 9.30am-8pm Mon-Sat)

Coffee Shop & Restaurant
● Eurobar

Consistency has been the keynote of Eurobar over the
years, as Gerry Kenny and his team produce excellent
drinks and light eats and do so with charm and, thankfully, consistent excellence. (Gerry Kenny, Stephen St.
car park, Sligo ☎ 071-916 1788 🖎 eurobar@eircom.net
🖰 www.eurobar.ie – Open 9am-5pm Mon-Fri, 10am-
5pm Sat)

Food-To-Go
● The Gourmet Parlour

In 2010 Catherine and Annette will celebrate 20 years
in business, and we can recall shopping in here back in
1990 as if it was yesterday. They opened up fresh out of
the Ballymaloe school, and we wrote that the GP "combines the precise execution and accessible tastes familiar
to Ballymaloe cookery with the girls' own spontaneous
and direct styles". Twenty years on, we could say the
same thing – we just did – and it would ring true as a

bell. The GP is a great traiteur, and whilst others have come and gone from Sligo, the girls – the women! – have remained steadfast, devoted to the deliciousness of their calling. Local heroes! (Catherine Farrell & Annette Burke, Bridge Street, Sligo ☎ 071-914 4617 ⏚ www. gourmetparlour.com – Open 9am-6pm Mon-Sat)

only in Sligo
Carraig Fhada Seaweed

Bar & Restaurant
● Hargadon's

Joe Grogan fashioned considerable success whilst work-ing out in Rosses Point, so his move into the centre of town to the legendary Hargadon's bar is a healthy jolt for Sligo eating. The bar has been meticulously restored, and also features a wine shop, on the Johnston Court entrance. Aside from lunch, the main food offer is a tapas menu, but Mr Grogan uses the term tapas lightly – somewhat like Ilia Tapas in Mullingar – so what you are offered are light eats rather than little tastes of Iberia: warm crab cake on tomato salsa, chorizo sausage with crispy potatoes, chicken spring roll with herb polenta cake, portobello mushroom with spinach and goat's cheese. (Joe Grogan, 4 O'Connell Street, Sligo ☎ 071-915 3709 ⏚ info@hargadons.com ⏚ www.hargadons. com – Open noon-3.30pm Mon-Sat, 4pm-9pm Tue-Sat)

Wine Shop
● Hargadon's Wine Shop

Hargadon's have more than 250 wines on offer with the majority imported directly from producers and with some even emanating from their own vineyards in the Languedoc. If you are going to eat in Hargadon's bar then this is the place to pick up a bottle, for you can bring it in and drink it for a small corkage charge. (Joe Grogan, Johnston Court Shopping Mall, Sligo ☎ 071-915 3709 ⏚ info@hargadons.com ⏚ www.hargadons. com – Open 10.30am-6pm Mon-Wed & Sat 10.30am-8pm Thu & Fri)

Delicatessen
● Kate's Kitchen

The Kate of Kate's Kitchen is now Kate O'Hara, and Ms O'Hara, along with her sisters Beth and Jane,

Sligo

has continued the distinguished tradition in Kate's of making this shop one of the best in the North West. "Everything you could or might need is here" the locals say, and that is absolutely true, so Kate's is not merely a fine kitchen, it is also an emporium of all the good things you could desire to eat. We love the fact that the produce of local bakers and butchers and growers is welcomed to Kate's, from Bluebell organic quiches to Woodville eggs, from the McHugh sisters' cupcakes to Sarah Murphy's tea bracks. All this lovely doorstep stuff is then haloed by classics like Ortiz tuna or san marzano tomatoes or Filligan's preserves or Murphy's ice cream, and it makes for the most irresistible experience. (Kate, Beth & Jane O'Hara, 3 Castle Street, Sligo ☎ 071-914 3022 ⏚ www.kateskitchen.ie– Open 8.45am-6.15pm Mon-Sat)

Café
● Lyon's Café

"He's really good!" is what the locals say about Gary Stafford's up-for-it cooking in the Lyon's department store, one of the icons of Sligo retailing. Mr Stafford makes lip-smackin', ruddy food: belly pork with Lyon-naise potatoes; Moroccan spiced lamb; a fine lasagne with ricotta and spinach, "and if he makes a meatball, it's a good meatball". In fact, everything Gary produces for lunchtime service is something you would happily eat anytime, especially those lamb burgers with pine nuts and that raspberry bakewell. Very fine. (Gary Stafford, Lyon's Department Store, Quay Street, Sligo ☎ 071-914 2969 ⏚ www.garystafford.com – Open 9am-6pm Mon-Sat)

Café & Wine Bar
● Ósta Café & Wine Bar

Brid Torrades' café and wine bar showcases the simple but spot-on food that has always characterised Ms Tor-rades' cooking. With a little crostini of Tullynascreena goat's cheese from County Leitrim, for instance, she adds a little caramelised onion, whilst with a different riff with the same cheese she mixes the cheese with roasted vegetables and serves it on olive bread with salad. Simple, crucial, pivotal details, and with a glass of Bergerac sec, we couldn't be happier, could we? (Brid Torrades, Unit 2, Weir View House, Stephen Street, Sligo ☎ 071-914 4639 ✉ info@osta.ie ⏚ www.osta.ie – Open 8am-7pm Mon-Wed, 8am-8pm Thu-Sat)

Sligo

Restaurant
● Poppadom

Did you know that "Fish Amritsarsi... this shack special
is the bestseller outside every off-licence in the Punjab region". Ho, fantastic! This sort of wit and deep
background is what makes Poppadom a cut above the
rest, from their Mammy's veggie and potato curry
to the Nepalese veggie momos, you can't go wrong.
(Amjad Hussain, O'Connell Street, Sligo ☎ 071-914 7171
🖰 www.poppadomsligo.com – Open 5pm-10.30pm Sun-
Thur, 5.30pm-11.30pm Fri & Sat)

Restaurant
● The Silver Apple

"French bistro cooking" is what Louise and her team
aim to achieve upstairs in The Silver Apple, so they
have the Jean Paul Belmondo posters and the cooking
has some nice, agrestic moments: perfect caramelized
apples with foie gras parfait, steak with good chips
and a tasty aioli for dipping, good mashed potato, and
a lovely unctuous warm chocolate brownie. Still early
days, but there is lots of promise. (Louise Kennedy,
Gateway Bar, Lord Edward Street, Sligo ☎ 071-914 6770
🖭 silverapplesligo@gmail.com 🖰 www.silverapple.ie –
Open 5pm-10pm Wed-Sun, 1pm-4pm Sun)

Farmers' Market
● Sligo Farmers' Market

The Origin Sligo market has an excellent array of produce from top-notch producers and it has added a vital
slice of new energy to food shopping in Sligo. From fish
to meats, from organics to home baking, from fresh fruit
juices to farmhouse cheeses, it's all here and sold by a
most personable bunch of traders. (Sligo IT Sports Field
Car Park, Saturday 9am-1pm)

Wholefood Shop
● Tir na nOg

Tir na nOg is one of the greatest wholefood shops, and
one of the great Sligo destinations for good things of
every hue and cry. Certain shops transcend themselves,
and become not just shops, but also pivotal elements in
their local food culture: Tir na nOg is that shop.
(Mary & Norah, Grattan Street, Sligo ☎ 071-916 2752 –
Open 9am-6pm Mon-Sat)

Sligo

Restaurant
● Tobergal Lane

Brid Torrades' second Sligo venture, along with Osta café across the river, is the place to go for Galway Hooker beer, foie gras tapas, fresh fish and good savoury hits like duck confit, and then some of the best sweet baking in the region. There is jazz upstairs at the weekends, and Ms Torrades, as usual, achieves her ambition of serving relaxed, modern cooking in a relaxed modern space. (Brid Torrades, Tobergal Lane, off O'Connell Street, Sligo ☎ 071 914 6599 ✆ www.osta.ie – Open 10am-10pm Mon-Sun)

Restaurant
● Café Victor

Good sandwiches and nice soups – mixed bean and lentil; mushroom and pesto, for instance – are what bring hungry eaters back to the Riverbank time and again, though if the sausage and onion quiche is on offer it's almost certainly got your name on it, whilst that breakfast porridge and that chocolatey muffin also seem to be speaking to you. (Nora, Millbrook House, Riverside, Sligo)

Wine Merchant
● The Wine Buff

Tom and Linda Ryall opened the most north-westerly branch of the Wine Buff in 2005, having spent many years working in the 'States, before they moved to Ireland in 2004. They were devising plans to open a restaurant in Galway, plans which were revised when they first came across the Wine Buff stores in Ireland, and which led directly to Sligo's WB coming into existence. Tom has a particular passion for Mexican food, so if you are planning the chimichanga for dinner, make sure to ask Mr Ryall what you should drink with it. (Tom & Linda Ryall, Bridgewater House, Rockwood Place, Sligo ☎ 071-914 0020)

Strandhill

Fishmonger
● John Dory Fish Merchant

"I learned about fish on a Norwegian factory ship. We

were supposed to be on the boat four weeks on, four weeks off, but on my first time out I spent three months on board. We sailed around Norway, the Faro Islands and the Western Isles of Scotland." Maura O'Boyle is a first-generation fish retailer, which is unusual in Ireland. But her passion comes from a love of the sea, and an ability to enjoy the wild and the remote. "When I wake up, if I couldn't see the sea I'd go mad. It gets into your blood". Nowadays, with fish sourced from all over Ireland, Maura sells from her mobile retail shop. She's in Ballyhaunis on Wednesday, Ballaghaderreen on Thursday and Castlerea on Friday. (Maura O'Boyle, Strandhill, Co Sligo ☎ 087-648 9783 – Find her @ Ballyhaunis, Co Mayo, 8am-3.45pm Wednesday; Ballaghaderreen, Co Roscommon, 7.30am-5pm Thursday; Castlerea, Co Roscommon, 7.30am-1pm Friday)

Fish

County Tipperary

Ardfinnan

Restaurant
● **The Riverside**

Ardfinnan is such a sweet little village, with the Suir
River babbling through, so French in style. Luckily for
Ardfinnan it has just the restaurant a French-style town
like this needs, a French-style restaurant. Rodolphe
is – you're right – from France – and he cooks some
things French-style – lamb with haricots; tortellini with
wild mushroom and ricotta; crab and shrimp galette;
a classy lemon tart – whilst others are tailor made for
Tipperary appetites – good sirloin with champ; glazed
parsnips; chicken with bourguignonne sauce; a bounte-
ous chocolate gateau. Sweet and lovely, and Dianne's
service completes the charm of this singular and, because it's so unassuming, rather special place. Value for
money, incidentally, is excellent. (Rodolphe Meyrand &
Dianne Conway, Main Street, Ardfinnan ☎ 052-746 6998
✉ rodway@eircom.net – Open 6pm-9.30pm Thu-Sat,
5pm-9.30pm Bank holiday Sun & group bookings taken
any other day)

Ballymacarbry

B&B with Dinner
● **Glasha Farmhouse**

PJ McKenna and his Dad did the summer 2009 visit to
Olive O'Gorman's country house. After they checked
in and checked out of their comfy room and had some
tea, they did the circuit walk all around to the village
and back, and they did the walk down to the pub at the
bridge for a pint of stout and a glass of pop. Then they
ate that great country cooking for which Olive is famous
– fresh bread, fresh vegetable soup, good lamb with
fresh vegetables, a creamy, dreamy pud – and then they
slept the sleep of the just. Next morning, they walked
the circuit again to build up an appetite for breakfast,
and then laid waste to copious fine pork products, farm-
fresh eggs, juices, cereals and bread and pancakes. Then

they said goodbye, and drove home via West Water-ford, happy as sandboys. And why wouldn't they be, after a night in this fab destination. (Olive O'Gorman, Ballymacarbry ☎ 052-613 6108 ✉ glasha@eircom.net 🖰 www.glashafarmhouse.com)

only in Tipperary
Inch House Black Pudding

Beef
● **Omega Beef Direct**

"Organics With Altitude!". Don't you just love Joe Condon's latest initiative, as he seeks to spread the word about how you create the most superb beef products by putting the right breed of animal on the right upland pastures and letting nature and breed get on with creating the most distinctive and delicious products that Ireland can produce. Mr Condon is a pioneer, a man who understands the acute interplay of breed and feed, a farmer who understands the unique gift of terroir that upland pastures contribute to, for instance, his own Galloway cattle reared in the high altitudes of West Waterford on the Knockmealdown mountains. Meet Joe at the Dungarvan market to buy his superb meats, butchered by the legendary Michael McGrath of Lismore, and you can also buy them on line and at the fabulous Ardkeen quality food store. "Organics with Altitude!" Aiming for the stars is the right place to aim. (Joe & Eileen Condon, Clashavaugha, Ballymacarbry ☎ 087-273 5447 ✉ info@omegabeefdirect.ie 🖰 www. omegabeefdirect.ie)

Borrisokane

Organic Farmer
● **Michael Seymour**

"When it was time to cook the beef for the 2009 Tipperary "Blas an Fhómhair" festival in Nenagh, whose beef was it that Hugo Arnold of *The Irish Times* cooked? Michael Seymour's beef, that's whose. And that says all you need to know about this benchmark organic food, that it should be the meat of choice here in the beef heartland of Ireland at a traditional food tasting festival.

Mr Seymour is a most perspicacious farmer, and you can buy his benchmark beef direct from the producer himself at the weekly Nenagh market. You won't get better anywhere. (Michael Seymour, Finnoe Road, Borrisokane ☎ 067-27182)

only in Tipperary
Beef with Altitude

Cahir

Orchard
● **The Apple Farm**

It's ten years now since we first came across Con Traas and his ground-breaking work in Cahir's The Apple Farm. The farm originated in 1967, with Con's parents, and Con had begun making apple juice in 1995, from James Grieve, Karmijn de Sonnaville and Bramley's Seedlings. The next year they acquired their own production process, using a rack and cloth press system. Since we first got to know the Apple farm, they have just gotten busier, and better. Today, these most handsome orchards grow up to 60 varieties of apple, along with beautiful strawberries, plums, raspberries, cherries and pears. The variety of apple juice mixes has grown, and most recently Con has added a sparkling juice to the range. Everything is as good as it can be, because that is the kind of man Con Traas is: intellectual, restless, a perfectionist. It's no exaggeration to say that knowing the Apple Farm for a decade has made life better for the McKennas for the last ten years. (Con Traas, Moorstown, Cahir ☎ 052-714 1459 ✉ con@theapplefarm.com ⌂ www.theapplefarm.com)

Farmers' Market
● **Cahir Farmers' Market**

Just a bit down from the square is where you will find local heroes such as Con Traas and Pat O'Brien and other brilliant Tipp food specialists. There is a particularly lovely atmosphere in the Cahir market, and the sun always seems to be shining. Optimists? Us? Wouldn't you be an optimist if you were chewing a Cate McCarthy cookie, filling your basket with Keith and Jim's organic veg, thinking on what Love 2 Eat savoury pastry to buy from Emma, and mulling over the contents of Leo's Ballydavid meats. (Craft Granary near the Square, Cahir, 9am-1pm ✆ www.tipperaryfoodproducers.com)

Potatoes & Apples & Farm Produce
● O'Brien's Farm Shop

Here's what we bought last time we stopped at Pat's farm shop: floury Golden Wonder spuds. A big head of cabbage and some parsnips. A jar of Redmond William's honey, a truly excellent honey at that. We got a wedge of Baylough cheese, and a bottle of apple juice along with some apples. We had a great chat with Pat, about potato types, about his stall at the Cahir market, and about the world in general. We walked down to see his gorgeous free-range pigs, who were making a mighty muck-up of the orchard. It was a lovely, authentic, shopping experience, and we are looking forward to doing it again. (Pat O'Brien, Outrath, New Inn, Cahir ✆ 086-648 2044 ✆ http://www.tipperaryfoodproducers.com/markets/obriens_farmshop.html – Honesty box at farm)

Café & Deli
● The River House

Sheena Buttimer has a good looking room where she serves breakfast and lunch and weekend dinner. We dropped in for a coffee and a scone for an 11am snack last time, and both were excellent, and served charmingly, making for a lovely pause in a busy day. (Sheena Buttimer, 1 Castle Street, Cahir ✆ 052-744 1951 ✉ info@riverhouse.ie ✆ www.riverhouse.ie – Open 9am-5pm Mon-Wed, 9am-9.30pm Thur-Sat, 9am-7pm Sun)

Carrick-on-Suir

Tipperary

Wine Merchant
● Approach Trade

Rafael Alvarez scored an amazing coup at the first Spanish Rising Stars competition when his Mantel Blanco Verdejo was picked as best white wine, whilst his Les Terrasses was picked as the best red wine. A double victory is quite some victory, but then anyone who knows the Spanish wines imported by Approach Trade will not be the least bit surprised, for Mr Alvarez picks winners every time. He has superstar winemakers on his list, and superstar prices from wines that are coming out of places like Priorat, but fundamentally his list is a portfolio of choice, terroir-led, individualistic wine-making and more than any other merchant he shows the dynamism and creativity that are now the signature of the Spanish wine world. (Rafael Alvarez, Mill River Pk, Carrick-on-Suir ☎ 051-640164 ✉ info@approachwines.com ✌ www.approachwines.com)

Farmers' Market
● Carrick-on-Suir Farmers' Market

With five years of happy trading under its belt as we go to press, the Carrick market is not just a wee beauty of a market, it's a successful wee beauty of a market at that. Get to the Heritage Centre early for the choice stuff. (Heritage Centre, Friday 10am-2pm)

Cashel

Hotel & Restaurant
● Bailey's Hotel

This former guesthouse has morphed efficiently into a medium-sized hotel with a restaurant and a swimming pool complex, and it's an excellent choice in Cashel, and much better for food and value than other longer-established addresses. (Phil Delaney, Cashel ☎ 062-61937 ✉ info@baileys-ireland.com ✌ www.baileys-ireland.com)

Café
● Café Hans

"Best? Café Hans in Cashel". That's what Ian and Lorraine from Belfast wrote after a wonderful gastronomic tour of Ireland using the Bridgestone Irish Food Guide. We quote it to show you the level at which CH is operating, for Ian and Lorraine stayed at lots of cutting-edge places, and yet Hansie and Steffie's daytime café beat all the superstars to take the top spot. That is some achievement for what the brothers are doing, but to be honest they have not put a foot wrong in Hans from the day they opened a few years back. This is a small room with beautiful cooking, a volcanic atmosphere, and not enough tables, so if you can't get here early, then get here later for anytime around lunchtime it is simply chock-a-block. Whatever you order – salmon with new potatoes and green beans; coronation chicken sandwich; tagliatelle with smoked salmon and cream; gnocchi with pancetta and spinach – it will be, well, the best. (Hansie & Steffie Matthiae, Moor Lane, Cashel ☎ 062-63660 – Open noon-5.30pm Tue-Sat)

only in Tipperary
Karmine Apple Juice

Restaurant
● Chez Hans

Chez Hans opened in 1968, and would it be fanciful to suggest that the revolutionary spirit of that annus mira-bilis in European history explains how this iconic restaurant remains so energised, so radical, so up-for-it? Jason Matthiae and his crew run this restaurant as if every night is a first night, and every service is a performance. Add in one of the most vividly atmospheric rooms in the country – it's in an old deconsecrated church – and that's how you get one of the best restaurants in Ireland. The cooking is lush and satisfying, with classic warhorse dishes such as Caesar salad, or chicken and foie gras paté, cooked to perfection, whilst Jason's riffing on more modern dishes is brilliantly realised: mussels on toast brings Rossmore mussels to a tomato and fennel velouté and excellent garlic bread; Dunmore East lobster is baked with butter and samphire; salmon has a super parsley and Parmesan crust. If it's a special occasion, there are wallet-bustin' wines on the list, but truthfully every evening in Chez Hans is a special occasion. (Jason & Louise Matthiae, Moor Lane, Cashel ☎ 062-61177 ⌂ www.chezhans.net – Open 6pm-10pm Tue-Sat)

Sheep's Milk Cheese
● Crozier Dairy Products

Harry Clifton-Browne's and Jane and Louis Grubb's sheep's milk cheese is one of the most favoured farm-house cheeses used in the creation of signature dishes by younger Irish chefs, which is tribute to its uniqueness

– it is somehow sweet and piquant all in one, quite an organoleptic feat to achieve – and also to its versatility. Crozier is also particularly consistent, and doesn't alter and vary through the seasons as much as farmhouse cheeses made with cow's and goat's milk. This is a cheese that graces every dish it touches. (Harry Clifton-Browne & Jane & Louis Grubb, Ballinamona, Cashel ☎ 062-61120 ✉ cliftonbrowne@eircom.net ⌂ www.cashelblue.com/crozier.htm)

only in Tipperary
Apple Farm Sparkling Apple Juice

Bakery and Café
● The Spearman

Cashel is looking a little tired and deserted these days – that's what happens when you let people build out-of-town supermarkets! – so thank the heavens for great local shops like Spearman's. Elaine Spearman and her family bake friendly, delicious things, and serve them in a friendly way in a friendly shop and café that is a pivotal part of the community. Pure darling. (Elaine Spearman, 97 Main Street, Cashel ☎ 062-61143 – Open 9am-5.30pm Mon-Sat)

Clogheen

Farmhouse Cheese
● Bay Lough Farmhouse Cheese

Do you know what is a great Tipperary food experience? Call into Con Traas' Apple Farm on the road between Cahir and Clonmel. Buy some juice and some nice, tart, crisp apples, and pick up a small truckle of Dick and Anne Keating's Baylough Cheese. Go and find a nice picnic spot, overlooking a mountain or some handsome part of the Golden Vale. Slice some apple, slice some cheese, taste the two, and see how the dairy and the orchard belong together. Tipperary cheese and Tipperary apples, nothin' like them, boy. Baylough is a beautiful cheese, mild and creamy on the palate, but resonant with flavour as you would hope with a handmade territorial-style cheese. The Keatings understand food: one bite of Baylough tells you so. (Dick & Anne Keating, Clogheen ☎ 052-616 5275)

● **Una O'Dwyer Fine Foods**

Una O'Dwyer has an epicurean's imagination when it
comes to creating sausages. True, she makes conventional pork bangers, and some black and white puddings,
but what about smoked bacon and cheese sausage? Or
black pudding and thyme sausage? Or sundried tomato
and basil sausage? Funny enough, those funky concoctions remind us of the sort of crazy, inspired mix of
things that Bernadette O'Shea used to pair together
on her legendary pizzas in Truffles in Sligo all those
years ago, so Ms O'Dwyer is a talent to watch. (Una
O'Dwyer, Cashel ☎ 062-65889)

Restaurant and Accommodation
● **The Old Convent**

"How's this for a parade of deliciousness: Ardsallagh
whipped goat's cheese and honeycomb with beetroot
and pistachio; Connemara Smokehouse organic smoked
salmon with sushi rice, crab, pineapple and cucumber
pickle; butternut squash velouté with thyme flower oil;
beech wood cured duck breast with barbecue pork,
melon mojito salad, Crozier Blue and pecans; lime sorbet
with blackcurrant and apple jelly; roast Goodherdsman
beef with truffled ricotta whipped potatoes and
yellow oyster mushroom dumpling and, finally, a trio of
desserts: lemon posset, Traas' farm raspberry meringue
and hot chocolate. The calmness with which each
course of such a parade of food arrives to every table
simultaneously should not be overlooked. Staff are
exceptional. Breakfast the next morning just puts the tin
hat on what has been, truly, a near perfect experience".
That's Eamon Barrett reflecting on his stay in Dermot
and Christine Gannon's cutting-edge country house in
late summer 2009. "A near-perfect experience". How
often can any of us say that. Funny thing is, it's exactly
what we would say about this landmark destination,
presently one of the most exciting places to eat and
stay in Europe. (Dermot & Christine Gannon, Clogheen
☎ 052-616 5565 ▢ info@theoldconvent.ie ⊕ www.
theoldconvent.ie – Open for dinner at 8pm Wed-Sun,
with different hours during low season)

Tipperary

only in **Tipperary**
Pat O'Brien's Records

Clonmel

Restaurant
● Befani's Mediterranean Restaurant

Befani's is where you eat when in Clonmel, simple as that. Fulvio and Adrian have been making people happy since the end of 2005, and four years on this bright and busy room serves the good stuff in the best way and does so seven days a week. You can just drop in for coffee, nibble some early evening tapas, or make the big night of it with your friends, and the food, the ambience and the service all adapt perfectly to every occasion. Adrian Ryan likes the sweet, summery tastes of the Mediterranean – seafood and saffron soup; baked hake with salsa verde; tuna with gazpacho dressing; scallops with Romesco sauce – so it's a Grand Tour through the great tastes of southern Europe. (Fulvio Bonfiglio & Adrian Ryan, 6 Sarsfield Street, Clonmel ☎ 052-617 7893 🖃 info@befani.com ⊕ www.befani.com – Open 9am-11am Mon-Sun, 12.30pm-2.30pm Mon-Sat, 12.30pm-7pm Sun lunch, 6pm-9.30pm Mon-Sat)

Farmers' Market
● Clonmel Farmers' Market

Joe Condon's unique Omega beef is one of the newer artisan arrivals at the Primary School market here, a favourite spot in Clonmel on Saturday morning. (St Peter & Paul's Primary School, beside Oakville Shopping Centre. Saturdays, 10am-2pm)

Cookies
● The Cookie Jar

Chocolate Chip. Nutty Buddies. Monster Cookies. Oat-meal & Raisin. Bring them on! Boston Brownies. Magic bars. Whoo Hoo! New York-style cheesecake. Is this a Homer Simpson moment I see before me?! Boston-born Cate McCarthy knows how to push the buttons with these American classics. We're speechless. And grateful. (Cate McCarthy, Poulmucka, Clonmel ☎ 052-613 5448 ⊕ www.thecookiejar.ie)

only in Tipperary
Chez & Café Hans

● **Hickey's Bakery & Cafe**

They take their barm brack seriously in Clonmel, and Nuala Hickey's barm brack is one of those cakes that will feature in every animated "who makes the best barm brack" conversation. Ms Hickey has the advantage of experience when it comes to getting barm bracks, and breads and cakes right, for the bakery has been here for almost 110 years. But don't just come to buy bread, take the time to grab a chair in the deli and sip a little coffee and enjoy some salads. (Nuala Hickey, West Gate, Clonmel ☎ 052-612 1587 ✍ hickey.nuala@gmail.com – Cafe Open 9am-6pm Mon-Sat)

● **The Honeypot**

A busy wholefood shop with lots of good things to discover. (The Honey Pot, 14 Abbey Street, Clonmel ☎ 052-612 1457 – Open 9.30am-6pm Mon-Sat)

● **Red Nose Wine**

Gary Gubbins is doing something interesting here with Red Nose, a new wine warehouse where Mr Gubbins sells the good wines from good growers that he has sniffed out from all over the globe. "Our winemaker skills lie more in wine making than marketing," says Gary, a vital distinction in the modern world of wine where so many mass-market brands are just alcoholic cola. (Gary Gubbins, Clonmel Business Park ☎ 052-618 2939 ✍ www.rednosewine.com – Open 2pm-7pm Mon-Tues, 11.30am-7pm Wed-Fri, noon-6pm Sat)

● **James Whelan Butchers**

Pat Whelan is a fifth generation butcher, but he is first generation in terms of devising new ways of retailing meat, both in his shop – which is not like any other butcher's you know – and on-line, through a swift, efficient ordering and delivery service that can bring these Tipperary meats straight to your door. Mr Whelan thinks about retailing meat in very different terms from everyone else – meat selling in Ireland is actually extremely traditional, which is one of its strengths, but which should not be its only strength – and it would be a brave writer who would predict the ways in which

Tipperary

this dynamic entrepreneur will build and diversify his business in the coming years. For now, whether you shop in Clonmel or just go on line, the products are quite superb, and include rarities such as Inch House black pudding. (Pat Whelan, Oakville Shopping Centre, Clonmel ☎ 052-612 2927 ⏚ www.jameswhelanbutchers. com – Open 8am-6pm Mon-Wed & Sat, 8am-6.30pm Thu, 8am-7pm Fri)

Wine Shop
● The Wine Buff

Aodhan O'Farrell is the man with the good Wine Buff bottles in Clonmel, so drop in on the hunt for something to go with dinner and we bet you won't emerge with less than a commodious collation of varietals. (Aodhan O'Farrell, 2 The Westgate, Clonmel ☎ 052-618 0494 ⏚ www.thewinebuff.com – Open 11am-7pm Mon-Sat, 'till 8pm Fri)

Dundrum

Meat Processor
● TJ Crowe

John Paul rears the piggywigs, TJ processes them, and Ned delivers the brilliant Crowe Farm produce to the four corners of the globe, or at least the four corners of the country. These are beautiful, respectful products, foods that celebrate the uniqueness of the pig in the spectrum of eating well and living well. You can't single out any one of the products as being better than the rest, for whether you have sausages, rashers, bacon or their fine puddings, you are getting something that re-flects husbandry, charcuterie and agriculture. (TJ, Ned & John Paul Crowe, Dundrum ☎ 062-71137/087-824 7394 ✉ info@crowefarm.ie ⏚ www.crowefarm.ie)

Fethard

Farmhouse Cheese
● Cashel Blue Cheese

Jane and Louis Grubb's daughter, Sarah Furno, now heads up the iconic and dynamic Cashel Blue operation, and Ms Furno brings to the enterprise not just the fact

Tipperary

that she was involved in it as a child right from the start back in 1978, but also a deep background in wine appreciation, pretty much the perfect organoleptic grounding for anyone who works making a blue-veined cheese. Cashel is, by Irish standards, a large-scale cheese, with 200 tons produced annually. But don't imagine that anything has been done to lessen its fragility in the process of achieving that output. The cheese is still made by hand by a team led by Geurt Van den Dikkenberg, and aside from its overall excellence and uniqueness, what always impresses us about Cashel Blue is its delicacy. Almost more than any other farmhouse cheeses, this is the one that must be bought from a good cheesemonger who has minded it well. Get that Cashel Blue – at 10-11 weeks old, in perfect shape – and you get one of the great Irish taste experiences. (Sarah Furno, Beechmount, Fethard ☎ 052-613 1151 ✉ jlgrubb@eircom.net ⌨ www.cashelblue.com)

only in Tipperary
Bay Lough Farmhouse Cheese

Kilgarvan Quay

Restaurant
● **Brocka-on-the-Water**

Can you find the world in a meringue? You might think not, but we think you can. Consider Ann Gernon's meringues in the unique Brocka, this private-house-cum-restaurant Anne runs with husband Anthony and mum Nancy. Anne's meringues are state of the art, and they reflect not just the work of a talented cook, but the work of a woman driven by an aesthetic need to get everything right. That's why Brocka is so special. It doesn't work like a commercial restaurant. What it is really is the passionate work of three passionate people for whom anything less than perfection in every detail is not quite good enough. So, consider that meringue, and consider its perfection, and consider the animus that made it so perfect, and now you understand the out-of-the-box Brocka. (Anthony & Anne Gerson, Nancy Burns, Kilgarvan Quay, Ballinderry ☎ 067-22038 – Open 7pm-10pm Mon-Sat. Reservations only)

Tipperary

Nenagh

Country Shop
● Country Choice

Since the publication of the last *Bridgestone Irish Food Guide*, Peter Ward has become the best-known grocer in Ireland, whilst previously he was simply the best grocer in Ireland. His journey into the public sphere has added polemic into the daily practicality of running a brilliant business in Country Choice. "His pork terrine and country butter are delicious", said Caroline Byrne after a first visit to CC to load up with good things, and that sort of attention to the simplest detail – good butter, a good terrine – are the measure of this landmark shop. The café at the rere serves fabulous, simple Irish country cooking, and Country Choice shows that, when it comes to food, the personal is also the political, and the practical also needs the polemical in an age when vested interests are squeezing the life out of Irish agriculture and Irish ruralism. Peter Ward fights the good fight. (Peter & Mary Ward, 25 Kenyon Street, Nenagh ☎ 067-32596 ✉ info@countrychoice.ie 🖱 www.countrychoice.ie – Open 9am-5pm Mon-Sat, coffee shop closes at 5pm)

only in Tipperary
Hickey's Barm Brack

Craft Butcher
● Hackett's

Michael Hackett's shop is a changeless butcher's shop. Don't know about you, but we find it enormously reassuring to walk into a butcher's store that has precious little meat on display, but where the man of the house will be able to facilitate any request you could possibly have, just by picking up his knives, and switching on the Butcher's Boy, and heading back into the cold room to emerge with some pristine piece of country beef or lamb that will expertly be transformed into the very thing you want for dinner. (Michael Hackett, 94 Silver Street, Nenagh ☎ 067-31340 – Open 9am-6pm Mon-Sat, closed Wed)

● Hanlon's

Gregory and Michael Hanlon's shop showcases a team
of butchers who are right at the top of their calling.
Superbly sourced meats are shown sharp charcuterie
skills in a handsome shop, and whether you are the
confident cook who is looking for the strange stuff, or
the novice who wants something good but which has to
be simple, then Hanlon's is the place for you. Excellent
service brings it all home. (Gregory & Michael Hanlon,
14 Kenyon Street, Nenagh ☎ 067-41299 – Open 8am-
6pm Mon-Sat, 8am-7pm Fri)

Craft Butcher
● Larkin's Bar & Restaurant

Isn't it nice to be able to go to a thatched Irish pub on
the lakeshore and eat bacon and cabbage, and then
listen to a spot of top-notch traditional music. Well
you can do all of these in Cormac and Maura's beautiful bar. There is bar food during the day and a broader
menu in the evening and it's classic cooking: Slaney
Valley lamb with rosemary champ, sage and apple stuffed
pork, Hereford T-bone steak. (Cormac & Maura Boyle,
Portroe, Nenagh ☎ 067-23232 📧 info@larkinspub.com
🖰 www.larkinspub.com – Open pub hours. Food served
10.30am-9.45pm Mon-Sat, noon-9.45pm Sun with more
limited hours off season)

Farmers' Market
● Nenagh Farmers' Market

Nenagh is a great town, and it has a great farmers'
market, a place where A-list artisans bring their good
things to sell on a Saturday morning. This is classy stuff,
from organic beef to rare-breed pork, from apple tarts
to sweet, crumbly confectionery. Fab. (Teach and Leinn,
Kenyon Street, Nenagh, Sat 10am-2pm)

Café
● The Pantry

"The team from The Pantry Café, led by Frances
Kennedy, cooked and served their legendary organic
beetroot and also piping hot buttered colcannon to the
capacity audience". Ah, isn't that the ticket? Legendary
beetroot. Piping hot buttered colcannon. How could you
get enough of that good food, eh? Grainne Moylan and
her team do the good thing here in The Pantry, and we

Tipperary

should have found them a long time ago, just so we could have enjoyed earlier the sort of deliciousness that *The Nenagh Guardian* reported on when the team cooked for the town's Blas an Fhómhair festival. Away from the festival, in this stylish room on Quentin's Way, they make their legendary hot belly sandwiches, lovely salmon fishcakes with organic leaves, fresh salads with loin of bacon and Dijon sauce, and a trio of good pizzas. Smart food, smart people. (Grainne Moylan, Quentin's Way, Nenagh ☎ 067-31237 ✍ info@thepantrycafe.ie ⊕ www. thepantrycafe.ie – Open 8.30am-6.30pm Mon-Sat)

Bakery Cafés
● Quigley's

We like food people with a taste for chutzpah. "Our Pink Slices are as evocative as Proust's madeleines", say Quigley's. Wow! Now that's confidence, and it's well merited with John and Margaret O'Connor's company, for these guys do things the proper way, and they have been rewarded with a small chain of nine very successful shops and cafés which sell their food. We toured their kitchens a few years back, and were amazed at the hands-on nature of everything, for one can have the idea that any chain is relying on industrial processes to make their foods. Not Quigley's: this is proper food, as Marcel Proust might have said himself. (Margaret O'Connor, Lisbunny Business Park, Nenagh, branches at: 9 Kenyon Street, Nenagh ☎ 067-36445 also Athlone Town Centre, Co Westmeath ☎ 090-647 7017; Roscrea Shopping Centre, Roscrea, Co Tipperary ☎ 050-523313; Liberty Square, Thurles, Co Tipperary ☎ 050-424397; Patrick St, Tullamore, Co Offaly ☎ 057-936 0353; MacDonagh Junction, Kilkenny ☎ 056-772 2606; Cruises Street, Limerick ☎ 061-411050; Crescent Shopping Centre, Dooradoyle, Limerick ☎ 061-228688; Parkway Shopping Centre, Limerick, Parkway Shopping Centre, Limerick ☎ 061-418407 ✍ quigleysbakery@eircom ⊕ www.quigleys.ie.)

Relishes
● The Scullery

There is something very wholesome about Florrie Purcell's work. When you are enjoying one of her Christmas puds you can just see the girl herself surrounded by fruit and flour and butter and brandy, concocting a little slice of happiness for somebody's special Xmas day. She is one of those artisans who

Tipperary

manages to coax all of the primary flavours out of every ingredient she works with, so the sauces, pickles and relishes are just as moreish as the ham glazes and the plum puddings. (Florrie Purcell, 7 Springfort Industrial Park, Stream, Limerick Road, Nenagh ☎ 086-174 4402 ☐ florrie@thescullery.ie)

only in Tipperary
The Scullery Plum Pudding

Roscrea

Farmhouse Cheese
● Boulabane Cheese

Michael and Kate Cantwell have been racking up the awards for their ice cream and sorbets over the last couple of years. They begin with the headstart advantage of having the milk of their own pedigree Holstein-Friesian herd, and then they just let their imaginations take flight: apple sorbet with Calvados; toffee ice cream with toffee pieces; mulled wine sorbet; Xmas pud ice cream. Phew! These are to ice cream what Pixar is to animation. Look out for the ices and sorbets at farmers' markets and in some Supervalus and good restaurants. (Kate & Michael Cantwell, Boulabane, Roscrea ☎ 0505-43430 ☐ kmcantwell@eircom.net ◌ www.boulabanefarms.ie)

Templemore

Artisan Beer
● White Gypsy Brewery

Cuilán Loughnane's White Gypsy is a new brewing company, which is using the kit of the defunct Kinsale Brewery to fashion Mr Loughnane's range of beers. Currently in barrel is Vintage Imperial Stout, which will be wood barrel aged, a thrilling drink to look forward to, whilst lagers and ales have so far appeared only at festivals, but watch this space carefully for Mr Loughnane is one of Ireland's most distinguished brewers. (Cuilán Loughnane, 14 Priory Place, Templemore ☎ 086-172 4520 ◌ www.whitegypsy.ie)

Tipperary

Terryglass

Gastropub
● **The Derg Inn**

Mick and Joyce Soden's gastro-pub is a real gastro pub: a bar that cooks and serves real food, and where you can see and enjoy the evident care and expertise of a talented kitchen. When they do the classics of pub food – battered hake and chips; bacon and cabbage; medallions of pork with wholegrain mustard sauce – they do them right, and the food is correct, satisfying, logical, not messed about with. So, a day sailing on the waters of Lough Derg, and then the thirst for a pint, and the hunger for pan-fried crab claws, and then a Hereford sirloin with mash and creamy shallots. Ah. (Joyce & Mick Soden, Terryglass ☎ 067-22037 🖅 derginn@eircom. net 🖰 www.derginn.ie – Food served noon-9.30pm Mon-Sun)

Thurles

Artisan Cheese maker
● **Cooleeney Cheese**

Breda and Jim Maher are sports of nature in Irish cheesemaking, for where others make a single cheese, and maybe smoke a version of that cheese, the Mahers have an incredible variety of cheeses produced on their farm. Cooleeney, the original of them all, is a mould-ripened semi-soft cheese made with raw milk from the Mahers' own herd. Dunbarra comes in three varieties and is made with pasteurised milk. Gortnamona is a soft, pasteurised goat's milk cheese. Darú uses vegetarian rennet in a semi-hard cheese. Maighean uses raw cow's milk from the Friesian herd, and you should let this magnificent cheese age to 10 weeks. Chulcoill is a soft goat's milk log which uses pasteurised milk. Finally, two new arrivals: Tipperary Brie, a mellow buttery, grassy cheese, and Gleann Oir, a fresh goat's milk cheese. Eight distinct cheeses from a single farm! What an achievement. And when you consider their individuality, their differences, their distinctiveness, then you say: what genius! Genius indeed, for the Maher family's achievement is amongst the pinnacles of Irish cheesemaking. (Jim & Breda Maher, Moyne, Thurles ☎ 0504-45112 🖅 info@cooleeney.com 🖰 www.cooleeney.com)

● **Crossogue Preserves**

Veronica Molloy was born in Kenya – as was Sally
Mckenna, so there you go: it is a small world – and
when she landed in Ireland she established Crossogue
Preserves as well as rearing six children. Recently, she
has taken to returning to Africa to work in Tanzania as
part of Tracey Piggott's Playing for Life project where
volunteers pass on skills to local women. So, a mixed
farm, a range of preserves that numbers no fewer than
85 products, six kids, and practical missionary work in
Africa. Superwoman or what? And you can taste that
energy for life in every one of the Crossogue range, so
don't miss them. (Veronica Molloy, Ballycahill, Thurles
☎ 0504-54416 ✉ info@crossoguepreserves.com
🖰 www.crossoguepreserves.com)

Country House & Restaurant
● **Inch House**

There is energy in Inch, as the go-ahead Egan family
branch out from the core business of their country
house and restaurant and begin making a terrific range
of specialist foods, including an ace black pudding which
is fashioned for them by the ever-smiling TJ Crowe of
Dundrum. In addition to the pudding, there are fine fruit
sauces and true-tasting relishes – mango chutney, plum
chutney, red onion marmalade and red pepper relish.
This is a logical and smart move, for Inch is one of the
standard bearers in Tipp for hospitality and dedication
to cooking and service that is selfless and devoted. So,
come and stay for the night in clamorous comfort, eat
delicious country cooking in the grand restaurant, and
after breakfast the next morning, fill up a basket with
good things and take the taste of Inch House home with
you to savour the experience a little longer. (Mairin
& Nora Egan, Thurles ☎ 0504-51261 ✉ mairin@
inchhouse.ie 🖰 www.inchhouse.ie – Restaurant open
7pm-9.30pm Tue-Sat)

Tipperary

Country House & Restaurant
● **Mitchel House**

The somewhat conventional initial impression of the
menus in Michael O'Dwyer's Mitchel House – roulade of
pork fillet; fillet of salmon; supreme of chicken; shank of
lamb; sirloin of beef – can seem a reflection of conservative local tastes in a conservative country town.

But look closer at Brendan Sheridan's menus and you
see lots of subversive little gestures: there is a saffron
butter with the salmon, angel hair potato with the pork,
a red pepper and spinach mousse with the chicken, a
black pudding and red onion parcel with the beef. It's
because of this modest subversion that food lovers have
already recognised that Mitchel is where you eat when in
Thurles, for the cooking is correct and professional, and
so is everything else. (Michael O'Dwyer, Mitchel Street,
Thurles ☎ 0504-90776 ✉ mitchelhouse@eircom.net
🖰 www.mitchelhouse.ie – Open 5pm-10pm Wed-Sat,
12.30pm-2.30pm, 6pm-9pm Sun)

Farmers' Market
● **Thurles Farmers' Market**

Saturday mornings at the greyhound track is where the
fleet of foot get all the best stuff. (Saturday 9.30am-1pm)

Asparagus and strawberries

County Waterford

Ardmore

Restaurant
● Cliff House Hotel

Cliff House has enjoyed nothing but rave reviews since opening in 2008, and you can list the reasons why. A stunning design set into the cliffside at Ardmore, with every room overlooking the bay. Brilliant style which takes boutique hotel-keeping to a new level. And a very dynamic, elemental style of cooking from Martin Kajuiters that draws all the creative and free-spirited ideas of this hotel together into one luscious feast at dinnertime. Simple details used with profound effect describes what Mr Kajuiter tries to do: shamrock sorrel to counterpoint scallops; ribbons of cottiers kale with pigeon; fennel with black pudding, truly a touch of drama with every bite. The cooking is both artful and elegant, and quite different to what anyone else is doing in Ireland right now. A must-visit, and one of the finest new destinations, simple as that. (Adriaan Bartels, Ardmore ☎ 024-87800 📧 info@thecliffhousehotel.com 🖰 www.thecliffhousehotel.com – Restaurant open noon-3pm, 6.30pm-9pm Mon-Sun – residents only Fri & Sat)

● White Horses

What a smashing lunch all the McKennas had in this lovely room the last time we visited. It was high summer, the sun was shining, and Ardmore was at its busy, bustly best, which means, inter alia, that White Horses was at its best. And that means tasty savoury cooking, nicely domestic, well measured, followed inevitably by some of the best baking to be found in these parts. The cakes and pastries here are amongst the very best, and we cannot sing their praises highly enough, so detour down to the sea and the tower and down to the main street, and get a slice of some scrumptiousness. (Christine Power & Geraldine Flavin, Main Street, Ardmore ☎ 024-94040 📧 whitehorses@eircom.net – Open 11am-11pm Tue-Sun, with more limited hours off season)

Ballymacarbry

Country House & Restaurant
● Hanora's Cottage

The Wall family's restaurant with rooms is cosy, friendly and beautifully tucked away at the side of the river just down from Ballymacarbry village. It is a haven for walkers, but for anyone who wants to ferret out the delights of West Waterford, this is a fantastic place in which to base yourself, and to return to each evening to eat well and sleep well. (Eoin Wall, Judith Hovenden & Mary Wall, Nire Valley, Ballymacarbry ☎ 052-6136134 ✉ hanorascottage@eircom.net ◌ www.hanorascottage.com)

only in Waterford
Ardkeen Quality Store

Cappoquin

Bakery and Coffee Shop
● Barron's Bakery

Barron's is one of Waterford's finest traditional bakeries, with breads and blaas all made in the traditional oven, with the bread allowed lots of time to develop and ferment, and with the final result nothing but sheer goodness. Simply wonderful. (Esther & Joe Barron, Cappoquin ☎ 058-54045 ✉ barronsbakery@eircom.net ◌ www.barronsbakery.ie – Open 9am-5.30pm Mon-Sat)

Apple Juice
● Crinnaghtaun Apple Juice

Consistent excellence is often the most difficult thing for artisan food producers to achieve, but Julia Keane's Crinnaghtaun apple juices never veer from a path of consistent, satisfying, excellence. High-quality fruit is the answer: we buy David Keane's apples whenever we see them in our supermarket, and they are peachy sweet and delicious. From this, Mrs Keane fashions a delicious, thirst-slaking juice that is a treasure. (Julia & David Keane, Cappoquin ☎ 058-54258 ✉ sales@irishjuiceco.com ◌ www.irishapplejuice.com)

Waterford

● Knockalara Farmhouse Cheese

Wolfgang and Agnes make the best-known sheep's milk cheese in Ireland, and in addition to the rich complexity of Knockalara, they also fashion some very vividly flavoured fresh cheeses, sold under the Dromana label. Believe it or not, but they have been making these superb cheeses for almost twenty years now, and in all that time their work has been characterised by the fact that they have stayed small-scale, but just gotten better and better. Pretty much the ideal trajectory for any artisan company. (Wolfgang & Agnes Schliebitz, Knockalara, Cappoquin ☎ 024-96326 ✉ wschliebitz@eircom.net)

● Richmond House

Paul and Claire's country house and restaurant is one of Ireland's best. There is a calm, a generosity, an almost uncommercial ambience in Richmond that really does make it feel like a visit to a friend rather than a visit to a country house hotel. Mr Deevy's cooking is subtle, pure, satisfying, and he has such knowledge of and respect for his local foods that every meal we have eaten here over the last fifteen years has been memorable and delicious. A great, great country destination. (Paul & Claire Deevy, Cappoquin ☎ 058-54278 ✉ info@richmondhouse.net ✆ www.richmondhouse.net – Open for Dinner for non-residents 7pm-9pm Mon-Sun, closed Sun off season)

Cheekpoint

● McAlpin's Cottage Bistro

Aidan and Marian McAlpin's poular restaurant continues to attract and please the many locals and tourists who flock to this pretty village in the summer months. The menu doesn't change much, and for a very simple reason: there would be a revolt amongst the Cottage Bistro's customers if even one of Marian's signature dishes were to disappear. Son Duncan joins the team occasionally, and despite his tender years has shown himself to be both a capable f-o-h, and a dab hand with the pots and pans in the kitchen too, so succession is assured in a sweet, smart food business. (Aidan & Marian McAlpin, Cheekpoint ☎ 051-380854 ✉ info@cottagebistro.com

Waterford

www.cottagebistro.com – Open 6pm-9.30pm Tue-Sat. Open Bank hols and Sun evenings, 5.30pm-8.30pm, Jul-Aug)

Bistro
● McAlpin's Suir Inn

There have been some changes to the venerable McAlpin's and this long-established restaurant now opens for Sunday lunch, a small change, but one which has been a huge success. The menu is based around a list of popular dishes that have been served here for years: seafood pie; chicken curry; fillet of beef, and a list of indulgent desserts – including a really lovely Queen of Puddings – that will leave you needing a walk down Cheekpoint's quayside after you've eaten. (The McAlpin family, Cheekpoint ☎ 051-382220 📧 suirinn@ mccalpins.com www.mcalpins.com – Open from 6pm Mon-Sun and Sun lunch)

Dungarvan

Bagel Bakers
● Broadway Bagels

Des and Rosie Sheehan are one of those unstoppable forces of nature right now, with their original bagel selection recently joined by a range of brownies, bagel chips, pretzels and cookies. This pair have the suss to achieve whatever they want, but their success is achieved through patient perfection and maintaining super-high standards. (Des & Rosie Sheehan, Dungarvan Business Park, Dungarvan ☎ 058-23843 📧 info@ broadwaybagels.ie www.broadwaybagels.ie)

Shop
● Country Store

This is a good food shop, with a strange aesthetic that places it somewhere between a supermarket and an old-style greengrocers. But there are lots of good local things – Baldwin's ice creams; Eunice Power's gorgeous baking and preserves – to bring you in the door, and to bring you back again and again, especially the foods bought in from Tipperary's Country Choice. (Conor Lannen, 3 Shopping Arcade, Mitchell Street, Dungarvan ☎ 058-43061 – Open 8am-6pm Mon-Sat)

● Dungarvan Farmers' Market

With more than five happy years of trading under
its belt, the Dungarvan market powers ahead every
Thursday. It's a sign of its success that marketeers
like Louise Clark have moved on to open their own
successful restaurants, as Louise has done with Nude
Food, though we rather regret that you can no longer
ask a friend if they would like to "Do a Naked Lunch?"
A great hardcore of traders make the market brimful
of energy and good stuff. (Gratton Square, Thursday
mornings. Contact Síobhan La Touche, ☎ 086-394 0564
📠 contact@dungarvanfarmersmarket.com 🖱 www.
dungarvanfarmersmarket.com – Open 9am-2pm
Thursdays)

● Gortnadiha Lodge

With only three rooms, it isn't easy to get into Eileen
Harty's house during the high season, but keep on trying
if at first you don't succeed, because Mrs Harty is a
great hostess, and her breakfasts are the stuff of legend.
(Eileen Harty, Ring, Dungarvan ☎ 058-46142 📠 info@
gortnadihalodge.com 🖱 www.gortnadihalodge.com)

● Nude Food

Marketeer Louise Clark has joined the ranks of the
Dungarvan Dynamos with the opening of her super
little café and restaurant, Nude Food, on O'Connell
Street, following on from her huge success with The
Naked Lunch in the market. From Naked to Nude:
well, it's a career path of sorts. It's an eclectic space:
mismatched furniture, old living room lamps and a
chandelier made from old bottles, but it all works and
the place has a lovely ambience. The food never misses
the spot: pork belly with roasted butternut squash,
couscous and hummus and char-grilled sourdough bread
is outstandingly good. Hederman's smoked salmon with
cucumber and cream cheese on brown bread is ace, the
salmon cut into nice thick pieces, and that bread and
butter pudding bubbling in the oven has your name on
it, if you can but resist the pear and almond tart with
Glenilen clotted cream. Good coffees, good service, low
prices - what more can one possibly want? A new star.
(Louise Clark, 86 O'Connell Street, Dungarvan

Waterford

☎ 058-24594 📧 info@nudefood.ie 🖰 www.nudefood.
ie – Open 9.15am-6pm Mon-Wed, 9.15am-9.30pm Thu-
Sat. Open Sun during summer months and three weeks
before Christmas)

Butcher
● John David Power

The queue will be out the door on Saturday mornings
at JD Power's smashing butcher's shop. We come here
for the bacon in particular, but everything in this special
shop is special. (John David Power, 57 Main Street, Dungarvan ☎ 058-42339 – Open 9am-5.50pm)

Country House
● Powersfield House

Caterer, Cook, Teacher, B&B keeper, Food producer.
Eunice Power is all these things, and more, but the
secret of her success is that she is not only good at all
these callings, she is positively distinguished. There is an
elemental generosity to her cooking that shines through,
and she loves the quotidian things: breads; porridge;
jams, simple stuff done superbly. Catch her classes at the
Tannery School, look out for her baking in the Country
Store in Dungarvan, enjoy her classy B&B just outside
the town. (Eunice Power, Ballinamuck West, Dungarvan
☎ 058-45594 📧 eunice@powersfield.com 🖰 www.
powersfield.com)

Café & Bar
● Quealy's Café Bar

A stylish bar with stylish modern bar cooking and good
service. (Andrew Quealy, 82 O'Connell Street, Dungarvan West, Dungarvan ☎ 058-24555 – Quealy's Bar
open noon-3pm, 5pm-9pm. 📧 info@quealys.com)

Restaurant
● The Tannery

Even among the good restaurants, there are those who
are not only better than the good, they come very close
to being 'the best'. Paul and Maire Flynn's The Tannery
is such a place. Open since 1997 the restaurant feels as
fresh and innovative today as it did back then - there
is not one hint of tiredness in Paul Flynn's cooking as
he continues his dogged pursuit of using the best local
ingredients as simply as possible to produce food of

Waterford

sublime satisfaction. Mr Flynn understands his food perfectly – buttered asparagus to start, seared lamb for main course, rhubarb with marshmallow and sorbet for dessert - with each and every detail perfectly executed. Or maybe chicken and foie gras sausage to start, then scallops with garden peas and chorizo croquette for mains - all just as perfect. Words can scarcely do justice to the absolute perfection of each of these dishes, for to add or remove a single component would have compromised the success of each course. Nobody else cooks like this and nobody else could cook like this and that such a sentence is undoubtedly true, twelve years after opening, is testament to Paul Flynn's unique talent. (Paul & Maire Flynn, 10 Quay Street, Dungarvan ☎ 058-45420 📠 info@tannery.ie 🖰 www.tannery.ie – Open 12.30pm-2.15pm Tue-Fri & Sun, 6.30pm-9.30pm Tue-Sat, 6pm-9pm Sun)

Townhouse & Cookery School
● Tannery Townhouse & Cookery School

"A quite extraordinary space that is so cutting edge, so well designed, that it could almost be described as futuristic. The restaurant also now has its own herb and vegetable garden behind the cookery school. The entire enterprise - restaurant, fourteen bedrooms, cookery school and vegetable garden – can only be described as an amazing achievement." That was Eamon Barrett's reaction to a first look at Paul Flynn's new townhouse and his new cookery school and gardens. Frankly, it is everyone's reaction, for Mr Flynn has hit the jackpot once again and, once again, he has raised the bar in terms of what a school can achieve. The rooms are svelte and sexy, the entire experience of taking a cookery class, staying in the Townhouse, and eating in the restaurant, is one of the great Irish adventures. (Paul & Maire Flynn, 10 Quay Street, Dungarvan ☎ 058-45420 📠 info@tannery.ie 🖰 www.tannery.ie)

only in Waterford
Tannery Cookery School

● **Tara's Handmade Quality Foods**

Tara Breen's company supplies lusciously good things to delis and shops, and the quality of their baking has garnered scores of awards over the years. Über-professional. (Tara Breen, 18G Dungarvan Business Park, Dungarvan ☎ 058-41912 ✉ tara@tarascookies.com 🖰 www.tarascookies.com)

Dunmore East

Organic Chickens

● **Born Free Organic Chickens**

There is no greater pleasure than sitting down to a roast of one of Paul Crotty and JJ Aherne's marvellous birds for Sunday lunch, that gorgeous aroma of roasting chicken permeating through the house. Add in some roast potatoes, cauliflower cheese and some glazed carrots with saffron, a glass of something invigorating to sip, and you have a traditional dinner which will never go out of fashion as long as there is chicken this good, and boy but these BF chickens are good. (Paul Crotty, Ballymabin, Dunmore East ☎ 087-279 2613/051-383565 ✉ paul_crotty@eircom.net)

Traiteur & Cafe

● **The Lemon Tree**

Joan Boland-Power's little place has grown and grown over the years, but the standard of cooking and catering in the LT has always been high, whether you are just grabbing a slice of rhubarb crumble and some custard – rhubarb and custard, aah! – or you are here for the newer evening menus, offered on Friday and Saturday evenings, and which show the style of a dedicated cook: warm duck and lentil salad with mixed leaves and pine nuts; cockles and mussels tossed in lashings of garlic butter; sardine fritters on toast with roast red pepper marmalade and for mains: sea bream Provençale; fricassee of monkfish with mussels and saffron; duck and Irish gourmet sausage cassoulet. With all of these main courses under €20, it is no surprise Joan's Lemon Tree is always a hive of activity. (Joan Power, Dunmore East ☎ 051-383164 ✉ lemontreecatering@eircom.net 🖰 www.lemontreecatering.ie – Open 10am-6pm Tue-Sat, 10am-4pm Sun with occasional Fri & Sat evening menus)

Waterford

● **The Spinnaker Bar**

The focus is firmly on food at Niall and Maria
Edmondson's popular Dunmore East bar, and in the
peak of the summer it can be hard to get a table
here. Sensibly, the menu sticks to the kind of food you
hanker for after a day on the waves: seafood chowder;
crab claws in garlic butter; beer battered fish and chips;
homemade lamb burger with relish and fries. Quality
is high and it's no wonder the place is such a hit with
families. (Niall & Maria Edmondson, Dunmore East
☎ 051-383133 ⌂ info@thespinnakerbar.com ⌂ www.
thespinnakerbar.com – Open pub hours, food served
12.30pm-4.30pm, 6pm-10pm Mon-Sun with more
limited hours off season)

Ferrybank

Boutique Hotel
● **Athenaeum Hotel**

Stan and Mailo Power's stylish boutique hotel is tucked
away on the north side of Waterford's River Suir, on a
lovely site that overlooks Waterford City. The public
areas are very well designed and exude luxury while the
long dining room treats you to a view of the twinkling
lights of Waterford City through the trees. Bedrooms
are quite large and many feature bespoke furniture
designed by Mailo herself as well as quite striking
colour schemes. Staff are extremely friendly and Stan
runs the hotel 'hands-on' and is full of local knowledge
and advice: no matter where you are travelling on
to, Stan will doubtless know somebody there. (Stan
& Mailo Power, Christendom, Waterford ☎ 051-
833999 ⌂ info@athenaeumhousehotel.com ⌂ www.
athenaeumhousehotel.com)

Glencairn

Restaurant with Rooms
● **Pastis @ Glencairn Inn**

"Brilliant place to stay overnight; great food." That
was how our mates Barbara and Trevor felt about an
overnight and dinner at Pastis, and this charming inn has
charmed many customers since Fiona and Stéphane

took up the reins. The cooking is French-accented and polished, and the Inn has a truly unique charm: there are few true inns in Ireland which makes Pastis someplace special. The rooms are lovely and inviting, and an overnight is always special. (Fiona & Stéphane Tricot, Glencairn, Lismore ☎ 058-56232 ✉ info@glencairninn. com 🖰 www.glencairninn.com – Restaurant open 7pm-9pm Thur-Sat, 1pm-3pm Sun)

Kilmacthomas

Porridge
● **Flahavan's**

We eat Flahavan's organic porridge almost every day of our lives. That's not just because it is an exemplary product – which it is – it is also because Flahavan's is the sort of sustainable, sensible, energy-conscious food producer that Ireland needs more of, and when we find virtue not just in the food, but also in how the food is sourced and developed, then it explains why Flahavan's gets our money, every time. Brilliant. (John Flahavan, Kilnagrange Mills, Kilmacthomas ☎ 051-294107 ✉ oatmail@flahavans.com. 🖰 www.flahavans.com)

Knockanore

Farmhouse Cheese
● **Knockanore Cheese**

Eamonn Lonergan's cheeses are popular and accessible, and many chefs in particular make use of his smoked cheeses. (Eamonn Lonergan, Ballyneety, Knockanore ☎ 024-97275 🖰 www.knockanorecheese.com)

Lismore

Butcher
● **Michael McGrath**

The quintessential traditional butcher's shop, with precious little meat on display, pristine scrubbed surfaces, and a little booth where you pay the kindly lady for the lovely meats Mr McGrath prepares for you. Once upon a time, all butchers' shops looked just like this. Charming. (Michael McGrath, Main Street, Lismore ☎ 058-54350 – Open 7am-6pm Mon-Sat)

Restaurant
● O'Brien Chop House

Justin Green knew exactly what he wanted to achieve
when opening O'Brien Chop House in the old Barça
premises in Lismore. The miracle is that he got those
intentions and ambitions so right, straight from the
start. The food is simple, but beautifully sourced and
finished: that little note of chilli in the sauce for devilled
kidneys judged just right; the perfect wobble of the ham
hock terrine; the sheer exuberance of the porterhouse
steak with bearnaise. Meats come from the peerless
McGrath's butchers just across the road, the staff know
their jobs inside out, and the setting is aesthete's heaven.
Lismore has waited a long time for a restaurant of this
quality, and here it is. (Justin & Jenny Green, Main Street,
Lismore ☎ 058-53810 ✉ info@obrienchophouse.ie
🖰 www.obrienchophouse.ie – Open 12.30pm-9.30pm
Mon-Sat, open from 11.30pm Sun)

Passage East

B&B
● Parkswood House

Throughout the summer, take a pit stop at the lovely
Parkswood for afternoon tea on the lawn, buy some
of Roger's superlative organic eggs, book the wife in for
one of Terrie's sewing classes (Terrie is a master dress-
maker), and just soak up the good life while overlooking
the much underrated Waterford estuary from the garden of this glorious B&B. Roger and Terrie just get better and better at what they do in this immaculate house,
so for eating and staying, it's hard to beat Parkswood,
one of the stars of the zone. (Roger & Theresa Pooley,
Passage East ☎ 051-380863 ✉ info@parkswood.com
🖰 www.parkswood.com)

only in Waterford
Waterford Blaa

Tramore

● Banyan

Chef Eugene Long and his partner, Sinead Frisby,
have gotten off to a flying start in Banyan, creating a
glammed-up space with top-notch cooking right from
the day they opened their doors. The cooking reads
modern-conventional, but Mr Long puts his mark on
it: crab tart with whole-grain mustard; beetroot and
Ardsallagh goat's cheese salad; ravioli of salmon and
langoustine; organic chicken with chorizo; duck confit
with red cabbage, and classy puddings like apple and
berry crumble with cinnamon ice cream, or orange and
passion fruit cake. There is a slick bar for drinks to begin, and a modest bill at the conclusion. Seriously good.
(Eugene Long & Sinead Frisby, Main Street, Tramore
☎ 051-330707 ✉ reservations@banyan.ie ✆ www.
banyan.ie – Open 6pm-10pm Thu-Sat, 1pm-4pm Sun)

Caribbean Traiteur
● Taste of the Caribbean

You need to be a confident, talented person to bring out
a book entitled "Caribbean Cooking for Culchies" but
Jennylynd James, Ph.D is both confident and talented,
and her little cookery book is a joyous romp through
the sauces, seasonings and specialities of the food this
gifted lady makes. Look out for Jenny's foods at farmers'
markets in and around Waterford and good shops. After
all, who could resist a girl who can make a Rasta Pasta
Sauce! Wicked! (Jennylynd James, Caribbean Enterprises, Tramore ☎ 086-871 3480 ✉ jennylynd@caribbean-
ireland.com ✆ www.caribbeanireland.com)

Waterford

Shop
● Ardkeen Stores

The Jephson family's super supermarket is one of the
treasures of the county and the country. Last time we
shopped here, virtually everything we bought came from
the counties of Waterford and Cork, with just a little bit
of our money going further north, thanks to a superb
Sheridan's duck confit, which was produced in Cavan.

Few food miles, superlative Irish produce, and a magical experience, thanks to brilliant staff. It seems ridiculous, but everything sold here is good. In particular, look out for the foods of the season, like Mairead Halley's fantastic fruits – her greengages are amazing – or the San Marzano tomatoes which Currids of Grantstown grow exclusively for Ardkeen. Irish apples arrive in from O'Dwyers of Piltown, and there is a great array of vegetables from Tom Cleary of Wellingtonbridge, a grower also highly praised by Michael Quinn of Waterford Castle. In a perfect food retailing world, every supermarket would be like Ardkeen. (Kevin Jephson, Ardkeen Shopping Centre, Dunmore Road, Waterford City ☎ 051-874620 ✉ QualityFood@ardkeen.com 🖰 www.ardkeen.com – Open 8am-9pm Mon-Sat, 9am-6pm Sun & hols)

only in Waterford
Eunice Power's Porridge

Producers' market
● Ardkeen Producers' Market

Sinead Cheevers handles the brilliant market that so aptly complements the brilliant Ardkeen Stores. (Sinead Cheevers ✉ market@ardkeen.com 🖰 www.ardkeen.com – Open 10am-2pm on the second and fourth Sun of every month)

Restaurant
● L'Atmosphere

Arnaud Mary is not only a great chef, he's a great restaurateur, fully understanding the commercial reality of keeping your tables full, offering the most lip-smackingly good food, and keeping prices keen. He does this by not buying just fillets and sirloin from his suppliers, he buys the whole beast and uses as near as dammit every single bit. So while you may not know which part of the cow an *onglet* or a *bavette* come from, you can trust Arnaud that they will be super flavoursome. Desserts are very strong thanks to Arnaud's partner, Patrice, and this inspiring restaurant just never puts a foot wrong. (Arnaud Mary & Patrice Garreau, 19 Henrietta Street, Waterford ☎ 051-858426 ✉ restaurant.latmosphere@gmail.com 🖰 www.restaurant-latmosphere.com – Open 12.30pm-2.30pm Mon-Fri, 5.30pm-late Mon-Sun)

Waterford

Deli & Coffee Shop
Berfranks

There are lots and lots of USPs to draw you to Frank
and Bernadette's brand new deli and coffee shop, but
one of the biggest attractions is surely the fact that they
are the only people who stock Mary McEvoy's incredible
Slice of Heaven cupcakes. Alongside these slices of the
hereafter, Berfranks has lots of great local foods and
the finest national artisan foods, which makes this the
best and brightest new destination in Waterford. (Frank
& Bernadette Treyvaud, Street, Waterford 086 844
6460/087 985 6791)

Restaurant
Bodega!

Cormac and Donagh Cronin's great restaurant continues
to pack in the crowds thanks to its amazing atmosphere,
and wonderful hospitality from Cormac and manager
Frank. This is what Bodega is all about: snappy food,
great friendly service and an atmosphere that just cannot
be equalled. On most nights the bar will be packed with
happy diners and the buzz is simply electric, thanks to
that good cooking: nice breads, crabmeat and shrimp
salad on grilled blaa, fine goat's cheese tart, Thai fish
cakes are delicate and full of fish, the Omega beefburger
is ace, the Comeragh lamb burger perfect, all served
with huge piles of cracking fries. If only every bar could
be as hip and smart – and as much fun – as Bodega.
(Donagh & Cormac Cronin, 54 John Street, Waterford
☎ 051-844177 ✉ info@bodegawaterford.com ✍ www.
bodegawaterford.com – Open noon-5pm Mon-Fri,
5.30pm-10pm Mon-Wed, 5.30pm-10.30pm Thu-Sat)

Restaurant
La Boheme

Christine and Eric Theze's formal French restaurant in
the basement rooms of the Chamber of Commerce
building in Gladstone Street is one of the most beautiful
dining rooms in the country. In keeping with the
flamboyant nature of the room, the cooking is classical
and luxurious: if you thought no one cooked quail
with foie gras scented with sauternes, or croustillant
of caramelized golden apple with frangipane and salty
caramel sauce, you will find them here. The set menus
are very good value indeed, though prices from the a la
carte can add up quickly. But this is serious cooking, and
service matches the class of the cooking. (Christine

Waterford

& Eric Theze, 2 George's Street, Waterford ☎ 051-875645 ✆ labohemerestaurant@eircom.net ⌂ www.labohemerestaurant.ie – Open 5.30pm-late Tue-Sat)

● Downe's Bar

250 years young, that's how old Downe's bar is. There is always a bottle of their own blend of whiskey, No. 9, waiting here for you with your name on it. (8-10 Thomas Street, Waterford ☎ 051-874 118)

only in Waterford
Downes' No 9 Whiskey

● Espresso

Sister restaurant to the popular La Palma, Espresso specialises in good pastas and pizzas. (Adriano Cavaliere, Parnell Street, Waterford ☎ 051-874141 ✆ info@espresso.ie ⌂ www.espresso.ie – Open 12.30pm-2.30pm, 5pm-late Mon-Sat, 1pm-9pm Sun)

● Full of Beans

Frances and Barry Coffey's super little shops are a treasure trove of good things: Doves Farm Flour, Solaris Teas, Sonnentor organic spices, Maldon Salt and a great range of pulses, rice, gluten-free products – everything you need for the good life, really. (Frances & Barry Coffey, Georges Court, Waterford City Centre, ☎ 051-843653. Also Full of Beans 2, Ardkeen Shopping Centre, ☎ 051-844644 – Open 9.30am-5.30pm Mon-Sat)

● Granary @ Waterford Treasures Museum

Take a simple lunch in Peter Fowler's café: roast chicken with honey and hazelnuts and saffron rice. So: how was it? Perfect. Just perfect. That's what Mr Fowler does: simple things, done with elegance and exactitude, and it has made the Granary into one of the key Waterford city addresses, the treasure in the Treasures museum. (Peter Fowler, Waterford Museum of Treasure, Hanover Street, Waterford ☎ 051-854428 – Open 8.30pm-5pm, 6pm Summer, Mon-Sun)

Waterford

● Harlequin Café & Wine Bar

The plain exterior and spartan interior of Simone Giorgi and Alessandro Lopez's little Italian restaurant close to Waterford's city centre make it an easy restaurant to miss - which would be a mistake. This is authentic Italian cooking with the emphasis squarely on flavour: tonnarelli con salsiccia e piselli is fresh pasta with Italian sausage and peas served in a simple white bowl and tasting wonderfully clean and fresh, the only accompaniment some grilled bread drizzled with olive oil - perfect. Gnocchi carne e verdura del giorno is equally successful and that bread is perfect for mopping up the delicious sauce. The restaurant serves some of the best coffee in Waterford, and value is amazing. A little gem. (Simone Giorgi & Alessandro Lopez, 37 Stephen St, Waterford. ☎ 051-877552 ✉ info@harlequin-cafe.com ⏱ www. harlequin-cafe.com – Open 8.30am-8.30pm Mon-Wed, 8.30am-10.30pm Thur-Fri, 9.30am-10.30pm Sat)

only in Waterford
Barron's Stonebaked Pans

● Hickey's Bakery

Hickey's are producers of the legendary Waterford Blaa, that square shape, flour-dusted burst of yeasty deliciousness that is one of the most important regional breads in Ireland. Due recognition to that importance was given when Hickey's was awarded a Eurotoques prize celebrating their distinguished championing of Waterford's signature food product. (Brian Hickey, 59 Barrack St, Waterford 051-375388)

● Jay Bees

The low-key nature of this little store is right in keeping with the low-key nature of the Mennonite Amish community that run it – indeed you could easily drive past the little filling station and shop without ever realising the quality of wonderful baking that is contained within. That drive past would be a shame because that baking is of the highest quality – fresh scones every morning, brown bread, fruitcake, carrot cakes, tarts and choco-

Waterford

late brownies; all absolutely delicious. The community also attend the Waterford City Farmers' Market as well as being makers of high-quality garden furniture. A little piece of goodness. (Campus Station, Ballinakina, Woodstown ☎ 051-382305 – Open 8am-7pm Mon-Fri, 8.30am-7pm Sat)

Country Market
● Jenkin's Lane Food & Craft Market

Traders wish to move to John Roberts Square, whilst the Council is urging a move to Blackfriars. Watch this space! (Jenkin's Lane, off Georges Street. Saturday 10am-4pm)

Butcher
● Tom Kearney's Family Butchers

Tom Kearney's traditional family-run butcher's produces meat for meat lovers, indeed meat aficionados. Top quality fillet and sirloin, of course, from their own animals, but also great topside of beef, lamb's liver of such delicious sweetness, lamb's kidneys from animals just slaughtered that morning and for that special event, how about a couple of monster T-Bones? Nothing better. (Tom Kearney, 37a John Street, Waterford ☎ 051-874434 ✉ tkearney@gmail.com – Open 8.30am-6pm Mon-Sat)

Bakery
● M&D Bakery

M and D are Michael and Dermot Walsh, third generation bakers and producers of Waterford's magisterial blaa, amongst a range of very fine breads. You will find their breads in many shops throughout Waterford, and those blaas, winner of a Eurotoques award, are worth hunting down anytime you are in the south east. (Michael & Dermot Walsh, 34 Mount Sion Avenue, Waterford ☎ 051-378080 ✉ mdbakery@eircom.net)

Butcher
● O'Flynn's Butcher's

Bernard O'Flynn's traditional butcher's shop right in the centre of Waterford City is a great source of top-quality beef from the family's own farm. It's not unusual for there to be a queue out the front door on Friday mornings – a great sight indeed. (Bernard O'Flynn, 17 Georges Street ☎ 051-874409 – Open 8.30am-6pm Tue-Thu, 8am-7pm Fri, 8am-4.40pm Sat)

Restaurant
La Palma on the Mall

A beautiful cocktail bar and a slick restaurant explains
La Palma's popularity with locals. The menus are kept
concise, and the execution of the food is consistently
fine and deservedly popular. They also operate the simpler Espresso restaurant in town. (Claudio Cavaliere, 20
The Mall, Waterford. ☎ 051-879823 ✉ info@lapalma.ie
🖰 www.lapalma.ie – Open 5.30pm-10.30pm Mon-Sat)

Restaurant
La Taverna

Cristian Casagrande and Alessandro Lopez's super little
slice of Italy is flavour of the month in Waterford right
now. Customers are welcomed like long-lost friends
and the food is the real deal, from thin and crusty pizzas baked in a proper brick oven to a great selection
of pasta dishes and more substantial meat choices. An
antipasto selection for two brings forth an amazing array
of cured meats, cheeses with honey, salads and hot tuna
with smoked cheese. The pizzas - including one where
the base has Guinness added - are super tasty and each
one comes with its own little scissors so you just cut
your own slices. Tagliatelle papalina with mushroom,
peas and Italian sausage is right on the money; caramelle
ricotta e spinaci, pomodoro e basilico is clean and full of
tomato and basil flavour. Superbly, there is just one dessert choice - a masterful tiramisu – and then some really
good coffee. Value for money is very strong. Mighty.
(Cristian Casagrande & Alessandro Lopez, 54 High
Street, Waterford ☎ 051-852 609 – Open noon-4pm,
6pm-10.30pm Mon-Fri, noon-10.30pm Sat, noon-10pm
Sun)

Country House & Restaurant
Waterford Castle

Michael Quinn is one of the best cooks in Ireland, and
it's a mystery that he hasn't become better known via
the medium of television, for he has an engaging, open
personality, which shows in the generosity and passion
of his cooking. That cooking is simply top notch, a
brilliantly realised personal vision of what sophisticated
modern Irish food can be: tongue and cheek salad (ha
ha!) with horseradish mayonnaise; home tea-smoked
quail with celeriac rémoulade and watercress; the

brilliant trio of lamb where parsnip accompanies braised shoulder, spinach accompanies roast loin and aubergine accompanies lamb fillet. All the details chime together in this grand room, and Mr Quinn is King of the Castle. (Michael Quinn, The Island, Ballinakill, Waterford ☎ 051-878203 ⌁ www.waterfordcastle.com – Open 6.30pm-9pm Mon-Sun)

Wine Shop & Wine Bar
● The Wine Vault

David Dennison no longer serves food at this long-established High Street location, but it's still a lovely premises to visit and David's expertise in wine, and genial, patient, unassuming manner, will ensure that you leave with just the right bottle for you. (David Dennison, High Street, Waterford ☎ 051-853 444 ⌁ www.dennisonwines.com – 10.30am-9pm Mon-Sat)

Wine Shop
● World Wide Wines

Winner of the Munster Off Licence of the Year for 2009 and no surprise, Claire and Declan Brady's great wine and liquor store on the Dunmore Road in Waterford is a wine lover's dream. The staff are super knowledgable and the selection of wines, whiskeys, spirits and beers is just amazing. If you've been hankering after a bottle of the difficult-to-find George T. Stagg bourbon or Papa Van Winkle, or maybe some beautiful Eroica Riesling from Washington State or a classic vintage Bordeaux or Burgundy, this is the place. It must be mentioned that the variety and selection of beers is just as impressive. A grand cru shop, alright. (Declan & Claire Brady, Cove Centre, Dunmore Road, Waterford ☎ 051-878798 ⌁ worldwidewines@eircom.net – Open noon-10pm Mon-Fri, 11am-10pm Sat, 12.30pm-10pm Sun)

Blaas

County Westmeath

Athlone

Farmers' Market
● **Athlone Farmers' Market**

The early birds get the best produce from an array of gifted artisans every Saturday morning at the market square. (Market Square, Athlone, Saturday 9am-2pm)

Restaurant
● **Kin Khao**

Adam and Janya's Kin Khao has proven such a success in Athlone that they have already opened a second branch in Gorey in County Wexford. In direct contrast to those Thai restaurants that operated under franchise systems and offered what was in effect fast food, Kin Khao, with its crew of Thai chefs delivers the real thing. This isn't international Thai cooking, but instead it is food influenced by village cooking, mother's cooking and domestic cooking. (Adam & Janya Lyons, Abbey Lane ☎ 090-649 8805 ✉ info@kinkhaothai.ie.com ⊕ www.kinkhaothai.ie – Open 12.30pm-2.30pm Wed-Fri, 5.30pm-10.30pm Mon-Sun, lunch from 1.30pm Sun. Also at 3 Main Street, Gorey ☎ 053-943 0677 – Open 5.30pm-10.30pm Mon-Sun)

only in Westmeath
Westmeath Beef

Restaurant
● **The Left Bank Bistro**

Annie and Mary's Left Bank serves genuinely Left Bank food, so whilst I can be enjoying spinach and ricotta tortellini in a pesto cream, you might very well be making short work of Thai-spiced chicken on egg noodles with chilli, lime, lemongrass, coriander and coconut milk. But Michael Durr's cooking isn't train crash cuisine, instead it's a reflection of the influence of Annie's Australian upbringing, and any tensions in such an eclectic sounding menu are always seamlessly and soulfully resolved. The room is quite beautiful, and the Left Bank should be recognised as one of the most important

Westmeath

Midlands restaurants during the last fifteen years, maintaining stellar standards of food and service and doing it all with great wit and humour. (Annie McNamara & Mary McCullagh, Fry Place, Athlone ☎ 090-649 4446 ✏ info@leftbankbistro.com ✆ www.leftbankbistro.com – Open 10.30am-9.30pm. Lunch served noon-5pm, dinner served 5.30pm-close Tue-Sat)

Restaurant
● The Olive Grove

Garry and Gael's Olive Grove is now a riverside Olive Grove, since they moved into slick new space hard by the river. Good fun and a lack of pretention has always characterised their work in Athlone, so bring along a crowd and kiss tomorrow goodbye. (Garry Hughes & Gael Bradbury, Custume Pier, Athlone ☎ 0902-76946 ✆ www.theolivegrove.ie – Open noon-4.30pm, 5.30pm-10pm Mon-Sat, noon-9pm Sun)

Fishmonger
● Rene Cusack

The Westmeath branch of Limerick's legendary fishmongers. They are legendary because the quality of the fish is peerless. (Paul Cusack, 8 Belhavel, Golden Island, Athlone ☎ 090-642 0355 – Open 10am-6pm Mon-Sat)

Organic Farm
● Terryglass Organics

Jens Krumpe rears some of the finest beef and pork that you can buy in Ireland and that explains why the queues for his speciality meats at the various Dublin markets he attends are always so lengthy. The queues may be lengthy but the people queueing are patient, a reflection of the slow maturing manner in which Mr Krumpe brings his meats to the pitch of culinary perfection. (Jens Krumpe & Jackie Gorman, Portanenna, Ballykeeran, Athlone ☎ 087-6597313/090-9747341 ✏ terryglassorganics@eircom.net)

Colinstown

Country House
● Lough Bishop House

"In spite of the weather we have managed to press apple juice from the earlier varieties in the orchard

Westmeath

(Worcester Pearmain, James Grieve and Sheep Snout) and make plum and damson jam so we will again have home produced apple juice and jam for guests. Our first Moile bullock is nearly ready for the butcher, so with any luck we will have some good rare-breed beef as well." Isn't that a lovely note of good tidings from Christopher Kelly of Lough Bishop House, this most handsome, hand-restored farmhouse in Colinstown? A glass of Sheep Snout juice for breakfast! Plum and damson jam on your toast! A day touring the countryside, then back for dinner of Moile beef – one of the original Irish breeds, and as rare as hen's teeth these days. Bring it on! Bring it on! The Kellys run the most lovely house, and they run it with care and circumspection. It has the lovely feeling of being deep in the middle of nowhere, a true rural escape, a true farmhouse, and it's the kind of house where other guests are instantly your new best friends. Blissful. (Helen & Christopher Kelly, Derrynagarra, Colinstown ☎ 044-966 1313 ⌨ enquiries@derrynagarra.com ⌂ www.derrynagarra.com)

only in Westmeath
Lough Bishop Sheep Snout

Glasson

Pub and Restaurant
● Farrell's Village Inn

Kathleen and Joe Farrell's eponymous inn is another good Midlands destination for proper cooking in a handsome pub. (Kathleen and Joe Farrell, Glasson ☎ 090-648 5208 – Food served 5.30pm-9.30pm Tue, 12.30pm-9.30pm Wed-Sat, 1pm-7.45pm Sun)

Bar & Restaurant
● Grogan's of Glasson

Grogan's is open breakfast, lunch and dinner, and is another of those Midland pubs that is responding to the crisis in rural pubs by giving people a pretty, comfortable room in which to enjoy good food, and nice drinks. In fact, they responded to the crisis even before it began,

Westmeath

which is proof of how smart this crew are. (Miriam Grogan, Glasson ☎ 090-648 5158 – Open 9am-noon, noon-5pm, 5pm-9pm Mon-Sat, 9am-11.30pm, 12.30pm-3.30pm, 4.30pm-8pm Sun)

Restaurant with Rooms
● **Wineport Lodge**

Wineport is on a roll. Our last dinner here was probably the best ever enjoyed at this fab lakeside retreat, and was one of the dinner highlights of the year. The sheer culinary confidence– heck, culinary bravado – seen in dishes like warm terrine of potato and Corry Lane smoked eel with dill, shallot and Pedro Ximenez dressing, or chump of lamb with roast aigre-doux plum tomatoes or halibut with celeriac mash and pickled lemon hollandaise was wondrous. Add in a room that glowed with the energy of happy diners, and you have a mighty destination, which is precisely what Wineport is. We slept the good sleep in massive beds with snow-white sheets, and next morning soaked in the rooftop tub. It felt like a dream, but it was just reality at pleasure pitch. (Ray Byrne & Jane English, Glasson, Athlone ☎ 090-643 9010 ✉ lodge@wineport.ie ◈ www.wineport.ie – Open 6pm-9.30pm Mon-Sat, 3pm-9.30pm Sun)

Horseleap

Country House, Spa and Restaurant
● **Temple**

Temple is well-named. "Edifice dedicated to accommodation or service of god(s)", says our old Concise Oxford, and in this most singular retreat and spa the god being accommodated and enjoying their resplendent services is: you. Relax: you're worth it. Temple is a true spa, by which we mean that it is motivated by an holistic, healthful vision of life. It's not just a place for the wives of the bourgeoisie to spend money – "women's golf" being the nickname given to that sort of place – instead it is a place dedicated to wellness in every manner. The comfort is here to make you feel well, the spa is here to make you feel well, the delicious, healthy cookery is here to make you feel well. At the centre of all this are Declan and Bernadette Fagan and their crystal-clear vision of health, wellness, and enjoyment. They are a most singular couple, blessed with great gifts and great

Westmeath

generosity and they are that rarity these days: they are wise people, and wisdom has no price. (Declan & Bernadette Fagan, Horseleap, Moate ☎ 0506-35118 🖅 relax@templespa.ie 🖰 www.templespa.ie – Restaurant open for dinner Wed-Sat & Sun lunch. Reservation advised)

only in Westmeath
Moonshine Milk

Mullingar

Café
● Gallery 29

The Gray sisters, Emily and Ann, open their café on Thursdays, Fridays and Saturdays, so that's the time to enjoy some good home baking and nice lunches. (Ann & Emily Gray, 29 Oliver Plunkett Street, Mullingar ☎ 044-934 9449 – Open 9am-5.30pm Thurs-Sat)

Cáfe & Food Shop
● iLiA

Three iLia destinations in one town? 'Fraid so. Julie Magan has created dynamic destinations in the three iLias, but it was always predictable that this smart woman would read the market in Mullingar so confidently, for the original iLia was a success right from the day they first started to serve good snacks and drinks and lovely light lunches. (Julie Magan, 28 Oliver Plunkett Street, Mullingar ☎ 044-9340300 🖅 info@ilia.ie 🖰 www.ilia.ie – Open 9am-6pm Mon-Sat)

Artisan Food Shop
● iLiA Gourmet

Gourmet is the iLia food and wine offer, and what a smart food and wine offer it is. All the experience and knowledge Julie Magan has collected working with food is distilled into a judicious selection of foods and wines, and lots of great foods to go, from the simplest sandwich to a party catering service. (Julie Magan, 25 Oliver Plunkett Street, Mullingar ☎ 044-9347182 🖅 info@ilia.ie 🖰 www.ilia.ie – 9am-6pm Mon-Sat)

Westmeath

Restaurant
● iLiA Tapas

"The food certainly hit the mark", said Eamon Barrett
after a first visit to this hip, modern space with its stylish
design and handsome bar area. Crab and Dublin Bay
prawn linguine is sure-fire delicious, whilst an unusual
nut-crusted goat's cheese with red pepper relish is
perfect. Everything on the menu has your name on it:
lamb tagine; rosemary-skewered chicken livers with Serrano ham; baby squid with prawn mousse with tomato;
Moroccan sweet lemon chicken. But, we have to ask,
is it tapas? Not strictly speaking, for you can order
Tormey's fillet of beef, for instance, but it is light eating,
and the tapas bit refers more to the ability to have as little to eat, or as much, as you like. Chances are, you will
have more to eat than you intended. (Julie Magan & Joe
Shields, 31 Dominic Street, Mullingar ☎ 044-934 5947
✆ info@ilia.ie ✆ www.iliatapasandmore.ie – Open
12.30pm-2.30pm Tue-Fri, 6pm-10pm Tue-Sat)

Dairy Products
● Moon Shine Dairy Farm

Mary and Gerry Kelly's Moonshine Dairy has been one
of the unstoppable forces of nature in Irish food for the
last few years. Their brilliant organic milk won the National Organic Award in 2009, but then every year brings
new acclaim for the amazing dairy products they fashion,
from the ground-breaking yogurts and smoothies they
began with to the latest organic emmenthal-style cheese
which complements their range of soft cheeses. "Our
products are created with the greatest of care on
favourable days in the Moon's cycle", they write, and you
have never tasted bio-dynamic farming principles put
into such delicious results as in Moonshine. And now,
you can visit their Cheese Barn at the farm and get your
hands on some of the most exciting dairy products in
Ireland (Mary & Gerry Kelly, Lough Ennel, Ladestown,
Mullingar ☎ 044-934 4631 ✆ www.kellysorganic.com)

Farmers' Market
● Mullingar Farmers' Market

Moonshine Dairy is just one of the local food stars at
Mullingar's market, and we would turn up just to buy their
milk, sold in a big, thick glass bottle. And we will also snap
up Ann Hamill's products, and John's smoked fish. (The
Fairgreen car park, Mullingar 10.30am-2pm, Sun)

Westmeath

Restaurant & Takeaway
● Oscar's

Noel and Tony's restaurant is the local champion, no
doubt about it, a sure-fire success story that feeds the
local people well, and makes no song and dance about
it. The food is modern, straightforward and energeti-
cally executed, and the energy of the room is almost
as much of an attraction as the cooking. If you want a
quiet night in, as opposed to a lively night out, Oscar's
also do a very busy food-to-go offer, (Noel Kennedy
& Tony Maloney, 21 Oliver Plunkett Street, Mullingar
☎ 044-934 4909 – Open 6pm-9.30pm Mon-Wed,
6pm-10pm Thu & Sat, 12.30pm-2.15pm, 6pm-8.15pm
Sun)

Butcher
● C. R. Tormey & Sons

The meticulousness you see in Tormey's shop is just the
tip of the iceberg for this family business, for meticulousness extends here all the way back to the rearing and
breeding of the beef on their farm, and then its treatment all the way down the line as it makes its passage to
the shop and then into your kitchen. The beef we have
bought from Tormey's over the last two decades has
been some of the very best meat we have eaten, simple
as that, the very essence of what Irish rain and Irish
grass and fine butchering can achieve. (James Tormey,
Harbour Place, Mullingar ☎ 044-934 5433 ◌ www.
crtormeys.ie – Open 8am-6pm Mon-Sat, 'till 8.30pm on
Thur & Fri)

Wine Importer
● Wines Direct

Paddy Keogh is one of the great figures of Ireland's contemporary food culture. A larger-than-life figure himself,
he is blessed with an almost manic energy, so when he
isn't tearing around Ireland visiting clients, he is tearing
around the globe visiting winemakers and vineyards. And
he loves it, he loves the whole crazy culture of wine and
restaurants and food, and because he is no snob, he finds
the good stuff, and brings it back to Mullingar, where he
has a beautiful shop in the Lough Sheever park, just up
from the hospital. If you drank nothing but WD wines,
you would drink well and live well, for the wines Mr
Keogh finds share his zest for life and his passion for the
culture of wine. There are so many sure-fire specials on

his list that we recommend you simply pledge to work your way through it, slowly, pleasurably. Nice work. (Paddy Keogh, 49 Lough Sheever Corporate Park, Mullingar ☎ 1890-579 579/044-934 0634 ✉ sales@winesdirect.ie ✍ www.winesdirect.ie)

Multyfarnham

Bar, Restaurant & Accommodation
● Weir's Bar & Restaurant

Certain places seem to suddenly get the wind in their sails, and then they are unstoppable. Weir's is that place. Pat and Una Weir are doing the good thing, and the culinary citizenry are loving it. This is the kind of cooking that you always feel like eating: Angus steak with onions, mushrooms, pepper sauce and chips; tempura of cod with tartare and coriander sauce; Thai green chicken curry with basmati rice. Listing the dishes like this makes them sound like the sort of thing every pub offers, but in Weir's the ingredients are sourced and cooked with care, and then served in a fine high-ceilinged room, with a tiny but just-right selection of wines to make the eating even more pleasureable. Really fine, and should you be smitten by the beauty of this lakeland zone, they have a holiday house for rental. (Una & Pat Weir, Multyfarnham, Mullingar ☎ 044-937 1111 ✉ weirs@eircom.net ✍ www.weirsmultyfarnham.ie – Open noon-3pm Mon-Tue, 1pm-9pm Wed-Sat, 1pm-7pm Sun)

Rathowen

Fish Smoker
● Rogan's Real Smoked Fish

John Rogan understands fish, and it shows. Whether you are having his smoked trout, eel, mackerel or salmon, his signature is not just the grace of beechwood smoke, but also a certain wildness, a certain sense of the feral, of man connected to nature. Many fish smokers want to be posh, but Mr Rogan reminds us of Sally Barnes of Woodcock Smokery: he wants a certain elemental fire in his flavours, he wants the whole deal, and it's pretty wonderful. (John Rogan, Corry Lane, Rathowen ☎ 043-76264 ✉ info@rogansfish.com ✍ www.rogansfish.com)

Westmeath

County Wexford

Arthurstown

Country House & Restaurant
● **Dunbrody Country House**

Here's our man Eamon Barrett on Kevin and Catherine Dundon's Dunbrody Country House: "A seriously sumptuous place to visit. The champagne bar is a cosmopolitan space that hits all the right notes in terms of design. The food is perfectly pitched – Kilmore crab cocktail with lime mayonnaise; Hook Head haddock smokies; chicken liver parfait with apricot compote; beer-battered fish and chips with tartare sauce and pea shoots; crock of mussels in saffron and tomato broth. Service is not as strong as everything else but nonetheless the achievement shouldn't be underestimated and the building is a truly beautiful place to spend some time." (Kevin & Catherine Dundon, Arthurstown ☎ 051-389600 🖰 www.dunbrodyhouse.com)

only in Wexford
Kilmore Crab

Bridgestown

Apple Juice
● **Ballycross Apple Farm**

The Von Englebrechten family use the traditional rack and cloth method to press their juices, so the individual character of the apples, and consequently of their blends, is beautifully captured in each bottle. They do Elstar, Jonagold and Bramley single varieties, and also mix the apple juice with carrot juice and blackcurrant juice. Really good, healthful drinks. There is a smashing shop at the farm, with a waffle bar and an interiors shop, so take some time out to enjoy a handsome, picturesque farm that produces lovely foods. (The von Engelbrechten family, Bridgestown ☎ 053-35160 🖰 info@ballycross. com 🖰 www.ballycross.com – Farmshop open Aug-Feb, 2pm-6pm Sat & Sun)

Bunclody

Home Bakery
● Sugar and Spice

Mary Murphy's home bakery is a quaint, classic country baker's shop and you will find it up at the top end of the town past all the pharmacies. Homley, domestic-style baking, and happy, maternal service make it a wee treasure. (Mary Murphy, Main Street, Bunclody ☎ 053-937 6388 sugar_spice@eircom.net – Open 8.15am-6pm Mon-Fri, 8.15am-5pm Sat)

Carne

Seafood Bar
● The Lobster Pot Seafood Bar

The Lobster Pot is as atmospheric a bar and restaurant as you will find in Ireland, a tabernacle of moody lighting, interlinked rooms, snugs and bars, flickering fires and old commercial signage. The proof of its legendary status is the fact that whenever anyone nearby is selling a house, they will give details of how proximate it is to this restaurant. In truth, it's worth the status: the fish and shellfish cookery – which is what you should have – is cleverly, simply done and right on the money, and allied with the charm of the setting it's hard not to feel that it's just the right time for another pint or another glass of wine and sure what's your hurry? and let's have the seafood platter. (Ciaran & Anne Hearne, Carne ☎ 053-31110 – Bar open noon-8.45pm Mon-Sun. À la Carte Restaurant menu 6pm-9pm Tue-Sat & 12.30pm-8.30pm Sun. In winter closes 7.30pm on Sun)

Dunbrody

Farmers' Market
● Dunbrody Abbey Market

The Sunday market at Dunbrody operates in conjunction with the Pierce and Valerie McAuliffe's cookery school. The tea rooms open for soups and snacks. (Dunbrody Abbey Cooking and Visitor Centre, Sunday noon-2.30pm)

Cooking Centre

● Dunbrody Cooking Centre

Pierce and Valerie McAuliffe's cookery school is a genial, happy place, thanks to their genial, happy personalities. A group of four people can even book an a la carte cookery day, when the concept of bespoke cookery gets taken to new heights. The McAuliffes were splendid restaurateurs in their own right before opening the school, so professionalism is at the core of this lovely place. Look out for their lovely relishes at local farmers' markets. (Pierce & Valerie McAuliffe, Dunbrody, Campile ☎ 051-388933 ⏁ www.cookingireland.com)

only in Wexford
Hook Head Haddock

Duncannon

Restaurant and Accommodation

● Aldridge Lodge

Aldridge Lodge has attracted lots of attention since opening, and they are steadily acquiring a distinct culinary signature. Service is friendly, the room is pleasant and value for money is very keen. (Billy Whitty & Joanne Harding, Duncannon ☎ 051-389116 ✉ info@ aldridgelodge.com ⏁ www.aldridgelodge.com – Open 7pm-9.30pm Tue-Sat, 5.30pm-8.30pm Sun)

Restaurant

● Sqigl

Cindy Roche's bistro is in a barn at the rere of her folks' bar – Roche's – across from the seafront, and whilst it's a bright, simple space, don't let the simplicity blind you to the fact that the fish cookery here is serious and delicious. Yes there are classics like ketaifi prawns and seafood chowder, but other fish dishes show true understanding – scallops with white onion mousseline and beetroot tempura; poached salmon with braised fennel and bisque; hake with Parmesan butter. Vegetarian dishes and children's dishes, incidentally, are equally serious. There is simple food served in the bar. (Cindy Roche, Quay Road, Duncannon ☎ 051-389700 ✉ sqigl2003@eircom.net ⏁ www.sqiglrestaurant.com – Open from 7pm Thu-Sat. Bar open 12.30pm-9pm Mon-Sun)

Enniscorthy

Country House
● Ballinkeele House

John and Margaret Maher's fine old country house
enjoys stellar standards of housekeeping and some very
apt country cooking, so your base for the opera festival
is in the bag. (John & Margaret Maher, Enniscorthy
☎ 053-913 8105 ✉ john@ballinkeele.ie ⬦ www.
ballinkeele.ie – Open Feb-end Oct)

Farmhouse Cheese
● Carrigbyrne Farmhouse Cheese

We think Paddy Berridge's Carrigbyrne cheese has
been getting better and better in recent years. It was
always a special cheese, but the cheeses we have been
buying over the last two years seem to have sharpened
their focus and their taste parameters, delivering the
Carrigbyrne lushnness with more alacrity and definition,
especially in the St Killian, and very successfully in the
small St Killian that has become so popular. They also
make the St Brendan and Emerald Irish brie cheeses, and
over the last decade they have developed an expertise in
minimising the environmental impact of cheesemaking,
using anaerobic digesters to make methane to fuel the
generator and developing various methods of sustainable
energy. Forward thinking, and forward looking, in every
way. (Paddy & Juliet Berridge, Adamstown, Enniscorthy
☎ 053-924 0560 ✉ info@carrigbyrne.ie ⬦ www.
carrigbyrne.ie)

Farmers' Market
● Enniscorthy Farmers' Market

From fancy fungi to goat's milk soap, from Tinnock Farm
to Green's Berry Farm, from Killowen Yogurts to The
Lavender Lady, the Enniscorthy Market, one of a quartet
of superb Wexford markets – the others are in Gorey,
New Ross and Wexford – has all the good stuff. (Abbey
Square, Enniscorthy ⬦ www.wexfordfarmersmarkets.
com – Open Saturday 9am-2pm)

Yogurt
● Killowen Yogurts

Killowen are very, very fine yogurts, and their USP is a
tart, defining sharpness of acidity that makes them

wonderfully refreshing, and particularly suitable for savoury cooking. Unlike other yogurts which have gone the low-fat route, Killowen is full fat, which still means, however, that it is 97% fat-free. But that sort of hands-off approach, the philosophy of letting the milk from their herd express itself with minimum interference, is what makes Killowen so special. (Nicholas & Judith Dunne, The Beeches, Courtnacuddy, Enniscorthy ☎ 053-924 4819 ✉ killowenfoods@eircom.net 🖰 www.killowenyogurt.com)

Hotel and Spa
● Monart

Monart has been a beacon of good taste and good tastes and good health ever since Liam Griffin opened the doors of his super-slick adults only spa. Beautiful design sets the calm, contemplative mood, but above all it is the ability of the service to read your mind, to predict your desires, that sets Monart at the top of the pile. Everything works to make you feel good and they actually manage to do that literally from the moment you drive in the gates, until the moment you leave. Healthful, holistic and happy, an ideal spa resort. (Liam Griffin, The Still, Enniscorthy ☎ 053-923 0999 🖰 www.monart.ie)

Country House
● Salville House

A demure and pleasingly simple country house, which is home to some of the best country house cooking you will find, thanks to Gordon Parker's assured culinary skills. (Jane & Gordon Parker, Enniscorthy ☎ 053-923 5252 ✉ info@salvillehouse.com 🖰 www.salvillehouse.com)

Ferns

Craft Bakery & Coffee Shop
● Noirin's Bakehouse

Noirin and Vincent Kearney used to be based in County Kildare, but their move south has seen this dynamic bakery continue to produce their stellar range of breads and cakes, sold at markets and in good shops in the south east and in Dublin, and they have also opened a coffee shop in Gorey, on McDermott Street. "Honest baking" was how we described their work in the last Food Guide, but that is only part of the story, Yes, this is honest baking – no rubbish, top-class ingredients, oodles of skill to extract the very best from everything from banana bread to chocolate chip cookies. But the baking is also organoleptically acute and aware, with the bakers looking to define each product precisely. Lovely stuff. (Noirin & Vincent Kearney, Newtown, Ferns ☎ 053-936 7335 ✉ info@noirins.ie 🖐 www.noirins.ie)

Dry Cure Bacon
● O'Neill Foods

Pat O'Neill cures a good bacon, and you can tell it's a good bacon because of the way in which it behaves in the pan: you heat the oil or butter, slide in the rasher, and it crisps and doesn't curl or exude any gunk or do any of that nasty stuff. And then, you have a wonderful cooked, tasty, salty rasher for your breakfast. (Pat O'Neill, Bolindrum, Ferns ☎ 087-677 9803 ✉ oneillfoods@eircom.net)

Gorey

Farmers' Market
● Gorey Farmers' Market

The Gorey market takes place on Saturdays from 9am, so grab the bags and we are off to get Killowen yogurts and organic chickens and farmhouse ice cream and organic vegetables and dry-cured bacon and, if the sun is shining, some bounteous Wexford soft fruits. Whew, I'm wrecked! Do you mind carrying the bags? (Gorey Community School 🖐 www.wexfordfarmersmarkets. com – Open 9am-2pm Sat)

Thai Restaurant
● Kin Khao Thai

Having blazed a trail for authentic Thai cooking in Ath- lone since 2003, Adam and Janya Lyons have opened in Gorey to acclaim equal to that enjoyed by their Midlands outpost. Mr Lyons is the only Irish man amongst the all-Thai crew, so the food has the true zinging attack of real Thai cooking, and is a million miles away from the franchised-restaurant rubbish that has dragged down the reputation of one of the world's greatest cuisines. They offer not only the great classics of Thai food, but also a small selection of signature dishes – Lao curry, their own version of Ho Mok Gai; Crying Tiger with hot chilli sauce – alongside lots of regional specialities. The real thing, so simply accept no substitutes and, if you live in Gorey or Athlone, there is a home delivery service available. (Adam & Janya Lyons, 3 Main Street, Gorey ☎ 053-943 0677 www.kinkhaothai.ie – Open 5.30pm-10.30pm Mon-Sun)

Butcher
● Tomas Kinsella

Kinsella's is an impressive, classy butcher's shop, with expertly prepared and presented meats in a swish store. (4 Esmonde Street, Gorey ☎ 053-948 1863 – Open 8am-6pm Mon-Sat)

Bistro & Delicatessen
● Partridge's

Christian Pauritsch has a really fine speciality food shop at the front of the house, where all of the hippest Irish artisan brands are featured alongside great wines, and a bistro and tea rooms, serving proper afternoon tea, at the rere. The cooking is simple and unpretentious and fulfills Mr Pauritsch's ambition of letting the quality of carefully sourced raw ingredients speak for themselves. Paintings by local artists are featured on the walls, which adds to the air of a local artistic hub, and Partridge's is a key destination in Gorey. (Christian Pauritsch, 93 Main Street, Gorey ☎ 053-948 4040 info@partridges. ie www.partridges.ie – Open 9am-5.30pm Mon-Sat, open till 9.30pm Wed-Sat in summer, and more limited evenings during winter, noon-5pm Sun)

Butcher
● Terry Redmond Butchers

Alan Redmond's prize-winning sausages are the main attraction in the simple, but always busy Redmond's butcher's shop. (Alan Redmond, John Street, Gorey ☎ 053-942 1344 – Open 9am-6pm Mon-Sat)

only in Wexford
Kelly's Hotel Flowers

Kerlogue

Cookery School & Catering Service
● Phelim Byrne

Phelim Byrne is one hard working chef. As well as his
cookery classes, he runs a catering company, and has a
relationship with Glendine House where he cooks dinners at the weekend for guests of the house. He is also
a busy media chef, with newspaper cookery columns
and radio slots, so we're not sure how much sleep he
manages every night. Best of all, he is an enthusiast:
he is hung up on the beauty of introducing people to
good food, and the culture and adventure of good food,
but his passion is genuine, and not slick or ersatz. So
whatever way you get this busy young man's food culture
into your life, via classes, dining or the media, he is a player.
(Phelim Byrne, Wexford Enterprise Centre, Strandfield
Business Park, Kerlogue, Rosslare Road, Wexford ☎ 053-
918 4995 info@phelimbyrne.ie www.phelimbyrne.ie)

Killinick

Farm Shop
● Karoo Farm Shop

"The Conservatory ranks very well with Grangecon,
The Forge, In a Nutshell, Karoo etc". That was how
our mate Niall summed up Mignon Fochessati's brilliant shop, and he could have simply said: if it ranks
with Karoo, it's one of the very best in the south east.
Everything Mignon has for sale here is here on merit,
because it is good, local, Irish, delicious, and because you
need it in your life. The shop has something of the feel of
a French country store – smart but relaxed, elegant, hip
and knowing but not at all self-conscious. It's a peach.
(Mignon Fochessati, Killinick ☎ 053-915 8585 info@
karoo.ie – Open 9am-6pm Mon-Sat, 11am-5pm Sun)

Kilmore Quay

Restaurant
● Le Poisson d'Or

We have been following Dominic Dayot around the

county for the last several years as this peripatetic chef has moved from place to place. We do this simply because he is a super cook, and if he finds himself cooking above a fish shop opposite the kids' playground in Kilmore Quay, well, no matter. What matters is his food: mussels mouclade; tempura prawns; monkfish with chorizo in a provençale sauce; lemon sole with pesto breadcrumb; risotto with prawns. It's a simple, straightforward room, and the food is spot on. (Dominique Dayot, Crossfarnogue, Kilmore Quay ☎ 053-914 8853 ⌨ www.lepoissondor.ie – Open noon-3.30pm, 8.45pm-close Wed-Sat, noon-5.30pm Sun)

Restaurant
● **The Silver Fox**

Shane and Gopal have been doing the good stuff in the Silver Fox for as long as we have been writing the *Bridgestone Guide*, since they opened first in 1991. Seafood is what you are here for: fisherman's pie; scampi with chips and tartare sauce; Wexford oysters; Kilmore Quay plaice. A cosy, calm room in a pretty village. (Shane Carroll & Gopal Kawander, Kilmore Quay ☎ 053-912 9888 ⌨ info@thesilverfox.ie ⌨ www.thesilverfox.ie – Open from 5pm Tue-Sat, from 12.30pm Sun)

New Ross

Farmers' Market
● **New Ross Farmers' Market**

The New Ross market takes place in Conduit Lane on Saturdays from 9am, and it is every bit as fine as the three other Wexford markets, though locals will no doubt tell you that theirs is, all things considered, at the end of the day, going forward, the best of the lot. Just agree with them. (The Quay, New Ross ⌨ www.wexfordfarmersmarkets.com – Open 9am-2pm Sat)

Café & Wholefood Shop
● **In A Nutshell and Café Nutshell**

"A beacon of all things good and wholesome". That's what food lovers say about IAN, Philip and Patsy Rogers' dynamic, spotless, brilliant, café and shop in New Ross. Philip and Patsy work real hard, which explains the perfectionist nature of this shop, and the perfectionist, inquisitive nature of the cooking: sweet potato, butternut squash and tomato soup with homemade bread; trofie Liguiri with basil pesto; bread and butter pudding that is as soft as a baby's skin. The value for money this food offers is amazing, because the care in the sourcing of ingredients means you would happily pay any amount for it. The shop, if you haven't time for lunch, will also afford a great lunch to go, as well as selling everything you could possibly need. Wonderful. (Philip & Patsy Rogers, 18 South Street, New Ross ☎ 051-422777 📧 inanutshell8@gmail.com – Cafe open 9am-5pm, Deli/shop open 9am-6pm Tue-Sat)

only in Wexford
Whelan's Fresh Fish

Farm Produce
● Tinnock Farm Produce

Peggy and John are the hardest working farmers in the south east. As well as minding the farm, they sell their lovely products – country butter and buttermilk; lamb; beef; eggs – at an amazing number of markets each week: Enniscorthy; Carrick-on-Suir; New Ross; Wexford; Kilkenny and Dun Laoghaire. Mr Murphy takes it all in his stride. (John Murphy & Peggy Gaffney, Tinnock, Campile, New Ross ☎ 087-417 0506/087-220 3300)

Rosslare

B&B
● Churchtown House

"It's so nice that they will cook a full Irish breakfast for early ferry travellers", said our mates Mark and Millie after their latest Irish jaunt and trip back to the UK on the Rosslare boat. What they also loved about their last night in Churchtown was the comfort of the house, particularly in the bedrooms, and the beautiful gardens that surround this handsome historic home, which total eight acres. Austin and Patricia Cody maintain a beautiful house, but it's the hospitality and the thoughtfulness of the care that you remember after the boat has docked and you are unloading the car and the holiday is done. (Austin & Patricia Cody, Tagoat, Rosslare ☎ 053-913 2555 ✉ info@churchtownhouse.com 🖰 www. churchtownhouse.com)

Resort Hotel
● Kelly's Resort Hotel

In the most recent piece of journalism we wrote about Kelly's Hotel, we didn't write about the wonderful cooking, or the amazing contemporary art collection, or the state-of-the-art spa, or even their century and more of legendary hospitality. No, what we wrote about was the flowers, as they are arranged throughout the hotel every day by Sheelagh Kelly. Ms Kelly has been arranging the flowers here for more than forty years – and that's a fairly typical length of service in Kelly's – and each day the flowers look fresh as daisies, and a darn sight prettier. So you see, the flowers show how Kelly's operates, with every element – right from the flowers – determined to be an example of subtle excellence. That is how Bill Kelly and his team work, and that is why Kelly's Resort Hotel is one of Ireland's leading luxury brands. So, as you are busy having a wonderful time with great food and benchmark wines and irrepressible hospitality, do take a minute just to sit down and gaze at the flowers, to gaze at Sheelagh Kelly's artistry, to gaze at the work of people who understand how to capture beauty. (Bill Kelly, Rosslare ☎ 053-913 2114 ✉ info@kellys.ie 🖰 www.kellys.ie – Closed early Dec-late Feb)

Restaurant
● La Marine

Of all the great alumni who emerged from Paul and Jeanne Rankin's kitchen in Belfast's Roscoff in the early 1990's, the modest Eugene Callaghan remains amongst the least-known, and remains amongst the most accomplished. A quiet, pensive chef, married to a quiet, pensive wife – Elizabeth – who also worked in Roscoff, Mr Callaghan doesn't turn up on the telly – though we did film with him once on a programme of McKennas' Ireland: he was a natural, and the camera liked him, so a smart producer should get down to Kelly's for a few days and get some becoming modesty onto the small screen. His food talks loudly, just as he chooses not to, and several of his dishes are *the* benchmark when it comes to judging salt and pepper squid, or crispy duck confit, or Irish stew, or pike with beurre blanc, or pavlova with Wexford strawberries. The hunger that was in the young Eugene Callaghan who won the first Roux Brothers' scholarship burns brightly, creating perfection. (Eugene Callaghan & Bill Kelly, Rosslare ☎ 053-913 2114 ✒ info@kellys.ie ⏱ www.kellys.ie – Open 12.30pm-2.15pm, Snack Menu 12.30pm-5pm, 6.30pm-9pm Mon-Sun. Closed early Dec-late Feb)

Saltmills

Fish Monger
● Suzie and Patrick Whelan

Only a wee sign saying "Fresh Fish" on the side of the R733 between Arthurstown and Wexford town gives some idea of what lies inside the converted van and chill cabinet that acts as Suzie and Patrick Whelan's fab fish shop. "What's good?" asked Eamon Barrett. "Well, hopefully everything", said Suzie, and so it was: scallops; plaice; black sole; lemon sole; naturally smoked haddock; hake; monkfish; and their own brilliant fishcakes, and the prices are more than super-keen. You will also find Pat and Suzie's van at different days at Tramore, Ferrybank in Waterford and in Kildare. (Suzie & Patrick Whelan, Curraghmore, Saltmills ☎ 051-562158 – Open 9am-5.30pm Mon-Sat)

Wexford

Restaurant
● La Dolce Vita

Roberto Pons has begun to cook at weekend evenings in LDV, trying to satisfy the insatiable hunger for his cooking amongst the good folk of Wexford. His cooking is packed with tiny gestures that transform simple things into special things – the slow-roasted tomatoes with gazzetto of prawns and cannellini beans; perfectly roasted and perfectly oozing roast garlic with lamb chops; perfect red wine sauce with wild venison; as good a tiramisu as is made in the Northern hemisphere. (Roberto & Celine Pons, 6-7 Trimmer's Lane, Selskar, Wexford ☎ 053-917 0806 – Open 9am-5.30pm Mon-Thur, 9.30am-9.30pm Fri & Sat)

Restaurant
● Forde's Restaurant

Liam Forde is one of those cooks who has defined
Wexford eating throughout the years, always serving
food that has its roots in classical techniques, but which
is always packed with vibrant, modern, umami, flavours.
(Liam Forde, Crescent Quay, Wexford ⏁ www.
fordesrestaurantwexford.com ☎ 053-23832 – Open
6pm-9.45pm Mon-Sun, 12.30pm-5pm Sun)

only in Wexford
Bridgetown Potatoes

Butcher
● T Furlong & Sons

"Est. 1621" it says on the wall of Furlong's butchers
shop, and Furlongs do exactly what it says on the wall:
the family have been trading in the town for almost
four centuries. Today, Furlong's is a modern butcher's
shop, with excellent meats and a large deli-counter
section with a great range of prepared foods including
many varieties of their own cooked meats. They have
a second store at Common Quay Street, and one at
the Gorey Shopping Centre. (The Furlong family, The
Bullring ☎ 053-912 2885 – Open 9am-6pm Mon-Thu,
9am-6.30pm Fri. Also at Common Quay St, also Unit 14
Gorey Shopping Centre, The Avenue, Gorey ☎ 053-
943 0428)

Wine Merchant & Delicatessen
● Greenacres

"The shop is like a library of wine", says our wine-
loving editor, Eamon Barrett, of the stunning selection
of world-class wines that you will find at Greenacres.
Wine lovers with a few euro to spare should note that
Greenacres is one of relatively few merchants who offer
an en primeur service, so if your boat has come in, this
is the place to start your cellar. A small new bistro, serving textbook French cooking under the direction of chef
Jacques Carrera is the latest addition to this essential
Wexford address, which is as notable for its

architectural grandeur and its superbly curated art exhi-
bitions, as for its brilliance as a source of great wines and
foods. One of the stars of the south east. (James & Paula
O'Connor, Selskar, Wexford ☎ 053-912 2975 ✉ info@
greenacres.ie 🖰 www.greenacres.ie – Shop open
9.30am-6pm Mon-Sat, Bistro open noon-3pm Mon-Sat
lunch, 9.30am-5.30pm Mon-Sat coffee, 6.30pm-10pm
Tue-Sat dinner)

Wine Merchant & Delicatessen
● **Kate's Farm Shop**

It's an incongruous-looking building at the side of the
road, but don't judge this gem by its modest exterior:
Kate and Ollie O'Mahony's magnificent shop is a place
that gladdens the heart, and delights the table. Inside
is a warren of rooms, each containing the veritable
bees' knees of superb foods. On the vegetables, little
notes tell you the source of everything: potatoes from
Bridgetown; celery from Bannow; carrots and turnips
from Foulksmills; cabbage, sprouts and parsnips from
Baldwinstown; carrots from Screen. The queue of happy
shoppers is neverending, and Kate's is simply not to be
missed. (Kate & Ollie O'Mahony, New Line Road, Wexford ☎ 086-172 7116/ 053-91 39848 ✉ ollieom@eircom.
net – Open 9am-6pm Mon-Sat, 11am-5.30pm Sun)

Restaurant
● **Le Tire Bouchon**

Arnaud Clement and Kevin Carley have met with early
success having opened their restaurant above the
famous The Sky and The Ground pub on South Main
Street. The pair are graduates of Dunbrody House, and
Mr Carley's food has a characteristic richness and savour
to it – pan-fried foie gras with toasted brioche and fig
chutney; supreme of chicken stuffed with a chorizo and
lardon farce; lobster with Cognac and butter sauce.
They like the depth of flavours that you associate with
true Cordon Bleu cooking, and there is a cute 70's-style
retro feel to the way in which the dishes are presented.
These are serious and ambitious young men, and Eamon
Barrett's summation –"Lovely place, good service and
cooking which is good" – shows that Le Tire Bouchon
is already well on the right track. Value for money is
extremely keen. (Kevin Carley & Arnaud Clement,
112 South Main Street, Wexford ☎ 053-912 4877
✉ letirebouchon@eircom.net 🖰 www.letirebouchon.
ie – Open 6pm-9pm Sun-Thu, 6pm-10pm Fri & Sat)

Townhouse
● McMenamin's Townhouse

They are people people, are Seamus and Kay McMenamin, and they have always been so. They have an ease with their guests that quickly – immediately! – makes you feel as if you are one of the family, rather than a paying guest, and their unpretentious informality means that their B&B is one of the stars of the South East. Ace hospitality, pristine housekeeping, and one of the very best breakfasts you can enjoy anywhere in Ireland, make a mighty trio of attractions. (Seamus & Kay McMenamin, 6 Glena Terrace, Spawell Road, Wexford ☎ 053-924 6442 ⌨ info@ wexford-bedandbreakfast.com ⌂ www.wexford-bedandbreakfast.com)

Farmers' Market
● Wexford Farmers' Market

The Friday Wexford farmers' market is held at the Mailin Street Car Park. Look out for local heroes such as Fancy Fungi, Tinnock Farm; Jim Whelan's beef and Killowen Yogurts amidst a cluster of admirable artisans. (Mailin Street Car Park, Cornmarket, Wexford ⌂ www. wexfordfarmersmarkets.com – Open 9am-2pm, Fri)

only in Wexford
Jim Whelan's Beef

Yoletown

Food Producer
● Stable Diet Foods

Katherine Carroll and Vincent Power's Stable Diet company has grown and developed over the years, and has most recently opened a café and patisserie at the quiet end of Wexford's Main Street. But whilst Stable Diet has grown, so that you find their products most everywhere, the song remains the same, even if the scale has changed. Stable Diet make wholesome products, and they make them carefully – they mind them. They are a medium-sized company, but they think like artisans, quietly innovating, keeping in contact with customers from the early days, meticulously attending to quality. Everything has changed, and yet nothing has changed, and the best way to see the excellence of their range is to walk into the café, and introduce yourself to healthfulness, and some really friendly staff. (Katherine Carroll & Vincent Power, Yoletown, Broadway ☎ 053-913 1287 Café & Patisserie, 100 South Main Street, Wexford ☎ 053-914 9012 ✉ katherine@stablediet. com ⌂ www.stablediet.com – Café and patisserie open 9am-6pm Mon-Sat)

Asparagus and strawberries

County Wicklow

Arklow

Farmers' Market
● **Arklow Farmers' Market**

Friday morning is the day, but get there early for the
best produce from local organic superstars such as Gold
River Farm. Why? Because organics are better for you,
and better for your planet, that's why. (Abbey Lane,
Arklow, Friday 10am-1pm)

Bakery
● **Nubo**

They care about what they are doing in Nubo, they put
their hearts into their daily work, and it shows. Conor
Spacey and his team are up early to fire up their stone
oven to bake the breads and scones, the tarts and buns
and cakes, before they move on to creating the savoury
foods that will be sold in the shop for people to eat
there, or to take away for dinner. The good pastry on
a vegetarian quiche is reassuringly real, the soup and
sandwich offer is excellent value and right on the money.
There is a real ethos of caring service at work here,
and you can both feel it and taste it. (Conor Spacey,
16 Main Street, Arklow ☎ 0402-32712 ⌨ info@nubo.
ie ✆ www.nubo.ie – Open 9.30am-7.30pm Mon-Fri,
9.30am-6pm Sat)

Farmhouse Cheese
● **Wicklow Farmhouse Cheese**

John Hempenstall's Wicklow Blue farmhouse cheese
has become perhaps the most successful of the second
generation of Irish farmhouse cheeses, and it is now
so well known that it comes as a shock to realise it
was only born in 2005. It has been quickly joined by
the brie-style Wicklow Baun, along with the cheddar-
style Wicklow Gold, a goat's milk log and a goat's milk
gouda, and the St Kevin brie, made for the catering industry. There is also a fine buttermilk. They pasteurise
the milk of their own herd of 60 cows to make these

deliciously creamy, seductive cheeses, and the cheeses are splendidly consistent and pleasing. (John & Bernie Hempenstall, Curranstown, Arklow ☎ 0402-91713 ✉ wfcheese@eircom.net ❀ www. wicklowfarmhousecheeseltd.ie)

Ashford

Country House & Cookery School
● Ballyknocken House

"Give this woman a television series!" we demanded in the last edition of the *Bridgestone Irish Food Guide*, calling for the capacious skills and charms of Catherine Fulvio of Ballyknocken House to be brought to a wider audience. Well, maybe because we asked so politely, it is indeed about to happen as we write, and "Catherine's Italian Kitchen" will soon make the brilliant Mrs Fulvio even more well-known than she already is. She doesn't need the telly series of course, for her best work has been and always will be done in Ballyknocken House, where Catherine is host and teacher, and has shown herself gifted at both. Ballyknocken is a special house. And, of course, sure we knew Catherine before she was famous! (Catherine Fulvio, Glenealy, Ashford ☎ 0404-44627 ✉ info@ballyknocken.com ❀ www. ballyknocken.com)

only in Wicklow
Buttery Café Gooseberry Fool

Wine Shop
● Caprani Off Licence

Most folk bypass Ashford nowadays, but if you are searching for a good bottle of wine, then the Caprani wine shop in the hotel is worth the detour into the village to pick up something wet and delicious. (The Caprani family, Chester Beatty Inn, Main Street, Ashford ☎ 0404-40682 – Open 10.30am-10pm Mon-Sat, 12.30pm-10pm Sun)

Cafe and Gardens
● Mount Usher Avoca Garden Café

The Garden Café is run by Simon Pratt of Avoca, adding

another reason to visit the beautiful Mount Usher gardens, "a collection of felicitous natural plantings according to (William) Robinson's principles". The Café also opens for dinner on Friday and Saturday evenings. (Simon Pratt, Ashford, ☎ 0404-40116 ⌂ www.mountushergardens.ie – Open 10am-6pm Mon-Sun)

Wicklow

Aughrim

Farmers' Market
● Aughrim Farmers' Market

Handsome Aughrim enjoys a busy market each Saturday, where you can harvest the produce of Wicklow's growers and producers, folk blessed with the gift of good land. (The Pavilion, Aughrim, Saturday 11am-2pm)

Organic Farm
● Gold River Farm

The Pierce and Winterbotham families of Gold River Farm are key practitioners of County Wicklow's organic aristocracy. They have revolutionised the way in which Dublin's leading chefs source and use organic vegetables and salads. Chefs call Gold River in the evening, vegetables and salads are dug in the morning, and delivered straight away. Alan Pierce and Mark Winterbotham also sell their beautiful produce at local markets, so it's not just for chefs, and we have to applaud the stunning quality of their work, where every vegetable and salad leaf is not just vigorous and healthy, but also aesthetically delightful. We know that organics is better than chemicalised farming, but when you combine organics with the aesthetic supremacy of Gold River farm, you get something else altogether: agricultural produce as art. (Alan Pierce & Mark Winterbotham, The Sycamores, Tinakilly, Aughrim ☎ 0402-36426 ⌂ goldriver@eircom.net)

Restaurant
● The Stonecutter

Fresh, simple food is what Ken Reddin aims to serve in The Stonecutter, and that is exactly what he achieves, and he achieves it along with excellent, enthusiastic service that makes the place sing with laid-back energy. Salads are fresh and clean-tasting – couscous with fresh herbs and cherry tomatoes; organic baby leaves in vinaigrette – and the savoury dishes are straight and true: gourmet burger with fries; slow-roasted Portobello mushroom with rosemary; marinated chicken on ciabatta. Locals have taken to the place with evident enthusiasm, and it's buzzing during the day. There is dinner service also on Fridays and Saturdays. (Ken Reddin, Main Street, Aughrim, ☎ 0402-94547 ✉ thestonecutter@hotmail.com – Open 9.30am-5.30pm Sun, Wed-Thur, 9.30am-9.30pm Fri & Sat)

Wicklow

Ice Cream
● Three Wells Farmhouse Ice Cream

Enda and Tracey Byrne's ices and sorbets have many champions, in particular the fine brown bread ice cream. (Enda & Tracey Byrne, Three Wells, Aughrim ☎ 0402-36570 ✉ info@threewellsdairy.com 🖰 http://threewellsdairy.com)

Baltinglass

Baking
● Ballyhubbock Home Foods

Olive Finlay told the *Sunday Business Post* that "I was born and reared on a farm and what I ate was homemade. That's the type of food I like to bake – tasty, simple and wholesome". Fantastic! What a trinity of ambitions: tasty; simple; wholesome. So, seek out those Ballyhubbock apple tarts and mince pies and jams in good Wicklow shops and stores and get that trinity of goodness in your life. (Olive Finlay, Stratford-on-Slaney, Baltinglass ☎ 045-404706)

Blessington

Ice Cream
● Goldenhill Farmhouse Ice Cream

Damien and Aoife Clarke's Goldenhill ice cream had its very own classic ice cream van at Electric Picnic 2009, evidence of the dynamism of this farmhouse company. They use the milk of their own cows to make the ice cream, and then source the fruits and other ingredients from the locality. You will find their ice creams and sorbets in a good range of very good restaurants and shops, and in farm shops such as Castlefarm in County Kildare. (Damien & Aoife Clarke, Goldenhill Farm, Golden Hill, Manor Kilbride, Blessington ☎ 01-458 2017/086-364 0135 ✉ info@goldenhill.ie ⌂ www.goldenhill.ie)

only in Wicklow
Sweetbank Farm Spring Lamb

Café
● Grangecon Café

Richard and Jenny Street do things their way, their own way, and nobody else does things the way they do them. Their food is incredibly simple, and if you arrived here with any sort of grand notions, you would be disappointed. But if you enter their world, if you can catch what it is that they are doing, then the simplicity of this café and foodstore will blow you away. Basically, they believe in goodness, and they want to capture that goodness in their work, in their cooking. If that sounds ridiculous, then frankly you don't know what good food is, and you don't know that good food must encompass goodness. That goodness is here, so take a bite, and let it blow you away. Heaven in a slice of bread? You'll believe it so. (Richard & Jenny Street, Kilbride Road, Blessington ☎ 045-857892 ✉ grangeconcafe@eircom.net – Open 9am-4pm Mon-Wed, 9am-5pm Thu-Sat)

Health Food Store
● Harvest Fare Health Food Shop

Mary Davis and Deirdre Mallitte's shop is packed with good things, but there is more to HF than just a shop, for they also offer a treatment centre and vegetarian cookery classes. The shop evolves, develops and improves all the time, driven by spirited owners. Mary is also developing an organic dairy farm with her husband, a hugely promising new venture for artisan dairy products. (Mary Davis & Deirdre Mallitte, Main Street, Blessington ☎ 045-891636 ✉ harvestfare@eircom.net ⌂ www.harvestfarehealthshop.com – Open 10am-6pm Mon-Sat, 'till 5pm Sat)

Bray

Farmers' Market
● Bray Farmers' Market

A Coco market organised by the dynamic Jackie Spillane,
the Heritage Centre is the place to be on Saturday
morning to get the good stuff from great producers.
(Bray Heritage Centre, Main Street, Bray – Open 11am-
3pm Sat)

Restaurant
● Campo de Fiori

As compact as a Fiat Cinquecento, this tabernacle of
good Italian eating shoves you in sardine-style beside
your neighbours, but the bustle and the Italian-accented
babble means you will quickly have eyes only for what
is on the plate. Real regulars start with an aperitivo
across the street in Sapori di Campo de Fiori, then get
stuck into gnocchi with Gorgonzola and walnuts, or
their special of linguini with lobster. It's major fun, and
it's the original of the species that has grown to include
Pinocchio in Ranelagh and a cookery school and catering service. (Marco Roccasalvo, 1 Albert Avenue, Bray
☎ 01-204 2514 ✆ campodefioribray@msn.com – Open
5pm-10.30pm Mon, Wed & Thu, 5pm-11pm Fri & Sat,
2pm-9pm Sun)

Coffee and Tea Merchant
● Clive McCabe & Co

You find them in good stores and delis here, there and
everywhere, the golden bags of Clive McCabe's coffees,
the green bags of his speciality blend teas. At a time
when we have gone coffee roasting and tea sourcing
crazy, we should remember the steadfast work of this
pioneer, who was creating bespoke blends when today's
coffee kids were in short trousers. Lovely work, always
understated, truly classy. (Clive McCabe, Unit 56,
Newtownmountkennedy Business Enterprise Centre
☎ 01-287-5835 ✆ www.clivemccabes.com)

Yogurts and Soft Cheeses
● Old MacDonnell's Farm

The McDonnell family's very fine yogurts and fresh
cheeses are excellent dairy products, their clean acidity

and refreshingly pure lacticity reflecting the high-quality milk that comes from their farm. Along with the dairy products we are also big fans of their hummus, which has a nice toothy, slightly coarse texture that makes it a real pleasure to add to sandwiches and wraps. These are high quality and naturally healthful foods and you'll find them in the best shops and good supermarkets. (The McDonnell family, Glen of the Downs, Bray ☎ 01-282 8992 ✉ sales@oldmacdonnellsfarm.ie ✎ www.oldmacdonnellsfarm.ie)

only in Wicklow
Amy Caviston's Fish Pie

Brittas

Cookery and Gardening Courses
● Hunting Brook Gardens

Jimi Blake is a visionary gardener and he was the man who transformed the Airfield gardens in Dublin over a ten-year period. In Hunting Brook he has created superb gardens, and in recent times has fashioned allotments. Vegetable growers can benefit hugely from Hunting Brook classes, but even the briefest tour here will provide years of inspiration. (Jimi Blake, Hunting Brook, Lamb Hill, Blessington ☎ 01-458 3972 ✉ jimi@huntingbrook.com ✎ www.huntingbrook.com)

Delgany

Butcher
● Farrelly's Butchers

The Farrelly brothers shop is recognised as the best butcher's shop in Wicklow, which is really saying something. Padraig and Anthony's dad opened the shop more than fifty years ago – 1958 to be precise – and that half century of skilled sourcing and skilled charcuterie is what blesses this business. Local meats, and local organic meats, are handled with a level of skill that is stratospheric. Superb. (Anthony & Padraig Farrelly, Main Street, Delgany ☎ 01-287 4211 – Open 9am-6pm Mon-Sat. Closed for lunch 1pm-2pm Mon-Fri)

Donard

Organic Vegetables and Herbs
● Castleruddery Organic Farm

The organic growers of County Wicklow were at it
before almost anyone else in Ireland, and Dominic Quinn
and Hilda Crampton have been producing superb food at
Castleruddery ever since we wrote our first book, way,
way back in 1989, taking good advantage of the richness
of Wicklow soils to produce exemplary foods. Twenty
years a growin'! Happy birthday! You can buy their
beautiful produce from their farm shop on Thursdays
and Fridays, and at the busy Naas farmers' market on
Saturday. (Hilda Crampton & Dominic Quinn, Donard
☎ 045-404925 ✉ casorg@eircom.net – Farmshop open
Thur & Fri)

Enniskerry

Café
● Avoca Powerscourt Terrace Café

The mighty Avoca has one of the most glorious locations
in the grand, dreamy Powerscourt. Lunch on the terrace
here is some kinda wonderful, one of the great Irish
pastoral pleasures from Ireland's leading luxury brand.
(Simon Pratt, Powerscourt House, Enniskerry ☎ 01-
204 6070 ✉ info@avoca.ie 🖱 www.avoca.ie – Open
9.30am-5.30pm Mon-Fri, 10am-6pm Sat & Sun)

only in Wicklow
Ballyhubbock Apple Tart

Glenealy

Organic Lamb, Poultry & Eggs
● Crocker's Organic Farm

The Crockers produce lamb, chickens, eggs, turkeys,
beef and potatoes, and produce superb examples of all
those foods, on a south-facing farm with fine, free-
draining soil. (The Crocker family, Ballydowling Farm,
Glenealy ☎ 0404-44854 ✉ crockerorganics@eircom.net)

Organic Store
● OOOOBY Store

A new store with the grooooviest name – it means
Out Of Our Own Back Yard – is where you will find
the organic produce of local growers. Masterminded by
Mike and Suzie Cahn, it's a not-for-profit venture that
dovetails with their Carraig Dúlra eco and sustainability
centre. Saturday morning is when you can get the best
foods at the shop, along with other eco products. (Mike
& Suzy Cahn, Glenealy Landscape Centre, Glenealy
⁂ www.dulra.org/ooooby – Open 10am-5pm Tue-Thu,
11.20am-3.30pm Sat)

Greystones

Restaurant
● Backstage @ Bel's

Jeff Norman cut his teeth at Roly's Bistro in Ballsbridge
before heading south to open up Bel's with his wife,
Tara. They are big players in the vibrant local food
community, and great supporters of local artisans in the
most practical way; they buy their produce, cook it and
put it on the menu: Butterly salmon; Gold River Farm
leaves; Synnott's meat; Wicklow Blue cheese; Three
Wells ice cream. Right through from breakfast to Sunday
dinner it's a welcoming place, two people working hard
at something they love. (Jeff & Tara Norman, Bel House,
Church Road, Greystones ☎ 01-201 6990 ⁂ www.bels.ie
– Open noon-4pm, 5pm-10pm Tue-Sat, 1pm-8pm Sun)

Traireur
● Butler's Pantry

Eileen Bergin's vital chain of traiteur shops now numbers
no fewer than nine stores, with two shops in County
Wicklow, where their main kitchens are also based in
Bray. The store on Church Road is open seven days a
week, and it is no exaggeration to say that having a BP
on your doorstep gives you a one-stop culinary solution
for any and every occasion. For more than twenty years
Ms Bergin has pursued a vision of true, real cooking, the
sort of food that has professional finish but domestic
soulfulness, and she achieves this ambition each and
every day of the week. (Eileen Bergin, Burnaby Buildings, Church Road, Greystones ☎ 01-201 0022 ⁂ www.
thebutlerspantry.ie)

Grangecon Sausage Rolls

Fish Shop, Delicatessen & Café
● A Caviston

Yes, Amy Caviston is one of the legendary Caviston's
of Glasthule, and with her beautiful new store and café
she is advancing the Caviston legend southwards into
Wicklow. With husband Shane and Shane's brother
Ronan they have hit the ground running, offering not
just superlative seafood, but also a fantastic selection
of foods in the deli, and a busy café where the cookery
is just spot on: Boston shrimp sandwich; Cajun salmon
burgers; fish pie; Toulouse sausage and chickpea stew.
A Caviston is, in effect, a one-stop solution shop for
whatever culinary demand or desire you could possibly
have. Brilliant. (Amy Caviston, Shane & Ronan Willis, No
1 Westview, Church Road, Greystones, ☎ 01-287 7637
✉ info@acaviston.ie 🖱 www.acaviston.ie – Cafe open
9am-5pm, Deli open 9am-6pm Tue-Sat)

Restaurant
● Chakra by Jaipur

Sunil Ghai has gone on to win huge acclaim for his
cooking in Ananda, and has been succeeded in Chakra
by Dinesh Chander, who trained under the brilliant
Mr Ghai. You can expect the same modernist, creative
twist on Indian cooking – minced lamb with cardamom;
coriander-crusted scallops – that has made the Jaipur
chain a staple of so many people's lives. Great service
completes a slick offer. (Dinesh Chander, 1st Floor, Me-
ridian Point, Church Road, Greystones ☎ 01-201 7222
✉ info@chakra.ie 🖱 www.jaipur.ie – Open 5.30pm-
11pm Mon-Sun)

Traireur
● Donnybrook Fair

Joe Doyle's brilliant super-supermarket gets out-of-
town with a hip destination in Grattan Court. We are
unabashed admirers of this man and his handsome
aesthetic, but above all we admire the fact that every
decent artisan wants their food on DF shelves, and finds
space there alongside the best food in Ireland.

(Joe Doyle, Grattan Court, Greystones ☎ 01-287 6346
✉ info@donnybrookfair.ie 🖰 www.donnybrookfair.ie –
Open 7am-8pm Mon-Thu & Sat, 7am-9pm Fri, 8am-8pm
Sun)

Wicklow

Green Shopping
● **Ecoshop**

Jane Hall's Ecoshop moved from Glen o'the Downs
into Greystones in 2008, bringing a swish collection of
Fairtrade and eco-friendly products along with foods
and great, eco gardening products. (Jane Hall, Merid-
ian Point, Church Road, Greystones ☎ 01-287 2914
🖰 www.ecoshop.ie – Open 9am-7pm Mon-Fri, 9am-
6pm Sat, noon-5pm Sun)

Kitchen Shop
● **Gourmet Gadgets**

Who could resist a shop called Gourmet Gadgets? Not
us, so Toni Dowdall's store is one of those places where
maintaining self-control is well-nigh impossible. So, if
you seek an Atomic coffee machine or a Garlic Twist by
Nextrend – the shop's bestseller – then Hillside Road
is the place for you. (Toni Dowdall, 2 Hillside Road,
Greystones ☎ 01-287 0044 🖰 www.gourmetgadgets.ie –
Open 10am-5.30pm Mon-Sat, noon-4.30pm Sun)

Cafe & Deli
● **The Happy Pear**

Steve and Dave Flynn are an identical pair, who run The
Happy Pear, and do so very happily indeed. They are a
focal point for lots of Wicklow's best growers, which
gives their hip vegetarian cooking a real edge of freshness and goodness, and we love the slightly madcap,
left-field, communitarian, utterly idealistic and holistic
ambience of the shop and smoothie bar and the restaurant upstairs. Unique, and quite brilliant. (Stephen &
Dave Flynn, Westview House, Main Street, Greystones
☎ 01-287 3655 🖰 www.thehappypear.ie – Cafe & Shop
open 9am-6pm Mon-Sat, Cafe only open 11am-6pm Sun)

Restaurant and Wine Bar Bistro
● **The Hungry Monk**

After more than two decades making the good folk of
Greystones happy, the new generation has moved in to
continue Pat and Sylvia Keown's legendary work in the

Hungry Monk. Julian Keown has joined the folks and works the upstairs restaurant, where the wine list provides almost as much of an attraction as the cooking; this list is special, and there is some amazing value in great bottles that Pat has collected over the years. Downstairs the cooking is simpler in the wine bar – kidneys Dijonnaise; Bombay chicken curry; lamb burger with jacket chips – whilst upstairs the emphasis on sourcing – Mullingar beef; Castletownbere scallops, Ballon pork from Carlow – is the guarantee of a good night out. (Pat & Sylvia Keown, Church Road, Greystones ☎ 01-287 5759 ✆ hungrymonk@eircom.net ⌂ www. thehungrymonk.ie – Restaurant open 6.30pm-11pm Wed-Sat, 12.30pm-8pm Sun. Wine Bar Bistro open 5pm-11pm Mon-Sat, 4pm-9pm Sun)

Food To Go
● Indian Spice Co.

Ronan Fleming's take-away produces some of the most authentic Indian cooking you can find, which might seem a surprise coming from an Irishman. Mr Fleming's secret is a sympathy and understanding of ethnic cooking, and a lack of pretension: he loves street food, and his cooking is very direct, whether you have his clay-oven specialities or good Punjabi curries. Great food, great value. (Ronan Fleming, 19a Church Road, Greystones ☎ 01-201 0868 ⌂ www.indianspiceco.com – Open 5pm-10.15pm Mon-Thur, 5pm-10.45pm Fri & Sat, 4pm-10.15pm Sun)

Fishmonger
● Moran's Seafood Specialists

Greystones' lovely fish shop is a vital address in the town not only for good fish and shellfish, but also because owner Suzanne O'Keefe also stocks superb wild Wicklow game, when in season. (Suzanne O'Keefe, Latouche Place, Greystones ☎ 01-287 6327 – Open 8.30am-5.30pm Tue-Sat)

Wholefood Shop
● Nature's Gold

One of the great and enduring Greystones destinations, and today Brod Kearon's shop continues to provide a vital service to this expanding town, with a great range of organics and essential wholefoods. (Brod Kearon, Killincarrig Road, Greystones ☎ 01-287 6301 ✆ natgold@iol.ie – Open 9am-6pm Mon-Sat)

Butcher's Shop
● The Steak Shop

Barry King sources from the family farm and hangs his steaks for 21 days before selling them to happy customers. (Barry King, Trafalgar Road, Greystones ☎ 01-255 7737 – Open 8am-6pm Mon-Sat)

Café
● The Three Q's

"It works perfectly, with real inventiveness and style". That's how John Wilson, wine correspondent of *The Irish Times*, described the work of Brian, Paul and Colin Quinn, and it's spot on, for whilst the menus can read a little complicated here, and whilst the guys like rich food, the brothers have lots of discipline, and getting everything to work perfectly is their ambition. You can have home-made baked beans on toast with mature cheddar all the way to rabbit stuffed with black pudding, but don't overlook the African-influenced dishes which are one of their specialities. Lovely smart room, lovely smart destination. (Brian, Paul & Colin Quinn, Gweedore Church Road, Greystones ☎ 01-287 5477 ✉ thethreeqs@gmail.com – Open 9am-11.30pm, noon-4.30pm Tue-Fri, 6pm-10pm Tue-Sat, 9am-3pm Sat & Sun)

Kilmacanogue

Café
● Avoca

The big news at Avoca Kilmacanogue is the opening of the Fern House Café for dinner on Thursday, Friday and Saturday evenings. A beautiful room, and beautiful food from Matt Murphy and Giorgio Romano: wild mushroom and soft polenta tart; Moroccan mezze with slow-cooked leg of lamb; 28-day sirloin with horseradish creme fraiche; raspberry cheesecake and chocolate brownie. Aside from dinner, the Sugar Tree café serves classic Avoca dishes to thousands of people every week, and not only do standards never waver in Avoca, standards in fact only ever seem to rise. Ireland's leading luxury brand, and no competition. (Simon Pratt, Kilmacanogue ☎ 01-286 7466 ✉ info@avoca.ie 🖰 www.avoca.ie – Open 9.30am-5.30pm Mon-Sun)

Chutneys & Relishes
● Janet's Country Fayre

Janet Drew's relishes were amongst the first artisan products to become conspicuous in Ireland, both because of their deliciousness, and because Ms Drew worked so hard to get them into the best delis and shops in Ireland. Today, with their extravagantly styled calligraphy on the labels, they remain amongst the most recognisable specialist foods, and their organoleptic excellence is as sharp as ever. Frankly, we keep a large pot of red pepper relish in the fridge at all times, for no sausage roll or savoury, porky product can be eaten without this defining relish. Everything else Janet makes is, of course, every bit as good. (Janet Drew, Copsewood Farm, KIlmacanogue ☎ 01-204 1957 🖃 janet@janetscountryfayre.com 🖰 www.janetscountryfayre.com)

Kilpedder

Organic Shop & Café
● Marc Michel Organic Life

Marc Michel was the first certified organic grower in Ireland, getting his papers way, way back in 1983, before it was profitable or fashionable. Well, in the intervening years, Mr Michel, more than any other grower, has made organics fashionable (and for him, we hope, profitable), thanks to his own extrovert character, and to the brilliant work he has done in Kilpedder, initially as a grower of wonderful organic foods, and then as a restaurateur. The café is presently closed due to some carry on with the local Council, but Mr Michel has hopes that his brilliant cooking venture can get back up and running: let's all hope so. Visionary, as we say, but then Marc Michel was visionary way, way back in 1983. (Marc Michel, Kilpedder ☎ 01-201 1882)

Kiltegan

Organic Farmer
● Denis Healy's Organic Delights

Denis Healy's Organic Delights. Yes indeed! Delights it is, whenever you encounter Mr Healy and his band –

his tribe!– of helpers, volunteers and family, selling at oodles of markets throughout Dublin and Wicklow. Mr Healy is not just a visionary, like so many other Wicklow organic growers have shown themselves to be. He is a visionary who is also a man of action, which is why he works so many markets, and grows so much splen-diferous foods on his 20 organic acres. For Mr Healy, organics is the baseline, organics is for everyone, organ-ics is the alpha, and the omega. He is one of the great figures, and not just in Irish food, for Denis Healy is one of the great figures in Irish public life. (Denis Healy, Talbotstown Lower, Kiltegan ☎ 059-647 3193 📠 info@ organicdelights.ie 🖑 www.organicdelights.ie)

Bio-Dynamic Produce
● **Penny & Udo Lange**

Penny and Udo Lange have been growing and selling vegetables since 1987, and in that time have established themselves as the philosopher king and queen of Irish agriculture, no mean feat in a field that is crammed with philosophers. Today, you can find their foods at Brighton Square in Rathgar on Thursdays, as well as the Dublin Food Co-Op and the Supernatural Market on Pearse Street on Saturdays, and the goodness and energy of their produce truly has to be sampled to be believed. If the people of Ireland all ate produce of the same quality as that grown by the Langes we would have no need of a HSE, we would have no childhood obesity, we would have a healthy, well population, a people who could recover naturally from illness, should it strike. There is a dynamic in this bio-dynamically grown food that is the very essence of life, the chi of our being. (Penny & Udo Lange, Ballinroan House, Kiltegan ☎ 059-647 3278)

Kilternan

Country Market
● **Kilternan Country Market**

A market that is a legend in its own Saturday morning, Kilternan is one of the best country markets, and has been active since 1964. If you can't get there early – very early – then phone in an order for baking and vegetables in advance, otherwise you haven't got a chance of getting them. "A hub of warm chatter and friendliness... a community that knows how to guide the future with

Wicklow

values that, happily, have not been left in the past"
is how Joyce Hickey described the market in *The
Irish Times*. Quite right, so make time for tea in the
coffee shop after the shopping is done. (Golden Ball,
Enniskerry Road, Kilternan ☎ 01-282 2182)

Laragh

Restaurant
● The Conservatory

Now, this is special. Lisa de la Haye's restaurant and
country house has the sort of qualities that you don't
come across very often, for there is an elegance, an attention to detail, in the aesthetic of this operation that
is simply disarming. "This will become one of Wicklow's
gems" says Caroline Byrne, and the mix of style and
service, and the lightness of touch in the right-on cooking is certainly going to achieve that: prawns in garlic
butter; Cashel Blue and leek tart; chicken with wild
mushroom and tagliatelle; wild venison and beetroot
casserole. Everything, from breads and soups to savoury
dishes and excellent treats such as apple and ginger
crumble or apple and blackberry tart, are beautifully
executed. Plans to open for dinner are in development,
and with six guest rooms, the Conservatory is going to
be one of the hottest destinations for the forseeable
future. (Lisa de la Haye, The Old Schoolhouse, Laragh
☎ 0404-45302 📧 lisa@theconservatory.ie – Open
10am-6pm summer, 11am-4pm winter)

Macreddin

Country Hotel
● The Brook Lodge Inn

The opening of La Taverna Armento, a restaurant with
a vivid southern Italian feel and ingredients, shows the
patient, organic way in which Evan Doyle has developed The Brook Lodge through its first decade. When
Deirdre Doyle met and married Michele Canosa, it gave
the Brook Lodge the chance to source organic Italian ingredients needed for the hotel's Strawberry Tree
restaurant – the hotel is the only organically certified
destination in Ireland. A connection sprang up between

Macreddin and Armento, hence the name, the inspiration, and the food: Armento antipasti plate of cured meats, olives and mozzarella with grilled organic vegetables; venison ravioli with red wine jus; oyster mushroom with blue cheese risotto; grilled sardines with leaves; and some funky pizzas: salsiccia sausage with spring onion; two cheese Margherita; vegetable calzone. Armento makes this brilliant hotel even more of a destination, along with the Strawberry Tree restaurant, their monthly organic farmers' market, the Wells Spa, the Brook Hall wedding and corporate venue, and you can even spoil a good walk on the golf course, Mr Doyle is – no question – the sharpest tool in the shed. (Evan Doyle, Brook Lodge Inn, Macreddin ☎ 0402-36444 ✉ brooklodge@macreddin.ie 🖱 www.brooklodge.com – Restaurant open 7pm-9.30pm Mon-Sat)

Organic Market
● Macreddin Village Organic Market

You just can't beat the atmosphere at the monthly Macreddin market. With families eating, kids playing on the lawn, music popping, shoppers strolling, a throng of sellers and exhibitors with foods and crafts, the sun shining (trust us!) it is a mighty panjandrum of good times and great foods. (Evan Doyle, The Brook Lodge, Macreddin Village. 🖱 www.brooklodge.com – Open 1.30pm-6.30pm on the 1st Sun of each month from Mar-Oct)

Organic Bakery, Smoked Foods, Preserves
● The Store Rooms

The Store Rooms at the Brook Lodge offer an organic bakery, a range of smoked foods from their smokehouse and lots of good pantry foods created with wild and organic ingredients. (Evan Doyle, The Brook Lodge, Macreddin Village ☎ 0402-36444 ✉ brooklodge@macreddin.ie 🖱 www.brooklodge.com)

Newcastle

Country Market
● North Wicklow Country Market

This is one of the great, legendary Wicklow Country markets, as opposed to the more recently arrived farmers' markets. Get there early on Saturday morning from

11am in the Newcastle Community Centre, for lots of good local foods, and a lovely, community atmosphere. (Newcastle Community Centre, Newcastle, Saturdays 10.30am-12.30pm)

Farm Shop
● Sweetbank Farm

David and Debbie Johnston are another pioneering pair of Wicklow producers. They have led the way in creating an excellent farm shop as a store front for their beautiful foods, a feature of empowered agriculture that is still all-too-rare in Ireland. And they have shown how one can attract an audience, thanks to top-class produce, in the case of Sweetbank that is their wonderful seasonal fruits and juices, and their spring lamb and Angus beef. They also support other local producers by selling their foods in order to supplement their own range. Brilliant. (David & Debbie Johnston Tiglin, Newcastle ☎ 01-281 9280/086-173 0497 ✉ sweetbankfarm@iolfree.ie ⊕ www.sweetbankfarm.ie)

Newtownmountkennedy

Café
● The Buttery Café @ Fishers

Aimée & Claire run "a doll's house of a café, with cutesy furnishings and little touches everywhere to create the perfect ambience for this girly establishment", says Caroline Byrne. Caroline enjoyed the food just as much as the space: Portobello mushrooms stuffed with creamed leeks and blue cheese; brie and tomato tart, and there was also bangers and mash and Dijon beef casserole on the blackboard that day. The sweet baking is tremendous: Tuscan plum tarte tatin; gooseberry fool; sublime cupcakes. "Genuinely yummy food. Go girlies!", says Caroline. (Aimée Tyrrell & Claire O'Brien, Fishers, Newtownmountkennedy ☎ 01-281 2892 ⊕ www. thebutterycafe.com – Open 10am-5pm Mon-Sat, 1pm-5pm Sun)

Wine Shop
● Claudio's Wines

Claudio of the smiling face will be much-missed in Dublin's George's Street Arcade, where he has happily sold happy wines for many years. But now, those happy wines are in a happy new store in Newtownmountkennedy, so a great new wine chapter begins. (Claudio Meneses, Newtownmountkennedy ☎ 01-281 0221 claudio@ gmailcom – Open 10.30am-7pm Tue-Wed, 10.30am-9pm Thu-Sat)

Rathdrum

Restaurant
● Bate's

Marino Monterisi is the sort of cook who doesn't just source ingredients: he curates them, he cares for them, and then he sends them out to the dining room in wonderfully evocative and creative dishes: tagliata of beef with rosemary potatoes; hake fillets with clam sauce; sausages with borlotti beans, potato gnocchi with Wicklow venison ragout; Tipperary pork belly with butternut squash; saffron risotto with pork cheeks; a tiramisu which is to die for. Bates made it into our 100 Best Restaurants in 2009, which gives you the level of accomplishment shown here, and the restaurant and the cooking is actually getting better all the time. A true star. (Marino Monterisi, 3 Market Street, Market Square, Rathdrum ☎ 0404-29988 batesinn@yahoo.ie ⚹ www. batesrestaurant.ie – Open 12.30pm-2pm, 6.30pm-10pm Tue-Sat, 12.30pm-3pm, 7pm-9pm Sun)

Butcher
● Synnott's

Synnott's is always one of our stops when we find ourselves touring through Wicklow. John and Richard do the good thing, the old way, so don't be fazed by the simple style of the shop, just pay attention to that superb beef, which is as good as it gets. (John & Richard Synnott, Rathdrum ☎ 0404-46132 – Open 8.30am-6pm Mon-Sat)

Game Producer
● Wild Irish Game Ltd

Michael Healy's company is your only man if you cherish the wild, wicked, feral flavours of rabbit, grouse, partridge, woodcock, wild duck, pigeon and venison, all of them beautifully prepared. Mr Healy sources from licensed hunters during the seasons, so unless you have a gun and a licence, this is your gateway to the superlative flavours of wild foods. (Michael Healy, Glenmalure, Rathdrum ☎ 0404-46773 📠 wigltd@eircom.net)

only in Wicklow
Kilternan Country Market

Rathnew

On-line Butcher
● Simply Sourced

Nigel Cobbe's company offers a superb service where they source top-class meat – free-range saddleback pork; long horn beef – and then deliver it in the Dublin and Wicklow region. The quality is superb: some breakfast gammon was amongst the best we have eaten, and the beef is succulent and tender, and they have cuts like rump steak – and the prices for such quality are superbly keen. You order through their site, placing the order on Monday, with delivery on Friday. The site lets you shop both à la carte or by selecting one of their box ranges, and it is simple to navigate. Mr Cobbe is keen and ambitious, and Simply Sourced is set to be a major culinary player. (Nigel Cobbe, Fourwinds Cottage, Cuckoo Corner, Ballymerrigan, Rathnew ☎ 087-057 0000 📠 info@simplysourced.net 🖱 www.simplysourced.net)

Roundwood

Country Inn
● The Roundwood Inn

Jurgen and Aine Schwalm's ever-popular inn is a Wicklow legend, a place for good, gutsy food with lots of potatoes and lots of cabbage and good pints of porter. Nothing changes here, save perhaps for whichever movie character Daniel Day-Lewis is inhabiting as he imbibes his stout. (Jurgen & Aine Schwalm, Roundwood ☎ 01-281 8107 – Open noon-9.30pm Mon-Sun)

Wicklow

Traiteur
● The Butler's Pantry

The county town address of Eileen Bergin's visionary
chain of traiteur shops. (Eileen Bergin, Abbey Street,
Wicklow ☎ 0404-66487 ⌁ www.thebutlerspantry.ie)

Café
● Halpin's Bridge Café

We knew Robert Doyle years ago when, in another
life, he was a news photographer. Now, like so many
interesting people in the food business, he has morphed
into a restaurateur, and opened up Halpin's, and the
good folk of Wicklow town have been queueing up to
get a table here from day one. Chef Ross Quinn makes
good savoury specials each day – beef cannelloni;
spinach and ricotta tortellini; really ace pork in a cream
and mustard sauce with basmati rice – and there are
fine sweet bakes as well, especially old retainers like
an excellent tea brack and a demon rice crispy square.
"Good food, friendly service and reasonable prices" is
how Caroline Byrne sums up Halpin's trinity of winning
qualities. That will do nicely. (Robert Doyle, Bridge
Street, Wicklow ☎ 0404-32677 – Open 8.30am-6.30pm
Mon-Fri, 8pm-6pm Sat, 10am-4pm Sun)

Organic Herbs
● The Organic Herb Company

Paul Pritchard and Michael Martin's company produces
the most beautifully packaged and presented organic
herbs, spices, snacks and oils, so handsomely put
together that just buying them seems as if you are giving
yourself a gift. Look out in particular for their elegantly
flavoured oils. (Michael Martin & Paul Pritchard,
Wicklow Enterprise Park, The Murrough, Wicklow
☎ 0404 66433 ⌁ organicherbco@eircom.net ⌁ www.
organicherbco.ie)

Organic Vegetables and Meat
● An Tairseach

The farm shop at the Dominican Convent enjoys the
produce of 70 acres of organic and bio-dynamic farm-
land, producing beef, pork, lamb, eggs and vegetables.

Aside from the shop at the convent itself, you will find their brilliant produce at farmers' markets in Dalkey and at Bray and Greystones markets. Their ecology centre runs courses on organic growing, cooking, nutrition and much else. This is an inspiring place, and a brilliant example of the garden of Ireland at its most deliciously productive and sustainable best. (The Dominican Sisters, Dominican Farm & Ecology Centre, Wicklow ☎ 0404-61833 ✉ ecenw@eircom.net 🖳 www. ecocentrewicklow.ie)

Wine Shop
● Wicklow Wine Co

For a decade now, Ben Mason and Michael Anderson have run one of the best bespoke wine businesses in the country. They don't do fashion, so brilliant – but unfashionable – wines from countries like Germany and Portugal find space here, and you need only trust to their expertise and experience to discover something new and delicious. Their wines are featured as best selections by wine writers so regularly that you would almost suspect something was going on, but when you try the wines you understand that these guys can simply pick winners every time, and we suspect it is the diversity – the disparity indeed – of their characters that gives them such nous when it comes to sourcing. Superb shop, superb service, superb experience. (Michael Anderson & Ben Mason, Main Street, Wicklow ☎ 0404-66767 ✉ info@wicklowwineco.ie 🖳 www.wicklowwineco.ie – Open 10.30am-7pm Mon-Wed, 10.30am-8pm Thu-Fri, 10.30am-7pm Sat, 12.30pm-6pm Sun)

Mountain Lamb

Northern Ireland

Belfast

Restaurant
● **Alden's**

Alden's is just a gorgeous space, the epitome of a sophisticated city restaurant, and a place we love returning to. They tweak it a bit – this year they're extending their opening times, and offering a speedier lunch menu, plus they've made it a little more casual – but the character of Alden's will always be urbane and svelte. They match the atmosphere with smart cooking, and you get dishes here that can really be described as "very Alden's": roast haunch of rabbit with lentils and salsa verde; rump of lamb with creamed French beans and bacon; mushroom curry with braised rice; sea bass with bubble and squeak. Jonathan Davis was born into the industry and he has such command of his role that he makes it look easy, and for value and class there is no-one to beat Alden's. (Jonathan Davis, 229 Upper Newtownards Road ☎ 028-9065 0079 ✉ info@aldensrestaurant.com ⏻ www.aldensrestaurant.com – Open noon-2.30pm, 6pm-10.30pm Mon-Sat, 'till 11pm Fri & Sat)

Restaurant
● **Alden's in the City**

What is there to love in Alden's in the City? Well there's the lovely green decor for a start. Urban dining reduced to a pale yellowy lime, with pretty bucket chairs and banquettes in the same tones, echoed again in the food labelling and the typography on the menu. This green declares that Alden's in the City is a class act. The restaurant is in the heart of Belfast's shopping zone. There was always a restaurant here, it was run by the present owner's mother, and while it was good, it was a much simpler, less sophisticated place. The staff from the old restaurant remain, but instead of serving Ulster frys and cups of tea, they now offer pastrami, Emmental, rocket and wholegrain mustard sandwiches with berry smoothies or roibos. Thankfully they've kept the formality and dignity of this long-established restaurant space, and even though it has changed utterly, it still feels right. There is also a small shop where you can buy pastas, wines, olive oils and all the accoutrements of city cooking to take home. (Jonathan Davis, 8-14 Callendar Street, Belfast ☎ 028-9024 5385 ⌐ www. aldensinthecity.com – Open 8am-5.30pm Mon-Wed, 8am-6pm Thu, 9.30am-6pm Fri)

Delicatessen
● The Arcadia

Just because Arcadia has been around for more than seventy-five years, don't make the mistake of taking it for granted, because this is a shop that innovates, updates and improves. So if you want Tickety-Moo ice cream, or Gubbeen bickies or Fermanagh black bacon, it's all here, in a shop that has a most handsome livery. (Willie Brown, 378 Lisburn Road ☎ 028-9038 1779 ⌐ info@ ardcadiadeli.co.uk ⌐ www.arcadiadeli.co.uk – Open 8am-6pm Mon-Sat)

Asian Supermarket
● Asia Supermarket

Nowhere else comes near to the Asia Supermarket, Saturday morning in here is like being in the centre of Shanghai mixed with the St George's market, all bustle and clamour and noise, and trolleys and vans, and boxes and happy shoppers getting just exactly what they want. The range of ethnic goods is phenomenal, but AS is particularly special for their fresh vegetables and herbs. It's also a place where you can buy a mah jong board, a cleaver and a Bruce Lee video. Enter the dragon. (The Pau family, 189 Ormeau Road ☎ 028-9032 6396 – Open 9.30am-6.30pm Mon-Sun)

Café & Home Store
● Avoca

The Avoca crew thought long and hard before they opened up in Belfast, and when they finally got the doors open on Arthur Street, it was as if they were the only banana seller in the city after rationing. We have described Avoca as Ireland's leading luxury brand, and everything in the Belfast store confirms this, from the knockout food in the café to the too-cool-for-school foods and home objects in the store. (Simon Pratt, 41 Arthur Street, Belfast ☎ 028-9027 9955 ⌐ www.avoca.ie – Open 9am-4pm Mon-Fri, 9am-5pm Sat, 12.30pm-5pm Sun)

Bagel Bar
● Bagel Bagel

The bagels in Bagel Bagel have names and titles that are as hip and amusing as all getout. So you can actually turn up at the counter and ask for a Fandango or a Big Blue, and nobody will think that you have been drinking. Good authentic bagels and lively service. (Joan & Paul Barr, 60 Donegall Street ☎ 028-9024 2545 ✌ www.bagel-bagel. co.uk – Open 8am-3.30pm Mon-Fri, 10am-3pm Sat)

Gastropub
● The Barking Dog

The Barking Dog is almost painfully fashionable, but don't let that put you off. This space used to be Rain City, owned by Paul Rankin, now it's owned by Samuel Spain, and chef Michael O'Connor, and it still cuts the mustard. The food here, well there's no better word to use to describe it than: delicious. Every dish is sculpted for flavour, whether it's the amazing burger, which is made from prime meat enveloping a braise of a long-cooked so-called lesser cut of beef, giving you *the* most flavourful, juicy patty imaginable. This is served with wedges of chips and an almost bitter coriander aioli which perfectly foils the sweetness of the meat. Memorable. It's the lightness of the cooking we like, herb gnocchi, peas, broad beans, asparagus, sun-dried tomatoes and a pea velouté. The boys' favourite: roast free-range chicken with bread sauce. How good is that! Or make that roast sirloin with horseradish, or roast leg of lamb with mint, they will both be perfect too. Or the girls' favourite: passion fruit and coconut sorbet, sublime. Brunch here at the weekend is packed, and why wouldn't it be if you could go and get a North Donegal bacon sandwich with a glass of Mimosa. Pub food at its best. (Samuel Spain & Michael O'Connor, 33-35 Malone Road ☎ 028-9066 1885 ✉ barkingdogbelfast@ googlemail.com ✌ www.barkingdogbelfast.com – Open noon-10pm Mon-Thu, noon-11pm Fri, noon-11pm Sat, 11am-4pm Sun)

Bistro
● Beatrice Kennedy

Jim McCarthy's restaurant is beside Queen's University, and consequently is a popular place for graduation celebrations. So, just imagine you have tossed the mortar board in the air, have your scroll, and now it's time for carpaccio of scallops with crab meat, basil and black olive oil and pea cress, and then roasted rack of pork with porcini braised potatoes, sautéed spinach and salsa verde, and then a mille feuille of lemon mousse with rhubarb compote. And, of course, plenty of bubbly. Now, wasn't all that studying worth it just for this celebration? 'Course it was. (Jim McCarthy, 44 University Road ☎ 028-9020 2290 📠 reception@beatricekennedy.co.uk ⁑ www.beatricekennedy.co.uk – Open 5pm-10.15pm Tue-Sat, 12.30pm-2.30pm, 5pm-8.15pm Sun)

Belfast

Tea Room & Coffee & Tea Merchant
● SD Bells

Robert Bell's tea company is also a coffee roasting company, and a cute tea and coffee bar, so they cover all the bases when it comes to making life's vital drinks. Whilst best known for their teas, which are superb in terms of the care of sourcing and the skill of blending, their coffee expertise is just as capacious and considered, and you could spend a lifetime drinking Bell's products and enjoy a terrific range and variety of flavours. Today, Robert Bell is the fourth generation to head up this proud firm, for us one of the outstanding food companies not just in Northern Ireland, but on the island of Ireland. So, meet you in the Leaf & Berry bar at their headquarters on the Newtownards Road, it's your shout and mine's a pot of China White Monkey. (Robert Bell, 516 Newtownards Road ☎ 028-9047 1774 📠 sales@sdbellsteacoffee.com ⁑ www.sdbellsteacoffee.com – Open 8am-5pm Mon-Fri, 8.30am-2pm Sat)

Diner
● Bennett's on Belmont

Colleen Bennett's second restaurant, sister to Holywood's Fontana, is a hip room with a hip soundtrack and hip modern food. We really like it at breakfast when the food manages to ease you painlessly into the day ahead. (Colleen Bennett, 4-6 Belmont Road ☎ 028-9065 6590 – Open 8am-9pm Mon-Fri, 8am-10pm Fri & Sat, 8am-3pm Sun)

Mexican Fast Food
● Boojum

In Boojum you firstly choose your base, then choose what you want it to be filled with, then choose the salsa you want to top it with and you can add jalapenos, guacamole and various sides to the Mexican equation. It sounds like fast food, but it isn't and that's why there's a queue out the door. "We need one in every town in Ireland" said our friend Sile. Sile lives in Ennis. (73 Botanic Avenue ☎ 028-9031 5334 ⁘ www.boojummex. com – Open 11.30am-9pm Mon-Fri, noon-9pm Sat)

Belfast

Diner
● The Bo Tree

"In Belfast this place is hard to find in quality. The staff are brilliant. We had a big amount of food. There was chicken, rice, squid, prawns and many more. The desserts were ice cream, bananas, rice, custerd and many more. The food is brilliant. And I recommend it. 5 stars! :-)" So ran PJ's first review of The Bo Tree in Belfast, the restaurant that was the firm favourite of all the family during our trip up north. This is a beautiful Thai restaurant, all orchids, buddhas and goddesses with delicately carved furniture and leaf-shaped plates. The owners originate from the UK, and the restaurant has a sort of confident London chic that is hard to beat. We did indeed have a big amount of food: dumplings, skewered chicken, red duck curry, chicken and coriander with garlic, prawn green curry, vegetables in peanut sauce, squid and crisp-fried bean curd. The atmosphere is calm, the wine list is carefully thought out, and the dumplings, according to notable hair-stylist Patrick Mulholland, who first recommended it to us, are legendary. Now you know. (31 University Road, Belfast ☎ 028-9024 7722 ⁘ info@botreethai.com ⁘ www. botreethai.com – Open noon-2.30pm, 6pm-11pm Mon-Sat)

Café
● Cafe Nosh

"Thanks from Nosh for spending your dosh!" Well, thanks to Nosh for helping us spend our dosh in such a nice way in such a nice busy place. This is a thoughtful little eaterie – they have rugs to drape over your knees if you want to sit outside for instance – and their sandwiches and salads punch way above their weight, which is why everyone from solo eaters with laptops to families are all here. And here's a question: just what do you think they put in their "Honey, I'm home" sandwich. We'd love to tell you... (Phil & Emma Andrews, 64 Comber Road, Dundonald ☎ 028-9048 9199 ⁘ phil_ andrews@tiscali.co.uk ⁘ www.cafenosh.net – Open 8am-4.30pm Mon-Fri, 9.30am-4pm Sat)

Café & Pizzeria
● **Cafe Renoir**

A very popular pizzeria and restaurant is the format
on Botanic Avenue, whilst on Queen Street the food
offer is simpler, but has stood the test of time as they
edge towards two decades in business. Careful sourcing of good ingredients means that CR has a head start
when it comes to delivering food with true flavours and
textures. Friendly staff bring the whole offer together.
(Lindsay & Karen Loney, 95 Botanic Avenue ☎ 028-
9031 1300 ✉ info@cafe-renoir.com – Open 8am-10pm
Mon-Sat, 9am-10pm Sat. Also 5-7 Queen's Street, ☎ 028-
9032 5592 – Open 9am-5pm Mon-Sat, 'till 7pm Thu)

Café & Delicatessen
● **Cargoes**

Rhada Patterson's café is, according to our mate Ian,
"the place to meet, to enjoy their pancakes with a twist,
the best traybakes in Ireland, and lunches always served
with imaginative salads". Indeed, and add to this the fact
that Cargoes has been making these superb foods for
more than 16 years and you get some idea of how and
why Belfast food lovers will nominate Cargoes as one
of the most vital destinations in the city. Essential fine
foods, beautiful cooking, every day. (Rhada Patterson,
613 Lisburn Road ☎ 028-9066 5451 🖱 www.cargoes-
cafe.com – Open 9am-4.30pm Mon-Fri, 9am-5pm Sat,
10am-3pm Sun)

Restaurant
● **Cayenne**

One of these days we will go into Cayenne and order
something like roast peppered rump of venison with
potato and celeriac croquettes, or breast of duck au
poivre with mushroom risotto cakes. But not yet. We
find it too hard to resist heading east and choosing their
inimitable fusion food - and that's the reason we love
Cayenne so much. So of course we will order the black
cod miso with radish salad and pickled ginger slaw, or
the Thai fish cakes wrapped in crispy noodles with lime
mayo, or the blackened monkfish with roast aubergine,
indian rosti and spicy lemon dressing, or the roast
organic salmon with Szechuan pickled cucumber, sticky
rice and teriyaki sauce. It is interesting that Paul Rankin
has always been in Cayenne (though we wish there was
more sign of him in the kitchen). He has owned other

restaurants, but this space will always be identified with him and Jeanne, and only the Rankins. As a result this room is full of history, full of the personality of the Rankins. There is a special atmosphere here and everyone who comes in feels it. You feel you've made the smart choice just by going through the doors. Belfast citizens should feel proud of Cayenne. (Paul & Jeanne Rankin, 7 Ascot House, Shaftesbury Square ☎ 028-9033 1532 ☐ belinda@rankingroup.co.uk ⟡ www. rankingroup.co.uk – Open noon-2.15pm Tue-Fri, 5pm-late Sun-Fri, 6pm-late Sat)

Belfast

Kitchenware
● The Chef Shop

Vincent McKenna's shop has all the gear and kit you could ever need to cut the mustard in a pro kitchen, but he doesn't stop there, for Chef Shop also hosts cookery demos by leading chefs. (Vincent McKenna, Bruce House, 29 Bruce Street ☎ 028-9032 9200 ⟡ www. thechefshop.net – Open 9am-5.30pm Mon-Thu, 9am-5pm Fri & Sat)

Restaurant
● CoCo

There's a humour and confidence to CoCo that we really admire. It's a dressy-uppy sort of place with a mirror ball, and jazz playing in the background. You'd come here and drink Tattinger and laugh, and enjoy superb cooking to boot. Chef Jason More has some confidence, because he first took over the building that was Shanks, following on from the legendary Robbie Millar, and then took over the building that was Roscoff Brasserie, following on from the legendary Paul Rankin. Wow, that takes courage, but we suspect he just throws it off with the confidence of youth. So in this lovely room, with its pop art posters (you spend hours looking at them wondering is that Bruce Lee or Jimi Hendrix) and its spacious tables, you can love the seared quail with peas, fava beans, herb salad and red wine balsamic jus, wonder at the Massaman soup, a rich coconut broth with mushrooms, peanuts and coriander. If you choose it, you'll always remember the duck breast with parsnip purée, roast spuds and thyme jus, because duck is supposed to taste like that. You can also hugely admire the dish of veal, which is served almost like a pasta sauce, with cocotte potatoes instead of pasta, lovely fava beans just out of their pods, and braised chicory all served in a bowl with the veal on top. The staff are only brill, sharing in the good-natured humour of the place - and do note the poster which reads "This is not the toilet" is actually the entrance to the kitchen. (Jason More & Yvonne Gray, 7-11 Linenhall Street, Belfast ☎ 028-9031 1150 🕮 www.cocobelfast.co.uk – Open noon-3pm Mon-Fri, 6pm-late Mon-Sat, noon-4pm Sun)

Butcher
● Coffey's

Philip Armstrong's shop is as top notch as Northern Irish charcuterie gets and Northern Irish charcuterie is the top notch. The staff exhibit seemingly effortless creative abilities and are always riffing on new ideas with sausages and prepared dishes. A Lisburn Road icon. (Philip Armstrong, 380 Lisburn Road ☎ 028-9066 6292 – Open 8am-5.45pm Mon-Fri, 8am-6pm Sat)

Café/bar
● Conor Cafe Bar

"On Sunday afternoon we ate in Conor's on Stranmillis Road just opposite the entrance to the Botanic Gardens – perfect after a stroll around the Rose Garden there (or the Palm House or the Tropical Ravine). Lovely airy room, friendly welcoming staff, and we both had delicious duck. Very good coffee afterwards too." That's our mate Sile strolling around leafy Belfast with her mate Conor, which may explain why Conor and Sile wound up in Conor café. They chose well: this is a lovely spot, whether you are having the soda bread, bacon, sausage and egg breakfast, or some lipsmacking crispy pork belly with bubble & squeak and a touch of cider cream. Manus and William also operate Greens pizzeria on the Lisburn Road, opposite Marlborough Park. (Manus McConn & William Clarke, 11a Stranmillis Road ☎ 028-9066 3266 🖰 www.cafeconor.com – Open 9am-11pm Mon-Sun)

Deli & Restaurant
● Deane's Deli

For many food lovers, the Deli is their favourite of Michael Deane's various addresses. Chef Stephen Alexander has been firing out red-hot cooking here for the last while, and you can't argue with the confident deliciousness of Lough Earn lamb with barley and vegetable broth or Walter's smoked salmon with pea and potato cake. If there is a risotto on the day's blackboard then it has your name on it. The room has a sublime ambience, and it's a great destination (Michael Deane, 44 Bedford Street ☎ 028-9024 8800 ⁀ www.michaeldeane.co.uk – Open 11.30am-3pm, 5.30pm-9pm Mon-Fri, 'till 10pm Thur, 11.30am-10pm Sat)

Restaurant
● Restaurant Michael Deane

"Rigorous thinking-through of ideas, with nothing on the plate superfluous to flavour or composition", wrote Sally McKenna after dinner at Michael Deane's restaurant in central Belfast. Those are exactly the chef's gifts: Mr Deane is always chasing a purity that encompasses the idea of the dish and then its execution, whether he is cooking a risotto of courgette flower, making a rich foie gras and chicken liver parfait, or triple-cooking chips. Ally this to sheer hard work and you get some idea of how Mr Deane has built up a chain of successful restaurants in the city. In the restaurant, the modern menu archetypes – pork belly with langoustine; confit of lamb with sauce niçoise; poached, roasted and braised beef; halibut with pea shoot salad – are shown dextrous skill and a classic imagination. A new Seafood Bar is opening on Howard Street as we write and, out of town, Mr Deane has opened Simply Deane's at The Outlet in Banbridge. which has yet to acquire the standards that characterise the Belfast addresses. (Michael Deane, 36-40 Howard Street ☎ 028-9033 1134 ✉ info@ michaeldeane.co.uk ⁀ www.michaeldeane.co.uk – Open noon-3pm, 5.30pm-10pm Mon-Sat)

Brasserie
● Deane's at Queens

A really slick room is home to Michael Deane's take on slightly more informal food, though don't imagine that it's any sort of studenty fare just because it's in the university zone: the cooking is cool, measured and fun. (Michael Deane, 1 College Garden, Belfast ☎ 028-9038 2111 ✉ info@michaeldeane.co.uk ⁀ www. michaeldeane.co.uk– Open 11.30am-9pm Mon-Tue, 11.30am-10pm Wed-Sat)

only in Ulster
Scullion's Ale

Wine Merchant
● Direct Wine Shipments

So, the McAlindon boys are presenting some of their superb wines at a Bridgestone dinner in Belfast, and chatting away with John McKenna, when the trio discover that they are all... Joy Division fans! So, Peter and Neal are superb wine merchants, and guys who know all the riffs and lyrics to "Unknown Pleasures" and "Closer". But even if your heart is closer to Wham! than 1980's Manchester, these guys will still get you sorted for the right bottle, and do ask about their own wines from Spain, Capenela and Creu Celta, from their own vineyards. Their wine educational classes in DWS are particularly compelling. (Peter & Neal McAlindon, 5-7 Corporation Square ☎ 028-9050 8000 ✉ shop@directwine.co.uk ⌨ www.directwineshipments.com – Open 9.30am-7pm Mon-Fri, 9.30am-8pm Thu, 9.30am-5.30pm Sat)

Accommodation and Brasserie
● Dukes at Queens

The former Duke's Hotel has been buffed up and turned into Dukes at Queens. "We were blown away by the welcome at reception" said our mate Sile, "genuine smiles, genuine interest in welcoming us to Belfast, nothing was too much trouble. The room was very comfortable, great bed, good linen, spotless. The bathroom had a big bath and a really good shower." A little more work on the breakfast offer could see D@Q emerge as a really significant player in Belfast's hotel culture. (65-67 University Street, Belfast ☎ 028-9023 7177 ⌨ www.dukesatqueens.com)

Kitchenshop & Café
● Equinox

Can you believe that Kay Gilbert's Equinox has been bringing the icons of the design world to Belfast for a full twenty-five years now? It seems incredible to imagine that a shop so focused and so knowing could have existed in Belfast back in the mid eighties, and it seems equally incredible that Equinox has remained the most stylish shop in the city despite many new arrivals over the last fifteen years. Ms Gilbert's secret has been to always focus on what she knows and is confident about delivering, whether it's the simple food in the café or finding the perfect pair of bedroom slippers. (Kay Gilbert, 32 Howard Street ☎ 028-9023 0089 ✉ contact@

equinoxshop.com ⁀🖰 www.equinoxshop.com – Shop open 9.30am-5.30pm Mon-Sat, 8.30am-9pm Thur, Cafe open 9.30am-4pm Mon-Fri, 9.30am-4.30pm Sat)

Belfast

Fishmonger
● **Walter Ewing**

There will be a big party on the Shankill Road in 2011 when Walter Ewing's peerless fish shop will celebrate a century of selling the best fish you can buy. One of the easy things about being a chef in Northern Ireland is that you don't have to decide which fishmonger to work with: Walter Ewing is the man, whether you are looking for his own smoked salmon, or just the best wet fish delivered each day. Even if you aren't a chef, and are just a culinary civilian, Ewing's is still your first port of call. (Walter Ewing, 124 Shankill Road ☎ 028-9032 5534 🖰 ewings.seafoods@btconnect.com – Open 9am-5pm Tue-Sat)

Hotel
● **The Fitzwilliam Hotel**

Notable for the involvement of superstar chef Kevin Thornton in its Menu restaurant, and Mr Thornton has brought some of his signature dishes up from Dublin – bacon and cabbage terrine with leek purée; duck braised in Calvados with Savoy cabbage – to a menu that is otherwise quite straight-ahead: crab cakes with coriander and sesame dressing; rib-eye steak with gratin dauphinoise; lamb shank with mashed potato. Still very early days for this sister hotel to Dublin's Fitzwilliam. (June Burgess, Great Victoria Street, Belfast ☎ 028-9044 2080 🖰 enq@fitzwilliamhotelbelfast. com ⁀🖰 www.fitzwilliamhotelbelfast.com – Open 7am-10.30pm Mon-Fri 7am-11.30pm Sat & Sun)

Take Away and Restaurant
● **Gaze**

The problem in Gaze is simply deciding what to order: do you go for Hong Kong metropolitan, Malaysian, Japanese, Korean or Japanese? Most people agree you should start with their famous duck kimchi, and then take it from there. There are only four tables, which you share, and you bring your own wine, but many more people use their services as a takeaway, so the atmosphere of the place is a little frantic. But along with their great chipper institutions, Belfast do these pan-Asian restaurants really well. There is a very well-established Asian community in the north, and it has blessed the country with some splendid cooking, and Gaze is more of the same. (415 Ormeau Road, ☎ 028-9069 4293)

Market
● St George's Saturday Market

So, Jakki Owens goes to the Saturday Market, and what's new? "Lavender Cupcakes by Alison Kane – look wonderful and taste fabulous. Delicious foods by Ann Keane: chick pea cakes, salmon cakes and fantastic wheaten bread. Magael McLaoughlin has been here since February with chicken liver paté that is from her mum's recipe and is absolutely delicious. Barnhill apples were selling bunches of dahlias at £2 per bunch and they were flying off the stall. And Love Olive had wonderful tapenades and they have great staff." So that's just a few of this year's new arrivals joining superstars like Trevor and Irene Barclay, Ann Stone, SD Bell's, the Mullen family, and all the rest of the eclectic bunch who have made the St George's Saturday market into one of the two or three best markets in the entire country. "Packed and buzzing as usual" says Jakki. As we expected. (4-10 Linenhall Street, Belfast ☎ 028-9032 0202 – Open Saturday, 9am-3pm)

Market
● St George's Street Friday Market

Don't imagine that the Friday market in Belfast is simply home to bric-a-brac and whatnots, because a lot of the principal traders, especially the fish merchants do their major work in the market on Fridays rather than Saturdays. The weekday market is less festive and more serious than Saturday's, but it's still a mighty panjandrum of great food, and that raucous Belfast wit which is the lingua franca of the marketeers. (Linenhall Street, Belfast ☎ 028-9032 0202 – Open 6am-1pm Fri)

Restaurant
● Ginger Bistro

Simon McCance is the ideal Bridgestone chef. He does things in an entirely individual way. Everything that comes out of the kitchen has his signature style of sharp flavours, accessible textures and a handsome visage. His room is unpretentious, his choice of music is excellent, he offers great value for money, and there is no non-

sense to him and to Ginger Bistro. That's what we like
at Bridgestone Central. That's what we would call "fine
dining". If you want "fine dining", then first get rid of
the tablecloths, and write your menu with expressions
such as "dauphinoise on the side", or "fish and chip shop
haddock" or "home cut fat chips", and confine your wine
list to one line descriptions of the wines, such as "low
yields and hand-harvested". Mr McCance does all of
those things, which is why Ginger is one of Belfast's best
restaurants, and why this bistro offers one of the most
satisfying experiences you can enjoy anywhere. (Simon
McCance, 68-72 Great Victoria Street ☎ 028-9024 4421
⌁ www.gingerbistro.com – Open noon-3pm, 5pm-10pm
Tue-Sat)

Belfast

Restaurant
● The Ginger Tree

Chef Shotaro Obana is from Osaka, which is what you
need to know about the authentic nature of the food
in the Ginger Tree. If the almost austere nature of true
Japanese cooking rings your bell then this is your one
and only destination. (Shotaro Obana, 23 Donegall Pass
☎ 028-9032 7151 – Open noon-2.30pm Mon-Sat, 5pm-
9.30pm Sun-Thur, 5pm-10.30pm Fri & Sat)

Bistro
● Gourmet Burger Bank

Bring the kids, who can do spectacular collapses of
Jenga bricks on the tables, enjoy the Banksy posters,
the blackboard wine list. Sit in the banquette booths
with their characterful café-style salt, pepper, sugar
tableware, and it'll be venison burger with brie, onion
rings, rocket and cranberry for Sally, bacon and cheese
for Sam and PJ, goats' cheese, avocado, sun-dried
tomato for Phoebe, chicken burger with herb pesto for
Portia, falafels for Connie and bacon and brie burger
with avocado for Belinda. Yum. (Samuel Spain, 20-22
Belmont Road, ☎ 028-9047 3333 – Open 11am-10pm
Mon-Fri, 9am-10pm Sat, 9am-9pm Sun)

Restaurant
● Hill Street Brasserie

How long does it take before you can describe something as "retro"? Definitely anywhere in Belfast that
serves salt and chilli squid and slow roast belly of pork –
two foods that have dominated the Belfast scene for

the last decade – is in danger of this description. And Hill Street Brasserie somehow has a turn of the century retro feel to both the design (black floppy rubber place mats - SO eighties – brown leather banquettes, black lacquer tables, and the food – goat's cheese bruschetta, bread, oil and tapenade, lime crème fraîche with grilled salmon. Of course, there's the open kitchen, the Chilean sauvignon blanc, the jazz compilation CD that plays John Coltrane one minute, Keith Jarrett the next. The thing about retro though, is it becomes retro because it's classic, and even though it may not be original, Hill Street Brasserie certainly knows how to interpret the zeitgeist. This is a good space with zappy tasty foods. (Harry Readman, 38 Hill Street, Belfast ☎ 028-9058 6868 ✉ info@hillstbrasserie.com ⁷ www.hillstbrasserie.com – Open noon-2.30pm Mon-Sat, 5pm-close Tue-Sun)

Restaurant
● James Street South

The cooking in JSS is daringly pure, with firecracker flavours illuminating the drama. Purity is found in a crab salad with a pomegranate dressing. Then comes the firecracker stuff: a bone marrow gratin - served in a piece of bone! - as part of a dish of Antrim beef. Or the rocket tortellini served with wood pigeon. Or a vivacious carpaccio of pineapple served with a perfect blueberry jelly. JSS is the restaurant in which to stray as wild as your courage will allow. If you choose loin of lamb or breast of duck, you will have a good meal, but you won't be rewarded with the dynamic flavours that you will get from Crossgar wood pigeon, or saddle of rabbit. The sourcing of the food is exemplary, from the pea shoots in the salad to the marvellous wine list. But, even though there are firecracker tastes, subtlety and purity win out. The flavours you will remember will be things like the taste of new asparagus, or a stringent olive oil - foods that usually stay in the background. Niall McKenna is a cook who gets excited by ingredients, so in JSS go for the wild stuff. (Niall McKenna, 21 James Street South ☎ 028-9043 4310 ✉ info@jamesstreetsouth. co.uk ⁷ www.jamesstreetsouth.co.uk – Open noon-2.45pm, 5.45pm-10.45pm Mon-Sat, 5.30pm-9pm Sun)

Fish and Chips
● John Dory's

If you think making perfect fish and chips is a simple matter, just talk to Mark and Stephen Polley about the lengths they go to in order to ensure that your fish dinner is truly epicurean. They source 90% of their potatoes from southern England to get the perfect chip, as they find that Irish potatoes cannot deliver the levels of consistency through the seasons that they want to achieve. They are also addressing the question of fish sustainability by using varieties such as basa and pollock in addition to the traditional favourites. The upshot of this level of care is pretty perfect fish and chips as the McKenna family can testify from the last time they visited Holywood Road and enjoyed fantastic fish and fantastic chips. (Mark & Stephen Polley, 220-230 Holywood Road, Belfast ☎ 028-9047 3535. Also at 1a Ballygowan Road, Belfast ☎ 028-9040 1674. Also at Carryduff Shopping Centre, Church Road, Carryduff, Co Antrim ☎ 028-9081 4595. Also at King's Square Shopping Centre, King's Road, Belfast ☎ 028-9079 9914 – Open 9am-10pm Mon-Sat, 1pm-9pm Sun ⌂ info@johndorys. co.uk ⌂ www.johndorys.co.uk)

only in Ulster
The Asia Supermarket

Gastropub
● The John Hewitt

Ten happy years serving proper grub and good ales, such as the Whitewater Brewery's Belfast lager, and the John Hewitt sails socialistically on. Quite how they do such proper food at such knockdown prices, we just don't know, but whether you are having a bowl of chowder for £3.95 or the steak and Belfast ale pie with mashed root veg at £7.25, what matters is the quality not the cost. Awesomely cool. (51 Donegall Street ☎ 028-9023 3768 ⌂ www.thejohnhewitt.com – Food served noon-2pm Mon-Sat)

Home Bakery
● June's Cake Shop

June's is brilliant. Simple as that. That's all you need to know, for what they do here is to bake and cook the Ulster classics such as fadge, soda bread, Xmas cakes and chocolate fudge cake that sustained your mammy and her mammy before her. Nice food to go at lunchtime. (Loraine Hindley, 376 Lisburn Road ☎ 028-9066 8886 – Open 7.30am-5.30pm Mon-Sat)

Restaurant
● Macau

The good things about Macau are Sue Ling's friendly
service, the fact that you can bring your own wine and,
best of all, the scallion and ginger oil they serve as a little
appetiser with prawn crackers before the meal starts. You
can order slightly more unusual dishes here, like scallops
in their shell and various hot pots. (Sue Ling, 271 Ormeau
Road ☎ 028-9069 1800 – Open 5.30pm-10pm Tue-Sun)

Hotel
● Made in Belfast

Rustic gastro-cookery is how they describe their
ambitions in MIB. They could also add "we are almost
impossibly hip" to that CV, for this has been the
tumultuous success in Belfast over the last year. Emma
Bricknell's restolounge, with Gerry O'Kane in the
kitchen, is shabby chic and campishly theatrical – the
Eddie Izzard of Belfast eating. And whilst it's extra
wacky, it's terrific fun, and the food is real. The burgers
come on a wooden board, soup comes in a jar, and the
chips come in an enamel mug, and the cutlery is rather
blunt. Do you care? Not a bit. (Emma Bricknell, 1 & 2
Wellington Buildings, Wellington Street, Belfast ☎ 028-
9024 6712 ☐ emma@madeinbelfastni.com ☐ www.
madeinbelfastni.com – Open noon-8pm Mon-Tue, noon-
10.30pm Fri & Sat, noon-9pm Sun & Wed-Thu)

Hotel
● Malmaison

Part of the UK chain which specialises in theatrical decor and dimly lit bars and restaurants. Fantastic location
means it is one of the best destinations in the city, and
we would love it even more if they wouldn't play Radio 2
at breakfast-time. (34-38 Victoria Street, Belfast ☎ 028-
9022 0200 ☐ www.malmaison.com)

Butcher
● Thomas McCreery's Butchers

A typically classy Belfast butchery, which is notable not
just for very fine meats but also for the very tasty take-
away foods that attract droves of lunchtime and evening-
time eaters to the shop. (Nigel McCreery, 439 Ormeau
Road ☎ 028-9064 4911 – Open 7.45am-5.45pm Mon-Fri,
6.45am-5.45pm Sat)

Butcher
● McGee's Butchers

"It's the sandy loam soil, full of clover and buttercup, and the soft mizzly rain that gives the grass, and our meat, their sweetness." Joe McGee knows that good beef and lamb starts with first principles and that above all else beef needs grass. The lush Tyrone pastures produce superb quality meat that McGee's carefully mind all the way down the line, with careful slaughtering, hip hanging and dry aging. (Joe McGee, Forestside Shopping Centre ☎ 028-9064 8885 ✉ mail@mcgeesfood.com ⏏ www.mcgeesfood.com – Open 9am-6pm Mon-Wed, 9am-8pm Thu & Fri, 8am-7pm Sat, noon-6pm Sun. Also at Bloomfield, Bangor ☎ 028-9145 5463; Asda Westwood, Belfast ☎ 028-9060 3644; Quarry Lane, Dungannon ☎ 028-8772 6620; Ards Shopping Centre, Newtownards)

Butcher
● Owen McMahon Butchers

McMahons are famed for producing especially fine sausages, amongst the best you can buy in Belfast. (Owen McMahon, 3-5 Atlantic Avenue ☎ 028-9074 3535 ✉ owen@owenmcmahon.com ⏏ www.owenmcmahon.com – Open 8.30am-6pm Mon-Sat)

Restaurant
● Me:nu

Sandy and Gerard worked with all the contemporary local masters – Deane's, Cayenne, Shanks – before taking the plunge and opening Me:nu. They like the sort of unmediated, up-front flavours that match the colourful room – salt and pepper squid with shaved fennel salad; wok-fried seafood hotpot with Asian greens and jasmine rice; saddleback pork belly with celeriac and cauliflower purée; sirloin burger with smoked bacon and cheddar. Typical of their thoughtfulness is a fine vegetarian menu, a nice gesture in a restaurant that concentrates on meat and seafood – potato gnocchi with truffled leeks and wild mushrooms; polenta crouton with sweet potato, peperonata and black olives; broad bean risotto with black olive oil croutons and Parmesan. Lots of character and very promising. (Sandy Plumb & Gerard Donnelly 15-17 Donegall Pass, Belfast ☎ 028-9024 4257 ⏏ www.menubelfast.co.uk – Open noon-2.30pm, 5pm-10pm Tue-Fri, 5pm-10pm Sat, 5pm-9.30pm Sun)

● Molly's Yard

With the beers of the College Green Brewery – Headless Dog; Molly's Chocolate Stout and Belfast Blonde – as an irresistible calling-card, Molly's Yard then turns up the local quotient as high as it can, with a menu that includes Finnebrogue venison; mussels in Belfast Blonde lager; duck with Bellingham Blue dressing; Ulster fadge with smoked salmon; Ditty's oatcakes; chocolate stout soda bread and chocolate stout ice cream. (Siobhan Scullion, 1 College Green Mews, Botanic Avenue, Belfast ☎ 028-9032 2600 – Open noon-9pm Mon-Thu, noon-9.30pm Fri & Sat)

Seafood Bar & Fish Shop
● Mourne Seafood Bar

"A lunch at the Mourne Seafood Bar, which I thought was just terrific all around", reports the great American writer Colman Andrews. And "terrific all around" is pretty much what everyone who gets up close and personal to Andy Rea's smashing cooking says. They have done things quietly in The Mourne, and Mr Rea, unlike other Belfast chefs, is a quiet, retiring kind of guy. But their sure and steady pace has meant that the food has fallen perfectly into place, exhibiting signature style, and, in particular, a signature succulence – curried cream with baked gurnard – one of our favourite fish; punchy chorizo and cannellini beans served with monkfish; clean, sweet tomato and prawn vinaigrette with grilled fillets of sole; the particularly brilliant match of skordalia and frizzled leeks with organic salmon. Served in a glitzier place, this dramatic cooking would be fêted by the media, but Mr Rea is his own man, and works his own way. (Andy Rea, 34-36 Bank Street, Belfast ☎ 028-9024 8544 – Open 1pm-6pm Sun, noon-6pm Mon, noon-9.30pm Tue-Thur, noon-4pm, 5pm-10.30pm Fri & Sat)

Butcher
● Murphy's Butchers

Murphy's has the reputation as the butcher's shop that locals at the top of the Lisburn Road use, and certainly the excellent service and the personal touch from the staff would bring anybody back here. Well hung beef and exceptionally good barbecue food make Murphy's well worth a detour. (400 Lisburn Road ☎ 028-9068 2442)

Restaurant
● Nick's Warehouse

Kathy Price is an Arsenal football club fan. Which has to make Nick Price the Arsene Wenger of the kitchen. How so? Simple. He motivates somewhat unlikely players to over-deliver for him: many great chefs have learnt under Nick and then gone their own way, for he is a fine teacher. He gets results: this is one hell of a busy restaurant. He is unclichéd: just look at the way he writes his wine lists: funny, expressive, truly explanatory, the product of serious study and work. And he is a true intellectual, in that he is a cultured man with a sense of humour and a sense of proportion, and he supports the good causes: Slow Food; A Taste of Ulster. Above all, he has that rare gift of making something special, truly memorable. Recently, travelling on the Dublin-Cork train, we chatted with a lady who hadn't lived in the North for many, many years. What did she remember most about her time there? The cooking at Daft Eddie's in Sketrick, when Nick and Kathy Price ran the kitchens. Thirty years ago, and just yesterday. (Nick & Kathy Price, 35-39 Hill Street ☎ 028-9043 9690 📠 info@nickswarehouse.co.uk 🖰 www.nickswarehouse.co.uk – Open noon-3pm, 6pm-10pm Tue-Sat Anix. Upstairs restaruant open noon-3pm)

Wine Merchant
● Nick's Wines

This isn't the only wine company that Nick Price is involved in, for he is also a player in Harry's Road wines. Nick's list is choice, described in grown-up witty language, and anything we have ever drunk from it has been a real cracker. (Nick Price, 35-39 Hill Street ☎ 028-9043 9690 📠 info@nickswarehouse.co.uk 🖰 www.nickswarehouse.co.uk)

Restaurant
● Number 27

No 27 is a party place. We first discovered it after Granny graduated with merit on her course, and we called in for a late night glass of Cava. We returned the next day with the kids and sat between a twenty-first birthday crowd and a hen party – it's the sort of place where you need to GHD your hair before you visit. The food is as fun as the room, char-grilled ribeye, home-cut chips, baby spinach, green peppercorn cream, Taleggio, Stilton, and smoked Gubbeen tart with broccoli, herb salad and grilled potatoes, roasted rump of lamb, braised sherry lentils, cauliflower purée, chantenay carrots, rosemary jus. Adrian Lowry has the staff pumped up and motivated, and the place buzzes. (Adrian Lowry, 27 Talbot Street ☎ 028-9031 2884 ⌁ www.no27.co.uk – Open noon-3pm Mon-Fri, 6p-10pm Tue-Sat. Bar menu 3pm-6pm Mon-Fri)

Delitcatessen & Café
● Olive Tree Company

Downstairs you buy all the choice Mediterranean palette of ingredients that will bring zing to your culinary thing – pesto, Lombardi peppers, Kalamata olives, marinated artichokes – and upstairs you can enjoy the all-day breakfast and some very choice and rustic soups, salads and pasta specials. A particularly friendly place. (Conor McCann, 353 Ormeau Road ☎ 028-9064 8898 – Open 8.30am-5.15pm Mon-Sat)

Coffee and Sandwich Bar
● Rowallane Garden Kitchen

David Semple made a mighty reputation when he was cooking in Espresso Soul in Belfast's Gasworks and he has brought this expertise to the more tranquil set-ting of this beautiful National Trust garden. Using the ceramic pots from on-site potter Matthew Liddle, David creates soups and sandwiches, quiches and home-made pasta lasagnes, plus specials like mutton stew using the meat from Churchtown Organics, or wheaten bread made in flower pots. "I'm really mucking around," he says "it's fantastic to be here." (David Semple, Saintfield ☎ 028-9751 0131 – Open noon-4pm Wed-Sun during winter, 10am-5pm Mon-Sun during summer)

Chinese Canteen
● Same Happy

We spend our time in Belfast looking for, and quizzing our sources about exactly who is firing out the most authentic ethnic cooking at any given time. The answer usually is that it's somewhere different than the place that was red hot just six months ago, so the search is never ending but full of fun. And that's how we wound up at this little canteen where the staff smile all the time they are serving, and where John McKenna had the spicy chicken feet, and the seasoned jellyfish with marinated pork knuckle, and his children didn't. What they had was char siu and chicken noodles in broth tossed noodles and soup noodles, whilst Sally had the Peking-style beef shin. We all shared spring rolls. For our money, the most echt Chinese cooking in Belfast – for now... (Eric Cong, 40b Donegall Pass, Belfast ☎ 028-9031 0507 – Open noon-8.30pm Sun-Fri. Closed Sat)

Belfast

Delicatessen
● Sawyer's Deli

John McKenna can remember shopping in Sawyer's after taking a bus trip down the Falls Road from Andersonstown almost fifty years ago. Almost fifty years later and Sawyer's do their inimitable thing, packing this tiny store with all the good stuff they can get their hands on and serving it in a quiet and professional manner. (Kieran Sloan, Fountain Centre ☎ 028-9032 2021 – Open 9am-5.30pm Mon-Sat)

Restaurant
● Shu

The food in Shu is intense, and the customers apply an equal intensity in their determination to enjoy it. You might have seen similar dishes on other menus but, in Shu, everything tastes as if chef Brian McCann has said – this is MY version. There are layers of flavours here so, whilst a crispy piece of pork, rolled tight, then sliced and grilled to melt-in-the-mouth tenderness, will be the centre-piece, it will be the sublime cauliflower purée – so light! – or the yellow raisins steeped in cider, that you will remember. Mains are book-ended with snappy, taste-loaded starters and desserts, and complemented with the side dishes: salt'n'chilli squid pairs crispy squid with three dips, wasabi mayo, chilli sauce and a ginger, spring onion and soy dip. Risotto of asparagus is pea green in colour and chlorophyll-charged with flavour. Newly in-season strawberries with vanilla ice cream is a celebration of a dessert. A great place, and a great cook. (Alan Reid, 253 Lisburn Road ☎ 028-9038 1655 📧 eat@shu-restaurant.com 🖱 www.shu-restaurant.com – Open noon-2.30pm, 6pm-10pm. Two sittings on Fri & Sat, 7pm & 9.30pm)

Shop & Café
● Smyth & Gibson

Richard Gibson does things right, whether he's making a custom-grade shirt, which you can buy in the S&G shop on the ground floor, or brewing a cup of coffee, which you can buy in the S&G café on the first floor. S&G is really popular with lawyers – they make specialist barrister's shirts – and who also like the good simple lunches and the vital hit of an espresso to get you through the afternoon. (Richard Gibson, Bedford House, Bedford Street ☎ 028-9023 0388 ✉ info@smythandgibson.com ✌ www.smythandgibson.com – Open 7.30am-5.30pm Mon-Fri 10am-5pm Sat)

Kitchenware & Homeware
● Still

Whether you want a Normann collapsible strainer or one of Nigella's baby blue lemon squeezers, Still is the store that has them all. Just remember you have to repay that VISA bill at the end of the month. (Maurice & Sharon Rankin, Royston House, 34 Upper Queen Street ☎ 028-9023 0494 ✉ info@stillforlife.com ✌ www.stillforlife.com – Open 9.30am-5.30pm Mon-Sat, 9.30am-8pm Thur)

Restaurant
● Sun Kee

Some restaurant relationships get so passionate that when the object of your affection ups and moves across the street and gets all posh on you, you get really miffed and find it very hard to forgive them. Well, forgive us, but we can't forgive the Sun Kee from upping and moving across the street and getting all posh, thereby renouncing the wonderful canteen-style ambience and service that made it the hottest place to eat in Belfast in the 1990s. It's still a fine Chinese restaurant, and the cooking is good. But we're just jilted lovers, so don't mind us. (The Lo family, 42-47 Donegall Pass ☎ 028-9031 2016 – Open noon-11.30pm Mon-Sun)

Café
● Swanton's Gourmet Foods

Gloria and Stewart Swanton bring an exacting eye to everything in their deli, whether it's what they place on the shelf or place in the oven to serve from breakfast through to lunch. The quality of the baking in particular is just as fine as you would expect in Belfast, and they complete the offer with good gifts and choice hampers. (Stewart & Gloria Swanton, 639 Lisburn Road ☎ 028-9068 3388 ✉ swantons@aol.com ✌ www.swantons.com – Open 9am-5pm Mon-Sat)

Sandwich Bar
● Tang Sandwich Excellence

Tang do the classic sandwiches right, BLT, pastrami with caramelised onion, egg and spring onion, but they also like to do some funky stuff such as Bang Bang chicken with spicy peanut sauce, or tuna with coriander lemon and crispy cos lettuce. Eat in, or take away is up to you. (Libby McCartney, 246 Ormeau Road ☎ 028-9066 4451 ⌨ tang.com@amserve.net – Open 8am-3pm Mon-Fri, 9.30am-4pm Sat)

Restaurant
● Tedfords

Alan Foster's restaurant is modest, a modest premises, a modest proprietor, which explains why it gets so much less attention than the headline hitting names in Belfast. But this is a professional, comfortable restaurant and the level of detail in the sourcing and cooking of the food is always impressive: Dundrum mussels with garlic and chive cream, Angus Sirloin with triple-cooked chips, cod in filo with horseradish mash and roast beans, an all-Irish cheeseboard with Ditty's oatcakes. Quietly impressive. (Alan Foster, 5 Donegall Quay ☎ 028-9043 4000 ⌨ www.tedfordsrestaurant.com – Open noon-2.30pm Wed-Fri, 5pm-late Tue-Sat)

Noodle Bar
● Thai-tanic Noodle Bar

"Every Thai is interested in food. Because we believe that life should be *Sanuk*, or fun, the pleasures of eating are very important to us." That's how Vatcharin Bhumichitr introduced Thai cooking in his book *The Taste of Thailand*. In Thai-tanic they really know what *Sanuk* is all about. So turn up here for beautiful chiang mai, or pattaya paradise or Samui island noodles. Everything is lovely and relaxed and informal, and yes, *Sanuk*. (Thanidtha & Joseph Allen, 2 Eglantine Avenue ☎ 028-9066 8811 ⌨ www.thai-tanic.com – Open 5pm-11pm Tue-Sun)

Wine Shop
● The Vineyard

Tony McGurran's shop has been selling good drinks to the people of Belfast for far more than fifty years now, so there's nothing they don't know about good wines and, in particular, spirits. The range of hootches available here is genuinely amazing. (Tony McGurran, 375-377 Ormeau Road ☎ 028-9064 5774 🖅 info@vineyardbelfast.co.uk 🖰 www.vineyardbelfast.co.uk – Open 9.30am-10pm Mon-Thu, 9.30am-11pm Fri & Sat, 11.30am-9pm Sun)

Delicatessen
● The Yellow Door

"When I opened the Yellow Door deli fifteen years ago, the whole idea was to provide customers with the food I like to eat every day" Simon Dougan told *The Irish Times* in 2009. "Not stuffy, not overly lavish, just gutsy, flavoursome, honest food – proper patés, delicate desserts with buttery pastry, and, of course, really good bread." Mission accomplished then, Simon. And accomplished every day of the week. (Simon Dougan, 427 Lisburn Road ☎ 028-9038 1961 🖅 info@yellowdoordeli.co.uk 🖰 www.yellowdoordeli.co.uk – Open 8am-5pm Mon-Sat)

Restaurant
● Zen Japanese Restaurant

There is more than just Japanese dishes on offer in the Zen, so if you really want to get close to the real thing try their Bento boxes. They have three types of boxes, in silver, gold and platinum standards where you can enjoy sashimi moriwase, chicken tempura, Japanese spring roll, diced steak ninhonjin style. Zen is a very stylish series of rooms and they make a feature of being particularly child-friendly. (Eddie Fung, 55-59 Adelaide Street ☎ 028-9023 2244 – Open noon-3pm, 5pm-late Mon-Fri, 5.30pm-late pm Sat, 1.30pm-10pm Sun)

Restaurant
● Zen Two

This is the modern fusion-style Japanese food offspring of the city centre Zen. They use the traditional Robata Charcoal Grill, but the food is anything but traditional: roasted duck samosa, soft shell angry crab with curry leaf, shredded duck, Japanese-style, lemon sole with ponzu sauce. There are some Thai dishes as well as Hong-Kong influenced food, so don't expect purist Japa-nese austerity. And the room itself is more glam than zen. (Eddie Fung, 92-94 Lisburn Road ☎ 028-9068 7318 🖰 www.zenbelfast.co.uk – Open noon-2pm, 5pm-late Mon-Sat, 1.30pm-9pm Sun)

County Antrim

Ballycastle

Fishmonger and Fish and Chip Shop
● **Morton's**

Morton's is a popular local store with good wet fish.
(Patrick McLernon, 22 Bayview Road, Ballycastle ☎ 028-
2076 2348 – Open 10am-5pm Thu & Fri. Closed 1pm-
2pm. Open other days during July & Aug)

Butcher
● **Wysner Meats**

Heading toward half a century of superbly prepared
charcuterie, and everything in Wysner's isn't a whole lot
different from the way it was in 1962 when they opened
their doors. The ethos of a hands-on family enterprise is
triumphantly evident, both in the shop and in the adjoin-
ing café. (18 Ann Street, Ballycastle ☎ 028-2076 2372
– Open 8am-5pm, Mon-Sat. Closed Wed. Cafe opens
9am-3pm Mon-Sat, 7pm-8.30pm Fri & Sat)

only in Ulster
Yellowman

Ballyclare

Organic Farm Shop
● **Ballylagan Organic Farm**

Tom Gilbert is in every sense a pioneer. He was the first
certified organic grower in county Antrim, the first to
open a farm shop, and he is that very rare fish indeed, a
man with an interesting farm website. Like the very best
philosopher farmers, Mr Gilbert sells you not only the
fruits of agriculture, but the culture of agriculture. (Tom
Gilbert, 12 Ballylagan Road, Straid, Ballyclare ☎ 028-
9332 2867 🖭 ballylagan@aol.com 🖰 www.ballylagan.
com – Open 9.30am-5pm Wed & Sat, 9.30am-6.30pm
Thu-Fri)

Antrim

● Errol Jenkins Butchers

Errol Jenkins is one of the original members of Northern Ireland's Elite Butchers Association, and shares the exemplary charcuterie skills and standards of his colleagues in the Guild. (Errol Jenkins, 41 Main Street, Ballyclare ☎ 028-9334 1822 – Open 8am-6pm Mon-Sat)

Ballymena

Artisan Cheese
● Causeway Cheese Company

Damian and Susan McCloskey have been making their hexagonal-shaped cheeses in a range of five styles since 2001. Three of the cheeses are flavoured, including Coolkeeran which is flavoured with dulse and in addition to the original Drumkeel there is a goat's milk cheese Ballyveely and Castlequarter, a cheddar-type cheese that can be matured for up to 18 months. (Damian & Susan McCloskey, Loughgiel Millennium Centre, Lough Road, Loughgiel ☎ 028-2764 1241 🖑 www.causewaycheese. com)

Coffee bar
● Ground Espresso Bar

Serious coffee and yummy things are the core ingredients of Ground, who have always shown themselves to be ahead of the local competition, ever since they opened up firstly in Coleraine and Ballymena. Comfortable rooms and committed staff mean that Ground can take the grind out of your day. (Karen Gardiner, 30-32 Ballymoney Street ☎ 028-2565 0060 🖑 www.groundcoffee.net – Open 9am-5.30pm Mon-Sat. Also at 44 Fountain Street, Belfast ☎ 028 9032 8226; 4 High Street, Ballymoney ☎ 028-2766 2625; 52 Main Street, Portrush ☎ 028-7082 5979)

Guesthouse
● Marlagh Lodge

Renovated from being a virtual ruin just a few years ago, Marlagh Lodge shows both the temperament of Robert and Rachel Thompson – determined, dogged, meticulous, and gifted with true aesthetic vision – and also shows their otherworldliness. The time frame of

Antrim

Marlagh doesn't belong in this century, with its foolish freneticism. Instead, the time frame here is maybe mid-Edwardian, maybe E. M. Forster, maybe early W.B. Yeats. When you stay here, you step out of time, and that is just one of the charms of the house. The other prodigious charm of the house is Rachel's stunning cooking, with its gracious flavour notes cascading from every dish. Mrs Thompson's food puts us in mind of Diana Henry's cooking, bullet-pointed with herb accents from starter to pud, the cherry on the icing of a great confection. (Rachel & Robert Thompson, 71 Moorfields Road, Ballymena ☎ 028-2563 1505 ✉ info@marlaghlodge.com ✌ www.marlaghlodge.com – Open all year)

Antrim

Ballymoney

Preserves and Catering
● Causeway Chutneys & Minor Events

We are big fans of anyone who does their deliveries in a vintage Morris Minor estate car – frankly only a vintage Volkswagen camper van is cooler – so Virginia Maxwell gets our vote for the chutney maker with the ideal mode of transport. Her chutneys are pretty ideal also, and she really likes to spice things up, using ginger, chilli and lemon grass, along with Indian spices in her spiced apple with raisins chutney. Look out also for a wild elderflower cordial, in season. Minor Events is the name of Virginia's catering company. So if you are planning a major event, you need Minor Events. (Virginia Maxwell, 19 Semicock Road, Ballymoney ☎ 028-2766 6394)

Ballyrobert

Restaurant
● Oregano

Dermot and Catherine Regan's restaurant looks sober and Victorian from the outside, but in reality is a pretty in pink dining room that is modern and elegant. Modern and elegant also suits the cooking, though there is a love of richness running through Dermot's food: roast rack and slow roast shoulder of lamb with potato gratin, chicken, foie gras and wild mushroom broth, smoked haddock and prawn risotto with poached egg. There is a very nice sense of a couple working hard to define themselves and their food and if Ballyrobert seems a little bit out of the way, then food and service of this quality makes it well worth the detour. (Dermot & Catherine Regan, 21 Ballyrobert Road, Ballyrobert ☎ 028-9084 0099 🖰 www.oreganorestaurant.co.uk – Open noon-2.30pm, 5.30pm-9.30pm Tue-Fri, 6pm-10pm Sat, noon-3pm Sun)

Ballyvoy

Herb Garden & Tea Room
● Drumnakeel Herb Garden

You can detour off from your gentle dander around the lovely North Antrim Coast in either July or August and stop at Drumnakeel to enjoy a cup of tea and nice simple cooking from Maria Patterson: potato and lovage soup, or tomato tart with basil pesto, with a lovely garden salad dressed with edible flowers. For the rest of the year the Pattersons open the herb garden, and sell their chemical-free herbs and vegetables. You can also buy some of their produce – breads, jams, oils and vinegars – in the Moyle Country Market. (Jake & Maria Patterson, Drumnakeel, Ballyvoy, Ballycastle ☎ 028-2076 3350 – Open 11am-5pm Mon-Fri, Mar-Oct, otherwise by arrangement)

Bushmills

Garden Centre Cafe
● Bushmills Garden Centre

The Creative Gardens company runs both the Bushmills and the Donaghadee Garden Centres, and has won a mighty reputation for the cooking in both destinations. "Good, old fashioned, homestyle cooking of the very highest quality", is their ambition, and it's one on which they overdeliver. So whether or not you intend to get your garden into shape, you have the best possible excuse to visit the garden centre. (Jane Segasby, Ballyclough Road, Bushmills ☎ 028-2073 0424 🖂 bmgc@creativegardens.net 🖰 www.creativegardens.net – Open 9.30am-5.30pm Mon-Sat, Cafe open 10am-5pm, 12.30pm-5pm Sun, Cafe opens 12.30pm-5pm)

Hotel & Restaurant
● The Bushmills Inn

As much of an institution in North Antrim as the Bushmills Distillery itself, this is the place to come to for real
Ulster-Scots cooking: Brotchan, a hearty daily soup, onion and Guinness soup, apple and herb stuffed pork fillet
with cabbage, fillet steak flambéed in Bushmills whiskey,
Dalriada cullen skink, smoked haddock on new potatoes
with poached egg and spring onions. (Alan Dunlop, 9
Dunluce Road, Bushmills ☎ 028-2073 2339 ⌨ mail@
bushmillsinn.com ⌂ www.bushmillsinn.com – Open
noon-5pm Mon-Sat, 12.30pm-2.30pm Sun, 6pm-9.15pm
Mon-Sun)

Distillery
● The Old Bushmills Distillery

The *Bridgestone Guides* don't do iconic tourist destinations, but the Bushmills Distillery is one iconic tourist
destination that we do consider worth your while. You
really do enjoy sipping whiskey a lot more when you understand the ancient, and alchemical process by which it
is made. Our choice is the Bushmills single malt, but the
legendary Black Bush isn't too far behind that. (Bushmills
☎ 028-2073 1521 ⌂ www.bushmills.com)

Glenarm

Organic Farmed Salmon
● Glenarm Organic Salmon

With stocks of salmon decimated by mauve stinger
jelly-fiish back in 2007, Glenarm organic salmon is back
in production, good news in particular for the many
cutting-edge chefs who made Glenarm's reputation
many years ago as one of the finest salmon with which
to work. Their organic status will only serve to cement
the reputation of this iconic produce amongst Northern
Ireland's food culture. (John Russell, Glenarm ☎ 028-
2884 1691 ⌨ northern.salmon@btclick.com)

only in Ulster
Black Bush

Glengormley

Butcher
● Thompson's Butchers

David Thompson does things nice and slow, hanging his sirloins for all of twenty-two days before he'll let you get your hands on them. Mr Thompson is a typically creative and imaginative butcher, so his sausages and chicken products are all top notch. And when the sun is shining he has everything your Weber needs. So you only need to chill the beer. (David Thompson, 7 Ballyclare Road, Glengormley ☎ 028-9083 2507 – Open 8am-5pm Mon, Wed & Sat, 8am-5.30pm Tue, Thu & Fri)

Lisburn

Cafe
● Café Square & Bistro

Stephen and Cristina run one of those bistros that people become genuinely fond of. It's also, however, the kind of place the critics like, which is why it's in the *Bridgestone Guide*. The cooking and service are both unpretentious and genuine so it's the kind of little place you'd take for granted if you found it in Italy, but which is all too rare in Ireland's towns and cities. They work hard in the evenings to create atmosphere, so if the guitarist sits down and starts to play *Champagne Supernova*, do remember that it's polite not to sing along. (Stephen & Cristina Higginson, 18 Lisburn Square, Lisburn ☎ 028-9266 6677 – Open 9.30am-4pm Mon-Tue 9.30am-late Wed-Sat)

Home Bakery
● Country Kitchen Home Bakery

Chris Ferguson is one of those wonderful bakers who are up at the crack of dawn – 3am! – to start to prepare the breads and cakes for the Country Kitchen. Once the baking is under way the chefs arrive to start to prepare the foods that will be sold at their busy breakfast and lunch service, and then it's go!go! in here as the hungry arrive. Go for the shortbread and flakemeal biscuits. (Chris & Audrey Ferguson, 57-59 Sloan Street, Lisburn ☎ 028-9267 1730 – Open 8am-5pm Mon-Sat)

Asian Restaurant & Takeaway
● Ginza

Beside the cinemas in the Lisburn Leisure Complex, opposite a Subway, and next to a KFC, you'll find a bit of a surprise. Ginza restaurant is a large open space with black lacquer tables and chairs, huge artificial bamboos and loads of fresh lilies, big-screen TVs and a massive open kitchen full of impressive black-hatted Asian chefs, fanning the flames underneath colossal woks. This is a Teppanyaki restaurant, and it's great theatre. Chris Kwan, their executive chef is half Chinese and half Japanese and the pan-Asian food here is a dynamic mix of both cultures. They even make their own desserts, which is very unusual in Asian restaurants, and it is symbolic of the level of care that is evident in both the food and the service. (Sally Yuen, Lisburn Leisure Complex, Lisburn ☎ 028-9266 6639 – Open noon-3.30pm, 5pm-10.30pm Mon-Sun)

Brew Pub
● Hilden Brewing Company & Tap Room

Owen Scullion manages the brewery, whilst Frances Scullion manages the Tap Room restaurant, and it's wonderful to see Ireland's original craft brewery flourishing under a new generation of hard-working talented people. There are five cask beers in the Hilden range – the original Scullion's is an amber ale; Hilden is a hoppy Irish ale; Silver is a light ale; and Hilden Halt a full malty ale with a whopping 6.1ABV. Molly Malone, then, is their dark red porter. Two new bottle beers are Titanic Quarter, a pale ale, and Cathedral Quarter, a full-bodied red ale. The third, Queen's Quarter, is due to arrive any day now. Terrific stuff. (Owen Scullion, Grand Street, Lisburn ☎ 028-9266 3863 ⌂ www.hildenbrewery.co.uk – Tap Room Open 12.30pm-2.30pm, 5.30pm-9pm Tue-Sun)

Restaurant
● Sabai Thai

Sabai is a good local Thai restaurant. Although the menus for both the restaurant and the take-away include some European dishes, it's really their own specialities that are the best recommendation. (Robert Mack, 71-73 Bachelors Walk, Lisburn ☎ 028-9264 0202 ⌂ www.sabaithai.co.uk – Open 5pm-10pm Sun-Thu, 5pm-midnight Fri & Sat. Closed Mon)

Portrush

College Canteen
● **The Academy**

The Academy is the Restaurant of the Portrush Catering College and it's where the students first get the chance to cook for dinner guests. The students cook lunches, as well as four dinners, and then it's out into the real world to become the next Jamie or Gordon. Let's hope it's Jamie. (Portrush College, Portrush ☎ 028-7032 3970 ☞ www.ulster.ac.uk/portrush/academy)

B&B
● **Maddybenny Farmhouse**

Maddybenny is a comfortable family home where B&B will mean a great breakfast after a good night's sleep. Long experience has given a professional sheen to the White family's work, and they are very much to the manner born when it comes to Northern Irish hospitality. (Karen White, 18 Maddybenny Park, Portrush, Coleraine ☎ 028-7082 3394 ☞ www. maddybenny.com)

Restaurants and Wine Bars Complex
● **Ramore Restaurants**

Nobody told George McAlpin that Portrush is no longer a holiday destination, but thank heavens they didn't, for whilst his sextet of restaurants and bars are more worthy of San Sebastian or Brighton, here are these slick, hip, happening rooms in dear old Portrush, There's a pizza restaurant, Coast, an oriental restaurant, The Ramore, a wine bar, Ramore Wine Bar, and a bistro, the Harbour Bistro, plus lounges and bars. Everything is characterised by a fantastic sense of style, and by George's endlessly enquiring culinary imagination. In summertime the buzz is awesome, and you might need to queue for an hour to get a table. (George McAlpin, Ramore Restaurant ☎ 028-7082 6969 – Open 6pm-9.30pm Wed-Thu, 6pm-10pm Fri-Sat, 5.30pm-9.30pm Sun; Coast ☎ 028-7082 3311 – Open 5pm-9.30pm Wed-Fri, 4pm-10.30pm Sat, 3pm-9.30pm Sun; Harbour Bistro ☎ 028-7082 2430 – Open 5pm-10pm Mon-Fri, 5pm-10.30pm Sat, 4pm-9pm Sun; Ramore Wine Bar ☎ 028-7082 4313 – Open 12.15pm-2.15pm Mon-Sat, 5pm-10pm Mon-Thu, 5pm-10.30pm Fri, 4.45pm-10.30pm Sat, 12.30pm-3pm, 5pm-9pm Sun ☞ www.ramorerestaurant.com)

County Armagh

Armagh

Home Bakery
● **The Cake Shop**

A thriving community shop making everything from wedding cakes to wee buns. (Pamela Johnston, 20 English Street ☎ 028-3752 2883 – Open 8am-5.30pm Mon-Sat)

Butcher
● **A Flanagan & Son**

David Flanagan's shop has been selling top-class meat from their own farm for almost eighty years. In common with many of the Elite Guild of Butchers the shop also has a very impressive delicatessen wing which shows that their mastery of cooked foods is as complete as their mastery of fresh meat. Look out for the home-made pies, quiches and bakes, and be sure not to miss their classic pork sausages. (David Flanagan, 1 Scotch Street, Armagh ☎ 028-3752 2805 – Open 9am-5.30pm Mon-Thur, 8.30am-6pm Fri & Sat)

Craigavon

Tea Room & Pottery
● **Ballydougan Pottery**

The Linen Barn Coffee Shop in this pottery workshop is a good spot for Ulster cooking. (Sean O'Dowd, Bloomvale House, 171 Plantation Road ☎ 028-3834 2201 info@ballydouganpottery.co.uk www. ballydouganpottery.co.uk – Open 9am-5pm Mon-Sat)

Artisan Charcuterie
● Newforge House

The Country House revolution inaugurated by Ballymaloe House in the 1960s has never really caught on
in Northern Ireland, so staying at Newforge is a rare
opportunity to enjoy a Georgian country house deep in
the Northern Irish countryside. John & Louise are serious about their food, and source from many of the best
Northern Irish artisans, so the standards of cooking at
breakfast and dinner are very high, and the house itself
is meticulously maintained. (John & Louise Mathers,
Magheralin, Craigavon ☎ 028-9261 1255 ✉ enquiries@
newforgehouse.com ✆ www.newforgehouse.com)

only in Ulster
Vegetable Roll

Crossmaglen

Tea Room & Pottery
● Old Tarts

Sarah Jane McGrath is an up and coming artisan in
Northern Ireland — she bakes sweet and savoury tartlets
and they have found a welcome audience in the St
George's market in Belfast, Fresh the Good Food Stores
in Dublin and their own new store in the Buttercrane
Centre in Newry. Watch out for this new talent. (Sarah
Jane McGrath, Crievekeeran, Crossmaglen ☎ +353
(0)86-816 2451)

Lurgan

Butcher & Coffee Shop
● John R Dowey & Son

3,000 customers a week can't be wrong! That's how
many punters come through the doors of Doweys
looking to buy not just well-matured beef, but also any
number of the huge range of deli products that they sell
in this emporium. There's a coffee shop next door to the
butchers, which serves their own scones and shortbread
as well as simple lunches. (John Dowey, 20 High Street,
Lurgan ☎ 028-3832 2547 ✉ john@johnrdowey.co.uk
✆ wwwjohnrdowey.co.uk – Open 8.30am-5.30pm Mon-
Sat)

Portadown

Artisan Cider
● Armagh Cider Company

Kelly Troughton's cider company is the only producer of cider from Armagh apples, and along with
the popular Carson's Cider they also produce AJ apple
juice, as well as seasonal products. (Kelly Troughton,
Ballinteggart House, 73 Drumnasoo Road, Portadown
☎ 028-3833 4268 ✆ info@armaghcider.com ⌂ www.
armaghcider.com)

Apple Juice
● Barnhill Apple Juice

Ken Redmond is one of the stars of the Saturday St
George's market in Belfast where he sells truck loads
of his splendid apple and fruit juices. These are proper
drinks, naturally cloudy, and the mixed drinks: apple and
blackberry, apple and elderflower, apple and blackcurrant, and so on, are rasping and refreshing. Ken has also
been known to sell dahlias in the market, so bring home
a bunch for your best girl, or boy. (Ken Redmond, Barnhill, Portadown ☎ 028-3885 1190)

Butcher
● Knox's Food Court

Barry Knox and his sons do everything from individual
birthday cakes through buffet parties, right down to
the humble sausage. It's not so much a butcher's shop
as a food market and all-in-one emporium. Who would
go near a supermarket when you get shops like this
providing not only high quality meats, but also excellent
service and advice. If you want to know how Northern
Ireland's Elite butchers have prospered you'll find the
answer here. (Barry Knox, 388 West Street, Portadown
☎ 028-3835 3713 ✆ knoxfoodcourt@mail.com – Open
8.30am-5.15pm Mon-Sat)

Delicatessen
● The Yellow Door Deli & Patisserie

It's a mark of just how important a figure Simon Dougan
is in Northern Ireland's food culture that he is the chef
who has written the outstanding book *The Yellow Door –
Our Story Our Recipes*. The story and the recipes are the
work of a man who understands how to make food

that is sumptuous yet modest, professional yet never slick, generous but never indulgent. "Being a chef is not just a job to me, it's an all-consuming way of life" Simon told *The Irish Times* when his book was published, but that way of life includes a very holistic appreciation of the philosophy of food and cooking. Add to this the fact that every venture he has been involved in has been a success and you can understand why The Yellow Door is so important to Northern Ireland's food culture. (Simon Dougan, 74 Woodhouse Street, Portadown ☎ 028-3835 3528 ✉ info@yellowdoordeli.co.uk ⌖ www.yellowdoordeli.co.uk – Open 9am-5pm Mon-Sat)

Tandragee

Tradition Breeds Farm Shop
● Forthill Farm

This quaint wooden farmshop sells the Gracey's own Saddleback and Old Spot pork, and Galloway and Longhorn beef. If you find yourself enjoying some superb beef in Pier 36 in Donaghadee, part of the reason for its quality is because it has come from Kenny and Jennifer's farm. "The steaks melted in our mouths" is what John's sister Jakki wrote after tasting the Forthill beef. This is the real stuff. (Kenny & Jennifer Gracey, 80 Ballymore Road, Tandragee ☎ 028-3884 0818 ✉ info@forthill-farm.co.uk ⌖ www.forthillfarm.co.uk – Open 9am-5pm Mon-Sat, late opening till 8.30pm Thur)

County Down

Annalong

Fish and Chip Shop
● **Galley Fish and Chip Shop**

For a really good "fish supper" head to the Galley where
they know that the secret of superlative chips is that you
have to fry them in dripping. (Aileen & Joey Chambers,
43 Kilkeel Rd, Annalong ☎ 028-4376 7253 ⏱ www.
thegalleyannalong.co.uk – Open noon-8pm Mon & Tue,
noon-10pm Wed & Thu, noon-10.30pm Fri & Sat)

Ardglass

Restaurant & Bar
● **Curran's Seafood & Steak Restaurant**

Curran's Bar is a friendly inn standing at the junction of
five country roads, where it has been home, over the
centuries, to story-telling, music, dancing, match-making
and all the other social services of a country pub. It
has remained in the same family since the eighteenth
century and unsurprisingly the design of the pub today is
slightly eccentric – a mix of wooden Corinthian columns,
beams, carved marble, heavy velvet curtains, gilt-framed
prints Dadaistically mixed with bare tables and paper
napkins all overlooked by puppet mannequins. It's a good
value, cheerful hostelry close to the characterful pier-
side town of Ardglass. It is definitely a family location,
so there's plenty for children to do and eat, while for
grown-ups the short menu lists classic things you want
to eat in a pub: fish'n'chips, scampi, burgers, sausage and
mash, steaks. The fish is local, the steaks are dry hung
and the potatoes, hand cut, come from a local farmer.
(Paula Mahon, 83 Strangford Road, Chapeltown, Ardglass ☎ 028-4484 1332 ⏰ info@curransbar.net ⏱ www.
curransbar.net – Bar open 11.30am-11.30pm. Restaurant
open 12.30pm-9pm Mon-Sun, last orders 8.50pm. Sunday carvery 12.30pm-4pm)

Fishmonger
● S&P Milligan

S & P Milligan are processors and exporters of herring and mackerel from their factory in Ardglass, but from the point of view of a *Bridgestone Guide* user, they are useful for their fish vans, whose fine selection of fresh fish attracts a healthy queue wherever it lands. Find it in Lisburn on Tuesday, Ballynahinch on Thursday, Cookstown on Friday, Ballymena on Saturday and in the Belfast Saturday St George's Market. (Seamus Milligan, 20 Downpatrick Road, Ardglass ☎ 028-4484 1595 ✉ sales@sp-milligan.co.uk ♒ www.sp-milligan.co.uk)

---

only in Ulster
Soda Farls

Ballynahinch

Fish and Chip Café
● Ginesi's

Hugely popular Ulster institution, serving fish and chips and Ulster frys. All you need to enjoy it is an appetite inspired by a hike in the Mournes. (Gillian & Romano Ginesi, 34 Main Street, Ballynahinch ☎ 028-9756 2653 – Open 9am-8pm Mon-Tue, 9am-8.30pm Wed, 9am-9pm Thu-Sat, 2.30pm-9pm Sun)

Banbridge

Butcher
● Bronte Steakhouse

It's in the middle of absolutely nowhere, you step in the door and step into a vernacular interior from the early 1970s, and the menus read as if they were formed at the same time. But the cooking in the Bronte, from chef James Richardson, is really spot on: chicken liver pâté, terrine of melon, smoked salmon & prawn cocktail, beef stroganoff, pepper-crusted fillet with Cashel Blue cheese and red wine gravy, pavlova with fresh cream and fresh fruit. As out of the age as the Brontes themselves. (Ian & Roy Clyde, 69 Ballinafoy Road, Banbridge ☎ 028-4065 1338 ♒ info@brontesteakhouse.com ♒ www.brontesteakhouse.com – Open 5.30pm-9pm Mon-Sat, 5pm-7.30pm Sun)

Butcher
● MA Quail

Many of the finest food businesses in Northern Ireland enjoy a service culture that would rival that of the Japanese, and the Quail family's century-old business is one of the very best examples of this service culture at work. Everything they do here is based on trust and experience, and it gifts their food with a level of quality and confidence that is joyous. Whether you are buying their award winning baked ham, or twenty-eight day aged Limousin heifer beef, or having lunch in the cafe with its array of contemporary artworks, Quail's exudes class. A Northern Irish luxury brand. (Joseph Quail, 13-15 Newry Street, Banbridge ☎ 028-4066 2604 ✆ www.quailsfinefoods.co.uk – Open 8.30am-5.30pm Mon-Sat)

Coffee Roaster
● Ristretto

It's great to see Gregg Radcliffe getting in on the bespoke coffee roasting revolution that has had such an impact on how people think and drink coffee in the Republic. It's still early days yet for Ristretto, but we look forward to seeing how the commitment and professionalism of this coffee company develops with time and experience. (Gregg Radcliffe, Unit 49 Banbridge Enterprise Centre, Scarva Road, Banbridge ☎ 028-4062 3242 ✆ www.ristrettocoffee.com)

Home Bakery
● Windsor Bakery

"We strive to make what the customer wants, and we feel that if we make tasty food and serve it with a smile then we will be busy" says Gordon Scott, and that is exactly what the Windsor has been doing with its home bakery and its bright, busy café, for many years now. Northern Ireland's home bakeries are the jewel in its culinary crown and the Windsor might be called the Koh-i-Noor of this distinguished baking culture. Go to the café for chicken, vegetable and potato pie, or mushroom vol au vent, or Irish stew, and then bring home a fruit soda bannock, and a Genoa slab, and all is well. (Gordon Scott, 36-38 Newry Street, Banbridge ☎ 028-4062 3666 – Open 7.30am-5.30pm Mon-Sat. Also at 30 Bridge Street, Banbridge ☎ 028-4062 5177 Café open 8am-4.30pm, bread counter open 7.30am-5.30pm ✉ winbake@btconnect.com)

Mutton pie

Bangor

Butcher
● David Burns Butchers

Brian and George Burns' butchers' shop is all about
quality, from their classic pork sausages through to the
best Xmas turkeys. We suspect that there are people
in Bangor who have never bought a piece of meat in any
other shop, and why would they? That explains those
early morning openings at the weekends, for this is an
astonishingly busy shop. But the guys aren't just busy:
they are also curious, and if we don't actually bump into
George when he is off on some jaunt checking out new
ideas – last time it was London – then we always enjoy
being back in the shop and hearing what he has learnt
whilst travelling. Vital energy, and a vital address. (Brian
& George Burns, 112 Abbey Street, Bangor ☎ 028-
9127 0073 ⌂ www.burnsbutchers.co.uk– Open 7am-
5pm Tue-Thur, 6am-7pm Fri, 6am-5pm Sat)

Restaurant
● The Boat House

Brothers Joery and Jasper Castel run the destination address in Bangor. Joery cooks, Jasper manages everything
else, and these are original and distinctive talents, with
a compelling take on modern food: beet leaf and ricotta
cannelloni, for example, or beignets of salsify with veal
steak, or pollack with gremolata fried beans, all offer
something distinct, clean and vibrant, with flavours that
riff smartly, perhaps seen best of all in their chicken,
lobster and shiitake sausage with Dutch mustard. Clever
work, and a nice room and very sharp value lift the
Boat House out of the norm of Bangor eating. (Joery
& Jasper Castel, The Boat House, Seacliff Road, Bangor
☎ 028-9146 9253 ⌂ www.theboathouseni.co.uk Open
noon-2.30pm, 5pm-9.30pm Wed-Sat, 1pm-9pm Sun)

Delicatessen and Café
● **Café Strudel**

Fritz Machala only has a small café space in which to cook, but his ambition is to achieve restaurant quality food with his breakfasts and lunches, and he gets there with gas to spare. Tomato and courgette soup is very fine, and smoked fish on crushed potatoes is even better. Salads such as crab and a classic Caesar, are right on the money, and with people coming to and fro getting take-aways and food-to-go for dinner it's a busy and important new address for Bangor. (Fritz Machala, 7-9 Market Street, Bangor ☎ 028-9147 7666 – Open 8am-4pm Mon-Sat)

Yogurt
● **Clandeboye Estate Yoghurt**

Clandeboye Estate yoghurt is one of Sally McKenna's favourite new foods. Why so? Because the balance of acidity and texture reminds her of yoghurt eaten decades ago in Istanbul. The Clandeboye secrets are to take the milk of prize-winning Holstein and Jersey cows and then to culture the milk slowly for 20 hours before it is strained through cheesecloth. The result is a million miles away from the commercial gloop that sits beside the Glandeboye products in supermarket chill cabinets. This is the real deal, a natural health product that is also a defining epicurean food. (Bryan Boggs, Clandeboye Estate, Bangor ☎ 028-9185 2966 🖅 bryan@clandeboye.co.uk 🖰 www.clandeboye.co.uk)

only in Ulster
Clandeboye Estate Yoghurt

Gastropub
● **Coyle's**

Coyle's gastropub is a place where they really enjoy their grub. They like cooking it, and you will like eating it, and there is an energy and lack of self-consciousness here that is very winning. All the classic modern culinary riffs are here – ham hock salad; goat's cheese tart; braised ox cheek; Moroccan lamb stew – but they don't just churn out the dishes. Instead there is real engagement and thought here, and you get that in every bite of really smart cookery. The food in the bar is simpler – soups, sandwiches, ciabattas, burgers and some savoury mains – but they show the same level of attention to detail. (Kyle Marshall, Mark Coyle, 44 High Street, Bangor ☎ 028-9127 0362 ◌ www.coylesbistro.co.uk – Open 11.30am-midnight Mon-Thur, 11.30am-1am Fri & Sat, 12.30pm-11pm Sun)

Home Bakery
● The Heatherlea

Bangor's champion bakery has a restaurant on one side and a coffee shop on the other and a busy, busy bakery – they bake 1,000 scones here on market days! – in between. The Belfast baps fly out of the shop almost as fast as the scones, and their classic wheaten breads and fruit loaves barely get a chance to cool down before they are packed up and taken away. "Good quality, wholesome, traditional food" is how Paul describes the cooking in the restaurant and coffee shop, and whether you are here for breakfast with fadge and soda bread or some fresh Portavogie fish, the consistency is unerring and the quality always sky-high. (Paul & Patricia Getty, 94 Main Street, Bangor ☎ 028-9145 3157 ◌ paulgetty@ btconnect.com – Open 8.30am-5pm Mon-Sat)

Restaurant
● Jeffers by the Marina

Stephen Jeffers has a new venture in the Castlereagh Hills golf club, Jeffers Bar & Grill, with a menu divided according to implements – spoon, fork, knife and fork, and pizza, (which should, surely, be classified under "fingers"?) It's smartly sourced and organised food from a smart operator, and that smartness has kept Jeffers in Bangor busy for many years now, with food that is modern and, above all, moreish. The sort of relaxed food that you could eat every day – 5-hour cooked Dexter beef; smoked cod with crushed potatoes; risotto with Strangford prawns (he does good risotto). There is a cookery book in the pipeline, and whilst we are sure we will love cooking the signature dishes at home, eating them here in situ is hard to beat. (Stephen Jeffers, 7 Grays Hill, Bangor ☎ 028-9185 9555 ◌ info@ jeffersfood.com ◌ www.jeffersfood.com – Open 10am-10pm Tue-Sat, 11am-8pm Sun)

Fishmonger
● McKeown's Fish Shop

This is where you buy fish in Bangor, both wet fish and
their own smoked fish, of which they are extremely
proud. (Sean McKeown, 14 High Street, Bangor ☎ 028-
9127 1141 – Open 8.30am-5.30pm Tue-Fri, 8.30am-5pm
Sat)

Preserves
● The Offbeat Bottling Company

Offbeat is just the right name for this funky and imaginative preserves company, who like to work their own riffs
on jams, preserves and marmalades. You'll find them in
good delis, even as far south as West Cork, and they
also have a lively stall in the George's market on Saturdays. (Unit 73 Enterprise House, 2/4 Balloo Avenue,
Bangor ☎ 028-9127 1525)

Butcher and delicatessen
● Primacy Food Village

Do you know of any other butchery/bakery/coffee
shop/ vegetable shop that produces a glossy, four-page
newsletter? No, we don't either, but Nicola Bowman's
Primacy Food Village does, and it tells you all about
their latest adventures, and who supplies their veg –
Raymond Rankin, well done Raymond – and all about
their new cake range and their Xmas turkeys and their
carvery lunches. The newsletter testifies to a dynamic,
creative organisation that is founded in the unbeatable
logic of a farm shop fed by a local farm, reducing food
miles, anticipating the needs of the community and
evolving imaginatively and intelligently. Top class. (Nicola
Bowman, 26A Primacy Road, Bangor ☎ 028-9127 0083
🖰 www.primacymeatsfoodvillage.co.uk – Open 8am-
5.30pm Mon-Fri, 8am-5pm Sat, Coffee shop open
9.30am-4.30pm Mon-Sat)

Garden Centre Café
● Rambling Rose Restaurant

Fresh potato bread, made from freshly mashed potatoes,
made every morning: that's the sort of dedicated excellence that explains the success of the Rambling Rose
Restaurant at Dickson's. David Perkes and his team pack
culinary care into everything, using Carrowdore eggs
for their omelettes; baking the wheaten bread for their
prawn open sandwich, sourcing those prawns

from Portavogie for their scampi, and they preserve the great tradition of high tea, with a menu that offers fish, grills and other cracking savoury dishes. (David Perkes, Dickson's Garden Centre, 79 Cootehall Road, Bangor ☎ 028-9185 3001 – Open Mon-Sun day time, High Tea on Fri & Sat evening)

Comber

Vegetable producers
● **Mash Direct**

How do Mash Direct manage to make prepared foods that taste real and true? The answer lies in what Martin and Tracy Hamilton do before they cook their various vegetable products, and that answer is quite simply that they are dynamic, talented farmers who grow exceptionally fine vegetables. Those veg, then, only travel out of the fields and into their production unit before emerging as Mash Direct foods – champ; neeps and tatties; carrot and parsnip; leeks in cheese sauce, and so on. It's the quality in the growing and the shortness of the production journey which makes them work so well, and it is worth noting that before MD, many other companies tried, and failed, to make acceptable cooked vegetables a reality. This is a big, successful company and, as they would say in West Cork, fair play to them! (Martin & Tracy Hamilton, 81 Ballyrainey Road, Comber ☎ 028-9187 8316 📧 info@mashdirect.cm 🖥 www.mashdirect.com)

Down

Farm Shop
● **Pheasants Hill Farm & Butcher's Shop**

Alan Bailey runs one of the most important shops in Ireland. His concentration on the breed of meat which he rears, sources and prepares is unmatched by any other shop in Ireland. So if you hanker after the particular flavours of Wensleydale sheep, or Berkshire pork, then this is the place to come to get it. There are also lots of other wonderful organic and speciality foods, but it's the meat products in particular that make Pheasant's Hill so vital. (Alan & Janis Bailey, 3 Bridge Street Link, Comber ☎ 028-9187 8470 📧 info@pheasantshill.com 🖥 www.pheasantshill.com– Open 9am-6pm Mon-Sat)

Crossgar

Down

Wine Merchant
● James Nicholson Wine Merchants

In his Xmas 2009 flyer Jim Nicholson actually revealed half a dozen of his own chosen wines to drink at home. There was a Riesling QbA from Helmut Donnhoff, the excellent Chateau Tour de Mirambeau, Le Pigeoulet from Daniel Brunier of Vieux Télégraph, John Forrest's Pinot Noir from Marlborough, the Morellino di Scansano from Morisfarms and finally Kevin Mitchell's Killermans Run Shiraz. So, what does this tell us about the most innovative and cutting-edge wine merchant in Ireland? Firstly, that he has diverse tastes, and that he is no snob, so the ethereal Riesling can share a table with the muscular Shiraz. Secondly, that his conduit to good wine is always through the ambitions and intentions of the producer: in choosing the wine, Nicholson is choosing the mind of the winemaker. Finally, he has an eye for value that is even keener than that of his customers: buy the Nicholson case and it will cost an average of a tenner a bottle. Just think about that: hand-picked wines made by some of the greatest vignerons in the world at ten pounds each. It's for these reasons that Nicholson's is such a vital part of the culinary culture of Ireland, and an indispensable part of your quality of life. (Jim & Elspeth Nicholson, Killyleagh Street, Crossgar ☎ 028-4483 0091 ✉ shop@jnwine.com 🖱 www.jnwine.com – Open 10am-7pm Mon-Sat)

Donaghadee

Garden Centre Café
● Donaghadee Garden Centre

Jimmy Hughes and his team are serious about their food, and everything they make and bake shows real TLC and a determination to make the very best things that they

only in Ulster
Finnebrogue Venison

can. So you go and choose the begonias, and I'll just sit here and have something nice to eat. (Jane Segasby, 34 Stockbridge Road, Donaghadee ☎ 028-9188 3237 ✉ ddgc@creativegardens.net 🖱 www.creativegardens. net – Open 9.30am-5pm Mon-Tue, 9.30am-8pm Wed-Fri, 9.30am-5pm Sat, 12.30am-5pm Sun)

Gastropub & Accommodation
● Pier 36

Margaret and Denis Waterworth have been making delicious food for as long as we have been writing guide books, and for the last decade their focus on good food in Pier 36 has seen them win numerous awards. Part of their secret is the hard work of their sons Lewis and Jody, but their real USP is simply an understanding of the deliciousness of domestic-influenced cooking. Everything works, because everything is fundamentally simple, from Portavogie prawns with a Parmesan crust and house breads, to rib-eye steak with bacon and leek rosti and crisp onion rings. The opening of their comfortable bed-rooms upstairs means that Donaghadee should be on your destination hit list when exploring County Down. (The Waterworth family, 36 The Parade, Donaghadee ☎ 028-9188 4466 ✉ info@pier36.co.uk 🖱 www.pier36. co.uk – Open 11.30am-9.30pm Mon-Sun)

Downpatrick

Gastropub
● Denvirs

Dating back to the mid 17th century, Denvir's is some-thing of a local legend in Downpatrick. Stick with the simpler dishes and you will fare well, and there are six rooms upstairs for the traveller. (English Street, Down-patrick ☎ 028-4461 2012 ✉ info@denvirshotel.com 🖱 www.denvirshotel.com – Open noon-9pm Mon-Sat, noon-8pm Sun)

Venison
● Finnebrogue Venison

When Denis Lynn carried around a plate of his rare-cooked venison steak at a *Bridgestone Guide* launch in Belfast it was the only thing that anyone who tried it could talk about. We have a feeling that the new Finnebrogue artisan pork sausages are going to achieve exactly the same sort of mesmerising impact as Mr Lynn's peerless venison. There are four varieties of sausage: pork with sage, pork with scallions, pork and apple and pork with sweet chilli. Needless to say, the pork is organic and free range. More than any other farmer, Denis Lynn has democratised his product, bringing venison into everybody's supermarket and everybody's kitchen and also managing to put it on every decent restaurant menu in Northern Ireland. In this regard he is a pioneering example of how farming that is orientated towards producing top-quality food, rather than commodity produce, is the only way forward for Irish farmers. You'll find Finnebrogue on the best restaurant menus and even in some burger joints: Finnebrogue for everyone! (Denis Lynn, Finnebrogue Estate, Downpatrick ☎ 028-4461 7525 ✉ sales@ finnebrogue.com 🖰 www.finnebrogue.com)

Local Shop
● Hanlon's

Down

A lovely, old-style general store packed with lots of good things. (26 Market Street, Downpatrick ☎ 028-4461 2518 – Open 8am-5.45pm Mon-Sat)

Bakery & Café
● Oakley Fayre Café & Bakery

The Kearney family's bakery and café has been trading happily for thirty years now, but since son Darren came into the operation a few years back there has been new drive and impetus here, and it shows in the revamped interior and the steadily expanding food offer. Mr Kearney worked in good professional kitchens before returning to the family, and he is ambitious to achieve the most he can in this charming bakery and café, thanks to "hard work and dedication". (Darren Kearney, 52 Market Street, Downpatrick ☎ 028-4461 2500 - Open 8am-5pm Mon-Thur, 8am-5.30pm Fri & Sat)

Mushrooms

Farm Shop & Guesthouse
● Pheasant's Hill Guesthouse

Janis Bailey's guesthouse is famous for the fact that Mrs
Bailey uses her own brilliant free-range, rare-beed pork
products at breakfast, and these pork products are as
good as it gets. And, once you have a taste for them, you
can buy the very same products in the family's speciality
shop in Comber and bring that taste of Pheasant's Hill
home. (Janis Bailey, 37 Killyleagh Road, Downpatrick
☎ 028-4461 7246 ⥁ www.pheasantshill.com)

Dromore

Restaurant & Pub
● Boyle's of Dromore

Raymond Murray has one of the best cvs of any chef in
Northern Ireland, and he cut quite a swathe in Dunmur-
ray's H2O before making his way to this colourful old
pub in Dromore where, with foh Martin Darwin, he is
cutting more culinary swathes. His food has the richness
of cuisine grand-mere and the swagger of Northern Irish
bravado – saddle of rabbit cooked in a champagne sauce;
Suffolk pork with Armagh cider and apple compote; Dover sole with brown shrimps. There is an excellent tasting menu which is a culinary tour of the region, which
shows just how smart and tuned-in these guys are. Out
front, Mr Darwin keeps everyone happy, and Boyle's
is a hugely significant new arrival. (Raymond Murray &
Martin Darwin, 8-12 Castle Street, Dromore ☎ 028-
9269 9141 ⥁ info@boylesofdromore.com ⥁ www.
boylesofdromore.com)

Dundrum

Restaurant
● The Buck's Head Inn

Writing about Alison Crothers' dish of scampi and chips,
Joris Minne in *The Belfast Telegraph* used the adjective
"extraordinary". Well, now: "extraordinary" is a term
that gets used about once every seven years when it
comes to writing about food, and it's not the sort of
term one expects to hear about scampi. But then, that's
what Alison does in The Buck's Head: she makes

the ordinary extraordinary, and she does it in the most modest fashion imaginable. Her food is blessed with that lovely domestic signature that shows infinite care, infinite patience, the intention to ennoble good local products with the benediction of good cooking. So, let yourself into this modest cooking, and see how the ordinary can, truly, become the extraordinary. (Michael & Alison Crothers, 77 Main Street, Dundrum ☎ 028-4375 1868 – Open noon-2.30pm, 5pm-9.30pm Mon-Sun)

Guesthouse
● The Carriage House

A pioneering restaurateur in her day, Maureen Griffith originally ran the superb Buck's Head Inn, before creating the ravishing visual palette that is the Carriage House. We use the term palette because everything here is painterly, and painterly perfect. Ms Griffith has the aesthete's eye, and the perfectionist's rigour, so house and garden and cooking are all of a superb standard. Add in the mix of places to eat in the village, and Dundrum offers all you need for a superlative base as you discover the delights of south Down. Mind you, after breakfast in the Carriage House, you may feel like doing not much of anything at all. (Maureen Griffith, 71 Main Street, Dundrum ☎ 028-4375 1635 📠 inbox@carriagehousedundrum.com 🖰 www.carriagehousedundrum.com)

Seafood Bar
● Mourne Seafood Bar

Here is what we want in the Mourne: half a dozen oysters, and a glass of oyster stout, made for the restaurant by the brilliant Whitewater brewery. OK. Now order it again. Twice is probably enough, but once is definitely not. Now that our zinc levels have ascended into the stratosphere it is time to move on to some rollmop herrings with pear chutney, or maybe a fillet of hake with chickpea and chorizo. With a new seafood cookery school in Kilkeel, and the third Mourne Cafe opened in Newcastle, Bob McCoubrey is fast becoming the Rick Stein of Northern Ireland. (Bob McCoubrey, 10 Main Street, Dundrum ☎ 028-4375 1377 🖰 www.mourneseafood.com – Open noon-late Mon-Sat, noon-8.30pm Sun)

Greyabbey

Butcher
● Angus Farm Shop

Noel Angus does things the old-fashioned way in his
farm shop. Cutting meat to order, refusing to sell
anything that is not ripe and ready for the oven, and
making sure that everything sold in the shop is of the
best pasture-reared quality. As well as meats Noel has
local eggs, and local vegetables, so the Angus is a true
local hero. (Noel Angus, 42 Main Street, Greyabbey
☎ 028-4278 8695 ⌂ www.angusfarmshop.com – Open
8.30am-5.30pm Mon-Sat)

only in Ulster
The Ulster Fry

Helen's Bay

Organic Farm
● Helen's Bay Organic Farm

Organic farmer John McCormick is one of the best
growers we know, and being on his delivery route for
a weekly box of good things is the best guarantee of
the good life that you can possibly get in North Down.
He is, in particular, a passionate potato grower, so
expect the most perfect spuds you have ever steamed.
(John McCormick, Coastguard Avenue, Helen's Bay
☎ 028-9185 3122 ⌂ organics2u@f2s.com ⌂ www.
helensbayorganicgardens.com. Office: 13 Seaview
Terrace, Holywood)

Down

Hillsborough

Wine Merchant
● Harry's Road Fine Wines

Neil Groom is one of the best known wine figures in
Northern Ireland and heads up Harry's Road, which
principally supplies to the 'on' trade. The list is consistently updated with new arrivals from Western Australia
and planned additions from Burgundy, the Loire Valley
and the Rhone Valley in 2010. (Harry's Road, Hillsborough
☎ 028-9268 2818 ⌂ www.harrysroadfinewines.co.uk)

Bistro
● Prima Gusto

Your first taste of Richard Nelson's slick venture is likely to be delight at the Italianate-style of this handsome deli and restaurant, but the elegance of the room is matched by a very astute and direct food offer: Jerusalem artichoke risotto, rolled pork belly with cabbage, gourmet burger with focaccia bun. They have worked extra hard here on all the incidentals, so the coffee from Mokaflor is shown proper barista-style respect, and the wines are ace. Prima Gusto is worth a detour. (Richard Nelson, 5 Harry's Road, Hillsborough ☎ 028-9268 8574 📖 info@primagusto.co.uk ⦿ www. primagusto.co.uk – Open 9am-5.30pm Mon-Thu, 9am-9.30pm Fri-Sat, 9.30am-8pm Sun)

Holywood

Café
● The Bay Tree

It is the most outrageous piece of marketing we have ever seen. A beautiful box, with a Bay Tree logo and the proud information that the box contains "1 Cinnamon Scone". Has anyone else ever had the nerve to put a single scone into its own, tailor-made box? No way. But then, Bay Tree cinnamon scones, like the Bay Tree itself, are not the normal stuff of life. Bay Tree cinnamon scones are the best, and no rival comes near to these exquisite pieces of baking. Sue Farmer could coast by on her scones, but there is much else going on in the BT: they are now open for dinner five nights a week, and have opened Go! Bay Tree, just beside the café, where you can buy their fabulous baking and savoury cooking. Meantime Sue's cookery book, *The Red Bay Tree Book*, with illustrations by her daughter, Bridget, is a loving reflection on twenty years of work here in Holywood. Meantime, that loving cooking just goes on and on: poulet grandmere with mash; Mileens tartiflette; sirloin with garlic potatoes; Finnebrogue rump steak with blueberry and shallots. Beautiful work. (Sue & William Farmer, 118 High Street, Holywood ☎ 028-9042 1419 📖 info@baytreeholywood.com ⦿ www. baytreeholywood.com – Open 8am-4.30pm Mon-Fri, from 7pm-late Friday, 9.30am-4.30pm Sat, 10am-2.45pm Sun)

Café
Café Kina

Karen and Niko's Café Kina is part of the Holywood
foodie hub that sees this pretty town packed every
weekend morning with folk eating and chatting and
enjoying themselves and touring the town's food destinations. It's great craic, and it's built on the foundation of good coffee, good sweet baking – they do ace
speciality cakes – and then at weekend evenings they let
their culinary imaginations rip with a cool bistro menu
– prawn and crab fishcakes; coq au vin; smoked duck
and avocado, profiteroles with cream Chantilly – and
you should bring the junior set along with you early in
the evening to enjoy meatballs and couscous or sausage
sticks. A key Holywood address in the town that is
becoming the Kenmare of the North. (Karen Ferguson,
81 High Street, Holywood ☎ 028-9042 5216 ✉ niko@
cafekina.co.uk ⌂ www.cafekina.co.uk – Open 8.30am-
5pm Mon-Fri, 9am-5pm Sat, 9.30am-5pm Sun)

Organic Shop & Bakery
Camphill Organic Farm Shop & Bakery

Rob van Duin's brilliant shop describes itself as "a small
urban community" so, it's much, much more than just
a shop, bakery and café, though it is utterly brilliant
in all these departments. Their soups, in particular,
are vegetarian concoctions that could feed the nation,
packed with goodness and energy. The vegetables they
sell are of sublime quality, the shop is packed with
good things to eat, and the special needs adults who
work here add to the jollity and unique nature of this
brilliant venture. (Rob van Duin, Shore Road, Holywood
☎ 028-9042 3203 ✉ camphillholywood@btconnect.
com ⌂ www.camphillholywood.co.uk – Shop open 9am-
5.30pm Tue-Sat. Cafe open 9am-4.30pm Tue-Sat)

Coffee Shop
The Coffee Emporium

What about Sumatra Extra Fancy? A Union Spirit? Or a
Sidmo Sun-dried Super lot Special Organic? David Chil-
vers has all these extraordinary exotica from Africa, the
Americas and the Pacific. And if these exotic brews don't
capture your imagination, then maybe you need a cup of
Taishan Buddha's Eyebrow, or maybe an Angel's Kiss. Mr
Chilvers' passion for the bean and the brew is evident in
his amazing teas and coffees. But there is also some nice

food, with organic scrambled eggs with smoked salmon, or Clandeboye yogurt with granola for breakfast, or a classic croque monsieur for lunch. (David Chilvers, 59 High Street, Holywood ☎ 0778-988879 ☐ davidchilvers@coffeeemporium.co.uk ⌂ www.coffeeemporium.co.uk – Open 7.30am-10.30pm Mon-Sun)

Kitchenshop
● La Cucina

A nice mix of good kitchenwares which it complements with the latest electrical products for the kitchen. Dualit, KitchenAid, Magimix, Global, Victorinox, Microplane et al are all here in their shiny perfection. (Peter Nicholl, 63 High Street, Holywood ☎ 028-9042 2118 ☐ lacucina.ni@yahoo.co.uk ⌂ www.lacucinacookshops.co.uk – Open 9am-5.30pm Mon-Sat. Also at Lisburn Road, Belfast)

Restaurant
● Enigma

A short, rock-solid modern food offer has seen Enigma – which for many years was Sullivan's restaurant – get off to a flying start in Holywood. The menus are a cat-walk of modern classics: lamb with roast garlic and rosemary jus, crab and Portavogie prawn cocktail, goat's cheese tart with red onion marmalade, salmon with asparagus hollandaise. The food matches the style of the room hand in glove – modern, simple, inviting. (Leslie Armstrong, 2 Sullivan Place ☎ 028-9042 6111 ⌂ www.enigma-holywood.co.uk – Open 8.30am-10pm Mon-Sun)

Restaurant
● Fontana

With Didier out front of house and a new livery in this upstairs room, Fontana is reasserting its position amongst the Holywood hierarchy as one of the great neighbourhood restaurants. (Colleen Bennett, 61a High Street, Holywood ☎ 028-9080 9908 – Open noon-2.30pm, 5pm-9.30pm Tue-Fri, 6.30pm-10pm Sat, 11am-3pm Sun)

Wholefood Shop
● The Iona

A good destination in particular for herb plants, and cut herbs, plus a small array of wholefoods. (Heidi Brave, 27 Church Road, Holywood ☎ 028-9042 8597 – Open 9am-5.30pm Mon-Sat)

● **Koi**

Sally's mother first discovered Koi, and what a great place it is too, a real addition to Holywood. It may be a fusion of all types of Asian cooking, but they are very clear in their own minds what it is about. If, for example, you order coconut rice with roast duck, they will tut tut under their breath and advise you not to mix Cantonese with Korean, for it will be too sweet. The Coconut rice needs the ferment of their kimchi sauce, the plummy duck will just need plain boiled rice. So while the choice might seem a little broad church - teriyaki Japanese dishes, Malaysian satays, Phad Thai from Thailand and a few European dishes thrown in – it is all very considered and, most importantly, extremely authentic. The room is simple, but stylish and the food is excellent value for money. Every town needs a Koi. (Sam, **10-12 Shore Road, Holywood, ☎ 028-9042 4238** – Open noon-11pm Mon-Sat, 2pm-10.30pm Sun)

● **Orr's**

There are loads of classy things to buy in this butcher's shop/deli and wet fish store. So look out for potted herrings, SD Bell's teas, their own cooked meats and fine wet fish. The shop reflects its own fifty year history with a timeless interior. (Gerry Orr, **56 High Street, Holywood ☎ 028-9042 2288** – Open 8am-5.30pm Mon-Sat)

● **The Yard**

There is something fiercely impressive about the Yard. It's quite a simple idea, but we've never seen a restaurant work like this anywhere else. Basically, it's a set of interconnecting rooms, some are good for slouching on sofas, some are good for having mini conferences with white boards and hard chairs, some are good for kids, and some are just like plain old restaurant tables. Likewise with the food, you can pick up a sandwich or order something from the counter. You choose and point, and pick from a breakfast/morning coffee/brunch/ lunch offering with terrific roast-filled sandwiches, or lovely scrambled egg, or a big ice cream pudding in a glass, or some nice Japanese tea, or a warming bowl of soup - it goes on and on. Then you pay for it, and the staff bring it to your table. You collect your cutlery on

Down

the way, and choose the manner in which you want to sit and talk. It works really really well, because the food is good, the system is clearly thought out and the various rooms are all, in their own way, comfortable. Next door is an art gallery which is owned by the same people, and it wouldn't surprise us if we were to see this formula repeated elsewhere. (J & M Beattie, 102-104 High Street, Holywood ☎ 028-9042 7210 ✉ info@ coffeeyard.com 🖱 www.yardgallery.com – Open 8am-5pm Mon-Sat)

only in Ulster
Clotworthy Dobbin

Kilkeel

Organic Farm and Accommodation
● Lurganconary Organic Farm

Lurganconary is a big restoration project which includes an organic farm, whose produce is sold to the public from the farm on Fridays, and through a box delivery scheme. (Helen Cunningham, 25 Lurganconary Rd, Kilkeel 🖱 www.lurganconaryfarms.com)

Brewery
● The Whitewater Brewing Company

We would walk a country mile, in the rain, for a bottle of Clotworthy Dobbin. Mind you, the judges who voted Clotworthy one of the 50 Best Beers in the World a few years ago would probably do the same also. In fact, we would walk that mile for any of Bernard Sloan's meticulously crafted drinks, and Whitewater is, we think, one of the most exciting breweries in the country. And what's that you say? There ain't no sanity clause? Oh yes there is, for Mr Sloan makes a Sanity Claus Xmas beer, spiced with nutmeg and cinnamon for that Christmas glow. Look out for the brews in their pub, the White Horse in Saintfield, where they also do some tasty pub food. But, above all, hunt down these magisterial brews in supermarkets and wine shops. (Bernard & Kerry Sloan, 40 Tullyframe Road, Kilkeel ☎ 028-4176 9449 ✉ info@whitewaterbrewing.co.uk 🖱 www.whitewaterbrewing.co.uk)

Killinchy

Restaurant
● Balloo House

Balloo is an ancient coaching house, appositely restored
by Ronan and Jenny Sweeney. The downstairs bistro is
wood-panelled and country-comfortable, whilst chef
Danny Millar's stage upstairs in the restaurant is plusher
and more gilded. Mr Millar has impressed us as one
of the very best chefs ever since we first ate his food
many years ago, and he has shown with stints in leading
restaurants that his fluidity around unusual taste combinations is utterly imperious – his dish of aromatic pork
belly with brandade, chorizo and salt chilli squid, for
instance, sounds impossible, and yet the chef pulls it off
with gas in the tank. Pulling in the finest local foods gives
Mr Millar the strongest of culinary bases, and he then
adds the magic with delicious surprises: scallops with
Jerusalem artichokes; old-spot pork with black pudding
beignet; sauerbraten venison. Irresistible stuff. (Jennie
Sweeney, 1 Comber Road, Killinchy ☎ 028-9754 1210
🖰 www.balloohouse.com – Bistro food served noon-9pm
Mon-Sun, 'till 8pm Sun. Restaurant open 6pm-9pm Tue-
Thu, 6pm-9.30pm Fri & Sat)

Down

Killyleagh

Gastropub
● Dufferin Arms

They have an imaginative menu in this venerable pub, so
expect the unexpected – butternut squash and ricotta
served with a pine-nut butter sauce; fruity couscous
stuffed courgette with red pepper sauce, beside the
more obvious cod with herb crust, or sirloin topped
with melted brie and chunky chips. It's the characterful
bar and the music sessions that bring in the crowds –
but don't overlook the food. (35 High Street, Killyleagh
☎ 028-4482 1182 🖰 www.dufferinarms.co.uk – Open
for bar food noon-7pm Mon-Sat, 1pm-8pm Sun)

Delicatessen and Café
● Picnic

Picnic is part deli and part café, so you can come for coffee while you shop, or have a delicious hot soup for

lunch and take home some choice cheeses for dinner. Best of all, buy a picnic and head off outdoors, for
this is a beautiful part of the world. (Katherine & John
Dougherty, 49 High Street, Killyleagh ☎ 028-4482 8525
– Open 7am-7pm Mon-Fri, 10am-4pm Sat, and Sunday
during summer)

Kircubbin

Restaurant with Rooms
● **Paul Arthurs**

Paul Arthurs and Danny Millar – of Balloo House – were
working together in Strangford many years ago when
we first encountered their work, and wrote about it
for *The Irish Times*. We were blown away by what these
guys could do, back then, and they have continued to
blow us away with fine cooking ever since. Today, they
are the kings of County Down, heading up two dynamic
restaurants that relish their different signature styles.
Mr Arthurs' cooking is based on superbly sourced
ingredients, and while it is crazy to overlook the superb
fish cookery, you should know that Paul comes from a
long line of butchers. We like the cheeky and appropriate native touches – potato bread with foie gras(!);
local pigeon with champ; hot-smoked mackerel – and
many dishes eaten here have been simply perfect. (Paul
Arthurs, 66 Main Street, Kircubbin ☎ 028-4273 8192
🖑 www.paularthurs.com – Open 5pm-9pm Tue-Sat,
noon-2.30pm Sun)

Lisbane

B&B
● **Anna's House**

Open up your *Guardian* Weekend, and there is Anna
and her house. Open *Mr Partner* in Tokyo, and there is
Anna and her house. Open the *Leipziger Tageszeitung*,
and there is Anna and her house. Switch on the telly, and
there are luminary chefs Nick Price and Danny Millar
enjoying Anna's House. It's official, then: Anna's House
is a global brand. Gucci. Bentley. Tiffany. Dior. Mandarin
Oriental. Hilton. Porsche. Anna's House. It's a good fit.
Mrs Johnson's B&B is celebrated because it is the B&B
of your dreams. A gorgeous, welcoming house. Beautiful

gardens. Superlative cooking. And the sort of maternal care for every guest that is beyond price, making Anna's not just a global brand, but a true global luxury brand. (Anna Johnson, Tullynagee, 35 Lisbarnett Road, Lisbane, Comber ☎ 028-9754 1566 ⌖ www.annashouse.com)

Café & Craft Shop
● The Old Post Office Café

There is a lovely out-of-time feeling to the Old Post Office, a place where you can take morning coffee or afternoon tea. The roof is thatched, the beams are bare and the fires are lit. You can eat in, or take home their tray bakes, pies and gateaux, or indeed do both. Having tea and cinnamon scones in the outside courtyard is one of the best things to do when summer comes. (Trevor & Alison Smylie, 191 Killinchy Road, Lisbane, Comber ☎ 028-9754 3335 ⌖ info@oldpostofficelisbane.co.uk ⌖ www.oldpostofficelisbane.co.uk – Open 9am-5pm Mon-Sat)

Moira

Restaurant
● Ivory Bar & Grill

This is a stylish, modern restaurant where fusion food is served on crisp white plates in an airy, elegant room on the main street of pretty Moira. The cooking puts us in mind of the Ozzie food writer Jill Dupleix, with main ingredients counterpointed by sympathetic partners. Roasted duck breast with savoy cabbage; salmon with watercress mash; salmon and crabcakes with wasabi lime crème fraiche. (William Crawford, Main Street, Moira ☎ 028-9261 3384 ⌖ www.ivorybarandgrill.co.uk – Open noon-2.30pm Fri-Sat, 5pm-9pm Mon-Thur, 5pm-9.30pm Fri & Sat, 12.30pm-3pm, 5pm-8pm Sun)

Butcher
● McCartney's of Moira

Is McCartney's an institution or a legend? We think it's probably both. For 140 years this family firm has produced the most meticulously executed charcuterie and with daughters Judith and Sarah now behind the counter they are sailing on towards 150 years of making the people of Moira very happy indeed. McCartney's is most famed for their sausage range, but in fact the sausages merely indicate the creative imagination that they apply to everything they make from the meat products to the deli products to their special seasonal foods. McCartney's is world class, by whatever standard you care to judge them, from the excellence of the foods to the exuberant beauty of the floral display on the exterior of the shop. (George McCartney, 56-57 Main Street, Moira ☎ 028-9261 1422 ▥ info@ mccartneysofmoira.co.uk ⌂ www.mccartneysofmoira. co.uk – Open 8.30am-5.30pm Tue-Thur, 8am-5.30pm Fri & Sat)

Gastropub
● Pretty Mary's

A pretty pub with pretty food that hits all the right notes is the formula for success in Richard Crooks' bar and restaurant. They source from the best artisans, including Maurice Kettyle, Pat O'Doherty and mushrooms from Hillsborough Forest Park. And then they don't muck about with the quality of the ingredients, adding smoked bacon and blue cheese to a Kettyle beef burger, or buttered brocolli to some Lough Erne lamb, or herbed and crushed potatoes to seared sea trout. Clever modern cooking. (Richard Crooks, 86 Main Street, Moira ☎ 028-9261 1318 ▥ prettymarys@hotmail.co.uk ⌂ www.prettymarys.com – Open noon-3pm, 5pm-9pm Mon-Fri, noon-9.30pm Sat, 1pm-8pm Sun)

Down

Newcastle

Deli & Bistro
● The Cookie Jar Bakery

James Herron's bakery, which he runs with his dad, is one of those classy characterful Northern bakeries that make everyone's life better. (James Herron, 121 Main Street, Newcastle ☎ 028-4372 2427)

Restaurant
● Mourne Café

The third of the excellent Mourne Seafood bars has chef Louis Mallon in the kitchen, and the same smart, nononsense seafood cookery that you will find in Belfast and Dundrum. Annalong crab with lemon and chilli mayonnaise, beer-battered fish and chips with tartare sauce, hot smoked salmon with avocado purée, Mourne seafood chowder. (Bob McCoubrey, 107 Central Promenade, Newcastle ☎ 028-4372 6401 ✆ www.mourneseafood.com – Open noon-8pm Mon-Wed, noon-late Thur-Sat, noon-8.45pm Sun. Closed Mon-Wed off season)

Newry

Home Bakery & Café
● The Corn Dolly Home Bakery

The Corn Dolly do the classic vernacular baking of Northern Ireland, from granary loaves to fruit bracks, to cream fingers, and meat pies, and they do it all with the dedication and pride that characterises Northern Ireland's great battalion of bakers. Make sure to pick up a lunchtime sandwich when you're in here for a treacle farl and a small trifle. (Jim & Anthony O'Keeffe, 12 Marcus Square, Newry ☎ 028-3026 0524 ✉ info@corndollyfoods.com ✆ www.corndollyfoods.com – Open 8.30am-6pm Mon-Fri, 8am-6pm Sat. Also at 28 Church Street, Warrenpoint ☎ 028-4275 3596)

Restaurant
● Graduate Restaurant

The students in the School of Hospitality and Tourism in the SRC are set the daunting challenge of having to cook lunch for the public, and a Tuesday evening dinner as part of their course. So if you want to discover the next Jamie or Rachel before the TV producers get their hands on them, this is the place to come for lunch or dinner. This is a proper, 60-seater licensed restaurant, so the students are really put on their mettle. (Southern Regional College, Patrick Street, Newry ☎ 028-3026 1071/028-3025 9611 ✆ www.src.ac.uk – Open for lunch, 12.30pm, Mon-Fri and Tue evening, 7pm, for dinner during term time)

Newtownards

Greengrocer
● Glastry Farm Luxury Ice Cream

Will Taylor is one of those dynamic blokes who doesn't let the currently depressed mood of the farming sector stand in the way of innovating, adding value, and making top-class food products, in his case, a range of luxury ice creams and ice cream cakes that use the milk of their 220 head pedigree herd. Glastry produce five true flavours, yellowman honeycomb, strawberry blonde, chocolate heaven, vanilla bean and rhubarb and ginger, and you can expect them to be the next Ben and Jerry's or Innocent. (Will Taylor, 43 Manse Road, Kircubbin, Newtownards ☎ 028-4273 8671 ✉ icecream@ glastryfarm.com 🖰 www.glastryfarm.com)

Greengrocer
● Homegrown

People love Homegrown, they like the look of the shop, the traditional style of service, and the wonderful mix of local veg that Trevor and Margaret offer for sale every day. A local star. (Trevor & Margaret White, 66b East Street, Newtownards ☎ 028-9181 8318 – Open 9am-5.30pm Mon-Thur, 8am-5.30pm Fri & Sat)

Home Bakery & Coffee Shop
● Knott's Cake & Coffee Shop

Michael Knott's craft bakery in the centre of town has a busy, bustling bread and cake counter at the front and a huge coffee shop and restaurant at the rear. The self service queue for the tasty savoury cooking never seems to slacken as people fill their trays with sandwiches, pies, beef olives, baked gammon and of course lots of sweetie things to go with that nice cup of tea. (Michael Knott, 45 High Street, Newtownards ☎ 028-9181 9098 🖰 www. knottsbakery.co.uk – Open 7.30am-5pm Mon-Sat)

Country Store & Restaurant
● McKee's Farm Shop

McKee's is an unbelievable place. You first notice something is different as you make your way up the newly gravelled road into what was clearly once a field that has been cleared to make space for an enormous car park. As the car park is absolutely full of cars, you wonder have you stumbled on some one-off agricultural show. You park, and walk through an entrance of pot plants and seedlings, and then, if you are lucky and have hit the right season, you'll come across big bags of new Comber potatoes, sold at premium prices for the gems that they are. Step in and you are faced with a cornucopia. And this is why McKee's is so clever.

Everything looks amazing, everything looks natural, everything, down to the flowers, looks local. If you are looking for the various Ulster specialities, you'll find them here, from the Comber spuds, to the farls, the bracks, even the pasties, which you only otherwise stumble across in fish'n'chip shops. And it's all laid out as if this is the food hall in Harrods, and these are the precious gifts of the earth. If you come here, be prepared to queue. Queue to buy the food, and queue longer to eat in the restaurant, in which you might be offered darne of salmon, beef curry, roast chump of beef with rich gravy or chicken liver pâté with wheaten bread and pickle. (Colin McKee, 28 Holywood Road, Newtownards ☎ 028-9181 3202 📧 orders@ mckeesproduce.co.uk 🖱 www.mckeesproduce.co.uk – Open 8.30am-5.30pm Mon-Sat)

only in Ulster
Pasties

Saintfield

Real Ale Pub
● The White Horse Inn

The White Horse is owned by Bernard and Kerry Sloan of the Whitewater Brewery in Kilkeel. So this is the ideal spot to try all their fantastic brews, and, as proper artisan beer is designed to be paired with food, you can have bacon loin with colcannon to go with your Clot-worthy Dobbin. Or maybe minute steak with chunky chips as the ideal foil for a bottle of Belfast Ale. (Bernard & Kerry Sloan, 49 Main Street, Saintfield ☎ 048-9751 1143 – Open pub hours)

Seaforde

Local Shop
● Brennan's Garage

Famous for their ice cream, and the way to show that you are in the know is to order an oyster. (149 Newcas-tle Road, Seaforde ☎ 028-4481 1271)

Strangford

Organic Farm Shop
● Churchtown Farm Organic Farm Shop

With their own Angus, Shorthorn and south
Devon cattle, with organic Saddleback pork from
Dundermotte farm near Ballymena, and with Lleyn
sheep providing their lamb and mutton, is it any wonder
that Churchtown is regarded as one of the finest farm
shops in these islands. Dale and John Orr are setting
new standards with their work in Churchtown, for the
meats are as superbly prepared as they are superbly
reared here, and given that you can order all their
products online, you have everything you need for the
good life at the click of your computer mouse, from
Angus beef to their own maple smoked leg of lamb.
Dale can also be found in the St George's Market, but
if you can't get there or to the farmshop, remember
that distance is no object to getting this incredible
food onto your plate. Outstanding. (Dale & John Orr,
Churchtown, Co Down ☎ 028-4488 1128 ⌒ www.
churchtownfarmorganicproduce.com – Farm shop open
Thur-Sun 9am-6pm)

only in Ulster
Weaver's Gold Blonde Ale

Guest Inn & Restaurant
● The Cuan Guest Inn

Peter McErlean wisely uses the good foods around him
to fashion his culinary style in the Cuan – Churchtown
farm organic lamb in a casserole with champ; Finnebrogue venison; Pinkerton's Armagh pork with wild
mushrooms; Eastcoast smoked haddock with parsley
cream; Noel Taggart's crab served in its shell; Dundrum
bay mussels. There are nine comfortable rooms upstairs,
and everything chimes so sweetly in this neat Guest Inn
that we would love a few days spent paddling kayaks on
Strangford Lough, with the promise of dinner and a good
night's sleep in The Cuan waiting for us. (Peter McErlean, The Square, Strangford ☎ 028-4488 1588 ⌒ www.
thecuan.com – Open noon-8.30pm Sun-Thu, noon-
9.30pm Fri & Sat)

Waringstown

Artisan Brewery
● Clanconnel Brewing Company

Here is a story about Mark Pearson's Weaver's Gold
Blonde Ale. Following a day spent failing to master the
devilish nature of dinghy sailing, John McKenna arrived
home despondent and exhausted. Seeking salvation,
he opened up a bottle of Weaver's Gold. Ten minutes
later he was in the kitchen cooking dinner, having been
brought back to life by a brew that can only be described
as a healthful life saver. If Mark Pearson's planned new
brews – he has an Irish ale and a stout in the Clancon-
nel pipeline – prove to be as good as Weaver's Gold,
then this will be one of the great trinities of Irish artisan
brewing. (Mark Pearson, Waringstown ☎ 07711-626770
✉ info@clanconnelbrewing.com ⌖ www.clanconnel-
brewing.com)

Warrenpoint

Home Bakery & Café
● The Corn Dolly Home Bakery

Sister to the wonderful Newry baking institution, so see
the entry described there. (Jim & Anthony O'Keeffe,
28 Church Street, Warrenpoint ☎ 028-4175 3596
✉ info@corndollyfoods.com ⌖ www.corndollyfoods.com
– Open 8.30am-6pm Mon-Sat)

Restaurant & Bar
● The Duke

Ciaran Gallagher is one of the very best cooks in Northern Ireland, and for more than ten years he has stuck
to his mantra of fresh fish and shellfish from Kilkeel,
and a few steaks, and he has won a devoted audience
for cooking that is elegant, intuitive and masterly. He is
a purist at heart, with a touch of the ascetic mingled in
with his culinary aesthetic, and this complicated mixture
makes for great eating: he will grill john dory and pair
it with queen scallops with a thermidor sauce, whilst
robust-tasting hake enjoys petits pois a la francaise with
baby gem lettuce and cream. Elsewhere he shows his
respect to the classics – prawns in beer batter with
tartare; smoked haddock with soft poached egg and

hollandaise. "Dad was a chef – I think I was condemned from a very early age!" Mr Gallagher told *The Irish Times* in an interview. Food lovers will be hoping, after a brilliant decade in business, that Mr Gallagher is doing a life sentence in this kitchen. (Ciaran Gallagher, 7 Duke Street, Warrenpoint ☎ 028-4175 2084 – Open 6.30pm-10pm Tue-Sat, 6pm-9pm Sun)

Restaurant
● Restaurant 23

Trevor Cunningham is doing the good thing in 23, firing out fine food at tasty prices. His USP is elegantly presented food that packs quite a taste punch. He takes a main theme – foie-gras terrine, let's say –and then hits home the message with jabs of complementary flavours – some quince purée, some gingerbread and a fig reduction. This is classic work in a modern guise, and it runs throughout the menus: fillet of Old Spot pork with 5-spice pork belly, creamy cabbage and Calvados sauce; john dory with coriander noodles and a prawn and coconut sauce; chocolate custard with Bailey's granita and cardamom foam. The devil that is in the detail is well taken care of: the room is comfortable and quite lovely, part of the Bennett's pub, the care shown in vegetable cookery is spot on, and staff know their stuff backwards. (Raymond McArdle, 23 Church Street, Warrenpoint ☎ 028-475 3222 ⌂ www.restaurant-23.co.uk – Open 12.15pm-2.30pm Tue-Fri, 6pm-9.30pm Tue-Thu, 6pm-10pm Fri, 12.15pm-10pm Sat, 12.15pm-8pm Sun)

County Fermanagh

Derrylin

Wine Merchant
● Blake's Fine Wines

Sam Brannigan has some serious bottles in stock in little
Derrylin and if your boat has come in and you urgently
need some Haut-Brion 2006, or the 2005 Chateau Palm-
er, then they are here waiting with your name on them.
Away from these wallet busters, there are fine wines
from all over the globe and the list is particularly strong
on French regional wines and Italians. (Sam Brannigan,
The Market Place. Derrylin, ☎ 028-6774 8550 ✉ info@
blakesfinewines.com 🖰 www.blakesfinewines.com)

---

only in Ulster
Fermanagh Boxty

Enniskillen

Home Bakery
● Leslie's Bakery

Breads, made by hand, using traditional recipes, practis-
ing regional techniques, make Leslie's Bakery special.
Look out for their famed Fermanagh fruit loaf and their
fadge and their farls. (Leslie Wilkin, 10 Church Street,
Enniskillen ☎ 028-6632 4902 ✉ wilkinsbakeryltd@
btinternet.com – Open 8am-6pm Mon-Sat)

Restaurant
● Lough Erne Golf Resort

The Bridgestone Guides have followed Noel McMeel
from place to place over the last twenty years, ever
since he first emerged as a major talent when cooking
in Derry's Beech Hill. Way back then there was a
delicacy and a deep affection for food evident in his

work, and those same qualities are just as evident today in the somewhat surprising setting of the Lough Erne Golf Resort. Mr McMeel has worked hard to stamp his signature on the food, and it shows: Irish crab with spiced couscous and roast beetroot, terrine of Fermanagh chicken with shallot soubise, beef Rossini with potato purée and truffle sauce. Typical of McMeel's sympathy for the customer is his splendid vegetarian menu, which includes a velouté of courgette with marinated brie and smoked garlic oil, and a red onion and spinach goat's cheese cannelloni served with heather honey and a fig chutney. (Noel McMeel, Belleek Road, Enniskillen ☎ 028-6632 3230 ✉ info@loughernegolfresort.com 🖰 www.loughernegolfresort.com)

Butcher
● **O'Doherty's**

"On Inishcorkish Island, the black pigs live wild for the duration of their life and form their own social structure and pecking order. At night they make their own nest under the trees and during the day they etch out a very good living from the widespread vegetation." Pat O'Doherty takes the whole business of bacon production as far as it can possibly go, as this quote, describing the lifestyle of the pigs he rears on Inishcorkish Island on Upper Lough Erne, vividly reveals. Mr O'Doherty is an unconventional bloke: he is actually an environmental science graduate who somehow got caught up in the butchering trade. But his scientific and environmental awareness have given his foods qualities that no other butcher can emulate, and he pairs up-to-the-minute techniques with a love of the ancient and local traditions of bacon curing that were commonplace a century ago. The result is Fermanagh Black Bacon. "The idea was to create a paradise for the pigs", Mr O'Doherty told *The Irish Times*. Paradise found. (Pat O'Doherty, Belmore Street, Enniskillen ☎ 028-6632 2152 ✉ sales@blackbacon. com 🖰 www.blackbacon.com – Open 8am-6pm Mon-Sat)

Restaurant
● **Café Merlot, Blakes of the Hollow & No 6**

One of the classic Irish pubs plays host to Gerry Russell and John Donnelly's pair of restaurants, the daytime Café Merlot, and the weekend No 6 Restaurant. The day time food in the cafe is big on flavours, especially in the pasta dishes, which are one of their signatures. But to see the real flavour of a talented chef like Mr Russell, you need to try No 6, where he has more space to work the Asian riffs that he likes to conjure up with his dishes. (Gerry Russell & John Donnelly, Blakes of the Hollow, 6 Church Street, Enniskillen ☎ 028-6632 0918 ⬚ rune. home@btopenworld.com – Cafe Merlot opens noon-3pm, 5.30pm-9pm Mon-Sun, 'till 9.30pm Sat. Restaurant No 6 opens 5.30pm-9.30pm Fri & Sat and for special bookings during the week)

only in Ulster
Kettyle Beef

Deli, Wine Shop & Café
● Russell & Donnelly

Gerry and John from Café Merlot hit all the spots in their new Enniskillen venture, where you will find hundreds of wines, scores of deli products and a small choice range of cooked foods, which you can eat sitting at glass-topped wine barrels. This is a particularly important destination in a region that has long been crying out for a top-class deli. (John Donnelly & Gerry Russell, 28 Darling Street, Enniskillen ☎ 028-6632 0111 – Open 9am-7pm Mon-Sat. Open for coffee, Sun 1pm-6pm)

Fermanagh

Irvinestown

Ice Cream
● Tickety-Moo Ice Cream

It all happens in Moo HQ. The pretty Jersey cows munch the grass and make the milk that makes the ice cream, thanks to a little bit of intervention from Steve and Gareth and their team. Tickety-Moo comes at you in an eruption of flavours, rhubarb crumble and custard, choc-a-lot, panna cotta & raspberry pavlova, or double caramel fudge chunk to name just a few. If you are in the zone do call in to see the cows being milked (4.30pm is the time, seven days a week). (Steve Gillies & Gareth Grey, Moo HQ, Oghill Farm, Kiladeas, Irvinestown ☎ 028-6862 8779 ⬚ www.tickety-moo.com – Open noon-6pm Mon-Sun from 11 April-28 September)

Lisbellaw

Cookery Schoolr
● Belle Isle Cookery School

Housed in the Duke of Abercorn's beautiful country
estate, Liz Moore's school has thrived over the years
and established itself as the leading cookery school in
Northern Ireland. There is a great range of courses from
four-week intensive courses, to more relaxed weekend
courses. And you can even bring your corporate team
here to do some team building around the pots and
pans. (Liz Moore, Lisbellaw ☎ 028-6638 7231 ⌁ www.
irishcookeryschool.com)

Lisnaskea

Specialist Beef
● Kettyle Irish Foods

Maurice Kettyle's ambition with his beef and lamb is
to rear and process "the best of the best". He could
also add that the best of the best chefs in Ireland and
UK all use Kettyle Beef. This is one of the defining Irish
products of its age, a summation of everything good
that careful breeding and lush pastures can create.
Mr Kettyle has solved the problematic areas in beef
production by ensuring that any manner of stress that
could befall the animal between the farm and the factory
is eradicated. And then his craftsmanlike preparation of
the beef means that what you cook is perfectly designed
for the grill or the oven.(Maurice Kettyle, Manderwood
Business Park, Drumhaw, Lisnaskea ☎ 028-6772 3777
⌁ maurice@kettyleirishfoods.com ⌁ www.
kettyleirishfoods.com)

only in Ulster
Fermanagh Black Bacon

County Londonderry

Ballykelly

Bakery and Café
● **Hunter's at the Oven Door**

Part of Sean Hunter's marvellous traditional and home-baking café empire. See Hunter's of Limavady. (Sean Hunter, 34 Main Street, Ballykelly ☎ 028-7776 6228 huntersbakery@aol.com – Open 8.30am-5.30pm Mon-Sat)

only in Ulster
Wee Buns

Castledawson

Home Bakery & Café
● **Ditty's Home Bakery**

Robert Ditty is the very personification of a food hero. His day to day work with the nuts and bolts of baking superlative breads and cakes establishes *the* benchmark that other Irish bakers have to live up to. In his community he is a powerhouse organiser, assisting local business, organising food festivals, and in his shops in Castledawson and Magherafelt he puts his philosophy of baking and eating into practice in the most practical and communitarian way possible. For Robert Ditty the baker is in essence the shaman of the society – wise, experienced, and daring. He is one of the most important figures in Northern Ireland's contemporary food culture, but his importance to the contemporary culture comes from his understanding of the historical culture and the values he places in what we can learn from the past. Of course, he also makes the best sody farls. (Robert Ditty, 44 Main Street, Castledawson ☎ 028-7946 8243 dittysbakery@tiscali.co.uk www.dittysbakery.com – Open 9am-5.30pm Mon-Sat)

LDerry

Claudy

Butcher
● O'Kane Meats

The O'Kane brothers are as good as butchers get, and
what is surprising about their surpassing excellence is
the fact that, unlike so many other butchers in Northern
Ireland, they don't have 50 or 100 years of family history
in the business. Instead, they are self-made butchers, which makes their incredible success even more
extraordinary. They have won every butchering award,
and won many of them several times over, yet their zeal
for competition is undimmed, and the guys themselves
are brimful of energy. So, turn off the main 'Derry road
into little Claudy, into this modest shop, and get ready
for some of the best meat products you have ever
enjoyed. (Michael & Kieran O'Kane, Main Street, Claudy
☎ 028-7133 8944 🖃 mail@okanemeats.com 🖱 www.
okanemeats.com – Open 7.45am-5.45pm Mon-Sat)

Coleraine

Coffee Shop
● Ground

Serious coffee and yummy things are the core ingredients of Ground, who have always shown themselves
to be ahead of the local competition, ever since they
opened up firstly here in Coleraine and then all over
the province. Comfortable rooms and committed staff
mean that Ground can take the grind out of your day.
(Karen Gardiner, 25 Kingsgate Street, Coleraine ☎ 028-
7032 8664 🖱 www.groundcoffee.net – Open 9am-
5.30pm Mon-Sat. Also at 30-32 Ballymoney Street, Ballymena ☎ 028-2565 0060 – Open 9am-5.30pm Mon-Sat.
Also at 44 Fountain Street, Belfast ☎ 028-9032 8226;
4 High Street, Ballymoney ☎ 028-2766 2625; 52 Main
Street, Portrush ☎ 028-7082 5979)

Home Bakery & Café
● Hunter's at Kitty's of Coleraine

Part of Sean Hunter's marvellous traditional and home-
baking café empire. See Hunter's of Limavady. (Sean
Hunter, 3 Church Lane, Coleraine ☎ 028-7034 2347
🖃 huntersbakery@aol.com– Open 9am-5.30pm Mon-Sat)

● The Watermargin

The Watermargin was a pioneer in Northern Ireland's Chinese restaurant history, opening a large theatrical East meets West dining room in the spacious first floor of the Coleraine boat club long before anyone else considered such a concept. Back in 1991, in our first *Bridgestone Irish Food Guide*, we wrote "All the theatre of Chinese food is at play in the Watermargin: the sizzling dishes, the spinning tasting tables, waitresses in long Hong Kong silks." – though we complained about them playing *The Hills Are Alive* on the music system. Since then this type of restaurant has been much copied, and indeed repeated, for they now have a sister restaurant in Belfast. The food, throughout its history has remained consistently good, and if you divert from the usual Western-style menus, you'll find much to enjoy here. (Tony Cheuk, The Boathouse, Hanover Place, Coleraine ☎ 028-7034 2222 – Open 5pm-10.30pm Mon-Sun)

Delicatessen and Cafe
● Willow Garden Tea Room

"Delicious herbal teas, good salads, cakes, and definitely worth knowing about along a coast which seems not to have too many places to eat," said our friend Maya after a visit to the Willow Tea Garden. There are lots of peacocks and hens running around the garden, so be careful where you step. (James Currie, Pretty Crafty Design Studio, 5 Springhank Road, Castlerock, Coleraine ☎ 028-7084 8146 📧 prettycraftydesignstudio@yahoo. co.uk – Open 10am-5pm Mon-Sat, 11am-5pm. Limited hours off season)

Desertmartin

Farm Shop & Charcuterie
● Moss Brook Farm Shoppe

It's been ten years since we met Trevor Barclay at the St George's Market at its first ever food festival. Pig prices had collapsed, all of Trevor's colleagues in the pork business had gotten out of it and, as a last ditch attempt to stay solvent, Trevor had made some sausages and brought them to the Festival. "We'll see you at the end of the day: keep us some bangers" we said as we headed off to introduce Josceline Dimbleby. We never did get those sausages: Trevor sold every last one that day, and Moss Brook was born. A decade on, and Trevor is one of the big cheeses of artisan food, his St George's stall now a veritable cornucopia unto itself, as Trevor grills – "The best sausage and bacon soda bap" regulars will tell you – and brews and shifts a mountain of delicious pork products and pies every Saturday. Saved by the bell! (Trevor & Irene Barclay, 6 Durnascallon, Desertmartin ☎ 028-7963 3454 📖 mossbrookbaconboys@btinternet.com – Open by arrangement)

Eglinton

Café
● Artisan In The Village

Having made a great success of Café Artisan in Derry, where it is calmly and comfortably tucked into the Bookworm bookstore, Rachel has set out eastwards to set up AITV in little Eglinton. Expect good music, a nice left-field ambience and great sandwiches and salad platters. (Rachel Doherty, 18b Main Street, Eglinton ☎ 028-7181 1682. Also at 18-20 Bishop Street, Derry ☎ 028-7128 2727 📖 dohertyrc@btinternet.com – Open 8am-5pm Mon-Sat)

Garvagh

Farm Shop
● Arkhill Farm Shop

Paul Craig sells the produce of their ten-acre organic farm, from the farm shop. Worth a detour for their fine eggs, and they also sell cakes, jams and chutneys. (Paul Craig, 25 Drumcroone Road, Garvagh ☎ 028-2955 7920 – Open 9am-5pm Mon-Fri)

Limavady

Home Bakery & Café
● Hunter's at the Oven Door

As they head towards half a century of invaluable service to communities in the North West, Sean Hunter's reputation for batch breads and buttery wheatens, hot plate muffins and buttermilk pancakes, has been extended

in recent times by their hugely successful tea loaves.
Jammed full of toasted hazelnuts and cherries, these are
one of the quintessential examples of Northern Ireland
vernacular baking, and even the smallest bite makes
you feel wonderful. Nice, simple food – stews, soups,
sandwiches, teas and coffees – complete the picture
of an ideal bakery and café. (Sean Hunter, 5-9 Market
Street, Limavady ☎ 028-7772 2411 ⊡ huntersbakery@
aol.com– Open 8.30am-5.30pm Mon-Sat)

Smoked Salmon

● Norman Hunter & Son

We have noted before that Ian Hunter has a famous
quote from John Ruskin on the wall of his butcher's
shop – we won't say what it is, it would spoil the fun of
visiting – and Mr Hunter puts the sane and sustainable
philosphies of Ruskin into practice every day in this
terrific deli, bakery, cheese shop and butchers. Sirloins
are hung for as much as four weeks and out of a
wonderful array of foods, their own pies are particularly
noteworthy. (Ian Hunter, 53-55 Main Street ☎ 028-
7776 2665 ⊡ normanhunterandson@yahoo.co.uk –
Open 9am-5.30pm Mon-Sat)

● Keady Mountain Farm

The Mullan family have been farming organically for a
decade now, and in that same period their chickens,
eggs and Sperrin lamb, have become some of the most
sought-after products in the St George's Saturday
market. They are products as nature intended, eggs with
vivid orange/yellow yolks, lamb that is Burgundy red in
colour, and which they hang for two weeks, and chickens
that roast to sweet perfection for your Sunday dinner.
(Michael Mullan, Limavady ☎ 028-7776 4157 ⊡ info@
mullansorganicfarm.com ⊖ www.mullansorganicfarm.
com)

● The Lime Tree

Stanley Matthews is the local champion, a chef who champions local foods – Ian Hunter's sirloin, Malin crab, local game, Atlantic fish – and alchemises the ingredients into handsome finely wrought dishes. Their seafood thermidor is perhaps the signature dish, but we very much like the way Stanley cooks the neglected and over looked rabbit, preparing it as a roast saddle, or in a Majorcan-style stew with sherry, onion and roasted garlic. Whilst there are dishes for more conservative palates, you really see Stanley's work at its best when he riffs on the Mediterranean influences that are close to his culinary heart. Maria manages front of house as to the manor born. (Stanley & Maria Matthews, 60 Catherine Street, Limavady ☎ 028-7776 4300 ✍ info@ limetreerest.com 🖰 www.limetreerest.com – Open from 6pm Tue-Sat)

Fish & Chips
● McNulty's Fish & Chips

We thought Brian McNulty's efforts to bring you the best fish and chips could not be topped – this is the man, after all, who having sourced the best potatoes for his chips then drove around in his car to road test them – but he's done it again. This time it's the bottling of their own vinegar to accompany said chips. Perfection, perfection, perfection. That's the name of the game in McNulty's, and that's exactly how you ennoble good fish and good chips into a true epicurean delight. We're just waiting to see what on earth Brian can do to further drive on this luxury brand chipper. (Brian McNulty, 84 Main Street, Limavady ☎ 028-7776 2148 🖰 www. mcnultysfishandchips.com – Open 9am-11pm Mon-Sat, 4.30pm-11pm Sun)

Londonderry

Hotel
● Beech Hill Country House Hotel

We are great admirers of Patsey O'Kane. She is one of the great figures of Northern Irish hospitality, incarnating that true hospitality that the Northerners exude, but framing it within both the tenets of extreme professionalism, and within the lovely aesthetic of Beech Hill

House itself. She is assisted in her desire to do things the right way by a dedicated kitchen crew, part of a team characterised by the fact that in the Beech Hill everyone over-delivers, everyone is always trying to do their best, to make sure that every detail is done right, done as well as it can be. That is the art of hotel keeping, and Ms O'Kane is mistress of that art, and she testifies to that art every day in her work in this beautiful, early 18th-century house. Beech Hill is only two miles from Derry, but truthfully it is a place of and unto itself, a place of hospitality. (Patsey O'Kane, Londonderry ☎ 028-7134 9279 ✉ info@beech-hill.com ✆ www.beech-hill.com)

Brasserie
● Brown's

Ivan and Elma Taylor have been the destination address in 'Derry for twenty five years now, with their menus evolving steadily to include modern flavours and tastes – loin of pork with warm noodle salad; sea bass with chilli chick peas – whilst classic dishes – lamb and rosemary sausages with mash and red onion gravy, salmon with champ and seafood nage – remain as people pleasing as ever. (Ivan & Elma Taylor, 1 Bonds Hill ☎ 028-7134 5180 ✉ eat@brownsrestaurant.com ✆ www.brownsrestaurant.com – Open noon-2.15pm Tue-Fri, 5.30pm-late Tue-Sat)

Café
● Café Artisan

Rachel Doherty's communitarian café has just the sort of laid-back ambience we like, with lots of well worn leather chairs, pretty flowers, good sounds and above all, good food. (Rachel Doherty, 18-20 Bishop Street, Derry ☎ 028-7128 2727 ✉ dohertyrc@btinternet.com – Open 8am-5pm Mon-Sat)

Restaurant
● Mange 2

They are a sincere and dedicated team, chef Kieran and foh John, and they have built a devoted following in Derry since opening in 2002. The cooking takes its cue from French cuisine: cod with chive mash and smoked salmon and spinach cream sauce; Glenties pork with champ, cabbage and gravy; medallions of fillet steak with pepper cream sauce. (Kieran McGuinness & John O'Connell, 110-115 Strand Road, Derry City ☎ 028-7136 1222 ✉ dine@mange2derry.com 🖱 www.mange2derry.com – Open 12.30pm-2.30pm Tue-Fri, noon-3.30pm Sun, 5pm-late Mon-Sun)

● The Merchant's House, Saddler's House

In addition to her two fine B&Bs, the Merchant's House and the simpler Saddler's House, Joan Pyne also has two self-catering houses in the city, Cathedral Cottage and Darcus Cottage. Ms Pyne is very sympathetic to the aesthetic of each of her houses, and it is this quest for correctness and appositeness that makes these houses such a vital alternative to the bland hotels that dominate town. (Joan Pyne, Saddler's House, 36 Gt James Street, Derry; Merchant House, 16 Queen Street, Derry ☎ 028-7126 9691 ✉ saddlershouse@btinternet.com 🖱 www.thesaddlershouse.com)

● Spice

Nicki and Darragh Cartmill like to spice it up a little bit in Spice, their colourful modern restaurant on Spencer road: chilli and coriander lamb shank shows the sort of funky spicing they like, and chicken is dusted with paprika and served with a spiced tomato sauce, whilst fillet steak gets both a shot of Jack Daniels and a blue cheese finish. We bet fifty percent of their customers go for the Malteser and hot toffee meringue. (Nicki & Darragh Cartmill 162-164 Spencer Road, Derry ☎ 028-7134 4875 ✉ info@spicerestaurantderry.com 🖱 www.spicerestaurantderry.com)

Maghera

● McKee's Butchers

Many of the best Northern Irish butchers are fortunate to rear their own cattle, and George McKee is one of those fortunate butchers. As befits a member of the Elite Guild of Northern Irish Butchers, he brings authoratative charcuterie skills to these wonderful raw ingredients, which are lovingly displayed in both the shops in Maghera. (George McKee, 26 & 78 Main Street, Maghera ☎ 028-7964 2559 ✉ mckeespies@btopenworld.com – Open 9am-6pm Mon-Sat)

Magherafelt

Home Bakery & Café
● Ditty's Home Bakery

See the entry for Ditty's under Castledawson. (33 Rainey Street, Magherafelt ☎ 028-7963 3944 – Open 8am-5.30pm Mon-Sat)

Brasserie
● Gardiner's G2

Sean Owens has a big personality and it shows in the big flavoured dishes that he puts on his big menus. Giant pork and leek bangers with mash and onion gravy, Lough Neagh Eels with bacon mash and parsley butter, roasted rump of Fermanagh lamb with roast garlic mash are typical of the unarguable assault of roasty sweet tastes that Sean likes to offer. They have made over the restaurant after a successful decade in business, so here's to the next ten years. (Sean Owens, 7 Garden Street, Magherafelt ☎ 028-7930 0333 ✉ gardiners2000@hotmail.com ⌂ www.gardiners.net – Open 5.30pm-10pm Tue-Sat, noon-3pm, 5pm-9.30pm Sun)

only in Ulster
Fadge

Supermarket
● JC Stewarts

This is a truly super supermarket, in fact Stewarts should reall be called a wondermarket, because it is pure, darn wonderful in every way. The design and ambience of the store is of a type that you only find in luxury brand boutiques in capital cities, and yet here it is in little Magherafelt, stocking and serving all of the best local foods that you can think of from McKee's pies to

Ditty's oatcakes. We have compared Stewarts to Field's supermarket in West Cork, but in fact we think it's somewhat close to the legendary Ardkeen stores of Waterford. The two shops both act as a focal point for local foods in the most meaningful and delightful way, and if all the issues about food miles and carbon footprint are keeping you awake at night, then you should know that shopping at Stewarts solves all of those issues in one delightful retail experience. (Paul Stewart, 1 Union Road, Magherafelt ☎ 028-7930 2930 🖰 www.jcstewart. co.uk – Open 8am-7pm Mon-Wed, 8am-9pm Thur & Fri, 8am-6pm Sat)

Portstewart

Bakery & Coffee Shop
● McLaughlin's

Stewart and Robert McLaughlin have been baking in Coleraine for many years, but their new bakery and coffee shop marks a return to their home town. Their pancakes and pastries are superb, as are their traditional griddle breads, and with a good cup of Illy coffee to pair with a fresh cream bun in the coffee shop, this is a great new destination for Portstewart. (Stewart & Robert McLaughlin, 91 The Promenade, Portstewart ☎ 028-7083 4460 🖰 sashenry@hotmail.co.uk – Open day time)

Butcher
● JE Toms & Sons

If you are heading up to the caravan in Portstewart for your holidays, then you need to know that when the rain stops and the sun shines you will find every possible ingredient for your ideal barbecue in Alan Tom's shop. They are also noted as particularly good sausage makers, and, as you would expect, their pies are really top notch. (Alan Toms, 46 The Promenade ☎ 028-7083 2869 – Open 8am-5.30pm Mon-Sat, from 7.30am Sat)

only in Ulster

Malin Crab

County Tyrone

Castlederg

Organic Delivery
● **Organic Doorstep**

OD is a visionary company that has developed from creating a market for their own organic dairy products into
a distribution and delivery company for a whole range of
organics. They deliver twice a week to more than 1,000
customers throughout Northern Ireland, and so this is a
brilliant example of how to solve the logistical difficulties of getting organics directly to the customer. (Glenn
Huey, 125 Strabane Road, Castlederg ☎ 028-8167 9989
☎ Freephone 0800-783 5656 ✉ info@organicdoorstep.
co.uk ✍ www.organicdoorstep.net)

Sheep's Cheese
● **Springwell Speciality Sheep's Cheese**

Linda Gourley makes Northern Ireland's only sheep's
milk cheese, milking a herd of 150 ewes on her farm,
and then fashioning the cheeses at the nearby Erganagh
Dairy in Castlederg. Although they look something like
feta cheeses the Springwell Cheeses are never brined.
The plain cheese has two flavoured counterparts, one
seasoned with red pepper, and the other with chives.
Look out for them at the local country markets in
Coleraine, Derry and Strabane. (Linda Gourley, c/o 29
Erganagh Road, Castlederg ☎ 028-8167 0626)

L'Derry

Cookstown

Seed Sprouters
● **Good4U**

There are are no fewer than two tubs of Good4u foods
in our fridge as we write – the lentil and bean shoots
we use in sandwiches, because we know that sprouted
seeds help you access more enzymes than any other
food, whilst the chilli mix of smart seeds are scattered
onto salads, giving us another nutritional powerhouse.

You will find these lovely products in all the major stores, and you really need them in your life. (Michelle Butler, 45 Tullywiggan Road, Loughry College, Cookstown ☎ 028-8676 1914 ✉ info@good4u.co.uk 🖰 www.good4u.co.uk)

---

only in Ulster
Potato Farls

Dungannon

Farm Shop
● Cloughbane Farm Shop

The Robinson family have made an amazing success of their farmshop on their farm, with fifteen people employed to prepare and process their own beef and lamb. They have recently won awards for their new range of pies, which ingeniously use all the tasty off-cuts to make savoury mince pie, steak, onion and mushroom pie, chicken, ham and leek pie, and turkey and stuffing pie. Northern Irish farmers are way ahead of the rest of the country when it comes to the question of securing farm incomes, creating a loyal customer base, and reducing food miles and carbon footprints, and in Cloughbane you see all of these essential objectives brought into delicious focus. (Lorna & Richard Robinson, 160 Tandragee Road, Dungannon ☎ 028-8775 8246 ✉ info@cloughbanefarm.com 🖰 www.cloughbanefarm.com – Open 9am-6pm Mon-Thur, 9am-8pm Fri, 8.30am-5pm Sat)

Guesthouse & Cookery School
● Grange Lodge

Norah Brown MBE is the archetype of the Northern Irish Domestic Goddess. Cook, hostess, cookery teacher and fount of culinary knowledge she has flown the flag of Northern Irish hospitality for decades and done so through the medium of Grange Lodge where you can come and stay for dinner, enjoy a cookery class, and truly get into the heart of mid Ulster. (Norah & Ralph Brown, Grange Road, Dungannon ☎ 028-8778 4212 ✉ stay@grangelodgecountryhouse.com 🖰 www.grangelodgecountryhouse.com)

● **Stangmore Country House**

A personable professionalism is the reason why Anne
and Andy Brace's guest house and restaurant continues
to attract a loyal local following. (Anne & Andy Brace,
65 Moy Road, Dungannon ☎ 028-8772 5600 ✉ info@
stangmorecountryhouse.com 🖱 www.stangmorecoun-
tryhouse.com – Open dinner Mon-Sat)

Wine Importers
● **Wattle Tree Wines**

Martin Forker's company imports bespoke wines from
seven family-owned Australian wine companies, and
they are thankfully far removed from the industrially-
produced wines that now besmirch the reputation of
Australia wine, and which fill the shelves of every supermarket. (Martin & Clare Forker, PO Box 1475, Dungannon ☎ 028-8776 9206 ✉ info@wattletreewines.co.uk
www.wattletreewines.co.uk)

Fivemiletown

Creamery Cheese
● **Fivemiletown Creamery**

The creamery makes eight handsomely packaged cheeses, of which the best known is their Ballybrie. There's a
panopoly of cheese here, from the soft O'Reilly's goat's
cheese, hand-rolled in snipped chives, to their mature
cheddars, and the famous Boilie cheeses preserved in oil.
There is also a blue, a goat's and an oak smoked cheese.
(Mervyn McCaughey, 14 Ballylurgan Road, Fivemiletown
☎ 028-8952 1209 ✉ welovecheese@fivemiletown.com
🖱 www.fivemiletown.com)

LDerry

Moygashel

Café
● **Deli on the Green**

The Deli is Claire Murray's second food outlet in the
Linen Green complex in Moygashel. Bob McDonald
cooks and wisely features lots of the best mid-Ulster
products from Kettyle beef to Lough Erne lamb. The

cooking style is very classic: velouté of smoked haddock, duck pastillas with tomato chilli jam, beef fillet with bacon and red wine sauce, quail with puy lentils. (Claire Murray, 30 The Linen Green, Moygashel ☎ 028-8775 1775 ✉ delionthegreen@btconnect.com 🖱 www.delionthegreen.com – Open 8.30am-5.30pm Mon-Wed, 8.30am-9.30pm Tue-Sat)

Café
● **The Loft**

The Loft is one of two food destinations in the Linen Green complex, so if you are here to get some Foxford throws or a smart Paul Costelloe jacket, do climb into the Loft because this is a really great café with a selection of irresistible scones in loads of different flavours, including raspberry and white chocolate. And if it's lunchtime and the tarts and quiches are coming straight from the oven then match them up with a couple of fresh salads and it's a lunch that just can't be beat. (Claire Murray, 10A Linen Green, Moygashel ☎ 028-8772 9929 – Open 9.15am-5pm Mon-Sat)

only in Ulster
Dulse

Omagh

Local Shop
● **Mr Eatwells**

Joe McMahon runs a bakery, a chipper and a hot food bar as well as his top class butcher's shop on Campsie Road. Quality is high in all the outlets, but it's the butcher in particular that is the star, and which is home to no fewer than twenty different varieties of sausage and the sort of quality levels you would expect from a member of the Elite Guild of Butchers. (Joe McMahon, 16 Campsie Road ☎ 028-8224 1104 – Open 8.30am-6pm Mon-Sat)

Strabane

Farmers' Market
● **Strabane Farmers' Market**

Look out for Springwell Sheep's Cheese and other local foods. (Last Sat of the month, Score Centre, Dock Rd – Open 9am-1.30pm)

Tyrone

Asparagus and strawberries